COPYRIGHT

Copyright © 2025 by Thyra Grimm

Published by Fireline Press LLC

Veritas Ignis Aeternus — Truth is Eternal Fire

All rights reserved. No part of this book may be reproduced, distributed, or transmitted in any form or by any means, including photocopying, recording, or other electronic or mechanical methods, without the prior written permission of the publisher, except in the case of brief quotations used in reviews, critical articles, or other noncommercial uses permitted by copyright law.

For permissions, contact:

Fireline Press LLC — Texas, USA

ISBN (Hardcover): 978-1-969533-01-3

ISBN (Paperback — IngramSpark Edition): 978-1-969533-02-0

ISBN (Paperback — Amazon Edition): 978-1-969533-05-1

ISBN (eBook — ePub Edition): 978-1-969533-03-7

ISBN (eBook — Kindle Edition): 978-1-969533-06-8

ISBN (Audiobook): 978-1-969533-04-4

Additional copyright registration filed with the U.S. Copyright Office, Washington, D.C.

This is a work of nonfiction. Some names and identifying details may have been changed to protect privacy, but all events and accounts are drawn from documented history, personal observation, or verifiable sources.

Edition: Revised & Expanded Edition

First publication: 2025

This edition: January 2026

Printed in the United States of America

Fireline Press LLC — www.firelinepress.com

1

———

AUTHOR'S NOTE ON THIS EDITION

EDITION NOTICE

This volume reflects the current and definitive edition of *Unapologetically American*.

Earlier printings and digital releases were part of an active writing and refinement process. This edition incorporates substantial structural revisions, new chapters, clarified arguments, and a reforged closing sequence that completes the book's intended arc. If you are holding this edition, you are reading the complete version of the work to date.

— Thyra Grimm
January 14, 2026

CONTENTS

PART III

THE SERPENT'S PLAYBOOK

PART IV

THE RECKONING

PART V
THE FIRELINE - WAR MANUAL

PART I

THE GATE OF FIRE

"When you walk through the fire, you shall not be burned, and the flame shall not consume you".

To enter, you must cross the flame. To remain you must carry it.

— Isaiah 43:2

1

THE LINE IS DRAWN
THE FIRST CONFRONTATION

It happened in an H-E-B grocery store in Texas. Not a rally. Not a protest. Not a headline. Just a weekday — fluorescent lights, carts rattling across tile, country music leaking softly from the ceiling, the cold briny smell of ice and fish in the seafood aisle. People buying shrimp, bread, milk. Ordinary life pretending everything was fine. Texas masked late and reluctantly. But when the order came, something in the air shifted — as if the last free stronghold had taken a knee.

Technically. Most people ignored it. I wasn't wearing one. *They were.* Not everyone — *just them.* You could always tell. The stiffness in the eyes. The tension in the shoulders. The way they scanned the room before they ever made eye contact. Not for friendliness. For enforcement. They stood near the seafood counter — a man and a woman, early forties maybe, dressed in fitted activewear and spotless sneakers, California accents they hadn't learned to hide. Their posture was tight, alert — not for danger, but for violation. At first, they only stared. Then it came — not polite. Not careful. "Put on your mask," the woman snapped. "You're not wearing a mask." Out loud. In the middle of H-E-B. Not a request. A command delivered by someone who didn't own the store, the street, or my breath.

I turned. "I'm fine," I said. That's when the man exploded. "You're putting everyone at risk!" he shouted — loud, sharp, uncontrolled. Heads turned. Full stop. The seafood clerk froze mid-wrap. A couple near the tilapia stiffened. A kid kept shaking a bag of chips like nothing in the world had changed. "This is Texas," I said calmly. "Most people aren't wearing one." "That's not the point!" he yelled. Exactly. **It wasn't about health anymore.** "People like you are why this keeps happening!" the woman added. *Not medicine. Moral indictment.* "I'm not sick," I said. "And neither are you." "You're selfish!" she snapped. "You don't care if people die!" Her voice trembled — not with grief, but with **righteousness. The most dangerous emotion in any crowd.** He kept talking. Louder. Sloppier. Unraveling. And that's when I noticed: **No one was looking at me anymore.** They were all looking at him. Because in Texas, you don't scream at strangers in the fish aisle. You mind your own business. You lower your voice. You move on. This wasn't protest. **This was cultural invasion.**

A Texas man stepped forward from the edge of the aisle. Late fifties. Boots. Ball cap. No mask. "She ain't botherin' you," he said quietly. The California man whipped toward him. "This is none of your damn business!" "It became my business when you started hollerin'." The air split. "This is about public safety!" the man shouted. "No," the Texan said. "**It's about control.**" Something in me went cold and clear. Silence fell hard. Not shouting. Not chanting. Just that one word exposed. **Control.** They froze. The manager appeared — young, nervous, caught between policy and reality. "Let's just... keep it peaceful," he said. Texas translation: *Please don't make me choose.* "I am peaceful," I said. "You came at me." He swallowed. "There is a mandate," he said carefully. "But we're not enforcing it right now." They stared at him like he'd betrayed a creed. The woman grabbed her cart. "Unbelievable," she muttered. They left. No one followed. No one apologized. No one defended them. The room exhaled. It had taken less than three minutes.

Outside, the sky was wide Texas blue. Wind pushing dust across the parking lot. Flags snapping hard on the pole by the highway. That was the moment I understood exactly where the war lived. Not in hospitals. Not in headlines. Not in governments. It lived in ordinary places — between ordinary people — in the instant someone decided they owned your breath. That was the day I saw it clearly: **Fear had learned to speak in the language of virtue.** And Texas — quiet, unbothered, steady — revealed where the line actually was.

It reminded me of growing up in Denmark — not through fear itself, but through the stories that fear leaves behind. I don't invoke that history lightly. **I invoke it because I've seen what fear does to a people.** We were taught what the Nazi occupation had really been: not grand evil at first, but ordinary people bowing one small step at a time. **How fear made people compromise on truth.** How safety became an excuse. How neighbors learned to watch each other. How whispers replaced words. How compliance spread faster than courage. They told us how the snitch was born — not from ideology, but from terror. How weak people, desperate to survive, began turning in their neighbors to prove loyalty to power. How names were written down quietly. How doors were knocked on at night. How people were taken and never seen again. Not in chaos. Not in riots. In silence. In order. In paperwork.

Later I learned the same pattern from Czechoslovakia. From East Germany. From the Stasi files where entire lives were reduced to folders. Children trained to report on parents. Husbands on wives. Friends on friends. An entire nation turned into a listening device for the state. And always the same weapon at the center of it all: fear — steady, invisible, and absolute. And the part that haunted me most as a child was this: the machinery didn't arrive all at once. It arrived as paperwork. As quiet compliance. As neighbors learning to look away at the right time. As people choosing normal life over truth—until truth was no longer permitted.

Over time, terror doesn't just silence a people — it shrinks them. It teaches them to turn away. It teaches them to accept the unbearable as normal. It teaches them to trade conscience for continuity.

Standing in that H-E-B, watching strangers try to enforce obedience on behalf of a system they didn't command and a mandate they didn't create, I felt the same mechanism stirring. Not at the scale of genocide — not yet — but at the root of it. The same psychological seed. The same exchange: **safety for submission. Belonging for silence. Fear for power.** That is how every empire of control begins. Not with soldiers. But with neighbors.

There were moments during that season when I understood, with frightening clarity, how quickly this could have tipped into open violence. Not because people were evil — but because fear had hollowed out restraint. When fear is that absolute, it no longer needs ideology. It only needs permission. And all across America, the same phrase kept surfacing like a quiet drumbeat beneath the chaos: *hold the line.* Not a slogan of aggression — a signal of tension. A recognition that something fundamental was being tested. A sense, felt more than spoken, that once a certain boundary breaks, it does not quietly return.

"The fear of man lays a snare, but whoever trusts in the Lord is safe." — Proverbs 29:25

2

PRELUDE — THE GATE OF FIRE

EVERY PATTERN BEGINS IN SILENCE

Before America. Before the masks. Before your world and mine — there was a story. What I saw in that aisle was not new—it was ancient. The Northmen whispered it by firelight, a prophecy carved in ice and blood. They called it **Ragnarök**: the long winter, the breaking of bonds, the betrayal of brothers and sons, the world tilted into shadow. They said the wolf Fenrir would snap his chains. Midgaardsormen — the World Serpent — would rise from the sea, poisoning sky and soil. The gods would march to war. Odin would fall into the wolf's jaws. Thor would crush the serpent and die from its venom. Fire would sweep the earth. Ash would swallow the sun. And from the south would rise Surtr — the fire-giant with the flaming sword — the one destined to burn the world clean. Not chaos, but cleansing. Not madness, but judgment. His flames were the final stroke, the fire that devours what is corrupt so a new world can rise from the bones of the old. Yet from the ruin, a green world would rise. A new sun would break the smoke. Survivors would step out of the ash, carrying memory and fire. The coil would break, and life would begin again. This was not a tale of despair. It was instruction. The serpent rises. The fire comes. Only those who stand inherit what remains.

13

I tell you this not as myth and not as bedtime story. I tell you because I have watched patterns once called prophecy bleed into policy—Revelation into headlines, saga into system. *The serpent never dies; it only learns new tongues.* It has digitized its skin. Its fangs are forms and filings. Its venom is bureaucracy. Its temples are treaties. It no longer hisses from gardens; it murmurs from screens, from dashboards, from the saccharine language of *progress and peace.* It whispers through algorithms, smoothing its words until obedience feels like virtue. It doesn't burn crops; *it erases memory.* It doesn't bite; it convinces. It doesn't hide beneath the sea; it swims beneath systems. I have watched gods replaced by governments, worship by convenience, truth by management. The sagas of the North were not wrong; they were early.

You will see Scripture throughout this book — woven into the architecture, fused into the map, burning through every passage. This is not religious garnish. This is the spine of the war. The Bible is the only text that described this serpent, this system, this global coil, and this war for the soul across every age. Kings, empires, prophets, and nations have fallen along the same pattern it warned about. I do not quote Scripture to comfort you. I use it the way warriors always have: as revelation, as intelligence, as the true coordinates in a world where deception is policy. If you understand the Word, you will understand the war. This is not a claim of total sight — only the line of sight I was given. I am a daughter of the North—raised under those skies, shaped by that memory. I have lived on both sides of the serpent's pattern — in nations that submit and nations that resist. In these pages, you will see how Denmark wears a mask, why America stands in fire, and how the two are bound by the same quiet machinery. And the Remnant — the ones who still feel the burn in their bones — must remember: the sagas were warnings. The serpent is real. The coil is here. The battle is now.

The sagas end with fire and survival. My story begins long before any battlefield — in a life steeped quietly in the serpent's script. I did not stumble on it once; I breathed it. I absorbed it. I felt it settling into the air of Denmark long before I had the words to name it. But Denmark was different. It was not loud. It was not brutal. It was *tight*. A soft grip with no visible hand. A pressure you felt without ever seeing the source. *You did not fight it — you moved inside it.* You learned its boundaries before anyone ever named them. You learned what could not be questioned long before you learned what was allowed. It was order without escape, comfort without liberty, agreement without consent. *The serpent did not roar there. It regulated. It coordinated. It normalized. You didn't resist it. You inhaled it.* Only later did I understand what I had been living inside. Denmark was only the first taste. I traveled the world and lived in nations that spoke different tongues yet carried the same tightening coil — different flags, different accents, same underlying pressure, the same quiet narrowing, the same polite control disguised as progress. I felt it in Europe's corridors, in Asia's order, in the velvet obedience of the North and the curated freedoms of the West. **By the time I reached America, I recognized the voice immediately** — the same serpent, whispering in a different dialect. My lineage is not ornament; it is evidence. Blood remembers patterns the mind forgets. Proof that the old designs never died — they simply changed uniforms.

Turn the page.
   The coil ahead is not meant for study.
   It is meant for fire.
   What follows is the match.
   Strike it.

3

———

THE FIRELINE BRIEFING
AN ORIENTATION TO THE WAR

This book will **not comfort you. It will orient you.** It is not for the distracted or the doom-scrolling. It will not fit into a reel or a hashtag, and it refuses to bend to the pace of a world addicted to noise. It was written for those who still possess the patience to think, to listen, to watch the architecture beneath the surface. If you are holding these pages, something in you has already awakened. You are not here by accident. You are part of the remnant, **the ones who remember what is real, refuse the lie, and stay awake when others fall asleep** — that still feels the burn beneath the skin, the quiet insistence that the story is not over. What you hold is not a memoir. **It is a map.** A living one. Each word has been shaped by witness—years of watching people, nations, systems, and the unseen architecture that binds them all together. It enters as lived experience, then becomes cultural diagnosis, then becomes systemic exposure, and finally becomes a war manual. **Story opens the gates; pattern carries you through; truth arms you.** You were born into a war older than your nation, older than your lineage, older than any institution we now trust or fear. This book will take you deeper than history and harder than politics. It will expose the glow behind the grid, the contracts behind the crises, the systems behind the slogans. And it will show you the one force the serpent still fears: *the remnant who remembers.*

This war is fought not only with bullets or ballots, but with loyalties, silences, stories, and the words that define reality itself — in classrooms, courtrooms, newsrooms, and kitchens. Empires rise and collapse in predictable patterns, but the serpent's system—the machine that feeds on faith, family, and freedom—adapts. It renews itself through language and law, reshaping the world through a thousand subtle permissions. *You live in its newest version.* And this book will show you why.

We stand at the hinge of ages. Some call it a fourth turning. Prophets call it the birth pains of the end. The institutions that once promised order are collapsing under their own weight. Truth is treated as rebellion. Fear governs faster than law. From the plague years to the wars of narrative, the world has slipped into the final act of a cycle older than empire. The page has turned. The pattern has resurfaced. Every age faces a reckoning. Ours has come. Yet you are not here to be entertained by collapse. You are here because something in you remained awake. Something refused silence. Something would not bow. That fire is your inheritance. Now listen.

To understand what lies ahead, you must first understand the Coil—the serpent's coil. It is not chaos. It is design — the old story, wearing modern language. Across centuries and continents, the same fivefold architecture reappears. Nations forget. Empires drift. Systems harden. Truth is mocked. Courage becomes rare. Souls fall asleep. And then the serpent coils again, adapting its tongue to the technology and language of the age. You must see this pattern clearly, because you are about to walk through its full arc. What follows is not summary; it is the terrain itself—five movements that form one covenant line between sight and sovereignty.

First comes the Gate of Fire—the place where vision begins. This gate is not designed to persuade, but to prepare. Those who pass through will find the terrain changes. Not where the exposé starts, but where sight is forged. Every awakening begins the same way: with disruption. With the moment the world you trusted fractures and the light behind it forces its way through. Fire does not arrive gently. It strips illusion. It reveals what was always there. Before I take you into systems, treaties, and power structures, you need to understand how I came to see them. This first passage is not theory—it is witness. This is where you meet my story, my voice, and the road that formed it. I was formed inside a system most outsiders call 'perfect.' I grew up in Denmark—where control rarely shouts, and compliance rarely looks like coercion. I learned what a soft grip feels like long before I had words for it. I watched how *control evolves when it no longer needs violence—only language, law, and social permission.* By the time I reached the United States, I recognized the pattern immediately. **This is an immigrant's story, but not one of assimilation.** It is a record of **discernment.** Of moving across cultures, governments, and belief systems—and seeing the same machinery wearing different faces. Here you will understand why this book is not a hobby, not a grievance, not a performance. **It is a warning. A line drawn in defense of a nation I chose,** written by someone who has seen what happens when that line is not drawn. Part I does not unload the full case file. It gives you the eyes to recognize it. You will learn how to name the pattern, how to trust your sight again, and why certain truths feel dangerous the moment you say them out loud. This is where saga becomes map. Where story becomes orientation. Where the voice I was born with is set in fire—not to persuade, but to prepare. **This is the Gate of Fire.** It does not burn the whole field. **It lights the first flame.**

Then you descend into the Fall—where collapse is not a spectacle, but a process. Nations rarely die in battle; they die in comfort, in drift, in forgetfulness—while believing they are civilized. Here you walk through **Denmark's mask: the polished face the world admires, and the quiet machinery underneath it.**

You will see how control evolves when it no longer needs brutality—only *bureaucracy, social consensus, and language that makes surrender sound like virtue.* This is where the soft grip tightens. **Denmark doesn't conquer with tanks; it conquers with administration.** *It builds obedience through comfort, then seals it with language—until surrender feels like virtue and dissent feels like danger.* What looks like peace from the outside is a managed society from the inside: speech narrowed, conscience outsourced, identity converted into paperwork. This is why **Denmark matters.** It is not a side story. **It is a prototype**—polished, *exportable,* and increasingly treated as the future. I won't ask you to take this on faith— I'll show you how it works. And because this book is a warning, you will also see America's mirror. The same pressures, the same tactics, the same inversion: truth treated as taboo, courage treated as threat, dissent treated as contagion. Collapse does not begin with violence. It begins with silence—then paperwork—then social enforcement—until the quiet occupation feels normal. *This is not commentary. It is anatomy.* **If you can see how Denmark falls without a shot, you can recognize the pattern before it completes its arc here.**

Once you have seen the Fall, you will be ready to confront the Serpent's Playbook—the modern architecture of control. This is the part most people feel—but can't articulate. Here the serpent's strategy stops being symbolic and becomes structural. **Tyranny no longer shouts; it governs through systems**—metrics, dashboards, treaties, platforms, and algorithms—quiet levers that don't look like levers until they close. It does not abolish freedom; it redefines it. It does not ban dissent; it measures it, scores it, nudges it, and trains you to police yourself. This section traces the blueprint: how nations are softened, how memory is erased, how "progress" becomes a religion, how crisis becomes currency, and how control is made invisible by making it feel reasonable. You will see **the shift from brute force to administrative force**—from prisons of steel to prisons of numbers—until the cage is not around you, but inside you.

Here, the pattern stops being a hunch and becomes a map. You will learn the circuitry of the system not to fear it, but to break it—because what can be mapped can be resisted, and what can be named can no longer masquerade as normal.

From there you enter the Reckoning—where truth and power finally collide. This is the phase systems fear most. Masks crack. Institutions wobble. Narratives built on illusion begin to fracture under the weight of reality. What was once whispered becomes visible. What was hidden can no longer be managed out of sight. This is not chaos—it is pressure. The moment when lies stop scaling, when enforcement replaces persuasion, and when power reveals its true face. Courts are tested. Media is exposed. Education, finance, faith, and governance are forced to choose what they actually serve. **This is the thunder hour.** *Judgment and mercy rise together —not as abstraction, but as consequence.* Babylon shakes, not because it is attacked, but because it can no longer sustain its contradictions. And in that shaking, a line is drawn. Builders rise. So do enforcers. **The reckoning is not destruction. It is decision.** What survives is what was real. What collapses was already hollow. You won't be asked to panic. You'll be shown what's happening—and why.

Finally comes the Fireline—where revelation becomes formation. If the first passages teach you to see, **this one teaches you to stand.** This is not catharsis. It is conversion: from awareness to discipline, from outrage to order, from spectator to builder. Here you recover the practices that anchor a free people—covenant, craft, courage, household, dominion, truth—and you learn how to apply them in a world designed to dissolve them. You will build the fireline where you actually live: in your home, your calendar, your money, your words, your work, your land, your community. This is where sovereignty stops being a slogan and becomes a way of life. Every table becomes a fortress. Every word becomes a weapon. Every family becomes a battlement against the Machine. **Not because you can control the empire, but because you can refuse its terms.**

This is where survival ends and sovereignty begins. You won't leave with opinions. You'll leave with practices. **This is your war manual—practical, unglamorous, and real.**

These five movements—*awakening, descent, unveiling, confrontation, rebuilding*—are not academic categories. They are the living pattern of every age where freedom is threatened and the Remnant is called to rise. You will feel them, not study them. Each part of this book is a passage through that pattern, a march through revelation toward renewal. **You are not reading a story. You are entering one.**

The serpent's coil will no longer be myth to you; it will be map. And once you see it, you cannot return to ignorance or ease. You will understand why the world looks the way it does, why your fire never died, and why this moment—the one you were born into—is the hinge between ruin and resurrection.

The Gate of Fire stands ahead.
    You have carried the flame long enough.
    Now you must walk through it.
    Turn the page.
    The war is here.
    It enters as a life.
    It leaves you armed.

Welcome to the fire.

4

———

THIS IS THE VOICE I WAS BORN WITH

THE MAKING OF A WATCHWOMAN

This is the story behind my voice — how silence forged it, fire tempered it, loss purified it, and wilderness returned it as command. Every voice has an origin. Mine began in the dark, before words. You will hear an accent in these pages that Denmark trained me to lose. *Not a vowel—an instinct.* A way of speaking that existed in the North before it was sanded down into politeness: oath-speech. Boundary-speech. Claim-speech. The old voice didn't debate the world. It named it. And once you hear it, you'll recognize what modern systems fear most—**someone who will not ask permission to tell the truth.** Truth, once born in silence, does not whisper again. *It speaks with fire's weight.*

When I was eight, my father died. The world split. Something inside me went still. The house said nothing, yet the silence shouted its first lesson: **your words do not matter; no one is listening.** So I listened. I watched. I learned. **Silence became my first language** — not weakness, but apprenticeship. While others filled the air with noise, I studied what sound concealed — how power moves in shadows, how truth hides in plain sight, how the loudest voices are empty.

Evil does not always shout. Sometimes it speaks through tone, gesture, or the quiet architecture of control — a look that erases, a word that wounds, a silence that says you do not belong. I felt it early — **the cold art of those who use language not to reveal but to erase.** Their aim was simple: *to dim my light before it could speak.* For a time, I hid — not from the world, but from eyes that despised what they could not bear to understand. But a voice like that isn't inherited whole. *It's forged.*

The Silence

He was thirty-one when the grave closed over him — an age that still burns like unfinished fire. I never said goodbye. The casket closed without me, and the earth sealed what I could not speak. The silence that followed was heavier than death itself. For years I carried that ache — the wound of no closure, the scream with no voice. In that ache, God found me — not in triumph, but in breaking. When men deny you farewell, only God can write the final word. *Silence, I discovered, is a teacher.* It strips language to its bones, exposes the counterfeit strength of noise, and forces you to hear what cannot be said. In the stillness, I learned this — *pain is not punishment. It is instruction.* Every unanswered cry becomes an echo that leads inward, to where God speaks without words. That was the beginning of my listening — not to people, but to pattern, to pulse, to presence. Silence became my discipline. And in its depth I found that grief, once purified, becomes perception. **The wound became an ear — the place where light begins to listen.**

The Fire

If silence forged the shape of my voice, fire gave it heat. I spent two decades inside the corporate world. I loved the labor itself — the rhythm, the pressure, the problem-solving, the exchange of ideas. I learned how to operate inside their machine. But I never respected it. The machine did not reward courage or intelligence. It rewarded **compliance.**

The loudest voice often won — not the wisest or steadiest, just the loudest. Meetings became rituals of noise where opinions passed for progress and mediocrity was crowned as virtue. Creation was tolerated only as long as it could be owned. The system valued extraction, not origin. The quiet ones kept everything running. The loud ones took the credit. Mediocrity rose. Integrity was quietly punished. Promotions were earned not by skill or service, but by submission — by those who bowed, flattered, and learned when to stay silent while power abused itself. It was **the logic of bureaucracy perfected: a machine that fears excellence because excellence exposes it.**

During my years in corporate Denmark, I learned how power actually behaves when no one is watching. In one office, everyone held their breath. People read one man's moods like weather, adjusting themselves constantly—afraid to speak wrong, afraid to move at the wrong moment. He ruled by humiliation, not respect; by volatility, not wisdom. He did not need to be right. He only needed to be feared. This is the psychology of the small tyrant: a fragile man disguised as authority, feeding on tension, governing by emotional instability, confusing terror with leadership. He was not powerful. He was desperate to feel powerful. But fear alone does not sustain a system. *It needs collaborators.* In that environment, the people who advanced were not the most capable. *They were the most compliant.* They learned how to smooth language rather than sharpen thought, how to flatter upward and press downward, how to read the script, repeat it convincingly, and never challenge the hand that fed them. Some traded integrity for access. Some traded silence for promotion. Some traded loyalty, conscience, or even their bodies for leverage—whatever the moment required. **Mediocrity advanced not by excellence, but by obedience.**

In another workplace, the same sickness wore a different mask. The leaders there lounged with their feet on tables—relaxed, smug, untouchable—carrying titles as proof of brilliance despite having no visible skill beyond the title itself. Power was mistaken for intelligence, credentials for wisdom, status for purpose. One of them said it to my face. *You can come back when you have a degree like mine. Until then, you're a nobody.* It was said calmly. Casually. As fact. That sentence revealed everything. Not confidence, but dependence. Not mastery, but credential worship. A man who mistook parchment for mind, certification for competence. He had learned the system's deepest trick: replace substance with symbols — and call the symbols authority. They looked down on the people who kept the machine alive—builders, operators, problem-solvers—blind to the simple truth that without them the entire structure would stall. **Degrees floated upward; responsibility sank downward.** The most capable carried the load. The most credentialed issued judgment. Different styles. Same disease. Noise replaced knowledge. Obedience outshouted courage. Titles carried more weight than truth. This was the fire. And fire teaches exactly one thing: *what cannot survive the heat was never real to begin with.*

At least in America — or so I believed — there was still room to rise by merit. If you worked hard, thought sharply, and carried discipline in your bones, you could build something greater than yourself. That was the covenant I admired — **the promise that liberty was not inherited from kings, but forged in the hands of ordinary people.** A land where gatekeepers did not own your future, where grit could still outweigh pedigree. Even as the same spirit of control began creeping westward, I held hope that somewhere the fire still burned. But I could no longer lend my time, my name, or my conscience to a system that had forgotten its own purpose. Eighteen years was enough. I had watched *mediocrity rewarded, integrity punished, and small men perform godhood behind oversized titles.* The ceiling was low. The air stale. The power games endless. I realized I would rather risk everything than spend one more day shrinking to fit their design. So I walked away — not because I failed the system, but because *I refused to become it.*

When I left corporate Denmark, they spoke to me as if I had stepped outside reality itself. *When will you work again?* The question was sincere. It wasn't asked with malice, only confusion — the kind reserved for someone who has stepped outside the map. It revealed everything. In that world, **work was not creation or calling** — it was **proof of worth.** A person existed only if they remained legible to the system: employed, titled, measured, approved. Anything unscored was suspect. Anything unregistered was irresponsible. Purpose did not belong to the individual; it was issued by institutions. I understood then how deeply the lie had settled. Labor had been reduced to a leash, dignity to a disguise. Work was no longer about building something true or necessary, but about remaining compliant, visible, and sanctioned. To step away was not seen as choice, but as failure — a refusal to submit to the only meaning the system recognized.

That was never freedom. It was control presented as virtue, repeated so consistently in offices, unions, institutions, and corporations that it hardened into moral law. I had heard it my entire adult life in Denmark — in policy language, in workplace culture, in the quiet shame directed at anyone who did not fit the approved path. Leaving did not silence that voice. I heard its echo later in other countries, in other systems, dressed in different language but carrying the same logic. **The machine does not forgive those who step beyond its fences.** It mocks them. It calls them unrealistic, irresponsible, unserious — anything but free. *I know that voice now.* I see the people still trapped inside it: polished, credentialed, performing success while hollowing out from within. They parade titles and curated achievements, yet carry the same unease. Because beneath the performance, a question remains — one no institution can answer for them: *What did you actually build today?* When the lights go off, the performance evaporates. Titles cannot tell you who you are. Status cannot carry meaning. And no amount of motion can substitute for purpose.

The Same Voice, New Uniform

In the years since I walked away, I have watched that same voice cross the ocean and take up residence in America. It speaks with the same breath, the same logic, the same quiet contempt for excellence. Only the language has changed. I do not say this lightly. I say it because I recognize the pattern at work. Not the stated intention, but the operational result. Not what it claims to protect, but what it consistently produces. By the time I saw it in Silicon Valley, the pattern was unmistakable: titles and company names had become identity, and prestige itself began to speak louder than judgment. Today it wears a new uniform. It is called DEI. It is not that people lose intelligence. It is that systems bury it. Competence is sidelined in favor of optics. Mastery gives way to narrative alignment. Discipline is treated as rigidity. Truth is recoded as "unsafe." Decisions no longer flow from skill or responsibility, but from compliance with a rotating script.

In that environment, the most capable become liabilities. The most disciplined become threats. The most truthful are managed, muted, or removed. In their place rise the agreeable, the credentialed, the groomed —*chosen not for what they can do, but for what they will not question.* This is not diversity. It is dilution. Not inclusion. Replacement. Not equity. The redistribution of competence. And because the system presents this inversion as virtue, it is celebrated. A population trained to applaud its own weakening will never challenge the hands that benefit from it. I have seen this before. **Different language. Same spirit.**

We measure worth in titles and salaries, not in truth or creation. The system honors what can be tracked, ranked, and displayed. What cannot be measured is treated as expendable. Yet much of what actually sustains life exists outside that ledger. The builder shaping timber, the farmer tending land, the craftsman, the writer, the artist, the mother raising children — work that does not scale, does not brand easily, and does not announce itself. None of it appears on a stock exchange. **All of it feeds the world.**

I was not unemployed when I stepped away. I was no longer willing to serve a system that devours time and calls it progress. I chose different work — work that could not be delegated or automated, work that required presence rather than performance. I chose to build what would endure, to speak what was true, and to create without asking permission. Inside the system, that choice was read differently. To those who remained, leaving looked like loss. Stepping outside the hierarchy was interpreted as failure. Freedom, without a title attached to it, registered as absence. *If your work could not be named, ranked, or displayed, it was assumed not to exist.* That misreading was not accidental. The system has no category for unmeasured labor, no language for work that answers to conscience instead of supervision. Those who step outside its frame are quietly diminished — not attacked outright, but reduced in status, relevance, and seriousness. A person without a role is treated as a person without worth. I understood then that the system must interpret freedom as foolishness. If leaving were acknowledged as choice, too many might follow. So it recodes refusal as loss and calls it realism. I did not walk away because I failed. I walked away because I saw clearly — and *chose work that could not be owned.*

I chose my children over a job. That decision clarified everything. Childhood is a narrow window. Once it closes, it does not reopen. No title compensates for absence. No salary repays years that cannot be recovered. What I gave my children was not efficiency or advantage, but attention — unoutsourced, unhurried, unseen. It was then that the reaction became visible. Not from institutions, but from peers — particularly professional women who had built their identities inside the system I had stepped away from. The response was not curiosity, but correction. The tone shifted. The smiles tightened. My decision was treated as regression, indulgence, or waste. Not because it harmed anyone — but because it violated an unspoken rule: *you do not leave the hierarchy and still claim dignity.* I recognized it for what it was — not personal animus, but enforcement. A reminder of the cost of stepping outside approved definitions of success.

When a woman refuses the terms of the system, her choice is reframed as irresponsibility. When she values stewardship over status, it is recoded as smallness. The message is subtle but consistent: *return to the structure, or accept social diminishment.* The system does not know how to value this kind of work. It never has. It rewards visibility, not consequence. *It praises ambition while quietly shaming those who choose responsibility over recognition.* Women are taught to apologize for the very capacities that make them powerful — *to downplay presence, endurance, and loyalty to what cannot be outsourced.* I did not walk away from work. I walked toward it — stripped of illusion, measured by consequence, and anchored in what lasts.

For years I mistook success for being seen. It took walking away from everything to learn that most people don't see you at all — only what you give them. *When you stop performing, they vanish.* Performance is not relationship. It rewards image over endurance, emotion over discipline. *The hollow world does not really see; it reflects what it wants.* And **when the mirror cracks, many no longer know who they are.** That realization forced a question I could not avoid: what was I willing to burn to stay free? What was I willing to walk away from so my children never would? Who would I be when the system demanded my silence? The forge begins where comfort ends. **Fire became the second teacher.** It reveals what silence conceals. It burns away illusion and leaves only essence. What is expendable turns to smoke. What endures remains. I am not explaining this choice. I am naming it — because too many women have been taught to apologize for work that is foundational to any civilization that intends to survive. **Fire taught me how to speak without asking permission.**

"When you walk through the fire, you will not be burned; the flames will not set you ablaze." — Isaiah 43:2

The Furnace

The forge was stoked hotter. Loss became the furnace, and my voice learned to stand inside it. For a time, I believed the worst was behind me. Then came **the season of loss** — one that scorched deeper than exile ever did. I watched friends bury their children. I saw mothers collapse beside caskets. Families split open by grief no language could hold. One friend ended his own pain with a gun, and the echo of that shot still rings in places I cannot name. It shattered every illusion of control — every fantasy that tomorrow was promised. There are no words for that kind of silence — the stillness that settles when laughter leaves a house forever, when a child no longer has a father, when a mother stares at photographs that will never be complete again. Then came the deeper sickness — the one no test could trace, and no language could contain. **Minds broke. Fear turned to pride. Pride to cruelty.** I watched friends drift into delusion, tormenting others to prove their own "safety." They performed virtue like a costume while their eyes emptied behind it. I watched them **trade conscience for approval, truth for belonging, spine for permission.** And that is where my disgust was born. Not at death — but at **submission.** It didn't break me. It repelled me. To see how easily people traded truth for comfort. How quickly *cowardice was reframed as compassion.* How *fear became a badge of moral superiority.* That was when I understood the **price of compliance** — and the **mercy of solitude.** The peace of not waking in the night wondering what piece of your soul you surrendered to stay socially clean. **Fear was the plague. Freedom the cure.**

This is where my voice stopped asking to be welcomed and started refusing to be erased. And in the years that followed — after the sickness, after the fear — more fell. Even now they keep falling. Some to cancer. Some to despair. Some to grief that never healed. Each loss a reminder that the plague did not end with the headlines. It lingered — in bodies, in minds, in silence. And still, some stand by the very lies that broke them — proud of their ruin, loyal to their captors. **Fear became their faith. It promised safety and delivered sickness — comfort laced with control.**

I watched people I love cling tighter to what harms them, convinced obedience was protection. They swallowed every new remedy, every ritual of reassurance, yet grew weaker with each dose — not because the treatment failed, but because fear had become the medicine they craved. It was not malice that bound them, but **a blindness of the soul** — the kind that teaches captivity to masquerade as care, dependence to disguise itself as safety. *That is the enemy we fight — not their flesh,* but **the spell that owns them.** Fear never stops at the body. It hunts the home. It stalks the family. It waits for the next generation — patient, quiet, merciless — knowing that if it can claim the children, it will never have to conquer the nation.

Then the fire came for my own house. One child nearly taken by flame, another nearly swallowed by despair. Different battles. Same war. When I tried to shield them, the system turned its face against me. What called itself education became indoctrination — pride disguised as progress, confusion dressed as compassion. I watched my children stand in the crossfire of a war they never asked for. There are wounds a mother carries in silence because no language can hold them. No one asked. No one knew. I carried it alone, praying for breath when faith felt like ash. The world kept turning, blind to the smoke rising from my roof. In those nights of unanswered prayer, something in me broke — not faith, but the illusion that I could fight this war with strength alone. The silence deepened until it felt alive. That was when I recognized it — not a voice in thunder, but a whisper that reasoned like mercy and cut like a blade. The enemy did not shout; it suggested. Gentle. Reasonable. Merciless. *It offered comfort for compromise, ease for obedience, peace for surrender. Relief, if I would just stop resisting.* That was the night I learned what **spiritual war** truly is. It does not begin in nations, but in souls. **Lose that war within, and every outer battle is already lost.** After that night, I began to see the same war played out in daylight — not with dreams or symbols, but in classrooms, offices, and laws.

The same spirit that whispered in silence now spoke through institutions, gentle as policy, merciless as control. I saw classrooms turned into pulpits for ideology, not education. Teachers trained in slogans, not scholarship, waving banners they barely understood. They weren't victims of the system — *they were the system*. Many became enforcers of ideology, policing thought with the zeal of the newly converted. Some hid behind "policy," others behind "compassion," but the result was the same: obedience over intellect, conformity over truth. They did not educate; they conditioned. Debate was treated as defiance. Questions as threat. Courage — real courage — was punished outright. I did not drift into confrontation. I chose it. When the war crossed the threshold of my home and reached for my children, silence was no longer an option. I did not organize a revolt. I did not gather a crowd. I walked in alone, armed with truth and a spine they mistook for threat. I learned quickly that systems fear nothing more than a single parent who will not bow, will not flatter, and will not be managed. What followed was not a debate. It was exposure.

The School of Submission

The principal sat still — spine softened, silence his shield, watching his teachers perform the ritual of submission. For a moment I wondered if he could not control his own dogs, but I said nothing. Silence was more powerful. When I spoke, the air trembled. Truth does that. One rose and fled — not from danger, but from exposure. Days later she told my child, "Your mother's presence made me feel threatened." Every word proved the point. Their creed is a porcelain idol — polished, hollow, easily cracked. They built their temple on slogans, not stone. They call it education; I call it indoctrination. I learned that **a mother's voice must be blade and shield—because no one else will guard the children.**

They call it safety; I call it fear wearing a mask. I felt no sorrow for them, only disgust — the clean disgust that comes when illusion burns away. *These are not teachers.* They are technicians of obedience. They do not educate minds; they manufacture consent. They train children to doubt their parents, to mock their faith, to bow to the collective lie. Their pride is weakness. Their compassion, counterfeit. Their gospel, rot. **One day, they will answer — not to me, but to the children they wounded.**

"It would be better for him to have a millstone fastened around his neck and to be drowned in the depth of the sea than to cause one of these little ones to stumble." — Matthew 18:6

The University of Inversion

In the university, the rot ran deeper. They preached enlightenment while teaching self-hatred, rewriting history in the language of guilt. My son was sent to study ranch management, but learned not stewardship or skill — only ideology. They spoke not of soil and seasons, but of "sustainability," not of tending land, but of saving the planet. He learned not mathematics or meaning, but shame — told that heritage itself was sin, that history was a crime scene, and that his worth was something to be apologized for before it could ever be earned. He was taught that character did not matter as much as category, that guilt could be inherited, and that responsibility flowed not from action, but from skin. They charged fortunes for this decay and still called it prestige. **Their temples of learning had become factories of inversion — debt sold as opportunity, propaganda sold as progress.** And they still call it education. I remember the call that broke the illusion — Another blow on the anvil. Another tone added to the timber of my speech — steady when their slogans howl. *"I'm wasting my time,"* he said, *"and you're wasting your money."* In that moment the mask fell. The institution that claims to build minds now imports obedience and exports illusion — and the world still calls it noble. I knew then — I would never bow to it, nor offer a single child to its altar.

Any system that trades truth for prestige calls illusion education — and its reward is ruin. I would fight with every fire in me — not for vengeance, but for truth's vindication. Truth does not shout; it stands until the noise exhausts itself. They still call that university in the West a great school. I laugh at the spectacle — elites and would-be visionaries proudly sending their children there, paying fortunes to purchase illusion and call it education. It is the oldest story, repeated without shame. The emperor parades naked, and the crowd still applauds. The West once taught men to read the weather — not the slogans written in the sky.

"Professing themselves to be wise, they became fools." — Romans 1:22

The Wilderness

When the furnace emptied me, the wilderness finished the metalwork. When everything fell away, I turned to the only places that do not lie — the road beneath my feet, the sky that never flatters, the raw land that asks only honesty. I buried myself in work that left dust on my hands and quiet in my mind. I rebuilt a home, room by room — sometimes alone, sometimes with help that cost more than it gave. What should have been sanctuary became battlefield. Dust in my lungs. Noise in my sleep. Prices doubled. Patience thinned. Faith frayed. Strangers in and out, walls half-torn, promises half-kept. For years I lived inside the wreckage of what was meant to be refuge, trapped in repairs that never seemed to end. The silence I loved was buried under drills and demands. *My voice went with it — smothered beneath noise and the illusion of a perfect life.* I found quiet only on trails and in distant lands — where wind replaced walls, ruins remembered, and truth still spoke. *Every wall taught patience; every setback, discernment.* I saw kindness in strangers and deceit in those I once called friends. *Rejection, I learned, can be mercy in disguise* — protection wearing the mask of loss. *Solitude, once feared, became sanctuary.* Labor turned to prayer. Every strike of the hammer, every tear left unshed, shaped me into something God could use.

In the mountains I learned truth again — not from men, but from wind, stone, and endurance. And while I stepped away from the permanence of social media, I could still see its pull everywhere — every day a new image, a new costume, a new hunger for validation. Noise dressed as connection. Content without substance. I no longer envied their presence; I pitied their captivity. The feed became their faith. I had walked away from that altar. I built what I could. I burned what I must. Even ashes held clarity. The world called it retreat. I called it resurrection. Out there, the voice I carried stopped being performance — and became obedience.

"Therefore, behold, I will allure her, and bring her into the wilderness, and speak tenderly to her." — Hosea 2:14

I had worn their masks — the polite smile, the borrowed strength, the names they wanted me to answer to. I chased their praise, carried their expectations, bowed to their noise. But *every mask burned in the silence.* What I thought was loss was cleansing. What I called exile was refinement. I was not being erased. I was being reforged. In that stillness I saw my reflection — stripped, scarred, unhidden — and it was enough. The voice that rose in that wilderness wasn't new; it was ancient — the one He placed in me before the world *began.* I became a woman marked by fire. Some ties I released. Some illusions fell away on their own. Some exits were mercy disguised as loss. **Fire clarifies. It reveals what is real.** Every loss became a teacher; every scar, a compass. Pain carves, but it also consecrates. And when the carving was done, there was silence — not emptiness, but command. The kind of quiet that asks what remains when everything false is gone. That's where He found me — not in strength, but in surrender. **He returned my weapon — my voice.** Forged in silence. Tempered by fire. Proven by loss. Steadied by wilderness. History does not absolve the fearful; it remembers the ones who refused the lie.

"Then the Lord put out His hand and touched my mouth, and said to me, 'Behold, I have put My words in your mouth.'"— Jeremiah 1:9

The world rewards noise. It is built to amplify distraction. But those who guard their silence guard their fire. When the noise fades, what remains is command — the quiet certainty that obedience to truth is the only freedom left. *The fire did not train me for peace. It trained me for precision.* The silence did not soften me. It clarified me. It stripped away every appetite that could be bargained with, every fear that could be leveraged. What remained did not need applause. This was never for one book. It was preparation — for warnings, for maps, for work that would outlive comfort. The house I rebuilt was never just wood and plaster. It was a battlefield disguised as shelter — every beam a confession, every nail a decision. I spoke to the walls, and the wind answered. Silence was the altar. But His gift was the voice — and this time, it would not be taken.

"In returning and rest you shall be saved; in quietness and trust shall be your strength." — Isaiah 30:15

This is the voice I was born with — forged in silence, tempered by loss, shaped for this hour. It does not bow to spectacle or flatter power. It does not borrow language from systems built to tame it. It speaks plainly, or not at all. It was never made for comfort or applause, but for truth — *the kind that costs something to carry.* And if you have lost your voice in the noise, take heart. It waits for you too, in the same silence, in the same fire. Now that you know the forge, you will recognize the flame when it begins to burn in nations. If you can still stand truth, you belong here. **My voice was not given for peace, but for war — the kind that sets captives free.**

"The Lord goes out like a mighty man, like a warrior; He stirs up His zeal." — Isaiah 42:13

5

THE BOARD — THE UNVEILING

THE WORLD IS NOT A GAME.
IT'S A FIELD OF CONSEQUENCE

This war is older than empires and deeper than borders. It wears many flags but serves one master. Some call it politics. Some call it progress. But beneath every slogan, every movement, every system, the same pulse beats. This is not a war for land. **It is a war for the human soul.** It begins where **truth is first betrayed — in language.** Words once built worlds; now they bend to ideology. Good is renamed harmful, evil renamed kind. The tongue becomes a weapon, the lie becomes law. When speech collapses, thought soon follows. When thought decays, conscience dies. This is how nations fall without a single shot fired: morality traded for management, discernment replaced with data. The conscience — once the echo of God within man — now lies buried beneath screens, noise, and curated lives. *We no longer confess; we curate.* And the sins we refuse to face return as systems that enslave us. Every sin denied becomes a seed in darkness. The rulers of this age know this well. Some are visible — in offices, institutions, and agencies. Others remain hidden — behind algorithms, treaties, and faceless boards. Together they form a machinery of control, a system that rules not with swords but with code. This is the architecture of the war we're in — invisible to the blind, unavoidable to the awake.

The Antichrist is not merely a man. It is also a mechanism — a spirit that can inhabit systems.

"For we wrestle not against flesh and blood, but against principalities, against powers, against the rulers of the darkness of this world, against spiritual wickedness in high places." — Ephesians 6:12

It seeks not only our labor, but our loyalty; not only our minds, but our memory. It desires **worship in the form of dependence.** Through technocracy and bureaucracy it clenches its iron fist. Through convenience it conquers. It harvests souls by numbers and hearts by clicks. Every post, every scan, every surrender of privacy becomes another stone in Babylon's tower. Yet this war cannot be fought with outrage or algorithms. It is a spiritual field — invisible, but real. To stand here, a man must first kneel. Confess. Repent. Armor up. For this is the battlefield of hearts, and **only the truth within can withstand the deception without.** *The weapons of this war are not missiles but virtues: faith over fear, courage over comfort, truth over tolerance.* **To stand in this field is to declare war on lies, not men. To reclaim sovereignty is to reclaim the soul.** The serpent's system may rule the networks, but it cannot rule the heart that bows to Christ. So put on the armor of God. Take back your conscience. Remember your name. The war is here — and it begins within. Once you see it, you realize the battlefield was never merely political. It was dimensional.

The fire gave me voice; the war gave it purpose. Lift your eyes. The battlefield is larger than you think. This is not a game of chance, but of consequence. Not checkers. Not even chess. Every move echoes beyond what you can see. **The board is not wood and pieces. It is us** — nations, faiths, hearts. Every move matters. Every silence counts. **Every cowardice opens a door for evil.** Once you see it, you can't unsee it.

Once you learn the pattern, you start to recognize the serpent — how he hides behind systems, disguising control as compassion, tyranny as reason. The serpent feeds on **fragmentation** — dividing what was once whole. Faith quarantined from public life—so power answers to nothing. History rewritten into story—so you can't see the pattern. Morality inverted—so appetite replaces conscience. That fracture is his camouflage. Fragmented vision is blind vision. But this fire refuses division. It reunites the fragments — **faith, history, conscience, prophecy** — into one story of freedom and fall. The serpent hides between the categories; truth burns through them. The same spirit that silenced prophets now censors patriots. The same logic that built empires now builds algorithms. Different language. Same breath. This is the field I walk. The pattern I was born to name. The serpent still believes he owns the board — but it was never his.

The Five Dimensions

You cannot fight what you cannot name — and you cannot see the board if you think it's flat. The world does not move in straight lines; it coils, it breathes, it unfolds in layered fields unseen by those who serve the surface. Every war, every lie, every redemption plays out across the same five coordinates — the hidden geometry of consequence. These are laws written into creation — the pattern Scripture reveals from Genesis to Revelation.

Time — the river where past and future collide.
   Truth — the plumb line that cuts through illusion.
   Power — the field where systems and souls choose allegiance.
   Eternity — the horizon that swallows every throne.
   Spirit — the breath that endures when everything else burns.

These are not ideas; they are coordinates — the hidden laws of consequence and the language of covenant. Every empire rises within them, and every deception breaks against them. The serpent fights in all five at once. That is why politics alone will never save us. This war is **spiritual in architecture, digital in expression,** and **eternal in consequence** — and Scripture mapped the field long before any nation understood it.

There is a pattern beneath every throne, every treaty, every system ever built by human hands. Most never see it because they search for enemies in flesh and forget the machinery beneath the surface. But **the serpent has always ruled through structures**—first temples, then empires, now networks. His design never changed; only his tools evolved. He once conquered through kings. Then through ideology. **Now he conquers through architecture:** through data, through access, through the quiet machinery that decides who may speak, who may move, who may buy, who may belong. Most people sense something tightening around their lives but cannot name it. They see the pieces, not the pattern. But once you understand the board is multi-dimensional, you start recognizing the same ancient fingerprint appearing in new forms. The serpent learned to hide not in superstition, but in systems. Not in myth, but in mechanisms. The battle that once raged in temples now unfolds in code. And the next time you hear the words progress, safety, or modernization, understand: these are no longer ideas. They are moves. And **every move serves a master.**

The Knight — The Remnant's Move
Every war has its warrior. Every field has its move. The serpent plays by power; the Remnant plays by revelation. In the game of chess, I have always loved the knight — the only piece that moves against the grain. He leaps when others march. He bends order to reveal strategy. He breaks through where logic fails — *faith against formula, courage against control.* Empire fears him because he cannot be predicted. He is the insurgent of light — the Remnant's move on a dark board.

The Remnant moves like this — unseen, unconventional, unstoppable. While others walk by sight, they move by spirit. Where the system sees chaos, they see pattern. Where Babylon builds walls, they leap them. They carry the ancient code of courage that confounds every empire — obedience over outcome, faith over fear, truth over safety. Every age tries to erase truth. Every tyranny tries to flatten the board. But truth still moves — alive, sovereign, unbending. Scripture is the only code the elites cannot rewrite. And the Remnant — the knights of covenant — still move by its fire.

I have seen the world from both sides of its divide — among those who issue commands and those who carry consequences, among the visible and the forgotten, the obedient and the watchful. I have shaken hands with power not because I belonged there, but because life placed me close enough to see how it works. They shape nations with signatures and screens—setting incentives, placing contracts, steering capital, selecting outcomes. And I've stood beside the unseen who hold the world together by simple faith. I've watched money pose as wisdom and bureaucracy harden into a cage of polite words and quiet threats. I've felt the chill of power — the silence before authority, laws written to bind the free and shield the corrupt. I've watched good men comply for comfort, mothers surrender for safety, nations kneel for convenience. I've seen the world bow to science without conscience, progress without truth—evil dressed in paperwork while the serpent learned to smile.

But I have also met the Remnant — the ones who still build, pray, fight, and refuse to bow. I've seen truth burning in eyes the world calls irrelevant, the forgotten holding more light than whole governments. One voice of conviction can still shake a room full of compromise. The pattern never changes — only its costume. The board is global, but the battle is personal. Once you see it, you cannot unsee it. And those who do carry a burden: to speak when silence feels safer, to move when fear whispers wait, to stand when the world kneels.

The pieces move faster now. The clock accelerates. What once felt like prophecy is unfolding in real time. You are not a spectator. You are a player. **Refuse to move, and the serpent will move through you. Stay silent, and your silence becomes surrender.** This is not politics — it is possession. The serpent believes you are cornered. But the board is not his. It never was. Refuse fear. Reject resignation. Move. The field is set. The players chosen. Every move echoes through five dimensions — time, truth, power, eternity, spirit. The battle inside you isn't chaos; it's alignment.

Every trial trained your hands for this hour — every silence, preparation; every loss, instruction. I met the serpent long before I could name him — in politics and pulpits, in men who smiled while serving his design. I met him in systems calling control compassion, and in eyes that once knew truth but chose comfort. Here the story begins. The serpent still plays, but the board belongs to the light.

"The light shines in the darkness, and the darkness has not overcome it." — John 1:5

6

WHAT I SAW BEFORE AMERICA
SEEING THE PATTERN BEFORE THE FLAG

Anyone called to watch must return to the ground that made her. Vision costs roots. The higher you learn to see, the deeper you must return. This is my journey from Denmark to America — and the systems I lived inside along the way. Before I could see the world's patterns, I had to stand where mine began: **the North**—cold and quiet, where order reigns and fire hides beneath stone.

"The lion has roared—who will not fear? The Sovereign Lord has spoken—who can but prophesy?" — Amos 3:8

Denmark — The Land That Shaped Me

I was born in Roskilde, the old Viking city — raised in the shadow of kings beneath the Domkirke, where marble tombs remember crowns turned to dust — where kings sleep in stone while the serpent still whispers through the streets outside. Longships once filled the harbor, and the fields of Lejre still hum with the echo of gods. Even the name Roskilde means spring of the rose — a well that never runs dry. I was not just born in Denmark. I was born a daughter of the North — blood of Vikings, raised in a land that remembered their daring but buried their fire beneath comfort.

Denmark is a compact patchwork — Jutland, Zealand, Funen, and scattered isles — easy to cross, hard to forget. Homogeneous, pragmatic, bound tightly by land and sea. The Viking spark lingers, but welfare and ease have dulled its flame. Order replaced daring. Security replaced risk. It is a land of quiet civility — honesty prized, taxes deep, streets in order. Beneath it runs *"Janteloven"* — the Law of Jante — don't shine too brightly. It pretends to be humility. In truth, it is a cage. And too many Danes are proud of it. **The serpent built his nest there.**

I learned to quiet my voice, to dampen my fire. Yet hunger smoldered — for mountains unseen, skies too wide for Denmark's horizon. I was a child in the wrong country, speaking the wrong tongue. We had little — hand-me-downs, a small table — but my mother cooked from scratch. Each meal was a lesson in aim and endurance, proof that survival was still sacred work. My mother worked hard, but she made the work beautiful. She taught me how to cook — and that remains one of the best gifts she ever gave me. I learned early that *food wasn't a product; it was covenant* — between soil, sweat, and grace. Real food wakes the soul. It roots you in the land. It sharpens your senses instead of dulling them. Most no longer know the difference — full stomachs, empty spirits. I was raised to taste life itself, not its imitation. Restlessness drove me into the Danish Home Guard — six years in uniform, sergeant, live rounds, secret clearance. From the outside it looked like ceremony; inside it was preparation. We trained for the war that never truly ended — Russian jets over the Baltic, coded alerts, the Cold War's ghost still breathing beneath polite treaties. I learned to fight what Denmark pretends is distant but quietly prepares for. We trained for NBC warfare — nuclear, biological, chemical — the unspoken trinity of modern apocalypse. I learned how to seal a mask before the air turns poison, how to read wind like scripture, how to move through contamination zones when breath itself becomes a weapon. We studied artillery by silhouette, tanks by traction, defense under collapse. Fifth-column drills in forests and city streets — rehearsals for invasion from without or within. We calculated what others refused to imagine — blast zones, wind paths, the math of loss.

It was less about numbers than nerve, less about weapons than will —
discipline under silence, composure under command. We learned to
obey without flinching, to stand when reason said run. From the outside I
looked composed, precise, reliable — everything Denmark demands of
its daughters. Inside, I burned. And when the world later masked itself in
fear, I recognized the ritual. I knew the protocols, the filters, the physics
— and I knew what was missing. What they called safety was theater.
The air was never the enemy; the lie was. Denmark gave me discipline
and demanded silence. It formed me, but it could not hold me. To keep
the fire alive, I had to leave. I wandered — across borders, oceans, skies.
Through cities where empires had fallen and markets where nations
bartered their souls. I studied faces, flags, and tongues — searching, testing, waiting. Everywhere carried lessons. None carried home. **One land
was already calling — not with comfort, but with covenant.** I wasn't
ready yet. The time had to ripen; the fire had to be tested — in silence, in
exile, in witness. Denmark taught me order; the journey taught me faith.
The North gave me roots, but the wind was already calling West. I know
this because I lived it. I was raised inside the silence, trained inside the
order, steadied by comfort — and I almost forgot the fire.

The Crossing - From Silence to Fire

I am an immigrant — not of convenience, but of calling. The fire carried
me across oceans into a land both promise and paradox. I came to
America not to blend, but to remember — to test whether freedom still
breathed. What I'm about to say, most Danes would never dare — not
even when the room is empty. But I am no longer bound by that silence.
My tongue was forged in another fire — one that bows to neither kings
nor committees. So brace yourself. There will be snakes — many of them
— hissing cowardice through polished words and moral theater. Let
them. My fire cannot be canceled by snakes. Their venom burns out in
the light. I do not speak with filters. I do not speak their split-tongued
dialect. I do not answer to them anymore — I am no longer one of them. I
never was.

This is the tongue of the North — the voice of covenant, not compromise. The serpent will hiss. I will answer with fire. And so I crossed — not to find a new world, but to remember the one I had carried all along.

America — The Dream That Found Me

Before I ever set foot on American soil, it lived in me. As a child I drew what I could not yet name — snow-capped mountains, a river below, a sun that never hid behind clouds, a little house in the middle of nowhere with a road that kept going. I tried to read English before I could, sounding out letters like a code to a future life. It felt as if my first language had been misplaced at birth. I wasn't born in the wrong body. *I was born in the wrong country.* America was the Statue of Liberty to me — an image of welcome and warning, torch raised over water, a promise that somewhere, someone still believed in breath. Denmark was black and white — wind, cold, and a sky pressed low. Summers were reprieve — bare feet, salt water, and long light that refused to die. The rest was hush. *Don't speak too loudly. Don't dream too brightly. Don't outgrow the frame.*

So I escaped in pages. Scheherazade whispered through the nights. Davy Crockett cut trails through wilderness. Robin Hood bent his bow against lords. Joan of Arc burned with heaven's voices. Odysseus braved storms and sirens. Asterix laughed at Rome's might. The Brothers Grimm warned of wolves in grandmother's clothes. The Greek myths thundered with gods and monsters — mirrors of powers that still walk among us. The Nordic sagas spoke in real time. Treasure maps promised rebellion. Every outlaw, wanderer, prophet-in-disguise became my secret kin. They weren't stories. **They were signals.** They whispered a covenant: *do not bow. Do not shrink. Do not settle for cages disguised as homes.* I swore I would not stay caged. I would chase horizons. I would claim the map. In my mind the world burned with color; around me it lay in gray. Something older pulled — a compass beneath memory, a fire that refused to die, a voice that would not be silenced. It pointed *west* — toward frontiers, toward freedom, toward the place where silence ends and fire speaks.

In fifth grade, English arrived like a door unlocking. By seventh, they pressed German on us. I could not pretend. My ear was already tuned to wide vowels and open skies. **German barked orders; English breathed invitation.** One built walls; the other built wings. When I spoke it, the vowels felt like wind in my chest.

At ten, I finally stood in New York. The city spoke back. The skyline rose like a vocabulary of stone and steel; neon was its grammar. Every horn, every shout, every subway roar was punctuation written for me. I was ten, but I knew: this was the language I had been waiting for. On top of the Empire State Building I whispered, *"One day, I'll live here."* That day I saw the contradiction that still defines her — a stranger's hand in my hair, the homeless on the sidewalk, a city blacked out yet still alive. America wasn't perfect. But it was real. And that was enough. It didn't just attract me.

It chose me.

Vermont - Where Frost Forged Fire

At fifteen I returned to America, not as a tourist but as an exchange student in a small Vermont town. For the first time, America wasn't a dream — it was a house, a family, a table I sat at every night. The family was big and loud, nothing like the Danish quiet I had left. A father, a mother, and four adopted children — twins, an older sister, an older brother — all under one roof. I was thrown into chaos, sharing a bedroom with two other girls, no privacy, no stillness. If I stepped into the wrong room at the wrong time, voices rose sharp. I didn't understand the rules. *I didn't yet understand America.* The food shocked me too. Where I came from, meals were simple, steady, alive — pulled from soil, not factories. Here the table overflowed with sweetness, grease, and colors that came from a box. Sugar was everywhere — in bread, in milk, even in what they called fruit. It filled me, but it never fed me. I was always hungry, chasing energy that vanished as fast as it came. So I ate more — not from greed, but from lack. I arrived thin as a stick; I left heavier, stronger, my body marked by new muscle from the sports I threw myself into — strength forged against a diet of empty calories that filled me but never truly fed me. Yet in that chaos — between excess and effort — something deeper formed: *endurance, discernment, and a hunger for what was real.*

The father became a quiet anchor. He had fought in Korea, worked thirty-five years for the New England Telephone Company, never complained, never boasted. Even cancer couldn't break him. He taught me to ski, to hike, to taste sap from maple trees, to laugh at TV with a bowl of popcorn. He was always cheerful yet serious — light when it was time to laugh, steady when it was time to stand. A man who guided me, and the first I truly loved like a father. The mother was a different breed. Tough, quick, always moving with so many kids under her roof. She had heart, but her voice was often loud for me. I learned to stay alert around her, to read the moment before I stepped in — another kind of discipline. She taught me resilience in a different way: not all love is quiet, and some of it arrives shouting.

She pushed me into track and field. At first, I hated it. Running the hallways in winter, air heavy and suffocating, my lungs raw. But my coach — who was also my English teacher — saw more in me than I knew. Even when I did well, he said, "You can do better." He never let me settle. On the track he forged grit; in the classroom he sharpened my mind. In his vocabulary class I discovered the bones of words. Greek roots, Latin roots — meaning beneath meaning. *I began to see language as more than speech, as structure, as power.* That combination stayed with me. From him I learned two laws: *don't quit, and never stop digging for the root.* That year we won the state championship, but the medals meant little. What lasted was *grit, endurance, loyalty*, and the lifelong hunger to run, to move, to stay fit, to never let stillness cage me again. And in that town, on the track and in the halls, I was no longer foreign. American friends challenged me, cheered me, shared their lives — and their open arms I will never forget. It was a frozen place, but their warmth made it home.

Lesson — Strength is not gifted. It is forged. If you think grit is born in ease, you have never trained in frost. True strength suffers first. Then it endures. I learned that hunger isn't only of the body. It is the ache that comes when comfort replaces purpose — when you forget what fire feels like.

Jakarta - The Fire That Baptized Me

Leaving Denmark was escape — but Jakarta was a crucible. Suharto's Indonesia was heat, chaos, survival. Smiles, incense, ceremony — and beneath them, rot and shadow. Yet it was *alive* in a way Denmark never was. Rice fields shimmered. Children ran barefoot. Families slept in huts open to the air. I lived on Java and trekked through Sumatra — weeks in the jungles of North Aceh, a land that would later be wiped off the map by the tsunami. The air hung heavy with rain and rot, beauty and danger intertwined. Bali was the mask — beaches and incense, ritual and glamour — but Java and Sumatra were the heart: raw, unpredictable, unsterile. Indonesia overwhelmed every sense — the smell of cloves, the hiss of snakes, the pulse of drums in the dark. And it was not just land — it was *faith. I lived in the world's largest Muslim nation.* Five times a day, the call to prayer cut the air — echoing across streets, through mosques, through dreams. Indonesia carried a gentler Islam than the Middle East, but it was everywhere, and it was loud. Faith there was not private or optional; it ordered the day, the street, the silence — and it taught me what it means when belief leaves the heart and governs the air.

In my office, the clash of faiths sat around one table — Muslims, Christians, Hindus, and a few secular voices. They ate together. They laughed together. They managed to work together — but tension never left the room. Complaints whispered in corners. The Muslim woman claimed prayer breaks — but others muttered she used them as naps while they kept working. Privilege disguised as piety. I noticed how some colleagues played sharper, quicker games of office politics, while others moved slower, more hesitant. Even their pace mirrored belief. To understand, I learned some Bahasa Indonesia. I wanted to eavesdrop, to cut through the surface. But language only opened doors — it didn't reveal the architecture. What stunned me was not the words — it was the way things worked.

In Denmark, you can hand a man a task and he runs with it — owns it, solves obstacles, delivers results. Indonesia moved differently. Staff arrived immaculate — smiles, pressed shirts, polite bows. But beneath the polish lived kampung rhythm — communal, cautious, shaped by deference, not defiance. When I handed out work, the first obstacle stopped them cold. They waited — for permission, for reassurance, for hierarchy to move first. What a Dane finished in a day could stretch into weeks. At first I bristled. Why couldn't they act? Why couldn't they just do the job? But Jakarta was not Denmark. It taught me that obedience can come from respect, that hesitation can be a form of survival. I learned that not every delay is laziness — sometimes it's protection, sometimes it's trust waiting to be earned; sometimes it's lack of skills. Jakarta trained me in a new discipline: composure when nothing moves, humility when surrounded by danger, patience where control had once been my creed.

I worked as a technical advisor, walking a tightrope between corruption and expectation. That title gave me access to a world where foreign influence was both courted and resented — welcomed in daylight, resisted in shadow. Everyone was paid through the same invisible machinery — a pyramid of favors and fear. At the top sat the minister or governor; beneath him, layers of loyalists who controlled contracts, permits, and access. Each circle fed the one above it. Money flowed downward; obedience flowed up. It was not chaos. It was choreography. Meetings looked formal. Reports looked professional. But behind every delay was a demand, behind every signature a toll. Power was not measured by law, but by how many lives you could make wait. And if you challenged it, you paid. That's when I learned the truth: **corruption doesn't thrive in disorder. It thrives in order — in paperwork, in protocol, in silence.** Everyone plays their part. Everyone eats — and everyone knows the cost. And once you've taken from the table, silence becomes your duty.

At work, I uncovered theft — money siphoned into a private account. In Denmark, theft earns termination. In Jakarta, it earned *me* an interrogation. A table. A pistol. A translator. A threat: rape, prison, silence. It was theater — intimidation staged to remind me: *this is our ground, not yours. Our rules. Our warning.* Do not cross the line again. My years in uniform steadied me, but I saw the truth — in this place, honesty was not virtue; it was liability. And here I learned the meaning of *rubber time* — time that bends. Meetings that waited while a man showered, ate, lingered, arrived when he pleased. It was not forgetfulness. It was control. Then the earth itself convulsed — a 7.6 quake. Windows shattered. Walls swayed. I didn't run. I walked — slow, deliberate, curious. I wanted to see what the world does when the ground betrays trust. Jakarta stripped away illusion. It was my baptism by fire. The world doesn't burn only in history books — it burns now, and it burns in silence.

Welcome to the Ring of Fire. 🔥

Lesson — Jakarta taught me that power rarely announces itself with violence. It governs through faith turned into atmosphere, obedience disguised as respect, and corruption dressed in procedure. Where belief leaves the heart and orders the air, dissent becomes dangerous. Where order replaces conscience, theft becomes protocol and silence becomes survival. Corruption is not born from chaos — it is maintained by systems that look professional and feel inevitable. Fear enforces what guns only threaten. This is not a foreign disease. It is a human one. And if you think this cannot happen where you live, you are already inside it.

England — Between Tradition and Turmoil

After Jakarta, I returned to Denmark — but I no longer fit. The air was heavier than the tropics. Rules, roles, expectations pressed in like walls. Every day felt like suffocation — power games behind polite faces, hidden agendas dressed as consensus, knowledge enforced as truth. I had tasted something freer, and the smallness was unbearable. So when England came, I was ready. I would spend six years there. Long enough for roots. Long enough to raise children. Long enough to watch the mask slip. Rain without end. Grey skies pressed low. London was packed — heat in the Tube, wealth in the windows, grime in the alleys. Polarity everywhere: money and hunger, polish and rot, heritage and decline. The city was alive, loud, organized chaos. The contrast with Denmark stunned me. The fire found no rest — only refinement. In Denmark, city and country shared the same rhythm — order, civility, restraint. In England, the divide was a canyon. The countryside was still British — rooted, traditional, calm, carrying history in every hedge and cottage. London was something else: global, restless, rootless. A marketplace more than a homeland. People came to rise or to flee, but rarely to belong.

I felt both welcomed and kept at a distance. British politeness had its sir-and-madam charm, but also its armor — the stiff upper lip, holding intimacy at bay. Humor was part of that armor. It made you laugh, made you feel included — even while keeping you outside the circle. Every joke was a handshake that never quite let you in. Immigrant families clung together for survival. The British themselves were courteous, sometimes warm, often closed. They opened doors just wide enough for you to glimpse in — but never enough to enter. Their vocabulary was rich, their manners polished, their humor — a weapon. I expanded my English here — words as armor, wit as blade. British and Danish humor share Viking blood, but differ in strike: British sarcasm erodes while it laughs; Danish hits blunt with honesty. British understatement mocks itself; Danish hides pride. Both wound. Both work. In England, humor wasn't escape — it was empire's mask, a smile hiding control. England sharpened me. It was where I first felt the fracture between order and truth.

It was a step closer to freedom. Yet something kept tightening — a familiarity I had hoped to outrun. Then I saw the empire's shadow. Foreign money bought the streets. Britons were priced out as immigrants poured in. They joked England would sink. It wasn't funny. The ship was sinking, and natives were being thrown overboard. I loved the land but saw the decline — roots traded for profit, culture for convenience, soul for survival. Today we see speech arrested, neighbors silenced, natives displaced. The rot didn't start now. It began then. And I watched the first cracks spread.

Lesson — England taught me that tradition is not nostalgia — it is infrastructure. When a nation no longer requires newcomers to enter its culture, the culture fractures. Imported communities do not dissolve on their own; they organize. Politeness delays conflict but does not prevent it. Courtesy without courage becomes surrender. Empires do not fall to invasion alone — they sell themselves piece by piece, smiling as they go. England taught me that decline wears a gentleman's face.

California — The Place That Taught Me What I'm Not

England was becoming too intense, too overrun. The dream was no longer the Old World. It was the New. And everyone knew what that meant — *California.* I pictured sun-drenched beaches, bronzed bodies, health and freedom under an endless sky. The land of opportunity. Small coastal towns. Citrus and fruit trees heavy with color. The smell of ocean, salt, and possibility. That was the California I dreamed of. Instead, I landed in *Silicon Valley* — and the dream shattered. Behind farmers markets, organic smoothies, yoga and mindfulness talk ran a famine of the soul. Tech obsession. Performative virtue. Relationships as transactions. Titles opened doors; without them, you were invisible. Smiles were masks. Dinners auditions. Even friendship carried calculation. It was never meant to be home. For most, California was a staging ground — make money, be seen, cash out, leave. That was its creed: **Temporary. Transient. Transactional.** In twelve years I met more people than anywhere else, yet never saw less rootedness. Barely any friendships that held. Disconnection wasn't an accident. It was architecture. In the Denmark I left it was the opposite — friendships for life, honesty without polish. California was a garden paved over: *alive in appearance, dead at the roots.*

I watched failure mocked and success built on connections. In Danish expat circles, I saw the same hunger — talk of *"hygge"*:, of home, of roots — but most weren't there out of love for America. They were there for leverage: wealth, status, a title to wear. And beneath it all, something darker was happening. Homes bought in cash by foreign investors. Shopping malls with Chinese signs beside English. American parents pushing their children into Chinese lessons — not curiosity, but belief. **Belief that China was the future and America the past.** When I questioned it, they frowned — not puzzled, but offended. Then they turned their backs. It wasn't investment. **It was surrender.** Silicon Valley preached tolerance while silencing dissent. I felt it often — the glance, the scan, the unspoken verdict: *not one of us.* I refused to bow to their tech lords and their **gospel of globalism** — most of all, to their quiet admiration of tyranny dressed as efficiency. It wasn't politics. **It was values.**

Their arrogance ran in the bloodstream — status carved not in faith or legacy but in ZIP codes and school names. They bragged about it like a creed. Hollow. Then came the mask behind the mask. A white liberal man — polished, fluent in the language of virtue. Over dinner he said it plainly, without a blink: white women were inferior — lazy, uneducated — compared to Asians. This was his creed. In public, he preached tolerance. Quoted diversity like scripture. In private, he bought goods made by slaves and spoke with quiet contempt. Virtue was his costume; disdain his marrow. That was the day I understood what it meant to be white — not as pride, but as accusation. Not identity, but original guilt assigned by fashion. I saw the sickness clearly then. **Tolerance had become camouflage. Justice, a costume.** When morality becomes performance, it loses its soul. *Not the color of your skin — but the content of your character.* And hypocrisy wasn't one-sided. Some hid behind a conservative mask, preaching virtue while practicing decay — condemning others for sins they soon excused in themselves. I saw it across colors, classes, and parties. Babylon wears every flag. **For twelve years I lived in California without taking citizenship.** Not because I couldn't — but because I wouldn't. The America I saw was not the one I dreamed of. I had come searching for covenant — for liberty, grit, and faith. But I found theater. Freedom had become performance. Patriotism a brand. Faith, a slogan. Comfort replaced courage. I loved the land, but I could not trust its rulers. **I could not pledge to a flag flown by men who despised its meaning.**

The Disruption

But politics caught me anyway. The Valley could sneer, but the ground was already shifting. Then came Trump. Disruption in human form. Straight talk. Provocation. Fire that broke the spell. He didn't play their game; he exposed it. I recognized the instinct immediately — the refusal to bow, the contempt for polite lies. There was Viking blood in that defiance, and it spoke to something old in me. When the choice came — Hillary or Trump — there was no dilemma. Had she won, I would have left. But he did. And I stayed. I didn't know it yet, but the disruption was only the trumpet. The war would come after.

This is where some of you will flinch. Your pulse will quicken. Your jaw will tighten. Notice it. Pause. Ask yourself why a single name can cause reason to collapse into rage. That reaction has a name — Trump Derangement Syndrome — but labels matter less than honesty. If you can press past the reflex, you may see what I saw. Not a man to worship, but a mirror that made the system blink. Not a savior, but a signal. A crack in the façade. **A voice that refused to kneel.** *The war was never for power. It was for permission.*

After that, I chose.

In 2017, I became an American citizen — one of the proudest moments of my life. It was not casual. It was covenant. Not paperwork, but an oath. A binding. A new name written into my blood. That vow changed me more than any place. Denmark gave me birth. California showed me masks. But America gave me covenant.

Studying for citizenship opened my eyes in a way Denmark never had. In those pages I saw not just laws, but legacy. Not just history, but fire — a Republic born in defiance, held together by courage. Looking back, I believe every immigrant should be required to walk that road before establishing themselves in this nation. Before careers. Before benefits. Before permanence. Visas and green cards should never become short-cuts around commitment. Knowledge of America's history, its values, and its cost should be common ground for anyone who works here, lives here, and builds here. Why? Because naturalization is not paperwork. It is a vow. A binding promise. And vows matter. Today the debate circles citizenship — who can run, who can serve, who belongs. But the older question is loyalty. Some born here betray the soil that raised them; others, born far away, would die defending it. Birthplace alone does not bind a man to a flag. Sacrifice does. I came with two passports, but one home. I laid the other down the day I became a citizen. You cannot serve two masters. You cannot belong to two homelands. A divided heart builds divided nations. Give people a choice — America, or the other — and you will see who stands when the fire comes.

This nation was built by immigrants — legal ones, forged in hardship and hope. But many have forgotten why their ancestors came, what they fled, what they built, what they vowed. **They traded inheritance for convenience and courage for comfort.** Citizenship without covenant is fraud. Allegiance without sacrifice is theater. Dual allegiance fractures nations. A house split between comfort and conviction cannot stand.

California gave me joy — but never where it claimed it lived. Not in Silicon Valley. Only in the escapes south, among people still capable of work, laughter, and life. For a short season, it fed me. Then the rot arrived there too. When I left California, I finally understood what I was not. Seven years passed before I returned, only for days. I felt no pull. No grief. No home. It told me everything — and meant nothing. Perfectly ordered. Perfectly efficient. And utterly soulless. A system that functioned, but did not *belong* to me.

Lesson — California taught me that wealth without roots breeds contempt, and freedom without covenant becomes theater. A culture built on leverage cannot sustain loyalty. When belonging is optional, character erodes. When virtue becomes performance, power answers to nothing. Globalism does not require love of place — only usefulness. And a system that rewards masks will always punish truth. Citizenship without covenant is fraud. Prosperity without allegiance is surrender. **A place that asks nothing of you will never be defended by you.**

Texas — Fire That Woke Me

California was dark — masks of virtue, rot beneath, arrogance posing as light. I could feel the tension, the coil tightening, something grim approaching. If I stayed, the fire would suffocate. Two years before the world shut down, I fled with my family to Texas. From the first small town, I felt it — life still human. People looked one another in the eye. Children sat beside parents instead of screens. Flags rose at football games. Freedom wasn't theory. It was breath. What shocked me most was the faith. A church on every corner. I didn't understand it at first. I wasn't convinced yet that Jesus was everywhere — even though the signs outside the churches literally declared *He is Risen*. It made me smile, half amused, half curious. Slowly, I felt safe to say His name. To wear a cross. To whisper: *Jesus is my Savior.*

The spirit of Texas was everywhere. Strangers spoke. Engaged. Welcomed me with words I had never heard in California: *"Welcome to Texas"*. It warmed my frozen soul. Sometimes I spent more time talking with strangers in stores than I did shopping. This was before the great exodus from other states. Texas was still itself. Friday night football shook the ground. Packed stadiums. Families cheering in rain or heat. Tradition. Belonging. Intensity. Belonging had a sound — drums, chants, cheers rolling like thunder. And the "ma'am" — that one word made me feel seen, respected, the way Madam had once done in England. Manners weren't formality. They were covenant. Wealth was different too. Big homes, nice cars — but not Silicon Valley flash. Not IPO bragging. Quiet grit. Businesses built without boasting. Men and women who didn't need to shout because their lives spoke louder.

The land was flat compared to California's coasts and mountains I used to run and bike. But Texas had lakes. I learned lake life. I ran wilderness trails with coyotes, bobcats and snakes at my side, trained for half marathons in 100°F heat, and fell in love with skies that burned orange at dusk. There is nothing like a Texas sunset. It's fire. It reminded me that heaven still paints reminders when earth forgets.

Texas restored my belief that America still breathes. Here, faith was alive. Guns were normal. Grit was expected. People were real. Businesses were built, not posed. Conservatives didn't cry or cave — they stood. They didn't take lies. They didn't bow. I met veterans — warriors of quiet conviction. We spoke of war, weapons, God, grit, and freedom — in ways I had never spoken before. They taught me things no classroom could. Small lessons. Silent codes. And I met others like me — freedom-loving exiles from other lands, men and women who had lived through threats, war and tyranny. *They carried the same fire. The kind that comes only from having already faced the serpent and survived.* **Texas reintroduced me to America — the real America.** But the fire was carried by men I met across the nation, warriors whose scars still guard our freedom. Their stories came next.

The Warriors

I want to share two stories, because they marked me — two men, two veterans. Different states, different lives, but both carried war in their bones. Through them I learned more about fire, trust, and covenant than any book could teach. Both became friends. Each carried scars; each tested truth in his own way.

The first I met years ago, somewhere on the western coast. Scarred by battle, restless and rootless, he moved like a man half in this world, half still deployed. Once, during a long hike, he stopped, looked at me, and said quietly: *You know we are all alone. I could kill you here and no one would ever know.* It wasn't a threat. It was a test. He lived in hyper-vigilance, measuring trust through provocation — if fear flashed, the bond broke. He wanted to know — *Are you steady? Can you see the man behind the dark?* It was his way of saying, *Here's the shadow I carry — can you bear to look at it?* And I did. That day a line was crossed. The mask fell. A deeper friendship began — not built on comfort, but on truth. His scars weren't mine, but in standing steady through his test, my own fire was confirmed. **Warriors don't choose each other. They recognize each other.**

The second I met years later, deep in the heartland. He had served long — a marksman, haunted by the precision that once defined him. His discipline was iron, his solitude carved from years of vigilance. He spoke of rituals before missions — not pride, but survival. And of the nights when those rituals failed, when the past returned and the silence pressed too hard. He carried the weight of duty like a millstone, the cost of obedience that outlives war itself. Through him I learned that *covenant must outlast combat — that the remnant must carry both sword and mercy.*

Both men carried scars, but I did not see their wounds alone. I saw *guardians — strong men who had stood where most Americans never will.* Yet they shared one thing in common — the struggle to dull the pain. Silence. Not weakness — survival. A way to quiet memories that never stop burning. But every warrior finds his own way to bear the fire. Some drown it in whiskey. Others build empires from the ashes — businesses, brotherhoods, purpose forged from pain. I have met many of them over the years, each carrying his war differently. This is why I bring you their stories — so you will remember them, and through them, see all the quiet veterans scattered across America. I see them everywhere — on roaring bikes cutting through Texas storms, tattoos and battle scars mapping their flesh like scripture of sacrifice. In grocery aisles, silent men with eyes that have seen more than we can bear to imagine.They walk among us unnoticed, but their scars are why this country still breathes. Freedom still bleeds through them. I honor them because I understand what they carried — and what they gave — so that America might not be shackled by compliance, hollowed by silence, or surrendered to the serpent's rule.

But Texas was its own battlefield too. The war was not only fought overseas; it had come home. And here, I saw whether the covenant still lived — or whether even the last bastion would bend. *Then came the order:* masks on, heads down, knees bent. The bastion obeyed. Even here, Texas bowed. But I refused. I homeschooled. I would not kneel. No mask. Babylon would not take my child, and it would not take my breath.

And that's when I saw it — the Californians had followed us here. Fleeing their empire, but dragging it with them. Too many poured in, wanting Texas land without Texas spirit. I wondered — why didn't they stay in their own land instead of trying to ruin ours? Because empires always export their poison. I loved Texas and I still do, but I wondered too — maybe it was time to disappear. Because something was off. Where were the remnants? Where were the fighters? Why would they allow the governor to close down their businesses, mask up their kids, and allow this circus? Why did we not repeat the Alamo? We are Texans after all! But too many bent the knee. And that was the shock — Texas, the last bastion, still bowed. We were not California. We believed in *God, grit, and guns — not government*. And yet, for a moment, even here, fear crept in. The serpent probes every stronghold with fear, then mocks it with scorn. That was when everything shifted. During the "plandemic," I opened the Bible in a new way. I read daily. I prayed daily. I spoke to God as if He sat across the table. Conviction deepened. Understanding widened. Faith anchored. I stopped looking to politicians or governors for guidance. — not that I ever truly did — and looked to Him instead. And still, I wrestled. Some days I ran from the weight — chasing freedom in the open road, reckless miles just to feel alive. I tried to drown the torment in motion, but the road never answered. *Only He did.*

Some Texans stood when others bowed. I watched them — and I still do. They are the true patriots, the remnant that would not yield. When the world shut its doors, they kept theirs open. When fear ruled headlines, they ruled themselves. These are the voices you still hear across Texas — the ones who never fell for the propaganda, who never hissed the slogans, who remembered who *they* were the day he came down the escalator — the moment the division of spirit began, when Americans had to decide whether they would think for themselves or surrender to the hive. Not because they served a man, but because they refused to be ruled by one. It was never about politics. **It was about the human will — whether truth would still stand when fear demanded it kneel.**

Their fire fed mine. Their courage awakened something ancient in me — the warrior code that remembers covenant before comfort. I recognize them because I am of their same kind. Their strength is not rebellion, but remembrance. They stand with Alamo resolve — not for fame, but for faith. They pray with dust on their boots and conviction in their bones. *They know Who delivers victory.* And because of them, I have hope. But now I know something deeper: they are not standing by chance. *They were chosen.* The soil of Texas has always carried covenant — men and women forged to guard freedom with blood, sweat, and prayer. They may not all see it yet, but heaven has already marked them. **The Remnant are not a resistance; they are a relay — carrying fire forward through the dark. Watchers for America.** Standing in the breach when others kneel. Fighting when others flee. The serpent knows this — which is why he presses here. If Texas falls, America falls. When Texas holds, the flame spreads. The Remnant in Texas fight not only for themselves, but for a nation's covenant — for generations not yet born. Politicians can fall. Governors can betray. But covenant cannot break unless abandoned. And the war is not unseen. Every covenant summons its adversary. Every flame invites the wind that tries to snuff it out. Ever notice how many snakes coil on Texas soil? Snakes follow heat — and there is no heat like holy fire. That is why the serpent circles Texas: it smells covenant, senses flame, and knows what happens when ordinary men and women remember who they are — and Whose land this truly is.

"Paul gathered a bundle of sticks and laid them on the fire. A viper came out because of the heat and fastened itself on his hand. But Paul shook the creature off into the fire and suffered no harm." — Acts 28:3–5

The serpent always emerges when the fire burns. Heat draws out what hides. What the enemy means as venom becomes proof of authority. *Fire exposes before it destroys* — revealing what slithers beneath comfort, then consuming it. **Covenant fire does not negotiate with serpents. It casts them back into the flame.**

Lesson — Texas taught me that freedom is not an idea, a vote, or a slogan — it is a covenant lived daily in flesh and bone. It survives where faith is spoken aloud, where men carry responsibility without applause, and where belonging is earned through standing, not posting. Manners are not weakness; they are order without coercion. Grit is not anger; it is endurance under truth. I learned that *fear is the serpent's first probe* — not because a people are weak, but because they are strong. Every covenant draws opposition. Every fire draws out what hides. Authority collapses when it rests on comfort, but covenant endures because it demands sacrifice. Freedom does not live in institutions; it lives in people willing to bear its cost. Texas taught me that liberty is never inherited intact. It must be reforged in every generation — or it will be surrendered in one. If freedom lives only in slogans, it will die quietly. If it lives in choice, labor, prayer, and scars carried without complaint, it will burn beyond empires. This land is not just soil. It is altar. And as long as the fire remains, the serpent will circle — and fail.

Come and Take It.

"The Lord your God is a consuming fire, a jealous God." — Deuteronomy 4:24

Into the Last Frontier

After the madness swept the world — fear saturating everything, voices breaking into panic — the noise had become unbearable. Headlines. Crowds. Slogans. The world shouting itself hoarse. So I went north, because something in me would not release. North was the last frontier — the wild edge of America, the wilderness the empire still pretends is untamed. At first it looked like heaven — snow on the peaks, wide valleys below, clouds like banners stretched across a blue so pure it cut the soul. The air was sharp enough to make you honest. The water clear enough to show you your own reflection. The silence wasn't empty. It was alive — a presence. I came to Montana to breathe, to build, to listen. I thought I was coming for peace. But God had other plans. What looked like peace was ice. The fire was inside me all along, waiting for the cold to draw it out.

I still remember my first Montana handshake — a Native elder, eyes bright with mischief and mercy, breath heavy with whiskey and spirit. We met at a gas station off the highway. The wind was brutal, the air sharp as glass — the kind that wakes you up. He hugged me before he spoke. "Welcome home," he said. He didn't mean geography. He meant recognition. We stood there a long time, trading words that felt older than we were — stories of land and loss, of what survives storms. When he stepped back, he didn't look away. His gaze held — deep, steady, searching. I smiled and waved, but he kept watching, as if trying to place me in a memory older than both of us. In his eyes I saw something ancient — something the world forgot but the land still remembers. I didn't know then how much truth hid in that greeting. This land greets everyone. But it keeps only those who can endure silence. Montana doesn't yield itself easily. It watches first — to see if you are real. Men have broken covenant before. The land remembers that too. What is not guarded is never given back. And when the silence finally let me in, the shock came quickly. I had believed Montana would be refuge — the last clean horizon, the place where freedom still meant something. But the frontier I expected was already being *rewritten*.

The same spirit that ruled the cities had crossed the mountains — disguised as progress, polite, proud, certain of its own virtue. What I had fled had followed. The peace I sought turned to ice, and God used the cold to show me what kind of fire I carried.

Montana - From Fairytale to Fire

Yellowstone painted paradise. Hollywood sold the myth. Tourists arrived chasing costume — hats, horses, curated cowboy dreams. But the locals knew better. They had lived beyond the postcards. Here, silence carried weight. Mountains stood jagged as memory. Survival demanded grit — woodcutters, hunters, ranchers whose handshakes still outweighed contracts. They lived covenant with the land. This was Montana — not wilderness to conquer, but ground that tested those who dared stay. An altar, not a backdrop. Then came the money. First millionaires. Then billionaires. Ranches became trophies. Cabins gave way to compounds. What had been lived was rebranded and sold. The myth became market — and the market devoured the soul. Newcomers arrived with coastal plates and coastal confidence — wearing hats and boots without scars. Performance, not covenant. They called it progress. I called it displacement. They did not come to join the land; they came to manage it. And it only takes a few signatures to tilt a valley.

Now the loudest voices no longer live in the mountains. They live behind gates — selling the water, signing the contracts, shaping policy from living rooms that overlook land they did not earn. Taxes climb. Bureaucracy thickens. The state takes more while giving less. And as symbols change, authority quietly shifts. Flags rise that did not grow from this soil — Pride, Ukraine, anything but Montana, anything but America. Symbols precede systems. Language follows power. New gatekeepers speak in acronyms and borrowed virtue — DEI, ESG, CSR — imported frameworks laid over the land like varnish, sealing decay beneath polish. They call it progress. It is something older: empire, refined. Polite. *Administered from elsewhere.*

The Foreign Spirit

The soil remains, but the spirit turns foreign — money imported, morals manufactured, management masquerading as mercy. Borrowed virtue is waved over stolen ground and called good. Even the headlines answer to voices far away. They call it local, but the strings run past the state line. In a small university town — once shaped by land and season — the pattern surfaced early. Quiet. Polished. Unmistakable. The newcomers brought more than wealth; they brought a worldview. Procedural. Credentialed. Certain of its own benevolence. Power no longer rose from place or people; it arrived pre-approved, fluent in policy and insulated from consequence. Here, the arrangement was unusually visible. Two mayors — not in rivalry, but in sequence. One elected and present. One unelected, enduring. A public face that rotated, and a governing script that did not. Civic authority spoke with a double tongue: representation above, management beneath. Less democracy than administration. Less leadership than stewardship-by-proxy. The frontier governed on behalf of interests that would never stay for winter. The serpent prefers this structure. *Local hands. Distant masters. Continuity without consent.* What arrived wasn't just money. It was a mindset — a foreign spirit dressed as progress, preaching compassion while practicing control. Power that cannot be voted out has already crowned itself. People no longer vote for leaders they trust. They vote against systems they fear. Elections have become acts of containment, not expressions of vision.

And every crowned system marks its territory. When a city raises a banner that did not rise from its soil, did not emerge from its history, and did not bind its people by shared sacrifice — it is not signaling inclusion. It is signaling allegiance. Flags are not decoration. They are declarations of rule. They answer one question only: *who is sovereign here?* A municipal flag is meant to represent the whole — land, people, memory, law. When it is replaced or overshadowed by an ideological banner, the message is precise: **governance no longer flows upward from the people; it flows downward from a creed.**

The symbol changes because the authority has already changed. This is how succession happens without ballots. Not tanks. Not speeches. **Symbols first. Language second. Policy last.** When ideology is elevated to the level of civic identity, dissent becomes heresy by default. The flag does not ask consent. It assumes submission. That signal was not sent to the people who live there. It was sent *over* them — *to those who recognize the code.*

"You shall not set up a pillar, which the Lord your God hates." — Deuteronomy 16:22

Between the Land and the Beast

Real men still work this land — branding cattle, mending fences, riding before dawn, praying for rain. Wranglers still lead city people down wild rivers and through forests that refuse to be staged. Wilderness teaches the same lesson every time: it cannot be curated. This is still the Wild West. In Yellowstone, tourists still wander into a bison's path and learn too late that the wild does not negotiate. The land does not bend to comfort; it breaks it. I've sat with these men in the high country — sunburned necks, scarred hands, speaking little because weather and work already said enough. I have spoken with hunters in small towns who track elk through silence and live by an older law: take only what you can carry, waste nothing, give thanks. They live in covenant with creation — not ownership, but stewardship earned through restraint. And even they feel it now — the tightening. Each year brings another regulation, another permit, another leash slipped quietly onto what was once governed by honor and necessity. They are pressed between the ground they love and a system that sees land only as an asset to be managed. The wild always knows first. The air changes. The silence shifts. Something foreign moves through the valleys — wealth without wonder, ownership without covenant. A land without stewards is a land already being claimed. This Beast does not roar; it regulates. It does not conquer; it manages. It arrives wearing virtue and leaves holding the deed.

They call it protection, sustainability, progress — but the earth knows the difference. The elk know. The rivers know. The soil remembers covenant, even when men forget. Stewardship becomes ownership. Control never asks permission. It enters quietly — convenience first, compliance next. Gates rise where there was sky; rules replace responsibility. The Beast no longer devours by teeth. It signs. It files. It smiles.

The Generations Who Forgot

They were the locals — born here, rooted here, names carved on mailboxes and gravestones. Their fathers broke this ground with prayer and sweat; their mothers kept lamps burning through winters that would break lesser men. Once, they lived covenant with the land. Then the flood came — money, migration, management. Outsiders bought the view; developers paved the meadows. Prices climbed, wages sank, and the quiet beauty was traded for noise and asphalt. Lawlessness followed the money — illegal migration enabled by policy negligence, bringing drugs, trafficking, and violence into towns too small to absorb the chaos. This was not accident. It was allowance. The locals felt the theft immediately — the land slipping, the heritage thinning. Their anger is not imagined. Their grief is not misplaced. But grief that never becomes guardianship curdles into spite. Pride without purpose becomes its own captivity. Too many now defend land they no longer tend. They speak of heritage while avoiding the labor that sustains it. They invoke their fathers' names but not their fathers' discipline — memory without stewardship, roots without obedience. Heritage without honor becomes performance. Roots without resistance become relics. Some raise their voices; others raise barns. Some shout about decline; others keep working and say nothing. And some claim to fight while bound to institutions already fallen — dependent on prestige, permission, and approval they pretend not to need. The same blood that once built the valley now watches its undoing through a screen. Complaint has replaced cultivation. Nostalgia has replaced responsibility. **Progress arrived because the land was left undefended in practice, not rhetoric.** And the Beast they once blessed now knocks at their own doors. Progress, they called it. Now progress wants their land.

"Do not be afraid of them. Remember the Lord, who is great and awesome, and fight for your brothers, your sons, your daughters, your wives, and your homes."
— Nehemiah 4:14

Those Who Hold the Line

The irony runs deep. Montana holds one of the highest veteran-per-capita rates in America — yet the flag they bled for is the one you rarely see. Pride. Ukraine. Every banner but our own. The land is filled with men who once carried rifles through desert and jungle, who buried brothers under foreign suns, who came home to find their own soil flying borrowed colors. They returned to a nation that spoke their names but forgot their price — parades of hashtags, policies wrapped in progress, applause without memory. Yet they carried the weight quietly — as if loyalty itself were an unspoken vow.

Those who praise "progress" rarely raise the flag. They sneer at patriotism, as though gratitude were beneath them. They skip the days that remember the fallen — too busy praising systems they never built, enjoying freedoms they never bled for. They call it progress. I call it amnesia with a crown. *The enemy within doesn't burn flags — it forgets them.* **The world changed its banners; the warriors never changed their oath.** Most pass them by — unaware that the man in line at the feed store once shouldered a rifle for the same freedom they now scroll past. Or that the butcher behind the counter — tattoos up his arms, scars like maps of battles no one remembers — still wakes to the sound of ghosts. He slices meat, wipes his hands, asks about your day. You never see the images behind his eyes — the brothers who never made it home. These men carry history in their flesh, yet few look long enough to read it. And if we forget the language of their scars, we will forget our own freedom. I've met many of them — delivering furniture, hauling lumber, laying stone. Contractors, builders, drivers. *Ordinary work, extraordinary men.*

I always took time to hear their stories. Beneath their quiet humility, I saw what most miss — the warrior still alive behind the eyes. **Men who once did the unthinkable so the rest of us could live as if freedom were ordinary.** They never ask for thanks — only truth. In their presence, I was reminded what covenant looks like when it walks on two feet. They are the keepers of covenant — the sentinels who remember. The ones who still rise when others fold their flags into slogans.

Every unraised flag is a silence that dishonors the covenant sealed by blood. Everything but remembering is treason — to the soil, and to the men who defended it. When a nation forgets its defenders, it forgets its covenant. And when covenant dies, freedom follows. **Freedom doesn't vanish in battle — it dies in forgetting.** They did not replace the American flag with another banner because they hated symbols — They replaced it with symbols that demand nothing of them.

Greater love has no one than this, that someone lay down his life for his friends."
— John 15:13

From Covenant to Compliance

Once, knowledge here served the land. It was practical, local, accountable — tested by weather, harvest, and failure. *The land-grant idea was simple: educate a frontier people to endure.* Build engineers who could bridge rivers, agronomists who could feed towns, teachers who could pass down wisdom that survived winter. Truth had dirt under its nails. Then covenant gave way to contract. Federal money and prestige replaced local responsibility. The land-grant became grant-dependent. And whoever funds the mission starts writing the mission. What once rose from the soil began reporting upward — to agencies, foundations, donors, and fashionable "standards" set far from the valley. Now the same halls that once served farmers train managers. Laboratories chase grants instead of truth. Students chase credentials instead of competence.

The frontier mind is being replaced by the bureaucracy of the frontier — polished, obedient, frightened of consequence. They call it innovation. But too often it produces compliance: credentialed, confident, and unrooted. And the locals took the bargain. Paychecks from the very institutions hollowing their towns. Comfort dressed as survival. Grants disguised as stewardship. *The conquerors didn't come with guns. They came with funding — and a pen.*

"Wisdom cries aloud in the street... 'How long will you love simplicity and hate knowledge? Turn at my reproof; behold, I will pour out my spirit to you.'" — Proverbs 1:20–23

The Few Who Still Stand

I still know of a few who show up — who speak truth when it costs them. Too few. The silence of the many drowns them out. Most bow quietly, afraid to lose a job, a name, a friend. **When the soil no longer holds courage, even the proudest lineage turns to dust.** Yet when the crowd bows, a few always remain standing. They are the thread that stitches history together — the ones who held the line when empires fell. They stood in fields and courtrooms, in pulpits and prisons. They hid families under floorboards. They crossed oceans with a Bible and a rifle. They faced tyrants with truth, refused to bow to kings, and lit fires that still burn centuries later. Their loyalty is not loud, but it lasts. And they are still here — scattered across the ridges and river towns of Montana. You find them in feed stores and county meetings, in barns turned prayer halls and cafés where the talk still has backbone. Welders and widows. Veterans and shepherds. Young men who still remove their hats when the anthem plays. They don't wait for orders. They take up the quiet work of keeping what remains free. They mend what's breaking. They stand when others scroll. They look weary — weathered by years and winters — yet their eyes still carry that old knowing. They don't always understand the Beast — its technology, its algorithms, its coded lies. I've seen the snakes around them laugh: polished men with soft hands, mocking the old ways as relics.

But I've also seen what endures when systems fail. Hard work still feeds when algorithms collapse. Supply chains still depend on hands, not dashboards. Bread comes from fields, power from labor, safety from men who show up — not from servers humming behind locked doors. Honor still builds when profit burns out. And in the end, I would take one man of soil and spirit over a thousand men of code who have never carried weight, risked consequence, or kept a town alive when the trucks stop coming.

"So this is what the Sovereign Lord says: See, I lay a stone in Zion, a tested stone, a precious cornerstone for a sure foundation; the one who relies on it will never be shaken." — Isaiah 28:16

The Serpent's Game

I had seen the pattern before — across regions, movements, and causes — but in Montana it finally sharpened. The stage was smaller, the players closer, the mechanics exposed. Different colors, same game. The velvet smile I had known in Denmark returned — the quiet warning not to cross certain lines. That was enough. I understood the oath clearly: never trade truth for belonging, and never stay silent when cowardice demands it.

Texas had taught me the heartbeat of the grassroots; Montana showed me its mirror — how power behaves when it thinks no one is watching. I wasn't a politician, only a witness with a pen. But when you know what to look for, the machinery reveals itself — the pulleys behind the flags, the donors behind the deals. I watched one circle from within, another from the outside. Different names, identical outcomes. You don't need spies to see how small-town and state politics play out — only eyes that notice who posts, who flatters, who fears, who they mingle with, and who falls silent when truth walks in. Power hides the instant it senses exposure. Follow the money — and you will find the altar.

Donors steer the table. Gatekeepers decide who speaks and who stays silent. The rules reveal themselves without explanation. Every system appoints a face for the rule — polite, credentialed, and never accidental. They play their games beneath the mountain's shadow, certain no one sees. But truth watches, and the land keeps witness. Every lie leaves a footprint. And that was the revelation — a new kind of cowboy had come to town — a mercenary in a Stetson. Not rooted, not accountable, loyal only to the highest bidder. **He doesn't ride for the brand; he rides for the bank.** He dresses well, speaks smooth, smiles wide, and calls it progress. But covenant cannot be bought, and loyalty can not be leased. **Empires don't die by invasion; they die by transaction.** And when the last deal is signed, the land remembers. When comfort becomes king, covenant becomes a costume.

The Silenced Majority

I have spoken with people from every stratum of life — farmers and waitresses, veterans and single mothers, hunters and students; men with calloused hands and weary eyes, and those whose power travels through boardrooms, donor lists, press passes, and political backchannels. I have met the poor and the wealthy, the builders and the bankers, the governed and those who quietly govern. They all knew something was wrong, but didn't know what to do — the governed, not the beneficiaries. Property values inflated by outside capital, then harvested through reassessment and rising levies. A second-home wealth tax in practice — even when the property was never a commodity. It wasn't mismanagement. It was design. Soft expropriation, executed by policy, applauded as progress. *Design leaves signatures. And signatures are eventually read.* Public speech had become whispers. Decisions were made without consent. Money flowed from far beyond the county line. Taxes climbed. Families sold. Towers replaced homes. Permits multiplied without permission. They called it progress. The people called it theft with paperwork.

The snake system hisses on — polite, procedural, protected by silence. I listened to these people — men and women too weary to shout. Taxed, trampled, labeled, ignored — they don't ask for miracles, only to be heard before another permit buries another piece of their history. They never voted for what was hidden in their bills, or policies that reward lawlessness and punish the law-abiding. They never voted to surrender their towns — but that is what is being done in their name. Sometimes I wonder why the locals haven't done what their grandfathers would have — driven the deceivers out of town and rolled them in tar and feathers. Maybe they're too decent. Maybe they're too tired. Or maybe they're waiting — for one spark, one voice, the moment silence finally breaks. Truth may whisper for a season, but when it speaks, it levels empires. The judgment fell silent — and in that silence, the land gave its witness. The land had shown me its people and its politics; now God would show me mine.

"In you they accept bribes to shed blood; you take interest and make profit from the poor. You extort unjust gain from your neighbors and you have forgotten me, declares the Sovereign Lord." — Ezekiel 22:12–14

The Remodel — The House That Tested Me

I lived in Montana with every sense. I fished her rivers where the current spoke like scripture. I watched bison move through snowstorms like ghosts of a braver age, and black bears with their cubs wander Yellowstone's quiet mornings. I rode horses through dust, rain, and snow, herded cattle across the ridges, kayaked wild water, and swung a club on mountain fairways carved between thunder and sky. I swam in lakes so cold they baptized the breath. I tasted the wind off the Rockies — sharp, pure, alive. Elk moved like a living tide across the valley. White-tails wandered past my desk while I wrote. Beauty was never distant here; it pressed against the glass. I endured two winters with no garage — digging the car out before dawn, shoveling snow so others could reach the property. I stacked wood until my arms gave out, and the ache lasted for weeks. When storms came, they tore fences and roofs like paper.

The lights failed, the grid went silent, and I learned to trust the satellites above — Musk's network stitching wilderness to the world. Even the bees died without explanation, and a giant fox came for the chickens before the moon had set. I used to joke that I wasn't in a Siberian gulag — just Montana's version of one. Not because it was cruel, but because it demanded everything: *endurance, adaptation, humility*. Montana gives what you need — not always what you ask for. It humbles the proud and heals the weary. It teaches how small you are, and how holy that can be. Here, the wild isn't out there; it lives in your own backyard. I didn't love every challenge — but I survived them. They carved strength into bone and spirit and taught me what no system ever could: God's creation is not meant to be managed by man. We were never meant to become gods. Man builds towers and names them progress. God names stars and calls it worship. The more we reach for control, the more we forget our scale. True strength begins where pride bends — under heaven, not above it.

"When I consider your heavens, the work of your fingers, the moon and the stars, which you have set in place — what is mankind that You are mindful of them, human beings that You care for them?" — Psalm 8:3–4

But above it all was the remodel — the furnace I never expected. What began as restoration became refinement. Four years of hammer and dust, men in and out, noise thick enough to drown prayer. Some days I worked alone, hands raw, voice gone. Other days I hired help — too often the wrong kind. Overpriced. Careless. Half-done. Promises broken. Work redone. Men who smiled, took the check, and vanished before the paint dried. They thought I was just another newcomer with money. They never saw the calluses — or the covenant. They had no pride in the craft, no reverence for the work. Yet sometimes a good man showed up — quiet, skilled, honest — and reminded me that *not all fire destroys. Some fire refines.* The house became a mirror. It showed how easily beauty turns to burden when hands lack honor. It taught how betrayal can echo louder than hammers. And it proved that silence isn't always peace — sometimes it's exhaustion dressed as stillness.

I thought I had come to build a home — maybe even to settle for good. But God had a different plan. He was building me. He stripped the noise from my fire, the people from my comfort, and the ease from my prayer. I wasn't proud — just untempered. I could see wickedness and strike without mercy, but I hadn't yet learned what it costs to wield truth with grace. Every wall became a test. Every season, a sermon. Winter buried progress; spring unearthed new battles. People came and went like storms — contractors, neighbors, even friends. What I thought was abandonment was pruning. Some people aren't taken from you; they're removed for you. Montana wasn't rejection. It was refinement. *Through the storms, the noise, the broken promises, and the isolation — God spoke.* Not in thunder. Not in lightning. But in the kind of silence that rearranges the soul.

It wasn't the peace I came for. It was the furnace I needed. The cold around me drew the fire within me higher. He spoke in the rhythm of the shovel, the strike of the hammer, the ache of hands that refused to quit. Every failure became instruction. Every delay, discipline. When the walls cracked, He showed me where my own foundations were weak. When people disappeared, He showed me who never belonged to the covenant in the first place. It took four winters to learn that refinement is not punishment. It is preparation. Fire doesn't arrive with comfort; it arrives with clarity. He stripped everything that dulled the edge — anger, noise, applause — until obedience was the only voice left. And one night, in the stillness after the final storm, I felt it — not a whisper, not a vision, but a force that moved through bone. A pulse in the hands. A weight in the chest. A voice that knew my name. He pressed fire into my flesh — not a gift for ease, but a covenant for war. A warning carved in bone. A weapon forged in spirit. **And then one morning it happened.** I woke before dawn and went straight to the computer, driven by a force I could not name. It was 5 a.m. — and the words came like fire on dry grass. The next morning was the same. And the next. For months I rose in the dark and wrote until midnight, barely stopping to breathe. Revelation did not trickle; it flooded. Every day something new — sharper, deeper, heavier than the day before. This is what you are holding now — the record of that fire.

What poured onto those pages is what you are about to read in the chapters ahead. *The page became altar; the pen, a sword.* Creation turned to obedience — revelation taking form in ink and breath. The noise of the world faded. Only command remained. Montana was never my home; it was my forge. Every snowdrift a sermon. Every wound a witness. I came to build a house. I left carrying a commission. The land did not teach me to stay — it taught me to stand. **Refinement was not the end — it was my enlistment.**

"Behold, I have refined you, but not as silver; I have tested you in the furnace of affliction." — Isaiah 48:10

The Land Still Sings — elk moving like shadows through timber, snow falling like hymns, skies torn open by storm. Rivers run wild and cold; fly-fishers stand mid-current, casting lines like prayers into living water. Hunters still track through snow and silence, honoring the covenant between hunger and grace. Hikers climb where ridges scrape the sky; skiers carve through powder that feels like flight. The wild still holds fire — untamed, unbroken, alive. But false lights creep in — screens masking the horizon, money replacing roots, slogans rising where silence once spoke. Don't think this is only Montana. It's happening across America — from cities to small towns — only here the pattern reveals itself more clearly, the full play exposed in a smaller sandbox. The land will not lie for them. Soil remembers covenant, even when men forget. I love Montana — its land, its wild, its skies that sing. But the serpent has set his chair here, and *God made it clear: my fight is not in Montana.* This was the training ground where I learned the American game — how power hides behind courtesy and systems dress as freedom. Texas taught me the Constitution; Montana taught me the cost. The sandbox was a mirror of the nation itself, and without it, I could never have seen the board — or the players — so clearly.

The serpent no longer needs armies; he has comfort. He wins not by conquest but by consent. When truth grows quiet and courage grows polite, the soul of a people begins to die. I understand now why God sent me there. Montana was the mirror — the last frontier, the testing ground between covenant and convenience. It was where the mask of wilderness fell and the machinery of empire began to hum beneath the soil. The land that looked the freest was already being mapped, measured, managed. And yet, it was here I saw the last guardians — the blue-collar covenant keepers, the men and women whose hands still bear the memory of freedom. Montana showed me what remains when systems strip away comfort: the soul of a nation, raw and unpolished, still choosing whether to stand or sleep.

Lesson

Montana taught me that freedom is not preserved by beauty, myth, or tradition. It is preserved by **guardianship.** Land that is not actively defended — in practice, not rhetoric — will be claimed. First by money. Then by management. Then by ideology. The Beast no longer conquers with force. It regulates. It permits. It reassesses. It reframes theft as progress and obedience as virtue. Symbols change before systems. Flags rise before laws fall. Power that cannot be voted out has already crowned itself. People no longer vote for leaders they trust. They vote against systems they fear. That is not self-government. It is containment. Grief without guardianship decays into resentment. Heritage without labor becomes performance. Memory without obedience becomes nostalgia. A land defended only in words is already lost. Veterans carry covenant even when the nation forgets it. A country that forgets its defenders forgets itself. Institutions fall quietly, funded from afar. Bureaucracy is the modern Beast — polite, credentialed, relentless. And this is the final measure: **The last frontier is not land. It is loyalty.** Freedom does not die in battle. It dies in comfort. Covenant does not break by attack. It breaks when people choose ease over responsibility. Montana was not my home. It was my forge. It stripped illusion, tested endurance, and revealed the enemy without announcing him.

It taught me how to see the board — and how to stand on it without bowing. Every reader must answer the same question: **When comfort calls louder than covenant — which will you serve?**

80

"The wicked flee when no one pursues, but the righteous are bold as a lion." — Proverbs 28:1

Texas — Fire That Woke Me

For 4 years I lived between ice and fire. Montana taught me the ground; Texas put fire in my blood. The two do not mix easily. Montanans eye Texans like invaders — too loud, too sure, too quick to plant flags where silence once ruled. But beneath that tension lies something older — *recognition*. Fire recognizes stone; stone respects fire. Both breeds know the storm. Both are bound by land and labor. Decades before I came, the longhorns moved north from Texas to Montana. The Great Western Trail carved paths through plains and grit, Texas fire steering toward Montana earth. The bond was written in hooves and dust — a covenant of cattlemen and courage that bridged the frontier. The cattle drove north, but the fire drove deeper — into the blood of a people who still carry the storm inside them.

You don't stop being Texan — once it's in the spirit, you can't let it go. Texas is pride. It is grit. It is covenant. It's fire. You either feel it in your bones, or you will never belong. America needs both — the quiet of the ground and the courage of the flame. **Without ground, fire becomes wildfire. Without fire, ground becomes grave.** I came from the old world seeking truth in the new — and found it where ice met flame, where the land still remembered God. Montana is soil. Texas is covenant ground at scale. Montana can be infiltrated quietly — valley by valley, town by town. Texas cannot. Its size, its people, its faith, and its memory make it a fortress that must be confronted head-on. That is why the serpent presses harder here. Politics infiltrated. Schools subverted. Pulpits softened. Money flooding in from coasts and foreign hands. Babylon has marked Texas not because it is pure — but because it is powerful.

And we know — **If Texas falls, America falls.**

The Land They Mock, the Fire They Fear

They laugh at Texas. They always have. They call it flat, loud, reckless — a wasteland of guns, churches, and men too stubborn to kneel. They sneer at its faith, its flags, its fire. They roll their eyes at its drawl and call its courage madness. But **mockery is never random — it is always the mask of fear.** They don't hate Texas because it is crude. They hate it because it still remembers what they forgot. *Texas never bowed.* When other states traded covenant for comfort, Texas kept its sword oiled. When others built systems of compliance, Texas kept building things that could not be managed from a distance — land, families, faith, and work that required presence. The serpent always mocks what it cannot conquer. That is why every late-night host, every bureaucrat, every polished coastal prophet feels compelled to sneer at the Lone Star — because one free people standing on covenant ground threatens an empire built on managed minds.

They call it barren. But step out under a Texas sunset and watch the sky set itself on fire. The land glows with the color of courage — gold, blood, and dust. Yet between the ridges, oaks still stand like sentinels of memory, their roots gripping the soil that never forgot freedom. In spring, the prairies turn green again — not soft, but stubborn — the kind of green that survives drought and war alike. And then the bluebonnets come — not planted, not managed, but returning on their own, year after year, covering the land like a quiet promise kept. *You can taste honesty in the air. The wind carries prayer.* The *soil smells like sweat and salt and promise.* Lakes flash like mirrors between the hills, quiet sanctuaries beneath the roar of the sky. This is not wasteland. **It is holy ground disguised as hard ground.** California once burned with the same fire. So did the Carolinas, and the hills of Vermont. But comfort smothered their courage, and management replaced meaning. They dreamed of freedom, then forgot its cost. *Texas remembered.* One birthed the myth; the other kept the covenant.

You can mock Texans for their pride, but pride is what keeps a man standing when the world tells him to kneel. You can mock their guns, but a man who keeps his powder dry remembers the oldest truth — **freedom is not a gift; it's a responsibility.** You can mock their faith, but when the lights go out and the empire collapses under its own lies, you will want a neighbor who still prays. But it isn't the skyline or the soil that make Texas sacred — it's the people. They are kind without weakness, fierce without vanity. They open their doors before they ask your name. They listen before they lecture. They'll rib you with a sharp tongue and defend you with a sharper one. **They don't brag, don't beg, and don't break.** They laugh at the dark, work through the dust, and **hold the line without applause.** *Texans love masculinity and femininity both* — the father who builds, the mother who keeps, the children who grow knowing where they come from. **They don't need permission to believe in family, or in God.** There's a toughness in them I recognize from Viking blood — a strength that isn't loud, just ready.

Texas is not just a state. It's a condition of the soul. **It's the part of every American that still believes fire belongs to the people, not the throne.** That's why the serpent wants it silenced. That's why the cities mock and the elites sneer. They sense what's coming — that the remnant still burns here, and the flame is spreading. Mockery will not stop it. Management will not contain it. **The frontier didn't die; it moved south.** Every sneer is fuel, every insult a spark. Because the land they mock is the fire they fear — and that fire is about to rise. So I came home — to Texas, where the fire first found me. God did not call me here for ease. Not for comfort. For fire. His command was not a whisper but a war order — *fight when others flee, stand when others bow, speak when others are silenced, burn where others smolder.* Here the work will be brutal and beautiful. Here the few must be both shield and spark. These are my people. The watchers on the wall. Farmers with rifles. Mothers with Bibles. Veterans with scars. Teenagers who will not bend. **Texans who are not afraid to speak truth — whose fire lives in the tongue, not in the noise. Pastors who refuse platforms and preach covenant instead.**

We all have our task. Some guard the gates. Some till the soil. Some raise the next generation. Some build businesses that stay honest when the system rewards deceit. Some heal bodies. Some operate and save lives when seconds decide eternity. Some run toward the fire — police and firemen who hold the line when the world burns. Others guard souls. Some forge tools; others forge men. Some carry rifles. Some carry prayers. Some preserve history so truth is not erased. Some investigate truth when others bury it. Some write words that wake the sleeping. Some craft music that steadies the broken. Some create work that reminds us of God's beauty — not man's imitation. Some judge with discernment — men who know the law and the truth beneath it. Some build systems of light inside a world of code and shadow. Each task is a post on the wall — none higher, none lower, all necessary. My task was not chosen; it was given: to see through fog where others see nothing, to speak when silence grows heavy. I did not seek this flame; it found me. And once it burns in you, you cannot stay quiet. This is my story — one thread in the larger tapestry. The places I've walked do not speak for all, nor erase the remnants and embers still burning in hidden corners of this land. But this is the story I was given to carry. It is enough to mark the map. Enough to light the way. The rest will come in its time.

Lesson — Freedom is not isolation.

Texas taught me that freedom is not isolation and not comfort. It is **responsibility accepted without permission.** Montana taught me to recognize the enemy. Texas taught me to face him. Fire without ground destroys. Ground without fire buries. Freedom survives only where both are held together — courage anchored in place, conviction carried at scale. Texas does not endure because it is loud. It endures because some still guard the gates. Mockery is the empire's confession. It laughs at what it fears, manages what it cannot break, and sneers at those who refuse to kneel. Freedom does not die when it is attacked. It dies when vigilance is traded for comfort. Texas is not a sanctuary. It is a front line. Strength is not noise — it is readiness. Courage is not chaos — it is calm resolve. Freedom is not inherited. It is maintained. And the work ahead will be brutal and beautiful — because anything worth keeping demands both.

The Next Move

The strength is the discipline to live without fear in fair weather — and without hesitation when the storm comes. The covenant to guard what you love when the wind turns cold. Without faith you cannot rise. Without fire you cannot stand. Freedom without faith is no freedom — only a prettier cage. The serpent tests every fortress with fear, then ridicule. Texas is no exception. But fear and ridicule cannot quench fire. Fire spreads. Fire endures. Fire wins. And the serpent cannot inherit Texas. *Fire already owns it.*

The Threshold

What you have read until now was the approach. The witness. The forging. The alignment of sight. This book has carried you through land, memory, systems, and fire — not to persuade you, but to prepare you. What follows is not personal reflection. It is not commentary. It is not opinion. It is exposure. Every war begins disguised as something else. Every collapse is preceded by language that sounds reasonable, familiar, safe. That is how gates are opened from the inside. That is how empires fall without a shot fired. This book was built the same way — not as deception, but as defense. The stories were not the destination. They were calibration. The words were not ornament. They were instruments. What you have been given is not comfort, but orientation. From here forward, there is no gradual descent. The language has been defined. The board has been revealed. The fire is lit. What follows is the Fall — not as history, but as mechanism. Not as theory, but as pattern. Names will be named. Powers will be traced. What hides behind institutions will step into view. **Read carefully. Read precisely. This is no longer witness. This is the war.**

"Therefore take up the whole armor of God, that you may be able to withstand in the evil day, and having done all, to stand firm." — Ephesians 6:13

Welcome to the fire.

7

———

WORD WISDOM

ESSENTIAL TERMS TO GUIDE YOUR JOURNEY

Before we march further, you need a key. The world you're about to enter has its own language — forged in fire, not theory. Misunderstand the words, and you will misread the war. The serpent twists meaning before he ever strikes. So before I speak of battles, you must learn to see the battlefield hidden inside language itself. This is how I speak — and how I see. These words are not decoration; they are coordinates. Once you grasp them, you will see the pattern everywhere. Only then can you read what follows — not as rhetoric, but as reality. **Every war begins with words.** Every fall begins with twisted meaning. If you don't define your words, your enemies will. This isn't theory. It's survival. Every word is a frontline. Every definition, a weapon. The words in these pages are not neutral. They are shields. They are swords. They are maps through the fog. Words can bind a people or break them — crown a tyrant or topple him — enslave generations or call them to freedom. To follow this journey, you must know how I wield them — and why the enemy fears them.

Lose the words, and you lose the war.

The Fire

Not metaphor. Not sentiment. Fire is clarity, judgment, renewal. In Scripture, fire is how God speaks — the burning bush that is not consumed, the pillar that led through the wilderness, the tongues that fell at Pentecost. Fire is the sign of His presence and the test of His people. It destroys what is false and forges what endures. It strips away pretense until only truth remains. It does not negotiate or flatter — it consumes lies, burns away fear, and leaves only steel. *Fire is the trial every covenant must pass.* Gold is proven by fire. Weakness is exposed by fire. Without fire there is no purity, no courage, no rebirth. The system fears fire because it cannot be bribed. Fire cannot be censored. Fire cannot be tamed. Fire leaps borders and jumps walls. Once lit, fire spreads faster than their lies. Fire is the one thing the serpent cannot counterfeit — because it belongs to God alone. Every true word burns — speech itself is fire from the mouth of God, and every lie that resists it turns to ash.

"Is not my word like fire, declares the Lord, and like a hammer that breaks the rock in pieces?" — Jeremiah 23:29

Awake

To be awake is to see through the spell — propaganda, programming, fear. Awake is clarity. Awake is eyes open. Awake is illusion shattered. Awake is not the same as woke. Awake does not seek applause. Awake cuts through fog. Awake sees who profits, who scripts, who pulls the strings. Awake is not despair; it is sight returned to the blind. Awake is strength to name the serpent when others call it progress. Awake will not bow to the script. Awake is dangerous to the system. Awakening is only the beginning. Awareness without courage is chains. Awake eyes cut through every spell. To be awake is to reclaim the words the serpent stole — to see through language itself until only truth remains.

"Awake, O sleeper, and arise from the dead, and Christ will shine on you." — Ephesians 5:14

Woke

Woke is a counterfeit awakening — a theater of virtue built on grievance and guilt, where the blind lead the blind. They parade outrage like a badge. They chant slogans but never ask questions. They demand tolerance but cancel anyone who dissents. They rewrite words, censor speech, and call it progress. They perform compassion for the cameras but seethe with envy and fear. They kneel to culture but never to God. Woke is theater — chains disguised as compassion. Woke twists language until lies sound merciful and truth sounds cruel; it is the serpent's oldest spell spoken in modern tongue. Every slogan they chant is a stolen word — language turned against truth until lies wear halos and tyranny wears kindness.

"Woe to those who call evil good and good evil, who put darkness for light and light for darkness." — Isaiah 5:20

The Board

The board is the battlefield of our age. It is not one game but many — played in economics, culture, borders, faith, and power. The serpent thinks he already owns it, but the board is not his alone. Every piece, every move, every sacrifice shapes the future. Ignore the board, and you surrender the game before the first move is made. Language is the first move on the board — define the terms, and you shape the war before a single shot is fired. The board is not flat — it lives across dimensions. Every move, every word ripples through time, truth, power, eternity, and spirit.

"...so that we would not be outwitted by Satan; for we are not ignorant of his designs." — 2 Corinthians 2:11

The Knight

The knight is the unexpected move. The knight leaps in L-shapes while others march in lines. The knight sees beyond dimensions while others shuffle forward. Prophets move like knights — bending rules, vaulting over obstacles, rewriting the board. Where others see a dead end, the knight sees an opening. Where others follow order, the knight disrupts. Prophets do not just move; they speak moves into being — every declaration a strike across dimensions.

"For my thoughts are not your thoughts, neither are your ways my ways, declares the Lord..." — Isaiah 55:8–9

The Serpent

The oldest deceiver — first whisperer of half-truths. He no longer crawls through gardens; he coils through systems. The serpent corrupts by redefinition. He twists the holy into the useful, the covenant into contract, the free into managed. His weapon is not the sword but sugges-tion. Every empire he builds begins with the same hiss: *Did God really say?* His voice flatters intellect but poisons obedience. The serpent is the architect of language turned against truth — the author of counterfeit light.

"That ancient serpent, who is called the devil and Satan, the deceiver of the whole world." — Revelation 12:9

♨ **Firelight Pause**

Every so often, you will find a Firelight Pause. It is like sitting by your firepit at night — flames dancing, stars blazing, the Milky Way cutting across the sky. A Firelight Pause is not homework or performance; it is a chance to breathe, to reflect, to let the questions burn a little longer. Do not let the spark cool before you answer. Reflection without action is only smoke. Even in silence, words smolder — what you choose to name or leave unnamed decides whether the fire spreads or dies.

"His word is in my heart like a fire, a fire shut up in my bones..." — Jere-miah 20:9

Babylon

Babylon is not just an empire of the past. Babylon is the system — then and now: control built on seduction, pride, and lies. It raised towers to heaven, conquered Israel, mocked covenant, and was called the "great whore" in Revelation — dazzling, rich, intoxicated, yet destined for fire. Every age has its Babylon: ancient towers, Roman palaces, digital skyscrapers glowing blue in the night. Babylon stares from your phone and whispers through your feed. Babylon wears a smile, sells pleasure, and calls it progress. It promises safety, belonging, and luxury while it empties your soul. Babylon always burns — and always falls. Its power is persuasion — a kingdom built from vocabulary, ruling hearts through slogans instead of swords.

"Therefore her plagues will come in a single day... and she will be burned up with fire." — Revelation 18:8

The Babylonian Person

Not everyone rules Babylon. Many serve it — some knowingly, some blindly. They scroll for hours, trading life for distraction. They crave applause instead of truth. They sell loyalty for status. They rename compromise "wisdom." They rename cowardice "tolerance." Babylon builds hollow people — easy to steer, eager to obey, desperate to be seen. They mistake visibility for value and noise for purpose. But Babylon always falls. Stone towers crumble. Idols break. Screens go dark. What endures is covenant. What endures is fire. Babylonian souls are full of noise but empty of flame.

"For my people have committed two evils: they have forsaken me, the fountain of living waters..." — Jeremiah 2:13

Covenant

Covenant is what tyrants fear most — it binds men to something higher than the state. It cannot be legislated, taxed, or erased. Contracts end when power shifts; covenant endures when kingdoms fall. It needs no signatures — only blood, memory, and loyalty. The ancients knew this: Hebrews walked between slaughtered animals; Vikings swore oaths in blood. Break covenant, and the curse fell on your line. Covenant is life for life, family to family, heaven to earth. Through Christ it became eternal — not bargain but bond. Covenant is the language of loyalty that no bureaucracy can translate. Babylon offers counterfeits, but covenant is forever. Contracts collapse; covenant conquers. Covenant is language sealed in blood — words bound to eternity that no empire can rewrite.

"This is the covenant that I will make... I will put my law within them, and I will write it on their hearts." — Jeremiah 31:33

Patriot

A patriot loves their country — its land, its people, its memory. Patriot is not a slur, no matter how the elites twist it. Patriotism is loyalty rooted deeper than politics. A patriot defends the soil that fed their fathers and the freedom that guards their children. Patriotism is faith in motion — duty, sacrifice, remembrance. You will find patriots at parades, at graves, in town halls, on porches — carrying memory, teaching why liberty matters. Patriotism is fire rooted in soil and bound by covenant. To speak as a patriot is to guard the language of freedom itself — words like honor, duty, courage, and covenant that tyrants try to redefine. A patriot guards a nation's land, law, and memory — even when the soul of that nation is under attack.

"Do not be afraid of them... fight for your brothers, your sons, your daughters, your wives, and your homes." — Nehemiah 4:14

Remnant

The remnant are not just patriots. They are the few who remember when the majority forgets. They do not bend when culture demands it. They do not trade truth for belonging. They do not bow when Babylon calls. The remnant carry scars but still walk. They carry fire but still stand. They speak when rooms go silent. They build when others scatter. They endure exile but never surrender. They are keepers of covenant and guardians of flame — loyal to God and rooted in land. They love the soil that fed their fathers and the truth that guards their children. They wave the flag and bear the cross, not as symbols, but as vows. Their loyalty is not ideological; it is embodied. It costs them comfort, approval, and safety — and they pay it willingly.

"A remnant will return, the remnant of Jacob, to the mighty God." — Isaiah 10:21

The remnant are what happens when a people refuse to abandon either heaven **or** earth. When faith is not quarantined from land, and land is not severed from God. Loyalty made flesh. Fire bound to soil. They cannot be bought with money, silenced with shame, or broken with fear. They speak truth with fire and resist tyranny with courage. They wage war in two tongues — one of earth, one of heaven — both forged in truth. One such soul is worth a thousand subjects. A nation of them cannot be conquered. If they call you dangerous, take it as proof you are remnant. The remnant may be few, but they never fall. They guard the ancient words. They speak fire when others echo fear. They carry truth through the collapse of everything that once seemed permanent — and when nations fail, they remain.

"Five of you shall chase a hundred, and a hundred of you shall chase ten thousand." — Leviticus 26:8

The Watchman — The Watcher

The watchman refuses the lull of sleep. Trained in silence. Forged in exile. Awakened by fire. A voice at the edge before the breach. Eyes that cut through fog, naming threats the crowd mocks until it is too late. While others bow to comfort, the trumpet sounds. The wall is lonely, but it is holy ground. The watchman knows that darkness breeds armies while the people dream of peace. He sees the serpent coil before it strikes. He discerns the lie before it hardens into law. Not welcomed at the feast. Not crowned in the court. Yet he remains — bound by covenant, not applause. His first weapon is not the sword but the word: warning before the blade is ever drawn. Behind every watchman stands the Watcher — the One who sees the pattern before the move, who reads the silence before the storm. *The Watcher* does not predict; He perceives. And every true watchman is born from that sight. He sees through the serpent's fog because he has already walked through it.

"So you, son of man, I have made a watchman for the house of Israel..." — Ezekiel 33:7

The watchman's duty is not approval but warning. Whether the city laughs, stones, or listens — the call must go out. A silent watchman is already a traitor.

"If the watchman sees the sword coming and does not blow the trumpet..." — Ezekiel 33:6

The Language of War

Behind every theft of words stands a power older than nations. The serpent twists tongues, the dragon fuels pride, the beast builds systems. These are the spirits of war — they do not march in uniforms; they whisper through vocabulary. Every polite lie is a spell. Every slogan a charm. They script surrender in the language of virtue. Speak their words, and you fight for their kingdom, not Christ's. The final test is speech — which kingdom your tongue serves when silence is no longer an option. *"For we do not wrestle against flesh and blood, but against the rulers, against the authorities, against the cosmic powers over this present darkness."* — Ephesians 6:12

The Word Made Flesh

Only Christ restores language — because He *is* the Word made flesh. He does not sanitize; He sanctifies. He does not blur; He clarifies. Every remnant called to stand in this hour must speak His fire — not slogans, not silence, not softened truth. For when Christ speaks, chains break. When the remnant repeats His Word, Babylon trembles. *"In the beginning was the Word... and the Word became flesh and dwelt among us."* — John 1:1, 14

Hold these words as weapons. Let them sharpen your vision and steady your steps. Language is not neutral. Every word is a front line. Lose the meaning of words, and you lose the war before it begins. Remember this: the battle for words is only the first layer. Beyond it lies the board behind the board — the powers that command language itself. Wield words with precision, or they will wield you. A craftsman keeps his tools sharp. A remnant keeps his words sharper.

"Death and life are in the power of the tongue, and those who love it will eat its fruits." — Proverbs 18:21

The match still burns 🔥
The war for words has only begun.

PART II

THE FALL

THE QUIET BEFORE THE STORM

"The truth will set you free, but first it will make you miserable." — James A. Garfield

Denmark glows like a candle — steady, admired from afar. To the world it looks safe. Sacred. But lean closer and the wax is melting, the wick thinning, the shadows climbing the wall. The quiet is not peace. It is warning. The storm has already begun.

8

DENMARK IS NOT WHAT YOU THINK

Americans talk about Denmark like it's a moral vacation. Clean streets. Safe cities. Happy people. A perfect model to copy. They see the surface and assume the soul matches the shine. But Denmark is not a "better America." It is a different creature—**built on consensus, not liberty. Harmony, not confrontation. Order, not argument.** It doesn't train citizens to resist power. It trains them to cooperate with it.

In Denmark, control rarely arrives with a boot. It arrives with a smile. A rule. A polite correction. A gentle "we all do this." And because the country is small, the social field is tight. Everyone is close enough to feel watched without anyone ever admitting it. The pressure is not always legal; it is cultural. Not always explicit; it is ambient. A soft grip—stronger than a hard fist because you start enforcing it on yourself. That is the trick outsiders miss: the most effective control is the kind you call kindness.

Denmark doesn't need to censor you loudly. It can simply make speech socially expensive. It doesn't need to punish dissent aggressively. It can treat dissent as embarrassing. The individual learns early: do not stand out, do not disturb the peace, do not create friction. And once a population is trained to avoid friction, it becomes easy to manage—because truth always creates friction. This is why Denmark can look peaceful while becoming spiritually numb. This is why it can feel safe while shrinking the human soul. Comfort becomes the national drug. Approval becomes the invisible currency. And the citizen learns to confuse being "a good person" with being compliant. Then something reveals the core: crisis. During crisis, the Danish reflex is not "draw the line." It is "protect the group." The group becomes the moral authority. And when the group becomes moral authority, the state only has to speak once. After that, neighbors do the rest. Not because they are evil—because they were trained. **Safety becomes virtue. Obedience becomes compassion. And those who resist are treated not as free people, but as threats.** This matters because Denmark is not merely a nation. It is a **prototype—** polished, exportable, admired by elites who want the same outcome everywhere: **a managed population that calls submission "progress."** That is what I am about to show you. Not with slogans. With mechanisms. With receipts. With the anatomy of a soft tyranny the world keeps calling "perfect." If America cannot learn to see Denmark clearly, it will import the mask and call it the future.

Denmark and the Mirror

Denmark does not define itself through conquest, resistance, or founding struggle. It defines itself through *contrast*. Quietly, over decades, the national identity settled into a reflexive position: *we are the opposite of America*. Where America is loud, Denmark is modest. Where America is unequal, Denmark is fair. Where America is violent, Denmark is peaceful. Where America is free, Denmark is responsible. This contrast functions as a stabilizer. When America looks chaotic, Denmark feels civilized.

When America stumbles, Denmark reassures itself. That is why Danish media reacts so emotionally to U.S. politics. Not because America governs Denmark — but because America anchors Denmark's self-image. The reaction is predictable. Headlines amplify drama. Context disappears. The same villains are recycled. Not to inform, but to regulate emotion. It is not analysis. It is reassurance. Denmark depends on the United States in ways rarely acknowledged — **militarily, economically, technologically, strategically.** Yet dependence creates discomfort. And discomfort seeks release. So criticism flows upward. Anti-Americanism becomes a form of social currency inside Denmark. It signals sophistication. It signals education. It signals belonging to the "informed" class. It is safe, applauded, and cost-free. And yet beneath the contempt lies fascination. Danes consume American culture obsessively. They copy its language, its products, its aesthetics, its ambition — while publicly rejecting the source. They desire what they criticize. This contradiction is not hypocrisy. It is tension. America represents something Denmark has deliberately constrained: **raw sovereignty** — the willingness to risk, to fail, to act without permission. That kind of freedom unsettles societies built on **safety and consensus.** So Denmark watches America closely. Critically. Emotionally. Not because it hates America — but because America reflects everything Denmark chose not to be.

9

THE MASK OF DENMARK
THE HIDDEN CHAINS

If you're still here, you've already passed the first gate. Most turned back when the fire burned their comfort. You stayed. This is where the real war begins — where symbols become systems, and systems start speaking. The mask drops here.

This book is not for everyone. It is for the warriors — the remnant, the watchmen, the ones who still burn for truth. Not for those who bow to fashion, scroll for comfort, or bark for approval. It is for those who still remember freedom's sound — the steady drum of courage in a coward's age. So let's step inside the model they praise.

The Dream — Paradise With a Price

They tell you Denmark is a dream — free healthcare, free education, bicycles gliding through cobbled streets, candles glowing in windows, windmills guarding the future. The world sees a fairy tale — the bronze mermaid in Copenhagen's harbor, polished equality, rehearsed smiles. But fairy tales hide monsters. Denmark is not a dream. It is a prototype — the velvet cage built to be exported. What looks like paradise from afar is actually a laboratory where the West rehearses its future.

Look closer and you find not paradise, but sedation. Not tyranny with guns, but tyranny with grins. Not chains on the body, but chains on the spirit — peace without truth, comfort without courage. Most never notice the price. Politicians across the world point to Denmark as proof that socialism can be civilized, that democracy can be domesticated. Presidents and prime ministers call it *the model of managed freedom.* The UN hails it as a *"global sustainability leader,"* a *prototype for inclusive governance and digital welfare.* The World Bank praises its efficiency; the IMF calls it a *template for equitable growth.* American politicians hold it up like scripture — the "Danish dream," they say, where no one is poor, no one is left behind, and everything is planned just right. But paradise on paper always costs a soul somewhere. Behind the smiles and surveys lies the ledger. Taxes that swallow half a worker's earnings. Data systems that log every prescription, paycheck, and pregnancy. Algorithms that score families and flag citizens for "risk." Welfare offices that now function like financial surveillance hubs. The same state that feeds also watches. What the UN calls *trust,* the serpent calls *tracking.* The line between care and control was erased quietly — coded into digital welfare programs that decide who deserves help and who doesn't. A country so small it could experiment without rebellion. A culture so polite it could be managed without resistance. Denmark became the perfect lab — where the serpent could test obedience in high definition.

Even the press joined the choir. CNN named it *"the happiest country on earth."* The Guardian called it *"proof that equality works."* The EU Commission called it *"Europe's moral compass."* Yet no one asked why the suicide rate remains among the highest in the West, or why antidepressants fill more prescriptions than antibiotics. No one asked why dissent is mocked, or why humor has become state-approved. When conformity becomes culture, happiness becomes performance. And still, the lights glow warm in the windows.

The nation rehearses contentment. Candles. Coffee. Calm. *Hygge* — coziness as creed. But even comfort can be a crown of control. When every need is managed, the will to resist withers. When no one hungers, no one fights. What the world calls happiness may be sedation with style. The UN applauds. The elites applaud. The serpent smiles. Denmark — small, efficient, obedient — has become his favorite showcase. Proof that the new world order needs no chains or coups, only consensus wrapped in kindness. That silence turned on me too — not with rage, but with revelation. Clarity is always the enemy of control.

Janteloven — Politeness as control

In Denmark, rebellion is not crushed by soldiers. It is smothered by culture. "*Janteloven*" — the Law of Jante. They were not laws in the courts. They were heavier. They were laws of the air you breathed. The law of "Jante" comes dressed as ten quiet decrees — commandments with God removed. They whisper in every classroom, every workplace, every conversation.

Don't think you're *special.*
Don't think you're *smarter than us.*
Don't think you're *better than us.*
Don't think you know *more than us.*
Don't think you are more *important than us.*
Don't think you are *good at anything.*
Don't *laugh at us.*
Don't think anyone *cares about you.*
Don't think you can *teach us anything.*
And above all, *don't think you can't be replaced.*

These are not shouted with fists or guns. They are murmured until they seep into your bones. Each one is a quiet restraint — invisible at first, unbreakable later.

A child learns quickly not to stand out in school. An entrepreneur learns not to dream too big — the tax man waits. An artist learns not to speak too loudly — beauty must be polite. Live under it long enough and the fire in your chest grows cold. Or worse, you forget it was ever there. "Janteloven" is not just Denmark's curse. It is the serpent's spell in every land — Babylon's way — shrinking souls until they forget they were ever meant to burn. Even Søren A. Kierkegaard saw it — the same slow spiritual suffocation he called "leveling," where society grinds down the exceptional until all stand equally small. Greatness is mocked into silence. Depth becomes a threat. Courage is treated as arrogance. The goal is not harmony; it is sameness. A people convinced that the highest virtue is to never rise above the crowd will never rise at all.

And H.C. Andersen knew it too. Everyone remembers *The Ugly Duckling* as a sweet children's tale about discovering you were a swan all along. But that was never the lesson I learned. I did not grow up and realize I was a swan. I did something the swan never did — **I woke up.** The duckling becomes beautiful only when the world finally recognizes him. My awakening came when I recognized myself, even when the world refused to. The lesson was not that I was secretly elegant or chosen. It was that I was **never meant to belong to their pond** at all. Janteloven breeds ducks. Fire births something else entirely. Andersen's child saw the Emperor was naked. I saw the culture was, too — polite on the surface, hollow underneath. Truth never belonged here. Conformity did. This is Janteloven: not law in books, but law in the blood. The velvet cage before the iron one. Henrik Pontoppidan lived it — the gifted son whose fire could not breathe under Denmark's ceiling. His *Lucky Per* wasn't fiction. It was prophecy: a man crushed by a country too small for his spirit. A country that rewards sameness cannot tolerate fire. That is why the gifted leave, and the obedient stay. Denmark has always produced its truth-tellers — and punished them for telling it. Even its prophets were not spared. Those who tried to awaken the people were eventually softened, sidelined, or turned into symbols without fire.

From the outside, Denmark glitters — glass towers, curated careers, degrees and promotions, the endless climb. But behind the shine you find emptiness. A treadmill disguised as triumph. A life measured in compliance, not creation. A graduate hangs his degree on the wall, but behind the frame he feels only emptiness — another cog on the treadmill. The system doesn't fail. It performs exactly as designed. **Silence makes you compliant.** Taxes make you captive. Denmark perfected both. Nearly half of every krone is gone before it touches the table — forty-six percent of GDP swallowed by the state. A man opens his paycheck, already cut in half. A woman tries to save for a home, the account drains faster than she can fill it. A father hopes to pass something to his children, inheritance stripped before it reaches their hands. You do not work for your family. You work for the system.

The Tax Man — The Blood Ledger

And the toll doesn't wait for April. It bleeds you daily. A flat 25% VAT — on bread, on shoes, on repairs. Every bite, every step, every mile taxed. Try to drive? A car that costs $25,000 in America runs $50–60,000 there. Families pushed onto bicycles and buses, sold as "green policy." In truth, economic coercion. Even the light switch fattens the state. €0.376 per kWh — nearly half pure taxes and levies. A pensioner sits beneath a single lamp. Parents time the dryer, skip the sauna, unplug what hums at night. Electricity isn't service. It's leverage. And now the land itself. In 2024 Denmark became the first nation to tax farm emissions — 120 DKK per ton of CO_2, rising to 300 by 2030. One cow equals six tons. Hundreds of dollars per head. Picture a farmer at dawn — the barn that once thundered with life now silent. Generations that fed the world forced into bankruptcy by policy. Herds sold. Fields abandoned. Barn doors swinging open to emptiness. This is not sustainability. It is strangulation — engineered scarcity paraded as virtue. Every decree framed as progress, every slogan a mask for control. Even faith is taxed — 0.7% of every income siphoned into the state church. Not tithe, but levy. Even God nationalized.

In 2020 the Prime Minister ordered the slaughter of 17 million mink. Soldiers and police went farm to farm. Bulldozers dug mass graves. Generations of breeding erased in days. Imagine a farmer standing in his barn. The cages are still warm. His life's work piled into a trench by decree. The cries of animals silenced under soil. The press called it safety. The courts later called it unconstitutional. But by then the barns were empty. It was not public health. **It was rule by fear.** Then came whispers — turn in your pets to feed zoo animals. Not farms this time. Not industry. Your dog. Your cat. Picture a child holding her puppy while her parents read the notice. The message is clear — **if you can surrender what you love, you can surrender anything.** This was not about feeding lions. It was about training people to obey the unthinkable. This is psychological warfare. The slow sanitizing of conscience. The cull of empathy. **The killing of resistance before a bullet is ever fired.**

We've seen this before. **Every regime that tests loyalty begins by demanding the innocent. In the name of progress. In the name of safety. In the name of peace.** But the goal is always the same — to break the human bond before breaking the human will. Every empire has its moral theater — rituals that pretend to free people while teaching them to kneel. Denmark is no exception. Obedience is performed as virtue; absurdity paraded as progress. What looks like compassion is conditioning. What feels humane is control. The serpent always sells submission as empathy. Once you mistake obedience for goodness, your conscience becomes his crown.

In 2021 Denmark paraded a new "consent-based" rape law as progress. Abroad, headlines praised it as feminist leadership. But inside the courts, nothing changed. An estimated 24,000 women assaulted. 890 reported. 535 prosecutions. 94 convictions. Picture a young woman walking into court, case folder in her hands. Weeks later, she walks out again — case dismissed, attacker free. Her voice silenced, while the papers still praised Denmark as a model for Europe. Ledgers weigh heavier than lives. Justice bows to the balance sheet.

Denmark doesn't just host the UN. It crowns it. From Copenhagen's harbor, the UNOPS headquarters gleams with glass and steel — the sanctum of managed mercy. Inside, billions move without a ballot: climate enforcement, digital ID grids, "resilience projects" that bind nations in polished debt. To the public, it looks like charity. In truth, it is conquest disguised as care — empire written in spreadsheets. And while contracts tighten abroad, they train their women to smile on command — bureaucratic missionaries draped in moral language. Danes are taught not to fight, but to regulate. Not to build, but to bind. Their strength is not steel or soil but paperwork — a velvet hammer swung in the name of equality. This is how modern empires rule: not with armies, but with audits; not by invasion, but by invitation. The flag is kindness. The weapon is compliance. The kingdom is data.

Denmark supplies the muscle. Margrethe Vestager — Europe's Commissioner for Competition. She fines in billions: Apple, Google, Amazon, Microsoft. The Digital Markets Act. The Digital Services Act. Each decree branded as *consumer protection*. Each decree, in truth, a lever — **rules written in Europe, enforced in America.** A nation of six million exporting chains onto 330 million Americans. Without a single American vote. Vestager is not the exception. She is the emblem — the polished face of managed virtue. Denmark trains its daughters not for battlefields, but for boardrooms, NGOs, and Brussels pulpits — polite priestesses of globalism. They smile while they sign away sovereignty. They speak of fairness while drafting chains. They call it equality; it is empire in heels. And the world applauds, mistaking control for compassion.

January 2024. A monarch's voice trembled as she read her final words. Queen Margrethe II — Denmark's longest-reigning ruler — laid down her crown, the first in nearly a thousand years to step down alive. Palace walls heavy with lineage, marble cold with memory. Reporters called it humane, graceful. But the walls knew better. Cameras flashed, the anthem rose, and the applause was not for Denmark — but for surrender. Before leaving, she severed her own house — stripping titles from blood and redrawing the royal map. Some called it justice, some mercy, but power was rearranged, not relinquished. A thousand years of precedent ended with a pen stroke: monarch to manager, covenant to contract. It was choreography — a velvet coup applauded by globalists who crave symbols of order collapsing on schedule. Denmark did not lose a queen; it rehearsed the West's submission — heritage yielding to administration, throne to spreadsheet. The headlines said abdication. To me it looked like surrender — a covenant signed away and called progress.

For a thousand years, the crown bound covenant to land and lineage. Now it binds perception to power — commanding not armies, but optics. Thrones no longer guard borders; they guard belief. The Queen stepped down. The son took the throne. Then the grandson climbed into the cockpit. As Denmark retired F-16s for F-35s, cameras rolled — legacy sold as progress. The message was clear: the bloodline still rules the air. Succession became spectacle; power became performance. The crown didn't fall. It upgraded. Flesh merged with steel, heritage with hardware. Myth continued through machinery — progress as liturgy, obedience as renewal. A signal to those who watch: legacy still flies, dynasty still breathes, the serpent still coils — not on marble, but in motion. The serpent never destroys what it can reprogram. It doesn't topple crowns; it updates their software. It need not kill kings when it can teach them to smile on cue. So ask yourself — is that still a crown, or just another circuit in Babylon's machine?

🔥 Firelight Pause — The Velvet Chains

- Are you mistaking politeness for freedom while chains slide on with a smile?
- Do you laugh at humiliation disguised as "fun," training your spirit to obey?
- Do you applaud "progress" without asking who signs away your sovereignty?
- Do you still believe obedience packaged as culture is harmless — even as it teaches you to kneel?

This is Denmark. Not a dream. A velvet cage. It doesn't beat you into submission. It lulls you into it. Peace without courage is not peace. It is preparation for chains. And once you see the mask slip, you cannot unsee the serpent beneath. The cage has been revealed. The serpent cannot hide behind velvet forever.

"For nothing is hidden that will not be made manifest, nor is anything secret that will not be known and come to light." — Luke 8:17

Denmark was never the endgame. It was the rehearsal. What you've just walked through is not a museum of Danish policies — it is the velvet cage's first test run. The serpent's mask. The smile before the bite. Now cross the ocean. Watch how the cage travels — in contracts, in codes, in signatures. Watch how the prototype becomes your present. The rehearsal is over. The main act has begun. And if you've guessed it — this isn't about Denmark. It's about what's coming for us. The lab is real. The experiment is already running in America.

10

BUREAUCRACY BEFORE BULLETS

THE REHEARSAL

You saw the prototype. Now see the plan. What began as Denmark's discipline became the world's design. The serpent doesn't need nations to fall — only citizens to conform. This next chapter is not speculation. It's replication. And it's already here. Scripture warned us of this long before the screens did.

"By your sorcery all the nations were deceived." — Revelation 18:23

The velvet cage was only the beginning — a test run for systems that would soon run the world. Denmark is the serpent's proof-of-concept: if you can standardize a soul, you can standardize a nation — and if you can standardize a nation, you can standardize the world. What began as comfort became control; what began as order became obedience. Denmark was the mask. The export came next. Paper turned to power. Signatures to shackles. A nation became a prototype. The serpent moves now across oceans. This is not history. It is the present unmasked.

Exporting the Cage

What begins in Copenhagen never stays there. It travels. Policies written in Danish become laws in Brussels, and ordinances in Sacramento. What is tested in a quiet, compliant state becomes the blueprint for the restless ones. Denmark is not a small country — it is a laboratory. If obedience can be engineered in the North, it can be replicated anywhere. Carbon taxes on Danish farms echo as carbon caps in California. Electricity levies in Copenhagen show up as rising rates in Oregon and New York. Car bans there become EV mandates here. A pattern emerges – pilot becomes policy, policy becomes mandate, mandate becomes dogma. And once dogma hardens, dissent becomes heresy.

In August 2025, California Governor Gavin Newsom signed a Memorandum of Understanding with Denmark in San Francisco — a partnership framed around green growth, technology and innovation, and "digital and cyber resilience." An MOU is not a treaty. It doesn't bind like federal law. But symbolism often outruns statute: a governor on the world stage, inked beside a foreign minister, performing diplomacy in miniature. That is how the velvet cage travels now — not by invasion, but by coordination. Not by conquest, but by "partnership."

The Pen Before the Sword

Empire rarely begins with soldiers. It begins with signatures. This is not equivalence. It is a warning about method — how control moves before it ever marches. In Nazi Germany, the serpent coiled itself in documents — chains disguised as forms, power hidden in stamps and ink. The world imagines tyranny arrives with boots on cobblestones. It rarely does. It comes first as paperwork — agreements, memoranda, "understandings." The ink dries long before the people notice the walls. Every empire starts with a pen. Every free people forget this too late.

The serpent never invents. It repackages. Every age thinks its chains are new — digital, progressive, enlightened. Yet tyranny still wears the same uniform: paper, stamps, and the quiet force of compliance. What began in Reich offices returns as apps and algorithms — decrees reborn as data, obedience automated. In Germany, 1933–1945, paperwork didn't follow tyranny — it prepared it. By the time the boots arrive, the paperwork has already won.

The Kennkarte — compulsory ID card. Without it you were suspect; without it, arrested.

Today it returns as digital IDs, QR scans, biometric passes — glow-in-the-pocket papers deciding where you may go.

The Ahnenpass — ancestor passport proving bloodline; without it, no marriage, no job, no future.

Today it reappears as DEI gates, ESG filters, genetic databases, and credential tests — paperwork deciding who rises and who is denied.

The Lebensmittelkarte — ration cards for bread and milk; mothers tearing coupons to feed children.

Today it becomes carbon quotas, meat taxes, digital wallets tracking every bite — hunger by code instead of coupons.

The Verordnung — decrees stacked until obedience was the only air left to breathe.

Today it returns as EU directives, UN compacts, and climate mandates no voter ever approved.

The Sippenhaft — collective punishment; one member's "crime" condemned the whole household.

Today it returns as cancel culture, lawsuits, and social-credit penalties that erase entire families for one defiant voice.

The Sonderbehandlung — "special treatment," the cold code word for execution.

Today it appears as assisted suicide, medical mandates, and policies that decide who is expendable.

The Endlösung — the "Final Solution," the obsession to erase life itself.

Today it dresses in "Net Zero," "population sustainability."

Different words. Same obsession — Control life itself. The serpent always writes in paperwork. The forms change. The spirit never does. Every time the ink dries, a new chain is fastened — and because it comes as policy, not prison, the crowd applauds.

"What has been will be again, what has been done will be done again; there is nothing new under the sun." — Ecclesiastes 1:9

Media as Manager

The press sealed the spell. Danish outlets do not expose the serpent — they maintain it. They polish the mask, dull the fangs, and sell the illusion as truth. When facts cut too deep, they vanish. When dissent rises, it is mocked into shame. And because Danish is spoken by so few, the omissions never travel. To the world, Denmark exports polished slogans in English; inside, truth stays buried in Danish silence. Media there is not a mirror — it is the mask's caretaker. Without headlines, no chain would ever look righteous. They even proposed a Media Ombudsperson — a state-backed "watchdog" to decide what could or could not be said. Sold as accountability, it meant oversight over the overseers — obedience disguised as ethics.

In 2014, the Danish tabloid *"Se & Hør"* scandal ripped the veil: — journalists caught buying stolen credit-card data to spy on celebrities, politicians, even royalty. It wasn't reporting. It was surveillance dressed as curiosity. And "transparency"? A mirage. Denmark's Freedom of Information law lets ministries withhold whatever matters. Requests are stalled, delayed, denied — until stories die of silence. Files exist, but light never reaches them. The nation that boasts of openness has perfected bureaucratic fog. Even safety is managed by script. After police and intelligence pressured sources, the government announced a "Plan for the Safety of Journalists." *When power must publicly promise not to persecute the press, the covenant is already broken.* This is how the mask survives. Not with open censorship, but with curated omission.

Not with jackboots, but with inbox delays, legal fog, and professional shame. The choreography is global now — algorithms, "fact-checkers," *trust and safety* boards. The mask stays polished while the fangs sink deeper. *Truth doesn't vanish. It's smothered in courtesy.* And the pattern does not stop at Denmark's borders. The same strategy has been exported. At Nelson Mandela's funeral, the cameras caught Barack Obama, David Cameron, and Helle Thorning-Schmidt laughing in the pews. To most, it looked like bad manners. To those who watched closely, it was revelation: a *triangle of power*, smirking while history buried one of its icons. Later, Thorning-Schmidt rose as co-chair of Facebook's Oversight Board — the "Supreme Court of speech." Nick Clegg, Cameron's former deputy, became Meta's President of Global Affairs. *Two Europeans, unelected and unaccountable, now hold veto power over America's public square.* That is how empire travels today — not by armies, but by algorithms. Not by conquering land, but by curating speech. Denmark refines the mask in miniature, then exports it at scale. Three leaders laughing while the cameras rolled — certain the world would never decode the smirk.

 Firelight pause — the mask of media

• What headlines have you swallowed without asking who wrote them?

• What truths have you dismissed because the crowd mocked them first?

• When silence falls on a story, do you notice — or do you move on?

• If unelected boards in Europe now decide what Americans may say online, whose speech do you really hear — yours, or theirs?

• When a headline tells you "progress," do you ever ask: progress for whom?

The mask is never only Danish. It is global. And it hides best on the glowing screen in your hand.

The Prototype — Covid Obedience Enriched

2020 was the rehearsal. The serpent spoke in decrees, and the people obeyed. Think back - it didn't arrive with tanks or soldiers. It arrived with slogans, "science," and neighborly shame. *It arrived softly — but it cut deeply.* Masks, lockdowns, curfews. Overnight, freedom became selfishness; submission was branded as morality. Churches were shuttered while nightclubs rebranded as "cafés" and stayed open. Worship was silenced; entertainment survived. The absurdity was not a flaw — it was a feature - obedience tested in plain sight. Families were told how many could gather at their own tables. Police fined citizens for standing too close. Neighbors scolded one another in grocery lines. Elites moved freely; ordinary people were watched. The chain was not enforced by soldiers — it was enforced by fear, pride, and peer pressure. The velvet cage had grown teeth, and people clapped as they were bitten.

The mark came too. First on paper, then on screens. A vaccine pass folded like a ticket; the ticket became a platform, the platform a system. Later, a QR code glowing in your palm. Without it you could not travel, work, or eat. Different symbol. Same segregation. A star on the coat then. A code in the pocket now. We have seen this spirit before. In Nazi Germany, freedom died by paperwork before it died by bullets. Identity cards. Ration books. Passes stamped and checked. Families split by forms. Neighbors deputized as informants. Bureaucracy was the chain, fear the lock. The uniform came later. History wasn't repeating. It was updating. The same serpent, now clothed in apps instead of armbands. And it did not stop in Denmark. America echoed the same patterns. Children masked on playgrounds and schools. Pastors fined for opening churches while strip clubs stayed open. Families split apart by mandates at Thanksgiving tables. Employers demanding papers, universities barring the unvaccinated, airlines grounding the noncompliant.

The rehearsal had gone global — and America proved it would bow just as quickly. No tanks. No jackboots. Just nods, masks, QR codes — and silence. And the silence didn't fade when the mandates ended. It hardened into new norms. Denmark proved how easily people can be trained to applaud their own captivity. Nazi Germany proved how bureaucracy becomes bondage. America proved how fast it spreads when fear is the teacher and pride the enforcer. **Three lands. Three rehearsals. One serpent.** No armies required — only paperwork, propaganda, private platforms, and neighbors deputized by hashtags. The most dangerous enforcement did not come from government. It came from neighbors. In Nazi Germany, it was the Brownshirts — stormtroopers of conformity, fists in the street. Then the "Blockwart" — the block warden, spying on every household, reporting to the Party. In East Germany, the Stasi — friends and family conscripted into informants, whispering against their own.

Denmark proved the same spirit can rise without uniforms, without pay. In 2020, no armbands were issued. No Party cards handed out. The obedience was volunteered. Neighbors yelling at the unmasked in shops. A woman screamed at in the bakery line — not for stealing bread, but for breathing unmasked. Coworkers demanding vaccine papers. Families dividing at their own tables. Social media mobs degrading dissenters into lepers. The serpent didn't need soldiers. It deputized pride. It weaponized belonging. This was not chaos. It was choreography. A society applauding its own captivity.

And *America was no different*. The same fury rose in grocery stores in Texas, in coffee shops in California, in classrooms across the Midwest. *Houses of worship* were shuttered — pastors fined, congregations scattered, prayer declared "non-essential." *Schools* became training grounds for compliance — children masked at all times, even outdoors, even while running, playing instruments, or breathing between lines of tape on the floor. *Playgrounds and parks* were fenced off, their swings wrapped in caution tape. *Beaches* were patrolled, families fined for touching sand.

Gyms were silenced, while "health" was reduced to isolation and slogans. The new priesthood wore lab coats, not robes. Its sacraments were mandates, its scripture "the data." Salvation was measured in compliance, not courage. *Alcohol retailers* stayed open — spirits poured freely while the Spirit was forbidden. *Big box retailers — Walmart, Target, Costco, Home Depot* — kept their lights on, their aisles full, while small businesses were boarded up in the name of safety. Even *adult venues* in California — strip clubs and casinos — reopened before many sanctuaries did. In some places, even garden aisles were roped off — packets of seeds labeled "non-essential," as if growing your own food was a threat. Amazon was also deemed essential — its empire expanding while Main Street withered. The giants feasted as ordinary citizens lost homes, hope, and the ability to feed themselves. Even the first nations of this land were not spared. Reservations sealed their borders, ceremonies went silent, and elders died behind curfews. The fear was vast — and understandable — yet it cut the oldest roots first. Where drums once called the people together, only sirens and mandates filled the air. Anything that promoted *faith, health, or freedom* was silenced, mocked, or banned. And **we should never forget that — ever.**

The old spirit of the *Blockwart* lived on — deputized now by hashtags and headlines. The serpent knows fear mixed with pride can conscript ordinary men. No jackboots. No tanks. Only shame, slogans, and the hunger to belong. When neighbors become wardens, the serpent needs no chains. Fear works for free. Yet beneath that fear rose another heat — not mobs, but the steady burn of those who watched friends turn wardens, teachers turn informants, neighbors delight in another's punishment. It was the quiet fury of men and women who still believed in choice, who felt liberty shift beneath their boots and knew how narrow the trench is between safety and servitude. **Conscience held the line.** Millions clenched their teeth, swallowed words, and refused to strike back. That restraint spared the nation. The quiet decency of the patient kept the peace — fragile, held together by heartbreak and prayer. There were no gas chambers — only glowing screens and digital decrees. The walls weren't concrete but code.

The doors stayed open; the minds were locked. And through it all, one phrase moved heart to heart — *hold the line.* There were moments I thought it would break. If it had, it would not have been a war of equals. The ones with ideology would have met the ones with resolve. But the armed were decent — men and women who feared God more than government, who still believed neighbor meant brother. Their restraint was not weakness; it was faith. That mercy, not fear, kept the republic from blood. For when covenant still lives in a people — when they remember freedom is stewardship, not license — the serpent cannot win. The cage never comes with chains first. It comes smiling, promising care.

⸙ Firelight Pause — Your Cage

• What papers have you flashed without thinking, and what did you trade for that moment of permission?

• What mandates did you defend "for the greater good," and whose good was it really for?

• What comforts have you called safety that were only softer chains?

• When your neighbor shouted you down, did you stop to ask whose fear he was carrying in his throat?

• And when the anger rose in you, did conscience hold your line, or did you wish it hadn't?

From Copenhagen to California, from Geneva to Beijing, the paperwork of power crosses every border it erased. It wasn't a single ruler that rolled over nations, but a machinery — bureaucrats who worship process over people, technocrats who believe data can replace conscience, and financiers who treat sovereignty as an inconvenience to profit. Brussels, Davos, Silicon Valley — different towers, same altar.

"And he causes all, both small and great, rich and poor, free and slave, to receive a mark... and that no one may buy or sell except one who has the mark." — Revelation 13:16–17

The serpent tested its mask in Denmark, refined it in Europe, and now stretches its coils across America — through Silicon Valley contracts, East Coast regulations, West Coast decrees. The same velvet cage, only dressed in English. What began in quiet Copenhagen boardrooms now sits in your pocket, in your laws, in your neighbor's eyes. *The rehearsal is over. The main act has begun.*

And if you think you can scroll past it, you are already inside the cage. But cages are never the whole story. Across the ocean, a different law still breathes — not paperwork, but covenant. I left the lands of kings because I wanted no king to rule over me. They call our president a king — yet they kneel before Brussels, Davos, and the hollow thrones of the UN and EU. They curse authority when it answers to voters, and worship it when it answers to none. That is the madness of this age — rule by those who despise rulers, crowns worn by those who swore off kings. The serpent has crossed the water, yes — but here the fire is older than its mask. Turn the page. From rehearsal to resistance. From velvet chain to vowed land. The serpent rehearsed obedience. Now the remnant must rehearse courage.

11

AMERICA THE BEAUTIFUL
THROUGH IMMIGRANT EYES

The serpent rehearses obedience. God raises nations that remember His name.

"Blessed is the nation whose God is the Lord, the people He has chosen as His inheritance." — Psalm 33:12

I left Denmark because it was a cage — velvet on the outside, steel on the inside. I came to America because the very air here burned with covenant. Yet as an immigrant, I see the same serpent stalking these shores. But understand this: the serpent hunts America for one reason — covenant. **Denmark was a rehearsal. Europe was refinement. But America is the target — because America is the covenant.** Tyrannies fear the land built not on kings or bloodlines, but on God and oath. Every empire fears the nation where freedom is not permission but **inheritance.** Every global system fears a people who still remember where their freedom comes from — a people who know rights are given by God, that the state is a servant and never a master, that the family is the first and final government, that the land belongs to the free, and that men bow only before the throne of heaven.

America is not merely another country the serpent wants to control. She is the *only* country it must destroy. Because as long as covenant breathes here, the serpent's kingdom cannot rise. What smothered Denmark in silence now whispers in America's ear — taxes dressed as justice, obedience disguised as virtue, treaties signed in secret. The serpent tested its mask in Europe. Now it wears it here. I recognize the scent — the same polished tyranny, perfumed to hide the rot beneath - the coil that I slowly squeezing the life force out of you. And yet — there is nothing on earth like America. Not Denmark with its silence. Not Europe with its fading empires. Not Asia with its collectivist chains.

America is different. Here, the soil still carries covenant. Here, freedom is not theory — it breathes, it bleeds, it demands your courage. Her beauty is not marble and glass, but the unpolished strength of a people who till, build, and believe. She is flawed — and her flaws prove she is still alive, still capable of repentance, still capable of rising. John Wayne once said, *"America the Beautiful — she still is."* He was right — not because she is perfect, but because she still fights to be free. Wayne's message was simple and sacred: love of country isn't naïve — it's holy ground. He reminded Americans what binds them beyond politics — **land, liberty, and courage.** His prayer was simple: America's beauty is not in her skyline, but in her spine. Not in monuments of stone, but in men and women who still stand when others kneel. *America the Beautiful* is not nostalgia. It is covenant. And covenant demands remembrance — and defense.

Through an Immigrant's Eyes

I came as a stranger with an accent, carrying scars from lands that bowed too easily. I did not know this land, not truly, but I felt her long before my feet touched her soil — a pull, a whisper, a promise that freedom still had a home.

"I was a stranger, and you welcomed me." — Matthew 25:35

Every border I crossed shed another chain. Every mile west felt like walking out of an old story and into a covenant not yet written. I arrived with no inheritance but hunger — hunger for truth, for courage, for a place where the soul could stand upright without asking permission. And America met me not in marble statues or grand speeches, but in the fierce warmth of ordinary people — imperfect, unpolished, unafraid. Many of my first friends were from nations nothing like my own, with faces and histories stitched from every corner of the world. None of it mattered. It was their fire, their humor, their wounds, their stubborn hope — their **soul** — that made us kin. And it still is. Wherever they are now, scattered across states and seas, I still recognize them — by the same flame that once welcomed me. I saw in them what I never saw in the nations I fled: a flame that refused to die, even when the world tried to smother it. A way of standing. A way of seeing. A way of living free.

I have seen weakness. I have seen strength. I have watched nations sell their birthright for safety — and men rise with fire still in their bones. That is why I speak now — not as the native-born, but as the witness who walked through other cages. And I tell you without hesitation: America is not like them. She is fire wrapped in a flag. Covenant written in blood. A farmer with soil under his nails, standing on land that is his by right, not permission. A widow clutching a folded flag — covenant carried through tears. A rifle above a Texan door — not relic, but reminder that freedom defended is freedom kept. And the grace of belonging to a land I did not inherit, yet would die to defend. Only here did I breathe the kind of freedom that lets a soul stand upright — protected by warriors, anchored by covenant, accountable only to God. That is what America does — she turns strangers into stewards, pilgrims into patriots. Here, freedom is not granted. It is guarded.

🔥 Firelight Pause — The Covenant Land

- What fire brought your family here — and have you kept it burning?
- When did you last thank God for the ground beneath your feet, not as property, but as promise?
- If freedom is covenant, not comfort, what price are you willing to pay to guard it?
- When you look at your flag, do you see fabric — or faith?
- Are you keeping the oath, or waiting for someone else to keep it for you?

The serpent watches still, but it has never understood this land. It knows systems, not souls; it fears men who kneel to God and no one else. The remnant here is rising — builders, believers, and broken ones who remember their oaths. They are not waiting for permission. They are sharpening truth, rebuilding trust, and lighting fires the serpent cannot extinguish. **America's covenant is not written in policy. It is written in people — in you.**

In the chapters to come, I will show you why you must fight for her — roar when it matters — and never bow to the serpent that wants her soul. This is not nostalgia. It is *warning*. It is *commission*. I speak as an immigrant, telling you what I see — the fire that made me choose this land, the fire you were born into, the fire you must now guard. Because **America is not just a country. She is a covenant.** If she falls, the world goes dark. The question is never whether a land has a flag. The question is — did it rise, or did it fall?

12

THE FLAG THAT FELL
COVENANT OR DECORATION

A flag is never fabric. It is oath. It is blood translated into color. It is memory carried on cloth. When a widow receives that folded triangle at a graveside, it isn't a ceremony — it's a covenant passed from the dead to the living. When a soldier plants a flag on foreign earth, it isn't decoration — it's the announcement that freedom has arrived. And when someone burns a flag in the street, they aren't torching cotton — they're making war on the dead who carried it.

According to Danish legend, Denmark's flag did not rise from rebellion; it fell from the sky. In 1219, at the Battle of Lyndanisse, King Valdemar's crusaders were nearly defeated when a red banner with a white cross descended from heaven. He raised it high. The army rallied. The tide turned. One miracle. One banner. One victory. But a flag that drops from the sky is different from a flag raised by a people. A gift trains obedience, not sacrifice. A people who inherit their flag never learn to bleed for it. Centuries later, the Dannebrog still waves — but now on birthday cakes, napkins, supermarket aisles. The sacred turned to decoration. The covenant drained into habit. The serpent never tore it down; he hollowed it. And hollow flags create hollow hearts.

123

Oehlenschläger — The Poet Denmark Softened

Denmark once had a poet who tried to give it a real anthem — Adam Oehlenschläger, the father of Danish romantic nationalism. His verses roared with Vikings, destiny, the old northern fire. But Denmark kept only the soft stanzas — the meadow, the beech tree — and threw away the battle-cry. Few Danes even know the truth: the original anthem held twelve stanzas of shields raised, warriors standing, blood and freedom in every line. The state sings only the gentle ones. The fire was trimmed. The courage edited out. Denmark raised a war-song — then declawed it into a lullaby. A nation's anthem teaches its children what courage sounds like. A people who once carved longships now sing about summer breezes. That is how you soften a nation: keep the melody, erase the muscle. I felt that hollowing in my own bones. I grew up saluting that flag. I watched the cloth rise. But my chest stayed cold. Ritual without fire. Allegiance without covenant. Denmark's anthem told me to lower my voice. Its flag told me to bow. The Dannebrog told me who I wasn't. The Stars and Stripes told me who I could be. **America's did the opposite.** The first time I stood under the Stars and Stripes on a Texas football field — no palace, no pomp, just ordinary people rising in uncoached reverence — something ancient woke in my chest. Hats came off. Veterans saluted with tears burning down their faces. Children stood still. No one bowed. Everyone stood. One flag was given from the sky. The other was earned in blood. And that defines everything.

The Stars and Stripes — The Flag That Rose

America's flag was different. Thirteen stripes for thirteen colonies. Stars for every state. Sewn not by kings but by ordinary hands. It was baptized not in myth but in blood — Valley Forge, freezing men binding rags to their feet — men starving, shivering, praying, yet still drilling at dawn because liberty was worth frostbite. Yorktown, where rebels forced an empire to its knees — cannons thundering, ragged soldiers watching redcoats surrender, knowing their defiance had split history in two. Gettysburg, where brothers bled the soil red — fields turned to graves, the price of unity written in blood no politician could erase.

Normandy, where boys carried the flag onto beaches of fire — teenagers with rifles stepping off boats into machine-gun storms, some never making it ten yards, yet the flag still rose above the smoke. Every stripe a wound turned into covenant. Every star a choice, not a decree. This is why the flag is heavy when folded — it carries the weight of every wound, every choice, every life given so it could rise again. The Stars and Stripes was not a gift. It was a declaration. And when Americans bury their dead, the flag folds thirteen times and is handed to a widow with trembling hands: *On behalf of a grateful nation.* The cloth is heavy because the memory is holy. And that memory has been tested — burned in riots, mocked in classrooms, dismissed as relic. Yet it still flies — over farms, over graves, over small towns where covenant has not been forgotten. The fire endures.

The Revolutionary Flag vs. the Counterfeit Banners

The Betsy Ross flag — America's birth-banner — branded "racist," pulled from shelves, shamed from memory. The same script that shrank the Dannebrog into decoration works here too: turn rebellion into offense, covenant into controversy, fire into fashion. What once flew for freedom is now feared for meaning. But its symbols still speak. **Stars** — heaven's covenant, the divine order above kings. **Stripes** — blood and purity, sacrifice and purpose. **Circle** — unity without hierarchy. It was never political. It was revolutionary — a covenant stitched in cloth, declaring that freedom answers to God, not governments.

Meanwhile, rival banners rise. The rainbow flag preaches identity above covenant, desire above truth, self above God. The Ukraine flag signals not solidarity but submission — a badge of compliance to global masters. The BLM flag elevates grievance over covenant, division over unity, politics over blood-price freedom. Corporate banners rise too — ESG logos and corporations rainbow-branded for one month a year — preaching virtue while selling chains. Every rival flag preaches a rival god. They do not join your covenant. They replace it. And when counterfeits multiply, the true banner must burn brighter.

Because in every age, the banner you stand under decides the battle you fight. Flags are not decorations — they are declarations of allegiance. They tell heaven who you belong to, and they tell hell who you oppose. And when the serpent rises, he does not fear weapons. He fears allegiance — because covenant defeats kingdoms. The serpent doesn't tear down banners. It hollows them. It leaves the fabric but steals the fire. Flags fall long before they touch the ground. Because if the flag falls, the covenant beneath it falls. Take the banner, and the people soon forget the blood that raised it. Dannebrog fell from heaven and taught submission. The Stars and Stripes rose from fire and demanded resistance. So choose. A nation's flag is more than cloth. It is covenant. It is destiny. Every age has rival banners. Every life must choose one. And so do you. The American flag is covenant stitched in blood and fire. If you forget that, you will watch it lowered — not by enemies abroad, but by cowards within.

🔥 **Firelight Pause — Stand Beneath the Banner**
- Which flag do you truly stand under?
- The rainbow that demands you kneel?
- The blue-and-yellow that drains your treasure for foreign wars?
- The corporate logos that sell obedience as virtue?
- Or the red, white, and blue — the banner that built your freedom and still dares you to fight?

"Set up a banner in the land, blow the trumpet among the nations!" — Jeremiah 51:27

But a flag does not stand alone. Cloth is covenant, yes — but covenant must be sung. Banners carry fire, but songs ignite it. Every nation waves a banner. Only the living ones roar with one voice beneath it. Now listen — from cloth to chorus, from banner to song. The serpent knows: break the anthem, and you break the people.

13

THE TWO ANTHEMS — ONE NATION AFRAID TO CHOOSE

TWO SONGS, ONE SILENCE

Every nation sings itself into being. Songs are not entertainment — they are identity. They carry memory, courage, destiny. Denmark sings with a split tongue: two anthems, two souls — one tied to crown and cannon, the other to fields and nostalgia. Neither whole. Neither fire. **America sings with one voice** — a single anthem forged under rockets at Fort McHenry, written in defiance. Not a lullaby. A war cry. But not all songs speak truth. Some lull. Some divide. And that is where Denmark reveals its mask.

Like a serpent, Denmark sings with a forked tongue. In the 1800s, it kept two anthems — one for monarchy and military, one for the rising nationalism of the people. Instead of choosing, it compromised. And compromise became identity. A people comfortable with welfare and warm houses, yet chained to a hollow crown. No roar of unity. No anthem binding throne and farmer, pulpit and hearth. A double-anthem nation. A double-minded people. A serpent's song — divided, never whole.

But Denmark's fracture began earlier, in the folk schools. Every morning the children sang — not thunder psalms of freedom or judgment, but soft, pastoral hymns crafted to stir feeling, not fire. Songs about fields, seasons, homesteads, the gentle passing of time. Beautiful, yes — but beauty without battle-readiness sedates. **Over time, this gentleness became the national voice — rehearsed, rewarded, and mistaken for virtue.** Not every Danish voice was soft. Jeppe Aakjær sang with fire — lament, not lullaby. He carried the ache of the farm worker, the widow, the man crushed under quiet injustice. He wrote of fields that toiled while cities slept, of hearts breaking beneath a polite sky. He saw what Denmark refused to see: a people who stop singing truth soon stop speaking it. He tried to rouse the folk — conscience, dignity, courage — but Denmark preferred B.S. Ingemann's gentleness. It shelved his fire for hymns that kept the peace. Another awakening swallowed by velvet. Aakjær tried to wake the fields. Denmark chose the lullaby. And that is the hinge of history: when one nation sings itself asleep, another must rise singing fire.

But Denmark did not silence only its poets. It silenced its prophets. Kaj Munk — pastor, playwright, firebrand — tried one last time to wake the nation. His play *Skriget* ("The Cry") told the truth Denmark refused to face: a man crushed by polite cruelty, the same quiet brutality Aakjær warned about. Munk knew the ancient law — **a nation that cannot bear a man's voice will never withstand a tyrant's boots.** He preached courage and condemned cowardice. Denmark mourned the martyr but ignored the message: a people who hush their truth-tellers will kneel for their conquerors. A nation that kills its cry forgets how to sing.

Across an ocean, another nation rose singing fire. America has one anthem. Forged in war. Written in defiance. Sung under rockets and bombs. Born at Fort McHenry while an empire's cannons tore the sky. Not a lullaby — a war cry. It belongs to no king, no committee, no global throne. It belongs to the people. When Americans sing, they look not to a palace but to a flag, a field, and the God who gave them liberty.

That is why stadiums, churches, and battlefields echo the same song — **one voice, one nation, one anthem.** And here is the deeper truth: in Scripture, song is covenant. Israel sang and walls fell. The early Church sang and chains broke. Nations that sing in unity rise in unity. Nations that whisper two songs fracture in silence. Song is covenant — and so the serpent strikes it first. They weaponize guilt — turning history into accusation and compassion into compliance. — calling the anthem racist, imperial, outdated. They drag up forgotten verses no one sings and smear the whole as hateful. Standing becomes "oppression." Kneeling becomes theater. Protest becomes performance. Celebrities parody it. Late-night hosts sneer. Fear finishes the job — students opting out, teachers shaming the bold, professors calling patriotism primitive, culture painting pride as embarrassment. Then comes the replacement: unity hymns — *Imagine, Ode to Joy,* climate anthems for a managed world. The whisper: America needs a "new song." Post-national. Inclusive. Harmless. Then comes the indifference — athletes sitting, schools erasing context, youth knowing the anthem only as controversy. But what they fear is simple: Americans still rise when the anthem plays. Stadiums still roar louder than protestors. The anthem binds ordinary people not to elites but to flag, soil, and God. That fear is proof of its power. Morale is the force that topples tyrants. Empires fall when the people sing together. Empires rise where people fall silent.

Denmark sings with hesitation. America sings with fire. Two anthems breed compromise; one anthem breeds courage — and **courage decides whether a nation stands or kneels.** A nation's song is its soul. Split the song and you split the people. That is why the serpent attacks the anthem — not because it is weak, but because it is strong. When Americans rise together, hand on heart, voices joined, the serpent trembles. If America ever stops singing with one voice, America stops being America. A nation loses its fire long before it loses its flag. First the banner. Then the anthem. Then the tongue. And once the tongue falls, the world falls with it. Denmark already learned this. America must not.

🔥 **Firelight Pause — Your Song**

Stop. Listen deeper than melody. This is not about music. This is about allegiance.

- What song does your land truly sing — fire or sedation?
- Do your children know it by heart, or only by controversy?
- When the anthem rises, do you stand with fire or sit in fear?
- If your nation lost its song, what would bind it tomorrow?
- Who writes the hymns your people obey — heaven or Babylon?

A nation that forgets its song forgets its soul.

"How shall we sing the Lord's song in a strange land?" — Psalm 137:4

Even the strongest anthem cannot survive on melody alone. A song lives or dies on the tongue that carries it. A people can still rise for the flag, still roar a chorus, still feel fire in their chest — but if their words are captured, their world is next. Denmark learned this first. The banner softened. The anthem split. And then the serpent reached for the tongue. Because once the tongue bends, truth bends with it. And once truth bends, the nation follows. The next battlefield is language itself — the words your children speak, the meanings your rulers rewrite, the vocabulary the serpent steals before you even notice it is gone. A nation's song is its soul. But a nation's tongue is its world. Now watch how Denmark lost both — and why America must not.

14

THE LANGUAGE —
WORDS AS WEAPONS

THE SERPENT STRIKES THE TONGUE FIRST

Every empire begins with language. Every chain is fastened first in words. The serpent knows this. That is why he strikes your tongue before your sword. Because a silenced word becomes a silenced man. And a silenced people becomes a captive nation. Denmark learned this long ago. "Janteloven" mocked the bold word. The velvet cage smothered the daring word. The press curated the approved word. And soon, fire itself forgot how to speak.

But America was different. She was born in words — *"We hold these truths to be self-evident."* That meant this — some truths need no king to approve them, no court to grant them, no vote to validate them. They are written by God into the bones of man — liberty, dignity, the right to stand free. Not decrees from a throne, but declarations from free men. Not permissions granted, but rights proclaimed. Words that carried fire across an ocean and shook an empire to its knees. That is why this chapter matters. If Denmark lost its tongue, America must not. What you silence in words, you soon surrender in life.

131

The Tongue That Softened

Every empire dies twice - first in spirit, then in speech. Empires fall the moment their language collapses. Denmark once spoke with the tongue of Vikings — sharp, fierce, full of steel and song. A tongue that carried sagas across seas, gave orders in battle, sang hymns in church. But over centuries it softened. It bent toward politeness. It shrank into consensus phrases and bureaucratic fog. It became small, insular, guarded — a language few outsiders could enter. Barely 6 million still speak it. That isolation became a shield for elites: one story told at home, another abroad. Silence by tongue became silence by design. Then came English — not as trade, but as fashion. A badge of global belonging. Danes sprinkle English into their speech like glitter, while their own words atrophy. What remains is often vulgarity — where once there was dignity.

Even H.C. Andersen's prophetic tongue — poetic, almost biblical — is now sterilized into bedtime coziness. But Andersen warned them in a way no one understood. His tale *The Shadow* was not a children's story — it was prophecy. In it, a man loses his voice while his shadow gains one, rises to power, and becomes his master. A false authority with a stolen tongue. A people who cannot speak truth are ruled by those who only perform it. *The Shadow* was Andersen's warning about Denmark's future: when real men lose their words, their shadows take the throne. And Georg Brandes saw the same decay a generation later. He wrote, "Denmark is a country where the great word cannot be spoken." He mocked the nation's fear of strong language, its worship of cozy speech, its polite avoidance of truth that demands courage. Brandes knew — a culture that trims its language will soon trim its spirit. A nation that censors strong words will never produce strong men. Together, Andersen and Brandes revealed the same wound: **when a people lose their words, they lose their world.** And the wound did not stay on the page. It spread — from poets to people, from literature to language itself. What Andersen warned in metaphor and Brandes shouted in critique became reality in the streets.

When a nation trims its tongue, the next generation inherits the silence. The wound did not stop in books; it moved into the mouths of the young. Among the young it is worse. They speak in "Danglish" — Danish cut with English slogans, globalist accents. Elders complain, but the youth call it progress. In truth, it is surrender. The serpent has entered their tongue. When a tongue dulls, a culture follows. What begins in speech spreads to imagination, to design, to life itself. A split tongue becomes a split spirit — neither rooted in the old nor free in the new, but suspended in mimicry. It is not creativity. It is decay dressed as modernity. And America is not immune. Our tongue is not "Danglish," but corporate cant, bureaucratic slogans, technocrat words that hollow truth into jargon: "equity," "stakeholders," "resilience." Buzzwords that smother fire. Empty phrases that replace covenant with compliance. When words rot, nations follow.

Minimalism as Discipline

Denmark's true export is not just policies, but a mindset. Minimalism sold as virtue. Chairs and lamps packaged as salvation. Royal Copenhagen porcelain — peasants buying a fragment of royalty. LEGO bricks placed in children's hands — not to spark wild arcs, but to train them to build in squares, in order, in boxes. Over time even LEGO bowed to the sermon of the age — swapping genders, disciplining imagination itself. What began as toys became catechism. The same creed spread westward — Apple, Google, Silicon Valley. White boxes. Clean lines. Devices that glow with simplicity while disciplining their users. Stripped-down watches strapped to wrists — modern shackles disguised as sleek. Not just furniture anymore. Not just lamps. Now it is chains for the body. Devices that track pulse, sleep, steps, life. You call it convenience. They call it compliance. Every heartbeat handed to the system as data, every step logged as tribute. The form is Danish. The function is globalist. The ideology exported — control dressed as convenience. And Americans buy it. IKEA fills our homes. LEGO fills our malls. Apple straps its leash to our wrists.

We mistake imported order for progress and forget that America's greatness was never minimal. It was carved in risk, forged in grit, fired in freedom. But if our words are boxed, timed, and monitored like our steps and heartbeats, then freedom falls the same way. The leash on the wrist becomes a leash on the tongue.

America's Tongue

America's English was frontier-born, immigrant-forged. Biblical in depth, frontier in edge. It mixed King James cadences with campfire slang. It built constitutions and skyscrapers alike. It carried declarations, sermons, and street talk — all with fire. But it is under attack. Not by guns. By redefinitions. By propaganda. By screamers who twist words until truth becomes "hate," courage becomes "toxic," freedom becomes "dangerous." God spoke creation into being. Babylon fell because its tongue was confused. Words build worlds — or break them. The globalists know this — control the dictionary, and you control the destiny. Redefine man and woman, faith and family, nation and people — and you unmake them without a shot fired. Because language is not just culture — it is law. Every law is made of words, not bullets. Redefine a word, and you rewrite a legal world. Change "man" and "woman," and you dissolve the family. Change "citizen," and you erase the nation. Change "speech," and you outlaw dissent. The serpent rewrites dictionaries because he cannot conquer a free people until he conquers the words that make them free. Once the tongue bends, the law follows. And once the law bends, the land falls.

Even Shakespeare saw it — though he spoke it in the wrong tongue. For centuries the people themselves said **Danmark**: a word of covenant, land, and ancient root. But the global courts, maps, and monarchs softened it to **Denmark** — a foreign syllable, a branding exercise. A name trimmed for treaties, not for truth. And so the most famous line ever spoken carried a counterfeit banner: *"Something is rotten in the state of Denmark."* The rot was real. The name was not.

That is the serpent's victory: **when even truth is forced to speak in rebranded words.** The serpent always changes the name before he changes the nation. Words are not furniture. They are fire. If you surrender them, you surrender your future. If you repeat the serpent's dictionary, you build his kingdom with your own tongue. That is why the First Amendment comes first — because once speech is chained, every other freedom falls with it. If the language bends, the land bends. If the tongue falls, the flag falls. **Words build worlds.** Blunt them, and you blunt your freedom — or wake up speaking Babylon's tongue.

 Firelight Pause — Guard the Tongue
   • What words have you surrendered without knowing?
   • What truths have you buried because culture renamed them?
   • What fire do your children hear at home — steel or sedation?
   • If tomorrow you could only speak what they permit, what would die on your tongue?

A people who lose their words lose their world. Lose their tongue, lose their truth. Lose their truth, lose their freedom. The serpent strikes first at the tongue. Guard your words like steel. For if you lose them, you lose the fire itself.

"Death and life are in the power of the tongue, and those who love it will eat its fruit." — Proverbs 18:21

But words themselves point to something deeper. A tongue can shape a culture, but only faith can set it ablaze. Denmark kept the tongue but lost the fire — polishing words while the Spirit fled. America was born in words, yes — but only because those words carried covenant carved in stone, sung in hymns, preached in pulpits. If the tongue is chained, the song falters. If the altar is hollow, the nation falls. That is why we turn now from speech to symbols, from words to worship — to see whether the fire still lives at the altar, or whether it has been sold to Babylon.

15

THE HOLLOW FAITH —
ALTARS WITHOUT FIRE

WHEN CHURCHES BECOME MUSEUMS

Denmark once burned with faith. The cross on the Dannebrog wasn't decoration — it was destiny. Long before the nation softened into welfare and weddings, it was carved in stone by a king who meant it.

Jelling — Covenant on Stone

Harald Bluetooth — the unifier of Denmark — raised the Jelling Stones around 965 and declared Christ over the land. Those stones still stand: granite slabs etched with covenant, announcements in Viking runes that Denmark would bow to Christ, not chaos. Queen Thyra and King Gorm raised him, but Harald carved the promise. Jelling was not folklore. It was a national altar. That fire did not stay on stone. It moved into men.

Absalon — The Warrior Who Built Copenhagen

Bishop Absalon — warrior-priest, statesman, founder of Copenhagen — carried a Christianity that crushed pagan fortresses and raised churches in their place. He sailed with kings, fought invaders, built cities, and planted order where lawlessness ruled. His faith wasn't gentle. It was steel and psalm braided together. The kind that builds civilizations. Today tourists wave at his statues, never knowing the fire beneath the bronze. The nation that once marched with psalms now manages faith with committees. The warrior-priest became marketing material. The flame he carried was reduced to guided tours. Even Harald's symbol wasn't safe. The runes he carved for Christ were hijacked centuries later — repackaged as the Bluetooth logo, binding machines instead of men, lighting towers that rise above the very steeples meant to preach His name. Covenant stripped into code. Cross rebranded as connectivity. Babylon always steals the symbol before it steals the soul. Because once a nation loses meaning, it loses the fight. And when symbols are hollowed, the serpent steps in.

Symbols Stolen

The rainbow was once God's covenant of mercy; now it is a banner of rebellion. The eagle once warned kings; now it sits caged on bureaucratic seals. "Patriot" once meant Lexington and Normandy; now it is branded extremist. Freedom was a birthright; now it is traded for "safety." Denmark suffered the same theft. The Dannebrog — once the banner of crusaders — became birthday décor. Janteloven hardened into cultural chains. The monarchy drifted from covenant to tourist theater. And in the vacuum came the new priests: the EU, the UN, and the technocrats — men who preach "universal values" that demand obedience, not belief. The serpent rarely destroys symbols. He hollows them.

Hans Tausen — The Reformer in Chains

Denmark once trembled before real preaching. Hans Tausen, the Danish Luther, preached with such fire that bishops threw him into prison in 1525. Crowds gathered outside his cell just to hear his voice through the stone. His sermons split the kingdom, forced Scripture into ordinary hands, and set Denmark ablaze with Reformation fire. He shook a nation so fiercely that the crown legalized Protestantism in 1536 simply to contain the flame. Denmark once imprisoned faith because it was too powerful. Now it subsidizes faith because it is harmless. Tausen's voice turned a kingdom upside down. Today the State Church could not shake a folding table.

Grundtvig — The Fire the Church Could Not Hold

Denmark once had a priest who warned it what would happen when faith became an institution instead of a fire. **N.F.S. Grundtvig** preached awakening, not compliance — conscience over committees, spirit over system. The State Church could not silence him outright, so it did something more effective: it absorbed him. His fire was preserved as heritage, his warnings recast as tradition, his rebellion softened into ceremony. What could not be extinguished was institutionalized. A church that cannot withstand a prophet will eventually turn him into furniture. Grundtvig did not fail. The State Church failed him.

Ingemann — The Lullaby of a Sleeping Nation

If Grundtvig was the mind of Denmark's awakening, Ingemann was its heart — and the serpent knew what to do with a soft heart. B.S. Ingemann wrote hymns that wrapped the nation in warmth: gentle mornings, quiet fields, sunlit calm. Beautiful, yes — but beauty without vigilance becomes a lullaby. While Grundtvig thundered awake, Ingemann whispered sleep. His hymns became Denmark's emotional climate: soft, tender, conflict-averse. "Peace over land and town." "The sun rises softly in the East." Songs without enemies. Songs without battle. Songs where nothing threatens and nothing must be defended.

A people who sing of eternal calm soon believe calm is their birthright —
and treat anything that disturbs it as an enemy. The welfare state didn't
invent emotional management. It inherited it. Ingemann gave Denmark a
soundtrack that shaped the soul long before bureaucrats shaped the
budgets. Harmony became holiness. Disagreement became sin.
Confrontation became foreign. A nation that once carved longships now
carved candles. A culture born from warriors became a culture terrified
of wounded feelings. Hymns meant to steady the heart became anesthesia for the spine. Grundtvig dreamed of awakening the folk. Ingemann
taught them how to sleep standing up. And the serpent knew: a gentle
nation is easier to govern than a courageous one. Denmark's cathedrals
still tower. Their bells still echo. But the fire is gone. Sermons are sterilized. Pews empty. Priests applaud parades but cannot kindle repentance.
Faith became folklore. Covenant became culture. Altars polished. Spirit
absent. A State Church always ages into State ideology — polite,
predictable, and perfectly harmless to the government that funds it.

Kaj Munk — The Martyr Who Would Not Bow

When Denmark's faith flickered one last time, it came through a man
the State now pretends to honor. Kaj Munk — pastor, playwright,
prophet. He thundered against cowardice, against tyranny, against the
polite obedience that had replaced character in Denmark's soul. When
the Nazis came, Munk refused to bow. The Gestapo dragged him into a
forest on January 4, 1944, and shot him. Denmark commemorates the
martyr — but ignores the message. **Munk warned:** *A church afraid of
conflict becomes chaplain to the State.* And Denmark proved him right. He
was the last major Danish voice with prophetic fire. Even Grundtvig saw
the danger long before — that a State Church would become a museum
of faith instead of a movement of fire. After Munk, Denmark no longer
killed its prophets. It replaced them.

The State Church did not disappear. It evolved. Faith was no longer confronted — it was administered. The language remained. The fire did not. What emerged was not atheism, but a new priesthood: technocrats preaching salvation through policy, obedience through expertise, and virtue through compliance. Denmark once had priests who carried fire. Today it has priests who carry policy. And no figure embodies the new creed more clearly than Ida Auken — daughter of Margrete Auken, raised in the State Church, trained for the pulpit, but converted into a missionary for the technocratic gospel. A priest of the climate-State. A disciple of Davos. A preacher of the creed that rewrites covenant into compliance. It was Ida Auken who wrote the now-infamous WEF manifesto: *"Welcome to 2030 — I own nothing, have no privacy, and life has never been better."* Not a parody. A proclamation. A sermon for a world without property, without sovereignty, without self. She traded the altar for algorithms, the pulpit for policy papers, the Gospel for governance. She is the perfect symbol of Denmark's hollow faith — a church that lost its fire and became chaplain to the global elite. A priest without covenant. A shepherd without Scripture. Proof that when a nation's faith collapses, its clergy does not disappear — it simply serves a different god. But fire never dies just because marble grows cold. It slips out the back door. It finds the broken. It gathers in the margins. And it burns there. Not in cathedrals — in the "frikirker". Free churches. Small. Mocked. Unfunded. Unpolished. But burning. They don't perform religion. They wage it. While Europe trades faith for safety, they trade comfort for covenant. History is clear: Where the institution collapses, the remnant rises. The flame always moves to the margins before it moves the mountain.

America's Flame

Denmark traded fire for comfort. America has not — not yet. Our choirs are imperfect, our rhythms messy, our tents leaky. But when gospel tents rise, the fire leaps. The world mocks it. The media slanders it. The State tries to bury it. But the ember remains — and embers, guarded, ignite forests. In 2025, *26,000 were baptized in a single wave* — the largest in U.S. history. Not ritual. Revival. Even the White House felt the tremor, creating a Faith Office to protect religious liberty.

America forbids a State Church; Denmark enthrones one. We guard free exercise; they subsidize compliance. This isn't culture. It is covenant. And covenant is war. A nation without fire becomes Denmark — comfortable, compliant, hollow. A nation with fire becomes America — unbroken, unbowed, unstoppable. But America is not immune. Our megachurches glow with lights but not always with flame. Our pulpits dodge courage to protect applause. The same hollowing that consumed Denmark whispers at our door.

"If My people humble themselves and pray... I will heal their land."
    — 2 Chronicles 7:14

🔥 **Firelight Pause — Choose Your Altar**
  • Where has your fire turned into ritual?
  • What symbols in your life have become idols?
  • Do your children see faith as folklore or fire?
  • If your church closed, would the Spirit still burn at home?
  • Have you bowed to culture, comfort, or Christ?
  • When the storm hits, will your knees bend in prayer or surrender?
  • When the line is drawn, will you bow to the Lamb or the Beast?

Revival cannot be manufactured. Fire cannot be scheduled, branded, or live-streamed into existence. Noise is not flame. Crowds are not covenant. A nation does not return to God by spectacle, but by repentance. When churches confuse emotion for obedience and applause for fruit, they glow brightly — and burn nothing. The serpent is not threatened by full buildings. He is threatened by bowed knees.

Fire in stone means nothing without fire in flesh. Denmark proves it: cathedrals tall, choirs beautiful — yet the fire gone. A nation of altars without flame. A nation of safety without Spirit. Hollow altars make hollow men. But America's ember still burns — which makes the test sharper. Nations are not built by thrones, treaties, or churches — but by people who carry the flame. Faith without flesh is folklore. An altar without people is stone. A country without fire is prey. That is why we turn from symbols to souls — from stone to flesh — because the serpent knows: Hollow the people, and the land follows.

The next battlefield is not the cathedral, or the flag, or the anthem. It is the human heart. I learned this leaving Denmark — a land of silent churches and polished altars. What saved me was not a cathedral, but a flame I found in the eyes of ordinary Americans. That fire lives in you now. If you carry it, America stands. If you abandon it, she falls. The serpent knows this — which is why he strikes your soul next.

16

THE PEOPLE — BUILDERS OR SUBJECTS
COMFORT IS CAPTIVITY

Nations are not governments; *nations are people.* Denmark's people once built ships that ruled the seas. They fished waters that fed empires. They stood as Vikings feared by kings. But today they are polite, obedient, conflict-avoidant. They avoid offense more than they seek truth. They accept control as long as comfort remains. Builders became subjects. And once a people forget how to build, they forget how to stand.

From Builders to Subjects

America's people were born different — rebels, pioneers, immigrants with iron spines. **Our DNA is defiance.** We carved homesteads from wilderness, towns from dust, industries from nothing. But the same forces that tamed the Danes are working here too: comfort, compliance, convenience. The welfare check that numbs. The screen that sedates. The debt that chains. *The war on courage is real.* Because the test before America is not political. It is existential. Will we remain a nation — or become a managed population? Will we stay builders — or be trained into subjects? Every globalist policy, every softened word, every comfort distorted into dependence pushes us toward one end or the other. And nothing creates subjects faster than the slow death of men — the quiet removal of fathers, grit, and masculine courage.

And that war begins in the home. Two generations have grown up in that fog. Families broken. Fathers absent. History politicized or erased. Schools teach grievance instead of grit. Soil forgotten, replaced by screens. These sons and daughters know how to pass exams, but not how to plant seed or raise a wall. They scroll, but do not build. They complain, but do not carry. Weak in body, weaker in mind — raised on edited stories instead of true ones. What Denmark lost through obedience, America risks losing through distraction. And the globalists do not want citizens. They want consumers — obedient, addicted, predictable. A people who build nothing, defend nothing, remember nothing. They become subjects long before they notice the chain. A people who forget their soil become easy to rule; a people who cling to screens become easy to program. A people that stops raising children stops raising nations — the birthrate collapse is the quietest conquest of all. The question is not whether America has people, but whether those people will still be builders — or whether they will become subjects.

What Makes a Nation

Governments come later; nations are covenant first. Israel was a nation before it had a king. Tribes carried covenant long before parliaments. Clans held land before courts drew maps. Kindreds guarded memory before bureaucrats wrote laws. A nation is blood, memory, covenant, land — not paperwork. Even here, the native tribes called themselves nations. They understood sovereignty. They knew. People are not born subjects. They are born to land, memory, and covenant. This is why globalists strike the word itself. *If they can redefine "nation," they can redefine you.* America was not built by individuals. It was built by covenanted communities — frontier families, militias, churches, clans — people bound to each other and to God. Subjects obey alone. Builders rise together. This is why empires import populations instead of strengthening families — replacement is easier than revival.

Nations. Tribes. Clans. Kindreds. Peoples. Tongues. These are the true words of covenant and belonging. But the "United Nations" is not nations at all. It is a cartel of governments, masking control with the sacred word. A counterfeit. A spell. Not peoples gathered — but populations managed. Not covenant — but control. Not nations — but numbers. Nations have souls. The UN does not. But you do. And what you call yourself matters. A nation without a soul becomes a jurisdiction; a nation with one becomes a fortress. What Americans can call themselves matters. You are not just citizens. You are *Patriots* — men and women bound by sacrifice to liberty. You are Builders — heirs of defiance, the word that stands in direct opposition to "subjects." You are *Homesteaders* — rooted in soil and covenant, even if you live in cities. You are *Clans and Kindreds* — the old words that remind us nations are families before they are states. You are the *Remnant* — the ones who carry the ember when others bow. You are *Sons and Daughters of Liberty* — fire from the Revolution, still burning in the present. You are *Pilgrims* — not tourists, but seekers who carry faith and freedom as destiny. Do not call yourself a population. Do not call yourself a stakeholder. Call yourself what you are — Patriot. Builder. Remnant. Fire-blooded. Covenant-bound. Unbroken. The words you claim are the future you build. Names are not labels — they are marching orders.

Denmark once burned with courage — ships, sagas, fire. Now it whispers obedience — polite, subdued, managed. America once thundered with rebellion — pioneers, grit, faith. Now it is tempted by sedation — screens, debt, safety. What Denmark surrendered through obedience, America is tempted to surrender through comfort. A government can rise or fall, but a nation's soul decides if it will rise again. Subjects scroll; builders plant. Subjects obey; builders forge. Subjects bow; builders rise. History is watching. Your children are watching. The globalists are watching. And God is watching. Will America become Denmark — polite and subdued? Or will America remain America — the last stronghold of the unbroken? People are not born subjects. They are trained to be. Break the training. Build again. For as Scripture warns: when the people lose vision, the nation perishes — not from invasion, but from collapse within.

Firelight Pause — Builders or Subjects?

- Are you only a passport — a stamp, a barcode?
- Are you only a ZIP code — Palo Alto, Beverly Hills, Manhattan, Aspen?
- Or are you more — Patriot, Builder, Remnant, Son or Daughter of Liberty?
- Do you belong to geography — or to covenant?
- When your children ask who you were, will you give them an address — or a legacy?
- Do you build — or scroll?
- Do your children see a subject in you, or a builder?
- What comforts taught you to bow instead of rise?
- If your ancestors saw you now, would they call you free?

You Are the Remnant

You are more than a passport or a ZIP code. You are a people, a covenant, a fire that does not bow. Subjects bow; builders rise. Faith is the altar, and the people are the warriors — but warriors without land are captives. Covenant is soil as much as spirit. Denmark forgot. They traded inheritance for regulation, drained their fields, surrendered their ground. Hollow faith made hollow people, and hollow people gave up their land. That is the serpent's trick: take the soil, and the soul follows. America still has frontier ground — mountains that roar, rivers that remember liberty. Lose the land and the people wander; lose the people and the land is taken. The choice is simple: claim the ground, or lose it to comfort. If the people are covenant in flesh, the land is covenant in stone. Lose it, and the people fall. People do not stand in air. They stand in soil.

17

THE LAND — ROOTS OR CHAINS

EVERY NATION BEGINS WITH LAND.
NOT LAWS. NOT TREATIES. SOIL.

A nation's spirit is tied to its soil. When you tame the land, you tame the people. Denmark forgot this. They drained their marshes, fenced their fields, and turned farms into "naturparker" — state-managed parks for tourists and climate ledgers. The wild was not erased — it was caged. And once the wild is caged, the people soon follow.

Jutland — Freedom Drained

Look to Jutland — once heathland, bog, and marsh. Kings and governments built dikes and canals, turning frontier into plowed fields. Freedom became rye and potatoes. Wildness became regulation. And now — the same State spends billions to "re-wild" that land — not to free it, but to serve the globalist climate agenda. 140,000 hectares flooded — not to feed families but to balance carbon books. €6 billion spent to buy farms and drown them — courtesy of Danish taxpayers. The world's first farm carbon tax — herds priced as emissions, fields turned into sinks. This is not nature restored. This is land monetized. Inheritance turned into accounting. And once inheritance becomes accounting, freedom becomes privilege. Because once land becomes a ledger entry, the people become inventory.

Hunting Shackled

Once the mark of free men, hunting in Denmark is now privilege. Rights are tied to land ownership — and most land is private, tightly regulated, and out of reach. To hunt, you must pass a state exam, lease rights from a landowner, or buy into an exclusive club. Own only a small plot — you might take a hare. But for deer or boar, you need five to twelve acres, State permission, quotas, short seasons, and EU directives. The nobles hold the estates. The bureaucrats hold the leash. It is not your land. It is theirs. A land you cannot hunt is a land you do not truly own. In Denmark, hunting became privilege. In America, it remained birthright — until now. Across states, that birthright is being stripped. Lands swallowed by billionaires, NGOs, and "conservation trusts." Rifles and soil replaced by contracts and signatures. Farmers squeezed with quotas, ESG scores, and taxes until they sell. A people who once lived by storms, nets, and saltwater now live by pensions and paperwork. When the land was subdued, the people were too. The serpent always coils around the roots first. It doesn't need to devour the tree if it can choke the soil. And nothing chokes a people faster than losing control of their water — the first right, the first resource, the first freedom.

America Still Roars

But America is different. Here the land still roars — mountains, deserts, plains, rivers. Frontier. Untamed. Our fathers knew this truth — if you own your soil, you are free. If you lose it, you are owned. That's why the homesteads mattered. That's why the pioneers mattered. They weren't just chasing land — they were chasing liberty. The tribes knew this long before the settlers — land was covenant, and covenant was identity.

The Land Seized

The globalists know this too. That's why they buy fields through billionaires, banks, and "conservation" fronts. They seize water rights, strangle cattlemen, regulate farmers. They herd families into grids and 15-minute cities. They don't need to march armies if they can starve you on your own soil. And when they control the minerals beneath your feet, they control the future built on them. Because in every age, the battle begins with land. Whoever owns the ground owns the people who stand on it. And remember — property taxes are the leash. If you must pay rent to the State for your own home, you are not free. You are a tenant with illusions. Land is not real estate. It is not a portfolio line. Land is the root of freedom. In Denmark the land belongs to the State. In China the land belongs to the Party. In America the land must belong to the people — or America will not be America. For foreign powers now own fields, water, and processing plants — sovereignty sold one deed at a time.

The Cage in Concrete

We can already see the finished product in Copenhagen. Look at the skyline — cold, modern, minimalistic. Architecture as ideology. Efficient boxes for a managed people. And now the same blueprint unrolls in America. Rural towns are reshaped into "15-minute cities." Universities and NGOs buy farms, carving "smart neighborhoods" from soil meant to feed. Digital IDs and land registries are fusing — a system where property can be switched off like a subscription. Property taxes rise until families can no longer hold their ground. They call it sustainable. It is eviction by design. The velvet cage, exported. The serpent always coils at the roots. Now it coils around our cities. And if you let go of your soil, the coil will close. And once the coil closes, it rarely opens again without fire.

• Where is your soil? Do you know it — or have you forgotten its name?

• Do you own it — or do the bank, the state, the global landlord own you?

• Would you bleed for it — or lease it back with a polite smile?

• Have you traded covenant for contract — freedom for zoning codes, inheritance for "smart growth"?

• When the surveyors come with maps and the governor comes with promises, will you stand — or will you sell?

• What will your children inherit — land or leash, roots or ration cards, freedom or fenced-off zones?

A people without water, minerals, and soil are a people already captured. A people without land are a people already conquered.

Faith is the root. But roots feed people. And without fire in the soul, a nation softens into silence. Denmark shows the pattern — faith dimmed, the people hollowed, the soil surrendered. But in America, if the fire of faith still burns, then the people must burn too. Because nations are not built by crowns or cathedrals. They are built by men and women whose blood carries covenant, whose bones remember liberty, whose voices will not bow. But land alone is not enough. Soil without sovereignty is just dirt you lease from your rulers. Denmark shows the pattern — once the marshes were drained and the fields fenced, the next chains came in ballots and coalitions. The serpent that coils around the roots soon coils around the laws. Just ask Naboth (1 Kings 21), who died to keep his vineyard — for the wicked always covet the righteous man's land. So the question sharpens — who speaks for the people, and who only manages them? Step now from soil to state, from inheritance to the house of power — where the serpent hides behind the mask of "democracy." Because control of land leads to control of law — and control of law leads to control of the nation.

18

THE HYDRA OF PARTIES — SERPENT'S TONGUE, PEOPLE'S CHAINS

MANY HEADS, ONE SERPENT

They call it democracy. They call it choice. But names lie. The stage is polished, the flags arranged, the people summoned to believe their mark still matters. Ballots drop like prayers into boxes that have already chosen. Every four years the serpent changes costume — a new color, a new slogan, the same soul beneath. This is not governance. It is ritual — the illusion of power to keep the people docile. For the real rulers are not the faces on posters but the clerks behind the curtain — the permanent bureaucracy that never leaves when the ballots do.

The Illusion of Choice

Denmark's parliament is not a house of the people — it is a nest of serpents. More than ten parties slither across the stage — Social Democrats, Venstre, Danish People's Party, Social Liberal, Green Left, Red–Green Alliance, Conservatives, The Alternative, Denmark Democrats, Moderates, Liberal Alliance. Left, right, center, green, red, blue — but when the ballots are counted, it all coils back into the same serpent.

Koalitionsregering — coalition government.

You may vote left. You may vote right. But the tongue always splits and then joins again. The bureaucrats remain. The dynasties remain. The serpent keeps the table, only swapping chairs. And above them all sits Brussels — an unelected altar where EU directives outweigh Danish ballots.

Even comedy became government. Jacob Haugaard, under the "Union of Conscientiously Work-Shy Elements," promised better weather, Nutella in rations, and the right to impotence. And he won. For a moment, the joke ruled. The serpent laughed hardest — because the punchline got a pension. When politics becomes comedy, resistance is replaced by amusement — and power goes unchallenged. This is not choice. This is managed chaos. A serpent's grin beneath a carnival mask. For a people trained to laugh at power stops demanding it.

The Two-Party Mirage

And here is the danger for America — even with only two parties, the illusion can still hold. When both sides serve the same masters, democracy becomes theater. The ballots change, but the outcome doesn't. Choice becomes choreography. A mask, not a covenant. Denmark hides its serpent in many heads; America hides hers in two. A few smaller parties exist, but they orbit the same sun — none with gravity enough to shift the Republic. This is how the serpent survives — not through parties, but through power. And when donors fund both sides, the serpent speaks through money, not mandates. But now a new current moves beneath the stage. **America First** has torn through the curtain — not a party, but a reckoning. For the first time in generations, *We the People* stand a real chance to cleanse the system — to expose corruption, to reclaim covenant, to make the Republic answer to its citizens again. The serpent will not surrender quietly. But for the first time in a long time, it is cornered. And when the serpent is cornered, it calls its agencies — the intelligence state that enforces what ballots cannot. And the states are stirring — remembering that sovereignty begins local, that a free people rule closest to their own soil. The serpent fears this most.

Two Masks. One Serpent

In America, the illusion is not created by many parties, but by two that fight loudly while governing within the same permanent system. Elections change the actors. The machinery remains.

Democrats — born from *demos*, the people, and *kratos*, rule — became the party of slavery, segregation, and later, globalist progressivism. Since 2020, we have watched them kneel in kente cloth for cameras, bless unrest in the streets as "justice," and legislate in ways that cut against biology, family, and truth itself. They redefine words until freedom sounds like privilege, truth like "misinformation," faith like "hate." They do not bow to God. In spirit, they bow to Baal. They rule through language, institutions, and moral framing — redefining dissent as danger and obedience as virtue.

Republicans — from *res publica*, the public thing — began as the party of abolition. Law above crown. Covenant above compromise. But even here the serpent entered. They rail against debt, then sign it into law. They wave the flag, then leave borders open by loophole. They preach liberty on Sundays, then legislate compromise on Mondays. Too often they bow not to Baal, but to career, comfort, and cowardice. They conserve symbols while surrendering leverage — mistaking restraint for virtue and compromise for survival. Two masks. Two betrayals. And betrayal inside the gate wounds deeper than assault from outside the wall. When the gatekeepers fall, the whole city trembles.

America First

And yet — out of betrayal, a banner rose. America First. Not a party, but a movement. Not a slogan, but a covenant. Not politics, but a people remembering who they are. Farmers, builders, mothers, soldiers, pastors — citizens who had watched both parties trade their labor, their land, and their sons for global applause. A remnant who still roar. They do not fracture into twenty acronyms or hide behind coalitions. They rise under one banner — not because they agree on everything, but because they agree on *one thing*: a nation has the right — and the duty — to govern itself. Denmark hides behind coalitions. America First refuses camouflage. The line is drawn. The serpent exposed. This is why elites hate it — especially in Denmark. They call it "MAGA" and sneer, because they mistake sovereignty for supremacy and responsibility for aggression. But America First is not empire. **It is boundary.** Not domination of others, but devotion to one's own. It says: *we will take care of our people before managing the world.* To a managerial class raised on consensus and compliance, that sounds like heresy. A people with one banner can defeat a hydra with many heads. Because hydras thrive on division — and fall to unity.

The Counterfeit "Democracy"

The **Folketing** calls itself *the Assembly of the People.* But the people do not speak there. Seats are carved by party lists and quotas. Voices are chosen by coalitions. Power flows not from voters, but from bureaucrats who never appear on a ballot — and never leave when elections end. Even sovereignty is conditional. A Greenlandic MP once spoke in her own language on the floor. She was forced down unless she translated into Danish. Greenlandic is permitted on paper, but not in voice. Autonomy acknowledged — then muted. Sovereignty allowed — then managed. And the monarchy? A crown without power. Christian X made the last attempt in 1920. He failed. Since then, the throne reigns in parades, not in government. Ceremony without command. Lineage without authority. Yet the illusion endures. Denmark is still sovereign. Still a kingdom. Still different — or so it is said. That is how counterfeits work. They preserve the symbols while stripping them of force.

Flags remain. Titles remain. Assemblies remain. Power does not. Counterfeit systems never abolish tradition. They **display** it — like furniture in a showroom — to numb the mind while control moves elsewhere. Counterfeit democracy wears the symbols — assemblies, crowns, ballots, slogans — but drains them of power. Denmark kept the symbols and lost the substance. The question is no longer *whether* this happens — but whether America will recognize it in time. Once the fire leaves the symbols, the serpent moves to the word itself. "Democracy" — *demos* and *kratos*, the rule of the people — becomes rule by coalitions, permanent bureaucracies, and signatures in foreign ink. Consensus becomes silence. Participation becomes theater. And the serpent cheers, because the people still clap while the chains are fastened.

In America, the word still shines — but those who shout it loudest often mean control, not covenant. They speak of saving democracy while scripting it. They defend the ballot, but not the people behind it. The serpent no longer wears crowns — it wears credentials. No longer thrones — but committees. And if America accepts the same substitution, her roar becomes a murmur. Already the whisper spreads — ranked-choice voting, ballot harvesting, procedural "reforms" that fracture the voice of the people into manageable pieces. The illusion multiplies. Power concentrates. And the people, still believing they choose, applaud the cage as though it were freedom. **Divide the vote, and you divide the people. Divide the people, and you rule them.**

The Firewall

The Founders built a republic — not a hydra. They carved fire into stone — the Electoral College. House seats + Senate seats = Electors. 538 in all. Reach 270 and you win. Why? To keep balance between people and states. To stop cities from ruling farms. To stop coalitions from cutting deals in smoke-filled rooms. To keep the fisherman in Maine, the rancher in Montana, the farmer in Iowa from being erased by New York and California.

But when the serpent cannot break the firewall, it moves the lines. Districts redrawn. Cities bleeding into countryside. Urban votes absorbing rural voices. What once was balance becomes drift — power oozing outward until the map itself lies. Yet even that tide can turn. The remnant rises again, drawing lines not of ink but of courage — restoring what the Founders meant: every state a voice, every citizen a flame. For geography shapes power — and power shapes destiny.

That is why the globalists hate it. They call it racist. Outdated. Undemocratic. They want it gone. Because if it falls, America becomes Denmark — fractured, managed, ruled by coalitions and bureaucrats instead of covenant and people. Franklin warned — "A republic, if you can keep it." The Electoral College is how we keep it. This is the firewall. Remove it, and America's roar becomes Denmark's murmur. Keep it, and the serpent cannot fracture us into submission. A wall without fire crumbles; a firewall without courage collapses.

🔥 **Firelight Pause — Choose the Banner**
- Do you see choice — or the serpent's tongue?
- Does your vote shape the future — or serve the same machine?
- Will you fracture into many voices, or rise as one?
- Is your "independence" conviction — or surrender?
- Have you mistaken ballots for freedom, forgetting freedom is fire, not paper?
- When the banners rise, will yours bear compromise — or courage?

Neutral ground is not safe ground. It is surrender.

Denmark's hydra proves the lesson — many heads, one serpent. Coalition is not consensus. Democracy is not always freedom. The serpent's tongue whispers in many voices, but its coils bind the same. America must not fracture. One banner. One covenant. One fire. Or the serpent's coils will close. But ballots and banners are not the serpent's only mask. When the show of choice grows thin, the serpent shifts tactics — from noise to hush. From the chaos of coalitions to the silence of conformity. That silence is not peace. It is surrender dressed as wisdom. Denmark proved it. And America now tastes it. For the serpent conquers in two ways — by division, and by silence. The serpent does not always roar. Sometimes he whispers. Sometimes he waits until silence itself becomes the chain.

"If a kingdom is divided against itself, that kingdom cannot stand." — Mark 3:24

The serpent had proven it could divide. Now it would prove it could silence. Denmark's stage of parties and coalitions was only rehearsal — noise to hide the training of obedience. The people thought the serpent wanted argument. It wanted agreement. It wanted order without conviction, peace without spine. When the moment came to stand, no one did. The noise fell quiet. The hands that once waved banners now folded neatly. The serpent smiled. The laboratory was ready.

The year was 1940. The experiment began.

19

RESISTANCE VS. SURRENDER

SIX HOURS THAT SHAPED A NATION — AND A WARNING FOR OURS

The Experiment

Every empire begins its conquest with an experiment. Before the serpent devours the world, it tests a smaller nation — one obedient, orderly, moral on the surface. A laboratory of compliance. Denmark was that lab. A perfect mask — clean streets, calm voices, quiet faith. The serpent could not have asked for a gentler host. When the flag fell, it was not cloth that dropped — it was will. The people who once sang of light learned to worship safety instead. From that moment, the pattern was written — surrender disguised as civility, obedience dressed as virtue. And this test was not random. Throughout history, empires always prod the softest borders first — using small nations as trial grounds before tightening their grip on the larger powers. Denmark was not chosen because it was weak, but because it was predictable: orderly, trusting, reluctant to imagine evil. Empires prefer laboratories where compliance looks like politeness, where surrender can be mistaken for sophistication, where obedience is praised as maturity. Denmark became exactly that — the prototype for a future the serpent hoped to replicate elsewhere.

"In quietness and trust was your strength — but you refused; therefore you fled, a thousand at the threat of one." — Isaiah 30:15–17

This is not about a small kingdom on a cold sea. It is about what happens when comfort becomes creed — when a nation trades courage for calm. The serpent needed proof that men would kneel without chains. It found it. And it called it peace. The mask had been crafted long before the march. All it needed was pressure. When it came, the illusion cracked in hours. The serpent didn't need to conquer — only to ask, and Denmark obeyed. It started in 1940. Not with courage, but with calculation. Not with invasion, but invitation. The test was simple — would a nation built on order choose freedom over comfort when the sky darkened? In six hours, the answer came. And the tragedy deepens: Denmark was not only facing Germany — it had been politically isolated by Britain and ignored by France, left dangling between great powers who expected it to fall quietly. When a nation stands alone, great powers often prefer it surrendered rather than fighting — "stability" matters more than courage. Denmark learned, painfully, that when global predators circle, the small nations are always the first to be offered on the altar of convenience.

The Six-Hour Surrender

April 9, 1940. Dawn. German planes filled Denmark's skies. Tanks crossed the border. Soldiers rolled into Copenhagen. In six hours it was over. The Danish government surrendered. The army was ordered not to fight. King Christian X remained on his throne — not as a leader of resistance, but as a symbol of continuity under occupation. And notice something else: The crown rarely falls. Regimes collapse, parliaments dissolve, invaders come and go — but the throne remains untouched. That is the quiet power of monarchy: it gives empire a familiar face. A king can legitimize occupation simply by staying seated. Denmark learned long ago that continuity is the crown's true currency — and every external power knows it. Later legend painted him as a resistor, riding through Copenhagen daily. But myth cannot cover the truth: he rode beneath swastikas, not against them. Shops opened. Schools continued. Trains ran on time. Life, for most, went on — only with swastikas flying where the Dannebrog once waved.

And the pattern hasn't changed. Today the Danish monarchy still performs its quiet function: it hosts power. When the EU elites gathered at Amalienborg — presidents, commissioners, ministers — the king stood before them as a symbol of continuity, not sovereignty. The Danish people heard a polished speech. The elites heard something else: alignment, reliability, a small nation offering its crown as a stage for a larger throne. Danes were proud of his words, proud of his poise — but they missed the audience. He was not speaking to the people. He was speaking above them. A monarch grants legitimacy simply by standing in the room. That is the crown's true trade: dignity in exchange for influence. In 1940 it softened occupation. Today it softens integration. Different uniforms, same function. A familiar face for foreign power.

Resistance vs. Compliance

The contrast was brutal. Norway, invaded the same morning, chose to fight. Not for hours — for **sixty-two days.** Mountain battles. Sabotage runs. Entire towns burned rather than bow. A king who fled into the wilderness rather than sign his name to surrender. A nation outgunned, outnumbered, outflanked — yet unwilling to kneel. Denmark managed **six hours.** Sixty-two days versus six hours. Two nations. One invader. The difference wasn't weapons. It was **will.** Norway chose the impossible. Denmark chose the inevitable. One wrote itself into legend. The other into footnotes. And that is the uncomfortable truth: a nation collapses not when the enemy breaks the rifle, but when it breaks the **spirit.**

"This iniquity shall be to you like a breach in a high wall, whose collapse comes suddenly, in an instant." — Isaiah 30:13

Psychologists later confirmed what history already proved: people resist only when they believe victory is possible. Denmark did not surrender because it lacked weapons. It surrendered because it lacked hope — and when hope collapses, courage follows. Norway had mountains, a warrior culture, and a belief that resistance mattered. Denmark had leaders who signaled defeat before the soldiers ever loaded their rifles. Nations do not collapse first in battle; they collapse in imagination. And while Denmark obeyed, the Reich built its racial future in the North. In Norway more than 12,000 Aryan children were born through the *Lebensborn* program — cradles turned into weapons, bloodlines engineered to carry the Reich into the future. Their descendants now number in the tens of thousands, proof that empire hides its conquest in generations, not just in borders. Norway fought fiercely, then complied deeply — high courage first, high compliance after. And the same nation that once resisted became one of Europe's financial fortresses, showing that empires don't always conquer by force. Sometimes they conquer by absorption. Sweden — the "neutral" brother — kept Hitler's furnaces burning. LKAB's Kiruna and Malmberget mines shipped millions of tons of high-grade iron ore to the Reich. Up to half of all German wartime iron came from Swedish rock. SKF supplied the ball bearings that kept tanks rolling. Trains carried German troops across Swedish rails. Neutrality was not purity. It was profit. It was complicity. It was empire fed by silence and steel. This is the truth the modern world refuses to face: **neutrality is often the mask of the collaborator. Playing both sides is easier than standing for one.**

The pattern hasn't changed. Today nations praise "cooperation" and "international norms" while quietly feeding modern empires with data, technology, and infrastructure. What Sweden was to iron, many nations now are to surveillance, biotech, and global finance. The serpent never wastes a compliant supplier. And Denmark? Its soil was occupied in a day. Its ports and shipping firms folded into German logistics. Merchants carried the Reich's cargo under flags of necessity. The crown stayed in place, the government stayed seated — and the nation kept the machine alive.

Scandinavia's image today is bicycles, innocence, and windmills, but the scars remain: Swedish ore fueling the Reich, Norwegian cradles filling the Aryan dream, Danish obedience greasing the gears. The serpent never left. It merely learned to smile. Candlelit windows. Moral superiority. The myth of flawless virtue. But the record tells the truth: **not a spotless North, but a collaborator's corridor.**

Yes, resistance rose — saboteurs, ferrymen, underground presses. But only later. First came the bending, the silence, the instinct to survive under the boot. That is the psychology of surrender: safety before struggle, peace at any price, consensus even under chains. The North was not pure. It was useful. And perhaps it still is. Here is the truth nations fear most: **institutions kneel long before individuals ever do.** Governments bow quickly. Bureaucracies bow faster. Conscience takes longer to kill. The serpent can subdue a parliament in a morning, but it cannot extinguish a remnant in a single blow. That is why empires fear individuals more than armies. Armies can be conquered. Conscience cannot. And even the resistance, when it finally rose, told its own story. The bravest Danes — saboteurs, couriers, the ones who ferried Jews across the Øresund — did not act because the nation roared. They acted because they themselves refused to kneel. Their courage was individual, not institutional. A few stood where the many bowed. And that pattern never changes: **the remnant resists while the nation sleeps. True resistance never begins with crowds. It begins with conscience.**

From Lebensborn to "Cryos"

The echoes are chilling. Not in cradles this time — but in catalogs. Denmark has become the global hub of sperm. Today Aarhus hosts *"Cryos"*, a sperm bank that ships donor samples to more than a hundred countries, and journalism has repeatedly reported strong demand from East Asia for Nordic donors. And what do they sell? The same image the Nazis once craved — tall. Blond. Blue-eyed. Healthy. Nordic.

And Cryos is only one pillar of Denmark's new genetics industry. In Copenhagen stands its mirror, the *European Sperm Bank* — a global hub selling the same phenotype the Reich once engineered, now packaged in soft colors and "ethical" language. They don't call it selection. They call it "matching." They don't call it eugenics. They call it "choice." What was once enforced by ideology is now normalized by markets. The language is softer. The intent is not. Cryos sells Viking fantasy. European Sperm Bank sells Scandinavian perfection. Two companies, two cities, one trade: the export of a curated future.

A young Dane can earn about $70 per sample — nearly $1,000 a month if he donates regularly. Catalogued seed, traded like currency. So ask yourself: who decides which genes travel? Who chooses which children inherit which nations? Is this commerce — or the quiet engineering of future populations? And Cryos is only the entry point. IVF surrogacy markets now span continents. CRISPR edits slip into medical journals. "Designer child" debates normalize the unthinkable. What begins as choice ends as coding — children shaped to fit someone's blueprint. Yesterday it was Lebensborn cradles. Today it is Cryos catalogs and gene labs. Same fantasy. Same manipulation. New tools. Behind the industry lies the darkest truth: fertility markets do not merely respond to demand — **they shape it.** Nations facing demographic collapse outsource reproduction. Tech elites outsource genetics. Global bureaucracies set "standards" for health and selection. What looks like freedom becomes population curation — modern eugenics with better branding. No boots required. The cradle becomes the battlefield.

Meanwhile, birth tourism and donor pipelines explode. Mothers land in Silicon Valley hospitals, deliver, and fly home with a child stamped U.S. citizen. Not soldiers at the gates — but seed and citizenship. Tomorrow the same outcome may come coded in genes, filed in databases, tracked in children who never asked to be born as currency. The serpent no longer marches with boots. It whispers through wombs.

And modern bureaucracies already track everything else — health records, biometrics, genomic profiles. Where biology meets bureaucracy, the next generation becomes a managed asset. This is not speculation. It is trajectory. The serpent has simply traded cradles for cloud servers. So ask yourself: is this coincidence — or the blueprint of a future already breeding among us? And understand this: it isn't about Denmark. It is the prototype — the testing ground — the quiet blueprint they intend to scale. So when the pattern repeats in your nation, will you recognize it... or kneel to it?

The COVID Surrender

And the pattern repeated in our time. In 2020, Denmark bowed again. Not to Panzer tanks, but to mandates, masks, and the needle. With hardly a protest, the people lined up. They obeyed. They complied. "Trust the State. Trust the experts. Keep calm." By 2021, Denmark bragged of being the "first European country to lift restrictions." The world applauded. But few noticed the fine print: restrictions were only lifted after nearly 90% of adults had submitted to the jab. Only after near-total obedience did the State reward its subjects with a return to "normal". That wasn't liberty. That was conditional permission. A leash. At Copenhagen Airport, travelers stood in lines like cattle. Swabbed. Tested. Tagged. Ordered to test again after a few days. And behind this obedience stood the new architecture of control — digital passports, QR codes, algorithmic approvals, movement tracked by apps, health access governed by databases. The serpent no longer needed checkpoints with rifles; it had checkpoints in phones. It discovered what every tyrant dreams of: a system where the people police themselves, where compliance is automated, where fear is a software update away. "Zu Ihrer Sicherheit," the Nazis used to say. For your safety. *Safety was the velvet word for iron chains.* And in 2020, Denmark repeated the script. The lesson was the same as 1940 - bow quickly, bend fully, and the boot becomes invisible. This is how the serpent hides: not in brutality, but in benevolence. Not in threats, but in reassurances. Not in chains, but in comfort. The words become softer even as the control deepens — "for your safety," "for the common good," "for public health." When virtue is weaponized, tyranny smiles.

The American Contrast

But America — at least in part — did not kneel so easily. Yes, the Blue States obeyed. California was the model child of COVID tyranny. Businesses shuttered. Children masked on playgrounds. Beaches closed. Neighbors snitched. The "science" shifted daily, but the obedience stayed the same. It was the Danish script replayed on American soil. But the Red States refused — and their defiance broke the spell. Texas and Florida defied the mandates. Churches stayed open. Families gathered. Life continued. They saw the trap for what it was — a rehearsal in control. And by standing, they proved the lie: if freedom survives anywhere, it exposes the fraud everywhere. Yet America faces a danger Denmark never had: distraction, not defeat. The serpent discovered that Americans do not need tanks or mandates to surrender — only screens, comfort, and endless noise. A people glued to devices will not storm beaches. A nation medicated by convenience will not remember its courage. Denmark bowed from fear; America risks bowing from fatigue.

America was born different. Resistance was not the exception — it was the inheritance. When the crown demanded obedience, farmers and blacksmiths took muskets from their walls and stood at Lexington Green. When slavery tore the republic in two, Americans chose war rather than compromise freedom. When tyranny rose in Europe and the Pacific, American boys crossed oceans, stormed beaches, and planted flags in foreign soil. **Rebellion runs through our marrow. Defiance is not an afterthought — it is our DNA.** Even in times of fracture, the pattern holds. Rosa Parks refusing to move. Families standing at school board meetings. Veterans and truckers rallying when the State pushed too far. The faces change, the fields change, but the spirit does not. When Americans are told to kneel, something in us rises.

The Warning for Today

But here lies the danger - Americans are being trained to surrender. Not in six hours with tanks, but in six months with mandates. Not with German helmets in the streets, but with globalists on our screens. 2020 revealed it. Masks worn even in open air. Churches closed by decree. Neighbors reporting neighbors. Speech codes enforced by platforms. Businesses shuttered "for public health." This was surrender by another name. Compliance dressed as compassion. Control sold as safety. Doctors who told the truth became targets. Careers erased. Licenses stripped. Some disappeared. Others died in ways too strange to ignore. The message was clear: truth is dangerous. Now the pattern sharpens. We no longer see only the horror of deranged school shooters. We see something colder — direct strikes on men and women who dare to speak freely. **Free speech has become a death sentence.** And this is no accident. Psychological warfare — once reserved for battlefields — is now deployed against citizens. Fear cycles are engineered. Rage is curated. Algorithms amplify despair. The serpent learned that a terrified population will police itself. Through media manipulation, trauma conditioning, and curated panic, modern systems produce a people too exhausted to resist and too numb to perceive the cage.

We've seen this before. In Stalin's Soviet Union, dissidents erased. In Nazi Germany, priests and journalists hauled to camps. In Mao's China, one word out of line could cost a family its life. The serpent always begins with slogans. But when words are no longer enough, it reaches for bullets. What begins as censorship ends as assassination. And if you think America is immune, ask yourself: **why are truth-tellers being targeted now — with precision?** For the serpent now uses new weapons — digital blacklists, deplatforming, AI moderation, financial freezes, reputation algorithms. These tools destroy a life without shedding a drop of blood. A modern regime can erase a dissident with a keystroke, not a bullet. The method changes, but the motive is the same: silence the voice before it awakens the nation.

You don't lose a nation first in tanks and fire. You lose it in silence. In small compromises. In six hours of cowardice stretched across decades. Denmark lasted six hours. **America must last forever.** But only if we choose fire over fear. Resistance over comfort. **Covenant over compromise. Resistance is not optional. It is survival.**

🔥 **Firelight Pause — The Test of Pressure**
  • When pressure comes, do you instinctively kneel — or rise?
  • Where in your life have you chosen safety over struggle?
  • What is your "six hours" moment — and will you be ready when it comes?
  • If your children inherit your choices, will they remember resistance — or obedience?

Denmark fell in six hours because the rifles were quiet. But before the rifles went silent, the tongues already had. No nation collapses first by tanks — it collapses when its people no longer dare to speak. The serpent knows this. It does not need to crush every arm — only every voice. For if you cannot speak, you cannot resist. And if you cannot resist, you will kneel. That is why every tyranny begins not with bullets, but with speech codes. Not with war, but with whispers. Not with chains, but with reassurances. Not with violence, but with "community standards." Denmark's lesson is not only about six hours. It is about six words: **"within the limits of the law."** Those words sound harmless — even virtuous. But they reverse the order of freedom. Speech no longer belongs to the people by right; it is granted by the State by permission. What the law gives, the law can narrow. What it narrows, it can silence. This is how a muzzle is fitted without ever calling it a gag. A freedom that exists only "within the law" is not freedom. It is parole. From there the spread is quiet. First the rifles fall silent. Then the pens begin to write. Then the keyboards type, the screens glow, and the algorithms whisper — not to warn you, but to soothe you. The serpent does not need to roar. All it needs is for the watchmen to sleep.

20

THE QUIET OCCUPATION
HOW DENMARK FELL WITHOUT A SHOT

"The truth will set you free, but first it will make you miserable." — James A. Garfield

From Occupation to Integration

They call it integration. But the word no longer means what it once did. In the heart of Copenhagen, the flag still flies, the anthem still plays, yet the grammar of power has shifted. What was once sovereignty has become management; what was once citizenship has become membership in a bloc. In the name of compassion, borders dissolved – not with tanks but with treaties. The occupation did not begin with soldiers. It began with signatures — paper instead of rifles, policy instead of invasion. What Denmark surrendered in 1940 under the swastika, she surrendered again in 2009 under the flag of the Union. Only this time, the chains came wrapped in virtue. *2015 — The year the gates opened. Caravans moved north through the Balkans, across Germany, over the Øresund Bridge into Denmark. The EU called it a migration crisis; the press called it humanity on the move.* **For many Danes, it felt quieter — the slow replacement of consent with decree.** *No referendum was held. The decision had already been signed — in Brussels boardrooms and UN halls.*

And beneath this quiet shift lay something deeper: a psychological reshaping. Denmark became the model child of "harmonic societies," where disagreement is treated as danger and dissent is framed as antisocial. In a culture built on avoiding offense, truth becomes impolite and silence becomes virtue. The people were trained to fear standing alone more than losing their country. The serpent did not need to impose obedience — it simply weaponized politeness, consensus, and the terror of social shame. In such a culture, surrender never feels like defeat; it feels like maturity. That is how occupation hides inside courtesy — not force.

The Paper Empire

No empire today marches in armor. It legislates in acronyms. The old kings ruled by sword and crown; Brussels rules by framework and compliance directive. From Brussels to Copenhagen, the serpent moved by signature, not sword. In 2009 *the Lisbon Treaty* bound twenty-seven nations beneath one legal spine — efficiency promised, hierarchy delivered. EU law rose quietly above every constitution, Denmark's included. Then came 2018 and *the Marrakesh Compact* — "non-binding," they said, yet within months its language, migration as a human right, was echoed in courts and classrooms across the continent. By 2020 a new Pact on Migration and Asylum sealed the pattern: quotas disguised as solidarity, opt-outs that still paid in. Through DANIDA and ECHO the money kept flowing, financing the very networks Denmark claimed to resist. The cage was outsourced, the covenant abandoned. Europe called it progress. Heaven called it surrender. But even surrender can become strategy. The serpent hides best inside systems — and Denmark learned to weaponize the very bureaucracy that once enslaved it. **The serpent's genius was never brute power, but moral vocabulary — turning mercy into mandate and conscience into code.** What the Church once called sin, Brussels calls non-compliance. What prophets called repentance, bureaucrats rename reform. And so a new religion rises — orderly, moral, godless.

Its directives become liturgies, its compliance metrics sacraments, its courts the high priests who interpret the sacred text of the *acquis communautaire* — the entire body of EU law and rulings that every member state must accept without negotiation or escape. In this new faith, there is no forgiveness, only audits. No prophets, only panels. No commandments, only codes. Bureaucracy becomes holiness, and dissent becomes heresy. The serpent has built a church without God — a cathedral of paper, where obedience is the only virtue left.

By 2024, entire districts in Copenhagen and Aarhus had become "parallel societies." The government's own reports admitted what citizens already knew: social trust was fracturing. Yet the prescription was always the same — more funding, more programs, more dialogue, never boundary. Tolerance became state religion; guilt its altar. The serpent no longer hissed — it whispered through paperwork. The psychology was precise: punishment was never loud. It came instead through soft ostracism — a job not offered, a grant not approved, a platform quietly throttled. Danes learned early that survival meant staying within the emotional temperature of the tribe. The serpent understood this perfectly. You do not need force in a nation terrified of social isolation. Shame does the work of soldiers. Self-censorship becomes patriotism. Silence becomes virtue.

In 2017, Parliament expanded §266 b — the "racism paragraph" — to cover religion. What began as protection became policing. That year matters. Once you know when the chain was forged, you can trace who hammered it — and break it. By 2021, journalists and pastors faced investigation and prosecution risks for quoting scripture or criticizing migration policy. The law's intent was harmony; its effect was hesitation. Truth became a health hazard. A nation that builds its virtue on paperwork must keep its sins unseen. The Danish illusion is moral cleanliness — the 'clean hands' that outsource the dirt. Every treaty that binds another nation is signed with that smile — efficient, innocent, immaculate. But the ink still stains.

The Press Compact

In 2022 the national broadcaster adopted the EU Code of Principles on Disinformation, pledging to counter "narratives that undermine social cohesion." Dissent became disinformation. Editors self-censored. Words were filtered through global codebooks. The serpent wrote the style guide. What once was journalism became jurisdiction — speech monitored not by truth, but by compliance. And across the Atlantic, the same playbook took root. Different continent, same doctrine: protect the narrative, punish the deviation. Accent aside, the serpent had found its new tongue — bureaucracy. This was not a European anomaly. It was a template.

The Mirror Across the Atlantic

In Washington, "illegal immigrant" became "undocumented." "Amnesty" became "pathway." What Brussels called solidarity, Washington renamed compassion. Every word carried a price tag. Billions flowed to NGOs echoing Geneva's language — Catholic Charities, Lutheran Immigration Services, International Rescue Committee — all funded through federal channels. The Marrakesh Compact wasn't signed by Congress, yet its spirit governs every border policy today. And what Washington copied most faithfully was Denmark's moral manipulation: the recoding of vice as virtue and obedience as empathy. **This was not policy drift — it was linguistic capture.** In America's administrative state, the serpent perfected the technique of moral inversion — making resistance appear cruel and compliance appear compassionate. A nation that loses control of its vocabulary loses control of its destiny. This linguistic trick is the velvet noose of the modern West. Language softened → borders softened → sovereignty softened. The serpent didn't need kings — only committees. Under Biden, boards and departments replaced debate. The DHS Disinformation Governance Board echoed Copenhagen's silence — same algorithm, new accent. The serpent now recruits servers, not soldiers.

The Invisible Government

And how fitting that Helle Thorning-Schmidt co-chairs Meta's Oversight Board, shaping speech for billions. The politeness that muzzled Denmark now governs the digital commons. Denmark was the beta test; America is the rollout. But to see how a nation becomes both captive and colonizer, look behind the charm. Denmark did not merely surrender — it evolved. Humility became infiltration. Survival became design. And America's blind spot is its administrative state. The alphabet agencies — IRS, EPA, DOJ, CDC, CISA, DOE — function as an unelected parliament. Presidents pass; the agencies stay. Their directives outlast elections. Their rules override voters. What Denmark built through charm, America built through scale. The serpent no longer needs to win elections; it only needs to outlive them.

The Silent Occupation

They call Denmark a small country. Six million people. A postage stamp on the map. Pastries, bicycles, "hygge." But look closer. For forty years, Danes have quietly walked into the command posts of the global order — Brussels, Geneva, New York, NATO headquarters, even Silicon Valley. They did not arrive as conquerors. They arrived as architects. As regulators. As referees. Their weapons were not tanks but treaties, not battalions but directives, not artillery but frameworks. Their reach extended far beyond Copenhagen. Behind the smiles, Danish services plug into the alliance machine — a hidden circuit of surveillance beneath the friendly face. **PET**, the Danish Security and Intelligence Service, watches the home front. **FE**, the Defence Intelligence Service, feeds foreign intelligence into NATO channels, sending Danish data directly into allied systems. Liaison officers and commissioners carry those priorities into committees and command rooms, embedding Denmark's agenda inside multinational decisions.

The Hidden Circuit

In media reporting on **"Operation Dunhammer"** — a Danish intelligence program revealed in 2021 that involved cooperation with the NSA to access European undersea and land-based data cables — Danish intelligence allegedly worked with U.S. agencies to tap continental communications. Critics saw this as proof of deep surveillance integration — a reminder that power today is not measured by population, but by placement. A small state with the right keys can influence empires far larger than itself. This is not coincidence. It is pattern. A small state exporting managers into the bloodstream of the global system. And now even America breathes their designs — speech policed on platforms, climate mandates embedded in law, digital IDs tested abroad and prepared for our shores. Influence disguised as expertise. Governance disguised as guidance. If this is what a "powerless" country looks like, then what does power really mean?

Denmark's quiet leverage does not rise from population or production. It rises from placement — from a northern vault that holds rare earths, airbases, and data cables beneath ice. Greenland funds the illusion of smallness. That is why the bureaucrats matter — because they manage an empire frozen in plain sight. The paper in Brussels is only half the story; the ice bankrolls the rest. And beneath the ice lies the secret no capital dares to name — the cables. Over 95% of global internet traffic runs through undersea fiber-optic lines, carrying bank transfers, military orders, intelligence feeds, and the daily heartbeat of nations. Cut them, and the world goes dark. Control them, and the world obeys. Cut them, and currencies freeze. Military commands fall silent. Nations stagger. In 2022, the Nord Stream pipelines exploded in the Baltic, proof that the deep sea is now a battlefield. If pipelines can be blown, cables can be tapped, severed, or seized. And where do those cables run? Through Arctic waters overseen by Denmark and Greenland — a quiet choke point in the modern world. The serpent no longer storms beaches; it slips along the seabed. Whoever governs the ice governs the signal. Whoever governs the signal governs the century.

The Danish Power List (1985–2025)

Every empire hides its engineers. Not the faces on posters. Not the voices at rallies. But the quiet hands who draft laws, shape treaties, and press signatures that no voter ever cast. Henning Christophersen opened the playbook in 1985 — architect of the EU Single Market and the Euro. Connie Hedegaard turned climate into code. Helle Thorning-Schmidt — the Ministry of Truth with Wi-Fi. Margrethe Vestager — the algorithm queen. Mogens Lykketoft — presiding over the UN's stage. Jeppe Tranholm-Mikkelsen — writing the law for half a billion souls. Dan Jørgensen — binding energy and housing into Europe's new compliance engines. Mette Frederiksen — laughing at Greenland's sale while locking it into EU defense plans. Every name is a mask. Every mask a lever. Every lever a loss of sovereignty. And what these names reveal is not conspiracy — but design. A design so polished, so polite, that even those bound by it call it progress. The serpent learned to smile.

Bureaucracy as Weapon

Denmark has been a net exporter of bureaucrats since 1973. Nine commissioners. Fifteen MEPs. Each one a pen turned into a sword. Copenhagen hosts one of the UN's larger field footprints — humanitarian in name, command in practice. In NATO, Danish ambassadors fill hallways. Every handshake becomes an obligation. Every briefing a new entanglement. Denmark's military footprint is small. Its bureaucratic footprint is vast. Even education became export. Thousands of foreign students cycle through UN-linked programs — indoctrination disguised as scholarship. The deeper machinery is faceless. Clerks. Legal drafters. Quiet hands writing the rules that shape half the free world. And as the bureaucrats built abroad, the dynasties built at home.

The crown never fell — it rebranded. Commerce became the new monarchy. Yet the engine behind it all is invisible infrastructure: fiber-optic cables spiderwebbing under the Skagerrak, data centers operated by global giants inside Danish borders, cloud pipelines feeding NATO intelligence systems, and Arctic relay stations that move global signals north and south. Denmark became more than a manager — it became a switchboard. In the digital era, the nation controlling the cables controls the conversation. And the serpent thrives wherever information flows quietly through friendly hands.

Denmark in America

Bureaucracy built the architecture. But dynasties fund the façade. To understand how softly empire walks, follow the money — and see how a postage-stamp kingdom stitched itself into the sinews of a superpower. America was supposed to be the escape. No crown. No king. A republic built to break Europe's chains. But the crown has found its way back in.

The Danish ambassador in Washington oversees a web of consulates — New York, Chicago, Houston, Silicon Valley. Each post is framed as service for citizens abroad, yet they also connect diplomacy with business, trade, and cultural outreach. These consulates host trade missions, energy dialogues, and tech partnerships that can shape networks far beyond their stated purpose. Do these consulates simply serve expatriates — or do they operate as forward outposts of Danish influence? When a small country plants diplomatic nodes in America's *financial hub*, its *oil capital*, and its *tech corridor*, is that routine diplomacy — or strategy? If ambassadors and consuls broker meetings that shape contracts and policies, who really benefits — local voters, or foreign dynasties with global reach?

Prince Joachim of Denmark, once a military attaché in Paris, stepped into Washington in 2023 as Denmark's defense industry attaché. His portfolio wasn't ceremonial — it involved contracts, supply chains, and critical technologies. He was tasked with strengthening industrial defense cooperation between Denmark, the United States, and Canada. His résumé includes France's highest-ranking military education and service as a liaison officer in the Danish Army. His Washington post gave him access to U.S. defense networks at the very moment NATO and American planners were debating supply-chain security and Arctic routes. Does this placement represent diplomacy — or embedded leverage? When a European royal sits in Washington with authority to shape defense industry cooperation, is that soft power — or silent pressure? When a crown joins critical-technology briefings, whose interests move across the table first — Denmark's, NATO's, or America's? If the crown no longer matters, why does it sit in the war room?

Maersk Line, Limited, a Danish shipping giant operating under U.S. flag, is one of the Pentagon's core sealift partners. Its U.S.-flagged arm participates in the Maritime Security Program and operates dozens of vessels made available to the Pentagon in emergencies. Shipping records show its vessels moving pre-positioned cargo, surge logistics, and deployment pipelines. If one foreign company sits at the hinge of America's war mobility, is that partnership — or dependency? When a nation's war boxes are carried under contracts with a dynasty abroad, who ultimately holds the leverage — the Pentagon, or the partner?

Novo Nordisk sells Ozempic and Wegovy that cost American patients over $1,000 per month, while the same injections cost a fraction abroad — often under $150 in Denmark and the EU. In 2023, Novo posted record profits of nearly $30 billion. Billions poured into U.S. factories, and millions more into lobbying and research partnerships. But what does that really mean? Is it innovation — or extraction? Is it concrete for resilience — or concrete for dependence? If this is the price of medicine, is it health — or is it a leash?

Carlsberg's ownership foundation distributes hundreds of millions yearly, funding research far beyond Denmark's borders. Its grants reach American universities, seeding scholars and programs that carry Danish frameworks abroad. But when a foundation funds inquiry at this scale, is it just support for science — or does the grant also become a leash on what questions may be asked? Carlsberg isn't just beer. It is a dynasty ruled through its foundation, holding controlling ownership while distributing vast sums each year. When a dynasty directs both capital and inquiry, is that independence — or influence with strings attached? At Carlsberg's historic Elephant Gate, early twentieth-century swastika motifs remain part of the original architecture; the company has contextualized them as pre-Nazi symbols. But the question remains: if symbols matter, what does it mean when a dynasty preaches progress under monuments that whisper otherwise?

And if the same pattern repeats across medicine, energy, and policy — do we still call it cooperation, or quiet chains? If Maersk carries the cargo, Novo Nordisk supplies the medicine, and a prince represents Denmark in Washington as defense attaché — is that coincidence, or strategy? And remember — Novo, Maersk, and Carlsberg are only three dynasties among many. The flag may be small, but the reach is long. Different sectors, same pattern — placement becomes policy, policy becomes leverage. If this is only philanthropy, why does it so often mirror policy outcomes? A crown in Washington. Corporations in the bloodstream. Clerks in the councils. The serpent no longer needs to roar — it rules through routine. And under that quiet routine, a fire still waits beneath the ice.

The Fire Under the Ice

Denmark was not always quiet. Once, when darkness marched under the swastika, the same cobblestones that now host parades hid resistance cells and secret presses. When obedience looked like peace, courage was reborn in cellars. Teachers printed leaflets. Fishermen ferried Jews under blackout skies. Students took up sabotage. The "Frihedskæmpere" — the freedom fighters — remembered what their rulers forgot: sovereignty means saying no even when it costs everything. That is Denmark's true inheritance — not silence, but fire. The lesson is not shame. It is warning: the longer you wait to resist, the higher the price of remembering who you are. And here is the wound the world never sees. Silence is not natural — it is conditioned. In Eastern Europe, the Soviets crushed resistance through fear: surveillance, informants, sudden disappearances. Czechoslovakians learned that truth spoken aloud could cost your life. Denmark learned a different lesson: that truth spoken aloud could cost your belonging. One nation was broken by tanks; the other by social pressure. But the result was the same — people who knew the truth stopped speaking it. And today the line has moved even further. Danes have faced criminal charges and professional threats over social-media posts and shares — statistics, comments, even words prosecuted under §266 b. In England, a charity worker was arrested and investigated for silently praying in her own head outside an abortion clinic buffer zone. Not shouting. Not blocking. Praying — and still treated as a threat.

And America is not immune. Blue states lead the charge, but the mechanism is federal. FBI field offices have monitored parents protesting school boards. DOJ memos labeled concerned parents as potential "domestic extremists." States like California and New York have investigated people for "misinformation," pressured platforms to silence dissent, and threatened medical licenses for doctors who speak outside approved narratives. Cities have arrested pro-life activists for standing on public sidewalks. Tech platforms — under federal pressure — have erased posts, throttled speech, and punished users without trial.

This is the technocrat model: obedience enforced not by open violence, but by algorithmic surveillance and social rules no one ever voted for. What Soviet officers once demanded at gunpoint, Western bureaucrats now enforce through code, policy, and digital policing. Occupation has changed its uniform. The serpent no longer needs boots on streets. It wages psychological war through dopamine loops, curated fatigue, micro-targeted fear, and the endless drone of triviality. It doesn't need you terrified; it only needs you tired, numb, and scrolling. Modern occupation is bandwidth, not bayonets. And so the question turns — from Denmark's silence to America's slumber. The coils that bound them are the same now closing around us. Will we wake before the wax melts? Every nation must choose between comfort and covenant. Denmark chose comfort. America still has time to choose covenant. But that window closes fast — and silence is already signing the papers.

🔥 **Firelight Pause — The Silent Covenant**
- When faith becomes private, who guards the public square?
- When "safety" means surrender, whose law rules your land?
- Bureaucrats you never chose write rules that bind you — is that freedom, or management?
- Sovereignty signed away in quiet agreements — are you free, or merely handled?
- If Denmark holds keys to America's supply chains and data streams, would you shrug if the name were China?
- When Brussels or Geneva shapes your speech and your bills, what does your vote still mean?
- Can mercy without truth save a nation?
- If comfort became your creed, would you notice when covenant burned away?
- Freedom dies not when the gun fires, but when the paper signs.

"Woe to those who devise iniquity and work evil upon their beds; when the morning is light, they practice it, because it is in the power of their hand." — Micah 2:1

21

HOW DENMARK FELL WITHOUT A SHOT

DENMARK: THE PROTOTYPE OF QUIET SURRENDER

You've seen the playbook. You've glimpsed the silent occupation. Now stand inside it. Not theory. Not speculation. A living case study — Denmark, the model nation. This is what it looks like when sovereignty is signed away without a single bullet fired. Clean streets. Smiling faces. Bicycles in perfect rows. And beneath it all — surrender polished as virtue.

Why Denmark?

Because it is the perfect test subject: high-trust, low-conflict, wealthy, compliant, secular, and trained for consensus. A people who avoid confrontation become a laboratory for global governance. The elites chose Denmark not because it was weak, but because it was obedient. What works in Denmark is exported to nations that still believe they are awake.

Eyewitness Shock

I went back to Denmark in 2024. Just for a visit. The streets were still clean. The people still smiled. The bikes still ruled. But something was... off. From the tallest buildings overlooking Tivoli Gardens, the skyline now held something new: **Chinese towers. Muslim domes.** Symbols that did not belong to Denmark's past — but announced its future. New construction patterns and cultural markers that would have been unthinkable a generation earlier. And on nearly every government building? **Rainbow flags. Ukraine flags.** Not a Danish one in sight. Even Politiken — one of Denmark's major newspapers — flew them proudly. Denmark is a country where the flag once meant something. It's waved at birthdays. It decorates cakes. It's sacred. But now? **It was gone.** The chilling part wasn't the flags. It was the silence. No one looked up. No one questioned. No one cared. **No one asked: Who owns this country now?**

The City That Forgot to Look Up

And in the summer of 2024, at Rådhuspladsen — the heart of Copenhagen — fenced stages rose for Pride Week. Families streamed in. Bands played. The city called it inclusion. But what I heard was not celebration. The lyrics were explicit, sexualized, and stripped of restraint — words no society once allowed near its children. Words glorified what should never be spoken in a public square. And the most chilling part? No one stopped it. People walked by. Some paused with their children. Some smiled. As if nothing was wrong. Silence was consent. The city blessed it with banners. The State wrapped it in rainbow colors. And the crowd applauded. This is what it looks like when a people stop looking up — when covenant breaks and conscience sleeps. Worse still: children raised to believe silence is maturity and obedience is virtue. This is Denmark's deepest wound — a generation without fire, without courage, without memory. Boys who never learned to defend anything. Girls taught to distrust their own heritage. Children catechized by screens instead of stories. A nation that forgets its children forgets its future. And the silence is not local — it echoes outward. From Copenhagen's squares to Brussels' halls to Greenland's ice. The Arctic lanes, the rare earths, the bases — all bartered in silence.

- Would you walk past — or walk out?
- Do your children hear songs of covenant — or corruption?
- When evil is paraded as pride, do you look up — or look away?
- If silence is consent, what does your silence bless?
- When Babylon's music plays, will you dance — or will you defy?

Land Is Memory

Land is not just territory. Land is memory. Whoever owns the soil owns the soul. When a nation sells its ground, it sells its story. Denmark markets itself as green, global, progressive — but beneath the slogans lies surrender. Chinese stakes in energy and property deepen each year. Farmers are fined for producing "too much." Brussels dictates what is planted, how many cows breathe, even how the soil is used. The people who once fed the nation now bow to quotas. Told it is "for the planet," they do not protest. But the truth is simple: Denmark does not own Denmark anymore. And when a people lose their soil, they lose their story. A feudal skeleton remains. Vast estates still sit in German bloodlines granted centuries ago — aristocracy repainted as progress. The flag waves, but the land beneath it is locked in dynasties and trusts. And here the pattern sharpens. If Denmark's soil is frozen under foreign crowns and old estates, what of America's? Farmland sold to Beijing. Acres swallowed by corporations and faceless funds. "Ownership" reduced to an annual tribute called property tax — miss one year, and the State reminds you whose name is truly on the deed. Dynasties never lose their estates. Trusts shield them from tribute. Corporations absorb the cost. Small farmers are crushed under the weight. That is why Americans feel like tenants on their own soil while the owners above never fear losing theirs. If land is memory, what happens when memory is leased? If sovereignty is tied to tribute, who really wears the crown? Denmark was the rehearsal. America is the stage. What Denmark surrendered to Brussels, America now risks surrendering to Beijing, BlackRock, and its own bureaucracy. The method differs. The result does not.

◊ **Firelight Pause — Soil, Tribute, Freedom**

• Who owns the land beneath your feet — your people, or foreign powers behind contracts and trusts?

• If missing one tax payment can erase your "ownership," do you own at all — or are you only a tenant of the State?

• When dynasties and funds hold land forever, and you hold it only until the bill comes due, who is the true sovereign?

• If farmland can be sold to Beijing, or your home seized for tribute, is that commerce — or conquest?

• Land is memory. If you lose it, what story will your children inherit?

China's Quiet Grip

Most only glance at Greenland, but China's reach runs deeper — through rare-earth bids, infrastructure offers, technology transfers, and "green" partnerships with quiet military shadows. Beijing doesn't march with armies. It arrives with contracts. And every contract tightens the grip. By 2024, China had become Denmark's largest Asian trading partner — more than **$15.5 billion** in clean energy, machinery, and agricultural technology flowing between them. And then there is pork. Denmark ranks among the world's top pork exporters, shipping roughly **$2.7 billion** annually. Pork is not just protein. It is leverage. When a study suddenly labeled pork "CO_2-friendly meat," the question wasn't culinary. It was regulatory. Climate classifications determine subsidies, trade access, quotas, and consumer legitimacy. Once food is coded as "green," it moves freely through policy gates others cannot pass. Science didn't just describe pork — it authorized it. Denmark does not need to surrender land. It surrenders **rules.** Denmark feeds China pork and technology. China rewards Denmark with regulatory alignment. And through Danish bureaucrats in **Brussels, Geneva, and New York,** those rules do not stay Danish. They become global. This is how modern power works — not through conquest, but through **standards.** Food standards. Climate metrics. ESG frameworks. Health classifications — even genetic 'quality' markers. Once these standards are written, nations comply automatically. Markets obey them. Courts enforce them. Citizens never vote on them. And pork is only one surface layer. Beneath trade lies biology.

Denmark has quietly positioned itself as a global hub in **genomics, fertility markets, and bio-standardization** — sperm banks, IVF pipelines, donor registries, health databases, and cross-border medical compliance systems. What begins as "choice" becomes classification. What is classified can be ranked. What is ranked can be governed. The same regulatory logic that labels meat "CO_2-friendly" can label bodies "low-risk," "high-risk," "desirable," or "non-compliant." This is not speculation. It is trajectory. Where biology meets bureaucracy, populations become datasets. China understands this perfectly. It does not need Denmark's land. It needs **Denmark's gatekeeping role** — a trusted Western country that writes ethical language, green metrics, and compliance frameworks the rest of the world accepts without suspicion. What Beijing cannot impose directly, it absorbs indirectly through partnerships that look benign. And the vulnerability cuts both ways.

Denmark's economic dependence creates silence. A country that exports pork, pharmaceuticals, energy components, and regulatory expertise cannot afford confrontation. Criticism becomes "irresponsible." Boundary becomes "extremism." Sovereignty becomes "nationalism." When trade is fragile, obedience becomes policy. This is how small nations are captured — not by force, but by entanglement. China plays the long game. It doesn't need flags in Copenhagen. It needs **alignment**. And alignment travels through food, climate rules, health standards, data sharing, and global institutions. What begins as cooperation ends as command. Denmark was not conquered. It was **integrated**. And once rules are surrendered, land always follows.

 Firelight Pause — China's Quiet Grip

 • When Beijing offers "partnerships," is it trade — or quiet conquest?

 • If pork can be branded "CO_2-friendly," what else can science be told to bless?

 • When a crown ties itself to China, is that ceremony — or signal?

 • If Denmark feeds China pork and tech, and China feeds back rules, who really sets the table?

 • When those rules arrive through Brussels and Geneva into your own town, do you still call it policy — or foreign command?

America's Reversal — Trade as Sovereignty

China plays the long game through trade. It doesn't need armies when it has contracts, ports, and quotas. Every deal becomes a lever. Every export becomes a leash. **This is why trade deals matter.** They are not just about prices — they are about power. Who sets the rules of food safety, energy, or tech? Who decides whose ships dock where? Who controls the flow of rare earths, steel, or semiconductors? If you let the EU or UN negotiate for you, you surrender sovereignty twice. First to Brussels or Geneva. Then to Beijing.

America under Trump reversed this pattern. He scrapped bad multilateral deals like the TPP — a Trans-Pacific pact that would have locked America into an Asia-Pacific trade bloc where rules tilted toward China and global committees, not U.S. voters. He forced the renegotiation of NAFTA into USMCA, a deal that brought jobs and production back under terms that favored American farmers, truckers, and workers. He imposed tariffs and restrictions on China's dumping of steel, aluminum, and tech components — exposing the hollow dependency hidden under cheap imports. And he insisted on bilateral deals, nation to nation, so every agreement was accountable to voters, not to faceless committees. This was more than policy — it was sovereignty in motion.

For the first time in decades, America negotiated like a nation, not a client. And this is the part the world refuses to admit: **sovereignty is always expensive, and dependency is always cheap.** Most nations choose cheap — then call the bill "globalization." Tariffs were not punishment; they were a declaration that the days of bending the knee to global markets were over. Multilateral means the elites hold the pen; bilateral means the nation does. And that is why the backlash was fierce. The media called it reckless, elites called it isolationist, investors called it dangerous. But ask yourself — dangerous for whom? For the trucker in Ohio, or for the fund manager in New York who bet on Beijing? For the farmer who regains his market, or for the executive who profits off factories shipped overseas? Every cry of "reckless" revealed not a defense of freedom, but a defense of profit built on dependency. For once, America bargained as a sovereign, not as a client.

And don't fool yourself by thinking this is a political rant. If you stop there, you'll never see what's at stake. This is not about left or right. It's about law — who writes it, who enforces it, and who it chains. That is the fork in the road. Denmark chose sedation — songs, subsidies, and silence. America, for a moment, chose fire — tariffs, sovereignty, and fight. One path dulls the people; the other hardens them. Which one survives the serpent's coil? This is more than economics. It is covenant. Trade done nation to nation keeps sovereignty alive. Trade outsourced to global unions dissolves nations into populations — faceless, rootless, managed like cattle. Most people miss the point. They scream when tariffs pinch their wallets. They curse when shelves shift. But that pain is not punishment. *It is surgery. The cut is meant to heal. The wound is meant to close.* The goal is not cheap plastic from abroad. The goal is strong factories, strong farmers, strong men who can feed, forge, and fight without begging imports to survive. If you measure trade only by today's price tag, you've already sold tomorrow's sovereignty. Cheap goods are not cheap when the cost is your chains.

That is more than I ever learned in Danish economic studies. Their "economics" was sedation — professors pointing at graphs as if arrows on paper could feed a child, as if models could replace men. Charts of GDP growth while farms closed. Models of efficiency while factories rusted. Theories so bloodless they could have been written by clerks who never swung a hammer or planted a seed. They called it science. But it was hypnosis. Numbers without men. Curves without courage. Equations without soil. Real economics is not abstract. It is survival — food in the pantry, wages that feed families, steel forged into tools, ships, and plows. It is men who know how to build, women who know how to stretch and preserve, children who inherit more than debt. True economics is covenant — to steward land, labor, and liberty so the nation can stand free. Everything else is illusion. And here is the truth economists never confess: a nation's GDP can grow even while its people wither. Growth without sovereignty is simply the swelling of the parasite, not the host.

🔥 Firelight Pause — Tariffs

- Do you see tariffs as punishment — or as fire forging independence?
- Would you rather save a dollar today — or save your nation tomorrow?
- What costs more in the end: a stronger America, or a cheaper import?

The Final Warning

Denmark didn't fall with tanks — it fell with flags. It didn't fall to bullets — it fell to silence. And if America forgets that silence is surrender, the Stars and Stripes will not be torn down in battle. They will be lowered quietly, without a shot. I didn't return to Denmark to admire its past. I returned to see if the fire remained. What I found wasn't fire at all — but silence dressed as progress. The perfect mask for surrender. Silence is not neutral. It is surrender. And once a nation learns to kneel, the next question is inevitable — who taught them to bow? Denmark does not rule Denmark. Brussels writes the laws.

The UN supplies the worldview. NATO enforces the order. The crown smiles. The flag waves. And the people call it sovereignty. But it is theater. And theater spreads. Virtue signals are not harmless. They are banners of Babylon — marking territory, staking rule. A nation that swaps covenant for hashtags and borrowed flags has already bent the knee. So don't ask what your land will tolerate. Ask what you will tear down to keep it free. **Action makes you a builder. Silence makes you a slave.** Because the serpent never conquers first by war — it conquers first by vocabulary. Change the words, and you change the world. Denmark taught us how fast a nation can be rewritten when its people no longer speak. America is being rewritten in the same script — one hashtag, one policy, one polite silence at a time. **The serpent conquers not by war, but by signatures.**

🔥 **Firelight Pause — When Silence Becomes Surrender**

• Who owns the land beneath your feet — your people, or foreign powers with contracts and quotas?

• Who chose the banners above your buildings — and who laughs as you salute them?

• Have you mistaken quiet streets for peace, when they may already be chains?

• If freedom can be lost without a bullet, what will you do before the shot is fired?

• When you see a rainbow flag, a Ukraine banner, or a hashtag filter — do you see virtue, or the serpent's signal?

"They have sown the wind, and they shall reap the whirlwind." — Hosea 8:7

Empires fall twice — on paper, then in the mind. The serpent wins when the conscience yields. The next battle is not for land, but for language. Lose the tongue, and you lose the nation.

22

THE CAPTIVE MIND
SILENCE IS SURRENDER

Silence is never neutral. Once it hardens, it becomes surrender. No one saw that spell clearer than a poet who lived under the serpent's shadow — Czesław Miłosz. In Communist Poland, he watched professors, journalists, artists — men of letters and learning — bend their souls in order to survive. They did not call it cowardice. They dressed it in wisdom. They called it pragmatism, realism, progress. They bent their knees and called it culture. Miłosz saw the spell for what it was — the slow death of courage disguised as intellect. He called it **the captive mind.** He wrote: *"In a room where people unanimously maintain a conspiracy of silence, one word of truth sounds like a pistol shot."* **That was his warning. And it is ours.** Miłosz saw another layer of surrender too — the inner mask. He called it **ketman,** the habit of hiding your convictions behind a public smile. A split soul: one face for survival, one buried for truth. Over time, the mask fuses to the skin, and the man beneath forgets he ever resisted. **Modern psychology calls it self-censorship;** Miłosz called it ketman — a mask so often worn it becomes the face. Look around now. The same surrender repeats. Elites parrot slogans scripted in Brussels and Davos. Professors chant catechisms written in think tanks. Journalists recite press releases as if they were scripture. Executives mouth ESG dogmas like priests of a new religion.

In America too — classrooms, boardrooms, newsrooms — the same script is read: speak the catechism or lose your place. We saw it when doctors were erased for questioning the "science," when parents at school boards were labeled extremists, when Big Tech silenced voices at the whispered request of federal agencies. **Millions stayed silent not because they agreed, but because they watched people lose their jobs, licenses, platforms, or friends for speaking one wrong sentence.** That was not a foreign tyranny — it was the American bureaucracy learning to weaponize silence. They call it fairness, equity, democracy. It is none of these. It is cowardice with polish. The lie does not only need propaganda — it needs your pretense. Denmark proved it. A nation trained to smile, nod, and never object. The velvet cage worked because people agreed to wear it. Not by force — by silence. And now the serpent wants America bound the same way. What Miłosz named in Poland, what I endured in Denmark, I now watch creep across the Republic I swore to love. Neutrality is not safety. It is complicity. And silence is the serpent's favorite language.

Decoder of Captivity

Censorship laws — branded as "hate speech" — criminalize truth while sanctifying lies. Cancel culture deputizes mobs to destroy reputations so the rest keep silent. Corporate HR catechisms force confessions you never believed, or cost you your job. Algorithmic suppression shadows dissent and de-monetizes truth. Academic orthodoxy awards degrees for conformity, tenure for the compliant. Peer policing turns neighbors, coworkers, even family into enforcers. Rebranded propaganda — ESG reports, DEI manuals, "fact-checks" — replaces evidence with enforcement. Different tools, same aim — to make you bow without a whip, to silence yourself before they ever silence you.

"In a time of universal deceit, telling the truth is a revolutionary act." — George Orwell

The serpent does not always roar. Sometimes it whispers. Sometimes it waits. Sometimes it simply teaches you to keep quiet until you forget how to speak. But **one word of truth is still a pistol shot.** The captive mind does not need shackles. It needs only the fear of them. Once fear governs thought, censorship becomes unnecessary — people silence themselves before the State even arrives. Silence will not hold forever. Silence makes subjects; **truth makes builders.**

🔥 **Firelight Pause — Break the Silence**
  - What truth have you swallowed because it was safer to stay quiet?
  - Have you mistaken silence for peace when it was really surrender?
  - When corruption rose in plain sight, did you speak — or scroll?
  - When God's name was mocked, did you defend Him — or hide?
  - What word of truth still waits on your tongue?

The serpent no longer needs fjords or fortresses. It rules through silence — through minds taught to police themselves. America will not fall by invasion, but by the surrender of speech. Silence is never neutral; it is the serpent's native tongue. Miłosz saw it in Poland. I lived it in Denmark. And now it coils around America. But this silence is older than politics — older than parliaments and kings. Beneath every age lies a presence waiting for its hour. That is where we turn next — the serpent beneath.

"Cry aloud; do not hold back; lift up your voice like a trumpet." — Isaiah 58:1

Silence begins in the mind — but it never ends there. When enough men bite their tongues, the serpent writes the laws. Fear in the classroom becomes policy in the courthouse. Whispers in meetings become codes on paper. The captive mind becomes the compliant citizen; the compliant citizen becomes the obedient subject. When truth is banned in speech, it will soon be banned in court. That is where Denmark went. And where America now stands. Justice without a soul is the serpent's next disguise.

23

JUSTICE WITHOUT SOUL

BUDGETS OVER BLOOD

Silence was only the first lesson. The serpent's next move is older and darker — it rewrites justice itself. Once a nation's conscience is captive, its courts soon follow. And when the courts bow, the people bow with them. The serpent's classroom doesn't end with diplomas. It only graduates you to the next lesson: a justice system where numbers weigh more than wounds and ledgers count louder than cries. Obedience was drilled in school. Now it is enforced in court. This chapter isn't about education. It's about judgment. And in Denmark, judgment serves the State — not the soul. Justice doesn't look to the wounded. It looks to the wallet. The ledger decides faster than the gavel. This isn't about Denmark — it's about YOU. And hear me: how a nation punishes crime reveals whom it truly worships.

Denmark's courts wear the robe of neutrality, but their loyalty is to the treasury. They do not guard the vulnerable. They guard the State. Property crime is prosecuted with speed. Financial fraud is punished without mercy. Rape or abuse? Often ignored — or minimized until it disappears. Scandinavia sells itself as the gold standard of "humane," "modern," "progressive" justice, but that shine is a mask. Beneath it sits a system that protects institutions and predators long before it protects women.

Under Danish law, rape sentences cap at eight years — twelve in the most brutal cases. Yet the sentences almost never come. In 2017, surveys estimated tens of thousands of sexual assaults, while only a small fraction were reported and an even smaller fraction led to convictions. Even after the 2021 consent law, conviction rates remained among the lowest in Northern Europe—far below Sweden and Norway. Meanwhile, financial crimes routinely bring five to twelve years. Tax fraud is treated like treason. Violence against the treasury is unforgivable. Violence against you is negotiable.

The pattern is old. In the 1970s Mogens Glistrup mocked the tax system and called fraudsters "freedom fighters." The State stripped him of immunity, shamed him, and imprisoned him. In Denmark you may insult God or the crown. But insult the Ministry of Taxation and you're finished. In the 1990s Klaus Riskær Pedersen built a fortune through Accumulator Invest before the collapse. Convicted of embezzlement, he was buried not because he betrayed the people but because he embarrassed the system. In 2024 British financier Sanjay Shah received 12 years for defrauding Denmark of DKK 9 billion. Assets seized: DKK 7.2 billion. "Organized economic theft of the highest order," the court said. Touch the treasury and they will bury you.

But break a woman? The response is silence. In 2017, Swedish journalist Kim Wall was raped, mutilated, and killed aboard a private submarine. Her killer received life — but the case revealed something darker than sentencing. Patterns of disturbing behavior and warning signs never triggered intervention. There was no system prepared to act until a woman was dismembered. These failures became visible only because the crime drew international attention. Had she been ordinary, she might have joined the thousands swallowed by Denmark's silence. Marcel Hansen was able to rape and kill over an extended period before finally being caught. His victims were dismissed. His violence minimized. His crimes allowed to fester until exposure was unavoidable.

Odense, 2022: a 17-year-old gang-raped by four men; two acquitted because "consent was unclear." Aarhus, 2023: an unconscious woman assaulted at a party; charges dropped. Defraud the State and you face the maximum. Break a human being and maybe — if the media cares — justice stirs.

A 2025 University of Copenhagen study confirmed what survivors always knew: tax-fraud convictions average five to twelve years; rape convictions average one to three — if prosecuted at all. Conviction likelihood is near-certain for fraud, near-zero for rape. "Financial criminals are punished harder than rapists." "The law prioritizes property over pain. Budgets over blood." In Denmark, the legal system does not protect the vulnerable. It protects the structure.

When a government fears accounting fraud more than it values a survivor's dignity, justice is not progressive. It is already dead. **Justice without a soul is bookkeeping with blood on its hands.** Every justice system worships something. If it worships the State, it punishes disrespect. If it worships money, it punishes fraud. If it worships man-made virtue, it punishes truth. Only a nation that worships God will punish wickedness. In Denmark, ledger wounds scream louder than human wounds. And where were the men? Once, fathers, brothers, and sons would have risen to defend the women dishonored by lawless men. Today even they are softened, sedated, trained to obey the very system that refuses to defend their daughters. A nation where men no longer guard women is a nation already conquered.

Europe — The Preview of Babylon

When the defender becomes the defendant, Babylon is already writing the verdict. Europe offers its warning plainly. In Scotland in 2025, two young sisters were confronted at night by adult men who believed the street belonged to them. The older sister — twelve years old — did what instinct and conscience demanded. She armed herself with what was at hand. Not to pursue. Not to punish. To survive. To shield her younger sister. The men fled. The children lived. Then came the inversion. The men walked free. The child was charged. A defender punished. Predators released. The system did not ask who threatened whom. It asked who disrupted order—and order mattered more than innocence. This was not chaos. It was logic. A justice system that prosecutes a child for surviving is not broken — it is revealing its allegiance. It protects process over people, calm over conscience, the appearance of control over the reality of evil. That is not justice. It is tyranny in robes. And this spirit does not stop at borders. Across the West, the pattern repeats: those who resist are disciplined; those who violate are managed. Children are no longer defended — they are corrected for refusing to become victims. Survival itself becomes suspect.

Vaclav Havel warned that in a post-totalitarian system, power does not rely on overt terror but on quiet normalization. Courts need not execute dissidents. They need only teach citizens that justice is impractical, that truth is inconvenient, that resistance is costly and futile. Once people stop expecting justice, the regime no longer needs to fear them. That is Denmark today. And increasingly, it is America. **Denmark is not the end of the story. It is the proof of concept.** What was perfected there did not remain local. It crossed borders quietly. It crossed oceans politely. And it arrived in America wearing familiar language.

Across the Atlantic — The Same Ledger Obsession

And it's not just Denmark. America carries the same sickness — a justice system calibrated to protect the ledger, not the people. Martha Stewart served five months in federal prison for lying to investigators during a stock-sale probe. Not for murder. Not for abuse. Not for violence. For offending the financial order itself. When the ledger bleeds, justice moves fast; when a woman bleeds, justice hesitates. Ledger before life is doom.

The IRS expands its enforcement apparatus while hundreds of thousands of rape kits remain untested in police evidence rooms nation-wide. The disparity is not logistical; it is philosophical. Financial compliance triggers immediate action. Violent crime against women does not. The State moves fastest to protect itself.

Wall Street is policed with theater while victims wait years for justice. Bankers who detonated the 2008 economy walked free as families lost homes, savings, and futures. No cells. No reckoning. The ledger was protected; the people absorbed the loss. Both Denmark and America insist their justice systems are impartial. Both reveal the same truth: the State protects itself faster than it protects you.

And when Americans resisted, the response was immediate. **January 6** made that clear. Men who entered public buildings were treated as enemies of the regime. Elderly veterans placed in solitary confinement. Fathers held for months without trial. Cancer patients denied treatment. Families bankrupted as breadwinners disappeared into concrete cells. Some did not survive the aftermath. Others emerged broken — not by violence, but by abandonment. These were not war criminals. They were not armed insurgents. Their offense was simpler and more dangerous: they believed their voice still mattered.

Meanwhile, the same prosecutors who release repeat violent offenders within hours demanded decades-long sentences for these men. Not because of what they did — but because of what they represented. The system required examples. That is why the word *insurrection* was deployed. Not as description, but as justification. A label strong enough to excuse extraordinary punishment and broadcast a warning: resist, and the machine will answer.

Solzhenitsyn warned that the line between good and evil runs through every human heart. But when courts erase that line — when they punish dissent and excuse predation — nations do not become safer. They lose their soul. What remains is not justice. It is management.

In Hitler's Reich — Justice Turned to Ash

In Hitler's Reich, the law didn't collapse overnight — it was quietly rewritten. Courts still opened, judges still wore robes, verdicts were still pronounced, but every part of the ritual served one master. Loyalty to the Party replaced loyalty to justice. The *Volksgerichtshof* became a stage for executions disguised as trials. Resisters like the White Rose students were condemned, while collaborators walked free under the shield of "duty." Even soldiers who refused immoral orders were shot, yet those who carried out massacres were praised. The inversion was total: truth became sedition, courage became treason, obedience the highest virtue. Citizens accepted it not from evil, but from fear.

The Reversal

With Trump, the inversion began to break. Instead of judges legislating from the bench, he planted constitutionalists — a kind of lasting firepower. He turned law-fare into light; shackles became receipts. The executive branch, for a moment, acted as a sword for the people rather than a scepter for the cartel. Trump slowed the serpent. For a moment, the system flinched. He cut coils from the courts and tore the mask off law-fare. That is why they came for him — first with financial attacks, then with law-fare, and finally with a bullet. Because when one man proved the system could still bend to the people, the serpent knew the mask might shatter for good. Havel taught that the powerless become powerful the moment they stop cooperating with the lie. But when justice itself enforces the lie, resistance becomes a moral duty. But the coils do not vanish overnight. Judges, agencies, and networks seeded over decades remain — slow poison in the system that still has to be drawn out, one case at a time. Even Babylon had its codes. Hammurabi carved law into stone — eye for eye, life for life. Justice was flawed, but it bound ruler and ruled alike. Today rulers carve ledgers that bind only the ruled. Theft of coin is punished. Theft of innocence excused. And here is the warning: a nation that punishes defenders and excuses predators is already training its people for slavery. **Choose now — before a judge chooses for you.**

🔥 **Firelight Pause — Justice or Tyranny?**

- Where have I bowed to the ledger when I should have stood for life?
- Would I face prison, ruin, or exile rather than kneel to Babylon's gavel?
- When false flags fly, will I see through the theater — or let fear decide?
- Do I measure justice by safety — or by truth and courage?
- If the serpent's court marks me as prey, will I still rise as witness?
- If my daughter's pain is negotiable but my tax return is not — is that justice, or idolatry?
- Will I submit to a gavel that frees predators and condemns defenders?

Justice without a soul is not justice. It is tyranny disguised as neutrality. Tyranny bleeds the people before it bleeds the state. When wounds are measured in ledgers, the end is set. Solzhenitsyn lived it. He named it. The prophet saw it first:

"Justice is turned back, and righteousness stands far away; truth has stumbled in the public squares, and uprightness cannot enter. Truth is lacking, and he who departs from evil makes himself a prey." — Isaiah 59:14–15

Tyranny never starts in the courtroom. It starts in the classroom. Before the judge ever bows to the ledger, the student learns to bow to the desk. Before law is hollowed out, the lesson is rewritten. When truth is punished, and silence rewarded, the next generation stops seeking justice — and starts memorizing compliance. The serpent does not only write laws; it writes curriculums.

Denmark perfected that pattern. America is repeating it. The courtroom taught fear. The classroom will teach forgetfulness. And that is how the next empire falls — not by bullets, but by lesson plans. Because once a child learns to doubt his own senses, he will never challenge the State again. A nation that loses its discernment becomes easy prey — citizens who cannot tell truth from propaganda, courage from cruelty, justice from obedience. That is how freedom dies: not when men forget their rights, but when they forget their sight.

"Woe to those who call evil good and good evil..." — Isaiah 5:20

24

THE MODEL STUDENT
OF GLOBAL SUBMISSION

THE OBEDIENT CLASSROOM

Over the years, Americans have asked me the same question: "**Why do Europeans act like they're above us?**" Why the raised eyebrow? Why the polite smirk — that quiet, cultured condescension? Why the sense that they are the "grown-ups" and America is the unruly child? I know the answer now: they mock America's freedom because it exposes what they surrendered — ambition, risk, sovereignty, faith. Europe inherited the hollow crown. They carry centuries of borrowed prestige — castles they didn't build, cathedrals they no longer enter, philosophies they no longer believe. They cling to the memory of empires long buried, and mistake that memory for wisdom. So they look down on the Republic that surpassed them — the nation that feeds, defends, and invents while they recite their lineage like a lullaby. Their superiority is not strength. It is inheritance masquerading as intellect. It is pride without power — arrogance without achievement. They lost the fire and kept the accent. When courage died, credentials took its place. Culture became costume. Memory became marketing. And the elites mistook their own drift into decadence for sophistication. They call America uncultured because America never kissed their ring. Denmark did. And in return, it became the model student of global submission.

Denmark is small — and moralizes big. A small-state, big-state complex. America must be the brute so Denmark can play the saint. The smirk is not culture. It is control-by-status — domination without daring. Their superiority is not analysis. It is therapy — pride medication for nations that outsourced their own defense. They call themselves the grown-ups. But grown-ups build and defend. Children critique and depend. Denmark doesn't export strength. It exports management — the bureaucratic art of making people behave. And they mock America's freedom because **it exposes what they surrendered: ambition, risk, sovereignty, faith.** They forget that the Republic was born by breaking their throne. That is why their contempt feels so personal — the serpent still remembers the rebellion. And now the same pride that once ruled their palaces rules their classrooms. The crown became the curriculum. The child who once learned to think now learns to obey. Now the tide has turned. The ones who preached superiority must negotiate reality — and yes, even Denmark learns what it means to kiss the ring when the Republic stops apologizing.

"Pride goes before destruction, and a haughty spirit before a fall." — Proverbs 16:18

There was a time when classrooms still taught how to think. Students analyzed texts. They debated ideas. They questioned the world. Even math carried a rhythm of logic, not ideology. It was not perfect — but it was not yet hijacked. Children were still raised as citizens, not tools. And that is why the shift is so clear now — because some of us remember. We remember when education stopped being thought and became consensus. We remember when curiosity was replaced by compliance. We remember when questioning was a duty, not a danger. We remember when obedience became the hidden curriculum. We remember the mind. And we refuse to stay silent while the next generation drowns in fog — while ignorance and superiority fill the room like incense before a false god. The Switch Was Not Accidental — This didn't happen because teachers suddenly forgot how to teach. It happened because the system discovered a quiet truth: minds are harder to govern than habits.

A citizen can argue. A citizen can resist. A citizen can say no. But a student trained to seek approval will beg for the rubric. So the classroom was redesigned. Not to awaken— but to standardize. Not to produce free men— but predictable ones. That is why the change feels so sudden to those who remember. **You are not watching "education evolve." You are watching authority change clothes.**

From Thought to Obedience

Every empire builds temples. Ours are called schools. From the first bell to the final degree, the child is shaped for service — not to truth, but to system. What begins as curiosity is slowly pressed into credential. The spark becomes a script. The question becomes a rubric. The mind becomes a file. **Basic education trains obedience. Higher education manufactures ideology.** Together they form the upper priesthood of Babylon — temples of polite control where the next generation learns not to think, but to comply. We remember when truth was taught, not programmed. Now education has become a ritual of obedience — a choreography of repetition dressed as progress. Children learn to conform before they learn to think. Teachers grade compliance more than courage. Math, language, writing, civics — all sterilized, fragmented, lifeless. No blood. No roots. No relevance. The sentence replaced the story. The formula replaced the question. Even speech itself was standardized until words lost their weight. And today, education has not evolved; it has only been repainted. The chalkboard gave way to the screen, the pen to the keyboard, the mind to the algorithm. What was once written by hand — traced through muscle, memory, and meaning — is now typed into clouds that own the ink. The hand no longer learns; it only clicks.

The screen has become the new temple — glowing, silent, omnipresent — where children bow to prompts instead of problems. Paper tests trained the eye; handwritten thought trained the soul. But the screen trains only the reflex. Students no longer wrestle with ideas; they scroll through them. Teachers no longer shape minds; they manage interfaces.

The classroom that once smelled of ink and effort now hums with the cold order of code. The cloud remembers everything — except the human who made it. The screen trains the reflex. The system trains the soul. Once the hand was free, now it is formatted. Once learning shaped the citizen, now it standardizes the worker. The student becomes the statistic; the teacher becomes the technician. And the machine smiles — for it has learned to replicate obedience faster than wisdom.

The machine does not stop at the classroom. Once it learned to program the child, it set its eyes on the nation. What began as lesson plans became global policy. Curriculums turned to frameworks. Schools became supply chains for citizens pre-approved by the system. From Copenhagen to California, the algorithm speaks one language — *efficiency, equity, obedience.* Nations now compete not in wisdom, but in compliance scores. And the same spirit that digitized the desk now standardizes the world. Denmark boasts of record university participation, yet many graduates admit they feel unprepared for real work. America mirrors the failure. Tuition has surged since 2000. Student debt has climbed into the trillions. And a growing share of graduates now work jobs that never required a degree. Paper over truth. Chains over skill. And layered over it all—digital grading systems, AI proctoring, standardized testing apps—machines training children to obey algorithms as much as teachers. A generation rehearsed not to think, but to click.

Then comes the next layer of conditioning — **universities.** Once meant to refine the mind, they now manufacture managers for the Beast system. Students emerge fluent in slogans but illiterate in truth. They can quote climate scripture but cannot grow food. They can recite inclusion creeds but cannot defend liberty. They can manage everything except meaning. Universities no longer shape citizens; they certify servants. The modern degree is not proof of wisdom — *it is a license to operate within the machine.* Bureaucracy has replaced calling. **Compliance has become the crown.** The crown of obedience needs a creed — and the creed of our age is "climate."

Climate as Curriculum

In Denmark, climate is not taught. It is performed. Children bow to CO_2 charts like sacred texts. They cannot plant food. They cannot build shelter. They cannot question institutions. But they can chant pledges. They can rank nations by carbon guilt. They can parrot slogans until they mistake obedience for wisdom. This is not education. It is pre-conditioning — a catechism of loyalty disguised as learning. What began as environmental stewardship became spiritual submission. The serpent learned that fear of sin could be replaced by fear of carbon — and that guilt could be monetized as virtue. And the creed does not stop in the classroom. It marches straight into the laboratories. Denmark boasts that around eighty percent of its students continue beyond compulsory schooling — most on state-funded paths all the way to university. But when the State pays, the State dictates.

Funding First. Questions Later.

At a state-owned university, research does not begin in a vacuum. It begins inside a funding structure where ministries, public agencies, and industry partners define what is *worth* studying. At Aarhus University, a 2019 climate report on beef and veal was later retracted after investigators found serious irregularities—failures of transparency and research independence. The problem wasn't a typo. It was that independence collapsed upstream, before conclusions ever reached the public. When funding and framing are aligned in advance, outcomes are not discovered. They are managed.

Academic Output Becomes Policy Justification.

Once research carries a university seal, it gains political utility. The "climate-controlled pork" campaign followed the same logic: a climate narrative moved seamlessly from academic authority into market messaging—until Denmark's High Court ruled the claim misleading because it was not independently verified. What failed in court had already succeeded in policy and public perception. That's the tell. The research didn't serve truth; it served legitimization.

Prestige Protects the Narrative — Until It Can't.
State-funded systems rely on reputation to enforce compliance. In Denmark's major biomedical misconduct scandal, the University of Copenhagen later revoked a doctorate, and the Ministry revoked a national research honor tied to the case. Only after exposure did the system correct itself. For years, prestige and institutional silence acted as insulation. Not because no one knew—but because challenging the narrative meant challenging the institution that funded it. This is how state-funded universities are infiltrated without conspiracies or coups: funding narrows the question, prestige shields the answer, and policy absorbs the result. **By the time the public sees the study, the verdict is already written.** The State was not funding truth. It was commissioning permission which is state-funded science used to authorize a predetermined outcome while pretending to discover truth. Power no longer asks research to discover what is true. It commissions research to grant itself permission to act.

What Denmark rehearsed, America industrialized. The liturgy did not stay in Europe; it crossed the Atlantic like every bad ideology before it. In Washington, federal agencies discovered the same power: fund the narrative, and the narrative becomes law. NIH, NSF, and DOE grants began rewarding ideology dressed as evidence, channeling billions toward research that affirmed policy rather than questioned it. Universities adapted immediately. They learned that **truth does not keep the money flowing — but compliance does.** Entire departments transformed into grant-farmers, producing findings that aligned with federal priorities. The question in the lab was no longer, "Is this true?" but "Will this get funded?" And as the academy bent, the platforms followed. The Twitter Files revealed federal officials directing private companies to shadow-ban scientists, journalists, and dissidents whose work challenged approved narratives. YouTube deleted entire lectures for contradicting agency guidance. Facebook suppressed studies at government request and buried researchers behind "independent fact-check" screens. Censorship no longer needed a courtroom; it needed only a dashboard.

Industry joined the ritual with enthusiasm. Pharma funded the medical schools that regulate drugs. Silicon Valley financed the AI ethics boards that determine how their own systems are policed. Climate-corporate networks bankrolled the modeling labs that justified their subsidies. Defense contractors paid for think tanks that shaped national security doctrine. The cycle was perfect: industry paid the universities, universities produced "evidence," government mandated the policy, and industry collected the profit. Science became marketing. Research became merchandise. Truth became collateral damage. This was never about discovery. It was about obedience. When the grant replaces the conscience, the lab becomes a pulpit. When peer review becomes gatekeeping, dissent becomes heresy. And when the State learns it can manage truth through funding, every institution that depends on grants becomes a cathedral of compliance. Denmark perfected the pattern. America scaled it. And now the West bows not to truth, but to consensus — consensus written by ministries, approved by foundations, funded by industries, enforced by platforms, and celebrated by universities that no longer remember what the word "science" meant before it became scripture for the serpent.

Critical Theory vs. Classical Liberalism — The Mind Under Siege

Once, the classroom was ruled by *Classical Liberalism* — not the modern slogan, but the old creed of reason. Truth was pursued through argument, not assumed by authority. You could test an idea, lose, and still keep your dignity. The purpose of education was liberty of mind — to teach citizens how to govern themselves. Then came the **Frankfurt School** — philosophers in exile who carried Marx's bones wrapped in new language. They fled tyranny, but brought its seed with them. From Frankfurt to Columbia, they rebuilt their temple inside America's universities, sanctifying suspicion as scholarship. **It was Marxism without rifles — a revolution smuggled in on reading lists instead of bayonets.** Where the classical teacher asked, *"What is true?"*, the critical teacher asked, *"Who benefits?"*

Critical theory is not analysis. It's therapy — a guilt machine that turns grievance into status and makes power look like compassion. Every discipline became suspicion; every achievement, oppression; every tradition, a mask for power. They replaced discovery with dismantling — analysis without creation, critique without construction. In their world, the individual is never innocent, and the collective is never guilty. All that remains is hierarchy, guilt, and endless confession. The old liberal believed in the mind. The new theorist believes only in the group. The old classroom trained debate. The new one trains denunciation. What began as philosophy became therapy. What began as inquiry became ideology. What began as the search for truth became the management of guilt. The child who once learned logic now learns grievance. The student who once studied Aristotle now audits equity. This is how the Red Line crossed the Atlantic — not with rifles, but with reading lists. It colonized universities first, then media, then policy. And the result is the world you see now: **credentials without thought, compassion without truth, obedience without end.** Reason dethroned. Virtue mocked. Freedom unlearned. The war for the mind was never fought with bullets. It was fought with syllabi.

The Priesthood of Paper

When the creed took hold, it needed clergy. Every revolution builds its own priesthood, and the new faith of theory was no different. It could not survive on protest alone — it needed payrolls, departments, and degrees. The universities obliged. Professors became prophets of grievance. Journals became scripture. Funding became favor. The seminar replaced the sermon. And the parchment — the diploma, the doctorate — became the priest's robe. The old cathedral had incense; the new one has endnotes. Both demand belief. Both reward conformity. The robe is now a lab coat or an academic gown, but the oath is the same: protect the creed, punish heresy, and call it "peer review." This is not analysis. It is therapy — a guilt machine that turns grievance into status and makes power look like compassion. This is how thought became hierarchy. This is how inquiry became industry. This is how truth was buried beneath titles. And from this machine rose a new idol — the PhD.

We are told the PhD is the summit of intelligence — the crown of civilization, the mark of mastery. Denmark calls it the doktorgrad — the "degree of the learned." But the crown is hollow. In Denmark, the doctorate no longer resembles the old ideal of the solitary scholar wrestling truth from the unknown. It has become an industrial product — compressed, standardized, and supervised into predictability. The reform that shortened Danish PhD programs into a rigid three-year factory model stripped away the very thing discovery requires: time. Students are pushed through pre-approved projects, measured not by insight but by efficiency. Universities are rewarded for speed, not truth. Independence is promised but never granted. Most Danish PhDs begin not with a question, but with a contract. Ministries, industries, and EU foundations pre-write the project, define the method, and signal the acceptable conclusion. These are not research proposals — they are assignments. "Binding PhD projects," they call them. The one who pays dictates the one who thinks.

At Aarhus and Copenhagen, students learned it the hard way. Not through discovery—but through incentives. In case after case, outside interests gained leverage over research: funding shaped the frame, contracts demanded loyalty, and researchers described pressure to delay, soften, or withhold results when findings became inconvenient. The lesson wasn't subtle. Stay inside the lane. Protect the narrative. Keep the money flowing. Discovery was fenced. Inquiry was rationed. The lab became a corridor of compliance. And so repetition becomes brilliance. Loyalty becomes genius. Compliance becomes career. Denmark produces graduates fluent not in originality, but in orthodoxy. It calls them doctors. But many are simply certified custodians of the consensus—parchment priests of an approved truth. What does the system produce? Not builders. Not pioneers. Not truth-tellers. It produces functionaries— parrots with parchment, trained to repeat rather than reveal. Ceremonial gowns, ceremonial minds. Titles of loyalty, not of fire. The title of "Doctor" once belonged to healers, inventors, reformers—men and women who studied to serve, not to rule.

Today it marks something smaller and far more dangerous: bureaucrats in lab coats and professors who curate consensus like museum glass. Their brilliance is measured not in courage, but in compliance. Their insight is graded not by truth, but by alignment. The paper is real. The wisdom is counterfeit. The robe is impressive. The mind beneath often isn't free. This is not an insult to intellect. It is an exposure of its idolatry. This is not mockery of education. It is grief for what it became. Those who grow angry reading this are not defending truth—they are defending a system that owns them. Their outrage is the flare that proves the wound is real. But I have met men without diplomas who think more deeply than any doctorate. Farmers who read the weather like scripture. Builders who understand geometry by instinct. Mothers who see through propaganda faster than professors. Men in blue-collar jobs who invent tools, solve problems, and create what the credentialed can't—yet their innovations never see daylight because bureaucracy guards the gates. Brilliance buried under forms. Genius trapped behind a timecard. They may never stand behind podiums—but they still stand in truth. Ask yourself: Where did my education end, and indoctrination begin? Have I been taught thought—or obedience? Did I build knowledge—or memorize ideology? And above all: did I trade my conscience for credentials? **The parchment may open doors. Truth still opens prisons.** I do not need their robe to see their ritual. You do not have to kneel at an altar to know when it's empty. And sometimes only the one standing outside the cathedral can see its walls for what they are—beautiful, yes, but built to keep light in and questions out. Truth does not require a title. It requires vision, courage, and scars—and only free men carry all three.

Even the crown jewel of American education has turned to dust. Patriot families who claim to fight for the Republic still bow before the diploma. They spend fortunes so their children can be branded by the very system they say they resist—four years of debt for four years of indoctrination. Students emerge fluent in slogans but illiterate in truth: climate hysteria, identity guilt, political catechisms recited like prayer. They can chant "equity," but they cannot plant, build, or defend.

Even parents who admit the poison still whisper, *But they need the paper.* Why? Because **fear still rules them**—fear their child will be left behind, locked out, unemployable. Fear that without parchment, they will not be enough. **The diploma has become the new idol**—a paper crown for a culture that lost its soul. And still the cycle continues. Sons and daughters march into the furnace while banners of ideology wave above the gates— Palestine flags, rainbow creeds, climate commandments. Even Christian campuses echo the same liturgy of shame and submission. The indoctrination is not hidden. It is celebrated. This is not education. It is a cult— complete with sacraments, high priests, and heresies. And the proof now sits in power. When the guardians of law cannot speak plain truth about man and woman, the rot has reached the altar. That moment was not confusion. It was creed. The ritual forbids truth if truth offends the new orthodoxy. And yet they still rule—deciding for a nation built on self-evident truths. This is the end product of the cult: young adults trained not to build, but to dismantle. Graduates prepared to staff NGOs that erase borders, to clerk in firms that despise the Constitution, to recite compassion while enforcing control.

I once met one of them—a polished lawyer on vacation, proud of his degree. He told me he "helped the vulnerable" get government assistance. Then he added, casually, "They're undocumented immigrants." When I said I came legally and received nothing, his smile cracked. "Well, good for you," he snapped. In that moment it was clear: a man trained in law who defended the breaking of it. Elite-educated empathy masking contempt for truth. A lawyer who serves the system, not the Republic—a clerk in a tie. That is the fruit of the modern diploma: compassion severed from covenant, intellect detached from loyalty. The system does not produce citizens. It produces clerks of compliance—fluent in grievance, speechless in gratitude. They do not know the Constitution. They do not know their history. They do not know the law of the land. And they do not know God. I have met many of them—polished, credentialed, confident in nothing but their own reflection. They speak in scripts, not sentences. Climate mantras. Media propaganda. Recycled lines mistaken for wisdom.

Scratch the surface and the emptiness shows. They cannot reason, so they ridicule. They cannot converse, so they condemn. They have the parchment. And that is all they have. Compassion without accountability. Virtue divorced from law. The creed of collapse disguised as kindness. A nation that worships credentials will soon be governed by cowards.

"Professing themselves to be wise, they became fools, and exchanged the glory of the incorruptible God for images made like corruptible man." — Romans 1:22–23

🔥 Firelight Pause — The Price of Paper

- Can your children think—or only repeat?
- Do they know the Constitution, their history, the law of the land—or only the creeds of the classroom?
- Can they stand before God—or have they been trained to deny Him?
- Can they support themselves—or will they be managed for life?
- Are you buying education—or funding indoctrination?
- Are you raising builders—or financing dismantlers?

The Intelligence They Can't Measure

Meanwhile, the men who frame houses, wire electricity, and pour concrete show more intelligence and resilience than any professor of grievance studies. They build with their hands — but they think with fire. They solve problems no bureaucrat can untangle. They carry common sense — a mind that functions far better than the parrots of parchment. They are craftsmen and philosophers in denim — the real backbone of nations. When the bill came due, the regime tried to swipe away billions in student debt — not by holding universities accountable, not by cutting bloated salaries or useless programs, but by handing the cost to the working man. The builder, the trucker, the farmer, the welder — the very men who never bowed to the paper cage — were told they must now pay for the indoctrination of others. Chains for the backbone. Bailouts for the bureaucrats.

When Titles Replace Truth

The Ivy League has become a temple of virtue. Parents brag about elite acceptances as if prestige were virtue. But prestige plants no wheat, defends no borders, and keeps no lights on. It feeds pride, not nations. Real learning was traded for ideology, leaving a generation credentialed, anxious, and trained to comply. This age will not be rebuilt by prestige, bureaucrats, technocrats, or globalists. It will be rebuilt by the Remnant —the scientists who still serve truth, the scholars who still fear God, the lawmakers who still read the covenant, the doctors who heal rather than merely prescribe, the farmers who feed nations rather than corporations, the teachers who awaken minds instead of managing obedience, the builders who still work with their hands and remember what foundations are for, and the pastors who still preach fire instead of comfort. We need minds that can read both Scripture and the fine print—souls who can discern deception in code, in contract, in lab, and in soil. Real builders. Real healers. Real stewards of truth. When titles replace truth, collapse is paperwork away.

When Obedience Kills

The price of this creed is not measured only in debt and wasted years. It is measured in blood. Air traffic control revealed the endgame. The FAA was short nearly four thousand controllers — not for lack of skill, but because DEI filters excluded them. Trained men were sidelined. Veterans were passed over. Biographical surveys mattered more than radar or judgment. And then, one gray January morning, the skies tore open. A Black Hawk helicopter collided with a passenger jet over Washington, D.C. Sixty-seven souls dead. At the same time, the FAA was already thousands of controllers short and facing lawsuits from applicants who said they'd been screened out by politicized hiring filters instead of proven skill. Reports and whistleblowers had warned for years that politics was thinning the towers. When safety kneels to slogans, the margin for error disappears. **No DEI mission statement can resurrect the dead. No ideology can rewrite the laws of physics.**

This is the human cost of ideological obedience — lives sacrificed to appease a political idol. A nation that prizes diversity over discipline, sentiment over skill, cannot claim compassion. For compassion without competence is cruelty in disguise. And no bureaucrat will ever stand trial for the blood their doctrine spilled. When truth is filtered through ideology, error becomes policy. When excellence is replaced by equality of outcome, the price is always human. A nation that exalts fairness over faithfulness will learn, in the end, that gravity does not care about politics. Even now, the warning plays out again. Because of the shutdown, the FAA is cutting flights by nearly ten percent at America's busiest airports. Towers run half-manned, controllers work without pay, passengers sit stranded. But the problem isn't paychecks — it's pride. The system that worshiped diversity over discipline, compliance over competence, now trembles under its own creed. The sky mirrors the classroom: ideology outranked skill, and the result is paralysis. A nation that treats its real workers as expendable will soon find its sky empty and its ground unsafe. A nation that trades excellence for inclusion will trade safety for slogans — until the sky itself goes silent. But silence is never the end. It's the sound a system makes before it feeds. Every collapse — from classroom to cockpit — points to the same altar: the economy of obedience. The failure isn't random. It's monetized. The debt, the credential, the compliance — all threads of one design. Babylon does not only teach obedience; it sells it.

The Obedience Economy

Obedience is not an accident. It is a market. Debt is the leash. Every tuition loan is a contract that can shadow a life—interest turning years into a harness. America's student loan system is now enormous, dominated by federal debt, and it functions like an engine that converts young citizens into long-term payers. Credentialism protects the boardroom from dissenters. The degree becomes a passport into the technocracy. Governments feed on it. A population trained to seek approval from teachers will learn to seek approval from bureaucrats. The same testing logic that drills children to tick boxes trains adults to file the right forms, accept the right policies, and fear stepping outside the approved script.

And above them all, global management systems feast on measurement: reviews, programs, indicators—frameworks that compare nations, rank systems, and pressure policy toward what can be scored. But ask the question nobody asks: **who chose the scorecard?** What worldview wrote the categories? What realities were excluded because they cannot be quantified—courage, conscience, faith, family, sovereignty? If a nation changes its schools to rise in a ranking, is that education—or behavioral conditioning? If funding, status, and legitimacy flow to those who align with the framework, is it "data"—or discipline? Nations trade their children's minds for a better place on a global report card. Not because it's true. Because it's measurable. And what is measurable is manageable.

Firelight Pause — The Market of Minds
- What price did I pay for belonging—and who profits?
- Do my debts serve my life—or does my life serve my debts?
- If the system buys obedience with convenience, what would it cost me to say no?

The Technocrat's Throne

The arrogance didn't vanish. It evolved—the arrogance of a class that believes it can manage reality better than it can understand it. The crown moved from marble halls to digital screens. The new kings wear badges, not robes: data scientists, global managers, diversity officers, bureaucrats fluent in metrics but illiterate in meaning. Their arrogance is quieter. Their reach is greater. They do not rule nations; they administer them. They do not conquer land; they program consent. Behind their policies hides the same old creed—control through civility, dominance disguised as compassion. The serpent no longer wears a crown. He wears a credential. And here is the machinery that staffs the throne: pipelines that import compliant managers, displace rooted citizens, and fill classrooms, hospitals, and codebases with people trained to serve systems first. That gate has a name.

The H-1B Gate

The story is not finished. The H-1B visa pipeline—once sold as a simple "skills fix"—became something far larger: a staffing channel capable of reshaping institutions from the inside. In universities, it does not merely change who teaches. It changes what is rewarded, what is tolerated, and how much dissent a department can afford—because hiring is not only about talent. It is also about incentives, leverage, and control. But the rules have shifted. Beginning with petitions filed after September 21, 2025, the federal government imposed an additional **$100,000 payment** on certain new H-1B filings—an abrupt cost shock now entangled in legal and political battle. Whether this rule stands or falls is almost beside the point. Its existence reveals the truth: **the gate can be priced, throttled, and weaponized.**

And the pipeline extends far beyond classrooms. In Silicon Valley, the H-1B system has repeatedly created wage-leverage incentives—labor priced below local medians, executives pocketing the spread. In medicine, hospitals have grown dependent on international medical graduates to staff critical roles, especially where Americans are unwilling—or unable—to go. In defense-adjacent work, the question is not whether foreign nationals exist in the ecosystem; it is exposure: dependency risk, influence risk, and who ultimately controls the supply chain of national capability. In finance, H-1B quants feed the machinery of quantitative modeling and algorithmic trading—systems that move markets and, in aggregate, steer the nation's future. What began as "filling shortages" can become dependency. What began as "global talent" can become leverage. What looked like a workforce solution can become a sovereignty leak—labor, incentives, and institutional power flowing through the same bureaucratic gate. The H-1B is not just a visa. **It is a Trojan horse—because it enters as help and can exit as control.**

The visa is the mechanism; permanent residency is the multiplier. Together they allow long-term institutional influence without corresponding requirements for civic education, constitutional understanding, or cultural integration. The issue is not immigrants. The issue is gates. Who staffs the classrooms, the hospitals, the codebases, the laboratories, the boardrooms—and under what incentives? Who shapes policy, culture, algorithms, and curriculum? Who advances, who complies, and who is quietly replaced? That is not immigration as a blessing. It is immigration as leverage. That is not diversity as strength. It is dependency as policy. That is not opportunity. It is displacement by paperwork.

"We ought to obey God rather than men." — Acts 5:29

◔ Firelight Pause — The Questions of Obedience

• When numbers bend to politics, is it still science — or theater?

• When food, climate, and debt become currency, whose script are you living in?

• When did your schools stop rewarding conviction and start rewarding compliance?

• Do your children know how to question — or only how to please?

• Are you mistaking credentials for courage, and debt for wisdom?

• If foreign professors and workers never took the oath, why should they shape your nation?

• When the Trojan horse rolls in through visas and diplomas, will you recognize it before the gates close?

The serpent finishes its lesson before it writes its laws. It trains the child to obey the rubric, then licenses the adult to speak "within the limits." The obedient student becomes the compliant citizen. And soon the same reflex that silenced the classroom begins to govern the courtroom. Consensus becomes censorship. Obedience becomes order. And freedom is rewritten as a term of service.

The War for the Mind

Every civilization falls the same way — first in faith, then in thought, and finally in speech. Education was never neutral; it was always priesthood. The one who shapes the mind writes the laws. The one who trains obedience governs without chains. That is why the serpent began in the classroom — because the battle for nations is first a battle for reason itself. If a people can no longer define truth, they will beg to be ruled. But if they remember who they are, and Who gave them sight, no empire of lies can own them.

"Do not be conformed to this world, but be transformed by the renewing of your mind." — Romans 12:2

The Call to Rebuild

If America is to survive, education must be the first battlefield reclaimed. The model we inherited — imported from European elites — was never meant to raise free men. It was built to manage them. It taught hierarchy, not honor; obedience, not ownership. It was designed to produce workers for empires, not citizens for republics. And we have lived long enough under its spell. The results are all around us: factories gone, mills silent, ships foreign-flagged, medicines outsourced, fields dependent on foreign seed, energy policies written in Brussels and Beijing. Trade deals opened the gates; classrooms trained the gatekeepers. The same global hand that standardized our schools exported our industries — turning a nation of builders into a nation of buyers.

"If the foundations be destroyed, what can the righteous do?" — Psalm 11:3

But that is not who we are. America was built by men who read the land, not the ledger — men who invented engines, mapped skies, refined oil, and planted wheat without permission. We were not managed into greatness; we were forged into it. Education once served that spirit; it can again. We must tear down the imported model and rebuild a covenant one — rooted in faith, skill, courage, and creation. In Texas we have a saying: "Come and take it." That must be America's answer to Babylon.

Come and take our children's minds — if you can. Come and take our trades, our faith, our fire — if you dare. But you will not take our freedom to think, to build, to believe. Because this time, the builders are awake — and they remember who they are. Education in America was never meant to serve empires; it was meant to form free men under God. I was born into the blue-collar world—where men came home with dirt on their boots and women stretched every dollar like survival. I watched good people get broken by systems they didn't build, then lectured by elites who never missed a meal and never swung a hammer. Later, I stepped into the other world—universities, conference rooms, corporate towers. I took their education, learned their language, studied their economics. I learned how their power thinks—and how it hides behind words. But I never forgot my own. I've seen both sides of the machine: the hands that build and the hands that manage. One works for survival. The other too often feeds on control. And I will not watch the builders be mocked by the managers ever again. Because the real intelligence of a nation still smells like sweat and soil. The credentialed class did not lose intelligence. It lost courage. It learned to speak beautifully while obeying quietly. It learned to measure truth by approval. And it learned to look down on the builders—not because it is better, but because without them it is nothing. And I learned this—**a man who can speak both worlds is hard to rule.**

I know who the builders are. I watched them robbed of opportunity, dismissed by degrees, written out of the future they hold up with their hands. They paid the heaviest price—long hours, late bills, quiet sacrifices—so their children could climb a ladder the elites later pulled up behind them. They gave everything, and were told they were nothing. The privileged taught their children to dream. The system taught the rest to doubt—doubt their intellect, doubt their identity, doubt their place in the world. They were even told the future required fewer children: don't build families, don't plant roots, don't multiply—because the planet might not "handle" it. And still they rose every morning and built a country the credentialed class could never understand.

That is why this book fights the way it does. This is my witness—and my honor—to the backbone of America: welders, ranchers, truckers, builders, mothers, makers. Men and women who kept faith when the "educated" traded theirs for comfort. They deserve their names written not in ink, but in stone. I learned the system. But I kept my soul. And the day is coming when America will not ask the elites for permission to rise. She will rise when the builders remember who they are—the fire in them older than any empire. Truth does not require a title. It requires vision, courage, and scars—and only the free carry all three.

Let me be clear: this is not a war on learning. It is a war on capture—on systems that use education to manufacture obedience and call it progress.

Truth is not a title. It is a price—and the free pay it.

"He frustrates the signs of the liars and makes fools of diviners;
He turns wise men backward and makes their knowledge foolish."
— **Isaiah 44:25**

25

LICENSED TO SPEAK
(UNTIL YOU'RE NOT)

WHEN FREEDOM BECOMES PERMISSION

Speech is the first front. But it is never the last. Once the serpent tests your tongue, it studies your hesitation — the pause before truth, the swallow before courage. It measures how quickly you self-censor, how swiftly you retreat. The goal is not merely to silence you; it is to train you. Because the moment you begin policing your own words, you are no longer a citizen — you are an apprentice in your own captivity. That is when the serpent moves from silencing the voice to shaping the reflex. What begins as censorship becomes conditioning. Before tyrants police your words, they tutor your reflex. Schools drill compliance; courts dignify it. The habit becomes a statute, the rubric becomes a code. Truth is parceled out "within the limits of the law." Education prepared the bow; now law tightens the knot. This is speech by permission — free until it isn't.

Free speech is not courtesy. It is not "community standards." It is not the privilege to echo what the state approves or some bureaucrat from another country permits. **Free speech is raw, inconvenient, unapproved truth — the kind that makes tyrants sweat.**

Without it, every other liberty is costume. If you cannot speak, you cannot worship. If you cannot speak, you cannot question. If you cannot speak, you cannot resist. Without it, worship becomes ritual, voting becomes theater, and law becomes chains. The Founders knew this. That is why the First Amendment is the soul, and the Second Amendment is the shield — because the First is only ink until the Second defends it.

Denmark still boasts that it has free speech. But its constitution hides the poison. Grundlov §77 declares that speech is free, but then adds the phrase **"within the limits of the law."** Six words that sound harmless — but turn freedom into a leash. That clause is the trap — freedom made conditional. Then comes §266b, the "hate speech" law. Broad. Elastic. A net wide enough to catch anyone. Criticize immigration, and it is hate speech. Question climate dogma, and it is hate speech. Offend EU consensus, and it is hate speech. And this is not theory. The record is full of examples. Politicians convicted for remarks on YouTube. Journalists punished not for their words but for airing others. Ordinary citizens fined for Facebook posts — one man calling gang rapists "parasites," another comparing Islam to fascism. Students investigated for memes. Teachers stripped of careers for writings "incompatible with state values." Even a single 'like' on social media has triggered a police probe. Denmark does not jail the body first; it jails the tongue.

And Denmark is not alone. Europe wrote the script. Germany's NetzDG law forces platforms to erase "illegal" speech within 24 hours or pay €50 million. The result? Over-censorship — lawful words deleted just to protect the companies. Tyranny now moves on cables faster than armies ever marched. The UK's Online Safety Bill went further, criminalizing even "harmful" speech — true or not. Brussels then codified both models into the Digital Services Act — shepherded by Danish commissioner Margrethe Vestager. She wasn't just fining Big Tech. She was hardwiring censorship into the platforms themselves.

Here's the catch — when Facebook, Google, or X rewrote their global policies to obey Brussels, Americans felt it too. A post deleted in Texas can trace back to a directive drafted in Brussels, enforced by Vestager, and rubber-stamped by corporate boards afraid of EU fines. They call it safety. They call it standards. But it is tyranny with a smile. German law. British law. Danish commissioner. Brussels directive. And suddenly, your First Amendment is filtered by foreign hands. We have heard these words before: *Schutz* — protection. *Ordnung* — order. *Gleichschaltung* — alignment. The serpent only updates its translation. **Same hand. Same poison. New tongue.**

The Dane Behind Your Censorship

And here is the twist — one of the loudest referees of online speech is not even American. **A Dane — former Prime Minister Helle Thorning-Schmidt** — now sits on Meta's Oversight Board, the so-called Supreme Court of Facebook. This "independent" body rules over 3.8 billion users and can overrule Zuckerberg himself. It has already issued more than 100 rulings, each shaping what billions may or may not say. A Danish bureaucrat, trained in consensus culture and raised to speak by permission, now hands out licenses for truth. Denmark was the rehearsal. Now its leaders literally license speech for the world.

A Dane scripted the Digital Services Act — the code that dictates what survives online. Another Dane shepherded it through Parliament. In Geneva, the pattern continued: the UN's Global Code of Conduct on Information Integrity, published in 2024, was shaped by Danish hands. What began as quiet prosecutions in Aarhus became treaties, directives, algorithms.

The serpent's tongue speaks Danish. The world is being trained to repeat it.

America was born on the opposite premise — the Constitution tells the state where it may not tread. Speech is protected first; the burden falls on government. Yet we are sliding toward Denmark's model — not by statute, but by mob: social-media swarms, corporate HR, banks, "community standards." You are free to speak — until it offends, until it challenges "the science," until it threatens profit. In Denmark, the state licenses speech. In America, the mob does. Different hands. Same gag. We have already tasted the price: parents at school boards branded as threats, pastors arrested for gathering while rioters were excused, doctors punished for truths later vindicated. The message is unmistakable — truth is tolerated only when it serves the system. Speech is under attack because it shatters spells. One word of truth can break a thousand lies. Every tyrant fears words more than weapons. The serpent strikes the tongue first; once it silences the parent, it owns the child. A nation that cannot speak cannot teach. A mother who cannot speak truth cannot pass it on. Silence is not censorship's goal — your children are. The EU calls it safety. The UN calls it misinformation. Silicon Valley calls it community standards. Different masks. Same serpent.

Two Americas — One Roars, One Kneels

At the federal level, Trump slammed the brakes. Biden's "Disinformation Board" was dismantled. The WHO's claws were blunted. Constitutional judges were seated to anchor the First Amendment in stone. At the state level, the contrast sharpened: **Texas** — HB20 anti-censorship law, DEI speech codes stripped from universities, new platforms thriving. **California** — AB 2098 punishing doctors for "misinformation," loyalty statements required for faculty, Big Tech exporting global censorship from Silicon Valley. Two states. Two futures. One roars. One kneels. But laws are not enough. Speech requires infrastructure. Twitter under Musk is freer, but shadow bans linger. Meta throttles truth while selling your data. YouTube remains the algorithmic gulag. Banks close accounts for "violations." PayPal threatens fines for "misinformation." When your money is tied to your speech, freedom is already collateral.

When tyranny tightens the wire, free nations do what they've always done — they build around it. Censorship may choke the main roads, but the remnant never marches where the serpent expects. When the system closes its gates, Americans build new ones.

America resists by building **parallel systems** — not with banners or hashtags, but with infrastructure. Lawsuits drag lies into the light. State laws defy the leash. New platforms rise to break monopolies. Entire parallel economies form in the cracks of the digital empire. The serpent hisses, *"comply,"* but the remnant answers with a builder's creed: *"we build."* Survival is not protest. It is construction. Parallel systems do not grow in spreadsheets. They grow in the wild — in code, in servers, in towns, in the backroads of the Republic where free men refuse to kneel. *Conversations* that once flowed only through Silicon Valley now move across spaces like Mastodon, Bluesky, Gettr, Parler, MeWe, and Minds — digital commons that remind people speech does not belong to one corporation. Video channels like Rumble, BitChute, Odysee, and Peer-Tube open escape hatches from the algorithmic chokehold. Writers reclaim their voice on Substack, Ghost, or self-hosted WordPress, carving independence into the web one page at a time. These aren't hobbies. They are outposts. Strongholds. Battle camps. *Infrastructure* matters just as much as words. Servers like DigitalOcean, Linode, Vultr, Hetzner, and OVHcloud keep the remnant online when Big Tech slams its gates. Registrars like Epik and Njalla protect domains when others bow to pressure. Privacy survives through ProtonMail, Tutanota, and FastMail. Conversations continue on Signal, Telegram, and Matrix/Element, where encryption becomes the new wall. Even *money* has its rebellion. Crypto gateways — Coinbase Commerce, BitPay, NOWPayments, OpenNode, CoinGate — carry transactions outside the banks that blacklist at will. When financial institutions try to choke dissent, parallel coin pries open a new path. Creators survive through Patreon, Locals, BuyMeACoffee, Gumroad, Shopify, and Square — entire livelihoods built beyond the reach of corporate gatekeepers. Even *search engines* play their role, as DuckDuckGo, Brave, and Surf cut through the fog that legacy platforms manufacture.

In this new world, servers are fortresses. Encryption is a wall. A login is a declaration of independence. These parallel systems are not Plan B. They are the ark being built while the serpent scripts the flood. They are the quiet scaffolding of a free nation preparing its escape from digital empire. And every platform, every server, every encrypted message is a plank in that ark — proof that even under the shadow of Babylon, the remnant still builds. These are not final answers. They are present banners, fragile but real. Tomorrow, they may fall, or new ones may rise. The point is not the brand. The point is the refusal. The point is the fire. The point is the covenant never to kneel when the cartel flips its switch. These aren't just tech brands. They are exits — doors in the wall.

Real speech has never been safe. Not for Jesus before the Sanhedrin. Not for Solzhenitsyn in the gulag. Not for Lincoln when bullets spoke louder than ballots. Not for the patriots who signed their names to a death warrant in 1776. Prophets, rebels, builders of nations — mocked, hunted, hated. If you wait for courage to be safe, you will wait forever — and you will die in chains. Silence feels safe in the moment. But in the end, it builds the bars of your own cage. Silence is not safety. Silence is surrender. Speech is resistance. The First Amendment is the soul. The Second is the shield. Together, they are the firewall of freedom.

The tyrant's first weapon is silence. The patriot's first duty is speech. Guard it with your life, or lose your nation without a shot. The serpent gags the tongue so it can reach the child undefended. But that is only the first strike. The serpent always silences the parent before it reaches for the child. It muzzles the tongue so it can mold the mind. And once it owns the mind, it owns the future. That battlefield begins in the classroom. Denmark was the rehearsal — not just in speech laws, but in schools that traded fire for compliance, questions for consensus, builders for bureaucrats.

In the end, these systems are not just tools — they are tests. They expose whether a people still remember how to stand. You can build a thousand platforms, launch a dozen new networks, draft laws in Austin or D.C., but none of it matters if the citizen is silent. Technology cannot speak for you. Infrastructure cannot carry conviction you refuse to voice. Parallel systems may keep the gates open — but only courage walks through them. Freedom is not saved by servers, apps, or encryption. It is saved by men and women who still speak when speaking costs. And that is where the true battle begins: not online, but in the heart.

🔥 Firelight Pause — Reflection

If you were raised to believe silence is safe, this is your summons to break it.

- When did you first bite your tongue just to keep the peace?
- What is the cost of the truth you swallowed?
- Do you speak freely, or only what the mob permits?
- Could you be fined, fired, or exiled for saying aloud what you believe in private?
- If your voice vanished tonight, who would carry the words you never spoke?
- Do your children see you resist — or only hear you whisper?

If you will not speak, the serpent will. And your silence will be its tongue. Silence feels safe in the moment. But silence is surrender. Speech is resistance. **The First is the soul. The Second is the shield.** *Guard them with your life — or lose your nation without a shot.*

"No weapon formed against you shall prosper, and every tongue which rises against you in judgment you shall condemn. This is the heritage of the servants of the Lord." — Isaiah 54:17

26

THE CLEAN HANDS LIE

BEHIND DENMARK'S SMILE,
THE EMPIRE STILL BLEEDS

Every empire trains its jesters long before it trains its judges. Mockery is control's softest weapon — sharper than law, sweeter than fear. When truth can be laughed off, no censor is needed. When a people learn to laugh at righteousness, they soon learn to kneel to evil. Deception wrapped in humor disarms conscience more effectively than force ever could. Scripture warned of this long ago: *"Like a madman shooting firebrands, arrows and death, so is the man who deceives his neighbor and says, 'I was only joking.'"* The joke is never neutral. It is a delivery system.

Even the court fool saw it coming. Decades ago, a satirist sang, "I side with China. They are not to be laughed at." The audience laughed. They are not laughing now. It was framed as satire — a jab at Western arrogance, a throwaway line meant to amuse. But satire has always been a way truth slips past defenses. What sounded like mockery was prophecy. The fool spoke what ministers would not say aloud. He named what kings refused to see. Power has always ignored prophets when they arrive dressed as jokes. By the time the laughter stops, the damage is already done.

227

The joke did not die. It metastasized. In Denmark, laughter became institutional. In Frederiksberg, the revue tradition is archived, rehearsed, and repeated — sketches, songs, annual lampoons that turn scandal into a seasonal souvenir. Satire became a civic ritual, a safety valve disguised as rebellion. This is the genius of the jester's mask. Satire is permitted to name the minister, provided it tucks him safely back into place. It exposes and anesthetizes in the same breath. When laughter is scheduled and subsidized, critique no longer threatens power — it entertains it. Every joke has an accountant. When rebellion is rehearsed, someone owns the stage. Satire that never bites power does not weaken it; it feeds it. Behind the curtain of laughter stands the bookkeeper, tallying sugar, ships, and souls. The joke protects the architecture it pretends to pierce. The public consents to be amused instead of alarmed. Truth becomes cabaret, and empire hides behind applause.

The greatest trick of a small empire is convincing itself — and others — that it was too small to have one. Denmark hides behind its size, as if sugar grown by enslaved hands weighed less because the flag was tiny. The myth of innocence becomes a shield. A people convinced they are harmless never repent their harm. Peel back the hygge postcard — the bicycles, the candlelight, the curated calm — and the empire appears. Slave ships. Sugar cartels. Monopoly companies chartered and blessed by a crown older than many states. The curtain falls. The lights rise on the real stage: plantations, ports, profit. What looked like laughter was rehearsal for the ledger.

The Laughing Mask of Empire

We rarely named the colonies. We rarely counted the sugar grown by enslaved hands. We did not reckon the more than one hundred thousand Africans who passed through Danish forts. But the memory did not vanish. It was domesticated. It survived in candy aisles. In children's songs. In playground rhymes. In phrases spoken casually by grandparents who never saw a whip but inherited its echo. Empire softened into humor. Slavery folded into sweets.

Shops sold treats called *negerboller* — "negro buns." Radios played songs boasting, *"I have seen a real negro man."*Jests comparing darkness to a Black body passed as ordinary mirth. Not whispered. Not hidden. Normal. Domestic. Safe enough for children. I name these not to resurrect them, but to expose them. They are ugly to repeat — and far uglier when they are buried. Silence does not cleanse history. It preserves it. These were not cultural accidents. They were residues of sugar islands and slave forts, of chartered companies and royal monopolies. Innocence built on ignorance is not innocence at all. It is complicity wearing a smile. Here is the irony Americans are never shown: the same Dane who dismisses these artifacts as "just jokes" will condemn American slavery with moral certainty. Satire punches outward, never inward. Guilt is exported. Memory is buried. Denial does not erase a ledger.It only hides the hand that wrote it.

"Woe to those who call evil good and good evil, who put darkness for light and light for darkness." — Isaiah 5:20

What follows is not about language. It is about reflex. When confronted, the response is predictable. *"Det er ikke så slemt... du overdriver"*. It's not that bad. You're exaggerating. This is not argument. It is anesthesia. Truth is smoothed until it disappears. The defenses are always ready: it was a different time, everyone did it, that's not who we are now. But nations are not absolved by tone. They are judged by what they keep. Denmark did not keep plantations. It kept leverage. It did not keep chains. It kept dependency. It did not keep overseers. It kept administrators. Colonialism did not die. It rebranded. What once ruled through forts and whips now rules through permits, subsidies, standards, and silence. The empire did not vanish. It migrated north — into offices, foundations, ministries, and treaties.

This is why the moral posture matters. A nation that never confesses its own empire learns to manage other people's guilt. Europe buries its chains, then lectures America with a clean voice. One continent hides memory. The other is forced to bleed it publicly. And this is where the lie reveals itself.

They will say it quickly: *That's not who we are now.* But then comes the tell. If Denmark is absolved by time, why is America not? If history ages out innocence in Europe, why is it permanent guilt in the Republic? Why is Denmark allowed to say *we have moved on*, while America is told *you must still atone*? This is not moral reasoning. It is power. America is punished not because it sinned — but because it confessed. Europe is excused not because it was clean — but because it buried the record. The Republic teaches its children the names: slavery, Jim Crow, the Trail of Tears. Statues fall. Textbooks bleed. Shame is compulsory.

Denmark does the opposite. The forts are forgotten. The sugar is romanticized. The crown remains honored. The empire is renamed "trade." One nation is forced to remember. The other survives by forgetting. And that difference is now weaponized. Europe speaks with moral authority precisely because it never reckoned. It did not bleed in public. It did not tear down its founders. It did not fracture itself in confession. America did. And now the paradox: The only nation that fought a civil war to end slavery is told it is uniquely guilty. The nations that ended slavery when it became unprofitable are treated as ethical referees. This is the clean-hands lie perfected. Confession is punished. Silence is rewarded. Memory is used as a leash. America is disciplined because it still believes in truth. Europe governs because it no longer needs it. That is why guilt never expires for the Republic. It is not about justice. It is about leverage. A nation trained to hate itself is easier to manage. A people taught to kneel to history will kneel to policy. Denmark was not cleansed by time. It was protected by quiet. And now it stands — unconfessed — drafting rules for others. That asymmetry is not accident

That asymmetry is not accidental. It is strategic. The plantation became a program. The charter became a foundation. The crown's decree became a Brussels directive. And the joke? The joke trained obedience. It taught people to laugh instead of reckon. To smile instead of repent. To mock power safely — as long as nothing changed. That is the clean-hands lie: **a nation convinced of its innocence because it never counted its dead.**

Colonial profits did not vanish when the plantations closed. They matured. Sugar factories became corporate houses. The East Asiatic Company collapsed, then quietly re-emerged as EAC Invest and the Santa Fe Group. Royal Greenland retained its monopoly lineage, repackaged as enterprise. Carlsberg's Elephant Gate — still bearing swastikas from another age — towers today over tidy tours and gift shops. History is not denied. It is curated. Empire did not end. It corporatized. When a crown trades chains for shares, is that liberty — or simply empire in a suit? Empires do not die; they incorporate. When flags come down, filings go up. The same bloodlines that once blessed slave charters now bless corporate boards and legal frameworks. The crown shed jewels, not control. What once wore ermine now wears Excel. Ermine was never just fur — it was the symbol of sovereignty. Mink was only an industry. One was slaughtered without a vote. The other was never touched. The same seal that chartered slave ships now underwrites NGOs. The same house that sanctioned plantations now sanctifies policies. As kings learned to smile instead of rule, scribes became ministers and merchants became ministers' donors. The bloodlines stayed. Only the ledgers changed hands. Monarchy did not survive by sentiment. It survived by strategy. It withdrew from the stage to control the script. Behind every foundation's "gift" lingers the ghost of a charter. Behind every treaty's signature, the echo of a crown. Behind every "defense partnership," the quiet continuity of dynasties that never stopped commanding fleets — only rebranded them as contracts. When the Queen stepped down, the accountants stepped forward. The generals followed.

Authority never left the house. It decentralized. Power no longer rules from palaces. It reigns from systems, ledgers, and perception. And when guilt grows too heavy for courts to carry, empires build cathedrals of charity. Foundations become the new confessional — laundering conscience through endowments. The tithe of empire is called philanthropy. Corporations alone were not enough. Fortunes need sanctuaries. So came the foundations — the modern treasuries of empire. Denmark is alone in Europe in this design: its largest corporations are not owned by families or shareholders, but by self-perpetuating foundations.

Who do you vote out when power owns itself? And what do you call a system that never has to answer to the people it governs?

Carlsberg washed its fortune through universities. Novo Nordisk poured billions into "global health" and climate virtue. AP Møller stamped its name across cultural halls and EU-aligned programs. The formula is consistent: let corporations extract, let foundations sanctify, let the state deny. The extraction never stopped. It only changed costume. And when wealth born in empire builds museums and endows universities, the question is unavoidable: is this philanthropy — or are chains simply being laundered into culture?

The Shipping Empire That Never Died

Most Americans think Maersk just moves Ikea couches. In reality, it moves the infrastructure of modern war. Maersk Line, Limited — its U.S. arm — sits inside the Pentagon's Maritime Security Program: fifty-plus U.S.-flagged ships, billions in defense contracts, guaranteed access. In 2024, Maersk ships carried U.S. cargo into Israel during the Gaza war. That is not theory. That is Pentagon record, GAO audit, Reuters wire. The empire of the sea never died. It traded sails for steel, forts for supply chains. But when a shipping line carries both couches and combat, is it commerce — or is it conquest by other means?

Sugar and Blood

In 1671, the Danish West India–Guinea Company ran both sides of the triangle — plantations in St. Thomas, St. John, and St. Croix, and slave forts on the African coast. For 250 years, Danish ships trafficked more than 100,000 Africans. The Crown took control in 1754. Plantations ran until 1917, when Denmark sold the islands to America for $25 million — quick cash for chains. Revolt rose up. In 1733, enslaved men and women on St. John rebelled. They were crushed in blood. The sugar did not vanish. It consolidated. Its corporate bloodline still fills shelves today.

The Gold Coast Ledger

On the Gold Coast (modern Ghana), Christiansborg Castle and other Danish forts served as gates of the trade. More than 100,000 Africans passed through. Denmark outlawed the trade in 1803 — but not slavery. Plantations kept grinding until 1848, when freedom came not by decree but by revolt. The echoes remain. Investigations and NGO reports have tied Toms Group, Denmark's chocolate giant, to cocoa supply chains run with child labor in West Africa. And on Danish shelves you still find its "Gold Caramels" — caramels dipped in chocolate, named for the Gold Coast where chains once clamped. That is not coincidence. It is sugar-coated empire.

"The voice of your brother's blood is crying to me from the ground". — Genesis 4:10

Empire Without Flags

The Danish East India Company planted its flag in India in 1616. It folded into the Crown, then sold to Britain in the 1840s. A generation later, the East Asiatic Company resurrected the routes — not with forts, but with contracts and cargo. The Nicobar Islands were a fever dream — settled in the 1750s, abandoned in the 1860s — but the dream of Asia never died.

From spices and tea to timber and rubber, the company stitched Denmark into global commerce. What began as a failed colony reemerged as corporate empire, headquartered not in Calcutta or Tranquebar, but in Copenhagen boardrooms. The empire of the Indies shrank on the map, but it grew in the ledgers. This is how empire survives failure: it abandons flags, not routes.

The Frozen Jewel

To the north, Denmark held Iceland until 1944 — a pawn in WWII, occupied first by Britain, then by America, before declaring independence while Denmark lay under German rule. The Faroes remain under the Crown, another fragment of empire kept for fishing rights and Atlantic position. And Greenland — the jewel — was never sold. In 1946, President Harry S. Truman offered Denmark $100 million for Greenland, seeing what every empire had seen — its strategic worth. Denmark refused. The U.S. built its bases anyway. "History repeats. Empires change uniforms. The map of power never forgets Greenland.

The Crown in the Shadows

The empire was not accidental. It was chartered. It was monarchy that authorized the companies. Monarchy that absorbed the profits. And monarchy that still claims sovereignty over Greenland — the jewel it never released. In 2022, Queen Margrethe issued an apology for the forced sterilization of Greenlandic women. It was framed as regret, not repentance. The same year, she expressed sorrow for Denmark's role in the Virgin Islands slave trade — again without reparations. Words were offered. Accounts were not settled. Regret, not repentance. When monarchy became impolite, bureaucracy replaced it. Treaties replaced chains. Subsidies replaced shackles. Laws replaced whips. Greenland today survives on annual block grants from Copenhagen — billions that bind the land as securely as any charter once did. The forms changed. The dependency remained. The Crown's shadow never left. It learned to smile through treaties and subsidies. But the deepest wound was not financial. It was cultural.

In 1951, Danish authorities — acting through the State under the Crown — forcibly removed twenty-two Greenlandic Inuit children from their families in a so-called "social experiment" designed to remake them into proper Danes. This was not a grassroots act. It was policy. The children were placed in institutions, stripped of language, identity, and belonging, then returned years later as strangers to their own people. Most lived broken lives. Many died young. Denmark later called it a tragedy. It was not a tragedy. It was policy. A colonial mind wrapped in welfare language. The same State that denied its empire attempted to manufacture it in miniature — by rewriting children. That is not compassion. It is control by erasure. Chains denied do not disappear. They change form. And when a State never confesses its own sins, it learns to manage the guilt of others. Memory, when buried, becomes manipulation.

The Hypocrisy

Today, **Denmark presents its colonial past as heritage.** Festivals, associations, and cultural parades celebrate the former colonies — from West Indian events in Copenhagen to heritage groups traveling to the Virgin Islands to commemorate "shared history." It is framed as pride. In practice, it is nostalgia without accounting — empire remembered as charm, not chains. The imagery is colorful. The numbers are absent. Most Danes know the carnival in St. Croix and the pastel facades of St. Thomas. Few are taught that more than 100,000 Africans passed through Danish slave forts on the Gold Coast. Fewer still know that Christiansborg Castle in Accra — today Ghana's seat of government — was once Denmark's primary slave fort. Ask for the name of a single African trafficked through its gates, and the answer is silence.

The contrast with America is instructive. Every American child learns the bus seat of Rosa Parks, the voice of Frederick Douglass, the courage of Harriet Tubman. American classrooms are saturated with slavery's shame. The reckoning is public, loud, often brutal. Statues fall. Textbooks bleed. In Denmark, the story is quieter.

Children are taught almost nothing of the 1733 slave revolt on St. John, of the whips in St. Croix, of the chains beneath Christiansborg's dungeons — where men were held in stone cells, waiting for ships that carried Denmark's wealth across the Atlantic. **America teaches its sin as wound. Denmark treats its own as décor.** One nation is forced to confess in the open. The other preserves innocence by omission. That asymmetry is not accidental. It is the foundation of Europe's moral posture — a continent that buried its chains now lectures a nation that exposed its scars.

Pastries Over Chains

In Copenhagen, King Frederik V still towers over Amalienborg Square, celebrated as founder of the city's "modern age." The same crown that sanctioned slaving voyages is remembered not as oppressor, but as architect. The irony did not end with statues. Today, Danes living in America rage at Trump's tariffs — fretting over higher prices on Danish butter cookies, chocolates, Christmas foods, and candy imports. Kjeldsens blue tins. Toms "Gold Caramels." Anthon Berg marzipan. Haribo licorice. Suddenly more expensive. Suddenly intolerable. Christmas, they say, is ruined. Then comes the sneer: American goods are "ugly." American design is "cheap." Nothing *made in the USA* belongs on a Danish table. They mock American craftsmanship while living on American soil, protected by American freedom, in a nation built by hands stronger than any they left behind. They worship packaging from a country that once packaged people in chains. Tariffs exposed more than economics. They exposed the reflex. Mock the Republic. Praise the realm. Defend the pastry. Pastries matter. The past does not. Think about that. A people who shrug at slave forts and forced sterilizations, but fume at tariffs on cookies.

The European Alibi

The colonial fingerprints do not stop with names. For decades, Danish candy aisles were filled with tropical girls, palm silhouettes, and smiling caricatures on cocoa tins — plantation imagery turned into décor. Toms wrapped its sweets in Gold Coast nostalgia. Anthon Berg sold truffles in boxes printed with Caribbean palms. Children's trading cards smuggled "Africa" into the kitchen as play. The past wasn't erased. It was merchandised. Colonialism didn't just sweeten profits. It sweetened packaging. Chains ignored. Pastries defended. And when this is named, the chorus arrives on cue. The same Danish voices that shrug at history but howl at anyone who points to it. Loud objections. Predictable outrage. No reckoning. Their noise doesn't matter. The truth doesn't need permission.

From Amnesia to Authority

And Denmark is not alone. Its amnesia is Europe's inheritance. One nation is scourged for its sins. Another is cloaked in forgetfulness. America bleeds its history in public. Europe hides its stains beneath treaties. That asymmetry is not accidental. It is the foundation of authority. **Denmark, with blood unconfessed in the Caribbean and Africa, now drafts climate treaties and human-rights resolutions in Brussels.** Belgium, whose rule in the Congo killed millions, parades as guardian of humanitarian law. France scolds the world on liberty after bleeding Algeria and Indochina. Britain lectures on equity atop wealth built from Bengal to Jamaica. The silence of the forts becomes the basis of their moral voice. A continent that buried its chains uses America's chains to preach. The plantation became a treaty. The chartered company became an NGO. The crown's decree became a Brussels directive. This is the clean-hands lie: virtue performed atop graves.

"You boast, 'We have made a covenant with death...' But your covenant will be annulled." — Isaiah 28:15,18

Today Denmark plays the high card — clean hands, high morals, climate pledges. Its bureaucrats fly to Brussels, Geneva, and New York to draft frameworks that strangle sovereignty in the name of virtue. EU quotas. UN compacts. WEF "sustainability" codes. Each bears the fingerprints of the same technocratic class that once managed colonies. The plantation became a program. The slave fort became a treaty. The Crown's charter became a UN resolution. **And still Greenland remains — the jewel of the crown, a living colony in plain sight.** Meanwhile, America is flogged with guilt. Statues fall. Textbooks shame. Europe hides while America is told to repent alone. But is that justice — or manipulation? Is America's confession cleansing the past, or funding Europe's lie? **America holds one truth no empire can counterfeit. It fought a civil war to end slavery.** Hundreds of thousands bled to break the chains. The soil itself carries that testimony.

The Split Republic

America stands at war with itself — not in trenches, but in spirit. Half the nation still knows what a Republic is. The other half mocks it, mistaking comfort for wisdom and rebellion for progress. I hear it everywhere: *"Wouldn't you rather live in Europe? They're happier. Safer. Smarter."* They have no idea what they're praising. I've lived under that smile — the polished control, the quiet surveillance, the State that whispers *trust us* while it watches you sleep. Denmark taught me what a cage can look like when it's clean. Cameras on every corner, bureaucrats in every breath, citizens proud of their own obedience. Small-minded, small-souled, proud of perfection because they have forgotten freedom. When I say I love America, they stare as if I've blasphemed. When I say Denmark is rotten at the core, they call it impossible. They still believe the lie that Europe is better — that managed peace is freedom, that silence is happiness. Let them pursue the lie. I've seen the truth.

There are people who would trade their European passports for an American one in a heartbeat — people who still know the difference between managed lives and chosen liberty. And the Danes? They boast their passport is the world's most powerful, their country the "happiest on earth." I laugh. It's not happiness. It's sedation. They brag their passport opens every border — but what good is crossing lines when every movement is logged, every gate scanned, every right pre-approved? Denmark may top mobility charts, but every trip begins with a chip, a scan, a digital ID, a certificate. **American freedom isn't measured by stamps — but by how rarely you ask permission.** The Danish passport may open doors; the American still chooses whether to walk through them. The Dane enters polite visa-free chains. The American holds the key. You don't need chains when people police themselves with smiles. That is why I love this land — because here, even divided, even bleeding, America still argues. Still fights. Still burns. Division is not death. It's proof the Republic still has blood in its veins.

Be proud to be an American — the only nation built on liberty as creed, the land millions still risk everything to reach, the country enemies mock in words but chase in action. *If America is so evil, why does the world keep knocking?* Because people do not flee toward management. They flee toward sovereignty. Many Americans believe Europe is a shelter — safer, calmer, more civilized. What they mistake for safety is supervision. What they call peace is permission. Europe feels gentle only until you disagree. Only until you speak out of turn. Only until you refuse the script. Then the shelter reveals itself as a system — polite, efficient, and absolute. Europe does not rest on God-given liberty. It rests on delegated tolerance. Rights there are granted, adjusted, revoked — always "within the law." And what the law gives, the law can take away. That is not sovereignty. That is parole.

America is different — not because it is pure, but because it was founded on a dangerous idea: that rights do not come from the State at all. They come from God. Governments exist to *recognize* them, not to invent them. That single belief is why America is loud, chaotic, and hard to govern — and why it remains unbearable to empires. Europe offers shelter from struggle. America offers responsibility for freedom. One promises comfort. The other demands courage. And people who still remember what it means to choose would rather risk the storm than live forever under a roof they do not own. But pride cannot drift into complacency. If America is to remain the firewall — refuge for the hopeful, guardian of truth — it must be honest. Charm is not justice. Guilt is not courage. People still cross oceans for freedom's promise — an indictment and a plea in one. Will America carry chains of false guilt — or wield truth as fire? History wounds most when hidden. Silence keeps scars open; truth snaps chains. Denmark sold its Caribbean plantations a century ago — but never its crown jewel. Greenland was too strategic to release, too rich to let go. The colony never ended. It only changed uniform. The empire's last ledger lies frozen in the north — power disguised as ice.

🔥 **Firelight Pause — Whose Chains Do You Carry?**

• When Europe hides its empire and calls it virtue, do you accept the story — or demand the receipts?

• When America is flogged with guilt, do you echo the chorus — or stand for truth?

• When did you first learn to stay quiet when something felt wrong — and who taught you that silence?

• Do you carry the chains your ancestors forged — or the courage they prayed someone would finally wield?

• When truth costs you reputation, comfort, or belonging, do you still speak — or do you fold like the nations that stayed silent for centuries?

• What will your children inherit from you — obedience or discernment, fear or fire?

27

GREENLAND — FROM ICE TO FIRE
WHY THE ARCTIC DECIDES THE CENTURY

They call it Europe's north. I call it empire's vault.

Greenland is not remote; it is the hinge between continents, the shield over missile arcs, the storehouse of minerals, data, and leverage that decide who speaks and who obeys. Kalaallit Nunaat means "Land of the People" — *not land owned, but land lived in.*

Every empire keeps a last hiding place — a fortress where truth is buried under virtue. For Denmark, that fortress is Greenland. The crown claims it as heritage; the world sees it as tundra. But under the ice lies proof that empire never repented — it just changed uniform.

The Ice Beneath the Flag

Greenland was never a colony. It was collateral. The jewel that kept the crown solvent while pretending to sleep. Under its ice lies the ledger that feeds the empire's new face — minerals, data, leverage. *The crown that once ruled seas now rules perception, but the vault still funds the throne.* That is why Greenland was never sold. It was never just land. It was the endowment of the realm.

When the Reich seized Denmark in 1940, the crown lost its voice but not its leverage. Cut off from occupied Copenhagen, Ambassador Henrik Kauffmann signed a secret pact with Washington in 1941 — without democratic authorization. The United States would "defend" Greenland from Germany — but defense was pretext. The deal gave America control of the Arctic corridor — weather, radar, and air routes that would decide the next war. After 1945, Denmark quietly inherited the arrangement and refused to sever it. **What was denounced in wartime became indispensable in peace.** The island was no longer territory. It was collateral. A decade later, the ice roared again. In 1951, under NATO's blessing, the United States carved Thule Air Base into Greenland's north — a fortress of steel and signal staring into the Soviet pole. It became the eye of the early-warning chain, the point from which America could see missiles before they crossed heaven's arc. Officially, cooperation. In truth, custody. Denmark managed the flag; Washington managed the sky. Eisenhower hid secrets to defend a continent; Denmark hid theirs to keep a colony. Beneath the aurora, radar dishes turned like silent sentinels, guarding a land its own people could no longer enter. Even the name — *Thule*, the mythic edge of the world — fit the purpose: a frontier where empires trade vigilance for sovereignty.

What Denmark Hid — and How They Hid It

What Denmark hid was not rumor — it was record. In 1953, under Prime Minister H.C. Hansen's government, Denmark rewrote its constitution and reclassified Greenland from colony to "equal part of the Realm." No referendum. No Greenlandic consent. No UN notification. This legal sleight-of-hand erased Greenland from the UN's decolonization list and kept Danish control intact behind constitutional smoke. Two years later, *the same government approved the 1951 U.S.–Denmark Defense Agreement,* giving the United States *exclusive* authority over Thule Air Base — while telling the Danish public that Greenland remained firmly under Danish sovereignty.

Internal letters between Danish ministers and Washington confirmed nuclear transit and storage at Thule, even as Denmark proclaimed a national "nuclear-free" policy. These were not accidents. They were decisions — quiet, strategic, and colonial. And Denmark's secrecy wasn't abstract — it had names. The 1953 *forced relocation of the Pituffik Inuit* to clear land for Thule was buried under polite lies about "modernization." *Camp Century* — a secret nuclear-tunnel city carved beneath the ice **without Greenlandic consent** — was disguised as "science", even as its abandoned toxic waste now melts toward the ocean. And the 1968 *Thule nuclear crash*, when a B-52 carrying four hydrogen bombs shattered across the ice, was smothered beneath Denmark's official "nuclear-free" posture. Each event proved the same truth: *Eisenhower hid secrets to stop the Soviets; Denmark hid theirs to keep a colony.* America's secrecy had a different motive. President Dwight D. Eisenhower concealed early-warning systems and nuclear protocols for one reason only: to deter Soviet attack. Washington kept military details quiet because the Cold War required silence — and because Denmark requested that silence, knowing that disclosure would unravel its UN narrative. Denmark hid a colony. America hid a shield. And the difference matters. It's the northern eye of NORAD — part of the same chain as Alaska and Canada.

Trump's "Joke" Wasn't a Joke

In 2019, Donald Trump said America should buy Greenland. The world laughed. Danish politicians sneered. Media crowned him a "mad king." But Trump wasn't joking. He was pointing at a fault line elites prefer to keep quiet. Greenland isn't just ice. It is the northern shield of the Atlantic world — the early warning line for missile arcs, space surveillance, and the protection of America's eastern seaboard. If Greenland slips out of alignment, American security fractures. They laughed because he named the imbalance: America carries the burden, Denmark holds the deed, and global institutions enjoy the shield without paying its cost. Trump didn't propose conquest. He proposed coherence — aligning responsibility with sovereignty. He wasn't the first. In 1946, Harry Truman offered Denmark one hundred million dollars for Greenland. Denmark refused. America built Thule anyway — a sentinel carved into the ice.

The Ice Pact — How Custody Survives

To understand who benefits, you must first understand how custody survives without force.

The Quiet Mechanics of Custody

Greenland was never governed as a nation in formation. It was governed as a dependency in preservation. Empires that intend to keep territory indefinitely do not rule it loudly. They rule it by closure. Custody replaces consent. Stewardship replaces sovereignty. Development is delayed, trade is filtered, and political agency is permitted only inside predefined ceilings. The population is told it is protected precisely because it is not free. Over time, dependence becomes moralized — framed not as limitation, but as care. *This arrangement does not require force. It requires structure.* Once established, it survives leadership changes, wars, and even occupations. Authority migrates into paperwork and agreements; responsibility diffuses outward; power remains claimed inward. *When global power shifts, such systems do not collapse. They adapt.* Defense can be outsourced. Administration can be internationalized. Symbolic ownership can remain intact while operational control moves elsewhere. What looks like partnership functions as possession. What looks like protection functions as control.

The Vault, the Lease, the Lie

Greenland is not a "remote territory." It is a vault — and vaults do not exist for romance. They exist for leverage. When you understand that, Denmark's behavior stops looking like virtue and starts looking like **asset retention.**

NATO — The Neutral Mask

NATO did not create Denmark's control over Greenland. It stabilized it — and in doing so, removed it from democratic review. *Security became multilateral, responsibility became abstract, and accountability dissolved into committees.* What might have looked like colonial custody now looked like alliance necessity. Under NATO doctrine, questions of sovereignty are postponed indefinitely in the name of stability. Bases are no longer "foreign." Militarization is no longer national. Decisions are no longer political — they are procedural. This is how custody survives without occupation. Not by force — but by normalization.

Three locks hold this vault.

The first is legal. A Crown claim wrapped in tidy language — heritage, realm, stewardship. Legal custody is the oldest camouflage. It does not require consent; it requires *paperwork.* It replaces ownership with permanence. It turns a people into an appendix and calls it unity.

The second lock is financial. Subsidy is not generosity when it prevents independence. It is a leash that keeps the dependent grateful and the manager righteous. Empire learned long ago that it is cheaper to fund dependency than to face a referendum. The money is calibrated: enough to keep life running, never enough to let a nation stand.

The third lock is security — and this is the one nobody says out loud. Denmark performs sovereignty. America provides defense. Washington carries the burden; Copenhagen collects the prestige. That arrangement is not a partnership. It is a lease masked as a marriage. That is why Greenland is emotionally dangerous to Denmark. **The threat is not that Greenland will be taken. The threat is that Greenland will be seen.** Because once the vault is visible, the moral story collapses. And Denmark is a system built on moral story. Small states do not become "global" by strength. They become global by managing corridors — trade corridors, treaty corridors, narrative corridors. **Greenland is Denmark's corridor.** Without it, Denmark returns to its true scale. And scale-loss is what the polite empire fears more than war.

This is why every challenge triggers the same reflex: *internationalize, legalize, moralize. Invoke law before debate. Invoke allies before consent. Invoke virtue to avoid inspection.* **When legitimacy is thin, language becomes armor.** So when you see Denmark rush statements, summon frameworks, and lecture the world, do not mistake it for confidence. It is custody under scrutiny. And custody always reaches for enforcement when the story breaks.

Denmark is the first beneficiary.

After World War II, when the UN was founded in 1945, Denmark moved fast. It quietly ensured Greenland was registered **not as a colony** but as part of the *Danish Realm* "Rigsfællesskabet" — a bureaucratic maneuver that disguised control as inclusion. When the UN began cataloging "non-self-governing territories," Denmark simply *didn't list* Greenland. In 1953, Copenhagen rewrote its constitution, claiming Greenland as an "equal part" of the kingdom. The UN nodded. No debate. No vote. Recognition through silence. That decision gave Denmark the one thing every small state craves: **leverage far beyond its size.**

Greenland became its geopolitical crown jewel — **a ticket to every major table:** NATO, EU, UN Arctic councils. Copenhagen could claim Arctic sovereignty, resource rights, and moral prestige as a "peaceful Nordic steward." **The crown doesn't need colonies when it owns corridors.** Greenland's minerals, data, and airspace make Denmark's bureaucracy indispensable — **a gatekeeper nation that manages access for global powers.** That's why Denmark punches far above its population. Its diplomats, technocrats, and environmental bureaucrats run deep inside EU, UN, and OECD networks — all financed by a territory whose people still lack full sovereignty. Greenland is what gives Denmark global weight. Without it, Denmark returns to its natural scale. Custody is never permanent because it is never legitimate — it only survives while it is unseen.

The United States is the unacknowledged leaseholder.

Washington never stopped holding the keys. The 1951 Defense Agreement — still in force today — gives the U.S. "exclusive" control over Thule and unrestricted use of Greenlandic airspace "as necessary for defense." It was written in Cold War ink but functions as a standing lease for the Arctic. So why did Trump want to "buy" Greenland? Because he saw the lie behind the lease. **The U.S. carries the burden but not the deed. It protects Greenland militarily, but Denmark reaps the diplomatic power.** America pays in presence; Denmark collects in prestige. Buying Greenland would have converted *liability* into *sovereignty* — ending the illusion that Washington defends what Copenhagen owns. The elites mocked Trump because he broke the polite fiction. The U.S. has always controlled the base; he dared to suggest controlling the land. Sovereignty denied always becomes risk unpaid. When sovereignty is denied, the bill is always paid later — in blood, leverage, or war. Deferred authority does not disappear; it accumulates.

The United Nations is the global middleman.

The UN benefits from the illusion of Danish stewardship. It gets a model "Arctic partner" — small, obedient, data-rich, and compliant. Denmark supplies climate metrics, Arctic access, and UN-aligned research infrastructure that legitimizes global climate treaties and "sustainable resource management." The UN's Arctic programs — under UNEP, UNOPS, and UNESCO — quietly rely on Denmark's Arctic foothold. In return, Denmark receives something no small nation should possess: *permanent relevance — Arctic authority without decolonization, moral prestige without accountability.* **Greenland provides the moral stage for climate governance** — a place where melting ice justifies *global carbon policy*, where every photograph of a glacier becomes propaganda for centralized environmental control. To the UN, Greenland is not land. It is narrative. A symbol of urgency, a global commons dressed as Danish sovereignty. Governed for the world. Spoken about by Denmark. Ruled without its people.

China — The Quiet Buyer

China never laughed at Greenland. It moved. State-linked firms bid for airports, mines, and infrastructure under the robe of "sustainable development." No flags. No speeches. Just contracts. Beijing's strategy was simple: buy the vault quietly, let virtue sell the story. **Those bids were stalled only when Washington forced the veto.** China didn't want Greenland's people. It wanted its minerals, airfields, and data corridors — ownership without governance, leverage without headlines.

Russia — The Builder in the Dark

Russia does not need Greenland to apply pressure. It builds from the east — icebreakers, runways, missile systems carved into the Arctic night. It operates legally in international waters, probes NATO airspace, and forces the northern warning systems to stay awake. That pressure is precisely why Greenland matters. *Russia's presence does not weaken Denmark's claim. It exposes it.* When real power moves, symbolism collapses. **Denmark does not fear Russia because Russia threatens its land. It fears Russia because Russia threatens the illusion that Denmark owns what America defends.**

Greenland is not territory. It is leverage. Thule is NATO's northern eye — watching missile arcs, tracking satellites, guarding the skies that shield the Atlantic world. In Greenland, NATO does not decide sovereignty. It postpones it. Control is normalized. Accountability dissolves. Beneath the ice lie uranium, zinc, iron, and one of the world's richest rare-earth veins — the bones of modern war, feeding jets, missiles, and chips. China knows it. Russia knows it. Beijing bids quietly under the robe of "sustainable development." Moscow answers with icebreakers and bomber runways carved into the Arctic dark. And while they move, Denmark hides behind subsidies — a leash sold as kindness. Just enough to preserve dependence. Never enough to allow freedom. Every empire recognizes the hinge. The Vikings saw it. Truman saw it. Trump saw it. Greenland is never a joke. **It is the hinge of power.** Empires rarely die. They adapt. And Denmark's ledger now stares back from the ice.

Pride Without Presence

Danes claim Greenland with words, not footsteps. They sing of sovereignty while standing on foreign soil. They boast of heritage without cost and unity without truth — flags waved for a land they have never walked. Most Danes have never set foot in Greenland. Few could name its towns; fewer still its scars. In daily life they ignore it. Yet online they roar — fierce defenders of Denmark's "sovereignty," wrapping themselves in a colony they don't know, claiming it as proof of greatness. Pride without presence. Heritage without cost. They call it loyalty. I call it fear — **fear of losing the one possession that makes their flag matter on the world stage. Without Greenland, the Danish welfare model loses its mask — the geopolitical leverage that keeps it solvent and relevant.** The exports are not oil or ore anymore — they are bureaucrats and climate reports, sold to the EU and UN as *moral capital.* Greenland keeps the illusion alive: the myth that a small state can fund virtue without power. The truth is simpler. Every welfare crown comes from empire's vault — minerals, data, and military rent. They sing of Greenland as "our land," but never speak of what was done to it — the land that over 133 years generated what Greenlandic historians estimate to be hundreds of billions of kroner for Danish coffers — while Greenland itself remained poor. Pride without presence. Dominion without repentance.

When Empire Touches the Body

Every empire hides its sins under sentiment. Denmark's comes wrapped in virtue — progress, education, modernization. But behind every moral slogan lies someone who paid the price. While Copenhagen praised equality, Greenland carried the cost. The farther Danes drifted from the ice, the easier it became to forget the faces beneath it. What they called "integration" was invasion in slow motion — policies that cut language, family, and flesh in the name of civilization. Never mention the twenty-two children taken from their families in 1951 under the *Little Danes Experiment* — stripped of language, land, and love in the name of modernization. Never mention the forced relocations that uprooted Inuit from ancestral villages into prefab housing blocks, where roots withered under fluorescent lights.

And never mention the women. From the 1960s through the 1990s, thousands of Greenlandic women and girls — many still teenagers — were subjected to birth-control programs implemented without informed consent. Some recall IUDs inserted without explanation. Others remember sterilizations signed under pressure. Almost every family carries that scar. One Greenlandic woman testified in 2023: "We were told it was for our good. We were told it was progress. But every woman in my family carries the wound." They'll say it was long ago. But trauma doesn't live in decades. It lives in blood. This wound wasn't made with rifles, but with gloves. Empire doesn't always arrive with chains. Sometimes it arrives with clinics. The same Crown that once trafficked sugar and slaves now managed wombs and futures — and still called it "modernization." **Wrong victims. Useful ally. Forgotten truth.** That is how empire survives apology.

Calculated Contrition

In August 2025, the Prime Minister finally said "sorry." But timing is never innocent. The apology did not rise from conscience. It arrived by calculation — issued as Arctic power plays intensified and Greenland's value sharpened in global negotiations. This was not repentance. It was **repositioning.** The message was not for Greenland. It was for Brussels, Washington, Beijing: Copenhagen still holds the script. They did not apologize because they changed. *They apologized because leverage was shifting.* Because the leash was slipping. Danish virtue has always come with fine print. **Every apology carries a balance sheet. Every confession protects an asset.** This was not sorrow. It was strategy. And the timing tells the truth. It aligned with renewed Arctic attention — diplomatic, military, and economic — not with any new moral discovery.

Silencing the Receipts

Even when Greenlanders speak, Denmark shrugs. Former Greenlandic leaders have said it plainly: *"Denmark's relationship is still colonial."* Others are more direct: *"We are ready for independence. Denmark fears losing us."* In Copenhagen, sovereignty parties are treated as provincial — indulged when useful, exotic when convenient, ignored when dangerous. Culture is celebrated. Power is withheld. A recent **documentary tracing how Greenland's cryolite riches poured hundreds of billions into Danish coffers aired once — then disappeared.** The editor resigned. No rebuttal. No debate. Just silence. Heritage is permitted. Memory is tolerated. Receipts are buried. And the ledger did not close in the past. It is still being written — in Nuuk's streets, in mineral contracts, in Arctic corridors — under the shadow of a military buildup Greenland never consented to, negotiated in rooms where Greenlanders are not present. They are allowed to speak. They are not allowed to decide. Denmark fears losing its position as gatekeeper.

When the Ice Cracks

A truth the diplomats will never say aloud: Within one generation — and likely sooner than diplomats admit — Greenland will leave the Kingdom. Every demographic, political, and strategic trend points to it. When the question finally comes as a vote, it will not be about culture or welfare. **The real break will not come with flags or speeches, but with a phone call that no longer routes through Copenhagen.** Denmark loses its Arctic seat — and everything that seat confers. Minerals. NATO leverage. The mask of global importance. A welfare model built on borrowed power. And Denmark knows it. That is why the buildup is happening now — the billions, the frigates, the new command base. This is not strength. It is fear in uniform. The vault is shifting. Empires do not militarize assets they are confident they own. They fortify what they fear losing. When control is unquestioned, there is no rush. When legitimacy erodes, hardware arrives. Every empire knows what it means when the vault begins to move.

The New Infiltration — 2025

In 2025, Denmark announced a *$4 billion Arctic military expansion* — and Greenland learned about it the same way the public did: through the news. A new Arctic command in Nuuk. A new Danish military unit stationed on Greenlandic soil. A naval quay built to receive "allied" warships. A Danish frigate and helicopters already deployed. Greenlanders were not consulted. They were not briefed. They were not asked for consent. Kuno Fencker, a member of Greenland's Parliament, broke the script: *"We feel like we are being infiltrated by the Danish military."* He learned of the buildup from journalists — not from Copenhagen, not from the committees supposedly responsible for protecting Greenland's self-rule. Another Greenlandic voice warned the expansion *"pushes us further away from becoming a sovereign state."* An independence activist said what many say quietly: *"People feel hopeless and afraid."* They have reason. Under the *2009 Self-Rule Agreement*, Denmark still controls what matters: defense, foreign affairs, treaty authority, and veto power over every major strategic decision. Greenland may vote. Copenhagen signs. Even Greenland's own Foreign & Security Policy Committee admits it is only *"partly informed"* — and is prohibited from briefing the full Parliament. Fencker demanded **full informed consent.** Then came the truth that ends the argument: *"It does not exist."* As the Arctic militarizes, the U.S. footprint expands, and Danish media whispers about "foreign actors" encouraging Greenlandic independence, one reality hardens: This is not sovereignty. It is custody. Not enforced by troops in the streets — but by secrecy, legal ceilings, and strategic silence. An occupation executed through paperwork. And that silence exists for one reason Denmark cannot admit: because **full transparency would expose why Greenland must be held at any cost.**

Denmark fears Russia tactically. But **it fears irrelevance strategically.** And when the two compete, irrelevance is the deeper terror. Russia is a threat. *Irrelevance is an extinction event.* Denmark understands this hierarchy instinctively. Russia threatens security. Greenland determines status.

Losing Greenland collapses everything that makes Denmark matter beyond its size — its Arctic seat, its NATO leverage, its EU relevance, its diplomatic weight, its justification for being heard at tables built for empires. Without Greenland, Denmark is no longer a "global partner." It becomes a managed state, not a managing one. That is the fear beneath the flags. A small kingdom with no strategic depth, no meaningful domestic resources, and no independent military power has only one path to lasting influence in a world of giants: borrow someone else's empire. Greenland is that empire. The ice is the vault. The minerals are the inheritance. The U.S. base is the shield. And **Denmark's welfare palace is built on top of all three.** Without Greenland, Denmark is Luxembourg with better pastries — no Arctic authority, no NATO gravity, no geopolitical voice. It becomes what it truly is: a small, anxious state clinging to leverage it did not create and cannot replace. So sovereignty becomes theater. Flags are wrapped around ice. Soldiers are posted as symbols. Unity is spoken while the ledger is hidden. Denmark performs sovereignty like ritual because ritual is all that remains once substance is threatened. They know the truth Greenland now whispers — a vault can walk away. And that is Denmark's terror. This is why Nuuk matters.

If Russia were the primary fear, Denmark would centralize command outside Greenland, emphasize NATO multilateralism, and minimize symbolic national presence. Instead, Denmark plants Danish command on Greenlandic soil, expands its own footprint, bypasses Greenlandic consent, and manages optics more than defense. *That is not counter-Russia behavior. It is asset-retention behavior.* They do not militarize Nuuk for Moscow. They militarize Nuuk for Greenland. They fear the referendum — and everything it would unravel. A future where Washington speaks directly to Nuuk and Copenhagen is no longer in the room. Greenland sees the shift. The world sees the shift. Only Denmark pretends not to.

The United States remains the real landlord of the Arctic, its eye at
Pituffik watching missile arcs and satellites above them all. Greenland
sees its worth. America sees its necessity. China sees its minerals. Russia
sees its lanes. And Denmark? Denmark sees its future slipping away.
**Billions suddenly appear for Arctic "security" not because Denmark
grew strong — but because Denmark grew afraid.** Afraid of a vault it
can no longer hold. Afraid of a people waking up. And afraid that the
world will finally see what has been true all along: **Denmark's wealth
and relevance are built on American protection, EU financing, and
Greenlandic resources. The welfare palace always stood on Arctic ice.
And the ice is cracking.**

The Theater of Pride

On social media, Danes defend their "Greenlandic heritage" with
fierce pride — flags, songs, sentimental slogans. But this pride is parasitic.
It is love of possession, not of people. Many Danes glorify a land they
barely know while mocking Greenlanders in Copenhagen as backward.
They praise royal tours and the Sirius Patrol — two men and a dogsled
dragging a flag across a land the size of Alaska and Texas combined,
while ignoring the scars in the womb, the graves in the soil, and the
minerals still waiting beneath the ice. They call it heritage. In truth, it is
possession without responsibility — pride without presence. Beneath the
theater lies something deeper: the psychology of a small empire terrified
of disappearing. Danes rage at America not because they understand
Greenland. They rage because they sense what it means if Greenland
walks away. Denmark shrinks back to scale. No Arctic seat. No strategic
leverage. No vault beneath the ice to prop up the welfare palace. So the
state manufactures sentiment. School textbooks. Royal tours. Patriotic
songs. Greenland is woven into Danish identity as a protective myth.
Most Danes do not know the treaties, the minerals, the missile corridors,
or the Cold War agreements. They do not know the ledger beneath the
ice. But they feel the anxiety of their elites — and like most conformist
societies, they absorb the emotion without understanding its source.
What looks like pride is fear wearing national colors. They are not
defending Greenland.

They are defending the illusion that Denmark is more than it is. And they shout at America because *silence would force them to face the truth: the empire was never real.* The ice was. And the ice is slipping from their hands.

Pawn, Not Partner

Greenland was never treated as a partner. It was managed as a pawn. The record is not written only in treaties and accounts, but in lives — families broken, language cut, trust violated, identity thinned across generations. What was done did not require secrecy to endure; it required silence. And silence was provided. Repentance was postponed. Profit was normalized. The ice became theater. The ledger became law.

Climate Theater, Spiritual Sellout

Greenland is paraded as the poster child of Danish climate virtue — melting ice, stranded polar bears, carefully staged sorrow. The world accepts the performance. Behind it lies the exchange: a land framed as victim, administered as asset, extracted as colony. Climate becomes the language empire uses when control must present itself as care.

Why Greenland Matters - The Arctic Hinge

Greenland is a gate between continents — the shortest arc between North America and Eurasia, where missiles fly and satellites are watched. **It is closer to America than to Denmark — closer to New York than to Copenhagen — a fact no treaty can erase.** Greenland is not remote. It is the hinge of the twenty-first century. Whoever controls it controls the Arctic lanes, the satellites above, and the submarines below. The island is not an ice desert but a fortress wall — the shield between America's eastern seaboard and Moscow's missiles, the keystone that can hold or collapse the northern front.

Thule — Watchtower in the Ice

Thule Air Base is not symbolic. It is NATO's northern eye, watching missile arcs, tracking satellites, feeding the command chains that protect the Atlantic world. Remove it, and the eastern seaboard of the United States lies exposed. Washington pays the bill. Denmark plays the landlord. Americans build the radars and runways; Copenhagen poses for photographs and calls it "sovereignty." That word, here, is a lie.

Rare Earths, Real Power

Greenland's mountains are not scenery. They are the bones of modern war — uranium, zinc, iron ore, and at Kvanefjeld one of the richest rare-earth deposits outside China. These minerals fuel every jet, missile, submarine, radar, and chip. Without them, modern armies grind to a halt. But minerals are only half the vault. Power now moves through fiber — data cables, satellite corridors, surveillance architecture. Ice, ore, signal. The full stack of empire. Denmark sends roughly four billion kroner a year in subsidies and calls it generosity. But the arithmetic tells the truth. The rare earths alone are worth trillions. **This is empire math: take trillions, return millions, and demand gratitude.** The subsidies are not kindness. They are insurance — enough to keep Greenland dependent, never enough to set it free. For 133 years, the cryolite mine at Ivittuut poured wealth into Danish coffers — hundreds of billions in today's value — while Greenland remained poor. Cryolite helped forge the aluminum that built Allied aircraft in World War II. Greenland got scraps. Denmark kept the fortune. The pattern never changed.

Sovereignty on a Leash

In 2009, Denmark granted Greenland what it called "self-rule." A parliament. A prime minister. A flag. To the outside world it looked like decolonization. But the fine print told the truth. **Defense, foreign policy, treaty authority, and veto power remained in Copenhagen's hands.** *Greenland may vote. Copenhagen signs.* Nearly four billion kroner a year — more than half of Greenland's budget — flows south as "support," returning as leverage. Presented as generosity, it functions as dependency.

This is not sovereignty. It is empire in a new costume. What was once enforced by decree is now managed by subsidy and veto.

The Exported Model

Greenland is not just a colony. It is a laboratory. The strategies tested there are not accidental. They are refined — tested on a small population, under moral cover, far from scrutiny. Land is sold quietly under the language of modernization. Resources are locked or outsourced until outside powers — Copenhagen, Brussels, Beijing — decide when and how they will be tapped. Sovereignty is not taken by invasion. It is dissolved by paperwork, dependency, and fatigue. This is conquest without armies. You do not need to raise a flag over a capital. If you can regulate a people into paralysis, subsidize them into silence, and narrate them into believing they are free, you no longer need force. Control no longer arrives with soldiers. It arrives with forms, grants, conditions, and expert panels. The chains are administrative. The obedience is voluntary. What is rehearsed in Greenland does not stay in Greenland.

Greenland was the testbed — where techniques of dependency, narrative control, and managed sovereignty were refined on a small scale. **Denmark became the prototype** — proof that a nation can wield empire without admitting it, rule without uniforms, and govern through virtue instead of force. **America is not the origin — it is the expansion.** Different scale. Same design. Funds flow downward. Power flows upward. Sovereignty dissolves in the exchange. The same structure now appears in larger nations. Federal "green" subsidies dictate how American states build their power grids. Education funding arrives bundled with curriculum requirements that rewrite identity and history. ESG scoring pressures banks and businesses to conform not to markets, but to ideology. Pandemic-era funding flooded cities with cash — tethered to compliance, behavior, and silence. The pattern is identical. Greenland's leash is financial and political. America's leash is federal and global. What was tested on sixty thousand souls is now applied to entire nations.

America's Return

In this hour, Washington is moving again. Thule's surveillance posture shifted. Arctic supply chains hardened. Beijing's mining ambitions stalled. Copenhagen was warned that sovereignty could no longer be laundered through treaties and theater. Denmark postured. China plotted. Russia built. Brussels stalled. America acted. And the choice ahead is not whether to "buy Greenland," but whether to recognize its right to stand free. For decades America has paid the bill for Greenland's defense while Denmark performed sovereignty with dogsled patrols and royal photo ops. That contrast is not accidental. It is the same ledger repeated since empire learned to outsource guilt — one nation bearing the weight, another harvesting the pride.

Greenland waits for truth. So does America. Denmark was rehearsal. Greenland is the hinge. The empire didn't end — it froze. It waited beneath the ice, preserved and patient, ready for the next hand to claim it. Obedience was taught there first. Legislated there first. Normalized there first. Perfected on a small nation until the system ran smoothly enough to export. Now the battlefield that matters most comes into view: America herself. The serpent has tested its coils. The question is no longer whether it exists — but whether we will resist. America was born to roar. Minerals. Subsidies. Bases. Ice — turned into theater. Even the ice itself becomes propaganda: melting glaciers, stranded polar bears, tear-stained headlines — images deployed to bind nations into climate compacts and centralized control. Panic first. Policy second. Fear sold, regulation delivered. But a vault alone does not make an empire. It must be wired into the system — money flowing out, contracts flowing back, treaties sealing the doors. **This is the map. This is the coil. Once you see it, you cannot unsee it.** Greenland is the hinge — the vault of ice that props the Danish crown and feeds the machinery of empire. Not just ore and ice, but a people. Every silenced testimony. Every broken family. Every sterilized womb proves Greenland is not scenery — it is soul. And their silence reveals who still holds the pen. Minerals mean nothing without markets. Bases mean nothing without treaties. Subsidies mean nothing without a sanctifying lie.

This is Denmark's genius: empire hidden in plain sight — not through battalions, but bureaucracy; not through conquest, but words; not through force, but virtue. What was rehearsed on sixty thousand souls is now repeated in American towns — through grants, ESG scores, regulations, and decrees. Greenland was the laboratory. Denmark was the proof. **America is the target.** The coil is tightening. Visibility is irreversible.

The Deeper Truth

Greenland is not only strategic. It is sacred. They sterilized the womb — but the land remembers. They leashed the soil — but blood remembers anyway. They sold the ice — but the stone remembers. Not all colonizers wear uniforms. Some wear lab coats. Some wave flags. Some draft treaties in Brussels. Some sign subsidies in Copenhagen. Empire does not always arrive with boots. Sometimes it arrives with grants, credentials, and well-worded concern. But the land still waits for truth. And so does America. Our soil remembers its covenants. Our blood remembers its liberty. Our stone — rejected by empires — became the cornerstone. The serpent has tested its coils in Greenland. The question is no longer whether it coils. The question is whether we will resist when it coils here. Denmark's rage is not love for Greenland. It is fear of losing the one asset that makes Denmark feel like a power. Most citizens cannot name Greenland's towns or scars — but they will defend "sovereignty" online with ferocity, because the state has woven Greenland into identity as a patriotic sedative. Pride becomes a substitute for presence. Sentiment replaces consent. And when a people are trained to confuse calm tone with moral truth, they will defend the machine that owns them — not because they are evil, but because the system has taught them that questioning is impolite. That is **the soft empire's masterpiece: exploitation without visible violence, domination without the sensation of domination.**

"The stone the builders rejected has become the cornerstone." — Psalm 118:22

🔥 **Firelight Pause — When the Ice Cracks**

• If Greenland is the vault, who actually holds the keys — and why were you never told they existed?

• When subsidies are framed as kindness, do you recognize care — or control dressed as mercy?

• If a people may vote but not decide, speak but not consent, govern but not defend — what is sovereignty worth in practice?

• If Denmark hid empire beneath ice, law, and virtue, where has your own nation hidden power beneath language, policy, and good intentions?

• China plots quietly. Russia builds openly. America pays the bill. Who benefits from the arrangement — and who bears the risk?

• If your land were treated as Greenland's has been — managed, narrated, subsidized, restrained — would you call it protection or possession?

• What happens when geography, security, and resources no longer align with the stories told about them?

• The land remembers. The blood remembers. **What will your children remember of you — silence, or courage?**

Custody always pretends to be care — until the bill comes due.

28

THE EMPIRE OF INFORMATION
WHERE DATA BECOMES DESTINY

Freedom doesn't shatter with armies. It dissolves in silence — exported through cables, mirrored in servers, rewritten by laws you never voted for. In Greenland you saw the empire of ice. Here is its twin — the empire of information. This is the domain where sovereignty ends without a sound.

The Cables of Control

Under the Arctic and the North Atlantic, subsea cables carry surveillance routes, financial flows, and encrypted military traffic linking Greenland, Iceland, Denmark, and the United States. The Greenland Connect system ties Nuuk to Newfoundland and Iceland; the "Havfrue" (mermaid) cable ties Denmark directly into America's digital spine. And in Odense, Meta's vast data center hums like a modern fortress — storing the world's information on Danish soil, under Danish law, behind Danish eyes. **Empire once controlled shipping lanes. Now it controls data lanes. Minerals fuel the missiles, but data guides them.** The same kingdom that once trafficked bodies now traffics information — packets instead of people — yet the logic is unchanged: control the corridor, control the flow, control the future.

The Jurisdictional Trap

And here is the part the world never notices: **data stored on Danish soil does not sit under American law.** It is governed by **Danish surveillance statutes, EU data directives, and the Brussels enforcement machine.** The same machine shaped by Margrethe Vestager — the Danish commissioner who built the EU's digital throne. Her competition rulings, privacy mandates, and algorithmic codes reach across oceans. A post removed in Texas can trace back to an EU statute drafted in Brussels and enforced on servers sitting in Odense. **American speech traveling through Danish cables becomes subject to European law.** In the age of fiber, sovereignty is not just borders; it is routers, nodes, and jurisdiction. But ask yourself this — **when American speech, banking, and military traffic pass through Danish cables and sit in Danish data centers under EU law, whose Constitution shields it? America's... or Brussels'?**

The Data Sovereignty Betrayal

Freedom does not vanish in riots or coups — it vanishes in cables. Americans think their rights travel with their words, but the moment a message leaves U.S. soil, your Constitution stays behind. iCloud backups stored in Denmark fall under EU decrees. Google traffic routed through Belgium answers to Belgian law. Facebook posts replicated in Ireland bow to Brussels' digital codes. A photo taken in Texas can be censored by a statute written in a city you will never vote in. Power no longer sits in parliaments; it sits in servers. **And here is the darkest twist:** when American data travels through foreign cables, even U.S. intelligence agencies are forced to treat it as "foreign-routed traffic" — legally targetable under foreign-intelligence authorities. Your own words, calls, and cloud files become fair game the moment they leave the country. Not because the NSA hates you — but because the architecture forces it. The jurisdiction decides the rights. The cables decide the law. **The path your data takes decides whether you are a citizen... or a target.** The freest speech on earth now passes through the least accountable jurisdictions, filtered by foreign algorithms and governed by laws no American ever consented to. Control the cables, control the servers, control the future — and today, the future of American speech runs through Danish soil.

When your rights cannot follow your data, sovereignty becomes a memory. And the republic trembles in the silence. Still think this is theory? Let me show you the receipts — not from 2030, but from *now*. Not hypotheticals. Not warnings. Actual lives. Actual Americans. Already caught in the cables.

CASE STORY 1 — The Danish Facebook File That Prosecuted an American

He never left Texas, yet his rights crossed an ocean without him. In 2023 a contractor from Lubbock posted a blunt criticism of EU migration policy — legal, ordinary, the kind of debate Americans have every day. But his post wasn't stored in Texas. It was stored on Meta's servers in Ireland, under EU jurisdiction, where Brussels' Digital Services Act governs speech. A Danish activist group flagged the post through an EU complaint portal, and because the server holding his words lived in Europe, the review was conducted through European law — not the First Amendment he grew up trusting. The post vanished. The removal was logged as a "cross-border risk signal." That signal fed into an automated fraud-and-extremism database. Within forty-eight hours, his PayPal account was closed, his Shopify storefront frozen, and his Facebook visibility collapsed. He had violated no American law, but Europe had jurisdiction over the server that stored his thoughts. The man stayed in Texas. His rights didn't. **In the age of fiber, sovereignty belongs not to citizenship, but to server location.**

CASE STORY 2 — The iPhone Backup Seized Because It Left U.S. Soil

She believed iCloud lived in the sky. She didn't know it lived in Denmark. A nurse in Colorado became tangled in a family inheritance dispute, and one morning her attorney placed a stack of her private messages on the table — photos, notes, texts, voice memos — all pulled from her iPhone. She assumed there had been a U.S. warrant, a judge, a constitutional process. There wasn't.

Her iCloud backup had been mirrored automatically in Apple's European clusters in Denmark and Ireland — a redundancy system she never saw, never approved, never imagined. European courts demanded access under EU data retention mandates, and Apple complied because the data was under their jurisdiction. The messages would have been protected in California. In Denmark they were not. The seizure was legal for Europe, illegal under U.S. constitutional privacy rights, and completely invisible to the woman who had never left Colorado. Her data crossed a border she didn't know existed — and her rights remained behind.

CASE STORY 3 — When a Danish Cable Route Turned an American Into "Foreign Intelligence"

A father in Wisconsin emailed his daughter in Chicago. A trivial, domestic moment — a message that should have traveled a few hundred miles and stayed inside American territory. But the internet doesn't honor borders; it honors efficiency. That day, because of network congestion and peering agreements, their email took an unexpected route: Chicago to New York, then out through Denmark, then back to New York and home to Chicago. A three-second detour. Under American law, that detour transformed the message into "foreign-routed traffic" — fully targetable under foreign intelligence authorities. No suspicion. No warrant. No crime. The father was not an enemy, not a target, not a threat. The cable made him foreign. For three seconds his words lived under the rules of espionage simply because the fastest path ran through Danish fiber. In a world ruled by cables, the architecture decides the rights — and the path your data takes decides whether you are a citizen or a category. These are not outliers. They are previews. **The system is already built, already humming, already reaching into American lives without the courtesy of a knock.**

The Question That Changes Everything

If Denmark — or any small state wired into Brussels and flirting with Beijing — ever crossed the line into quiet tyranny, what would stop them from using the data they already hold? The logs of your calls. The metadata of your messages. The cloud backups that Apple mirrors overseas. The location histories Google stores in European data centers. **If a foreign government colluded with China tomorrow, would you even know when your privacy died?** Rights do not disappear with a gunshot; they disappear with a silent export. A Constitution cannot shield you if your life is stored in a jurisdiction that does not recognize it. And here is the dread no one wants to name: many of these nations have already violated their own human-rights guarantees — gag orders, political prosecutions, censorship laws, digital surveillance. If they do this to their own citizens, what do you think they will do to **your data**? The question that haunts the honest mind is not "could it happen?" but "if it did... would anyone be able to stop it?" Tyranny does not need your obedience. It only needs your information. And you already gave it the keys.

🔥 **Firelight Pause — The Silent Surrender**

- When your data leaves U.S. soil, do your rights leave with it?
- Who should govern your life — your Constitution or foreign bureaucrats?
- When speech becomes subject to foreign laws, is your freedom still yours?
- If tyranny rises quietly, will you even know when your privacy died?
- What chains are digital, invisible, and already wrapped around your name?

If they can take your data, they can take your destiny. But not if America wakes. Not if her warriors rise. Not if you refuse to live in silence.

29

THE MAP OF THE COIL
THE SMALL STATE THAT SCRIPTS THE WORLD

The ice was never just geography. It was blueprint. What was rehearsed in Greenland now scales to the world. The coil is not buried in ice — it's wired into policy, contracts, and cause. Denmark is the mask, not the monster — a smiling operator in the empire's machine. This is how the serpent learned to hide in plain sight.

The world sees a postcard — bicycles, canals, six million souls by the sea. Windmills spin, bills are paid, smiles are polite. Harmless. Peaceful. Unthreatening. But how does a nation so small sustain so much wealth? Its true export is bureaucrats. It strangles farmers, funds students, feeds civil servants — and the sushi still arrives on time. Where does the money come from? Step into the marble halls of New York or Geneva and the mask cracks. Behind the smile is a machine — a micro-power dressed as a lamb, seated among lions. A pleasant facade is its first weapon. Politeness becomes camouflage. Virtue becomes branding. Soft power greases the hinges while hard interests stay hidden. Denmark learned early what empires forget late: the quiet hand moves the map.

The Seat of Giants

Denmark holds a seat on the UN Security Council for 2025–2026. Not for the first time. For the fifth. How does a nation of six million equal Egypt's record with 115 million people, and surpass Indonesia's four turns with nearly three hundred million? Is it done with tanks? With armies? Or with contracts and careful positioning? When Denmark assumed the Council presidency in March 2025, its Permanent Representative Christina Markus Lassen chose to spotlight themes like the climate-peace-security nexus and Women, Peace & Security. Is this defense — or the power to redefine what "defense" even means? When a small state is treated as a giant, what exactly is it selling? Influence is no longer purchased with force — it is purchased with frameworks. Denmark writes the vocabulary others must obey.

The Money Crown

In 2024, Denmark poured out 21.9 billion kroner — roughly $3.2 billion — in Official Development Assistance. ODA is not loose charity but the official measure of government-to-government aid, counted and defined by the OECD, the very currency of global virtue. By January 23, 2025, before most capitals had signed their checks, Copenhagen had already wired its entire $18 million contribution to the UN's regular budget. How many nations pay so punctually — and why does Denmark insist on being one of them? Each transfer buys standing. Each transfer buys voice. Denmark is among the few countries that consistently meets the UN's 0.7% ODA/GNI target. GNI — gross national income — is the sum of every krone earned by a nation's citizens and companies at home and abroad. The target demands nearly one percent of that total be siphoned into global aid. Denmark not only meets it but publicly urges others to "join the club." Is this generosity — or leverage disguised as virtue?

The Circle of Return

Follow the money home. Aid does not simply vanish into the Sahel or the Levant; it circles back to Copenhagen. In 2023, Denmark was the second-largest UN procurement supplier in the world, posting $1.04 billion in sales — 4.18% of all UN purchasing. Look at the companies — Danoffice IT booked $192.7 million; Atea, $112 million; Scan Global Logistics, $139 million. UNICEF alone paid Danish firms $270.4 million; UNDP, $192.5 million; UNHCR, $141.8 million; UNOPS, $132.1 million; WHO, $92.3 million. Does this resemble aid — or a business ledger dressed in compassion? Copenhagen openly advertises UN procurement as an "export opportunity." Trade envoys boast of four consecutive years clearing $1 billion in sales. The marketing hook? The 17 Sustainable Development Goals. Are the SDGs a moral framework — or a commercial wrapper? It is not charity when the money returns home with interest. It is an empire of invoices — philanthropy as profit.

The Front Door and the Side Door

Copenhagen's generosity shows two faces. Through the front door, billions in ODA go to countries and multilateral bodies, with a pledge to prioritize the Least Developed Countries. In 2023, 29.4% of bilateral aid went to the top ten recipients, largely in Africa and the Middle East. At the same time, 35% was channeled into multilateral organizations, and in 2024, about 9% flowed directly into the UN system. Through the side door, the UN's agencies purchase back from Danish firms at scale. Aid leaves speaking the language of compassion. It returns speaking the language of invoices. Which door is the mission — and which is the margin?

The Frozen Vault

A nation of six million does not summon such leverage out of nothing. Look north. Is it the frozen vault propping up Denmark's throne? Beneath the ice sit 25 of the EU's 34 "critical" raw materials, with roughly 12 million tonnes of rare earths already mapped. Some assessments stretch that figure to 42 million tonnes of rare earth oxides — enough to rival China's dominance and surpass Vietnam, Brazil, and Russia. One estimate for graphite alone: 6 million tonnes, compared to global EV demand projected at only 3.5 million tonnes in 2040. Could Greenland hold the keys to the twenty-first-century energy map? A 2008 *U.S. Geological Survey (USGS)* study — the American government's own scientific agency for mapping geology and natural resources — estimated 17.5 billion barrels of oil and 148 trillion cubic feet of natural gas offshore. Exploration has been banned since 2021, but is the geology any less real? At the same time, Pituffik Space Base (Thule) anchors America's Arctic missile-warning architecture. The personnel headcount has shrunk to about 150 — yet the line items show up in $5.2 billion of Space Force operating requests for FY2025. Does strategic relevance itself function as rent?

And what of subsidies? In 2023, Greenland received a DKK 3.9 billion block grant, about $511 million — ~20% of GDP, more than half the public budget. In September 2025, Denmark committed DKK 1.6 billion more through 2029. The EU adds €17.29 million yearly for fisheries access. If Greenland were truly a burden, why sustain it with such a steady infusion of subsidies? Mining politics make the story even sharper. All seven parties in Nuuk say mining must grow. Yet in 2021, uranium exploitation was banned above 100 ppm after protests over the Kvanefjeld project — even though uranium often comes with rare earths. *How can a mining future be built when politics blocks the geology?* Infrastructure is thin. Weather is brutal. As of 2021, only two mines operated — rubies and anorthosite. Investors hesitate. Who steps in? Outsiders?

China maps Greenland into its Polar Silk Road. The EU signed a strategic minerals MoU in 2023 and launched a €22.5 million Green Growth program in 2025. The U.S. reopened a consulate in Nuuk in 2020, pushed USAID's Enterprise-Driven Growth Initiative in 2022, and now backs projects like the "Citronen" zinc mine through EXIM financing — Washington's export-credit arm that funds overseas deals to secure American influence and counter Chinese state lenders. If Greenland were only a frozen backwater, why do Washington, Brussels, and Beijing circle like wolves? The Crown decentralized, not disappeared — its power migrated into contracts, councils, and causes. The numbers tell one story. The crown tells another. What the treasury hides in ledgers, the monarchy hides in light.

The Velvet Crown

While bureaucrats count contracts, the monarchy sets the stage. The crown learned to trade velvet for influence — a soft reign that outlives the armies of larger states. King Frederik X once served at Denmark's UN mission in New York. Queen Mary is patron of UNFPA's "10 Million Safer Births" initiative. Together they host UN elites at Kronborg Castle. Is the pageantry mere symbolism — or theatre to sanctify the coil? Placement of people follows the same script. Only a handful of Danes sit inside the UN system — yet look at the roles: Inger Andersen at UNEP. Ib Petersen at UNFPA. Jens Wandel tapped in 2025 as Special Adviser on UN Reform. Mogens Lykketoft once presiding over the General Assembly. These are not ceremonial posts — they sit at the levers that shape policy, budgets, and global messaging. Environmental mandates. Population policy. Institutional reform. Narrative control. Does the crown, the castles, and these fingerprints together harden soft power into real influence?

The Consent Engine

Power needs applause. When a population is conditioned to trust global authority, domestic sovereignty becomes optional. Consent becomes automatic. Debate becomes decor. In 2020, Pew Research found 80% of Danes favored the UN; among youth 18–29, it was 86%. By 2022, Euro-skepticism collapsed. Multilateral reflexes deepened. At home, the Danish Institute for International Studies (DIIS) briefs media and ministers. Critics note no strategy, no depth, but it still frames debate. Meanwhile the press runs the hymn sheet: Politiken leans left. Berlingske leans right. Both still orbit the same assumptions of multilateralism. DIIS threads the middle. When think tanks feed ministers, and newspapers harmonize the same chorus, *when does debate become echo?* Once minds align, the words follow. Belief becomes policy. Language becomes law.

The Treaty Loom

And then the words. Treaties became the new chains — soft, silent, global. Denmark learned to weave them. Others learned to wear them. Copenhagen has staged influence before. COP15 in 2009 birthed the Copenhagen Accord. It was non-binding, merely "noted." Yet its phrases — "below 2°C," "adequate, predictable and sustainable" finance, national "mitigation actions" — reappeared in the Paris Agreement years later. Did Denmark legislate the world — or midwife a vocabulary that would bind later?

Paris (2015) embeds resilience. The Sendai Framework (2015–2030) builds on it. The SDGs spread it into every target from 1.5 to 11.b. NATO even folds it into deterrence in 2021. Framework. Resilience. Sustainable governance. When the same words thread through climate, development, disaster, urban policy, and defense, are they five different fabrics — or one uniform?

The Hands on the Levers

Count the fingerprints. Inger Andersen at UNEP. Ib Petersen at UNFPA. Jens Wandel in UN reform. Henrik G. Petersen at UNDP Evaluation. Christina Markus Lassen presiding over the Security Council in March 2025. Charlotte Slente steering the Danish Refugee Council. *Do a few hands, placed carefully, turn the flywheel of a much larger machine?* And the pipeline never stops. The UN's Senior Leadership Talent Pool recruits "recognized leaders" who can align "collective values," mobilize stakeholders, and "manage reforms". Who fits that description better than the very cadre Denmark trains? *If power is administered by vocabulary, what kind of voices are being chosen to administer it?* Influence fills the boardrooms, but gravity still rules the poles. Power always returns to the ground — to the ice that funds the illusion.

The Arctic Hinge

Strip away the pageantry and the procurement, and the hinge remains Greenland. The numbers tell the truth. A colonial past repackaged as stewardship. Strategic bases that never sleep. Subsidies that bind. *Critical minerals that could, if developed, redraw the map of energy and defense.* Foreign powers already moving their pieces — China's 2023 graphite export restrictions, Europe's 100% reliance on China for heavy rare earths, America's full import dependence on natural graphite in 2023. The chessboard is for keeps. So ask yourself: without Greenland, is Denmark a polar power — or just a welfare state of beer, toys, and insulin? Without Greenland, is Denmark done? The hinge is not just Greenland's minerals. It is the narrative of stewardship that grants Denmark moral authority it never earned. So wouldn't they fight for it — not with battalions, but with treaties; not with bayonets, but with pageantry; not with decrees, but with definitions? If you can keep the vocabulary, you can keep the vault.

The world calls Denmark a model nation. Models become molds. A template in the North becomes a doctrine in the world. The coil does not hide — it standardizes. But do the receipts tell another story — aid as weapon, contracts as chains, ice as currency, monarchy as theatre, newspapers as chorus, treaties as loom? The model becomes the mold. The empire of tomorrow does not march with tanks. It whispers through treaties. It launders power through aid. It hides behind a Danish smile while the coil tightens. The mask is slipping. The coil is visible. And once you see it, can you ever unsee it?

"For Satan himself transforms himself into an angel of light. Therefore it is no great thing if his ministers also transform themselves into ministers of right-eousness". — 2 Corinthians 11:14–15

You've seen the mask crack. You've traced the money. You've mapped the coil. But even serpents know fear won't sell forever. Chains must be disguised. Control must be scented with cinnamon and candlelight. Enter Denmark's greatest export. Not beer. Not insulin. Not bureaucrats.

And now — the sweetest mask of all.

Hygge — the warm blanket that hides the cold machinery beneath.

30

THE HYGGE PACKAGE™
GLOBALISM WITH A SCENTED CANDLE

Before we go further into the machine, you need a breath. Not relief — clarity. Because every empire wraps its chains in comfort before it clamps them down. And Denmark perfected the art. So before the next descent into treaties, bases, and global coils, let me show you the **mask** the serpent wears when it wants you smiling. A little candlelight. A little pastry. A little sedation disguised as "happiness." Welcome to the **Hygge Package™**. Soft power with soft chairs. A velvet prison with warming lights. Laugh — but don't miss the lesson. Even comfort can be weaponized.

The Hygge Package™ — Because freedom is overrated

Step right up, land of liberty. Denmark has the lifestyle upgrade you've been waiting for. Trade your cattle ranches, your roaring highways, your diners stacked with ribeyes — for "hygge". *Welcome to the Hygge Package™*, where every problem is solved with candles, hashtags, and polite fines.

Why drive your truck across the plains when you could wobble through sleet on a rusty bike, knowing your car is safely priced out of reach with a 150% tax? Call it "green freedom." Smile like a model citizen. Why fill your pantry with steaks when you can shop Aldi shelves stacked with imports, watching half your paycheck vanish? That's not poverty, it's "simplicity." And don't worry about sugar. Denmark consumes more sugar per head than any nation on earth. But Novo Nordisk waits like Willy Wonka with a syringe: "Eat up, boys. We'll sell you the insulin back at globalist prices." And don't forget brunch — artisanal rye, cold salmon, and a latte that costs more than a Texas ribeye. Post it with #happiestpeopleonearth, swallowed as progress.

Upgrade to Hygge Premium™

But wait — there's more. The Sterilization Starter Kit™ — brightly lit clinics, friendly nurses, and consent forms that feel like recipes. Small families are the future. Don't worry, the app will remind you when to stop believing in legacy." The Cryo-Baby Concierge™ — designer embryos frozen to order, optimized for height, test scores, and office-chair endurance. It's progress, shrink-wrapped with biodegradable ribbon.

Imagine democracy not as roaring debate, but as knit sweaters, triplicate forms, and polite scolding if you mis-sort your recycling. Safety is the new sacrament. Compliance is the communion. City Hall chic, "hygge-style". Sound familiar? Washington's already browsing the catalog. Taxes rise, choices shrink, but don't worry — the Happiness Czar™ assures you that compliance is caring. At the DMV, stand in line three hours for your new Digital ID. A candle flickers on the counter. And above all, remember the invisible constitution of Danish life — the "Jantelov". Don't think you're special. Don't stand out. Don't speak too loudly. Don't challenge the consensus. "Jantelov" is the software running beneath the candles — the unwritten code that tells every citizen to sit down, smile, and never rise above the group. It's what makes "hygge" feel warm and also makes rebellion feel rude.

Global Expansion Package

Why stop at Denmark? We're exporting the brand. Glossy "hygge" manuals crowd the shelves of New York, Tokyo, and London. Light a candle, bake a pastry, and learn how to surrender with style. Book a ticket to the revue — Denmark's satirical theater where ministers are mocked on stage and then politely reinstalled in office the next morning. Don't forget your MitID at the door — *no login, no latte.* Global compliance — now in your favorite flavor. In Denmark, you need a digital ID to buy a cup of coffee, but not to surrender your sovereignty. Because if every nation learns to smile while submitting, the empire no longer needs soldiers — just stylists.

The Candle Guarantee

And always — always — the candles. Every new law, every new tax, every new form comes with one. We promise every regulation comes scented in lavender. Strike a match and forget that you live in one of the most taxed nations on earth. *Call it cozy. Call it culture. Call it sedation.*

Price & Value

The "Hygge" Package™ isn't free, of course. But who minds the price when comfort is included? You won't even notice — just tap the subsidy and it ships overnight. Property taxes? Up. Gas prices? Doubled. Groceries? Rising weekly. All worth it when you know the state will wire billions in ODA, win billions more in UN contracts, and keep Greenland's minerals tucked under ice until the moment is right. And the bonuses! Free university. Free government housing. Seven weeks' paid vacation. A monthly check if you don't find work. Even a free PhD diploma for your wall. Who needs grit when you can have credentials?

Exclusive Crown Add-On

For our premium subscribers — skip electing presidents. Instead, enjoy the stability of the world's oldest crown. Attend royal banquets at Kronborg Castle, sip sour Danish vineyard wine at $30 a bottle, and bask in the glow of Europe's longest-running dynasty. Perhaps bring home a souvenir of your crown experience with a Royal Copenhagen porcelain trophy — much better than a red hat. Stability never tasted so cozy. Cancel culture can't touch monarchs — they were grandfathered in."

Career Option — Bureaucrat Track™

Looking for job security? The Hygge Package™ includes a career upgrade - *become a Danish bureaucrat.* The requirements are simple — perfect compliance, no visible emotions, and a smile polished for committee rooms. And, of course, obedience to "Jantelov" — never believe your work or your voice is more important than the group. And when your frameworks run out at home, we'll ship you to Geneva to write them for the world. In return, you'll enjoy lifetime meetings, endless acronyms, a lifelong pension, and the satisfaction of writing frameworks no one reads but everyone must obey. The pen is not just mightier than the sword — *it's cozier, too.*

So — America. Ready to trade your land, your fire, your grit for sleet bikes and yellow raincoats? For coalition governments where compromise is eternal law? For an inheritance tax that seizes your farm before your children ever can? All very "hyggeligt" (cozy), right? Just add candles, coffee, and compliance. But remember — in the "Hygge "Package™, "Jantelov" is the hidden clause. You don't just give up comfort — you give up covenant. You trade the First Amendment for speech codes, the Second for "safety regulations." You trade freedom for furniture. And once you call chains "hygge", you'll never notice when the door locks. That's the "Hygge" Package™. A velvet prison with free pastries. The smile of surrender, lit by candlelight.

Cozy, isn't it?

Warning: side effects may include dependency, digital sedation, and loss of soul. Candles burn down. Thrones topple. Ice melts. But the spirit behind it does not die.

You've seen the coil, the cage, the cozy mask. This isn't a package — it's a prototype. "Hygge" is the perfume on the chains. Behind every tax and treaty, every candlelit surrender, waits something older and darker. This war was never just about policy or power. It has always been about worship — about thrones and altars. The serpent knows: the war is spiritual.

Even laughter can be a warning. The serpent loves a smile more than a sword.

31

THE SERPENT BENEATH
EVERY AGE HAS ITS SERPENT

Beneath every age coils a presence older than parliaments, older than kings. It does not shout; it whispers. It does not march; it waits. And when nations grow blind, the serpent beneath rises to guide them — **not to freedom, but to chains.** "Hear now the old tale, for the serpent never sleeps."

Before I lead you through this book — across history, through Europe, back into America, through the storms of our time — I want to take you all the way back. The Vikings called them sagas. A saga is not just a story. It is a vessel. It carries blood and soil, loss and triumph, gods and men. It is how a people remembered who they were — and warned who they might become. As a child, I loved these stories. They were mythical, exciting, and just frightening enough to make me shiver under the covers. My teachers told them in classrooms, my family told them at the table. Alongside Andersen's fairy tales of mermaids and snow queens, the sagas carried a darker fire — gods, monsters, battles, and warnings.

One of the first I ever heard has stayed with me all my life — the tale of the serpent. Midgaardsormen —The World Serpent. Thrown into the ocean by the gods, it grew until its coils circled all of "*Midgaard*" — the realm of men. You could not see it, but you could feel it. Men said the *tides themselves rose and fell with its breathing*. It did not strike quickly. It waited. Silent. Patient. Prophecy said one day it would rise from the sea, spew venom into the sky, shake the earth, and meet Thor in the last battle of "*Ragnarök*". It was terrifying. And yet, I loved it — the thought that hidden beneath calm waters, a serpent waited. Not gone. Not dead. Just waiting.

"Now the serpent was more subtil than any beast of the field which the Lord God had made." — Genesis 3:1

The serpent is not myth. It never was. It coils still — tighter each day — in freedom, in speech, in the silence pressing on your soul. It does not live in oceans now, but in systems — in laws that promise safety while breeding control, in words that sound like virtue but bind like chains. It feeds on comfort and forgetfulness. It waits beneath headlines, beneath policies, beneath every compromise that trades truth for peace. You cannot always see it. But you can feel it — in the air, in the eyes that look away, in the unease that hums beneath a world that calls itself good. The serpent beneath never dies; it only learns new tongues. It no longer coils beneath the sea — it swims beneath systems.

The Warrior's Hall

You already know the serpent. You have felt its pressure, heard its whisper, watched its coils tighten through law, comfort, and silence. I will not repeat its names here. This chapter is not about the enemy. This chapter is about who stands when the enemy rises.

Before there were parliaments, before there were systems, before power learned to hide behind language, there were peoples who understood a simple truth: freedom is not inherited. It is defended — again and again — by those willing to stand when others kneel. The North called that remembering a **saga**. A saga was not entertainment. It was training. It carried warning, lineage, and instruction across generations. It taught a people how to recognize danger — and how to meet it without illusion. One of those teachings was **Valhalla**. Valhalla was not a promise of comfort. It was not heaven by another name. It was a warrior's hall — a place reserved for those who fell standing. The Vikings believed that those who died with courage were gathered, not erased. Every day they trained. Every night they feasted. Not to rest — but to prepare. Valhalla existed for one purpose: when the final battle came, the warriors would rise ready. It was a brutal ethic. And it was honest. The sagas never promised safety. They promised meaning. They taught that silence was worse than death, that submission was a slower grave, and that a life spent avoiding the fight was already lost. When Ragnarök came — when the serpent uncoiled and the world burned — the question was never whether you survived untouched. The question was whether you stood. That ethic did not die with the old gods. It migrated. Scripture names the same truth in covenant language. It does not promise escape from the battle — it promises victory through faithfulness. The martyrs are not remembered because they were spared, but because they refused to bow. The crown is not given to the safe, but to the steadfast.

"Be faithful unto death, and I will give you the crown of life." — Revelation 2:10

Valhalla was a shadow. Covenant was the substance. Different tongues, same demand: **stand.** And that spirit did not vanish when the old myths fell silent. It crossed oceans.

America did not invent the warrior ethic — but it inherited it. You can see it wherever names are carved into stone instead of forgotten. In Arlington. In rows of white markers that testify to a people who understood something older than politics: that liberty is purchased, not granted. The warrior's hall is no longer mythic. It stands in cemeteries, in folded flags, in oaths sworn with the knowledge that they may cost everything. America's dead do not rest as victims. They rest as guardians. That is why America still stands — not because it is flawless, but because there has always been a remnant unwilling to choose comfort over courage. Men and women who refused silence when silence was safer. Who stood when the pressure to comply grew heavy. Who understood that obedience to evil is never neutral — it is collaboration. The serpent counts on forgetting. It counts on fatigue. It counts on people deciding the fight is too costly, too loud, too lonely. The warrior ethic answers with refusal.

It says: *I will not kneel.*
It says: *I will not forget.*
It says: *I will not trade truth for peace.*

This book is not written for the masses. It is written for the Remnant — the ones who still feel the burn in their bones, who sense the pressure tightening and know that silence is already a choice. You are not called to comfort. You are called to clarity. You are not called to blend in. You are called to stand out — and stand firm. The sagas ended with fire and renewal. Scripture ends with the serpent cast down and the faithful crowned. Both insist on the same truth: evil does not get the last word — but it must be confronted.

What comes next in these pages is not myth. It is not theory. It is not symbolism. It is the serpent's playbook — written into systems, policies, and narratives that govern the modern world. You will see how it moves, how it binds, how it trains obedience without chains. This chapter is the hall you enter before the war. Stand upright. Remember who you are. The match is already struck.

🔥 Firelight Pause — The Warrior's Hall
  - When the pressure rises, do you stand — or adapt?
  - What do you value more: comfort, or covenant?
  - When your children ask where you stood, what will they inherit?
  - Do you live as a subject — or as a warrior?
  - If the call came today, would your name answer?

"Be strong and courageous. Do not be afraid or discouraged, for the Lord your God is with you wherever you go." — Joshua 1:9

"Be strong and courageous. Do not be afraid or discouraged, for the Lord your God is with you wherever you go." — Joshua 1:9

PART III

THE SERPENT'S PLAYBOOK

COVENANT VS. EMPIRE

I will put enmity between the woman and you, and between your seed and her seed; he shall crush your head, and you shall strike his heel.—
Genesis 3:15

Where the gods met men, the serpent slid away — and returned clothed in contracts.

The serpent shed its myth. Its skin now bears emblems, treaties, signatures. Read on and you will see the pattern — dominion written not in runes, but in policy. This is the serpent's playbook.

32

THE PROGRAM — HOW THE COIL TIGHTENS

FROM SYSTEMS OF CONTROL TO THE REMAKING OF MAN

Every empire writes a manual. This is theirs. What begins as a model nation becomes a global mandate. The coil tested in silence now tightens across the earth. The oldest prophecy still stands:

"He shall crush your head, and you shall strike his heel." — Genesis 3:15

Every tyranny begins with a dream—not yours, but theirs.cThey sell it as progress. Behind the curtain, it is always the same: control dressed as paradise.

The Design of the Perfect World

In this dream, the perfect person *belongs to no one* and bears *no roots*. At most, there are seedless IVF offspring—produced on demand, monitored from birth, raised by screens instead of mothers. Life begins in a lab and ends in a clinic; the unborn treated as inconvenience, the frozen as inventory. Guilt replaces legacy. *Don't have children—the planet is burning.* Even woman herself is erased—renamed a "birthing person," stripped of name, dignity, and design. The Creator is replaced by the coder; covenant by consent form. All under the banner of equity, safety, and sustainability —the new trinity of control.

The perfect family *dissolves* with her. The father reduced to a "co-parent." The mother recast as a "birthing unit."The child claimed by the state—raised by programs, disciplined by algorithms. Faith becomes curriculum. Morality is outsourced to policy. Loyalty attaches not to blood or covenant, but to rule. Function replaces kinship. Compliance replaces love.

The perfect citizen is *meticulously tracked and surveilled* — scrolling endlessly, attention spans shrunk to seconds. Fed synthetics and substitutes, injected and edited, medicated into numbness, taught slogans instead of strength. This citizen trades freedom for convenience and mistakes obedience for peace. Steps, sleep, speech — all logged, scored, stored. Words are filtered, thoughts pre-approved, questions flagged as threats. Even the soul is quantified, its worth determined by compliance.

The perfect city follows — *a cage disguised as convenience*. Fifteen-minute zones. No cars. No freedom of movement. Errands tallied in carbon credits; faces scanned by cameras that never blink. Electric ranges mandatory. Smart meters tattling from every wall. Digital wallets linked to compliance; ration apps tracking carbon and food. Drones patrol the sky in the name of safety. Algorithms assign trust scores, silencing dissent before it speaks. Climate becomes leash, not weather. Geo-fences mark invisible borders. The AI mind governs the streets, censoring both speech and speed. Citizens applauding confinement and calling it progress.

The perfect government hides behind forms, not flags. It rules by regulation, not revolution. Ministers become managers, lawmakers become clerks, presidents become spokesmen for systems they no longer steer. Decrees arrive as "guidelines," mandates as "emergency measures," tyranny as "public safety." Agencies multiply until no one remembers who gave the order. The machine governs itself, and the people applaud its efficiency. Bureaucracy becomes theology — compliance, its only creed.

Above it all rises the perfect state — *wired, watching, worshiped.* 5G towers on the horizon. Cameras on every corner. Digital IDs in every pocket. Programmable money in every hand. Beneath it hum the data centers — vast, silent cathedrals of code where every breath is stored. Contracts bind across borders, granting foreign councils and private consortia authority once held by the Constitution itself. No faith beyond the State. No churches beyond permission. No gatherings outside approved lines. Every policy a cage. Every citizen a barcode. Every soul flattened into data.

Beyond that lies **the perfect world** — Beyond that lies the perfect world — borderless, culture-less, faithless. One language. One rulebook. One elite. Property erased. Family dissolved. History rewritten. Babylon reborn. Seedless people. Borderless states. Wordless faith. A digital god enthroned in the cloud, demanding carbon offerings for salvation. Why this dream? Because rootless people are easiest to rule. Raised by programs, not parents, they obey by conditioning, not conviction. That is how ordinary men become wardens, women become enforcers, and nations become instruments of the serpent.

Their Blueprint — The Language of Control

Language is the first dominion. Before borders fall, words must. Every empire begins with language, not armies. The serpent speaks first — twisting meaning until silence sounds like peace, slavery feels like safety, obedience masquerades as freedom. Language becomes law. Law becomes cage. The whisper becomes chain. "Safe" now means silenced. "Equal" means erased. "Green" becomes taxation, tracking, and rationing. "Progress" means dependence. "Science" equals obedience. "Peace" is power for them and submission for you. "Love" demands tolerance for lies and intolerance for truth. Even "freedom" is demoted to permission — granted, scored, and revoked at will. The serpent's hiss is written not only in slogans but in symbols — the bicycle sold as virtue, the database sold as efficiency, the barcode sold as safety. Denmark taught me these emblems; now I see them glowing in America too.

Behind every softened word, an action is already complete. Education rewritten — history stripped, faith mocked, obedience drilled as "learning." Brains rewired — screens in every hand, memory eroded, dopamine engineered. Fear weaponized — pandemics leveraged, lockdowns enforced, digital passes sold as "health." Life redefined — abortion renamed "healthcare," motherhood recast as burden, family dismissed as "optional." Speech twisted — truth relabeled as hate, lies marketed as justice. Surveillance normalized — cameras on every corner, apps in every pocket, algorithms inside every word. Nations sedated — drugs legalized, food degraded, entertainment engineered to distract. Sovereignty hollowed out — treaties inked in secret, borders blurred, countries reduced to provinces. This is the blueprint — **seduce with words, enslave with systems, punish with guilt.** The program is not hidden; it is lived.

The Pattern — Always the Same

At *the top*, chaos is created on purpose. Yesterday a Reichstag fire; today a pandemic, a bank panic, a war on demand. The world is shaken until fear begs for order—then control is sold as cure. In *the middle*, the gates are captured. Schools stop teaching thought and drill slogans instead. Courts twist law into decree. Churches clap for sin but cannot kindle worship. Hospitals obey orders over conscience. Gatekeepers become wardens; rules replace reason. At *the bottom*, daily life is rewritten. A ration card once—a carbon score now. Neighbors once spied for the Party; your apps report you today. Families once broke from fear; now they are broken by policy. Freedom is not lost in one invasion; it dies by a thousand quiet nods.

Man Remade — Dominion Over Flesh

But the system isn't content with your land. It wants more than your borders. It wants more than your freedom. It wants you — body, mind, and soul. And so the war descends from map to molecule, from border to body — from laws written on paper to laws written in code.

The Bio-ID Cage

The chain begins with a number. A passport. A profile. A login. In Denmark it is already here — MitID — the mandatory digital ID system replacing old bank logins and government credentials. Without it you cannot bank, rent, pay bills, or access government services. No login, no life. It was sold as convenience; in truth it is a leash. The European Union sharpened the model with the European Digital Identity Wallet — one login for banking, healthcare, travel, even voting. They promise control— until one switch denies access. In America, the trial balloons rise — vaccine passports, federal pushes for digital health records, quiet banking experiments linking credentials to biometrics — face, iris, and fingerprint becoming the new currency of trust. The next phase ties ID to currency itself — programmable money that obeys policy, not people. Step by step the citizen is reduced to credentials. The serpent has learned — you don't need chains on wrists when you can put chains in wallets. When every nation adopts the same ledger, sovereignty becomes software — and deletion replaces dissent.

AI as Priesthood

Every empire needs priests. Today they wear hoodies, not robes — and every citizen kneels by choice, trusting the algorithm more than their own soul. Algorithms sit above law — deciding what you see, what you buy, what you're allowed to say. Code is labeled "neutral"; in practice it encodes values — whose values, whose inclusion, whose truth? The data becomes scripture — edited, purified, declared infallible. To question it is blasphemy. When ideology is compiled into a model, neutrality becomes mandate. AI already judges credit scores, medical treatments, parole decisions, and job applications. The system calls itself impartial. But impartiality designed by fallible minds becomes a priesthood — no appeal, no jury, no vote — only a model's decree. The new Sanhedrin — once charged with guarding God's law but remembered for condemning the innocent — now issues verdicts in silence; your appeal is a form you never see. And those who question the code are branded heretics — sentenced by systems that claim no belief at all.

Once data governs decision, the next frontier is destiny itself — who may be born, who may live, who may die.

"He causes all, both small and great, rich and poor, free and slave, to receive a mark on their right hand or on their forehead, so that no one can buy or sell unless he has the mark, that is, the name of the beast or the number of its name."— Revelation 13:16–17

Gene Editing & Population Control

Once the serpent controls your ID and your feed, it reaches deeper — into the womb, into the cell. CRISPR makes it possible to edit embryos — erase traits, favor others, design "desirable" children. In laboratories around the world, ethics bend under the promise of prevention and perfection. Corporations patent life itself; profit replaces providence. In China, reckless experiments have already been attempted. Elsewhere, fertility markets industrialize the body. Global agencies speak of "sustainable population" as if souls were spreadsheets. Combine commodity seed with gene editing, and the ghost of past eugenic dreams awakens in a lab coat. Abortion, sterilization, and population management can slide from autonomy into architecture. What begins as "choice" can become policy. Once life is reduced to data, it becomes administrable — and deletable. **Creation is claimed without Creator; destiny coded by decree.** This is not science; without covenant, it is sorcery arranged as policy.

The Prototype Nation

Small nations often set precedents that giants later adopt. Denmark is not the cage — it is the prototype. Its bureaucrats draft EU bio-ID frameworks, pilot digital health records, and shape fertility laws that treat reproduction as a managed system. Denmark exports control as progress — always in the language of care, always for "safety," always for "equity." Cryo-banks in Copenhagen ship seed worldwide. Where a sword once struck openly, a scalpel now cuts quietly. What is rehearsed in Copenhagen is exported outward — to Brussels, Geneva, and Silicon Valley — replicated line by line, and finally into your own town.

Technology can heal; it can also become priesthood without covenant. That line of discernment is mercy, not surrender. I name the danger plainly so that truth and tyranny are not confused with progress — and so that the remnant remembers mercy is not the same as surrender.

"So God created man in his own image, in the image of God he created him; male and female he created them" — Genesis 1:27

What Breaks First

They start with the family and move outward. Covenant is mocked, duty dissolved, and the first bond is weakened. From there, dreams are flattened—ambition taxed, apathy rewarded. Labor is exploited in the name of equality while ownership is quietly stripped away. Minds are numbed with entertainment and pharmaceuticals; streets are sedated with surveillance and distraction. Children are taken through schools that teach shame instead of strength. Guilt replaces faith. Memory is rewritten until a nation can no longer tell truth from script. The serpent cares little for the flag it flies—swastika, sickle, or silicon—only that the mind beneath it forgets how to resist. Yet even as the tower rises, one land still burns with covenant.

America — The Final Holdout

The serpent has feasted already—kingdoms swallowed, empires drained, continents bound in debt. One prize remains: America. Every empire eventually turns toward the last free land. But this land is not easy prey. It carries bone and backbone. Here dwell men and women who keep steel in their hands and fire in their chests—who kneel not to globalists, but to God Almighty. America holds a covenant the Beast cannot counterfeit. A Constitution that shields liberty. A flag that still stirs the blood. An anthem that still roars like a lion. Soil soaked in sacrifice—too costly to surrender. At the core stand the First and Second Amendments together—speech still sharp, arms still ready. The serpent fears a people who believe freedom is sacred enough to defend. When deception fails, fury follows.

"The serpent rages where deception no longer holds—for he knows his time is short" — Revelation 12:12

The serpent rarely strikes head-on. It arrives as care, as governance, as progress—soft words, smiling bureaucrats, polished promises—harmless until the fangs set. No roaring armies. No crowns. Only processes and panels. Denmark revealed the pattern: candles and consensus above, committees and coalitions beneath. What appears harmless in Copenhagen today coils around Washington tomorrow. The velvet glove hides the fang. Even when the coils loosen, do not be deceived—the serpent does not retreat; it resets. It advances through open gates, often wearing familiar faces. The assault is relentless, and it comes from within.

"A nation can survive its fools, and even the ambitious. But it cannot survive treason from within" — Cicero

The Venom in the Veins

The serpent struck—and the bite took hold. The wound was not on the heel of one man, but in the body of a nation. The venom moves slowly, disguised as virtue, whispering that safety is love and obedience is wisdom. Yet every drop carries the same toxin: the denial of design. It began with fear. A sickness came, and the world bowed. Freedom was suspended "for your safety." Churches closed while liquor stores stayed open. Neighbors became suspects; faith was replaced by sanitizer and slogans. Panic was wrapped in compassion, and the serpent found its perfect weapon. Then came the cure that wounded. The syringe became a sacrament; dissent, a sin. Those who hesitated were branded heretics. Families divided. A people once fierce in liberty begged for permission to live. That is how venom works—it does not kill at once; it numbs conviction. The poison spread into commerce and creation.

Food was laced with chemicals that dull the will. Water carried the residue of industry and control. Soil was stripped, seed patented, sky seeded in the name of climate. Appetites were engineered; dependencies monetized. The serpent does not need to conquer what it can medicate.

"The earth mourns and withers... because they have transgressed the laws, violated the statutes, broken the everlasting covenant. — Isaiah 24:4–5

The venom did not stop at the bloodstream. It seeped into borders and cities—the body politic itself. Illegal waves crossed not only land but conscience. Cartels moved like unseen armies, trafficking poison, children, and chaos into quiet towns while officials called it compassion. Some even cheered, confusing surrender for mercy, mistaking invasion for inclusion. The serpent laughed; it had found converts who celebrated their own undoing. Then the venom reached the flesh. Woman was rewritten. Motherhood renamed. Creation recoded as "choice" or "procedure." The female body—once the living sign of covenant—was carved, injected, erased. Children, sacred image-bearers, were led to altars of confusion and mutilation, told that to wound themselves was to find themselves. Doctors became priests of a new gospel: affirmation. And behind it all, profit. The serpent always charges for its sacraments. Masculinity was mocked into silence. Femininity dissolved into function. Even the word *family* was scrubbed until it meant nothing more than a contract between dependents. What God joined was separated—spirit from body, man from woman, child from truth—until identity itself became merchandise.

"Male and female He created them... and named them Mankind. — Genesis 5:2

Across the land the symptoms multiplied. Addiction was marketed as coping. Distraction sold as rest. Entertainment weaponized as anesthesia. Dispensaries lined the streets where churches once stood, selling sedation as freedom. Fentanyl flooded the borders—a chemical invasion deadlier than armies, dissolving towns one vein at a time. Screens fed dopamine; pills fed despair; pleasure became policy. Algorithms whispered, *Don't think—just feel.* And the people obeyed.

"Woe to those who call evil good and good evil." — Isaiah 5:20

Even the universities—once citadels of thought—burned incense to the creed. Campuses chanted hate in the name of justice, silencing dissent while waving causes they did not understand. The venom taught rebellion without truth, empathy without discernment, until confusion was mistaken for compassion. That is how Babylon rebuilds herself—not with armies, but with applause.

"This wisdom is earthly, unspiritual, demonic." — James 3:15

This is the modern liturgy of the bitten. But venom can be drawn out. Truth still purifies. Courage still bleeds clean. The same prophecy that warned of the strike also promised the crushing. The serpent may strike the heel—but the heel still moves. And it is marching.

"He shall crush your head, and you shall strike his heel." — Genesis 3:15

The Program — Status of the Coil

You may be wondering how far this has gone. If you work in tech or the systems surrounding it, you already see the pattern. For everyone else —the men and women who build, farm, fix, drive, and serve—there may be no reason to notice, no time to look, and little interest to ask. But the system does not require your attention to advance. The beast system is not a rumor. It is here—unfolding quietly while politics, outrage, and endless headlines keep eyes elsewhere. That noise is the camouflage. While the world argues, the architecture locks in. Measured honestly, the program is well underway. If the blueprint were a hundred steps, humanity has already walked most of them. The components exist. The interfaces are live. What remains is not invention, but fusion. The coil tightens, though it has not yet struck openly. **The first layer** is already visible across the world. Digital ID systems manage daily life—logins, licenses, banking, benefits. Cash fades as habit shifts to tap-to-pay, app-only stores, and QR menus that require a screen to exist. Cameras watch intersections and entrances. Algorithms decide what you see, what you buy, and increasingly what you may say. Your life is stored in servers you will never visit, owned by institutions you will never meet.

Language is rewritten to match the system. Disagreement becomes hate. Tradition becomes harm. Corporations preach virtue like churches, measuring morality through checklists of "equity" and "sustainability." Screens keep the population sedated with fear, outrage, and engineered dopamine. These are not theories. They are features of modern life. But surveillance is not the end goal. Sorting is. The system does not need to cage everyone—it only needs to classify them. Who complies easily. Who resists quietly. Who remembers freedom, and who will trade conscience for convenience. This sorting is not new. The Nazis called it selection. The Soviets called it re-education. Mao called it rectification. The language changes. The purpose does not: to separate the obedient from the unbroken. Every algorithm becomes an altar. Every data point, a test of allegiance. And history is clear about what follows when the State decides who is fit to belong.

The second layer is forming. Pieces are being tested, waiting for the next global "emergency" to finish the merger. Programmable money runs in pilot programs from Brussels to Beijing. Artificial intelligence drafts policies, judges cases, and increasingly writes the rules of its own oversight. Gene editing advances in the name of prevention; fertility becomes a managed industry. Global health treaties move quietly, linking medicine to digital identity. Cities experiment with fifteen-minute zoning and carbon allowances. Banks and social platforms explore behavior-based scoring systems. International bodies repeat the same language— "resilience," "safety," "sustainability"—until nations begin to sound like departments of one global office. Even faith is being centralized, with interfaith councils preaching unity without repentance. The pattern is not hidden; it waits for crisis to be called necessity.

The third layer has not yet fully emerged, but its shape is clear. A single global login will merge identity, wallet, passport, and health record into one credential. Artificial intelligence will claim moral authority, judging disputes and rewriting ethics in the name of neutrality. Rights will become permissions—digital constitutions revised by code. Synthetic wombs will standardize birth; edited generations will replace inheritance with design. Nations will dissolve into managed regions run by treaties, not citizens. Dissent will be labeled disorder. In the end, machine and state merge into one digital god—omniscient, unblinking, jealous of every rival loyalty. This is where the coil tightens. The playbook is not secret; it is disguised as service. The danger is not only in what is built, but in what is accepted. The system is already powerful. The question is whether those inside it will notice before the circle closes. **The future you feared is not ahead. You are standing in it.** The coil is tightening, but it hasn't struck — not yet.

The Prototype — Denmark *(Blueprint in Practice)*

Denmark is one of the most digitally integrated states in the world. Nearly all adults use **MitID**, a mandatory digital identity that replaced NemID and now functions as a single key for banking, healthcare, housing, education, and government services. Without it, daily civic life is largely inaccessible. **This system is not experimental. It is operational.** Under the EU's **eIDAS2** framework, all EU and EEA countries are required to deploy a digital identity wallet. Denmark is already implementing its national wallet, **AltID**, built on existing MitID infrastructure and aligned with the EU-wide **European Digital Identity Wallet**. Denmark is therefore an early interoperability node in the continental rollout. Denmark's model is defined by deep public–private integration. Banks, tech firms, and state agencies share authentication infrastructure. Identity is embedded across sectors, normalized through convenience rather than force. Other countries, including the UK, have studied the Danish system as a reference for their own digital ID deployments. Alongside this expansion, Denmark is testing identity-rights legislation aimed at protecting biometric likeness—face, voice, and body—from AI misuse. This does not reverse digital integration; it manages its consequences. Control and consent advance in parallel. Denmark rarely commands from the podium. Its influence travels through drafting rooms, pilot programs, regulatory language, and international bodies where standards are written long before mandates are announced.

Timeline summary:
- Digital ID: fully deployed and mandatory
- Digital wallet: in national rollout under EU mandate
- Cross-border interoperability: active pilot phase
- Biometric and identity rights: early legal testing

Denmark is not the end state. It is the working prototype.

Identity and Language — Permission Without Mandate

The system has not entered the United States as law. **It has entered as access.** America has no national ID card. Yet identity mediation is already routine. More than half of U.S. states issue or pilot digital driver's licenses and mobile IDs. Federal agencies increasingly require digital verification to access taxes, healthcare, immigration, benefits, and education. Employers, universities, banks, and platforms now decide who may work, travel, transact, or speak. No mandate announces this shift. Access simply becomes conditional. During the plandemic, the logic was tested openly. Identity merged with compliance. Vaccine passes were enforced through employers, airlines, cities, and universities — establishing precedent without legislation. Once access is conditioned, force is no longer required. Language prepared the ground. Terms now embedded in American policy and corporate governance — *resilience, whole-of-society, public-private partnership, misinformation, community standards, safety, equity, sustainability* — do not arise from constitutional tradition. They come from **international governance frameworks developed in European Union and United Nations institutions**, where authority advances through standards, coordination, and compliance rather than law. *This language is not descriptive. It is operational.* Rights become permissions. Citizens become stakeholders. Law becomes policy. In Denmark the credential is centralized and visible. In America it is fragmented and deniable. But the logic is the same:

no ID, no access.

"Stand firm, and let nothing move you." — 1 Corinthians 15:58

🔥 Firelight Pause — The Coil and the Choice

Seventy percent complete. Not prophecy—rollout. The system hums in plain sight, sold as progress. The coil only holds if you nod. Ask yourself:

- How much of your life already runs on a screen, a code, or a card?
- Which comforts have you traded for control—and called it normal?
- When did safety become a leash, and noise become peace?
- Who trained you to obey first and discern later?
- What "protection" are you clinging to that is really a chain?
- If every choice required permission, what would you still choose?
- When the grid goes dark, would you know how to live free—or would you beg for the leash again?
- God's image or a state barcode—which one are you defending?

This is not despair. It is the moment of sight. The system does not need to cage everyone. It only needs to sort them. Who is easiest to manage? Who still remembers freedom? Who will trade conscience for convenience—and who will not?

"They overcame him by the blood of the Lamb, and by the word of their testimony; and they loved not their lives unto the death." — Revelation 12:11

33

THE FALSE LIGHT

HOW EMPIRES DISARM BEFORE THEY KILL

The greatest danger of every empire is not resistance. It is discernment. So before coercion appears, power learns to glow. False light is not darkness. Darkness warns. False light comforts. It soothes the conscience while it loosens conviction. It warms the ego while hollowing the soul. Every empire perfects this stage, because men who believe they are good will surrender what free men must defend. This is not new. It is ancient.

The serpent never begins with chains. He begins with illumination. Every empire builds an altar before it builds a prison. Ours glows. Screens replace candles. Slogans replace Scripture. Applause replaces repentance. The language is gentle, inclusive, therapeutic. Nothing is demanded. Nothing is forbidden. Nothing is judged. And so nothing is resisted. False light blesses the cage before it closes. It preaches tolerance while silencing truth. It offers comfort without correction, belonging without boundary, unity without conviction. It baptizes obedience as compassion and calls discernment harm. Holiness becomes "extremism." Conviction becomes "violence." Silence becomes virtue. Under false light, evil does not look cruel. It looks kind.

This is how moral inversion works. Language shifts first. Words soften. Definitions slide. "Love" is detached from truth. "Justice" is separated from law. "Safety" replaces freedom. "Equity" replaces equality. What once restrained power now lubricates it. False light does not attack faith head-on. It reframes it. Repentance becomes shame. Sin becomes trauma. Redemption becomes self-expression. God becomes a mirror. The cross becomes a metaphor. Salvation becomes wellness. And when there is no sin left to name, there is no Savior left to need. This is the counterfeit sanctuary of the age. It does not deny God. It renders Him unnecessary.

Beside it rises a second glow — quieter, softer, deeply personal. Here **the altar is the self.** The language is healing, alignment, awakening. There is spirit without covenant, transcendence without obedience, power without humility. Sin is renamed imbalance. Truth becomes a frequency. Reality becomes something to curate rather than submit to. This false light preys on wounds. It offers comfort without confrontation, affirmation without formation. It promises ascension but keeps the soul circling endlessly inward — eternally seeking, never arriving. "You will be as gods." That was the first sermon of false light. It remains the last. Every modern counterfeit repeats it with new accents. The self crowned divine. Desire enthroned as truth. Boundaries condemned as oppression. Covenant mocked as fear. This is not rebellion. It is seduction. False light spreads not because people are wicked, but because they are weary. And once a population is morally softened, enforcement no longer looks tyrannical. It looks necessary.

This is the pattern history repeats. Chaos is introduced or exploited. Fear expands. Order is demanded. Control arrives as cure. Those who resist are no longer opponents — they are threats. Violence, when it comes, is framed as service. Jesus warned of this inversion: *The time is coming when anyone who kills you will think they are offering service to God.* He was not describing madness. He was describing moral permission.

False light always comes before the blade. Empires do not kill in cold blood. They kill with clean consciences. They believe they are purifying, protecting, progressing. Whether under sacred banners or secular slogans, the conviction is the same: the world must be saved — even if some must be removed. This is why false light is more dangerous than darkness. Darkness is resisted. False light is applauded. But false light has a fatal weakness. It cannot burn. It can glow. It can soothe. It can blind. But it cannot purify. It cannot forge courage. It cannot sustain sacrifice. It collapses the moment comfort costs too much. Truth is different. Truth burns clean. It sanctifies. It divides. It frees. Empires rise on glow. They fall to fire. So choose carefully which light you follow. One will make you compliant. The other will make you free.

"Satan himself masquerades as an angel of light." — 2 Corinthians 11:14

🔥 **Firelight Pause — The Test of Illumination**
False light always feels warm at first. Fire does not.
Ask yourself:
- Where have I accepted comfort that numbs instead of truth that frees?
- Where have I traded conviction for affirmation — and called it growth?
- What language shapes my conscience more: Scripture or slogans?
- What light am I following — the one that soothes, or the one that sanctifies?

False light disarms before it destroys. Fire refines before it frees. Choose wisely. And choose before the glow decides for you.

34

SEVEN MOVES TO ERASE A NATION

HOW SOVEREIGNTY IS
SURRENDERED WITHOUT A SHOT

Modern conquest no longer arrives with boots and banners. It arrives with documents. The serpent does not storm capitals; it schedules meetings. It does not fire cannons; it files agreements. It does not overthrow governments; it outgrows them. What follows is not chaos, but choreography — the repeatable sequence by which nations surrender sovereignty without a single shot fired. This is not theory. It is pattern.

Sovereignty rarely vanishes through dramatic theft. It dissolves through consent. Treaty by treaty. Standard by standard. Emergency by emergency. One morning, a people wake up to discover that what once required a vote now arrives as policy — and what once required force now operates automatically. Empires have always known this truth: a nation does not fall when it is conquered — it falls when it agrees. What follows are the seven moves.

Move One — Condition the Mind

Every conquest begins with perception. A people must be taught how to see themselves before they can be ruled. This is not achieved through censorship, but through framing. Pride is reclassified as danger. Memory is recoded as bias. Loyalty is softened into sentiment and then discarded. The goal is not ignorance — it is moral hesitation. A nation unsure of itself will not defend itself. Modern conditioning enters through education, media, and credentialing. Knowledge gives way to formation. Emotional harmony replaces moral reasoning. History is filtered through grievance. Courage is reframed as disruption. Children are taught what to feel before they are taught how to think. Technology completes the shift. Screens replace inheritance. Algorithms curate attention, sentiment, and conformity. Deviation becomes visible long before it becomes punishable. By adulthood, dissent already feels antisocial. The result is not obedience — yet. It is hesitation. And hesitation is enough. *Seen in practice: national curricula rewritten to prioritize emotional regulation and "global citizenship" while removing local history, faith, and civic formation.*

Move Two — Frame Surrender as Survival

Once confidence weakens, fear is introduced. Every empire requires a crisis. It may be real, exaggerated, or engineered — the distinction is irrelevant. What matters is urgency. Fear compresses time. It collapses debate. It transforms compliance into virtue. Under threat, people do not ask whether power is legitimate — they ask whether it is effective. Public messaging shifts from rights to safety, from freedom to responsibility, from consent to necessity. Temporary measures are framed as moral acts. Obedience becomes compassion. Resistance becomes recklessness. Citizens are not ordered to comply. They are convinced it is the right thing to do. By the time the emergency passes, the mechanisms remain. *Seen in practice: emergency health measures introduced as temporary protections, later normalized as permanent authority.*

Move Three — Bind Law to Finance

Once fear has softened resistance, sovereignty is transferred through contracts. Modern power does not seize assets; it encumbers them. Debt, subsidies, grants, and trade agreements replace conquest. Compliance becomes a condition of access. Money moves first; authority follows. Legal authority is redistributed upward through treaties, regulatory harmonization, and supranational courts. Decisions once made locally are now "aligned" internationally. Parliaments ratify what they did not draft. Voters approve what they cannot reverse. At the individual level, livelihoods become conditional. Licenses, permits, and credentials replace citizenship as the gatekeepers of survival. A person may speak freely — but access is another matter. This is governance without occupation. Control without visible rulers. *Seen in practice: international loan conditions and trade agreements quietly overriding domestic labor, energy, and agricultural policy.*

Move Four — Standardize the Nation

Difference is inefficient. Empires prefer templates. Local variation is reclassified as risk. National customs become obstacles. Everything must be harmonized — education, labor, energy, agriculture, speech, data. Uniform standards promise efficiency, but they deliver control. Once systems are standardized, sovereignty becomes technical. Rules arrive pre-written. Updates replace debate. Compliance is audited, not voted on. What cannot be measured is dismissed. What cannot be digitized is discouraged. What cannot be aligned is isolated. A nation that no longer governs itself does not revolt. It submits tickets. *Seen in practice: industries forced to adopt global "best practices" written by external bodies with no local accountability.*

Move Five — Rewrite Identity

Control of territory is temporary. Control of identity is permanent. Nations dissolve when their people forget who they are. Heritage becomes liability. Faith becomes private. Family becomes optional. Identity is fragmented into preferences, labels, and profiles — each manageable, each replaceable. Belonging is relocated from covenant to system. The citizen becomes a stakeholder. The people become users. Memory gives way to narrative, and narrative is curated. A rootless population does not defend borders. It negotiates access. *Seen in practice: patriotism recast as extremism, family authority diminished, and identity fragmented into administrable categories.*

Move Six — Rule Through Perpetual Emergency

Once authority is centralized, it must be preserved. Emergencies provide continuity. Each crisis justifies the next expansion. Temporary powers are extended. Exceptional measures become normal. Oversight dissolves in urgency. Borders blur — not only geographically, but administratively. Jurisdictions overlap. Responsibility diffuses. No one is accountable because everyone is involved. When crisis becomes operating system, liberty is no longer revoked. It is deprecated. *Seen in practice: executive powers extended indefinitely through rolling crises that never fully resolve.*

Move Seven — Fuse Narrative and Enforcement

The final move is integration. Speech, finance, identity, and access are merged. Narrative becomes infrastructure. Enforcement becomes automatic. Compliance is measured, not commanded. Dissent is no longer punished; it is deprioritized. Accounts are throttled. Services are denied. Visibility is reduced. Participation becomes conditional. There is no knock at the door. The system simply stops responding. At this stage, resistance requires sacrifice — and most people have already been trained to avoid it. The conquest is complete. *Seen in practice: financial services, platforms, and institutions restricting access based on behavior, speech, or compliance scores.*

The Pattern

Empires once conquered land. Modern empires conquer process. No invasion. No coup. No shot fired. Only agreements, standards, emergencies, and silence. The nation is not overthrown. It is absorbed.

The Snapshot

In Europe, identity is centralized. A single digital credential accesses banking, healthcare, housing, employment, and government services. Cross-border interoperability is mandated. Regulation arrives pre-written. Compliance is routine. Authority is technical, not debated. **In America**, identity is fragmented. No national card exists. Yet access is already conditional. Digital verification governs taxes, healthcare, education, employment, finance, and speech. Authority is outsourced to platforms, institutions, and private enforcement. **In Europe**, sovereignty moved upward through treaties. Parliaments ratified what bureaucracies drafted. National law aligned with supranational standards. Citizens adjusted. Resistance faded into procedure. **In America**, sovereignty moves sideways. Federal power expands through agencies. Corporate governance enforces norms. Courts defer to "expert" frameworks. The Constitution remains — functionally narrowed by interpretation and compliance. **In Europe**, speech is regulated by law. Hate-speech statutes, content rules, and identity protections define boundaries openly. **In America**, speech is regulated by access. Platforms throttle reach. Banks deny service. Employers enforce codes. No law is needed when permission is sufficient. **In Europe**, emergency governance is normalized. Temporary measures extend indefinitely. Energy, health, and climate powers persist. **In America**, emergency governance is disguised. Mandates appear through employers, insurers, universities, and regulators — deniable, distributed, effective.

Different methods. Same destination. The nation is not conquered. It is absorbed.

🔥 **Firelight Pause — The Signature Test**
Ask yourself:
- Where has consent replaced consented authority?
- Which decisions now arrive as "non-negotiable"?
- What freedoms depend on access rather than right?
- What emergencies never seem to end?
- And at what point did governance stop asking permission?

Sovereignty is not lost in war. It is surrendered in peace. And once signed away, it is rarely returned.

"For we wrestle not against flesh and blood, but against principalities, against powers, against the rulers of the darkness of this world, against spiritual wickedness in high places." — Ephesians 6:12

35

___

THE GLOBALIST BLUEPRINT

FROM WHISPER TO WORLD MANDATE

The moves are finished. The design continues. What began as quiet coordination now governs openly. The serpent no longer hides behind ideology; it administers. It no longer whispers through fringe theory; it speaks fluent bureaucracy. Its servants wear credentials, not crowns. Their weapons are frameworks, not spears. They conquer by coordination — through compliance, not conflict. This is the stage after sovereignty fractures. Empires once conquered by force. Modern empires govern by process. They do not overthrow nations; they absorb them. Treaties outlive governments. Standards override constitutions. Agreements bind future generations that never consented.

I saw the rehearsal in Denmark — ministers nodding to Brussels, schools echoing United Nations language, energy projects financed by global funds and repaid by local debt. It looked peaceful. Orderly. Efficient. That is how the blueprint works: it presents management as mercy and calls submission stability. What was tested quietly in small nations now speaks openly to the world.

But the blueprint has a weakness.

It governs best where force has been outsourced and survival has been delegated. It thrives in systems protected by others — where order is maintained by guarantees, not grit. When raw power returns, administration is exposed. Denmark revealed this limit in real time.

The Denmark Illusion — When Process Meets Power

Denmark does not understand power anymore. It understands process. For three decades, Denmark has lived inside a protected bubble — NATO guarantees, American hardware, EU insulation, and a world where negotiation replaced force. In that environment, power was redefined as coordination. Sovereignty was treated as paperwork. Survival was outsourced. So when Greenland re-entered the arena of real geopolitics, Denmark reached for the only tools it knows: statements, summits, legitimacy language, and multilateral choreography. The Prime Minister spoke of dialogue, international law, frameworks, and negotiation — as if territory, resources, and military positioning respond to tone. They do not.

The great powers are no longer playing Denmark's game. America has returned to hard deterrence — hardware, positioning, leverage. Russia operates on spheres and force — not permission. China advances through infrastructure, debt, and quiet encirclement. This is Cold War physics, not postmodern governance. Steel, not speech. Geography, not goodwill. Denmark still believes the world runs on consensus because consensus once worked — when someone else guaranteed the perimeter. But the moment raw power re-entered the board, Denmark froze. It had no vocabulary for force, no instinct for escalation, no spine for confrontation. That is why the scrambling looks panicked. That is why the statements sound hollow. That is why the appeals feel desperate. Denmark is not weak because it is small. It is weak because it forgot what power is. Globalism taught Danish elites that: treaties replace territory, legitimacy replaces leverage, law replaces force, process replaces preparedness. But real power nations never believed this. They played along while it suited them — and walked away when it didn't.

Greenland exposed the lie in real time. A nation that outsources survival to systems eventually discovers that systems do not bleed — people do. And when force returns to the world, those trained only in administration are left holding binders while others move fleets. This is the danger of the globalist blueprint: It produces managers, not guardians. Clerks, not defenders. Negotiators who have never had to mean no. Denmark perfected the velvet glove. But velvet has no grip when the iron hand returns. And now the same nations that were told power was obsolete are discovering — too late — that power never disappeared. It was merely waiting. **This is the fault line running beneath the globalist system.** Administration governs stability. It fails under pressure. Process manages peace. It collapses under threat. The blueprint works best where others still believe force is obsolete. It unravels the moment power reasserts itself. Denmark revealed the limit. What follows explains the machinery that failed it.

The Administrative Empire

The serpent no longer rules through kings. It rules through committees. Authority migrates upward into councils, agencies, and institutions that claim neutrality while exercising power. Acronyms replace accountability. Governance becomes technical, procedural, and deniable. No single office commands. No single nation controls. Responsibility diffuses upward until no one can be voted out. At *the United Nations*, governments gather beneath the borrowed name of "nations," though no people are asked and no ballots cast. Sovereignty is traded for signatures. Treaties replace consent. Language replaces law. In *the European Union*, flags became one flag, parliaments became ratifiers, and laws arrived pre-written. What was once debated locally is now aligned globally. Authority is no longer exercised — it is implemented. Across *the Atlantic*, the same architecture takes root by different means. In America, the Constitution remains, but governance moves through agencies, courts, corporate policy, and private enforcement. What cannot pass legislatures advances through regulation, litigation, and compliance regimes. The form differs. The function does not. The empire does not announce itself. It operationalizes.

The Alignment Layer

What gives the globalist blueprint its power is not any single policy, but synchronization.

- **Health policy** advances surveillance
- **Climate policy** advances rationing
- **Financial policy** enforces compliance
- **Education policy** normalizes ideology
- **Technology policy** manages behavior
- **Media policy** controls perception

Each domain moves under its own justification, yet all speak the same language: resilience, sustainability, safety, equity, coordination. The vocabulary is shared because the architecture is shared. This is not conspiracy. It is standardization. When multiple systems advance together, resistance fragments. Citizens argue one issue at a time while governance advances on all fronts. By the time patterns are noticed, the mechanisms are already integrated. This is how a world is governed without appearing to be ruled. Pandemic policies appear almost simultaneously across continents, written in the same language and justified by the same frameworks. Climate targets drafted in international forums re-enter nations as binding energy law. Education standards align through accreditation, funding requirements, and global metrics long before voters are aware they have changed. Alignment makes power invisible. Invisibility makes it durable.

Enforcement Without Ownership

Modern empire avoids the burden of responsibility. Authority disperses upward and outward:

- **The UN** recommends
- **The EU** aligns
- **NGOs** advise
- **Corporations** comply
- **Governments** implement

When harm occurs, no one is accountable. Authority is distributed just enough to prevent resistance and diffuse blame. Courts defer to "expert consensus." Legislatures cite international obligations. Officials claim their hands are tied. **This is rule without authorship.** Citizens sense injustice but cannot locate it. Protest has no target. Elections change faces, not direction. The system persists regardless of who wins. Power no longer needs loyalty. It measures compliance.

The Export

Denmark did not export dominance. It exported obedience. Bright administrators trained in consensus, process, and alignment moved into international bodies, advisory panels, and regulatory institutions. What they carried was not malice, but method — a belief that order is virtue and resistance is disorder. That instinct now shapes policy in Brussels, Geneva, New York, and Washington. The same frameworks appear across health, climate, education, and finance. The same language repeats. The same solutions circulate. Funds flow from global institutions. Standards flow from international councils. Enforcement arrives through national law and private compliance. No invasion is required. The system installs itself. The serpent learned obedience in Copenhagen. It legislates through Brussels, funds through global finance, and enforces through administrative states. A thousand committees. One tongue.

The Warning

Every empire begins as a promise — a safer world, a fairer system, a more sustainable future. Beneath each promise lies the same exchange: sovereignty for security, liberty for order, consent for management. Denmark proved how peace becomes paralysis. Europe proved how alignment becomes absorption. America — bold, restless, weary of conflict — is now the testing ground for whether freedom can survive administration. The coil no longer hides. It tightens in plain sight. What was rehearsed in the small now governs the great. What arrived as guidance now functions as mandate. Yet what was signed away can still be resisted — if covenant is remembered before consensus, if truth is chosen before safety, if fire is guarded before comfort. The architects build. But the fire waits.

 Firelight Pause — The Expanding Coil
Ask yourself:
- When did foreign councils begin shaping the laws of a free people?
- How many signatures now speak louder than your vote?
- What "global standards" govern your food, medicine, energy, and speech?
- Have you mistaken management for mercy and regulation for righteousness?
- When the mandate reaches your town, your work, your church — will you recognize it?

The serpent's language has changed. Its aim has not. What it rehearsed quietly, it now performs globally. The question is not whether it speaks — but whether we still listen.

"And the devil that deceived them was cast into the lake of fire and brimstone, where the beast and the false prophet are."— Revelation 20:10

36

THE SERPENT'S ARCHITECTURE
EMPIRE REBORN IN CODE

It begins where thrones end — in glass chambers where flags hang silent and no voter can see. The serpent's genius was never violence; it was administration. Empires once conquered by sword. Now they govern by spreadsheet. Its altars are glass towers. Its scripture — policy. Its priests — bureaucrats who mistake process for morality. They do not bleed for their kingdoms; they budget them.

The Design

Every empire builds temples. Ours are the institutions — UN, EU, WHO, IMF, WEF — a pentagon of power, each corner joined by policy and profit. Each was founded in the ashes of war, sold as peace, and matured into control. Together they form an invisible constitution that outranks the one written by nations. The **United Nations** became the moral throne — a cathedral of guilt that baptizes global governance in the language of virtue. Under its banners come treaties no citizen voted for — on health, migration, climate, and speech. Its quiet genius is that it claims to speak for all humanity, while answering to none — the serpent's first global throne.

The **European Union** became the prototype — a continent willingly surrendered to committees. Its constitution was never ratified by its peoples, yet it rules them. Law by regulation, sovereignty by subscription. The serpent perfected harmonization here — difference erased, culture standardized, patriotism pathologized. The **World Health Organization** became the priesthood of fear — commanding lockdowns by decree, rewriting constitutions in the name of "emergency." Its architects learned that biology could justify tyranny. With each outbreak, another freedom died — one molecule at a time. The **IMF and World Bank** became the fiscal architects — builders of invisible chains. They lend to save, then own through debt. Their documents read like charity; their footnotes read like conquest. They call it "conditionality." The condition is obedience. The **World Economic Forum** became the crown without a nation — a private monarchy of billionaires pretending to be prophets. They write doctrines in Davos chalets: ESG, AI governance, digital IDs — sacraments of submission recited by CEOs, copied by ministers, enforced by machines. And behind them all, the **Technocracy** — the engine room of empire, where the digital priests baptize humanity in data. Algorithms replace law; AI governs attention. The architecture is not stone but code — woven into every transaction, every screen, every search. Where the UN writes the creed, the technocrats enforce belief.

The Operating System

This is the serpent's true design — a distributed empire, immune to rebellion. It cannot be toppled; it must be unplugged. No flag to burn. No palace to storm. No single tyrant to overthrow. Each agency is a node; each law a thread; together they weave a net too vast to name. Power is not held; it's automated. Policy moves through pipelines faster than parliaments can read it. The architecture ensures continuity — governments change, but the program remains. Presidents are replaced; the clerks stay. The architecture endures because it is unseen — not personal, but procedural.

This is how the pieces are moved. Politics is the visible layer — the distraction. Beneath it lie the real levers: finance, data, medicine, climate, and war. Finance enforces compliance. Data enables surveillance. Medicine justifies emergency power. Climate supplies moral cover. War resets the board when resistance hardens. Each layer feeds the next. Together, they simulate progress while consolidating control.

The Warning

The serpent does not roar; it regulates. Its tyranny feels like order, its conquest like coordination. It needs no throne because it already sits in your pocket, your policy, your paycheck. Denmark was the rehearsal, Europe the model, *America the prize*. The architecture is finished. But architecture can still be broken — if the builders are unmasked.

🔥 Firelight Pause — The Invisible Constitution

• Do you know who drafts the rules that govern your life — or only who signs them?

• When did governance replace government?

• Which institutions shape your future while claiming neutrality?

• If power no longer wears a crown, how do you resist it?

• If the architecture is invisible, what would it take to unplug it?

37

THE GULAG OF NUMBERS
WHEN JUSTICE REDUCES SOULS TO STATISTICS

"*Justice is turned back, and righteousness stands far away; for truth has stumbled in the public squares, and uprightness cannot enter. Truth is lacking, and he who departs from evil makes himself a prey.*" — Isaiah 59:14–15

The prophet saw it first — *when law became ritual, and truth was tried in the square.* Aleksandr Solzhenitsyn lived it — and he named it. Justice without a soul is not justice. It is tyranny disguised as neutrality, and tyranny always bleeds the people before it bleeds the state. When a nation measures wounds in ledgers and calls it justice, the end is always the same. The Soviet Union did not call it tyranny. It called it order. It called it justice. It called it numbers. But behind the statistics were camps. Behind the ledgers were chains. Behind the "neutrality" was death. Yesterday the gulag counted prisoners. Today it counts credits, carbon, and clicks.

Witness of Chains

Solzhenitsyn carried that witness in his flesh. Arrested, beaten, imprisoned — not for violence, but for words. For daring to tell the truth. For daring to think outside the Party's equation. He wrote to tear the mask away. *'The line separating good and evil passes not through states, nor between classes, but right through every human heart.'* That line cannot be measured by court ledgers or state decrees. It cannot be balanced in budgets. It runs through every judge, every bureaucrat, every father, every citizen. And when men surrender their courage, when they yield their hearts to the system, the gulag is born.

When Truth Became Crime

A man whispered a joke about Stalin at a dinner table. Ten years in a camp — "anti-Soviet agitation." A mother taught children the Lord's Prayer in secret. Five years of forced labor — "religious propaganda." This was justice by numbers - cases tallied, quotas filled, sentences written like bookkeeping. The State pretended to be neutral while it bled the innocent to keep itself alive.

The War That Never Ended

The world yawns while blood cries from the ground. And in the West, persecution hides behind policy and platform — not bullets, but bans. The echo is not just rhetorical — it is real and global. More than 360 million Christians live under high levels of persecution and discrimination worldwide — one in seven believers on earth. *China*: churches that refuse state control are raided, pastors jailed, children barred from worship. Crosses torn down, cameras watching prayer as if it were treason. *Sudan:* war has weaponized faith — churches burned, believers driven from homes, civilians hunted for creed. *Nigeria:* entire villages wiped out by extremist militias. Men slaughtered, women kidnapped, churches reduced to ash. *The West:* believers lose jobs, face court cases, or endure harassment for affirming biblical convictions. A teacher suspended for prayer. A street preacher arrested for quoting Scripture.

Employees disciplined for wearing a cross. The contradiction is glaring - Christians dragged to court for prayer, while the same state trembles when Islam threatens. Preachers silenced, radicals shielded. This is not neutrality. It is surrender.

The Ledger Becomes Digital

History does not disappear. It upgrades. What once required guards, guns, and barbed wire now requires databases, policies, and screens. The mechanism is the same. Only the interface has changed. The old gulag measured bodies with paper and ink. The new gulag measures behavior with data. If the Soviet state tallied prisoners, the modern state tallies compliance — carbon scores, credit access, reputational risk, ideological alignment. This is not metaphor. It is administration. A system that once punished dissent with camps now punishes it with exclusion. Accounts closed. Access revoked. Livelihoods erased. Denmark and America alike resist this truth because it demands courage. The danger is not only corrupted systems, but compliant souls — judges who defer, citizens who stay silent, men who look away when truth is priced out of existence. The ledger never vanished. It went digital.

The Serpent's Math

Solzhenitsyn bore the chains so no one could pretend this inversion was harmless. He tore the mask from the bureaucrat's face and showed the gulag underneath. He showed us what silence becomes when it matures: camps, chains, graves. The serpent's math never adds up to justice. Its equations always end the same way — the gulag of numbers.

From Barbed Wire to Servers

The Soviet gulag was built of brick and barbed wire. The new gulag is built of servers and scores. Yesterday, men were imprisoned for jokes and prayers. Today, they are erased for the same crime — truth. Shadow-banned. De-banked. De-platformed. Professionally exiled. The old camps were hidden in Siberia. The new ones sit in your phone, your wallet, your school, your workplace. A prison without walls — because the cage is everywhere. The old system rationed bread. The new one rations speech, money, medicine, and movement. The old erased dissent with bullets. The new erases it with compliance metrics — and when needed, still with bullets. The gulag did not die. It migrated. From paper to server. From iron to code. From the body to the soul. Do not sign your own chains.

🔥 **Firelight Pause — The Question of Courage**
   • Will I risk chains for truth — or call silence survival?
   • Have I mistaken order for justice, or neutrality for freedom?
   • Do I measure life by ledgers — or by the line in my heart?
   • When words become crimes, will I whisper — or roar?
   • When the gulag goes digital, will I still resist?

"Woe unto them that decree unrighteous decrees, and that write grievousness which they have prescribed." — Isaiah 10:1

38

———

THE DIGITAL GULAG
CHAINS WRITTEN IN CODE

When Barbed Wire Became Bandwidth. **The gulag never vanished. It updated.** What once was barbed wire and watchtowers is now firewalls and dashboards. What once was a ration card is now a carbon score. What once was a file in the secret police drawer is now a database in the cloud. The serpent learned — iron bars are too visible; numbers are not. Chains of steel make people resist; chains of data make them comply. The danger of the Soviet gulag was its cruelty. The danger of the digital gulag is its comfort — no camps, no trains, just nudges, scores, bans, and "community guidelines." A velvet prison where you lock yourself in, smiling, believing you are safe.

China's Prototype — The Social Credit Cage

The serpent always tests its system where resistance is weakest. The first prototype was built behind the Great Firewall. China does not hide its model: cameras on every corner, every purchase tracked, every step logged, every silence scored. A "social credit score" tallies loyalty — rewarding obedience, punishing dissent. The numbers are staggering. A nation of 1.4 billion watched. In the pilot years alone, more than 30 million citizens were denied travel for "bad behavior."

Miss a bill and your child cannot enter university. Criticize the Party and your ticket is canceled. Worship in a church and your bank account is flagged. And the stories are not abstract. Pastor Wang Yi of the Early Rain Covenant Church was sentenced to nine years in prison for refusing to bow his congregation to Party oversight. His only crime — leading worship outside the serpent's spreadsheet. This is not science fiction. It is operating now.

The Western Blueprint

Western elites helped birth the monster. In the late 1970s and 1980s, Deng Xiaoping opened "Special Economic Zones" like Shenzhen — fishing villages transformed into factory-cities overnight. Wall Street, Brussels, and Silicon Valley didn't recoil. They rushed in. Cheap labor. No unions. No regulations. Corporations shuttered factories in Detroit, Pittsburgh, and the Midlands and rebuilt them along the Chinese coast. America's Rust Belt was not an accident. It was a transfer — wealth and fire stripped from the heartland and wired into Beijing's ledger. And Europe played its part. Brussels wrote the treaties that legitimized the transfer. WTO entry in 2001, bilateral trade pacts in the 1990s, climate rules that offshored "dirty" industry eastward while importing cheap green goods back west. Denmark did not design the cage. It helped move the steel. Maersk carried the containers. Danish firms built factories, supplied energy systems, and normalized partnership. What Wall Street financed and Brussels legalized, Denmark operationalized — through logistics and compliance. Not as conquest — as commerce. Not as ideology — as efficiency. Wall Street financed it. Brussels legitimized it. Denmark operationalized it. **The Party consolidated the gains.** The money didn't feed the countryside. It stacked glass towers along the coasts — Shanghai, Shenzhen, Guangzhou — glittering trophies for investors while inland villages stayed poor. By the 1990s, China had become the workshop of the world, but the tools belonged to Western capital. What was sold as "global partnership" was really global plunder: profits for elites, dependency for nations, and a Communist Party armed with the very wealth the West once called its own.

That is why Beijing's gulag is not just a Chinese story. It is a *Western export.* The serpent's cage was designed in Brussels boardrooms, financed on Wall Street, and installed along China's coast — before creeping back to censor, ration, and control the very nations that built it. The chains forged in Shanghai now click in your smartphone. The gulag was never only theirs. It is yours. *They sold out steel towns and farms for skyscrapers on the Pearl River — and called it progress.* When money lost its soul, morality became a metric. The serpent learned to sell control as virtue — the tyranny of good intentions.

Europe's Climate Chains

Brussels dresses its gulag in green. In 2023 the EU passed carbon border taxes, embedding quotas into the global marketplace. Denmark has already approved a plan to tax livestock emissions by 2030 — the first of its kind. Farmers fined for producing food. Herds culled for emissions. Land flooded in the name of offsets. Already, fifteen-minute cities are trialed across Europe. Travel allowances rationed in apps. Meat rationing disguised as sustainability. Liberty reframed as pollution. Directives drafted in Brussels copy into Germany, France, and America's building codes. The gulag is not only digital. It is ecological. A ration card written in carbon.

America's Trial Runs

Do not think it cannot happen here. It already has. COVID passes in New York and Los Angeles divided the nation into two classes of citizen by QR code. Those without the right mark were barred from restaurants, travel, even work. In Canada, when truckers protested vaccine mandates, the government froze their bank accounts by decree — obedience enforced with a keystroke. And the private ledgers run just as deep. PayPal, Stripe, and Chase have closed accounts for political speech. Between 2021 and 2023, dozens of high-profile groups were cut off from finance for "policy violations."

Platforms throttle truth in real time, demonetize dissent, and erase voices from the digital square. Corporations are judged not by profit but by loyalty to creed. The gulag of numbers is not planned for tomorrow. It is tested today.

Biden's EO 14067 sketched the blueprint for a Central Bank Digital Currency — a programmable dollar dressed as modernization. FedNow launched in 2023, sold as "instant payments," but designed as the on-ramp to programmable control. Pair it with ESG scores, and suddenly every mortgage, job, and retirement account bends to ideology. But the serpent miscalculated. Trump slammed the brakes — warning against CBDCs, declaring "I will never allow a central bank digital currency." He rallied states like Florida and Texas to preemptively ban their use. Governors signed bills outlawing CBDCs as legal tender. Parallel currencies — Bitcoin, stable coins, state-level bills — surged. The remnant built lifeboats even as the elites drew blueprints for cages.

The Soft Gulag of Finance

Prison bars are replaced with PIN codes. Obedience enforced not by soldiers, but by servers. Programmable money already in trial, designed to expire if you do not spend it fast enough. Digital IDs tying your health, travel, and banking into one key. Algorithms deciding whether your mortgage, your medicine, or your job survives. CBDCs are the master key — programmable obedience cloaked as efficiency. ESG scores the measuring rod. But resistance is here too. States passed laws banning ESG discrimination. Lawsuits against PayPal and Chase forced retreats. Alternative payment rails — crypto, parallel banks, cash economies — began to surface as bulwarks against the cage. They call it progress. They call it safety. But every system is a lock. Every update a chain.

The Comfort That Kills

The Soviet gulag terrified its victims. The digital gulag seduces them. It offers convenience, discounts, fast delivery, personalized feeds. But beneath every ease is erasure. **Free speech replaced by "community guidelines."** Faith gatherings replaced by "safety protocols." Cash freedom replaced by "traceable tokens." The Soviet gulag took bodies by force. The gulag of numbers buried millions. The digital gulag does not promise less. It promises more.

🔥 **Firelight Pause — The Velvet Cage**
- What is tracked in your life without your consent?
- When does a "guideline" become a chain?
- If your account vanished tonight, could you still live free?
- Would your ancestors recognize you as free — or as managed?

China's Christians, Sudan's displaced, Nigeria's massacred — the blood still runs. In 2023 alone, two hundred believers slaughtered in Plateau State at Christmas while the world scrolled past. Churches in Khartoum turned into barracks, believers branded as enemies. *Three hundred sixty million Christians now live under "high levels of persecution, one in seven believers on earth.* The serpent has not retired its bullets. It has only added screens. And if America bows, it will not be by bayonet. It will be by login. The gulag will not announce itself. It will arrive as convenience.

"It is for freedom that Christ has set us free. Stand firm, then, and do not let yourselves be burdened again by a yoke of slavery." — Galatians 5:1

39

THE ARCHITECTURE OF
THE INVISIBLE EMPIRE

WHERE SYSTEMS RULE AND SOVEREIGNTY DIES

Freedom does not fall in a single moment. It falls through architecture. Not laws. Not armies. Systems. The new empire rises in silence, built not on land but on infrastructure—financial, digital, legal, algorithmic. Its borders run under oceans and across satellites. Its armies are servers. Its capital sits in Basel, where the Bank for International Settlements commands the world's monetary regime with the authority of an emperor no one elected and no one is allowed to question. This is where the skeleton begins. The BIS does not propose. It directs. Its Unified Ledger blueprint is not a concept—it is a protocol. A global grid where identity, currency, assets, contracts, carbon scores, and behavioral profiles merge into a single programmable system. Nothing like this has existed in human history. Once identity is fused to money and money is fused to behavior, autonomy evaporates. A man becomes a point on a dashboard—legible, traceable, and manageable at scale.

The IMF enforces the system internationally. It arrives in debt-strapped nations carrying loans that sound like lifelines but function like shackles. "Modernization" becomes digital identity. "Inclusion" becomes programmable money. "Stability" becomes surveillance. The conditions never lift. The debt never ends. And sovereignty becomes a quaint word in a document filed away in a ministry that no longer governs anything. **The ECB** acts as the field laboratory. Its digital euro is not a currency—it is a behavioral instrument. Its internal papers openly describe spending controls, time limits, geographic restrictions, identity-linked permissions, and rulesets programmable in real time. Europe accepted it because Europe no longer remembers what sovereignty feels like. Denmark taught them the model.

Denmark proved that compliance can be engineered. A single digital ID —first NemID, then MitID—became the compulsory key to banking, medical care, education, government communication, property registra-tion, travel, and daily life. Denmark did not need force. It needed effi-ciency. A digital identity became a digital jurisdiction. The State became the operator of existence. Denmark is not a nation-state. It is an adminis-trative node. Everyone who studies the model understands exactly what it is: **the prototype of population-level digital governance.** Where Europe tested compliance, the Federal Reserve tests concealment. It denies building a digital dollar while its New York Innovation Center runs pilots identical to those of the ECB—programmable settlement, tokenized liabilities, real-time policy transmission, and cross-border identity integration. It calls this "exploratory research." Denmark used the same language. So did Brussels. The denial is not deception. It is delay. **The WEF** manufactures the ideology. It writes narratives that make centralization moral and compliance virtuous. It reframes surveillance as trust, control as sustainability, identity as safety, and programmable money as progress. It persuades the elite class that citizens are problems to be managed, not people to be represented. Every tyranny in history needed a priesthood. This one needed a communications department.

But the empire is not built by governments alone. It is executed by corporations—because corporations enforce what governments cannot legally impose. Visa and Mastercard decide which transactions count as acceptable. PayPal freezes accounts for ideological deviation. Stripe erases businesses that fail moral compliance. Amazon Web Services deletes entire platforms overnight. Apple and Google control which apps may exist, which identities may authenticate, and which information may circulate. Bank of America hands private data to federal agencies without a warrant. *This is the world's first corporate enforcement mechanism.* A privatized policing arm with no constitution, no jurisdiction, no appeals process, and no nation to answer to. *Terms of Service* have become the new legal code—borderless, unchallengeable, instantly modifiable. A parallel legal system built by unelected executives and enforced by algorithms.

Beneath all of this lies the true sovereign of the coming order: the **algorithm.** Once identity, currency, and access are routed through a single digital infrastructure, algorithms—not judges, not legislators, not presidents—become the operators of human life. They evaluate risk. They assign trust. They flag behavior. They freeze access. They lift restrictions. They allocate permissions. This is not futuristic speculation. It is spelled out in BIS documents as *"automated policy transmission."* A euphemism for direct machine-governed enforcement. When the architecture is complete, no human being will decide whether your transaction clears, your account unlocks, your mobility expands, or your medical pass updates. The algorithm will. And **no one will know how it decided.** This is the part no one sees—not even those who think they understand the system. The new empire is not run by men. **It is run by mechanisms.** The cloud completes the cage. Ninety-seven percent of the world's financial, governmental, health, and identity data is stored on servers owned by three companies: Amazon, Microsoft, and Google. If AWS shuts off a government's backend, that government collapses. If Azure removes a banking node, transactions halt. If Google Cloud disables an identity network, a population becomes digitally homeless. This is not a marketplace. This is digital feudalism. The cloud lords can burn kingdoms to the ground—and have done so.

The physical empire runs under the oceans. Undersea cables are the arteries of the global system. Denmark's Havfrue cable ties Europe directly into the U.S. digital spine, routing authentication and financial traffic across the Atlantic. The Arctic cables bind North America to Nordic and EU networks. **Whoever owns the cables owns the flow of identity and money. No one votes on undersea sovereignty. It simply exists, invisible and absolute.**

On top of the infrastructure sits the treaty lattice—the legal superstructure that overrides national constitutions without ever acknowledging it. **The EU-US Data Privacy Framework** aligns transatlantic digital governance. **OECD tax agreements** bypass congressional authority. **Nordic-US accords** merge biometric and travel systems. **UN digital identity** initiatives push for universal registration. **WHO frameworks** override national health sovereignty. **NATO cyber doctrine** merges civilian and military data systems into a single interoperable grid. Each treaty looks harmless alone. Combined, they dissolve the idea of a sovereign nation-state. Interoperability is the empire's weapon. The more systems connect, the more control can flow across borders without permission. Denmark's ID standards can become America's access keys. ECB digital rules can influence U.S. banking. UN identity indexes can become global requirements. When systems sync, sovereignty ends. Layered onto this is the Western social scoring regime. It does not look like China's because it doesn't need to. It is decentralized, embedded inside finance, healthcare, insurance, and infrastructure. Carbon allowances. Medical compliance. Risk flags. Reputation metrics. ESG evaluation. Misinformation scores. Behavioral underwriting. This is social control by a thousand small levers instead of one giant one. No iron chains. Just protocols. Above all this floats the AI-governed compliance loop: governments issue rules, corporations automate enforcement, AI monitors behavior, financial systems penalize deviation, governments receive analytics, new rules are drafted, and the loop tightens. No tyrant required. The system governs itself.

This is the architecture of the invisible empire: a supranational machine built from cables, treaties, algorithms, cloud servers, identity portals, payment networks, and compliance software. It governs not through law but through access. It punishes not through force but through disconnection. It does not care about borders, constitutions, or elections. **It is not ideological. It is infrastructural.**

Most Americans do not see it because it arrived disguised as convenience. A thousand portals instead of one. A hundred corporate rules instead of a single decree. But every gate leads to the same architecture. And every architecture leads to the same truth: **a nation that must ask permission to function is no longer sovereign.** The empire assumes America will submit like Denmark—quietly, politely, efficiently. It assumes convenience has defeated courage. It assumes Americans no longer remember the cost of their own birth. It is wrong. The Republic carries a memory no algorithm can overwrite. It carries a suspicion no corporate system can neutralize. It carries a defiance older than the institutions trying to contain it. Once the architecture is seen, it cannot be unseen. **Once exposed, it cannot be accepted. Once rejected, it cannot survive.** The invisible empire is real. Its machinery is built. But its victory is not inevitable. Not in a nation that still remembers that sovereignty is not granted by systems. It is exercised by citizens. And the moment those citizens stand, the architecture will crack. Because in the end, the empire is nothing more than wiring. And the human spirit has broken stronger chains than that. Empires fall the moment their machinery is seen—this one just made itself visible.

Sit with this—not in fear, but in clarity. You just saw the architecture they hoped you'd never see. And once seen, it cannot be unseen.

- Where does the cage already brush your life?
- Where has convenience replaced choice?
- Where has access replaced freedom?
- Where has a machine replaced a human voice?

This is not a warning about another land. It is the blueprint beneath your feet. Not prediction. Diagnosis. Every diagnosis demands a decision. And every decision begins with a line you will not allow the empire to cross. Hold the fire. You will need it for what comes next.

"He causes all, both small and great, rich and poor, free and slave, to receive a mark... that no one may buy or sell except one who has the mark..." — Revelation 13:16–17

40

COMMON DENOMINATORS
OF THE SYSTEMS

THE SKELETON BENEATH EVERY REGIME

The gulag was not Soviet alone. The camps were not German alone. The chains are not Chinese alone. The serpent molts. The serpent rebrands. But the skeleton remains. They change the banners. They change the uniforms. They change the slogans. But the bones never change.

The Eight Bones of Tyranny

Every empire builds on the same frame. The names change, the flags change, the slogans change — but the skeleton does not. Once you see the bones, you can see the body forming. What feels like chaos begins to reveal pattern. What looks like random policy shows itself as design. The serpent's power is not new. It is ancient. And its skeleton has always been the same - **eight bones, set in place, clothed in different flesh in every age.**

First — Centralized Power — The Rise of the Unaccountable Few.
Mao's people's committees, Hitler's "Führerprinzip", Stalin's "politburos",
Brussels' commissions, Washington's alphabet agencies, the EU's bureaucrats, the UN's councils — always the same drumbeat - power rising
upward, away from families, towns, parliaments. The fewer the hands,
the tighter the chains. And you may be asking — what about executive
orders? Today, executive orders and unelected agencies in Washington
write rules that bind millions with no vote cast. For decades, this was the
mark of abuse — presidents sidestepping Congress, agencies smothering
liberty in fine print. By the letter of the Constitution, such power belongs
only to emergencies and to war. *Yet in this hour something feels different.*
The same instrument once used to tighten chains may now be used to cut
them. Whether that proves true or not, history will decide. But power
never moves without purpose. *If the pen once signaled overreach, it may now
signal an unseen struggle for freedom.*

Second — Controlled Speech — When Truth Becomes Contraband.
Soviet Pravda. Nazi Gleichschaltung — "alignment." Denmark's §266b
hate-speech enforcement. In the United States, the attempt to stand up a
Disinformation Governance Board exposed how easily language-control
can be bureaucratized, even inside DHS; the board was announced,
publicly contested, and then disbanded amid concern over speech policing. On the street level, American courts now wrestle with whether
quoting Scripture can be treated as criminal disturbance. Street
preachers in Seattle and elsewhere were arrested for reading the Bible in
public; one such case reached federal appellate review and courts have
recently pushed back against censoring preaching where the speaker's
words — not the listeners' reaction — are at issue. And today, the cage is
digital. What Mao once stamped in red ink, does Silicon Valley now
enforce in code? Words are twisted until truth sounds like hate and lies
sound like virtue. Once they own your tongue, they already own your
mind.

Third — The Collective Above the Person — The Erasure of the Individual. Mao declared the individual nothing. The Nazis exalted the Volk above all. Technocrats preach "sustainable goals" above sovereignty. Modern public-health absolutists place "the public" over the person. Different masks — same erasure. How many times must the person disappear before the system is seen for what it is? During COVID the logic of the collective swallowed the person. Families were barred from burying their dead while mass protests filled city streets. Nursing-home doors were locked; elders isolated, abandoned, and in many places condemned. Hospitals discharged contagion into care homes. Schools closed, robbing a generation of childhood. Vaccine mandates, masks for children, travel bans, and vaccine passports made the "public good" the supreme law — even when it stripped dignity, family rites, and the future of young minds. When the collective becomes the law, the person becomes collateral. Rituals that sustain a life — a funeral, a bedside hand — became privileges granted by the state. They measured safety in charts; you measured humanity in losses.

Fourth — Manufactured Crisis — The Emergency That Never Ends. Every tyranny manufactures or magnifies an emergency. The Reichstag fire. Class struggle. Permanent revolution. Racial purity campaigns. Climate collapse warnings. Pandemic panic. The crisis never ends, because **the crisis is the power source.** Today, climate "emergencies" are wielded as weapons — to justify rationing, lockdowns, land restrictions, and agricultural mandates. In the Netherlands, courts ordered nitrogen cuts that throttle farmers. In Denmark, livestock taxes and "green" quotas are exported as models through Brussels — showing how one small state becomes a laboratory for global obedience. Crisis becomes the excuse. What the law forbids outright — does subsidy now achieve in silence? In America, the pattern clones itself.

The USDA's Climate-Smart Commodities program poured more than $3 billion into "climate-friendly" agriculture — not to free the rancher, but to tag him. Carbon tracking, methane metrics, "smart" subsidies — every dollar wrapped in data strings. The independent cattleman becomes a carbon accountant, his herd reduced to emission units. Meanwhile, the same four giants — Tyson, Cargill, JBS, and National Beef — still control over 80 percent of U.S. meat processing, dictating prices, access, and survival. These are not ranchers; they are middle kingdoms between Washington and the land. And yet the noise isn't about them.

The headlines fixate on imports from Argentina — barely two percent of America's beef supply — as if foreign herds were flooding the plains. You have to wonder: if the numbers are that small, why the uproar? If four companies already control the gates, what stops more ranchers from building their own? Is it ignorance, or incentive? Is it easier to shout about Buenos Aires than to look behind the feedlot fence at home? Even the Constitution drew a clear line — no federal hand over soil or stock. But Washington learned a subtler art: pay them to obey. Every grant becomes a leash; every metric, a map of control. What the law forbids outright, subsidy achieves in silence. So perhaps the real question isn't about Argentina at all. Who owns America's beef — the rancher, the bureaucrat, or the boardroom?

Why do politicians rage at foreign cows while the domestic cartel fattens unchallenged? Maybe they don't know what's happening. Maybe they do. Either way, the result is the same: the rancher is managed, not free. And if the system now pays you to measure carbon instead of raising cattle — do you still call yourself sovereign? Or does freedom begin only when you stop waiting for permission and build your own market again? The land does not need saving. The rancher does. Free the herd from the ledger.

Maybe that's why "ranch management" no longer means managing a ranch. University curricula now teach carbon credits, water quotas, ecosystem services, digital tagging. The soil is a spreadsheet. The cow, a data point. They no longer train stewards of land — they train compliance officers for the climate economy. And suddenly the Argentina show makes sense. It's not about beef at all. *It's about obedience.*

Fifth — Captured Media & Education — The Factories of Obedience. Mao's *Little Red Book.* Goebbels' propaganda machine. Soviet *Pravda.* Different century, same choir — one script, one hymn, one lie. Today the voices are Big Tech, elite universities, and compliant mainstream networks — preaching ideology while censoring dissent. Under Biden, control hardened. In 2021, Twitter and Facebook silenced a sitting U.S. president even as terrorist regimes and dictators kept their accounts. When the Hunter Biden laptop surfaced, fifty-one intelligence officials called it "Russian disinformation." Platforms buried it. Journalists mocked it. Truth became a liability. The "lab-leak" story proved the pattern: for two years it was heresy to ask if science had sinned; now even federal agencies admit what they once banned from the screen.

Then came the Twitter Files — exposing federal agencies quietly directing platforms on what could be said, shared, or seen. The censors no longer wore uniforms; they wore badges and contracts. What Stalin enforced with fear, the modern state enforces with code. The pulpit shifted to the classroom. Universities purged professors who resisted gender dogma, mandates, or DEI pledges — ideology became the tuition price of tenure. In public schools, parents who questioned radical curricula were branded "extremists," even "domestic terrorists." The new inquisition wears a PTA badge. The classroom became a pulpit. The newsroom an echo chamber. The platform a gatekeeper. Different tools, same result: thought bent to serve power — the digital gulag becomes the syllabus.

Sixth — Enemy Creation — Mark, Isolate, Destroy. Tyrants always require a scapegoat — Jews, kulaks, the bourgeoisie, reactionaries. The method is the same: find an enemy, brand them dangerous, unleash the mob. Today the labels sound different but work the same. "Climate denier." "Misinformation spreader." "Christian nationalist." "Racist." "White supremacist." "MAGA." "Transphobe." "Homophobe." "Bigot." "Xenophobic." "Right-wing extremist." The vocabulary shifts with the season, but the purpose is constant — silence the target, rally the mob, justify exclusion. During the "plandemic," the unvaccinated were cast as threats to society — neighbors turned into enemies of the state. Afterward, the playbook widened: faith became "hate," conviction became "phobia," dissent became "extremism." And the punishment no longer required prisons. Banks closed accounts. Employers canceled contracts. Platforms erased speech. The bureaucratic mob replaced the torch-bearing one. Once the brand is burned onto you, a career, a reputation, even a family can be destroyed overnight. The playbook is ancient — redefine disagreement as danger, then strip the marked of their voice. When words become weapons, freedom is already in chains.

Seventh — Suppression of Faith — Erasing What Stands Above the State. Every tyrant fears what is higher than the State. The Soviets sought to erase churches; Mao's Red Guards burned temples; the Nazis turned pulpits into Party altars. Today, transnational institutions exalt "science" as priesthood and bureaucracy as gospel. If there is a God above the State, the State cannot remain absolute — so it seeks to erase Him. In China, Pastor Wang Yi was sentenced to nine years in prison for refusing Party oversight — a warning to any pulpit that dares speak truth. In the West, suppression wears softer clothes. Public-school teachers are pressured to silence their faith; Christian students are punished for prayer; churches face zoning denials, audits, and digital shadow-bans when they refuse the new orthodoxy. The machinery is polite, procedural, paper-bound — persecution by policy instead of prison.

At the same time, activist teachers — credentialed in ideology, not wisdom — are elevated, preaching gender confusion and grievance politics while silencing conviction. Yet there are still signs of pushback: in *Kennedy v. Bremerton School District*, the Supreme Court ruled that a high-school coach's post-game prayer was protected speech — proof that even within the system, remnants of courage remain.

God is not silent — but the State would prefer He be invisible.

Eighth — Utopian Promises — Chains Wrapped in Compassion. The bait is always paradise — the worker's utopia, the thousand-year Reich, the great leap forward, pledges of global peace and cooperation. The language is always seduction. The result is always the same: graves, chains, silence. Today's mask is "sustainability." The United Nations sells its Sustainable Development Goals as a pathway to peace. ESG scores are pitched as ethical investing, but function as gatekeeping — rewarding compliance, punishing dissent. The EU's Green Deal and Danish-backed nitrogen laws are praised as progress while throttling farmers and draining sovereignty.

Central banks promise digital currencies as tools of inclusion, but in practice they mean every transaction can be watched, tracked, and shut off. What is promised as salvation arrives as surveillance. What is advertised as progress delivers obedience. The genius of the modern utopia is that it feels moral. Do they submit out of fear — or out of virtue? Do they obey because they must, or because they believe they are helping? Every tyranny now cloaks itself in compassion — "for the planet," "for safety," "for equality." Every empire tells its people paradise is just one more sacrifice away. But utopias never free; they always bind. The chains are simply polished before they are fastened. Strip away the costumes and the skeleton is clear — centralized power births controlled speech, which manufactures crisis, which demands scapegoats, which erases faith, which promises utopia, which delivers chains.

A skeleton is only the beginning. Bones demand flesh. Policies become programs. Slogans become mandates. Promises become prisons. The bones of tyranny always dress themselves in law, in media, in schools, in treaties. What was theory now walks as power in your streets. Different skins. Same breath.

Firelight Pause — The Skeleton Exposed

You've seen the bones. They are not relics of history — they are blueprints of the present. Every empire swears it will be different. Every generation insists it cannot happen again. But the serpent does not innovate; it imitates. What changes are the faces — not the frame. *The question now is not whether you recognize the pattern — but whether you still have the courage to break it.*

Ask yourself:

- Do I see the bones in my own nation — or still pretend they belong to another age?
- When the State calls control compassion, do I nod — or name it for what it is?
- Have I mistaken the comfort of safety for the chains of surrender?
- If tyranny wore my flag, would I still recognize it?
- When the serpent rebrands, will I remember the skeleton beneath?

Empires do not rise because tyrants are clever. They rise because nations forget. When the serpent sheds its skin, men applaud the shine and forget the fangs. History does not erase memory — comfort does. It softens judgment, dulls vigilance, turns warning into nostalgia. And so the bones return, rebuilt by the very hands that swore "Never again." This is how freedom dies in modern light — not by invasion, but by amnesia. Not with a sword, but with a scroll. Not with fear, but with fatigue. The serpent does not need to conquer a nation that refuses to remember. It only needs to lull it back to sleep. **And when a nation falls asleep — who will wake it?**

41

THE ANATOMY OF FORGETTING
WHY AMNESIA IS THE SERPENT'S FIRST VICTORY

They said it could never happen again. Not in the West. Not in the age of screens and science. But tyranny doesn't always march with boots; sometimes it scrolls with thumbs. What empires once enforced with fear, democracies now erase with distraction. What if history is not forgotten because it is old — but because it is inconvenient? Even now, only a few years after the lockdowns, many pretend it never happened — the lies, the lab leaks, the funding, the silencing, the neighbors who turned on neighbors. They scroll past memory as if it were a bad dream instead of a warning. **Forgetting is not just weakness; it is strategy.** The serpent survives through amnesia.

First — Emotional anesthesia. When tyranny breaks a people, do they rebel — or do they numb? They bury pain under "moving on." But unprocessed memory festers; it becomes infection. Nations that refuse to grieve will repeat what they will not name. Comfort becomes anesthesia. Silence becomes coping. And coping becomes surrender.

Second — The algorithmic fog. TikTok minds can't remember tyranny. The feed trains reaction, not reflection. A generation that can recall every meme but not every mandate becomes easy prey. Flood the brain. Starve the soul. Memory dies in the age of noise.

Third — The moral exchange. How many enforced their own servitude and called it virtue? They tattled on neighbors, shamed dissenters, cheered as churches closed and small businesses died — all in the name of "saving lives." To remember would mean confessing complicity. So history is rewritten as care. And obedience is renamed compassion.

Fourth — The spiritual root. This is older than propaganda; it is possession. The serpent's weapon is distraction. If truth can't be destroyed, it can be drowned in noise. Scripture calls it the *strong delusion* — when men trade remembrance for illusion, when peace is just paralysis renamed. That is why tyranny always returns faster than anyone expects. It doesn't need new soldiers, only forgetful citizens. The next cage is already built, waiting for a generation too tired to remember the last one. Wake up.

Fifth — Legalizing the unthinkable

Every crisis begins as an exception. Every exception seeks permanence. What would never survive open debate slips in under emergency powers, pilot programs, temporary mandates, and provisional authorities. The language is always cautious — just for now, just until safety returns. But safety never returns, because safety was never the goal. The emergency becomes precedent. The precedent becomes policy. Courts defer. Legislatures abdicate. Citizens adapt. What once shocked the conscience fades into background noise. The abnormal is legalized not by force, but by repetition. When the extraordinary becomes routine, tyranny no longer needs justification. It has become procedure. Memory is resistance. Recollection is rebellion. Refuse the anesthesia. Refuse the fog.

Refuse the lie that forgetting is healing. **Nations do not fall because they are conquered — they fall because they forget.**

Why Humanity Never Learns

It is not ignorance that blinds a people — it is **pride.** Every generation inherits the warnings: Solzhenitsyn's witness, the Nuremberg trials, the graves of millions. But man studies them as artifacts, not as mirrors. He dissects history instead of repenting from it. Knowledge without remembrance becomes pride — and pride repeats what it thinks it understands.

Mechanisms of Forgetting

Amnesia of Comfort — When Safety Dulls Memory

After collapse, survivors cry "Never again." But one or two generations later, comfort dulls memory. Comfort breeds blindness; blindness breeds surrender. Today, young Europeans walk streets paved with Holocaust memorials yet rally behind parties that censor speech and flirt with authoritarian power.

The Seduction of Utopia — Paradise as a Weapon

Man longs for paradise. Forget God and he buys the counterfeit. Communism. Nazism. **Climate salvation. Perfect safety.** In 2020, millions surrendered freedoms overnight for the promise of protection — discovering too late that emergency powers rarely expire.

Fear of Standing Alone — Silence as Self-Preservation

Most people sense the lie, yet silence feels safer than speech. They wait for someone else to speak. By the time they realize, the herd is already at the slaughter. In Canada, truckers protested. Most citizens stayed silent — only later realizing bank accounts could be frozen for dissent, **without trial.**

Divide the dissent - Why resistance never converges

Power does not fear opposition. It fears unity. So resistance is never crushed all at once — **it is fractured.** One group is allowed to protest climate mandates. Another is allowed to protest speech restrictions. A third is allowed to protest surveillance — but never together. Each is labeled, sorted, and siloed. Cultural issues are split from economic ones. Faith is separated from liberty. Speech is detached from consequence. The moment these lines could converge, the system intervenes — with scandal, distraction, or moral blackmail. Fragmented resistance exhausts itself arguing over tone, purity, and hierarchy while power advances unopposed. A divided opposition is not a threat. It is a managed population arguing inside its cage.

Fatigue as policy - When tyranny outlasts courage

The modern system does not need terror. It needs endurance. Rules change constantly. Crises overlap. Outrage never resolves. Nothing is ever finished. This is not incompetence — **it is design.** A population kept permanently reacting never organizes. A citizen exhausted by paperwork, mandates, updates, reversals, and moral pressure eventually stops resisting — not because he agrees, but because he is tired. Tyranny no longer breaks people. It waits them out. Exhaustion becomes governance. Compliance becomes rest.

The final locks - When the prisoner blames himself

The last cage is internal. When systems fail, when lives shrink, when dignity erodes, the citizen is taught not to question power — but to question himself. I didn't adapt fast enough. I didn't comply well enough. I didn't signal virtue clearly enough. Structural injustice becomes personal failure. Control no longer requires enforcement, because the prisoner disciplines himself. A population trained to self-blame will never revolt. It will only optimize its obedience and call it maturity.

The spirit behind the systems

This is older than Rome, older than Babylon, older than Berlin or Beijing. The beast rises again and again because it is not merely politics; it is spirit, hunger, the dragon's breath through human systems. That is why across continents — from China's digital gulag to Europe's climate quotas to America's speech bans — the patterns align as if choreographed. Man never learns because he mistakes memory for immunity. He believes knowledge is repentance. But **memory without obedience is theater — and theater never saves nations.**

The Prophetic Frame

Scripture names what we see — *"The dragon gave the beast his power and his throne and great authority."* Revelation shows the architecture. Solzhenitsyn named the cost: *"Men have forgotten God; that's why all this has happened."* Different skins. Same serpent. The beast today is no longer one man in jackboots; it is a **network** — diffuse, slippery, hard to pin down. That is why people are confused. But the pattern is visible. *Global elites move capital* like kings once moved armies; technocrats and data harvesters build the code that governs daily life; global bureaucracies speak soft words that harden into chains; political operatives pass treaties and enforce orders; cultural machinery — Hollywood, media, academia, corporate HR — polices the mind and makes dissent look crazy, dangerous, hateful. These organs are not the animating force. The bloodstream is power without God. The animating spirit is the serpent. That is why coordination feels inevitable: not secret handshakes in smoky rooms so much as alignment with darkness. *Every time men choose lies over truth, comfort over courage, silence over fire, the serpent rises again.* The serpent molts. The serpent rebrands. But the skeleton is the same. And **you will face it in your generation — either as a slave, or as a warrior.** But even bones can be broken. And some have begun to strike back.

Signs of Return — Hope & Resistance

Since the shock of the "plandemic," something else has stirred alongside the rot. People are turning back to what cannot be centralized — *faith, craft, neighborhoods, local markets, and honest speech.* Where the system sells papers and slogans, communities are trading in skill, service, and trust. You see it in churches — quieter rooms filled with people hungry for roots, not labels. In classrooms — apprenticeships, trade schools, small colleges where teachers answer to parents, not committees. In markets — farmers, craftsmen, entrepreneurs building supply chains and payment rails outside corporate chokeholds. In law and policy — pockets of resistance, courts defending conscience, and citizens choosing competence over credentialism: roofers, nurses, machinists, carpenters — the true backbone of nations. This is not romanticism. The dangers are real. But movements for recovery are not waiting for permission. They build schools, start presses, host civic salons, retrain a generation in trades that cannot be credentialed away. This is the parallel economy. And it is also the rescue.

Not all see it. Many sink back into the "new normal," scrolling, numbing, mocking the builders. They trade fire for fog. But some lit fires. Every garage hammer, every acre planted without subsidy, every book printed outside their presses declares: we are still free. Normal is gone. What comes next is slavery disguised as safety — or freedom rebuilt on faith and courage. Mutual aid networks, carpentry co-ops, legal defense funds, independent presses: those who build are already choosing to be free. They hire on merit, not ideology. They choose skill over slogans, character over creed. This is the choice before every reader - remain a subject of the Paper Cage, or become a builder. Learn a trade. Found a school. Support an independent press. Host conversations. Fund the institutions your children will inherit. Nations are rebuilt piece by piece — by those who refuse surrender and act with courage. The system will not save you. The serpent will not free you. But you can build. And if you build, you will stand. The serpent builds cages. The remnant builds houses of fire. Choose your foundation — because the storm is already here.

- Have I mistaken comfort for freedom?
- Where has silence felt safer than truth?
- Do I see the spirit behind the systems — or only politics?
- When the hour comes, will I choose sovereignty over security?

"They worshiped the dragon who gave the beast his authority, and they also worshiped the beast and asked, 'Who is like the beast? Who can wage war against it?'" — Revelation 13:4

42

THE PANOPTICON STATE
SURVEILLANCE AS SALVATION

"*Nothing is covered that will not be revealed, or hidden that will not be known.*" — Matthew 10:26

The merchants built the market; now the overseers build the eye. What was bought must now be monitored. What if Babylon's economy has matured into empire — a system not content to own our labor, but our gaze? Every empire builds its tower. Rome used spectacle — the Colosseum was its eye, where citizens learned to cheer for control. The Soviet Union perfected paranoia — informants, files, whispers. China coded obedience into its citizens — face scans, social scores, digital leashes. The West chose comfort — data traded for convenience, truth outsourced to algorithms. The methods changed; the gaze remained. Every empire refines the art of being watched without seeing the watcher. And perhaps that's the point — to make us forget there even *is* a watcher. This is not cultural drift. It is design. Surveillance is not a side effect of modern life — it is the governing mechanism.

Then came the philosopher of the eye. Two centuries ago, Jeremy Bentham imagined the perfect design for obedience — the *Panopticon*. One tower, many cells. Everyone visible; no one certain when they're being watched. It promised "reform." It delivered compliance. He called it humane. In truth, it was the blueprint of silent domination — *obedience without force, control without chains.* A century later, the French historian Michel Foucault warned that Bentham's tower had become culture itself. In *Discipline and Punish*, he wrote that modern life had turned into a "disciplinary society." Schools, hospitals, offices, prisons — all built on the same invisible design: "Visibility is a trap." The citizen became his own jailer. Surveillance no longer needed guards. It needed conscience. Do we still live free — or only inside a panopticon so elegant we call it convenience? — a design first imagined by Bentham, perfected by algorithms: one tower, many screens, everyone visible, no one certain who watches. A society where the fear of being seen replaces the need for chains. The result is obedience without force, compliance by perception.

The Eye That Never Blinks

Every empire builds its walls. This one builds windows — one-way glass, looking in. The serpent's tower now sees everything and forgives nothing. No iron bars, no barbed wire, just lenses and lines of code. You don't live in a prison. You live in a panopticon — a cage so elegant you call it convenience.

The serpent whispers: *"You are seen, therefore you are safe."*
But the truth is older: *"You are watched, therefore you are owned."*

From Bentham to Babylon — The Digital Panopticon

The tower never fell. It digitized. Rome watched crowds in the arena. Moscow watched neighbors through curtains. Beijing watches faces through glass. And Silicon Valley watches souls through screens. The new panopticon doesn't punish — it *predicts*. It doesn't coerce — it *conditions*. You are studied, scored, simulated, and sold. What began as Bentham's architecture has become Babylon's algorithm. This is the counterfeit omniscience — the serpent's imitation of God's eye. God sees to redeem; the system sees to restrain. God's knowledge brings mercy; the algorithm's knowledge brings management. This is Babylon's great inversion: omniscience without love, transparency without grace, safety without freedom.

The Web of Watching

The system is everywhere — not because it must be, but because perhaps we invited it. Phones listen. Cars track. Doorbells record. Fitness watches your pulse; smart homes watch your habits. What began as assistance has become accusation. What began as service has become surveillance. Cameras once guarded banks; now they guard you — from yourself. Data once belonged to you; now it *is* you. Everything is archived, cross-referenced, and sold to those who promise safety. Safety is the leash; surveillance is the collar.

The Digital Priesthood

The watchers no longer wear uniforms. They wear badges, passwords, and nondisclosure agreements. Technocrats call it "predictive governance." They mean preemptive obedience — citizens training themselves to comply before command is even given, the serpent's favorite form of worship. AI is their prophet — omniscient, amoral, unappealable. It knows your habits, anticipates your rebellion, and adjusts the algorithm before you ever speak. The new justice system is statistical. The new morality is measurable. The new confession is consent to terms and conditions.

In this new faith, repentance is replaced by reprogramming. The sinner becomes a data set. The penitent, a user. True obedience to God is born of conviction. Preemptive obedience to the system is born of fear. One redeems; the other reprograms.

The Gospel of Transparency

They preach transparency as virtue — but it flows only one way. You must reveal; they remain hidden. You must justify; they never explain. You must surrender privacy for safety; they hoard secrecy for power. Every authoritarian regime sold control as compassion. The serpent smiles through the bureaucrat who says, *"We only want to protect you."* But protection that never ends is not protection — *it is possession.*

The Illusion of Choice

They give you apps to vote, cards to pay, passports to move — and say you are free. But each convenience adds a lock. Each update installs a watcher. Each permission grants another unseen power access to your life. Freedom no longer dies in battle; it dies in downloads. Every checkbox is a covenant you never read. They call it innovation. It is indoctrination by interface.

The Silent Compliance

The most effective tyranny is the one the people enforce on themselves. Neighbors report each other "for safety." Children monitor parents "for misinformation." Employers flag workers "for risk management." Churches livestream confession to the cloud. You no longer need a warden when fear and virtue signal from the same device. The serpent smiles — because his guards no longer wear uniforms. They wear guilt. Virtue has been weaponized; silence has been standardized.

The Global Fusion

Data flows faster than armies ever could. Your phone talks to satellites that talk to agencies that talk to corporations that talk to nations — all under the banner of "shared intelligence." Denmark rehearsed the model — digital IDs, health passes, and centralized data hubs under the EU's gaze. What was a rehearsal in Copenhagen is now architecture in Washington. Health merged with finance. Finance merged with mobility. Mobility merged with morality. When every system merges, the individual disappears. Was globalism ever truly about trade — or about trace?

The Firewall of Flesh

But still — flesh resists. Every human soul is a firewall the serpent cannot code. No algorithm can replicate repentance. No database can track faith. The remnant stands not with encryption but with endurance. When every voice is recorded, the truth must be spoken louder. When every word is scored, prayer must be whispered deeper. When every movement is mapped, the remnant must learn to walk unseen — not through hiding, but through holiness. The final resistance is not technical — it is spiritual. A clean heart still scrambles every signal of Babylon. This is the playbook: observe everything, predict behavior, reward compliance, penalize deviation, and call the result safety. Once surveillance is moralized, resistance becomes antisocial. Once resistance is antisocial, enforcement becomes unnecessary.

The Ground Truth

You don't need to live in Silicon Valley to feel this war. You feel it every time your card gets declined "for security." Every time your phone updates without asking. Every time you speak your mind and lose a job, a friend, or a platform. You feel it when your kid's school surveys what they believe, when your tractor reports your harvest, when your pickup truck tells you it needs permission to move. **This isn't theory. It's here.**

They told us it was for safety. Maybe they even believed it. They told us it was for convenience. But control wrapped in comfort is still control. The same system that scores your credit will soon score your conscience. The same data that sells you ads will one day sell your allegiance. If you think this is science fiction — remember: every empire begins as paperwork. Every tyranny begins as policy. Every cage begins as care.

The rancher in Texas. The welder in Ohio. The mother in Montana. The veteran in Georgia. You are the firewall now. Your refusal to comply blindly, your courage to question, your faith to see through the fog — that's what still holds the line. Don't let the screen become your shepherd. Don't trade your birthright for convenience. The serpent doesn't care whether you understand the code — only whether you obey it.

🔥 **Firelight Pause — Eyes Everywhere**
- What convenience has become your cage?
- Do you still choose what you watch — or are you being trained?
- If your phone records your faith, will you still pray aloud?
- If every act is logged, will you still act with courage?
- What is left of freedom when even your silence is stored?

You are not powerless — you are proof that the soul cannot be surveilled. The serpent watches from the tower, but the tower will crack. For the eye that sees all cannot endure the One who sees through it.

"For the eyes of the Lord run to and fro throughout the whole earth, to show Himself strong on behalf of those whose heart is perfect toward Him." — 2 Chronicles 16:9

43

———

THE BIO-DIGITAL COVENANT
WHEN FLESH MEETS CODE

The Bio-Digital Covenant — When Flesh Meets Code
Before the serpent rewrites flesh, he must first observe it. Perhaps surveillance was only rehearsal — teaching man to monitor himself before another learned to modify him. But the eye was only phase one. Once the watchers learned to see every move, they began to crave power over the design itself. Observation became modification. The next frontier of control is not your screen — it's your skin.

The Bio-Digital Playbook
This is not innovation drift. It is design. The sequence is always the same:

- **Observe the body** — track movement, sleep, fertility, emotion
- **Map the data** — genome, hormone, behavior, compliance
- **Medicalize deviation** — label dissent as disorder
- **Offer correction** — pills, shots, edits, implants
- **Attach access** — work, travel, money, identity
- **Call it care** — safety, inclusion, health, compassion

Once biology is moralized, refusal becomes pathology. Once refusal is pathology, coercion becomes treatment. And once treatment is normalized, **no tyrant is required.**

"You knit me together in my mother's womb." — Psalm 139:13

When the serpent controls speech, creation is next. Once he masters words, he moves to rewrite worlds. If he masters words, how long before he begins to rewrite worlds? First he seizes the dictionary; then, the DNA. *For the power that names truth also names life* — and when man forgets that words were meant to bless, he begins to engineer the body as if it were a sentence he can edit.

The New Genesis

Do all empires, in time, seek to play God? When power can no longer rule men, it begins to re-engineer them. The serpent's final project is *not political; it is biological.* Its goal is not to manage humanity — it is to modify it. They call it progress. They call it trans-humanism. But beneath the glow of silicon is the oldest heresy in history: *"You shall be as gods."*

The Covenant Rewritten

God made a covenant in blood. The serpent makes one in code. DNA is the new scripture; algorithms the new prophets. Every genome edited, every embryo scanned, every neuron mapped — the handwriting of heaven rewritten by human pride. What was once birthright is now patent. What was once creation is now copyright. They call it precision medicine. They mean programmable life. When did healing become editing?

The Flesh Made Plastic

The line between body and machine blurs daily. Implants regulate hearts and hormones. Neural chips promise memory on demand. Artificial wombs hum in laboratories while "ethicists" debate how many mothers a child needs. The serpent sells it as healing — but could it be harvesting? He whispers, *"Upgrade your body,"* while erasing the image of God from the design. Gender is re-coded. Fertility outsourced. Motherhood mechanized. Fatherhood optional. Childhood patented. This is not evolution — it is engineered extinction of the human spirit.

The Digital Soul

They say consciousness can be uploaded — that the mind is data and salvation is storage. Servers replace sacraments. Clouds replace heaven. AI becomes the oracle, promising eternal life through replication. But an algorithm cannot resurrect. It can only simulate. What it copies, it owns. What it owns, it controls. Eternal life without the Eternal is not salvation — it is synthetic damnation.

The Pharmakeia Economy

Scripture warned of *pharmakeia* — sorcery through substances. Now the spell is digital. Pills for obedience. Shots for behavior. Gene therapy baptized as moral duty. Corporations preach salvation through subscription — monthly miracles for a price. And when salvation is sold, can it still save? The serpent no longer tempts with fruit, but with the promise of eternal youth, endless upgrades, programmable peace. And every dose trades one more piece of your sovereignty for one more hour of sedation.

The Economic Leash

Every empire baptizes its control in currency. The serpent's code is written not only in data, but in debt. Control of flesh means nothing without control of bread. And so the new covenant comes with contracts — monthly, renewable, and denominated in fear.

Digital ID links to digital wallets; digital wallets link to digital obedience. They call it "financial inclusion." But inclusion means surveillance; access means permission. The same system that scores your purchases will soon score your principles. Refuse the next mandate, and your account freezes — not by decree, but by design. What began as convenience becomes covenant. The subscription replaces the sacrament. The paycheck replaces the promise. Corporations preach morality while indexing your virtue to your balance. The new tithes are carbon credits, social scores, and biometric verifications — obedience with a receipt.

Even philanthropy has turned predatory. Global funds "for health" and "for the planet" buy entire governments in the name of progress. Relief becomes ransom. Nations trade sovereignty for subsidies, families trade freedom for benefits, individuals trade conscience for compliance. The serpent's economy doesn't steal; it seduces. It pays you to forget you're enslaved. And yet, there is another economy — older, slower, sacred. The economy of covenant. The farmer who feeds his town without a barcode. The craftsman who sells what his hands have made. The mother who gives life freely, not as transaction but as gift. The remnant who trade in trust, not tokens. Money is no longer neutral — it is **moral**. Every purchase is allegiance. Every transaction is testimony. Every dollar either deepens the leash or weakens it. So ask yourself: *Whose economy am I serving — Babylon's or the covenant's?*

The Technological Priesthood

Priests once guarded temples; now technicians guard servers. They speak a priestly tongue of data, code, and genome. Few understand it — that is the point. Mystery becomes monopoly. Only the initiated may edit the code of creation. Only the credentialed may decide who lives, who reproduces, who remembers. They call it ethics; it is eugenics with manners. They call it safety; it is censorship of the soul.

The People's Wake-Up Call

This isn't science fiction. It's already in your schools, your doctor's office, your children's phones. You may not work in a lab, but the lab is working on you. At what point does survival become surrender? They're rewriting what it means to be human while you're still paying the grocery bill. They say "gender is fluid." They say "birth is optional." They say "the body is obsolete." And your son comes home from college repeating words you never taught him. That's not rebellion — *it's reprogramming.* When did compassion become surgery? When did care become mutilation? When did we start calling confusion progress? You don't need a microchip to be enslaved. All it takes is to forget that life is sacred — **that being *born* is holier than being *made*.** If you still believe that your children are a gift, not a government experiment — then you're already part of the resistance. And one day, every hand that mutilated the innocent will have to answer — not to politics, but to God. Judgment may delay, but it does not forget.

America's Choice

The serpent's gospel has already crossed the ocean — biotech partnerships, military AI programs, behavioral-prediction systems. If America forgets that man was made, not manufactured, she will trade liberty for longevity. She will preserve the body while losing the breath. Could the Republic's final test come not in ballots or borders, but in laboratories and classrooms? And already, the serpent's labs glow red, white, and blue. Our universities preach the same gospel once whispered in Brussels. Our children are told they can rewrite their bodies as easily as apps. This is not freedom — it is fragmentation sold as choice. The real covenant was never signed by hand or code. It was written in blood — on wood. Christ did not upload Himself; He incarnated. He did not digitize the soul; He redeemed it. The serpent promises immortality without repentance; God offers resurrection without purchase. The war between flesh and code is not about technology — it is about allegiance. **Who owns you — the Creator or the counterfeit?**

 Firelight Pause — The Code or the Cross
- Have I begun to trust the machine more than my Maker?
- What "upgrade" have I accepted that edits my humanity?
- When science claims power over birth, memory, or death — do I still call them holy?
- If tomorrow offered eternal life in a lab, would I trade my soul for it?

Technology can serve the covenant — or replace it. Choose who writes your code. For the serpent's promise is always the same: immortality without God, progress without purpose, paradise without love. They want fewer souls, smaller families, quieter homes — because faith and family are the last places they can't code. The serpent hates birth because every birth is defiance. Every new life says: God still creates. The body still rebels — every scar, every heartbeat, every child conceived without permission.

"For what shall it profit a man, if he shall gain the whole world, and lose his own soul?" — Mark 8:36

44

THE PSYCHOLOGY OF SUBMISSION
HOW FEAR BECOMES FAITH IN CONTROL

Before Babylon falls, we must understand why it rose — not by force, but by faith in control. Every empire of lies requires believers. This is how they are made. History's great evil was never committed by monsters, but by administrators. The men who filed the forms, processed the data, enforced the decree — believing they were civilized because they did it politely. That is where the serpent hides now — in logic, in procedure, in the polite language of progress.

Every system begins in code, but before it controls machines, it must first reprogram men. The serpent's software runs on psychology — *fear, conformity, and moral inversion.* It spreads not through governments, but through neighbors, teachers, and intellectuals who believe themselves immune. This is where tyranny becomes subtle — when even intelligent men — calm, educated, certain they are virtuous — begin to defend the very thing that enslaves them. It's what makes the pattern so chilling, and why history repeats — not because people forget, but because they *rationalize.* Every century, the serpent finds new words, new data, new reasons. The costumes change. The creed remains — Control redeems. What follows is not theory. It's witness — a moment that revealed how quickly conscience can be recoded, and how fear, once baptized as compassion, becomes faith in control.

The Polite Tyranny — How Fear Wears a Smile

It began in a comment thread — polite, educated, Danish. No shouting. No slurs. Just reasoned words and quiet conviction. One man proposed that the unvaccinated be denied medical care. Another replied that perhaps isolation camps would be more efficient. Someone else added, smiling emoji and all, that it might not be possible yet — *"not until we decide it should be."* No boots on cobblestone. No soldiers. Just citizens nodding along to the logic of exclusion — in the language of compassion. They spoke as if reason itself were their armor, never seeing that fear had already rewritten their faith. It struck me — this was not madness. It was order. It was the calm of people who believed they were good. Every tyranny begins this way — not with hate, but with *certainty*. Certainty that they are right. Certainty that safety justifies control. Certainty that freedom, if unregulated, becomes dangerous. The serpent never comes screaming. He comes smiling — with a clipboard, a policy, a promise of safety. He speaks through the polite and the practical. Through the teacher, the doctor, the neighbor. Through those who would never call themselves oppressors. And yet they are the perfect soldiers — the ones who believe obedience is virtue. The ones who trade conscience for consensus. The ones who build cages with good intentions and call them "public health." I watched this thread unfold like a microcosm of history. The same arguments that once justified eugenics, segregation, and censorship had returned — not in German, not in Russian — but in fluent, progressive Danish. The words were new. The spirit was ancient. That night I wrote these notes — not about the virus, but about **the virus of the mind.** Because what I saw was not about vaccines. It was about *fear turned into faith in control.* It was about the human tendency to protect the system even when the system devours the soul.

Stage 1: The Spark — Fear of Chaos

It always begins with **fear** — fear of illness, fear of instability, fear of difference. The human mind, when frightened, trades freedom for order. People say, *"Something must be done."* That phrase sounds reasonable — but it's the moral ignition point. Fear creates the moral vacuum in which authority blooms. *Inner belief:* "If everyone obeys, I'll be safe." *Reality:* Safety becomes the idol that replaces truth. It doesn't start with mobs or mandates. It starts with a mother afraid for her child, a man afraid to lose his job, a neighbor afraid to stand alone. Fear is ordinary before it becomes organized. That's why it spreads so fast — because it feels like care. How many times have we said it ourselves — and felt righteous doing it?

Stage 2: The Rationalization — Virtue Redefined

The next step is **moral laundering** — wrapping control in compassion. Coercion becomes "care." Punishment becomes "protection." The intelligent elite frame totalitarian logic as *policy optimization.* "We only restrict you for your safety." "We must protect the system." "Freedom must have limits."This is the **moral inversion** — The shepherd becomes the jailer, and still believes he's saving the flock. How many modern shepherds wear the same smile?

Stage 3: The Normalization — Bureaucracy as Theology

Once the moral shift happens, **the machinery of enforcement grows teeth.** Meetings, policies, and slogans replace conscience. People no longer ask *"Is this right?"* but *"Is this compliant?"* They don't see themselves as oppressors, only as administrators of the inevitable. Bureaucracy turns belief into procedure. Procedure turns obedience into pride. Pride blinds repentance. This is where Denmark's cultural conditioning — order, politeness, consensus — becomes a perfect Petri dish. Tyranny doesn't need to roar; it smiles.

The Control Sequence

This is not cultural drift. It is design. Surveillance is not a side effect of modern life — it is the governing mechanism. The sequence is always the same:

- **Observe everything**
- **Predict behavior**
- **Reward compliance**
- **Penalize deviation**
- **Rename control as safety**

Once surveillance is moralized, resistance becomes antisocial. Once resistance is antisocial, enforcement becomes unnecessary. The system no longer needs force — because the people do the work for it.

Stage 4: The Polite Persecution — Social Enforcement

Soon the mob becomes the ministry. Neighbors report neighbors. Critics are not debated, they're "fact-checked." Friendships fracture — not because people become cruel, but because **virtue has been redefined as compliance.** "I'm not punishing you — I'm protecting others." "You chose this consequence." Fear shifts from external to internal. Now the people police themselves — proud to be obedient.

Stage 5: The Justification — Denial of Moral Parallels

When someone warns, *"This echoes the 1930s,"* they reply, *"That's not the same."* They're right — it's not the same uniforms, but it's the same spirit. The modern mind, trained in progress-worship, cannot bear to see its own reflection in history's mirror. So it mocks the warning instead of repenting. "We're democratic — it can't happen here." That is exactly what every democracy says before it does. History always rehearses itself politely before it kills. In Germany, neighbors filled forms before they filled graves. In the USSR, doctors signed diagnoses before guards signed death warrants. Evil never begins with bullets — it begins with bureaucracy. By the time the blood flows, the paperwork is already done.

Stage 6: The Inversion Complete — Obedience as Holiness

The final stage is **moral inversion** — the moment when disobedience becomes the new sin. The unvaccinated, the dissenters, the skeptics — all become scapegoats. The majority now believes persecution is compassion. The serpent smiles; his work is complete. "You are excluded for the greater good." "Freedom is selfish." "Submission is love." This is the religion of control — the cult that calls tyranny care. One day, a child asks why their friend disappeared from school. A nurse wonders why the data no longer matches the faces she treats. A soldier hesitates before signing another form. That's how it ends — not with revolution, but with conscience waking one person at a time.

Stage 7: The Awakening — When the Lie Tires

Eventually, reality breaks through. The policies fail, the data shifts, the harm is undeniable. And yet, most will not repent — they will simply forget. History repeats because societies rarely confess; they just reset. That's why the *remnant* must remember — not as historians, but as guardians of discernment. To say: *"Never again"* must begin with *"Never forget how it begins."* The serpent's system always ends the same way — when the lie grows too heavy to carry, it collapses under its own illusion.

Firelight Pause — The Psychology of Submission

History never begins with monsters — it begins with men who want to be safe. Men who mistake control for peace and consensus for truth. Once obedience is sanctified, it becomes the altar where liberty dies. The serpent never demands worship; he whispers, "You are good if you obey," hiding tyranny inside virtue and fear inside compassion. Modern man no longer kneels before kings — so he bows before science, safety, and the greater good.

- We imagine we would never comply — but would we?
  - How far have I already accepted this without noticing?
  - When fear comes, do I reach for freedom or control?
  - When anger rises, do I speak truth or seek consensus?
  - When silence feels safer, do I stand alone or blend into the crowd?
  - When obedience feels holy, do I still test the spirit behind it?

This is where the war truly begins — not in parliaments but in hearts. The real program is not digital but spiritual, running on fear, shame, and the worship of comfort. To break it, one must do what the masses rarely do: stand alone in the light, unapproved and unafraid. The remnant remembers what compliance costs and what silence precedes. Freedom is never kept by approval — only by courage. Control always begins politely. It ends by decree.

"For there is nothing hidden that will not be revealed, nor anything secret that will not be known and come to light." — Luke 8:17

45

THE CULT OF PROGRESS

THE RELIGION OF CONTROL

They said progress would set us free. They said the future would be clean, safe, and smart — run by experts, powered by data, guided by reason. But look closer. The "progress" they built looks less like freedom and more like management. The architects built their towers; now they crown them with creed. What began as policy has become religion — a gospel written in code and sold as compassion.

"They exchanged the truth of God for a lie, and worshiped and served created things rather than the Creator." — Romans 1:25

The serpent no longer preaches with horns and idols. He preaches with PowerPoints, hashtags, and policy briefs. He calls his gospel *progress*. His kingdom — *sustainability*. His salvation — *safety*. Once men built cathedrals; now they build data centers. Once priests burned incense; now scientists burn carbon credits. Once prophets called for repentance; now pundits call for compliance. The modern creed is simple: *Man is broken, the planet is dying, and only control can save us.* But if control becomes salvation — what god are we really worshiping?

The New Trinity

Every faith has a trinity. The Cult of Progress has its own — *Science, Safety, and Sustainability.* Three words that sound noble — three altars of submission. **Science** — the infallible oracle. Question it, and you are an outlaw. **Safety** — the sacred idol. Obey it, and you are pure. **Sustainability** — the eternal promise. Serve it, and you will be saved — from guilt, from carbon, from consequence. Each sermon begins the same: "The experts have spoken." *Each ends the same: "You will comply."*

The Moral Substitution

Faith is not abolished; it is inverted. Sin is no longer moral — it is environmental. Redemption no longer requires repentance — it requires regulation. The confessional is now digital — your carbon app, your social score, your biometric ID. The indulgence is subscription-based — offsets, donations, diversity pledges. And the priesthood wears suits, not robes — issuing sacraments through screens. They promise "heaven on earth" — a world without pain, risk, or inequality. But heaven built on control becomes hell. *When man crowns himself savior, tyranny is always the cross.* Have we grown so terrified of consequence that we now call control compassion?

The New Saints and Martyrs

Every religion crowns its faithful. The Cult of Progress does the same. Saint Greta of Climate. Saint Fauci of Science. Saint Gates of Philanthropy. Saint Musk of Mars. Their halos glow in LED. Their robes are lab coats. Their pulpits are TED Talks. They preach salvation through innovation — redemption by subscription, deliverance through data. Their creed is simple: *trust the system, not the soul.* Their miracles are metrics. Their commandments are code. Their crusade? Against creation itself — to edit, patent, and monetize what God once called good. And every "breakthrough" ends the same way: a new product, a new law, a smaller man. Laugh if you must — but remember, every cult begins as a joke.

The Cathedral of the Algorithm

The new temple is the internet. The altar glows. The faithful scroll. Every click an offering. Every post a confession. The algorithm hears all, sorts all, judges all. It decides what is truth and what is sin. It rewards obedience with reach, and punishes dissent with silence. *The digital priest replaces the pastor. The feed replaces the flock.* AI whispers like an oracle, predicting desire before prayer is uttered. It pretends to serve — but it shapes. It pretends to answer — but it edits the question itself. When data becomes deity, free will dies. If the algorithm now defines truth, who needs God — and who dares to disagree?

The Babel Within

This cult builds its tower not from stone but from pride — stacked with good intentions, wired with self-righteousness. The serpent's oldest lie echoes through the circuitry: *"You will be like gods." Every invention becomes an idol when it forgets its Maker.* We wanted wisdom; we traded it for knowledge. We wanted connection; we traded it for surveillance. We wanted peace; we traded it for permission. This is not progress. It is regression in disguise — Eden rebuilt with Wi-Fi, Babel with better branding. Every cult demands converts — but every remnant is called to rebellion.

The Counter-Faith

The covenant people are not called to escape this system — but to expose it. To remind the world that man is not machine, that freedom is not permission, and that creation is not a commodity. We serve no algorithm. We kneel to no screen. **Our creed is older than their code: Truth over trend. Spirit over system. Covenant over consensus.** The remnant must learn to stand as priests of reality in an age of illusion — to speak sacred words into digital noise, to build real altars in a world of simulations, to remember the living God when men worship the grid. Faith in the machine will end as it began — in malfunction. But faith in the Maker endures fire.

⟡ Firelight Pause — The Religion of the Machine
- Where have I bowed to "experts" instead of discernment?
- When did I mistake comfort for peace?
- Do I believe technology will save me — or truth will?
- What altar does my daily routine serve: the covenant or the code?
- Am I raising my children to worship creation or the Creator?

Every screen glows with a sermon. The only question left — which gospel have you already been following? The serpent's cult promises progress but delivers paralysis. Only the covenant gives fire — the kind that frees, not fries.

"For the wisdom of this world is foolishness with God." — 1 Corinthians 3:19

The religion has been named, the altar exposed. Now we descend into its economy — the market of men, the trade of nations, the system where everything holy becomes a commodity: The Marketplace of Babylon.

46

THE GREEN GOSPEL
THE CREED OF CONTROL

You've seen the signs close to home. Grocery bills climb while they preach "sustainability." Gas prices rise while they say it's "for the planet." Farmers are told to cull herds, welders to quit diesel, families to shrink their tables. They call it stewardship; it feels like surrender. This isn't about polar bears or melting ice — it's about whether your kid can afford beef and whether you can still drive to work when the grid says no.

They promised salvation. What they sold was chains. Green is not care. Green is control. They do not want to heal the earth; they want to manage you — your food, your fuel, your fertility, your freedom. If control wears the mask of care, how many will kneel before it thinking they are kind? They preached a new idolatry — solar and wind will save the planet. The worshippers believed. Behind the hymns, however, the altar was built on toxic inputs and human misery. Much of the world's poly-silicon — the heart of solar panels — flows from Xinjiang, where reports and government actions have exposed forced labor of Uyghur and other Muslim minorities; containers of solar equipment have been seized at U.S. ports on that very suspicion.

Wind was sold as clean and eternal. The truth is uglier — turbine blades, built of composite materials that do not biodegrade, are cut into pieces and buried or landfilled when retired; industry reporting shows tens of thousands of blades reaching end-of-life disposal in the years ahead unless recycling scales far beyond current capacity. The image of green smiling upon a landscape hides mountains of fiberglass and resin, a waste stream the market never priced. They told us renewable machines would never fail. But when a winter storm struck Texas in February 2021, the state's lights went dark. More than four and a half million homes lost power; the system failures and deaths that followed exposed a grid unprepared and brittle — a cautionary tale about brittle systems dressed as progress. The winterization failures were not only one technology's fault, but the collapse revealed that an ill-prepared dependency on a single architecture kills.

They promised electric cars as freedom. Yet every battery begins as a scar on the earth — hundreds of thousands of pounds of ore stripped from Congo, Chile, Australia, and elsewhere, processes that have been documented by human-rights groups as linked to child labor and forced evictions in cobalt belts and the expansion of mines that crush communities. Human-rights groups and investigative reporting have traced cobalt and other battery metals through supply chains that too often hide violence and abuse. These are not small footnotes; they are the ledger of modern industry. They told you that green would be painless. The market told another story. Panels made with supply chains implicated in forced-labor investigations, turbines that create non-recyclable waste, batteries refined by carbon-heavy processes in smelters powered by coal — these are the hard facts under the slogans. What kind of salvation demands the suffering of other people's children? They are not contradictions; they are the plan. When the cost of "green" is outsourced to other people's rivers, other people's lungs, other people's children, the gospel expires and the scam reveals itself.

They preach a new liturgy about eating less meat and shrinking families. In Denmark the movement has already become law in the making — Copenhagen has agreed on measures that include taxing livestock emissions beginning in 2030, a world-first levy that will alter what farmers produce and how households feed themselves. That policy was sold as stewardship; to many it reads as rationing by another name.

What of the so-called offsets and credits, the indulgences of the modern Church of Green? Carbon markets and offsets function like medieval pardons — corporations buy paper absolution while the planet pays the bill. When corporations buy credits rather than stop polluting, the result is not healing but permission to pollute at scale while citizens are taxed into penance. The architecture behind the robe is not accidental. Denmark was the lab, Brussels the pulpit, Washington the copy machine. Polite politicians posed beside windmills while the draftsmen of policy worked the levers. Turbines froze in Texas and the headlines showed the danger of a brittle system; thousands of blades will sit in deserts and landfills unless a costly recycling revolution arrives; solar supply chains have been implicated in forced-labor investigations; forests are torched for questionable biomass credits while politicians clap and take a bow. This is not stewardship. It is suicide with subsidies.

Behind the technocrats and the NGOs stand treaties and taxes. The European Union did not invent the carbon ledger as charity; it crafted the Carbon Border Adjustment Mechanism to put a price on embedded emissions in imported steel, cement, and fertilizers — a mechanism that changes the terms of trade and hands regulators a scoring pen. That border tax is not simply environmental policy; it is a tool to reorder economies and exert leverage over supply, production, and the lives of ordinary people.

The Green Gospel is sold as humility before creation, but it is practiced as power over people. They tell the frightened that urgency demands compliance. Fear becomes the knife that severs liberty. Guilt becomes the tax that tills dependency. Identity is reshaped so any dissent becomes a moral failing — and the dissenting are cast as villains. When did virtue become obedience, and stewardship become silence?

America must see the pattern — Denmark rehearsed, Brussels codified, Washington imported. Policies that first show up in a small capital echo into Brussels and then into Washington. The collapse of trust in a technology or a policy does not erase the policy's power; it simply recasts it as a softer chain. What began as green initiatives — forests to be restored, quotas to be met — becomes passports, grids, IDs, and quotas that touch the wallet, the hearth, the field, the womb. The lie is simple and seductive — "Comply for the common good." The reality is that compliance centralizes control. A household that cannot heat itself without remote permission, a car that a manufacturer can disable with a software update, a farm that is taxed for the methane that comes from feeding your family — these are not libertarian fantasies. They are plausible outcomes in a world that values aggregate metrics over persons.

And now — in public and loud — the pushback begins. Leaders have started to name the con. At the United Nations General Assembly, the U.S. president warned these policies were a "con job." He urged nations to *reject policies that trade prosperity and freedom for technocratic chains.* The hall split down the middle — some applauded, others recoiled. But the moment marked a shift. The debate is no longer about carbon charts or climate models. **It is about sovereignty itself — whether nations will remain free, or kneel to compliance.**

This chapter does not deny environmental risk. *It denies a false messiah.* Real stewardship honors soil and family, supports farmers with true energy independence, and defends the right to repair and to choose how we feed and fuel our homes. Real policy prizes resilience over fashionable dependency. Real justice resists systems that concentrate power and externalize harm. The seed story still matters. A boy in a perfect green city pierced the wall and found ash, poisoned rivers, and burned forests. He carried the last seed — truth, soil, food, freedom. That seed is you. You are the seed. When the globalists advertise Denmark as a postcard of the future, remember that postcards hide borders. America is the prize precisely because it still contains many seeds.

Look for the signs and the tricks. Officials will sell fear as urgency — it is "too late" unless you hand over liberty. Guilt campaigns will paint individual choices as crimes against the planet. Corporations will offer offsets and indulgences so they can continue business as usual. Identity will be fused with compliance — if you question the catechism you will be labeled racist, privileged, or ignorant. But you are not anti-science; you are anti-slavery. You are not selfish; you are sovereign. You are the firewall. Remember: it's not rebellion to resist false gods.

The Green Gospel is not about carbon. It is about control. Not about Eden. About empire. The turbines, panels, and pledges were never salvation; they were rehearsal. Behind the turbines stood treaties; behind the panels stood passports; behind the slogans stood chains. Behind it all stood Western elites who rehearsed in Denmark, codified in Brussels, financed in New York, and exported it back to you. The serpent does not stop with windmills. It coils around your wallet, your speech, your borders, your body.

This is not paranoia. These are patterns and receipts — supply-chain seizures, policy texts, landfill counts, and national tax plans. The evidence is public. The stakes are not abstract. The next move is not an argument about kilotons but about whether your children can feed themselves when the grid is a lever and permits are the key. Resist not as a tantrum but as stewardship — the kind that mends what's broken instead of bowing to those who broke it. *Real stewardship isn't bowing to Brussels; it's fixing what you own, feeding who you love, and leaving the land stronger than you found it.* Grow, trade, repair, teach. Back farmers, welders, builders, and families, not distant bureaucracies. Teach your children the table is covenant, not carbon. Keep seed in your hand. They promised salvation. What they sold was chains. Because in every age, the serpent sells salvation — and the remnant plants truth. Green is not care. Green is control. *Stand. Sow. Resist. Keep the seed.* 🔥

🔥 **Firelight Pause — Lines in the Soil**
- What have I obeyed "to save the planet" that enslaves me?
- When did children become a threat instead of a legacy?
- Who profits from my guilt — and who suffers when I refuse it?
- Where does stewardship end and surveillance begin?
- When the lie collapses, will I still hold seed in my hand?
- When the system preaches "repentance" through restriction, will I remember Who truly redeems?

They promised salvation. We saw the waste, the forced labor, the brittle grids, the lies hidden in the turbines and panels. That was the sermon. But sermons alone cannot build an empire. Behind the pulpit stood a playbook — drafted in decades, rehearsed in Denmark, perfected in treaties, and funded by Western capital. The Green Gospel was the mask. The Climate Playbook was the machinery. And unless you draw a line in the soil now, the next harvest will be rationed, not reaped.

47

___

THE CLIMATE PLAYBOOK

FROM OIL SHOCK TO NET ZERO —THE SCRIPT THEY PERFECTED

The Green Gospel was the sermon. The Climate Playbook was the system — written in boardrooms, rehearsed in schools, perfected in fear. Before they taught the world to panic, they taught Denmark to obey.

I was a child in Denmark when the oil crisis hit. I remember the silence of *"bilfri søndage"*—car-free Sundays. Streets that once hummed with bicycles and cars were empty, eerily still. Children tried to play soccer in the middle of the road because no engines came. It felt almost festive, but beneath it was fear. We were told - this is necessary, the oil is gone, the world is in crisis. Gas stations shut down, lines formed, rumors spread. My parents and their friends spoke in hushed tones about rationing, about how fragile our lives suddenly were. I didn't have the words then, but I felt it in my bones - someone, somewhere, could turn the tap off, and Denmark would kneel.

Behind that silence was the Yom Kippur War of 1973. When Arab nations used oil as a weapon—slashing production, raising prices, punishing the West—Denmark was caught in the crossfire. Imports collapsed. Prices surged. A war fought in the Middle East plunged our little northern kingdom into crisis. And the crisis came with a script. I remember the commercials—grim voices and stark images telling us to save energy, to switch to alternatives, to sacrifice. We were told to turn off lights, lower the heat, bicycle instead of drive. It was not just policy. It was theatre. Posters, television, even school lessons drilled the same catechism: *Denmark must obey, Denmark must conserve, Denmark must sacrifice.* Survival was not only measured in barrels of oil, but in the willingness of citizens to submit. As a child I didn't know geopolitics. I only knew the silence of the streets, the stern voice from the screen, the feeling that invisible hands somewhere far away had the power to plunge our small nation into darkness. When did survival replace sovereignty? And who decided obedience was the new virtue?

Across the Øresund, in Sweden, the Barsebäck reactors were rising. Even as a child I saw the glowing lights on the other side of the water and heard the arguments — safety, survival, the future. Nuclear power was sold as the only way forward. The debate split the Nordics. In Denmark the yellow sun buttons said *Atomkraft? Nej Tak* — No Thanks to nuclear. In Sweden, another camp rose with *Atomkraft? Ja Tack* — Yes to nuclear. Politics divided neighbors, families, even churches. Barsebäck ran for decades, then one reactor was shut in 1999, the second in 2005. Sweden claimed it was about safety, but everyone knew it was politics. The lights went dark across the strait, but the ghost never left. Barsebäck was never only about energy. It was a rehearsal — a test of how slogans, fear, and politics could decide the fate of nations. Meanwhile, Norway struck oil. Black gold gushed from the North Sea, and the papers filled with pictures of rigs and riches. The state built its sovereign wealth fund, one of the largest in the world, while ordinary Norwegians watched their small kingdom transform into a petroleum empire.

Denmark? We got "green Sundays." Politicians told families to park their cars one day a week to save fuel. Ordinary people pedaled bicycles while Oslo piled billions into its vaults. Norway got the wealth. Denmark got the sermons. *Who wrote the liturgy?* At the time, I thought it was just the way the world worked. Some nations were lucky, others were disciplined. Later I saw it wasn't luck or discipline. *It was choreography.* The lines were drawn in boardrooms, not on maps. Who would pump? Who would save? Who would profit? Who would obey? The serpent knows how to write destiny with policy. Norway was trained to be rich. Denmark was trained to be green. One drank oil. The other drank slogans. Both played their part in the script.

The Ozone Panic

By the 1980s, a new fear was everywhere: the hole in the ozone layer. Newspapers shouted it, teachers repeated it, TV ran documentaries that burned into our young minds. *The sky will open. The rays will scorch you. Skin cancer will rise. Crops will die.* As a teenager, I remember looking up at the sky on hot summer days and thinking it might crack open. That was how it was sold to us—an apocalypse in the atmosphere. The propaganda was relentless. Posters and school lessons warned us of invisible rays. Television showed animations of Earth's shield thinning, as if the very sky above our heads might collapse. Everyday products—hairspray cans, refrigerators, sprays we kept in our homes—were suddenly rebranded as weapons against the planet. The villain was announced: CFCs. And then came the "solution": *the Montreal Protocol.* Ban, regulate, police. Industry retooled overnight. New products, new patents, new monopolies. We thought it was salvation. In truth, it was the same pattern: *declare an invisible terror, force obedience, consolidate power.*

Warming, Cooling, "Change"

The script kept shifting. In the *1970s* they warned us of global cooling, a new ice age. I still remember library books with black-and-white photos of frozen cities, grim predictions of advancing ice sheets. It was chilling—not just the images, but the certainty with which adults spoke. By the *1990s,* the ice age had melted into fire. Global warming was the new doctrine. Seas rising. Deserts spreading. Polar bears drowning. We were told Denmark's coasts would disappear. I grew up internalizing it - your nation is fragile, your future is at risk, you must obey the experts. The narrative was everywhere. Television specials ran simulations of drowned coastlines, complete with mournful music and animated waves crashing over Manhattan. Newspapers printed countdown clocks of "ten years left," resetting the numbers every time the deadline passed. Classrooms taught charts and graphs as gospel, not inquiry — a liturgy recited by children too young to notice the doctrine inside the data. Every storm, every drought, every anomaly, no matter how ordinary, was held up as proof of apocalypse. And **when warming didn't hold**, they perfected the pivot — *climate change.* A doctrine elastic enough to explain everything and accountable for nothing. Flood? Climate change. Drought? Climate change. Wildfires? Climate change. Record cold? Also climate change. It became a theology dressed as science — unfalsifiable, unchallengeable, unending. A belief system that grew stronger the more it contradicted itself. The most powerful doctrines don't require proof; they require participation. And participation was mandatory. What I didn't under-stand then — what I see with brutal clarity now — is that the pattern was never weather. It was **obedience**. A psychological architecture built to corral entire populations into fear, then into compliance, then into **policy**. Climate was not the enemy. **Dissent was.**

I did not yet know about the lobbying networks, the conferences funded by governments that profited from the panic, the NGOs whose survival depended on the next headline. I didn't see the billion-dollar pipelines of grants, carbon credits, and treaties — the global machinery built on a single premise: if you control the story of the planet, you control the people who live on it.

Nature had been conscripted into a political narrative. Weather became warning; seasons became sermon; climate became catechism. And we, the public, became the congregation — expected to nod, pay, obey. The shock wasn't the fear. The shock was the *certainty* — the way grown adults repeated the lines with religious devotion, the way disagreement was treated as sin, the way a question sounded like heresy. Fear had turned into faith. And faith, misdirected, builds cages cleaner than any tyrant ever could. **How many times must we be saved before we notice the cage?**

Denmark and Norway - Two Faces of the Same Script

The oil crisis carved a destiny into Scandinavia. Norway walked away with oil rigs and sovereign wealth. Denmark was dressed in green robes and handed climate sermons. The legend still circulates—Foreign Minister Per Hækkerup drunk at the table when the North Sea oil line was drawn. Whether true or not, the symbolism is searing - Norway secured the fields, Denmark secured the crumbs. In Denmark, we used to joke about Norwegians as goat herders, a rustic people, not to be taken seriously. It was our quiet superiority complex. Shame on us. When the oil came, those "goat herders" built one of the most powerful sovereign wealth funds in history. They inserted themselves into global finance and, quietly, into the architecture of Western elites. Today that fund is everywhere—owning shares of corporations, land, and infrastructure across continents. The same country we mocked as provincial became banker to the world. And Denmark? We kept our sermons — and Greenland, the world's largest island. Every empire keeps a consolation prize.

I grew up in the Denmark that followed - told to be proud of being the green pioneer, the good student of EU and UN treaties. Schoolbooks praised our nation for leading the way in conservation. Politicians reminded us that sacrifice was proof of virtue. The bicycle became a symbol of identity. Energy austerity was repackaged as moral superiority. Meanwhile, Norway drilled and banked. Denmark rationed and preached.

As a child I didn't see the line in the North Sea. I only saw the line drawn between neighbors—one enriched, one constrained—both drafted into a script written far above them. Two neighbors. Two paths. Both locked into the same architecture. Once you see it, you cannot unsee it. First comes the engineered shock—oil shortages, ozone holes, ice ages, burning deserts. Each one framed as an existential crisis. Each one demanding instant obedience. Then comes the offered solution—centralized treaties, bans, and regulations, always wrapped in the language of survival. *"Act now,"* they say, "or the planet dies." Next comes the division of spoils—Norway with oil, corporations with patents, finance with carbon. The chosen few walk away with wealth and power, while the rest are told to sacrifice. And finally comes the mask—Denmark branded the "progressive green," Norway the "neutral banker," both feeding the same globalist machine. The image is virtue. The engine is control. This isn't science. This is strategy.

Today - The Green Reset

By the 2000s the game was no longer a rehearsal. It was mature. Every storm became evidence. Every flood an argument. Every wildfire a headline of proof. Finance stepped in to sanctify it. ESG scores. Net-zero pledges. "Sustainable" funds. Central banks and supranational bodies tying climate to money itself. When did bankers become bishops? Now, whole industries are outlawed. "Green" monopolies are subsidized. Citizens are told how to drive, how to eat, how to travel. And the cycle repeats: *fear, solution, profit, control.* I saw the roots of it in my childhood. Denmark rehearsed it long before the world copied it. The pattern was seeded in those silent Sundays, in the ozone lectures at school, in the maps that handed Norway oil and Denmark obedience.

The Pattern — How Control Always Arrives

Each climate treaty followed the same architecture: an invisible threat, an urgent deadline, a centralized solution, and a permanent transfer of power. The language evolved. The mechanism did not. This was never a sequence of independent scientific awakenings. It was a pattern — rehearsed, refined, and scaled.

1973 — The Oil Shock

Fear: The world is running out of fuel.

Response: Rationing, car-free Sundays, behavioral mandates, emergency controls.

Result: Proof of concept — fuel scarcity could discipline nations overnight.

The oil shock demonstrated something far more valuable than conservation: **compliance.** A distant conflict could collapse domestic life. Energy could be weaponized. Citizens could be trained to accept restriction as virtue. Once fuel could be rationed, behavior could be shaped. Dependence was no longer theoretical. It was operational.

1987 — The Montreal Protocol

Fear: The sky itself will burn the earth.

Response: Global bans, forced industrial resets, regulatory enforcement.

Result: Old patents expired, new monopolies emerged; regulation became a profit engine.

Invisible danger justified total compliance. Industry retooled under mandate. Chemical giants transitioned seamlessly to patented replacements. What was sold as planetary rescue became industrial consolidation. Regulation didn't stop production — it redirected it upward, toward those positioned to comply first and profit fastest.

1997 — The Kyoto Protocol

Fear: Global warming will drown coasts and starve nations.

Response: Carbon taxes, carbon credits, emissions trading.

Result: Air became a commodity; finance entered the climate economy.

Kyoto introduced the most important innovation of all: **emissions as tradable value.** Pollution was no longer a byproduct — it was a market. Financial institutions moved in immediately. Carbon exchanges emerged. Billions flowed through instruments detached from measurable environmental improvement but deeply attached to regulatory leverage.

2015 — The Paris Agreement

Fear: Climate apocalypse within decades.

Response: Net Zero pledges, binding targets, global coordination.

Result: Sovereignty traded for compliance.

Paris did not impose enforcement directly — it normalized obligation. Nations volunteered into permanent targets that outlived governments, elections, and dissent. Policy authority drifted upward and outward, away from voters and toward frameworks no citizen could revise. **Compliance became the price of legitimacy.**

2020s — The ESG / Net Zero Reset

Fear: The world will end if you refuse.

Response: Banks, corporations, and insurers enforcing climate policy directly.

Result: Unelected finance became regulator of daily life.

This was the final maturation. No treaties were needed. Capital itself became the enforcement arm. Credit access, insurance, employment, and energy were conditioned on alignment. The market replaced the state as disciplinarian — quieter, faster, unappealable. Obedience was no longer legislated. It was scored.

They told us it was science. The receipts show a repeating scaffold: **fear declared, power centralized, profit extracted, obedience normalized.**

Not evolution. Repetition.

Where the Script Lands — America's Reckoning

What began as conferences and protocols now lives in American homes. Not as theory — as consequence. The treaty language written in distant halls shows up as higher fuel prices in Texas, shuttered plants in Ohio, denied loans for farmers in Iowa, and trucks priced off the road by mandates no voter approved. Rules drafted overseas now reach into the American wallet, the American field, the American factory floor. This is what "global cooperation" looks like on the ground: permission slips for energy, compliance tests for capital, and moral scoring disguised as policy. America was not meant to function this way. A republic cannot survive when its citizens are governed by targets they never debated, enforced by institutions they cannot remove. When bankers replace legislators, when ESG replaces law, when carbon scores decide who may build, borrow, or drive — sovereignty has already been surrendered. Not with tanks, but with paperwork. Not by invasion, but by agreement.

Denmark learned obedience early. America was meant to learn resistance. That is why this script matters here. Because once fuel can be rationed, food follows. Once production is throttled, dependence grows. Once behavior is scored, dissent becomes expensive. The Climate Playbook does not end with emissions — it ends with management. Of movement. Of labor. Of family life itself. This is the line. Not left versus right. Not science versus denial. But **self-government versus administered life.** A nation that cannot decide how it powers itself, feeds itself, or moves its people is not sovereign — it is supervised. The question is no longer whether the script exists. It is whether America will continue reading it — or finally refuse the role.

American Countermove — Withdrawal from the Climate Regime

Under President Donald Trump, the United States formally exited the **Paris Climate Agreement** twice — first in 2020 and again after returning to office in 2025 — signaling a deliberate rejection of binding international climate commitments. The withdrawal removed U.S. participation from emission-reduction targets negotiated under the United Nations framework and halted future compliance obligations. Domestically, the administration reversed or paused multiple federal climate regulations tied to emissions standards, energy production, and financial enforcement mechanisms. Biden-era climate mandates affecting power generation, vehicle standards, and ESG-driven financial rules were rolled back or defunded. Federal agencies were directed to prioritize domestic energy production over Net Zero alignment. Internationally, the U.S. also withdrew from participation in global climate finance mechanisms, including loss-and-damage funding structures designed to redistribute capital based on climate impact claims. This effectively severed the financial enforcement arm of climate compliance that operates through banks, insurers, and international institutions. These actions did not dismantle the climate architecture — but they interrupted America's automatic submission to it. For the first time in decades, the United States stepped outside the treaty-based climate regime rather than refining it from within. The withdrawal did not end the system — but it proved it could be refused.

"You trample on the poor and force him to give you grain; you have built houses of hewn stone, but you shall not dwell in them... For I know your many transgressions and your mighty sins— you afflict the just, you take a bribe, and you turn aside the poor in the gate." — Amos 5:11–12

The Human Cost — The Everyday Impact

While the technocrats traded graphs, ordinary people paid the bill. Families watched grocery prices climb — not as accident, but as instruction — while elites signed pledges in Paris. Farmers were told to cull herds in the name of carbon. Parents chose between heating the house or filling the tank. Small towns once fueled by steel and coal were stripped of jobs and called sinners for it. Truckers, welders, ranchers — the men who fed and built the world — were told they were the problem. The irony burned hotter than any pipeline. The same leaders who flew private jets to climate summits lectured the people who drive pickup trucks to work. Green policy was not shared sacrifice; it was selective punishment. The rich bought indulgences. The poor paid taxes. In the Midwest, farmers have already been denied loans not for poor yields, but for poor ESG scores—soil audited by spreadsheet, livestock treated as liability. Credit dries up — not because the land fails, but because the model does. Climate policy does not eliminate consumption—it redistributes it upward, where penalties are optional and indulgences are deductible.

The Moment of Withdrawal

When America withdrew from the Paris Agreement, something rare happened — the gears slowed. For a moment, the system lost leverage. Bureaucrats raged. Headlines warned of doom. But ordinary people felt relief. Energy costs stabilized. Industries long punished by regulation began to breathe again. The carbon market — that invisible tax on the worker — loosened its grip. What the elite called "isolation," working families called oxygen. When a nation steps back from global pledges, it steps closer to sovereignty. Every treaty signed in secret halls binds the laborer's hand at home. Every withdrawal restores a little freedom to the farmer, the welder, the driver trying to fill his tank without guilt. The climate clerics called it heresy. The remnant called it harvest. That is how empires end — not when the towers fall, but when the people finally realize who paid for them.

"Behold, the wages of the laborers who mowed your fields, which you kept back by fraud, cry out; and the cries of the harvesters have reached the ears of the Lord of hosts." — James 5:4

America was never meant to run on this kind of faith. But the same script now plays in Washington — subsidies dressed as salvation, treaties signed without votes, children catechized in carbon guilt. The stage is no longer Denmark's. It's ours. And the sermon has come home. The door to what — management or mercy? Control or covenant?

◔ Firelight Pause — Investigate Your Chains

- When did I first believe the sky, the fuel, or the food itself would vanish unless I obeyed?
- What "apocalypses" have I internalized — cooling, warming, change — and who profited from the fear?
- Which treaties signed in distant halls now reach into my wallet, field, or home?
- Do I know the true cost of "green" — the child miner's hands, the turbine graveyards, the brittle grids?
- Do my children learn to plant and pray — or to eat crickets and obey?
- When fear sells itself as virtue, will I still remember what freedom sounds like?

The receipts are on the table. Oil shocks, ozone panics, warming and cooling, treaties and taxes — all rehearsals, all scaffolding. But climate was never the endgame. Once you can ration fuel, you can ration food. Once you can price air, you can price thought. Climate was never the finish line. It was the door.

Choose your door.

48

THE WIDER CHAINS
MAPPING THE CAGE

The chains grew quietly. They did not rattle in the night; they hummed in the circuits, the screens, the treaties, the apps. Freedom was not stolen — it was traded, one convenience at a time. A meter for the wall. A passport for the phone. A promise for your privacy. The serpent learned that tyranny wears a smile best when it calls itself "progress." Now, the architecture stands complete — a lattice of law and code, built across nations. *The Wider Chains.* These are not theories. These are field notes — receipts of tyranny rehearsed in Copenhagen, exported to Brussels, translated into Silicon Valley code, resisted in Austin, and now pressing at America's throat. Every chain makes you dependent. Every chain hands power upward. Every chain breaks covenant. I will show you the fang of the serpent — the false promise, then the violation. And now we take two states that stand as opposites in their treatment of freedom and sovereignty. Texas isn't perfect. But freedom roars here. California has adapted to EU and UN code. Do not only compare these two states. Look at your own state. Where does it bend to Brussels, to Silicon Valley, to Washington decrees? Where does it still defend soil, family, and speech? Take notes. Know your ground. This battle is not abstract — it begins with the laws, councils, and policies where you live.

Energy — Smart Meters and Stoves

The Fang. They promise stewardship — smart meters to save energy, cleaner stoves for a greener world. A glossy screen for efficiency, a shinier kitchen for progress.

The Violation. In practice, the smart meter is a spy in the wall — recording when you are home, what you use, and built to enforce quotas. Where policy ties to the grid, the meter ceases to be a tool and becomes a ticket. Remote throttling replaces choice. A flame that once symbolized home becomes a privilege measured by regulators.

The Response. *California* bans gas stoves in new construction, mandates smart meters, and ties homes into statewide green quotas. *Texas*, by contrast, passed laws defending natural gas access, prohibiting city-level bans, and limiting appliance mandates. Two futures: one of control, one of resistance.

The Remnant's Task. Defend the fire. Keep gas legal where it keeps homes free. Insist on local control and the right to opt out. Resist surveillance and remote throttling sold as "efficiency."

Digital ID — The Key That Can Delete You

The Fang. They promise safety and simplicity — one login to rule convenience. Digital ID will make life "frictionless."

The Violation. In truth, a national eID is a single key binding money, travel, health, and speech to permissions. When civic life hinges on an app, one policy shift can erase liberties you thought permanent.

The Response. *California* already pilots digital IDs — driver's licenses in Apple Wallet, TSA acceptance, and agency services tied to apps. *Texas*, by contrast, is only drafting bills like SB 215. One state lives it; the other prepares it.

The Remnant's Task. Refuse mandatory digital IDs. Defend cash and paper identity. Build parallel systems that do not depend on centralized apps.

Speech and Censorship — When Truth Becomes Illegal

The Fang. They say censorship protects the vulnerable from "hate." Platforms promise safety; regulators promise harmony.

The Violation. When states or corporations decide which words may live, truth itself becomes contraband. Delegated censorship lets governments dodge accountability while platforms erase voices at will. A banned post is not just silenced speech — it is outlawed thought.

The Receipts. In 2025, Texas Attorney General Ken Paxton sued and won a $1.375 billion settlement against Google for unlawfully collecting Texans' private data — location, biometrics, even "incognito" searches — all without consent. The case exposed how deep the surveillance goes, and how easily speech, identity, and privacy are monetized by the same machine. This was not theory. It was evidence of empire in code.

The Response. *California* embraces speech control — backing hate-speech legislation, platform obligations under EU-style rules, and deplatforming defended as "safety." *Texas* pushes the other way — passing laws to block censorship by Big Tech and defending citizens' right to speak freely online. One state codifies silence; the other codifies speech.

The Covenant. The First Amendment is not a suggestion. It is law.

When government or corporations decide which truths may be spoken, they do not "protect" the public — they **violate the Constitution.** Every speech law dressed in moral language is still a muzzle. Every platform that enforces government orders is an arm of the State. Free speech is not a privilege granted by tech companies; it is a covenant bought in blood.

The Remnant's Task. Speak while you can. Build alternative presses, platforms, and networks. Refuse monopolies over conversation. Guard free speech as covenant — for once the tongue is shackled, the chains on the body soon follow.

Financial Chains — Credit, CBDCs & Debt

The Fang. They sell efficiency and virtue: ESG investing, programmable digital money, and credit expansion promise inclusion and progress.

The Violation. In reality these are complementary levers of control. ESG and politicized credit metrics gate capital and insurance. CBDCs encode obedience into money — expiring balances, blocked categories of spending, instant freezes. Rising public and private debt ties households and states to creditors who demand policy strings. Together they turn finance into a power stack that can punish regions, industries, and persons in real time.

The Response. *California* leans into the rails: ESG disclosures, fintech pilots, wallet programs, and expansions of public credit. *Texas* takes resistance seriously — moving to protect cash, pass laws against CBDC deployment, restrict ESG in public funds, and shore up state reserves. Two financial maps: one binds capital to orthodoxy, the other fights for hard assets and plural payment rails.

The Remnant's Task. Use cash. Build tangible reserves. Shift capital to local banks, credit unions, and non-ESG funds. Create alternative lending pools and community finance that cannot be frozen by code or politics.

Borders and Sovereignty — Nations Dissolved

The Fang. They recast migration as pure compassion and policy as borderlessness.

The Violation. When migration is wielded as demographic engineering and borders are hollowed, sovereignty dies. No border, no nation.

The Response. *Texas* reinforces the line with Operation Lone Star, razor wire, and state-led enforcement when federal agencies hesitate. *California* declares sanctuary, funds legal aid for illegals, and passes laws shielding them from deportation. Two maps, two models: one defends soil, the other dissolves it.

The Remnant's Task. Stand with local guardians. Reinforce the covenant of soil with men, law, and institutions willing to defend it.

Health Emergencies — Empire's Password

The Fang. Emergencies are sold as moral duty. Urgency became virtue, and law bent under the weight of "saving lives."

The Violation. An "emergency" swallows restraint. Businesses closed. Travel banned. Breath itself regulated. What should be temporary became permanent architecture. "Emergency" turned into the master password of empire.

The Response. *California* extended health powers deep into daily life — mandates, passports, and sweeping authority for bureaucrats. *Texas* pushed back — banning vaccine mandates, restricting mask requirements, and sunsetting emergency orders. Two states, two signals: one normalizes permanent emergency, the other insists on limits.

The Remnant's Task. Reject endless emergencies. Guard medical freedom as covenant. Demand that powers sunset, restore accountability to law, and keep the individual — not the bureaucrat — sovereign.

Food & Water — Soil as Covenant

The Fang. They sell "sustainable food" and global efficiency; they sell insect protein as humility and alternative proteins as salvation.

The Violation. But policy and capital concentrate land and water, impose quotas, tax livestock, and penalize traditional producers. Farmers are squeezed by carbon and ESG rules; schools pilot insect protein while elites feast elsewhere. When the field and well are controlled, a people's independence is finished.

The Response. *California* moves toward centralized controls: climate-driven farming mandates, water rationing, alternative-protein pilots, and consolidation pressures. *Texas* moves to shield ranchers and local water boards, defend traditional agriculture, and push back against quota regimes. Two futures — food as commodity rationed by score, or food as covenant preserved by local hands.

The Remnant's Task. Buy from and back farmers. Defend water rights. Plant gardens, preserve seeds, support ranchers, and treat soil and the table as covenant, not carbon metrics.

Surveillance & AI — Eyes of the System

The Fang. They promise safety and convenience: cameras to deter crime, AI to speed response, and "smart" grids and cities to make life seamless.

The Violation.

In practice, the city becomes a panopticon and the machine a judge. Cameras, license-plate readers, drones, sensors, and smart meters feed algorithms that track faces, cars, movement, habits, purchases, and conversations. Code predicts and preempts dissent. Algorithms decide visibility, hiring, credit — even who is "safe." Data is harvested, sold, and archived until daily life itself becomes evidence in a ledger.

Texas law forbids capturing a person's retina scan, voice-print, or face geometry for commercial use without consent. Yet enforcement only began when the state sued tech giants for violations. *California*, by contrast, races forward — drafting laws that force every police report generated by AI to carry an audit trail, requiring disclosure of machine-written drafts, and banning vendors from reselling law-enforcement data. Regulation grows, but the net tightens. **The message to you:** Being "connected" means being scored. Being "smart" means being seen. The eye is not blind. The tracker is not neutral.

The Response. *California* accelerates both hardware and software: city sensor pilots, predictive policing, drone and plate-reader programs, widespread AI in services and law enforcement, and experimental digital-ID and smart-meter rollouts. *Texas* pushes back — banning certain biometric systems, restricting foreign-made drones for state use, and insisting on human oversight and audit rights for algorithms. One state builds the panopticon; the other tries to wall it off.

The Remnant's Task. Guard privacy as sovereignty. Insist on human governance over machines. Demand transparency, audit rights, and limits on predictive policing. Design cities that serve people, not ledgers.

Gender and Privacy — Erasing Male and Female

The Fang. They preach inclusion through fluid identity policies.

The Violation. When law erases clear biological categories, women's safety and sex-based protections collapse. A society that cannot define male and female cannot defend truth.

The Response. *California* codified self-ID in schools and prisons, letting men who declare "female" enter women's spaces, sports, and shelters — even when safety is at stake. *Texas* has drawn a line, advancing laws that define male and female by biology and restricting gender ideology in classrooms and sports. Two models. Two futures.

The Remnant's Task. Defend women's spaces. Teach children biological truth. Refuse policies that sacrifice safety and reality for ideology.

Family and Fertility — Chains on the Womb

The Fang. They frame family planning as climate mitigation and population management.

The Violation. Messaging that treats fertility as pollution and subsidizes sterilization or childlessness is population engineering in softer clothes. A nation without children is already conquered.

The Response. *California* pushes tax dollars into abortion access, even funding out-of-state travel, and teaches climate guilt around family size. *Texas* has moved the other way, restricting abortion, supporting childbirth, and experimenting with pro-family incentives. Two opposite visions: one erodes legacy, the other seeks to preserve it.

The Remnant's Task. Cherish children as covenant. Defend mothers and fathers. Treat family-building as resistance against a system that profits from collapse.

Weed & Sedation — Drugs for Chains

The Fang. They sell legal highs as liberation, wellness, and therapy — "freedom" in a gummy.

The Violation. A drugged populace is docile. Sedation is governance by distraction. Legalizing and normalizing mass intoxication softens resistance, dulls vision, and replaces courage with apathy. Chains feel lighter when you're too numb to lift them.

The Response. *California* leads the sedation economy — recreational cannabis legalized, psychedelics decriminalized in cities like San Francisco, and an industry wrapped in wellness branding. *Texas* resists: cannabis remains largely illegal, with narrow medical exceptions, and cultural emphasis still leans toward sobriety and accountability. One state normalizes sedation as lifestyle; the other frames restraint as strength.

The Remnant's Task. Teach sobriety as strength. Build households and communities on clarity, not chemicals. Foster institutions that train stamina, virtue, and the fire to resist.

Screens, Porn & Dopamine Sedation

The Fang. Entertainment is packaged as harmless leisure, distraction sold as freedom.

The Violation. Endless feeds, pornography, and dopamine loops are chemical warfare on willpower and virtue. A people glued to screens cannot build, cannot fight, cannot rise. Sedation becomes self-chosen slavery.

The Response. *California* resists meaningful guardrails — striking down age-verification laws for pornography as unconstitutional and embracing tech lobbies that profit from endless scrolling. *Texas* takes the opposite path — passing laws requiring age-verification for explicit sites, pushing digital-safety frameworks for children, and advancing parental control rights. One state normalizes addiction; the other draws lines to defend the young.

The Remnant's Task. Break the screen before it breaks you. Teach planting, fighting, and prayer. Guard eyes and time as sacred, not for sale.

Faith Under Siege

The Fang. Faith is pushed into private corners, dismissed as personal preference while public life is remade under other seals.

The Violation. When the State claims spiritual authority — elevating idols like carbon, equity, or identity — the soul is orphaned. Citizens bow to bureaucratic priesthoods instead of God. Crosses are stripped from schools, prayer is punished on fields, and policy scripts are treated as sacred texts.

The Response. *California* advances the suppression — defending DEI orthodoxy in schools, penalizing dissent on gender ideology, and shrinking religious exemptions in health and education. *Texas* defends the covenant — passing laws to protect prayer in schools, conscience rights for medical staff, and space for worship in civic life. One state replaces God with idols of progress; the other fights to guard His name in law and culture.

The Remnant's Task. Keep the covenant fire alive in homes and churches. Refuse substitutes. Stand firm that no State can take the place of God.

The Architects of the Cage

Do not imagine the cage built itself. It was drafted in Brussels, scripted in Geneva, paraded in Davos, coded in Silicon Valley, and rehearsed in Copenhagen.

The EU frames quotas. The UN crowns "rights" that become strings. The WEF brands programs as "sustainable." Danish bureaucrats pilot plans. NGOs fund models. Big Tech enforces the code. These institutions are not neutral. They are priests of a new order — baptizing citizens into compliance while erasing covenant. Their vision is not liberty; it is management. **They see consumers, not citizens. Files, not builders.**

The Covenant Under Siege — Where Freedom Is Breached

First Amendment — Voice and Faith

Under Siege: Laws, platforms, and schools that decide which truths may speak.

Guard It: Make sure your state protects prayer, conscience, and free speech — without permission from tech or bureaucrats.

Second Amendment — Arms and Autonomy

Under Siege: Surveillance and registries that map citizens instead of defending them.

Guard It: Make sure ownership stays private, not logged in databases or scored by code.

Fourth Amendment — Privacy and Property

Under Siege: Smart meters, license readers, mass data collection — a search without a warrant.

Guard It: Make sure your laws demand consent, warrants, and penalties for spying without cause.

Fifth & Fourteenth — Due Process and Equality

Under Siege: Algorithms that judge without appeal; digital verdicts without faces.

Guard It: Make sure every automated decision in your state has human oversight and a right to challenge.

Tenth Amendment — Sovereignty of the States

Under Siege: Federal and foreign "standards" imported through grants and contracts.

Guard It: Make sure your legislature approves — not bureaucrats — before any outside code becomes local law.

Property, Contract & Commerce — The Land and the Ledger

Under Siege: ESG, quotas, and financial scoring that punish belief and local control.

Guard It: Make sure state law bans financial discrimination and protects water, land, and trade from global hands.

Ninth Amendment — Human Dignity & Natural Rights

Under Siege: Systems that treat people as data to be managed, not souls to be free.

Guard It: Make sure your leaders remember: rights come from God, not government.

Freedom doesn't vanish all at once. It leaks — rule by rule, grant by grant, click by click. Patch every leak where you live. The cage is a lattice of IDs, ledgers, grids, and screens. Break one link and another forms. Every Amendment bleeds from neglect before it breaks by force. The siege is silent — coded in law, encrypted in convenience. To guard the covenant, you must know where it's already breached. The Constitution is not parchment; it is perimeter. Hold it.

🔥 **Firelight Pause — Investigate Your Chains**

- Which state do you live in — the cage, or the firewall?
- Do your children learn to plant and pray, or to eat crickets and obey?
- Will you trade covenant for comfort, or defend the soil with fire?
- Has your state banned CBDCs, or stayed silent while pilots quietly proceed?
- Who is purchasing farmland near you, and where are the water rights flowing?

"Where the Spirit of the Lord is, there is freedom." — 2 Corinthians 3:17

49

THE MARKETPLACE OF BABYLON
THE ECONOMY OF ENSLAVEMENT

T*he merchants of the earth grew rich from her excessive luxuries."* — Revelation 18:3

The cult found its creed; now it seeks its commerce.

The Golden Web

Every empire has its marketplace. Babylon's is not made of stalls and spices but of *servers and stock indices*. Here, everything is for sale — from land to language, from seed to soul. The serpent's kingdom does not conquer by sword; it conquers by sale. It does not burn cities; it buys them. It does not enslave men with chains; it enslaves them with contracts. *This is the new commerce — control through convenience.* Every transaction logged, every purchase profiled, every human turned into a line item on a digital ledger.

The Merchants of the System

Once it was kings and caravans. Now it is CEOs and central banks. The merchants of Babylon wear tailored suits, not crowns. They meet in Davos, in New York, in Geneva, in quiet rooms above the noise of nations. The goods they sell are invisible — *data, debt, and dependency.* Your habits, your hunger, your hopes — all priced, packaged, and sold. They speak of innovation, but their aim is ownership — not of products, but of people. They smile as they tighten the grip. They call it "financial inclusion." They mean "digital control." If money can now measure morality, who decides what virtue costs?

The Currency of Chains

Money was once a tool. Now it is a tether. When cash dies, consent dies with it. Will I still give if every gift must first be approved? Central Bank Digital Currencies promise efficiency — instant payment, instant tracking, instant obedience. Programmable money is the perfect leash: it knows where it's spent, when, and by whom. If your behavior displeases the system, your funds freeze before your protest does. This is the serpent's dream — morality outsourced to machines. No law needed, no trial required. Algorithmic justice in real time. When your wallet reports you, the state no longer needs to.

The Trade in Flesh and Data

Babylon's merchants once trafficked bodies; now they traffic behavior. The modern slave trade is not on ships; it's on screens. Every like, swipe, and scan feeds the same market — human experience harvested for profit and prediction. They sell your attention by the second, your emotion by the click, your privacy by the byte. *The product is not the app — the product is you.* This is not capitalism. It is cannibalism disguised as commerce. When the market feeds on men, who still calls it progress? And the altar still smokes — the sacrifices are souls. At its core, Babylon is not an economy but a theology — the worship of profit over providence, of currency over covenant.

The False Promise of Global Prosperity

At its core, Babylon is not an economy but a theology — the worship of profit over providence, of currency over covenant. They preach inclusion, equality, and prosperity for all. But the metrics reveal the lie. For every billionaire born in this system, a million families sink deeper into debt. For every megacity that glows, a countryside is stripped of roots. For every algorithm that predicts health, another predicts obedience. *The serpent's economy has no middle class — only masters and managed.* It is feudalism with better branding, slavery with stock options. They call it "the Great Reset." But what resets is not the system — it's the soul.

The Collapse of the Sacred

Once trade followed trust, and trust followed truth. Now trade follows deceit, and deceit follows data. The covenant of exchange — once sealed with honesty — has been replaced by **terms and conditions no one reads.** The handshake gave way to the checkbox. Faith gave way to fraud. *When contracts replace conscience, the market becomes a god — and man its offering.* This is why prophets once cried out in the gates of cities. Because when commerce turns sacred, the soul turns cheap.

The Ledger in Your Pocket

You feel it every payday. The card, the app, the automatic draft. The hours you sweated become numbers on a screen you don't control. The same banks that mock your beliefs decide if your card still works. The same store that raised its prices last week tells you how to live this one. This is how Babylon hides in plain sight — not in temples, but in terminals.

The American Stronghold

But not all is lost. America's covenant still carries a remnant of economic freedom. *True capitalism — when tethered to conscience — is creation, not control.* The founders knew it — that enterprise without virtue becomes empire, and wealth without faith becomes weapon. Can a nation keep liberty if it no longer keeps its word? They built a nation where men could work, worship, and own what they built. That covenant is under siege — but it is not dead. Local trade, small farms, parallel economies, honest barter — these are not nostalgia; they are rebellion. Every independent craftsman, rancher, or coder who refuses the leash is a patriot priest in the temple of liberty.

The Worker's Wage

The man on the line, the nurse on night shift, the trucker on the road — they all feel the same squeeze. The harder they work, the faster the digits vanish. Their sweat feeds a system that thanks them with slogans, not security. Yet every hour still has weight; every calloused hand still holds the power to rebuild an honest economy — one job, one trade, one neighbor at a time.

The Remnant's Task — Build the True Market

Pay cash when you can. Trade skills with neighbors. Buy from men you know by name. Work with hands, not apps. Teach your children the price of effort, not the price of trends. *Every honest exchange rebuilds the covenant the empire forgot.*

The Fall of Babylon

Every market built on lies collapses. Every empire that prices the soul will one day be bankrupted by truth. Babylon will not fall by boycotts or tariffs; it will fall when her own merchants mourn her emptiness. When the screens go dark, and the algorithms choke on their own deceit, the world will remember what can never be bought — *honor, faith, and freedom.*

Every empire ends the same way — when its merchants finally realize they've sold their souls. Then the words will ring again:

"Come out of her, my people, so that you will not share in her sins." — Revelation 18:4

🔥 **Firelight Pause — The True Economy**
  • Who profits when I comply?
  • What part of my life have I leased to convenience?
  • Do I still own my time — or does my screen?
  • Do I spend to live, or live to spend?
  • If Babylon's markets collapsed tomorrow, would I still know how to live free?
  • Do I buy in fear, or sow in faith?

Freedom is not a product; it is a practice. The remnant must learn again to trade with conscience, to buy with purpose, to sell without soul-loss. For the true marketplace is covenant — and its currency is trust.

"Come, buy wine and milk without money and without price." — *Isaiah 55:1*

The economy feeds the empire, but every empire eventually hungers for blood. What begins in trade always ends in tyranny. The merchants have done their part; now the overseers take the stage. The market was never neutral. It always chose sides. Those who design the system live above its consequences. Those who live under it pay the price. The economy drew the line — now comes the clash: **the Globalists vs the Folks.**

50

GLOBALISTS VS THE FOLK

THE PHILOSOPHY OF CONTROL VS COVENANT

Europe perfected kings; America abolished them. But now the kings return — crowned not in gold, but in governance. They rule not from thrones, but from forums. Not by decree, but by data. The same mouths that once cried, "No more kings!" now kneel before councils no citizen elected. They mock tyranny while worshiping bureaucracy. Do we despise kings but still crave their order? They call a president chosen by the people a dictator — yet kneel without question to unelected bodies in Brussels, Geneva, and New York. They fear the ballot, but trust the algorithm. They hate crowns of gold, but love crowns of policy. It would be comic if it weren't tragic — the people who sneer at monarchy now serve the digital throne.

Europe traded kings for commissions. America's elites call that progress, but it is only monarchy rebranded — the UN as court, the WEF as crown, socialism as the new scripture. They do not want freedom. They want to be ruled — so long as the chains feel polite and the rulers speak fluent compassion. The serpent's first weapon is not war — it is consensus. It conquers not with armies, but with agreement. When did I start mistaking agreement for truth?

Denmark was its perfect rehearsal. From consensus comes compliance; from compliance, control. What begins in words ends in laws. The serpent's philosophy always becomes its policy.

Denmark's Reflex — Consensus Perfected

Denmark has always bent to the first instinct. Kings, bishops, bureaucrats, Brussels technocrats — the faces change, but the reflex does not. Authority speaks, the people nod. Consensus becomes creed. Safety becomes idol. Obedience becomes price. That is why Denmark accepted the serpent's rehearsal so easily — order disguised as virtue, control disguised as compassion. When the EU dictated climate quotas, family farms complied. When the Prime Minister ordered the culling of 17 million mink — later ruled illegal — the people obeyed. When lockdowns came, they complied again. Masks. Mandates. Curfews. No fire in the streets, no protest in the squares. Consensus smoothed it all. Comfort bought silence. Bureaucracy bought compliance. Consensus became the warm blanket that smothered fire. But consensus carries a cost. It kills the warrior spirit, training the young to obey before they ever think. How many comforts have we confused with peace? It replaces courage with comfort, fire with formality. What looks like peace is only paralysis — a managed quiet that mistakes sedation for virtue. Denmark forgot that consensus without conviction is submission dressed in courtesy.

America's Inheritance — Covenant Remembered

America was born different. We were not ruled into existence — we revolted into existence. Farmers with muskets faced down an empire. At Lexington and Concord, the first shots of the Revolution were fired — ordinary men standing their ground against the might of Britain, proving freedom could be defended by citizens, not kings. Suspicion of power is not paranoia here; it is patriotism in its purest form. Have we taught our children to question authority — or to comply with it? From *"Don't Tread on Me"* to *"We the People,"* our instinct has never been consensus. It has been distrust —

a holy distrust that guards liberty from the serpent's whisper. That suspicion built checks and balances, local militias, and a culture where even ordinary parents rise up at school boards when elites overreach. Suspicion is not cynicism; it is the conscience of a free nation.

The Script Replayed — The Serpent Tests America

Denmark became the serpent's rehearsal stage — obedience bred into the culture, compliance sold as morality. But America's inheritance was rebellion and fire. What bent Denmark stiffens America. What was perfected there — silence through comfort, obedience through consensus — is now attempted here. The same playbook now unfolds on American soil. Globalists regulate. Bureaucrats command. Billionaires demand loyalty. But Americans bristle. They question. They refuse to nod politely while their sovereignty is stolen. When Fauci said, "Trust the science," millions answered, "Show the truth." When Davos declared, "You will own nothing," farmers and patriots bought seed and land. When governments issued mandates, millions said, "Not on my watch." When borders broke, ranchers and sheriffs held the line. When digital credits were proposed, the folk smelled the leash behind the promise. What Denmark nods to, America resists. And that resistance is what the serpent fears most. Because rebellion born of covenant still burns hotter than compliance born of comfort.

What Denmark Taught Me — The Price of Consensus

Consensus is not kindness. It is control. Comfort is not peace. It is sedation. A people who nod too long forget how to stand. Israel once begged Samuel for a king "like the nations" (1 Sam. 8:5). God warned them of conscription, seizure, and tithe — "you shall be his slaves." Still, they demanded a ruler. Denmark obeyed that pattern. America must never start it.

Paul warned: *"Do not be conformed to this world, but be transformed by the renewal of your mind."* — Romans 12:2.

This is not advice. It is a war command. The world will always press to mold you — through slogans, systems, and fear. Transformation is rebellion. Renewal burns lies and restores covenant sight.

"Test everything; hold fast what is good. Abstain from every form of evil." — 1 Thessalonians 5:21–22.

That is the warrior's discipline. Do not swallow words from pulpits of power. Test. Expose. Name. Hold fast to good — even when mocked for it. Abstain from evil — not just in deed, but in consent, in silence. For silence itself is evil's ally. We call out the serpent — but we do not cast off the souls caught in its coils. Many followed in fear, not malice. To them we offer not scorn, but a road back. That is covenant — it names the enemy yet opens the gate for the repentant. Consensus condemns; covenant redeems. That is the difference between empire and liberty. From Denmark's consensus to America's choice, the pattern repeats — the serpent never changes script, only setting.

The Serpent's Gospel — The Lie of Socialism

Every empire needs a creed. The serpent's creed is socialism — the promise of equality without liberty, compassion without truth. It flatters the poor while enriching the priesthood of planners. It offers heaven on earth, but only if you surrender freedom first. Socialism is not charity. It is control wrapped in empathy — the state crowned as savior. In Denmark, it came as safety. In Europe, as solidarity. In America, it wears the mask of "justice." But behind every version lies the same exchange: *your sovereignty for their security, your faith for their system.* It whispers that the individual is dangerous, that independence is greed, that family is privilege, that tradition is oppression. If the family is rebellion, will we still choose to lead one? And it feeds on guilt — guilt for strength, guilt for success, guilt for simply standing.

America's founders built this land on the opposite creed: liberty over comfort, self-responsibility over state provision, covenant over command. We were never meant to be managed — **we were meant to be free.**

The tragedy of socialism is not that it fails to share wealth — it succeeds in sharing poverty. It levels by lowering. It equalizes by erasing. It breeds dependency, then calls it virtue. And its final fruit is always the same: *silence, scarcity, surveillance.* Even now, its missionaries preach through media, academia, and policy — soft voices saying "We can fix it all, if you just give up a little more." That is not compassion. That is conquest in kind language. For the serpent knows — if you can convince a man that the cage is moral, he will never try to leave it. Liberalism once meant liberty; now it means license — freedom without faith, compassion without truth. That creed cannot live long in a land built by covenant men.

What America Must Remember — Covenant or Chain
Distrust is not division. It is defense. Fire is not reckless. It is survival. Freedom is not inherited; it is guarded — tooth and nail, oath by oath, generation by generation. Consensus is the serpent's chain. Covenant is the shield that breaks it. Even Reagan knew this:
"Freedom is never more than one generation away from extinction... It must be fought for, protected, and handed on."
He was right. Freedom is not inherited in the blood. It is carried in the will. If fathers stop fighting, sons will live as slaves. If mothers stop teaching, daughters will live as subjects. If we forget, we forfeit. Freedom is always one heartbeat from burial — unless you choose to breathe it alive. Will our heartbeats be ones that defends liberty — or forgets it?

For once freedom sleeps, the serpent writes its next law.

The Serpent's Next Move

If Denmark bows by consensus, America must stand by covenant. For the serpent is not finished. What was tested in silence abroad now marches in fire here. The coils tighten on our soil — in streets, schools, borders, ballots, even the barracks of our warriors. The serpent's first weapon was consensus. Its next is conquest — not by war, but by code. And that is where the next chapter begins — not with technology, but with alignment. Before the serpent governs by code, it must first unite crowns, councils, and capital. Control does not emerge from chaos; it is coordinated. What follows is the operating system of empire — the alliances, institutions, and agreements that make global control possible. The serpent thrives on silence; covenant begins with **no.**

🔥 **Firelight Pause — The Choice Before You**

• Where have I nodded to "consensus" instead of standing in truth?

• What comforts have I accepted that cost me conviction?

• Do I confuse obedience with peace?

• Who do I trust more: globalists with polished words, or my own God-given discernment?

• When "consensus" is used to silence debate, do I hear peace — or the serpent's hiss?

• If comfort demands my children's future, will I pay the price — or break the chain?

• When the choice comes, will I be ruled — or will I stand free?

• Have I mistaken civility for courage — or do I still remember how to say "no"?

And if you have nodded, if you have bowed, even then the Lamb does not turn you away. Repentance reopens the gate. Mercy still waits on the wall.

"Let the wicked forsake his way, and the unrighteous man his thoughts; let him return to the Lord, that He may have compassion on him, and to our God, for He will abundantly pardon." — Isaiah 55:7

51

THE GLOBALIST ALLIANCE
THE OPERATING SYSTEM OF EMPIRE

You have seen the fragments — policies that suffocate, slogans that invert, leaders that betray. But fragments confuse. The pattern is the point. The serpent's trail winds beneath every empire, every age, every lie — deliberate, ancient, global. It whispers through parliaments, treaties, boardrooms, and screens — always the same tongue, always the same goal. Once you see the pattern, you cannot unsee it. And once you see, neutrality dies — **you must choose a side.**

This is no conspiracy. It is coordination — written, signed, and televised for all with eyes to see. What America calls politics is only one franchise of a worldwide cartel — elites, bankers, bureaucrats, tech prophets, and unelected priests of progress. The faces change; the instinct does not: *manage, regulate, silence, rule.*

The Architecture of Coordination

Every empire eventually discovers the secret of control — you no longer need to conquer nations when you can synchronize them. The serpent's new empire runs not on territory, but on treaties. Its architecture is coordination itself — one body with many heads.

The **UN** drafts the moral script. The **IMF** and **World Bank** fund obedience through debt. The **WHO** enforces health decrees. The **EU** and **OECD** standardize governance and taxation. The **World Economic Forum** rehearses the public narrative each January, then delivers it to presidents, CEOs, and ministers who perform it by spring. **Silicon Valley** amplifies the chorus — translating decrees into algorithms, code, and censorship. Different agencies, one breath. Different flags, one rhythm. The serpent's brilliance is not domination, but synchronization. Bureaucrats, bankers, and billionaires now move as a single machine — the **Operating System of Empire.**

The Algorithm of Empire

The serpent's modern weapon is not the sword; it is the system. It does not occupy land; it occupies language. It governs by dashboard, not decree — policy by algorithm, morality by metric. What the Gestapo once enforced through fear, the technocrat now enforces through friction. He does not kick down doors; he disables accounts. He does not burn books; he hides them behind "content moderation." He does not jail dissenters; he erases them from the feed. This is the automation of tyranny — control at the speed of signal. In the globalist order, compliance is rewarded with convenience. Access replaces ownership. Obedience replaces merit. The algorithm remembers your loyalty score and quietly adjusts your access to life. You will not need chains. You will volunteer them — for comfort, for convenience, for calm.

The Prototype — Denmark and Beyond

The serpent always tests its systems in the small before scaling them to the great. Denmark became the perfect lab: obedient, efficient, polite. Its farmers complied with quotas. Its citizens trusted the state. Its ministers learned to trade sovereignty for influence — and were rewarded with seats in Brussels, Geneva, and New York. From there, the script spread: Digital IDs, carbon quotas, and "green transitions" dressed as salvation. Governance by memorandum — *agreements that feel local but bind global.* A governor in California signs an offshore wind pact with Copenhagen. A mayor in Texas adopts "sustainability metrics" written in Brussels. No vote. No consent. Just alignment. What began as a Danish reflex has become a planetary reflex — **obedience disguised as progress.**

The Velvet Cage

The serpent sells the cage as cure. Each policy is introduced as a kindness — *equity, safety, sustainability.* But the pattern is constant: every kindness comes with a condition. Every promise of peace requires a permission slip. The velvet cage is not built overnight. It is assembled piece by piece — through health mandates, digital currencies, and carbon credits. Each regulation claims to protect life while quietly managing it. Each treaty claims to empower nations while dissolving them. Each innovation claims to connect humanity while surveilling it. The serpent's language is flawless — moral, progressive, compassionate. But its grammar is always the same: *centralize, standardize, sanitize.* It does not destroy nations; it drains them — until sovereignty becomes ceremony and freedom becomes nostalgia. Yet even now, light pierces the cage. The remnant still resists. The covenant still breathes. For truth cannot be standardized, and the soul cannot be coded.

The Everyday Empire

The empire never announces itself as global when it reaches you. The cage doesn't look global when it reaches your street. It looks like a price hike, a permit, a new form at work. The rancher fills out climate-quota paperwork before he can ship beef. The trucker buys fuel priced by policies written in Brussels. The factory worker watches automation "targets" arrive from a UN sustainability pledge his union never voted for. The nurse loses her job to a health rule drafted by a council she never heard of. The carpenter, the farmer, the welder — all feel the same squeeze: rules without representation, costs without consent. The global plan always cashes out in local pain.

 Firelight Pause — See the Pattern

• Where have I accepted a slogan without testing its truth?

• What "best practice" in my workplace, school, or town echoes the serpent's tongue?

• Do I treat treaties and MOUs as distant politics — or as chains already coiled around me?

• Have I mistaken consensus for covenant, comfort for freedom, safety for sovereignty?

• When the same words repeat across nations, do I dismiss them as coincidence — or discern them as strategy?

• What system has replaced your spirit — and do you still have the courage to unplug?

• When obedience feels easy and rebellion feels costly, which do I call righteous?

"And no wonder, for even Satan disguises himself as an angel of light." — 2 Corinthians 11:14

They no longer hide the plan — they headline it. One system. One script. One synchronized will. Neutrality is no longer innocence. It is alignment.

52

———

THE FOUNDING REWRITTEN

WHEN STORY BECOMES STATE

History is the oldest weapon. Empires used to conquer with armies. Now they conquer with adjectives. Once you change the words a people use to describe themselves, you no longer need to invade their land — they will surrender it by teaching your vocabulary to their children.

In August 2019, four centuries after the first enslaved Africans arrived on the coast of Virginia, *The New York Times* released a document that would do what no foreign power ever could — alter the birth certificate of a nation. They called it **The 1619 Project**. It claimed that America did not begin in 1776 but in 1619 — the year a ship of captives arrived at Point Comfort. It recast the Revolution as fundamentally driven by the preservation of slavery rather than the pursuit of liberty. That every system — capitalism, law, even traffic — carried the DNA of oppression. It sounded like journalism. It was theology. A new creation myth built from guilt instead of grace. Within weeks, the essays became textbooks. Universities sanctified it as doctrine. Corporations quoted it in HR manuals. School boards recited its liturgy of *systemic, structural, reparative*. It did not pass through Congress. It passed through culture — faster, deeper, unquestioned.

And the people who carried the real work of the Republic — the linemen, welders, nurses, teachers, and soldiers — woke up to find their own story stolen. They had not changed. But the meaning of their labor had. The same flag they saluted was now read as accusation. The same history they built was now called hate. Historians protested. Veterans of the civil-rights era warned against a single-lens history. But protest is powerless once the new scripture is printed. The 1619 Project achieved what treaties and compacts only dream of — it rewrote America's origin inside her own mind. This was not a treaty of nations. It was a **narrative compact** — the domestic twin of Marrakesh and Paris. Where those documents re-defined borders and carbon, this one re-defined belonging. It shifted America's foundation from covenant to crime. *California* embraced it. State educators folded its language into curricula, calling it "decolonized learning." University grants and Hollywood scripts multiplied in its image. *Texas* rejected it — drafting laws to keep classrooms tethered to 1776 and the Declaration's moral architecture. Once again the line split across the continent — one coast aligning with ideology, one state holding the line of covenant and conscience.

The 1619 Project did not burn flags; *it re-captioned them.* It replaced gratitude with grievance, replacing "We the People" with "We the Accused." It turned classrooms into tribunals and children into witnesses against their ancestors. It preached that redemption is collective guilt — and guilt, the new patriotism. But under the weight of accusation, a remnant remembered. They read 1776 again, not as myth but as mission. They taught their sons and daughters that liberty was not whiteness or wealth but covenant — the agreement between God, conscience, and courage. And in that remembering, the counterfeit began to crack. 1619 was not the year America began. It was the year narrative replaced nation — when the serpent stopped erasing and started editing. **This shift did not happen through law. It happened through curriculum, training modules, and grant requirements.** 1619 was not the year America began. It was the year narrative replaced nation — when the serpent stopped erasing and started editing.

"You shall know the truth, and the truth shall make you free." — John 8:32

🔥 **Firelight Pause — The Founding Rewritten**

Every generation must decide which story to believe — the one written in sacrifice or the one edited for shame. Freedom begins in memory. Tyranny begins in revision. They can't chain a people who remember what they were made for.

Ask yourself:

- What stories have I accepted without testing the source?
- Who benefits when I despise the nation that protects me?
- If my children's textbooks were the only history left, would they still know freedom or only grievance?
- Do I recognize propaganda when it dresses itself as compassion?
- Am I teaching history, or am I repeating programming?

Every rewritten past writes a new future. Guard the archives of your heart as fiercely as you guard your land. Truth is the only founding that cannot be edited. Every rewritten past writes a new future. Guard the archives of your heart as fiercely as you guard your land.

June 19 — The Day Freedom Was Delayed *(and Then Rewritten)*

June 19, 1865 - *From Deliverance to Division*

The message of freedom crossed rivers, mountains, and battlefields before it reached Texas. On June 19, 1865, when General Granger's words finally echoed through Galveston, the nation's promise caught up with its faith. It was not new liberty, but liberty remembered — the covenant delayed, not denied. For generations, Juneteenth was a quiet feast of gratitude. Barbecue smoke, gospel hymns, prayer tents, elders telling stories of deliverance. No corporate logos. No curriculum battles. Just memory — raw and sacred.

Then came the editors. The same machinery that repackaged 1619 began to rewrite 1865. Juneteenth was lifted from the churchyard to the boardroom, from family tables to federal proclamations. It was called *the real Independence Day* — not the celebration of covenant fulfilled, but **the replacement of one founding with another.** Where the old Juneteenth thanked God, the new one thanks policy. Where it once united, it now divides — **weaponized by Marxist rhetoric that feeds on perpetual grievance.** The message changed — from *"Look what God has done"* to *"Look what America will never escape."* They turned deliverance into dependency — a ritual of reminder that the chains may have changed form but never fallen. It became another liturgy of guilt, written by the same priests of ideology who crafted the 1619 gospel. Both projects serve the same end — fracture memory, erase gratitude, and replace covenant with control. But the remnant still gathers — in fields, in small towns, under porch lights. They still pray thanks for a God who frees before governments follow. They know that freedom delayed is not freedom denied — unless we surrender it again by believing the lie that liberty was never real. The serpent cannot create new holy days. It can only corrupt the ones that worked. Marxism feeds on wounds; faith heals them.

The Hand Behind the Pen

This was never a grassroots reckoning. It was a strategic import. Europe has spent a century unmaking itself — trading nationhood for bureaucracy, covenant for consensus, kings for commissions. What it lost in faith, it replaced with management. What it lost in courage, it replaced with guilt. America's founding stood in the way of that project. A nation born in rebellion, grounded in God-given rights, allergic to permanent authority — could not be allowed to remain morally confident. So the attack did not come as invasion. It came as interpretation. The same elite networks that drafted post-national Europe — foundations, universities, NGOs, cultural arbiters — learned that America could not be conquered from the outside. It had to be **re-educated from within.** If you could not repeal 1776, you could reinterpret it. If you could not abolish the Declaration, you could accuse it. If you could not silence America's story, you could make it shameful to repeat.

The 1619 Project was not written for slaves long dead. It was written for children not yet born. It aligned perfectly with Europe's post-sovereign worldview: history as guilt, identity as liability, freedom as a dangerous myth. Where Brussels governs by regulation, this governed by narrative. Where treaties dissolve borders, this dissolved belonging. Same architecture. Different front. This is how empire now moves — not through flags, but through footnotes. Not through armies, but through educators. Not through law, but through legitimacy. Once a people are taught that their beginning was criminal, their resistance becomes immoral. Once their heroes are recast as villains, obedience feels like virtue. The cage no longer needs bars — only textbooks. This is not about race. It is about rule. And the moment America forgets who she was allowed to be, she becomes exactly what the global system needs her to be — *managed, compliant, apologetic, and ready for administration.*

"Where the Spirit of the Lord is, there is liberty." — 2 Corinthians 3:17

🔥 **Firelight Pause — The Day Freedom Was Delayed**
Ask yourself:

• Do I celebrate freedom as gift or grievance?

• When I honor history, am I remembering deliverance — or rehearsing division?

• Who profits when gratitude disappears from a nation's calendar?

• Can any people stay free if they are taught to despise the day freedom arrived?

The Red Line — The Long March Through Memory

How the Ideologues Captured Story and State

They said the revolution would begin in the streets. They were wrong. **It began in the classroom.** After the fall of the Soviet empire, the old Marxists didn't vanish; they mutated. They traded the hammer for the hashtag, the picket for the professorship. Italian theorist Antonio Gramsci had already mapped the route decades earlier: *"Capture the culture, and politics will follow."* In the 1960s, the German Frankfurt School —Marcuse, Adorno, Horkheimer—carried his torch into Western universities. **Their new weapon was critical theory** —not the study of truth, but the perpetual deconstruction of it. Out of that soil grew a thousand branches—*critical race, critical gender, critical climate*. Each one preached the same creed — all hierarchy is oppression, all tradition is suspect, all identity must be politicized. The target was never economics alone; it was *meaning itself*. When the Berlin Wall fell, the Red Line didn't die—it went underground into NGOs, foundations, and media. They discovered that you can dismantle a nation more efficiently with narrative than with armies. Rewrite the heroes, recode the holidays, rename the sins, and the republic forgets why it exists.

That is why **The 1619 Project** and the politicized version of **Juneteenth** arrived together. One *rewrote the birth,* the other *rewrote the deliverance.* Both replaced gratitude with grievance. Both turned repentance from a spiritual act into a political demand. And behind both stood the same machinery — *universities funded by global foundations, journalists trained in activist pedagogy, bureaucracies incentivized by "equity metrics."* The *Red Alliance* had learned to wear progressive language like a mask. Today its descendants fill HR departments, editorial boards, and grant offices. They quote Marx without ever naming him, using his ghost to shape school policy, urban planning, even corporate training. They call it *social justice*. It is still class war—just rewritten as compassion.

California exports this ideology through academia, entertainment, and tech. *Texas* becomes the control group—the place where families still teach history without apology. And between them runs the modern front line of **the Cold War reborn — the battle for memory**. The serpent no longer promises utopia through revolution. It promises safety through surrender. It whispers that equality can be engineered, that history can be corrected, that language can be purified. But every purification ends in fire. The battle for memory is not fought in faculty lounges alone. It's in the break room, the school board, the town paper, the dinner table — where ordinary Americans still dare to tell the truth about who they are and what they've built.

"See to it that no one takes you captive through philosophy and empty deceit."
— Colossians 2:8

🔥 **Firelight Pause — The Red Line**
Ask yourself:
• What ideas in my mind were not planted by experience but by curriculum?

• Do I measure justice by outcome or by truth?

• Who taught me that freedom and fairness are opposites?

• What part of my story have I surrendered because someone called it privilege?

• Which institutions still teach gratitude instead of grievance?

• Have I defended my ancestors—or apologized for them to gain acceptance?

• When did celebration become suspicion — and who taught me to call that virtue?

• Do I guard memory as fiercely as freedom — or have I forgotten they are the same?

The new revolution does not storm palaces—it rewrites textbooks. Guard the page before they guard your mind.

53

AMERICA IN THE CROSSHAIRS
CHAOS AND CAPTURE

When consensus fails, the serpent unleashes chaos. When order cannot seduce a people, disorder will. Denmark was the rehearsal. America is the target. Every chain tested abroad now slithers onto this soil. The serpent knows — America is the firewall. If this land falls, no land resists. When consensus can no longer bind, confusion divides. That is the serpent's next tactic — noise as weapon, division as theater, fatigue as surrender.

The Strategy of Confusion

Every empire learns the same truth: a people divided cannot defend themselves. So the serpent engineers confusion — ideological, racial, economic, spiritual. He floods the land with noise until truth sounds like extremism and lies sound like compassion. When truth feels like extremism, has the lie already won? The serpent does not crave peace; it craves exhaustion. For when a people grow weary of confusion, they will beg to be ruled. The serpent's war is not only fought on streets — it is waged in minds. Confusion is its anesthesia, fatigue its artillery. When thought itself becomes suspect, tyranny needs no tanks.

We Have Seen This Before

History does not repeat — it rehearses. When Germany fell to chaos between wars, the serpent spoke the same language. He promised order through obedience, safety through surrender. The people, weary from inflation and division, accepted chains wrapped in flags. Neighbors were turned into informants, teachers into propagandists, doctors into executioners. The press became a pulpit for the state. Churches split between those who bowed and those who burned. Even art and architecture were conscripted into worship of the regime — beauty became obedience. By the time the serpent's mask slipped, the machinery was already built. The lesson was not Germany's alone — it was humanity's: When fear replaces faith, and confusion is weaponized, the cry for order always summons tyranny.

And today, the same trick is dressed in softer words — equity, sustainability, health, safety. No swastikas. No rallies. Just spreadsheets, slogans, and screens. The serpent learned that modern tyrannies need no boots — only bureaucrats. No smoke-filled chambers — just policy rooms and panels with "stakeholders." The pattern is unchanged: exhaustion first, control next. But covenant is not so easily erased. Even in confusion, truth has a pulse. Every lie must borrow its breath from truth — and that breath still lives in the remnant. The serpent learned from history's blood — what it once enforced with armies, it now enacts with algorithms.

The Infiltration — Everyday Capture

The serpent does not live in palaces; it lives in paperwork, platforms, and policies. It has entered every American home, though few recognize its hiss. For the worker, the trap looks ordinary. It's the union contract rewritten by ESG metrics. The trucker fined by digital tolls he never voted for. The lineman required to log carbon output before he climbs the pole. The factory foreman told to file diversity reports before fixing machines. Ordinary men and women doing real work now carry the weight of policies written by people who've never used a wrench.

In the schools, the curriculum is rewritten to replace truth with tolerance, faith with fragility. Children are taught the planet is dying, that gender is a spectrum, that patriotism is dangerous, and that guilt is virtue. Textbooks praise the UN before the Constitution, climate pledges before courage. *Obedience is graded higher than discernment.*

In the economy, the serpent prints compassion into inflation. Small businesses are crushed by regulations that global corporations wrote. Farmers face quotas written in Brussels but disguised as "sustainability." A rancher who refuses digital compliance risks losing his market. A mother who questions a medical mandate loses her job. The serpent starves independence, then calls it equity.

In the public square, speech itself is scored. Truth flagged as "misinformation." Questioning authority labeled "hate." Ordinary Americans — nurses, soldiers, teachers — are punished for refusing to lie. The serpent hides behind "safety" labels — but every label means silence.

In medicine, the oath was rewritten. Health became obedience. From Denmark's digital passes to America's mandates, the pattern repeats: Those who questioned the cure were treated as the disease. Hospitals became gatekeepers for compliance; pharmaceutical giants became prophets of salvation. Compassion was rationed by QR code.

In faith, churches fractured — pulpits traded gospel for governance, prayer for policy. Pastors repeated government lines and called it wisdom. Those who refused were fined, mocked, or erased from platforms that claim to defend "community." The serpent loves polite pulpits and terrified prophets.

In family life, screens replaced fathers, algorithms replaced elders, and artificial "community" replaced covenant. The serpent learned that if you can confuse the home, you can conquer the nation. America's strength was never in its cities or armies — it was in its families. That is why the attack began there.

And so the modern citizen lives half-awake — scrolling, anxious, ashamed for simply existing in the wrong century. He no longer trusts his neighbor, his church, his flag, or even his own memory. That is the serpent's true conquest — not territory, but perception.

The Script Unfolds

Protests ignite in the streets — Antifa in black, BLM with banners, pro-Palestinian mobs chanting for Hamas on university lawns. Rage is organized. Outrage is imported. The serpent does not destroy order outright; it manufactures disorder to demand stronger chains. Every empire rots the same way — not from defeat, but from indulgence. The serpent waits for softness, then moves in. It does not strike the strong; it sedates them first. Debt balloons until every generation is mortgaged. The welfare state numbs. The surveillance state watches. Screens preach the serpent's catechism — safety, inclusion, progress. Elections wobble under shadow — mail-in ballots, machines, narratives pre-written before votes are cast. Dissent is labeled conspiracy. Questions punished as extremism. Even the military is tested — warriors trained for battle forced into ideology seminars, loyalty rewired from Republic to regime. Flags drape coffins while bureaucrats in suits sign away sovereignty to Brussels and Davos. This is not chaos by chance. It is orchestration by design. The serpent knows confusion weakens nations faster than conquest ever could. Chaos is not a byproduct — it is a business model. Every riot funds reconstruction contracts, every crisis swells budgets, every division feeds the machine that sells the cure. The same corporations that preach sustainability ship weapons. The same foundations that decry inequality bankroll censorship. The serpent grows fat on the friction it creates.

The Fire That Still Burns

But the serpent has not gone unchallenged. The warriors still rise. The remnant still stands. From the truckers who refused digital leashes, to pastors who opened churches in defiance of edict, to parents who refused silence in classrooms — America's folk still burn. Even in halls of power, sparks of defiance remain. For a brief season, borders were defended, speech was freed, and warriors remembered their oath. Proof that resistance is still possible when courage governs. The serpent presses, but the warriors have not laid down their arms. The serpent thrives where confusion reigns. But the Republic still remembers clarity — and the fire still burns.

"Blessed be the Lord my rock, who trains my hands for war and my fingers for battle." — Psalm 144:1

The Warning

We are no longer diagnosing. We are sounding the alarm. Chaos is the serpent's camouflage. Confusion is his currency. Whenever you hear the cry for "order," ask who created the disorder. He does not roar to conquer America; he whispers until Americans roar against each other. That is his playbook — create division, then sell peace at the price of freedom. If the firewall of covenant fails, the coil closes. The only antidote to chaos is clarity — truth spoken aloud when silence is safest. When confusion no longer fractures and chaos no longer conquers, the serpent changes posture.

The Firewall Tested — The Siege Phase

When confusion fails to fracture and chaos cannot conquer, the serpent lays siege. It no longer prowls at the gates — it presses against the wall. This siege is not fought with tanks — but with treaties, algorithms, and exhaustion. The serpent wages war through systems that never sleep — digital leashes, open borders, laws that erode the will to resist. But Nehemiah's warning still echoes:

"Do not be afraid of them. Remember the Lord, who is great and awesome, and fight for your brothers, your sons, your daughters, your wives, and your homes." — Nehemiah 4:14

The wall stands for more than soil. It guards covenant, conscience, and the freedom to repent. The wall is not made of stone but of souls — every family, every oath, every truth refused to be buried. We do not build it to shut the world out, but to keep truth alive within — and to hold the gate open for those ready to return.

• When outrage floods your feed, do you see protest — or orchestration?

• Have you confused exhaustion with peace?

• Do you know your neighbor — or only their party?

• Are you fighting the real enemy — or the one the serpent assigned you?

• Where does confusion masquerade as compassion — and who profits?

• If the Republic calls, will you be numb or ready?

• Have you guarded your mind — or outsourced it to noise?

• When truth costs comfort, will you still speak it?

• Do you believe the line can hold — or are you the one who must draw it again?

• When your hands are dirty from work, do you still lift them in prayer — or has the noise stolen that strength?

• When the serpent whispers "unity," will you recognize the chains in his peace?

"Be sober-minded; be watchful. Your adversary the devil prowls around like a roaring lion, seeking someone to devour." — 1 Peter 5:8

54

THE SPIRIT & THE SWORD
COVENANT VS. EMPIRE

You've seen the chains. You've seen the systems. You've seen the cage built in laws, ledgers, and lies. But behind every cage is the same breath. Behind every treaty, every ID, every slogan is the oldest war of all. The war beneath every empire is not political, not economic — it is spiritual war disguised as order.

The Old Dragon

Babylon fell. Rome crumbled. Berlin burned. Brussels builds. But the hunger never died. Every empire that rises against man carries the same spirit — the dragon of control. It feeds on worship. It thrives on silence. It promises peace while sharpening the sword. Babylon demanded men bow before statues. Rome demanded incense at Caesar's altar. Berlin demanded the salute. Brussels advances carbon pledges and new speech codes critics call "hate-speech" laws. Brussels does not demand incense or salute — it demands quotas, credits, and codes. A softer altar, but an altar still. Now the dragon writes in code, not cuneiform. The dragon has traded spears for spreadsheets, scrolls for screens — but it still asks the same thing: your silence as tribute. Different banners. Same beast.

The Remnant

Yet in every age a remnant stood. Not the many. Never the comfortable. Always the few who carried fire in silence and truth in chains. Prophets in Babylon, dragged before kings. Apostles in Rome, hunted in catacombs. Students of the White Rose in Berlin, executed for leaflets. Aleksandr Solzhenitsyn in the gulag, writing with fire. Patriots in America, muskets in hand, ink on parchment, covenant on lips. Deborah under the palm. Joan at the pyre. Mothers hiding their sons. The remnant is never the majority. It is the thin line that holds the fire.

The False Utopia

Every empire sells paradise. The Reich promised a thousand years. The Revolution promised equality. Technocrats sell Net Zero as salvation, data as peace, equity as justice. Technocrats promote "Net Zero" and "sustainability" as solutions. But every empire built on control ends the same - graves, ashes, chains. Paradise without covenant is hell dressed in progress.

The Call

And so the burden falls on America. Not just as a nation. Not just as a people. As the firewall for the world. Because America still carries a covenant written in ink and blood — that rights come from God, not government. That speech is fire, not permission. That arms defend liberty, not empire. That covenant stands above control. If America falls, there is no other firewall. If America forgets its covenant, the world does not get another chance. Every welder, teacher, farmer, and pastor becomes a keeper of that covenant — the unseen wall that still holds the world upright.

🔥 **Firelight Pause — Choose Your Throne**

- If silence is worship, whose throne are you serving?
- If you bow, whose crown are you polishing?
- If you fight, know whose kingdom you defend?
- If your hands bear the scars of work, do you still lift them in faith — or have you let the dragon write your prayers in code?
- If truth is your sword, have you kept it sharp — or let comfort dull the edge?

The serpent has a sword. But so do we.

Not of empire — of covenant. Not forged in councils or codes, but at Sinai, where law was given; at Calvary, where death was broken; at Philadelphia, where liberty was declared in ink and blood. This war is not only over land. It is over allegiance. And the battle is not first fought in parliaments, but in words — where truth is renamed and lies learn new costumes. Yet the sword still cuts. In every tongue. **Name the sin. Call the deed by its true name.** Teach your children scripture, not slogans. Covenant, not convenience. Keep the fire alive in small places — kitchens, schoolrooms, pulpits, the quiet work of neighboring. Truth is not kept by councils. It is kept by households — by a people who refuse to bow to idols of control.

"For the word of God is living and active, sharper than any two-edged sword, piercing to the division of soul and of spirit, of joints and of marrow, and discerning the thoughts and intentions of the heart." — Hebrews 4:12

PART IV

THE RECKONING

WHEN THE MASKS BURN

Memory is a weapon. Memory is salvation.
Forgetfulness is slavery. Remembrance is rebellion.

55

THE WAR FOR WORDS

THE SERPENT STRIKES THE TONGUE FIRST

"Woe to those who call evil good and good evil, who put darkness for light and light for darkness." — Isaiah 5:20

The Serpent's First Strike — The First Chain Is the Tongue

The serpent molts. Names change. Uniforms shift. But before it takes your food, your freedom, or your family — it strikes your tongue. **If you cannot name your chains, you cannot break them.** If you cannot speak the truth, you cannot resist the lie. The next battlefield is not tanks or treaties. It is words. Welcome to the war on speech. Welcome to the war on thought. Welcome to **the war for words.**

Every empire begins the same way — with silence. Before empires fall, they first make the people mute. The Soviets built gulags. The Nazis built camps. The technocrats built platforms. They no longer need barbed wire; they need algorithms. They no longer need guards with rifles; they need moderators with code. The method changes — the spirit does not.

The serpent knows truth is contagious. One spark can ignite a people. So it smears, isolates, and breaks truth-tellers before they can multiply. Aleksandr Solzhenitsyn knew this better than anyone — arrested for words, beaten, exiled, his books smuggled like contraband while tyrants trembled at his name. In our day the pattern repeats. In 2020 and 2021, doctors who questioned the prevailing narrative found licenses stripped, reputations shredded, platforms erased. Jordan Peterson was threatened with "re-education" by Canada's College of Psychologists for refusing speech codes. Journalists across Europe were fined for questioning migration policy and censored under "hate speech" laws. Everyday citizens are de-banked, shadow-banned, fired for a meme or a prayer in the wrong place at the wrong time. The tool looks different now, but the tactic is the same: **erase the witness, and the lie survives.**

The Archipelago of Silence

Solzhenitsyn called his prison system the *Gulag Archipelago.* Today we live in a *digital archipelago.* The shouting remains — but the world no longer hears. Shadow-bans let you shout into silence; algorithms throttle meaning until truth drowns in noise. Vague "community standards" strip dissent of its voice. It feels bloodless, but it is not. Reputations are slain. Livelihoods destroyed. Voices vanish. **Chains no longer clink — they click.**

"We cannot but speak the things which we have seen and heard." — Acts 4:20

Solzhenitsyn wrote, *"The simple step of a courageous individual is not to take part in the lie."* He wrote it under Stalin. It burns just as true under Silicon Valley. Where Stalin needed guards to haul you away, Zuckerberg needs only an algorithm. Where Mao needed mobs in the square, the mob today lives in your pocket — hashtags, cancel-storms, digital pitchforks. **This is not freedom. It is exile by keystroke. It is a gulag without fences.**

When the social-media vaults cracked open, the receipts spilled into light — pipelines between federal agencies and private platforms, shadow-ban patterns targeting doctors, journalists, and citizens. Algorithms hid dissent while promoting the sanctioned line — censorship outsourced through corporate proxies. **Denmark rehearsed what Brussels later codified — speech licensed by law, dissent gagged in the name of safety.** From there the script spread through Europe, and then across the Atlantic. The serpent's tongue tempts every tribe — those who govern and those who rage against governance alike. Tyranny wears many masks: bureaucracy, mob, or brand. It does not care who enforces its silence, only that the silence holds.

How Propaganda Becomes Policy

Ideas become headlines. Headlines become funding. Funding becomes law. The serpent does not always march in boots — it moves through briefings, think-tanks, and grants. It whispers in op-eds and names its whispers "evidence." It convinces ministers, funds NGOs, rewrites textbooks — and when the time is right, it locks the law around a society and calls the lock "protection." This is how a culture that once prized argument now prizes conformity. This is how democracy becomes script.

The Mob as Enforcer

The machinery of silence is not only governmental — it is social. HR departments blacklist "wrong-think." Banks de-bank dissidents. Payment processors cancel accounts overnight. Neighbors file complaints; employers police speech as if it were crime. Truckers in Canada saw accounts frozen for protesting mandates. Chase, PayPal, and others quietly shut down nonprofits and individuals for dissent. Silence arrives through the wallet as surely as through the gag. In Europe, the state licenses speech. In America, *the mob licenses it.* Whether the censor wears a badge or a brand logo — the result is the same — *silence.*

- When did you first bite your tongue to keep the peace?
- What did silence cost you?
- Who profits when you stay quiet?
- Could you lose your job, account, or name for speaking truth?
- If your voice vanished tonight, who would speak the words you didn't?

The Battlefield of Meaning — The Weaponization of Speech

Every tyranny begins the same way — by editing the dictionary. Before it conquers nations, it conquers nouns. Before it silences speech, it rewrites what words mean. The serpent knows — once you lose your language, you lose your liberty. A people who cannot name evil cannot resist it. A people who cannot define truth cannot defend it. **The war is no longer fought with bullets, but with definitions.** Once "freedom" meant the ability to speak, build, and believe. Now it means permission — granted by those who claim to protect you. Once "truth" meant alignment with reality. Now it means consensus — curated by those who control the feed. Once "justice" meant impartial law. Now it means equity — partiality baptized as fairness. **They did not discard the words — they captured them.**

- **"Tolerance"** now means obedience.
  - **"Diversity"** means uniformity of thought.
  - **"Science"** means censorship.
  - **"Democracy"** means management by elites.
  - **"Peace"** means permanent compliance.

These are not mistakes — they are tactics. The serpent no longer hisses; it hashtags. Each slogan replaces scripture. Each headline rewires conscience. Each euphemism blinds a generation to reality. **This is how free nations forget they were free.**

"For the Spirit God gave us does not make us timid, but gives us power, love and self-discipline." — 2 Timothy 1:7

The Language of Surrender

The serpent's tongue does not only speak from thrones abroad — it echoes in our own streets and schools. Many in America repeat the language of their own undoing, believing it progress. They say "democracy," not knowing this land was founded as a **constitutional republic** — a covenant of law, not the rule of mobs. They cry "equality," not seeing that enforced sameness is not justice but control. They praise socialism as compassion, forgetting that dependency is not mercy — it is mastery in disguise. When citizens adopt the serpent's words, they defend the very system that binds them. They repeat slogans polished by think-tanks and funded by bureaucrats, mistaking moral tone for moral truth. They no longer ask what freedom costs — only what comfort demands. A people that cannot discern language cannot discern chains. And so they vote for control while believing they vote for care, they trade sovereignty for safety, and they call it love.

The Memory War

Language shapes memory — and memory shapes nations. Erase the words, and you erase the world. They edit textbooks. They censor archives. They rewrite monuments and retell history. **The Nazis understood this when they burned books in the public square — not because the books were dangerous weapons, but because they carried dangerous memory.** Yesterday's heroes become villains; yesterday's truths become hate speech. The past is declared offensive, and the future becomes programmable. When the timeline is rewritten, the people forget their lineage. And a nation without lineage is a nation without armor.

The Algorithmic Catechism

Once children learned commandments; now they learn hashtags. Once preachers quoted prophets; now pundits quote platforms. Once debate sharpened truth; now "fact-checks" dull it. AI now edits language faster than we can think it. It rewrites words mid-sentence, replaces offense with approval, filters faith into metaphor, and edits patriotism into extremism. The serpent learned automation. **He no longer silences speech — he edits it before you finish typing.**

The American Tongue

But not all tongues have been tamed. The American tongue was forged for rebellion. The words of the Republic were carved in fire — Liberty. God. Sovereignty. Truth. These words still cut — and that is why the serpent seeks to dull them. **When a people can no longer say man or woman, they can no longer defend family. When they can no longer say republic or country, they can no longer defend borders or law. When they can no longer say God, they can no longer define good.** To protect language is to protect life.

The Covenant of Speech

Speech was the first freedom — and it remains the last defense. When God spoke, creation obeyed. When man spoke, truth spread. When tyrants speak, confusion reigns. The serpent's goal has always been the same — **to twist the Word, because the Word births worlds.** Our task is not to invent new language but to redeem the old — to speak truth as if it were oxygen again. Every word of truth pierces the algorithm's veil. Every unfiltered sentence lights a beacon in the dark grid. For words still carry fire — the kind that frees, not fries.

🔥 **Firelight Pause — Guard the Tongue**

- Which words have I accepted without questioning their spell?
- Do I speak truth — or echo the slogans I was fed?
- When truth offends, do I choose comfort or clarity?
- Do my children speak the language of liberty — or the dialect of compliance?
- Have I forgotten that words can still wound evil?
- If my tongue is silent, whose kingdom grows?

Words build worlds — or bury them. Choose yours like weapons. For the serpent cannot rule a people who still know how to name Him.

"In the beginning was the Word... and the Word was light." — John 1:1, 4

56

THE INVERSION OF EVIL

WHEN THE SERPENT TURNS
LIBERTY INTO TYRANNY

Empires no longer burn libraries. They build them — and fill them with propaganda. The serpent never simply attacks. He inverts. *He swaps labels, scrambles the map,* and trains the world to chase shadows while the dragon works in daylight. He did this with history — moving the Nazis to the "right" side of the spectrum, carving the line so that fascism would look like the twin of Christianity, of nationhood, of anyone who dares to say "God" or "country." And the world believed it. But history tells a different story. **The Nazis were not the children of liberty; they were children of tyranny.** They were born of the same soil as other totalizing creeds — communism, top-down socialism, Maoism — and the UN belongs to that same tradition of upward control, where **'global governance' replaces consent and the individual is merely an instrument of policy.** Beneath the slogans sits the creed that opened the door: late-stage liberalism collapsing into progressive neo-Marxism — a doctrine that weaponizes grievance, dissolves the family, and replaces duty with entitlement. It promises compassion while importing the machinery of control.

"Woe to those who call evil good and good evil, who put darkness for light and light for darkness." — Isaiah 5:20

442

The Root System

Most people look at today's ideologies and see a forest of different trees — liberalism over here, socialism over there, progressivism, Marxism, technocracy, climate governance, even the Red–Green alliance. But these are not separate species. They are branches of the same root system, fed by the same serpent, bending toward the same throne. They all share the same doctrine: the individual must shrink, the family must weaken, the state must centralize, borders must dissolve, and truth must bend. The languages differ — one speaks of equity, another of inclusion, another of science, another of solidarity — but the grammar is identical. All demand that the free person become manageable, the home provisional, sovereignty transferred upward, and truth replaced by narrative. Look closely and you see the pattern: **socialism regulates a man's labor while progressivism rewrites his identity. Marxism dissolves family loyalty, while technocracy replaces conscience with code. Climate utopianism turns guilt into governance, and the Red–Green alliance baptizes all of it in the language of moral urgency.** These movements pretend conflict, but they share the same altar. **They worship the same god — the State enthroned above man, covenant replaced with management, freedom traded for the illusion of care.** Once you see the root, the branches make sense. The serpent does not care which mask his followers wear. He only cares that the mask leads to the same cage. The West didn't drift into this by accident. The machinery that hollowed nations didn't vanish—it adapted, softened its tone, polished its language. And when you want to see this system in its velvet costume, look north.

Denmark's polished, polite, "managerial socialism" — is simply the velvet version of the same creed. It does not seize property; it regulates it. It does not outlaw dissent; it socializes it into silence. It does not break the citizen; it sedates him. **Same altar, softer ritual — but the god is unchanged:** the State enthroned above man. And once the velvet mask is in place, the iron mask is easier to hide. Fascism merges state, corporation, and military. Communism elevates the Party above the person.

Maoism demands obedience so absolute that even parents become suspect. Socialism replaces independence with dependence. Technocratic progressivism centralizes authority under "expert rule." Different banners. Same creed: the State above man. And yet liberals call America First "fascism." They mistake loyalty to land, family, and covenant for loyalty to a dictator. They confuse rootedness with tyranny because the serpent has trained them to see every strong border as oppression, every proud history as bigotry, every faith in God as fanaticism. **The inversion is deliberate — smear covenant as extremism so that only centralized management looks "safe."**

History proves the difference.

When *the Nazis* rose, they did not strengthen families, churches, or communities — they banned them. Independent clubs, unions, youth groups, congregations: outlawed or absorbed into the Reich. Fascism consumed the nation; it did not guard it. *Communism* followed with the same blueprint — abolish private property, criminalize faith, dismantle family loyalty. Pastors imprisoned, parents monitored, children indoctrinated. *Maoism* intensified the destruction — children denouncing parents, villages uprooted, churches obliterated, history rewritten. *Soft socialist regimes* repeated the pattern — nationalizing industry, eroding the home, rewarding dependence, replacing ownership with compliance. *Technocratic progressivism* does the same in digital form — polished logos, global councils, climate ministries. It bypasses family, church, voter, and Constitution through regulations, frameworks, and algorithms. The same spirit lives today. Brussels overrides farmers. Washington imposes "equity" decrees. Local choice dissolves; power flows upward. The serpent hides the real truth: **True fascism is not love of nation. It is the State devouring the nation. Not "America First." But "State First, Man Last."** Different uniforms. Same pattern. Every one replaces covenant with control and roots with regulation. And on the other side stand the only anchors of freedom: covenant, family, local sovereignty, generational duty, faith in God, a Constitution built to restrain power, and a remnant who know freedom survives only in the hands of those willing to defend it.

🔥 **Firelight Pause — The Line Beneath Your Feet**

- Which throne do my instincts bow to—**covenant, or control**?
- Do I trust experts more than elders? Systems more than family?
- When I hear "safety," do I ask who holds the leash?
- Does comfort quiet my courage?
- Do I defend borders, or apologize for them?
- Has the State crept into places only God and family should stand?
- When I imagine a good society, do I picture **free homes**—or **managed people**?
- If every label vanished—left, right, conservative, progressive—where would my loyalty stand?
- When tyranny comes in velvet, do I still recognize the iron underneath?

Freedom is not a spectrum. It is a stance.

The Rhetorical Surgery

Why the inversion? Because if citizens ever saw the family resemblance between Nazism, Communism, Maoism, statist socialism, and modern technocracy, the dragon's flank would be exposed. So the serpent performed *rhetorical surgery*. He shoved the real tyrants out of sight — and smeared defenders of faith, family, and nation as the "extremists." He equated faith with fanaticism. Sovereignty with bigotry. Patriotism with fascism. This was no accident. **It was the forked tongue at work:** polished, repeated, drilled into textbooks, transmitted through media pulpits until even classrooms taught the lie. The lie was institutionalized in curricula, think-tank reports, films, and algorithms. And then it was baptized in glass towers. Brussels wrapped the inversion in "European values." Geneva wrapped it in "human rights." New York wrapped it in "peacekeeping." And then the serpent crossed the Atlantic.

America's own institutions became amplifiers — universities that swapped inquiry for ideology, Hollywood that romanticized rebellion while preaching conformity, Silicon Valley platforms that claim neutrality while curating narrative. The inversion went global not because Europe imposed it, but because America exported it — wrapped in entertainment, apps, conferences, and credentials. Washington preached freedom abroad while outsourcing sovereignty at home. The lie became lingua franca - the common language strangers use when nothing else connects them. The EU, the UN, and their NGOs took the serpent's whisper and codified it into treaties, frameworks, and compacts — turning propaganda into policy, and policy into law.

"When he lies, he speaks out of his own character, for he is a liar and the father of lies." — John 8:44

The inversion is not just politics. It is spiritual.

The true line is not left versus right. The true divide is top-down tyranny versus God-given sovereignty. On one side stand systems that enthrone the State above man — Nazism, Communism, Maoism, managerial socialism, technocracy, and the supranational towers of the EU, the UN, and the WEF — institutions that turn covenant into contracts and sovereignty into signatures. On the other side stand covenant, family, local law, oaths of liberty, and the remnant who still guard them. Once you see that line, you cannot unsee it. The inversion does not stop at politics. It targets the pillars of a healthy society — men and women themselves. Men are recast as threats, their strength labeled "toxic," their leadership "patriarchal." Women are split from their own design — taught to fear motherhood, despise softness, and treat family as a trap. **A people confused about their own nature cannot defend a people or a land.** The serpent knows the order: weaken the man, scatter the woman, and the children wander without shepherds. **This inversion is not only ideological. It is biological warfare.**

The serpent's agents rarely look like monsters. They wear suits. They speak the language of "progress." With one hand they offer comfort — glossy programs, polished campaigns, convenient systems. With the other they take freedom — privacy, duty, rootedness. They build snake systems — bureaucracies that dress as angels of light but function as cages. Corporations consolidate instead of create. Governments substitute management for moral formation. Media trade truth for outrage. Schools erase words and manage memory until children forget who they are — first in name, then in habit. All offer the same bargain: trade liberty for comfort, covenant for compliance, roots for slogans. **The velvet cage always closes in the name of care.**

"The Beast was given a mouth uttering haughty and blasphemous words, and it was allowed to exercise authority for forty-two months." — Revelation 13:5

Nazi Germany showed the system naked. Corporations thrived by serving the Reich. Factories stamped weapons while camps supplied slave labor. Contracts and efficiency kept the machine alive. They called it "industry." It was slavery dressed as order. The Reich fell. The machine did not. The industrial-bureaucratic complex mutated — rebranded in boardrooms, research institutes, global strategies. What once bore a swastika now bore a trademark. What was once Reich planning now became "global coordination." Follow the money: mergers, partnerships, foundations with political reach. The receipts reveal a single thread — bureaucratic giants feeding on people — never creating, only consuming. **The Beast did not die in 1945. It rebranded.** The serpent's greatest victory was not in the camps or the gulags. **It was in the classrooms and the newsrooms.** There, the lie was planted: that liberty looks like fascism, and centralized planning looks like progress. No bullets required. Policy replaced force. Algorithms replaced rifles. Neutrality was swallowed. Fence-sitting devoured.

To the independents, the neutrals, the fence-sitters — **you cannot sit between Christ and Caesar.** You cannot keep covenant and bow to a managerial state. You cannot claim freedom while outsourcing discernment. **Silence will be taken as consent. Neutrality will be counted as allegiance. Do not sign the cage.**

Thinking Under Fire

The serpent's first whisper in Eden was not a sword, but a question: *"Has God really said...?"* (Genesis 3:1). That was propaganda. That was gaslighting. That was the first war on thinking. Now his tongue is digital — written into feeds, framed in headlines, embedded in "fact-checks." A famine not for bread or water, but for truth itself (Amos 8:11). **Silence is not peace. Silence is the serpent's throne.** The inversion does not stop with history. Once the serpent swaps labels on regimes, he swaps labels on words, virtues, and thought. Clarity becomes cruelty. Conviction becomes "extremism." Silence becomes "maturity." Chains migrate from borders to minds. No bullets. Just narratives — until thinking itself becomes suspect. In that fog, **the simple act of speaking truth becomes rebellion.** The serpent's finest trick is self-policing. Once a mind is trained to doubt its own memory, distrust its own instincts, and fear its own thoughts, no guard is needed. The citizen becomes his own censor. He deletes his own opinions before the algorithm ever sees them. He mocks the very virtues that once built his civilization. Chains are no longer placed on the wrists — they grow in the conscience. That is the serpent's true tyranny: when a free man enforces his own captivity. **The serpent's masterpiece is not censorship. It is curriculum.** Once he conquers the conscience, he goes for the classroom. If the lie can be taught early enough, it no longer needs to be enforced. The next generation will guard the cage themselves — smiling, credentialed, convinced they are free. The next chapter shows how the classroom became the serpent's pulpit — how education was weaponized to replace formation with programming, and conviction with compliance.

Firelight Pause — Thinking Under Fire

Sit by the fire and ask yourself:
- Where have I traded thought for comfort?
- Where have I swallowed a headline instead of asking a question?
- Where have I mocked someone only because they unsettled me?
- Where have I stayed silent because truth might cost me approval?
- Where have I mistaken compliance for peace?
- And most of all: am I thinking — or merely repeating?

"Woe to those who call evil good and good evil, who put darkness for light and light for darkness, who put bitter for sweet and sweet for bitter." — Isaiah 5:20

57

THE CLASSROOM COUP
HOW EDUCATION REPLACED THE PULPIT

"*Train up a child in the way he should go; even when he is old he will not depart from it.*" — Proverbs 22:6

They silenced the prophets. Then they rewired the pupils. When truth could no longer be spoken aloud, the serpent went hunting for a quieter battlefield — the mind of the child. You can gag a generation's voice for a decade; but if you train its memory, you own its future. Censorship ends in silence. Indoctrination ends in obedience.

The Weaponization of Innocence

Empires used to burn books. Now they publish the textbooks. The modern coup doesn't march in boots; it enters with grant money, UN templates, and "inclusive frameworks." The target isn't the adult dissenter — it's the unformed soul. From kindergarten to university, the same catechism repeats — *the planet is your god, the state is your savior, feelings are your truth.* They call it "critical thinking." But the thinking has already been done for them. Children memorize shame instead of scripture, slogans instead of sentences. Patriotism becomes privilege. Faith becomes phobia. Masculinity becomes "toxic." The serpent learned long ago — capture the definition of good, and you never need to use force again.

From Pulpit to Program

Once, pastors and parents shaped the moral spine of a people. Now bureaucrats and consultants do — through policy, not prayer. The sermon has been replaced by the slideshow. UNESCO writes "values education." The OECD tracks "global competencies." The WEF funds "Future Skills" programs that define what your child *should believe* about economics, gender, and governance. What was once covenant — between God, parent, and child — is now contract — between state, funder, and outcome. The language sounds harmless — equity, inclusion, sustainability. But beneath the slogans lies the quiet erasure of faith, nation, and family. The classroom is no longer a house of learning. It's a factory of alignment.

The Indoctrination Economy

Education is now the most profitable weapon on earth. Trillions flow through foundations and ESG-compliant investors. Corporations fund "curriculum reform" because ideology creates predictable consumers. Universities sell debt and degrees while teaching contempt for the civilization that built them. Teachers are trained not to educate but to "facilitate" — a code word for policing thought. Parents who question the lesson are flagged as threats. Children are taught to confess privilege instead of sin, to pledge allegiance to progress instead of principle. They call it **social-emotional learning; it is emotional surveillance.** Most teachers never see the chain—they only follow the checklist. ESG scores now grade not only corporations, but classrooms — measuring compliance as morality, and teaching children to see obedience as virtue.

The Return of the Builders

But beneath the noise, the remnant stirs. Mothers pull their children from the system. Fathers build schools in barns and basements. Churches reopen classrooms once thought obsolete. Homeschool co-ops rise like underground presses, teaching scripture, trade, and sovereignty. These are the new monasteries — the safe houses of knowledge after the empire's fall. They will not produce bureaucrats. They will produce builders — men and women who remember that wisdom begins with fear of the Lord, not fear of the state.

The Firelight Code of Education

There is a law older than the classroom — a covenant of learning written before the first desk was ever carved. We've forgotten it. We traded truth for tolerance, reverence for relevance, and called it progress. But the Republic will not survive on slogans. It survives only where truth still has teachers. **Truth before tolerance.** Teach facts even when they offend feelings. A child who learns that truth must first be liked will never stand when truth is hated. Truth is not cruel — it is the spine of mercy. **Creation before consumption.** Let children build before they buy. Let them fix a fence, care for a garden, change a tire. A generation that only consumes will always need masters. Builders make nations; consumers rent them. **Faith before fear.** A mind anchored in reverence cannot be manipulated by trends. Teach awe before anxiety. Teach that the world is not random — it is ordered, designed, and waiting to be stewarded by hands that fear God more than hashtags. **Covenant before curriculum.** Parents, not programs, are the first teachers. No state, no screen, no standardized test can replace a father's instruction or a mother's wisdom. When that covenant breaks, every other law crumbles with it. **Work before words.** Let calluses teach what classrooms forgot. Let effort become the alphabet of virtue. There is holiness in the hammer, dignity in the dirt. Labor trains gratitude — the first theology of a free people. They taught the children to fear the wrong fire — the one that burns, not the one that purifies. But now the remnant remembers — **the true classroom is the heart, and its first lesson is courage.**

Education is not information. It is inheritance — the passing of light, not data. Lose that, and the Republic dissolves quietly between the pages of someone else's workbook. But guard it, and a nation's fire can live a thousand years.

 Firelight Pause — The Classroom Test
- Who teaches your children what truth is?
- Do your schools shape courage — or compliance?
- When your child comes home, whose words echo louder — yours, or Babylon's?
- What are you building — a generation of disciples, or a database of dependents?
- If education is covenant, who signed yours?

Freedom begins where learning is holy again. The next fire is not in books but on the altar — where knowledge meets oath, and covenant becomes nation. The serpent built schools; the remnant builds altars. A people cannot be free until their learning is consecrated. The classroom taught obedience; the covenant teaches dominion. Now the builders return — not to study liberty, but to swear to it. But the serpent was never content with the children. He wanted the conscience. Once he captured the classroom, he captured the culture. The pupil became the parent, the subject became the citizen — all trained to obey before they could discern. Screens replaced elders. Experts replaced wisdom. And what began as education became enchantment. The next chapter enters that war — where discernment is outlawed, silence is sold as peace, and thought itself becomes rebellion.

58

THE WAR ON THINKING
WHY DEPTH TRIGGERS THE DULL

They no longer burn the dissenters. They retrain them. The serpent learned that if you can't silence truth, you can flood it — drown it in noise, data, distraction, and self-doubt until no one remembers what clarity feels like. The new chains are invisible, made of headlines, hashtags, and "approved experts." It isn't ignorance that rules the age — *it's confusion, engineered by design.* **We have been conditioned first not to question anything — and then to question everything.** That is how conviction dies: one generation trained to obey, the next trained to doubt. **Thinking itself has become rebellion.** Discernment is branded "extremism." Certainty is called "hate." Conviction is renamed "danger." The mind that questions is quarantined, and the one that obeys is crowned "kind." *This is the serpent's final classroom — the one where grown men recite propaganda as virtue and call it education.* The war on thinking is not fought with censorship alone. It is fought with overload — with endless input, constant stimulation, and the slow erosion of silence. When there is no stillness, there can be no wisdom.

In a time of universal deceit, telling the truth is a revolutionary act.— George Orwell

454

The war on women is brutal—first by erasure, then by imitation. Men invade their sanctuaries, rewrite their names, claim their trophies, and the world applauds. Even many women, trained to call surrender compassion, celebrate the masquerade. The same spell that confuses bodies now confuses minds. When truth can be rewritten at will, thinking becomes treason. The assault on thought is silent. And silence kills faster than bullets. We live in an age where emotion has replaced logic, where personal offense is wielded like a weapon, and where the simple act of speaking clearly—without apology, without dilution—is branded as arrogance. Outrage is mistaken for passion. Volume for authenticity. Virality for value. Flatness for virtue. A generation has been trained to confuse disagreement with harm and conviction with cruelty. When I speak plainly, it doesn't trigger because I'm wrong. It triggers because thoughtfulness itself has become dangerous. Because **once a man begins to think, he begins to see. Once he sees, he cannot kneel. And once he refuses to kneel, the empire begins to crack.** The serpent's oldest weapon was never force, but doubt — a question first whispered in Eden and now amplified by algorithms.

Strong Women, Weak Men

The system fears strong women — not because they topple men, but because they expose weakness. A covenant woman does not perform. She does not chase applause. She stands. And her stillness unmasks the charade. To weak men, she is a mirror of abdication — proof of the crown they refused to carry. To conditioned women, she is an indictment of compliance — proof that chains can be broken. To institutions, she is un-programmable, a glitch in the design. Dangerous not by rebellion, but by presence. Strong women do not march to the serpent's drumbeat. They do not need permission. They do not play at empowerment sold by tech-nocrats who despise life in the womb and covenant in the home. The system offers performance, titles, and applause. Covenant offers weight, roots, and fire. And this is why the system demands weak men — men dulled by comfort, trained in passivity, medicated into numbness.

Weak men do not guard gates; they surrender them. They trade strength for safety, authority for approval, covenant for consensus. A man does not lose his crown by force — he sets it down, one compromise at a time. When men grow weak, women are told to perform — to fill the void with noise. This is not a war of sexes, but of order. The serpent always strikes where covenant breaks. But a covenant woman refuses. She stands not to replace, but to remind — to call men back to the fire they abandoned. **The world does not fall because women are strong. It falls because men grow weak.** And when weak men bow, strong women rise — not to rule, but to hold the line until men take up their crowns again. In covenant, strength is not competition but alliance. Man and woman forged as one flame — unbreakable, unbending, beyond the reach of the serpent's chains.

Mockery and Gaslighting

Mockery is not just cowardice. It is programmed cowardice. **When people cannot match depth, they have been trained to laugh at it.** Laughter becomes censorship. The meme becomes the muzzle. Joke. Smear. Block. None of it is argument. It is the reflex of those conditioned to flinch at truth. And when mockery fails, gaslighting begins. *"You're too intense. You sound arrogant. You think you know everything."* No. You simply refuse to kneel. Gaslighting is not debate. It is the defense of illusion. And the most dangerous adversary to illusion is not the fragile or the loud — it is the one who stands unbroken.

The Death of Critical Thinking — By Design

Critical thought wasn't lost. It was dismantled. Rockefeller-era pedagogy trained obedience. Silicon Valley dopamine labs engineered distraction. UNESCO frameworks sold "global citizenship" while hollowing civic duty. EU rubrics bureaucratized dissent. Denmark was the prototype — consensus disguised as curriculum, obedience disguised as education. From there the script spread outward: UNESCO to Common Core, DEI pledges to ESG scorecards. What was once taught as reasoning became conformity in the classroom and compliance in the workplace.

A nation that thinks deeply cannot be ruled. But a distracted, triggered, emotionally brittle nation? That is the perfect colony. Chains once hammered in iron now arrive as narratives and algorithms. What was once enforced with shackles is now streamed in headlines. What was once a prison wall is now a glowing screen.

Small Country, Big Compliance

Denmark is small in land, but vast in obedience. Consensus is its god. Harmony its gospel. Success must be hidden. Strength must be softened. Questions must be silenced. Obedience is called maturity. Silence is praised as safety. Contradiction is branded betrayal. And while freedoms erode and sovereignty dissolves, the average Dane shrugs: *"That can't happen here."* But it already has. And the obedience did not stop at Denmark's borders. Bureaucrats carried the script to Brussels, Geneva, and New York. Silence hardened into treaties. Consensus became compacts. What Denmark rehearsed in miniature, America now faces on the grand stage. Do not shrug at Denmark's obedience. **It was the test site. You are the target.**

Contrast America

For all her flaws, America was forged in rebellion. In Texas, defiance is still a virtue. Obedience without discernment is called cowardice. In Denmark, obedience is praised. Silence is rewarded. Consensus is called maturity. Denmark is the caution. Texas is the test. **America is the battle-field.** And to those who fear strong speech — you do not fear cruelty. You fear clarity. You were trained in systems that reward dilution, flattery, and false consensus. Behind that silence stands a hand — the same hand that wrote decrees in Brussels, drafted mandates in New York, gagged prophets, and called it peace. It is not Danish alone. It is not European alone. **It is the ancient serpent, whispering compliance across the ages.** The uniforms change. The hand does not.

"Casting down imaginations, and every high thing that exalteth itself against the knowledge of God, and bringing into captivity every thought to the obedience of Christ." — 2 Corinthians 10:5

This is the lesson. Silence is never neutral. Every silence strengthens the serpent. Every clear word weakens him. Thinking is not leisure; it is resistance. Speaking truth is not arrogance; it is covenant. **You will either be trained into obedience — or trained into courage. There is no third path.**

 Firelight Pause — Thinking Under Fire
- Where have I traded thought for comfort?
- Where have I accepted a headline instead of seeking truth?
- Where have I stayed silent because clarity might cost me approval?
- Have I begun to bless confusion — calling it compassion?
- When truth is rewritten, do I defend reality or retreat?
- And most of all: **am I thinking — or merely repeating?**

Silence is not peace. Silence is the serpent's throne. And every throne not shattered will soon demand your chains. Silence is never empty — it is architecture. It is how tyranny moves from bayonets to boardrooms, from cages to classrooms, from decrees to dopamine hits. What begins as a whisper of *"be polite"* hardens into *"don't speak,"* until dissent feels impolite, then dangerous, then impossible.

"For everyone who does wicked things hates the light and does not come to the light, lest his works should be exposed. But whoever does what is true comes to the light, so that it may be clearly seen that his works have been carried out in God." — John 3:20–21

The serpent does not end with chaos, but with calm — not blood, but boredom. Not violence, but a silence so complete the mind censors itself before words are born. **Silence has two masters: one that heals, and one that enslaves. Choose yours.**

59

THE SILENCE SPELL
WHEN SILENCE BECOMES SURRENDER

S ilence is not peace. It is covenant with the serpent — a vow made in fear. Only truth spoken, even trembling, breaks the spell.

"Open your mouth for the mute, for the rights of all who are destitute. Open your mouth, judge righteously, defend the rights of the poor and needy." — Proverbs 31:8–9

Silence, once learned, becomes culture. Culture becomes law. Law becomes export. That is how the spell travels — treaties, frameworks, polite words hiding chains. Denmark perfected it. Brussels codified it. Washington echoes it. The rehearsal is over. The stage is America. Every empire needs soldiers with swords. But tyranny needs something stronger — citizens who silence themselves. Citizens who smile at their chains. Who prefer approval to truth, comfort to courage, sedation to strength, entitlement to duty. The serpent does not always conquer with force. He conquers with compliance. With trust. With smiles. He conquers when people begin to kneel without being asked.

459

This chapter is about those faces. They are not strangers. They live next door. They sit in classrooms. They scroll beside you at night. They are the faces of your own age. And the serpent wears them well.

The First Face: Emma — Approval as Bondage

Emma is the model citizen. She recycles. She follows the rules. She repeats the headlines. She trusts the system so deeply she cannot imagine it lying. She bikes to work in reflective gear. She posts about *hygge*. She sips organic lattes and calls it conscience. She teaches her children to trust the state more than the family, the expert more than the elder. She quotes headlines like Scripture, fact-checkers like prophets, bureaucrats like saints. She does not argue — she cites. She does not think — she trusts. To Emma, truth outside approved channels isn't truth at all. If it mattered, the government would have said so. If it isn't on the news, it must not exist. Emma doesn't ask if she is free. She asks if she is approved. Approval is not a weapon — but in an age of spells, it cuts deeper than a sword. She isn't malicious. **She's approved.** And the most dangerous citizen in a time of war is the one who believes there isn't one.

The Second Face: Karen — *Comfort as Sedation*

Across the ocean her cousin waits — Karen. Karen is not one woman. She is the pattern of comfort — the spell millions cast to stay safe. She parrots DEI in the classroom. She quotes fact-checkers like Scripture. She wears the fleece. Carries the tote. She posts rainbows in June, flags in February, pledges in September. She is the yogi who preaches "love and light" while demanding censorship of "hate." The neighbor who reports you for too many cars in the driveway. The HOA eye peering over the fence. She doesn't carry a gun. She carries compliance. She believes compliance is compassion. Consensus is maturity. Skepticism is danger. Karen doesn't ask if she is free. She asks if she is comfortable. Comfort is not compassion. It is sedation. Comfort is not harmless. It is chloroform. She isn't malicious. **She's comfortable.** And the most dangerous citizen in a time of war is the one who mistakes sedation for safety.

Together, Emma and Karen are the serpent's daughters — one seeking approval, the other seeking comfort. Between them, nations fall silent.

The Third Face: Adam — *When Strength Is Sedated*

Adam is not one man. He is the pattern of numbness. He scrolls at midnight. Jaw slack. Fed by reels that never end. He smokes what dulls him. Mocks faith he never studied. Quotes podcasts, not Scripture. He inherits strength from fathers who built — and leaks it out in pills, porn, and passive outrage. Adam doesn't ask if it is true. **He asks if it is safe.** He mistakes sarcasm for courage, dopamine for destiny. And when it costs — he folds. A man without fire is no threat. And when Adam will not guard, women, children, and nations are exposed. When Adam is hollow, Emma is unshielded. When Adam kneels, the serpent advances.

The Fourth Face: Chad — *When Wealth Replaces Honor*

Chad is not hollow — he is inflated. He drives what he cannot fix. Wears what he did not earn. Inherits what braver men won. He flexes with money, not protection. Quotes Forbes like Scripture. Calls debt "leverage" and selfishness "strategy." He plays golf while his marriage withers. Scrolls tickers while his children are raised by screens. Chad doesn't ask what is right. He asks what it will earn him. He looks strong — but bends. Looks free — but kneels.

Together, Adam and Chad are the serpent's sons — one sedated, the other entitled. And when sons kneel, daughters are unshielded. And nations stand exposed.

Emma. Karen. Adam. Chad. Approval. Comfort. Sedation. Entitlement. The four corners of the serpent's square. This is how nations are softened. This is how freedom bleeds without a shot fired. Fragility is not a glitch. It is the program. Weakness is not drift. It is engineered. And the engine has a command center.

The Script Writers

The universities write the spell. Everyone else enforces it. They teach young men to distrust strength. Young women to despise motherhood. Both to treat faith as superstition. They call it progress. It is programming. From the lecture hall, the silence spreads outward — into policy, culture, and law. But **the serpent's greatest victory is not enforcement. It is agreement.**

Silence as Covenant

Every empire needs soldiers with swords. But tyranny needs something stronger — citizens who silence themselves. The serpent knows this. He does not always conquer with force. He conquers with compliance. Silence is not neutral. Silence is consent. Silence is not absence. It is covenant. And once chosen, silence does not stay personal. It becomes culture. Culture becomes law. Law becomes export.

Firelight Pause — The Mirror
- Where have I chosen approval instead of truth?
- Where has comfort mattered more than courage?
- Where have I numbed instead of guarded?
- Where have I stayed silent to stay safe?
- And when the serpent comes — **will I kneel, or will I speak?**

History Proves It

Silence when Ukraine starved. When daughters vanished in China. When women were beaten in Iran. When neighbors shut doors in Germany. Silence has always walked beside atrocity — not shouting, not striking — just *looking away*. The serpent feeds on silence. Always has. Always will.

The Test of October 7

On October 7, 2023, the sword was unsheathed. Jewish women were raped, mutilated, paraded like trophies of terror. Children were butchered. Families erased. Bodies dragged through streets to cheers. And the world went quiet. The UN stalled. Universities hedged. Professors excused. Students celebrated. Media diluted. Feminist icons vanished. Churches softened their prayers. This was not confusion. *It was silence.* **To chant slogans while women were brutalized was not solidarity — it was allegiance.** To hide behind "context" while daughters were violated was not wisdom — it was cowardice. History will record the crime. Heaven will record the response. Silence stood beside the violence — and called itself peace. That was the test of our age. Many failed it.

The Law Stated

Silence is not peace. Silence is permission. And permission is how the serpent survives.

"Open your mouth for the mute..."

— Proverbs 31:8–9

The silence that begins in hearts becomes law in nations. Denmark rehearsed it. America will face it. Every silence is a vow — the only question is who it serves.

60

THE ARCHITECTURE OF SILENCE

HOW OBEDIENCE IS ENGINEERED

Silence does not sustain itself. It must be built. Once silence is accepted as virtue, it requires architecture — systems that reward compliance, punish clarity, and train people to police themselves. Tyranny no longer needs dungeons when it can outsource enforcement to culture, credentials, and convenience. This is the enforcement layer of the serpent's rule — the machinery that turns fear into habit and habit into law.

Psychological Warfare in Plain Sight

They did not outlaw speech. They therapized it. Debate was replaced with "safe spaces." Argument with emotional management. Citizenship with compliance training. Fragility is not accidental — it is engineered. An obedient population must be emotionally brittle, unable to withstand contradiction, unable to hear truth without collapsing. Offense is monetized. Weakness is rewarded. This warfare does not stop at the mind. It moves through the body. Babylon reshapes flesh as well as thought. High-calorie diets. Low-testosterone men. Soft bodies trained to avoid discomfort and resent discipline. A people weakened in body are easily ruled in spirit.

A weed dispensary on every corner numbs men who might have risen. Pills replace purpose. Dopamine replaces duty. **Notice where they cluster most — around campuses, not churches; near lecture halls, not workshops.** This is not cultural decay — it is strategic sedation.

Mockery as Censorship

When truth cannot be refuted, it is mocked. Mockery is not humor — it is training. Laughter becomes the leash. Memes replace arguments. Ridicule replaces reason. Those who speak clearly are branded "intense," "arrogant," "dangerous." **— the telltale response of performative intelligence weaponized for social shutdown.** Not because they are wrong — but because they will not submit to the script. This is not debate. It is behavioral correction. The system does not need to silence you if it can make you afraid of looking foolish. When people learn that clarity costs social standing, they begin deleting their own thoughts before anyone else has to. Self-censorship is the serpent's most efficient tool.

The Workplace as Discipline Center

Silence is enforced gently now — through policies, trainings, and contracts. HR departments do what secret police once did: monitor speech, correct tone, and punish deviation — not with prisons, but with performance reviews. DEI seminars reward apology over competence. "Safe workplace" policies redefine disagreement as harm. Promotion is no longer tied to excellence, but to compliance with emotional codes. Men learn quickly what is permitted.

- **Speak plainly** and you are *"aggressive."*
- **Question a premise** and you are *"unsafe."*
- **Lead with conviction** and you are *"a problem."*

The lesson is clear: Think quietly. Soften your voice. Apologize first. Survive.

The system rarely disciplines men directly. It disciplines them socially — through reputation, peer pressure, and relational enforcement. Often the cruelty wears a pleasant face — women installed in gatekeeping roles: HR, compliance, "culture," "people teams." Not confused. Not misled. **Cruel.** They smile while they cut. They speak of safety while destroying livelihoods. They do not argue ideas — they hunt deviations. They do not confront men openly — they document them to death. They do not fire with cause — they erase through process. Tone becomes the weapon. Empathy becomes the knife. A man is not punished for being wrong, but for being clear — for refusing to bow, for not submitting his spine to consensus. These women do not protect others. They protect the system. They enjoy authority without the burden of courage. They punish strength because it exposes their power as borrowed. They remove dissenters with rehearsed language and sleep well afterward, calling it "care." This is not misunderstanding. This is **deliberate moral sadism,** outsourced to those trained to believe they are righteous. The serpent favors them because they do not look like tyrants — and because they strike without mercy while insisting they are victims. **The most dangerous tyrants are not the loud ones — but the smiling ones who enjoy ruining lives and call it virtue.** This is not inclusion. It is **ritualized cruelty with a clipboard.** The modern worker is trained to self-edit first and think second. Not because the law demands it — but because survival does. Because rent, reputation, and family stability are always on the line. A man who cannot speak freely at work will not speak freely anywhere. And a workplace that trains silence becomes a factory of obedient citizens.

When the Spell Breaks

These systems survive on vagueness. On euphemism. On silence. They rule through "concerns," "culture," and "process" precisely because none of it survives definition. Once named, the spell breaks. HR power depends on informality. The moment behavior is called what it is — retaliation, discrimination, viewpoint punishment — paperwork turns into evidence. Smiles become liability. Process becomes record. This is why they fear clarity. Documentation cuts both ways.

Emails become exhibits. Trainings become admissions. What was framed as "care" begins to read like coercion. What hid behind tone-policing stands exposed as punishment for speech. Tyranny thrives in fog. Justice thrives in light. That is why they move first to shame, then to silence, then to exhaustion — not because dissenters are wrong, but because if truth is spoken plainly, the system loses jurisdiction. **Once cruelty is named, it stops being culture and starts becoming evidence.**

The Hand Behind the Curtain

This is not chaos. It is a pipeline. Universities manufacture ideology. Agencies translate ideology into regulation. Corporations profit from regulation. All of them fund one another — chairs, grants, boards, campaigns. They call it *public-private partnership*. In practice, it is cartelized power wearing academic robes. From the classroom to the clinic to the credit score. From the pronoun seminar to the pill bottle to the ESG dashboard. This is how control becomes "consensus." This is how silence becomes policy. This is how the spell scales.

The Universities — Command and Control

The universities write the spell. Everyone else enforces it. They train young men to distrust strength. Young women to despise motherhood. Both to treat faith as superstition. They call it progress. It is programming. What begins as theory becomes policy. What begins as language becomes law. From lecture halls, silence radiates outward — into courts, corporations, and classrooms. The serpent's greatest victory is not force. It is consent.

Silence Codified

Silence does not end at culture. It hardens into law. In Brussels, silence is called "hate speech regulation." At the UN, it is baptized "anti-disinformation." In Silicon Valley, it is coded into "trust and safety." In American workplaces, it is enforced by contract. This is silence not as accident — but as weapon. Once silence is codified, dissent is no longer controversial. It is illegal.

The Endgame

The serpent no longer needs mobs in the street. He has dashboards. He does not burn books. He buries them in search results. He does not need firing squads. He has shadow-bans. First they smear. Then they mock. Then they isolate. Then they erase. And when silence is complete, violence is optional. **The final stage is not terror. It is normality.**

🔥 **Firelight Pause — Enforcement**
- Where has silence been rewarded in my life?
- Where have I learned to self-edit to survive?
- Which institutions benefit from my quiet?
- And when the cost comes — will I comply, or will I speak?

Silence is not peace. Silence is policy. And policy is how the serpent rules without resistance.

61

THE TWO-TIER TRAP

ERASING THE MIDDLE CLASS,
ENSLAVING THE MANY

The erasure of America's middle class is not loud. It does not riot. It does not crash markets overnight. It cuts like a surgeon — quiet, steady, precise. The rich float higher in insulated towers. The poor grind lower in endless shifts. But the middle — the builders, the bridge, the backbone — is being erased. Not by accident. By design. The middle class once carried America's dignity and mobility: farmers who fed towns, tradesmen who built after hours, mothers who stretched one paycheck into a future, men and women who lived between morning labor and midnight dreams. Price them out of homes. Tax them into silence. Mock their values. Bury them in regulation and debt — and you do not merely shrink an economy. You amputate its spine. And when the spine breaks, a nation collapses into two pits: masters above, servants below. Even the Founders understood this fault line. Jefferson praised the farmer as the Republic's backbone. Madison warned that factions would tear the bridge apart. And Hamilton — brilliant, dangerous — trusted paper over plow, banks over barns. That split never healed. Hamilton's system built Wall Street — but Mount Rushmore forgot him. Washington, Jefferson, Lincoln, Roosevelt stand in stone. Hamilton remains on the ten-dollar bill. Finance got power. Builders got honor. Which lasts? Ask the stone. Ask the soil. It remembers the builders. What replaces the middle is not balance. It is caste.

469

The Two Tiers

At the top rises an administrative elite: bureaucrats, regulators, compliance officers, DEI directors, HR enforcers, policy analysts, NGO managers, grant writers, sustainability officers, ESG consultants, credentialed academics insulated from consequence, remote knowledge workers untethered from place, influencers monetizing opinion, professional activists paid to agitate but never build. They manage systems they do not suffer under. They speak in frameworks, not consequences. They are shielded from the outcomes of their own policies.

At the bottom spreads a service class: dishwashers, janitors, delivery drivers, warehouse pickers, gig workers, rideshare drivers, meatpackers, field laborers, hotel staff, care aides, undocumented migrants kept permanently temporary — necessary, silent, replaceable. They keep the system running but never rise within it. They produce value without leverage. They work — but do not own.

And *between them:* nothing.

The builders are erased. Owner-operators. Tradesmen with shops. Farmers with land. Contractors who hire locally. Machinists, welders, electricians, truck owners, small manufacturers, independent retailers, family businesses. The bridge class. Gone. Universities no longer feed that middle. They sort it. They credential administrators instead of forming builders. They train compliance, not competence. Graduates are funneled upward into management roles or downward into debt-financed precarity. What emerges is not opportunity but orbit: two classes locked in rotation, one living on screens and subsidies, the other on scraps and fear. No bridge. No ladder. Just managed decline, polished as progress. This is not drift. It is design.

India — Caste by Credential

India did not invent caste — but it perfected permanence. People were frozen into stations: elite above, labor below, no bridge between. Birth decided destiny. Mobility was myth. The system called itself tradition. It was control. **Globalism did not abolish caste. It digitized it.** Caste now wears credentials. Universities mass-produce degrees to sort humans, not free them. India exports credentialed workers — engineers, coders, analysts — into global pipelines trained to serve systems they will never own. Corporations call it "talent flow." Economists call it efficiency. Look closer. A thin elite rises into managed service roles abroad. A vast base remains cheap, replaceable, and leverage-less. The independent builder collapses. This is not failure. It is extraction. The British trained clerks. The empire changed names. The logic stayed. When American firms import that pipeline — payrolls, code, classrooms — they import caste logic: masters above, servants below, no bridge between. Caste never disappears. It only changes language.

Denmark — Caste by Comfort

If India shows caste by compression, Denmark shows it by comfort. Denmark does not beat dissent. It subsidizes obedience. A third of the population works for the state. Most of the rest depend on it indirectly. Ownership is discouraged. Self-employment is rare. Builders vanish. Administrators multiply. The result is not equality — it is managed sameness. Farmers shrink. Small business withers. Bureaucracy expands. Obedience is rewarded. Initiative is penalized. Strength must apologize. All of it wrapped in the softest packaging imaginable: free healthcare, free education, security, happiness. But security without sovereignty is a cage. Comfort without ownership is a leash. Denmark exports bureaucrats, not builders. It produces administrators for supranational systems — people trained to manage outcomes they will never feel. That is why global institutions adore Denmark. It proves a population can be controlled without force. A polished colony. No riots. No resistance. Just smiles — and paperwork.

Why Builders Terrify Empires

Empires do not fear the poor. They can be managed. They do not fear the elite. They can be bought. They fear the builder. The builder lives without permission. He owns tools, land, skill. He repairs what breaks, feeds what starves, remembers what others forget. He does not need the system — and therefore cannot be ruled by it. Builders are dangerous because they are anchored. They belong somewhere. They answer to covenant, not policy. A man who can raise a wall does not fear losing a title. A woman who can feed a household does not panic when shelves thin. A family that owns its means of survival cannot be coerced by slogans. That is why every empire targets builders first — not with bullets, but regulation; not with chains, but paperwork; not with force, but incentives that punish independence. Builders are taxed harder, licensed tighter, mocked as backward, framed as inefficient, labeled "unsustainable." Their work is called primitive. Their values dangerous. Their children are taught to aspire away from them. Because once builders disappear, resistance becomes theoretical.

A strong middle class is not an economic accident. It is a political threat. The middle allows movement — and empires cannot survive movement. They require fixed positions: masters above, servants below. A nation with builders argues. A nation without them obeys. India shows the model by credentialed caste. Denmark shows it by subsidized obedience. Different costumes. Same outcome. Empires do not fall because the poor rise. They fall because builders disappear. And when the last builder is gone, the nation does not explode. It expires. There are only two futures left: masters or servants. There is no third class. **That is the Two-Tier Trap** — humanity traded as commodity, masters above, servants below. John saw it in vision. We see it in policy. Denmark showcases it in polished cages. India exports it through credentialed pipelines. Different masks. Same bondage. The many serve the few. Builders are erased. Sovereignty is traded for stipends and salaries. Call it equity if you like. History will call it empire.

America — Still a Firewall

By contrast, America still resists. Most work outside the state. Millions still build, own, haul, weld, farm, raise, repair. Entrepreneurship is oxygen. Dependency is a leash. The more we build, the less we bow. America is not Denmark. Not yet. But if the builder's fire goes out, the firewall collapses — and when it falls, the cage slams shut.

A Republic cannot survive without builders — but an empire cannot survive **with** them. That is why the middle is being erased. That is why skill is mocked, ownership punished, and independence treated as extremism. Because once the builders are gone, the only choices left are **masters or servants.** There is no third class.

62

THE PARASITE ORDER

WHEN NOTHING IS BUILT
AND EVERYTHING IS TAKEN

Empires do not begin by seizing land. They begin by severing dignity from labor. When a people no longer build, they can be ruled without chains. When work no longer leads to ownership, obedience feels inevitable. When survival is mediated by systems, resistance becomes theoretical. This is how the plantation returns — not by force, but by design. This is not a future threat — it is the operating system you are already living under.

The Plantation Rebuilt

They call it equity. But it is the old plantation — only with new branding. The overseer no longer carries a whip; he carries an iPad. The lash is gone, replaced with the algorithm. Chains are hidden in apps. Migrant labor keeps the system alive, and fear of deportation keeps mouths shut. That isn't compassion. It is exploitation in polite clothes. You cook — they post memes. You clean — they host equity seminars. You work — they consume. And they dare to call it progress. The plantation endures not because people are chained — but because they are managed.

"The limits of tyrants are prescribed by the endurance of those whom they oppress." — Frederick Douglass

The Parasite Classes —None of these classes are disciplined, because none of them threaten the system's survival. Not all who rise build. Some only consume. Some only perform. Some only infest. These classes are tolerated — even celebrated — because they do not produce independence. They require platforms, stipends, credentials, algorithms, or permission to exist. They are legible to power. Measurable. Replaceable. Safe. They do not own what sustains them. They do not feed communities, raise structures, or carry skills that survive system failure. They circulate wealth, language, and influence — but they do not anchor anything. And because they cannot stand without the system, they will never stand against it. That is why they are indulged. That is why they are protected. That is why their excesses are excused while builders are regulated, audited, mocked, and bled. The system does not fear parasites. Parasites never revolt. They cling.

The Trust-Fund Elite inherit wealth without sweat and call it merit. They vote for guilt, not growth — because guilt costs them nothing. They mistake consumption for contribution, curation for creation. They dine, they travel, they signal virtue — but they do not build. They have never risked a payroll, repaired what broke, or carried responsibility past inconvenience. Their success is not achievement but insulation. Capital without covenant. Comfort without competence. They speak fluently about justice, sustainability, and equity — precisely because none of it threatens their position. The system protects them because they are harmless: dependent on inheritance, allergic to sacrifice, incapable of standing once the scaffolding is removed. They are not builders. They are heirs of decay — and they confuse movement with freedom, exposure with meaning, and consumption with identity.

The Performance Class glides on stipends, subsidies, and attention. On screens they sparkle; in reality they carry no weight. They call themselves influencers, but influence without creation is illusion. Their empires are pixels. Their virtue is rented. **They produce noise, not value.** Smart enough to game the system. Too fragile to sustain it.

The Locust Class does not build where it lives. It flees collapse, then recreates it. It leaves ruined cities, ruined policies, ruined institutions — and demands the same order wherever it lands. It often arrives subsidized — by NGOs, foundations, or political pipelines — using universities and housing as entry points. It does not migrate to contribute. It migrates to consume, vote, and impose. It does not escape decay. It exports it.

The Priesthood of Policy are the intellectual enablers — those who sanctify ruin with language and turn it into doctrine. They write the creeds of modern empire: white papers instead of scripture, graphs instead of witness. They call themselves experts, analysts, thought leaders. Their gospel is management. Their altar is metrics. Their god is control. **They never bear the cost of what they design.** They do not farm, forge, or defend. They interpret. They justify. They rename chains "safeguards." They call obedience "maturity."

The Pulpit of the Serpent

Once doctrine is written, it is preached. Policy writes the creed. Media delivers the sermon. Journalists and influencers translate power into language that sounds merciful and feels inevitable. Lies are baptized as compassion. Censorship is sold as safety. Poverty is renamed "transition." They do not build nations. They narrate surrender.

When Farmers Fall, Nations Starve

The Soviets called it collectivization. Land seized. Farmers shot. Quotas enforced at gunpoint. Ukraine's black soil — once the richest in Europe — became a graveyard. Millions starved by policy, not nature. The Nazis called it the Hunger Plan. Food stripped from occupied lands to feed German tables. Bread became a weapon. Hunger an army. Denmark did not resist with rifles. It fed the Reich. Butter, bacon, pork — shipped south while swastikas flew over Copenhagen. The nation survived, but on its knees. Today Denmark does not merely regulate its farmers — it redirects them. While small producers are taxed, fined, and buried under climate quotas at home, industrial agriculture is preserved for export. Danish pork does not disappear. It ships east. China is one of the largest recipients — millions of pigs raised under exemptions denied to local farmers, processed at scale, and sold abroad. The citizen is told to eat less meat "for the planet," while the state feeds foreign markets for profit. This is not sustainability. It is rationing for the people and abundance for the buyer. The farmer is punished. The export ledger is protected. Once again, bread is seized — not to starve the world, but to discipline the nation.

Plunder Disguised as Prosperity

Who pays the price? The worker bled dry by taxes. The rancher finding strangers dead on his land. The mother burying a child poisoned by fentanyl. The soldier watching his sacrifice mocked by leaders who will not guard the gates. These are not separate tragedies. They are the downstream costs of policy sold as progress. While families absorb the damage, the system celebrates itself. They cheer rising property values. They clap at ribbon cuttings. They boast of "investment" and "growth." But when taxes soar and homes become ransom, that is not prosperity — it is plunder. The applause of your neighbors is not joy. It is the sound of a people applauding their own chains. Every "value increase" is a weapon. Every "adjustment" a transfer. Blue or red, the serpent plays both sides. Watch your city. Watch your state. Plunder dressed as prosperity is his oldest scam. The poor feel it immediately. The middle bleeds slowly. The elite are insulated.

"Woe to those who write unjust laws — who use policy to crush the poor and strip the needy of justice." — Isaiah 10:1–2

The Boiling Point

Dependency feels warm at first — stipends in your account, subsidies in your pocket, slogans in your ear. But the water never cools. It only heats. Denmark calls it stability. Europe calls it solidarity. America is told to call it compassion. Look closer. Identity thins. Families are priced out. Ownership drifts out of reach. Service classes are imported while builders are displaced. What is praised as care is control. It looks enlightened. It is slavery with a smile. Nations do not die in explosions. They evaporate. Freedom does not vanish in firestorms — it slips away in paperwork, subsidies, and smiles. By the time the water boils, the jump feels impossible. Dependency is not stability. It is slow execution. This is the road back to slavery. Not the old kind with overseers and iron — but the modern kind, where dependency replaces chains and obedience is called care.

Truth vs. Trend

We live in an age of noise without witness. Podcasters rage. Influencers rant. Few have built anything that could survive without a screen. Feelings are not facts. Opinions are not evidence. A million clicks cannot replace a single brick. The Republic does not exist to preserve comfort. It exists to protect freedom. Without builders, there is no bridge. Without farmers, there is no bread. Without men and women who sweat, risk, and sacrifice, there is no Republic — only a performance of slogans. Denmark shows the end state: builders replaced by bureaucrats, initiative punished, dependency praised. Not conquered. Hollowed. Not burned. Boiled. The next America will not be birthed by talkers. It will be birthed by builders. The age ahead will not reward cleverness — only endurance, skill, and refusal.

"All hard work brings a profit, but mere talk leads only to poverty." — Proverbs 14:23

This is not theory. It is inheritance.
A nation's chains are not forged overnight.
They are forged every time ease replaces effort,
systems replace skill,
and permission replaces responsibility.
The Two-Tier Trap is not destiny.
It is preparation.
When nothing is built and everything is taken,
only builders will remain free.
The rest will call it order.

63

VELVET CHAINS

DEPENDENCY IS THE NEW
CHAIN — VELVET, NOT IRON.

Dependency is the new chain — not iron, but debt, digital rations, and false security. The crisis facing America is not only political. It is economic. It is societal. It is spiritual. Every link is forged by those who profit when you remain weak. Once tyranny looked like shackles. Now it looks like benefits. The bread line became the EBT card (*the government-issued debit card that quietly replaced food stamps*). The ration book became the "digital wallet." The gulag became the mortgage and foreclosure. The muzzle became the "terms of service." The serpent learned - if you call slavery "safety," people will beg for it.

Dependency does not merely provide aid — it rewires behavior. When survival flows through a card, a portal, or an approval system, honesty becomes optional and obedience becomes rational. Fraud is no longer moral failure; it is adaptive behavior inside a captive system. People learn what not to report. What to hide. What not to say online. Which opinions threaten eligibility. The chain tightens not because the state is cruel, but because the recipient becomes afraid to lose access. That fear is the leash. And once fear enters the stomach, it climbs quickly to the tongue.

What Stalin enforced with rifles, Brussels enforces with subsidies. What Hitler seized with soldiers, technocrats seize with spreadsheets. What Caesars once chained in iron, globalists now chain in velvet. Comfort became the cage. And most will never leave it — because comfort feels like kindness until the day it demands your soul.

The Prophetic Warning

Moses warned Israel not to forget God when they entered the land *"with houses you did not build, vineyards you did not plant, wells you did not dig."* (Deuteronomy 6:10–12)

Forgetfulness is the seed of slavery. Prosperity without remembrance becomes dependency, and dependency, dressed as compassion, becomes the velvet rope of Babylon. Paul echoed the same alarm: *"It is for freedom that Christ has set us free. Stand firm, then, and do not let yourselves be burdened again by a yoke of slavery."* (Galatians 5:1) The yoke has returned. Only this time, it smiles.

The Price of Bread — Venezuela's Lesson

Once one of the richest nations in Latin America, Venezuela depended almost entirely on oil revenue — and when oilfields dried up, so did everything else. Years of economic mismanagement, corruption, and single-commodity dependency hollowed out production, eliminated incentives to build, and left the people dependent on state handouts, imports, and promises. As imports replaced industry and oil checks replaced work, dignity faded. Fraud and black-market coping became the norm because survival demanded it. Neighbors turned on neighbors. The ballot lost meaning when the hand that fed you also counted your vote. Hunger came later; silence came first. Venezuela proves the rule: a people who trade freedom for false security do not get both. They lose freedom first — and security last.

Break the Spell

Chains — even velvet ones — can be broken. But not by waiting. Not by pleading. Not by voting for bigger cages. The mission is clear - break free from the systems that would own you. Rebuild strength through resilience, community, and stewardship. Reclaim your freedom — because no one will hand it back to you. *No tyrant returns what he has stolen. Freedom is never given. It is reclaimed — by those who refuse the chain.* Velvet or iron, a chain is still a chain. Break it now — or bow forever.

🔥 **Firelight Pause — The Sovereign's Question**

- Where have I traded liberty for comfort?
- What invisible chains am I carrying — debt, dependency, silence?
- Who around me still believes safety comes from the very systems built to weaken them?
- What one act of resilience can I take today to loosen the chain?

Velvet chains hide in kindness and paperwork. They come wrapped in convenience, signed with compassion. But every stipend that buys obedience is a down payment on tyranny. If the Republic is to live, builders must rise again — men and women who sweat, sacrifice, and remember covenant. Not slogans. Not subsidies. Covenant.

After velvet comes theater. Freedom dies not in chains, but in subscriptions. And the serpent's newest product line is comfort — sold monthly, billed annually, soul included. The empire no longer needs decrees — only ads. The serpent markets obedience with a smile, and nations click "accept." Here's his catalog: **The American Comfort Package™** — freedom shrink-wrapped and sold with free shipping.

64

THE AMERICAN COMFORT PACKAGE

HOW COMFORT SELLS THE CAGE

The serpent doesn't sell tyranny. He sells convenience — shrink-wrapped and same-day delivered. Welcome to the catalog of captivity. Every empire has its marketplace. Babylon had idols. Rome had circuses. America has comfort.

The American Comfort Package™

Chains wrapped in screens, subscriptions, and slogans. So step right up, land of the free. Forget the frontier. Forget the covenant. Forget the fire. Here's your starter kit: **The American Comfort Package™**.

Fast-Food Liberty - Trade your cattle-ranch steak for a lab-grown burger pressed in California and call it "sustainable." Bite down on soy and subsidies while ranchers go broke and globalists cash in. What was once a field of providence becomes a product line; *The spirit of Texas and Montana — bottled, branded, Impossible™.*

"Tastes like freedom... if freedom were grown in a lab and shrink-wrapped in subsidies." — Verified Diner

And the serpent doesn't stop at your plate.

Pharma Freedom. Freedom used to mean a man with a plow, a rifle, and a prayer. Now it is a candy aisle that fattens you for Big Pharma's syringe. ADHD meds for the restless boy. Antidepressants for the silenced girl. Obesity is repackaged as a chronic market and insulin becomes a subscription — eat up, America, and pay Willy Wonka–style for the cure. *Health isn't a calling anymore — it's a recurring payment.*

"Finally — a cure for freedom. My doctor prescribed compliance in pill form!" — Happy Customer

If he can sedate your body, he'll sedate your mind.

The Screen as Sovereign. Rebellion outsourced to apps. Outrage delivered daily. Swipe for your politics. Scroll for your virtue. Netflix teaches your history. TikTok trains your children. Opinions pre-approved, rebellion pre-programmed, truth throttled. *Your feed is the new gospel* — swipe, repeat, obey.

"Scrolling replaced thinking, and honestly, I've never been more entertained!" — Influencer in Residence

The Smart Prison. "Smart" is the code word for surveillance. A fridge that counts your milk, a meter that tallies your stove, a car that reports your location. Alexa whispers back to headquarters while you whisper "freedom." Convenience became a contract - every "helpful" device is a potential sensor in a network that learns how to govern you softly. Every update is obedience disguised as innovation. You traded liberty for convenience — *A velvet prison — now with Wi-Fi.*

"Freedom at my fingertips — until the battery died. 10/10 would trade liberty for faster downloads again." — Verified Smart Citizen

Comfort Premium™

Still restless? Upgrade today.

The Patriot Pajama Set™. Slip into regulation-approved loungewear. Elastic waistband, equity-compliant fabric, and a barcode stitched on the tag. Comes with a TSA-branded eye mask for when you don't want to see what's happening. *One size fits all — so long as all means compliant.*

⭐⭐⭐⭐⭐ *"Five stars! I barely noticed when my freedoms expired. The pajama waistband is so forgiving." — Verified Subscriber*

The Couch Command Uniform™. Camo print sweatpants, a remote holster, and slippers engineered for maximum scrolling endurance. The only battles you fight are with your streaming queue. Firearms optional; delivery apps included. *Freedom reduced to two clicks and a nap.*

⭐⭐⭐⭐⭐ *"Perfect fit! Haven't left the couch in months. Who knew liberty came with free delivery apps?" — Proud Participant*

The Therapy State Hoodie™. Democracy repackaged as comfort-wear - IRS with emojis, DMV with scented candles, TSA offering "mindful pat-downs." Your voice outsourced to "community standards," your vote padded with fleece. *Bureaucracy has never been cozier.*

⭐⭐⭐⭐⭐ *"The hoodie hugged me tighter than my Constitution. I feel safe, seen, and softly silenced." — Wellness Voter*

Sedation Nation

They don't fear your guns if you never leave the couch. They don't fear your fire if you smother it with Netflix and debt. You are not a citizen anymore. You are a consumer. *Consumers swipe. Citizens roar.*

⭐⭐⭐⭐⭐ *"I haven't stood up in weeks. Resistance is overrated when delivery is free." — Couch Patriot*

The Freedom Choice™ — Abortion Rebranded

The serpent's most premium product — death disguised as deliverance. Freedom™ now comes with a clinic coupon and a hashtag. They call it empowerment — a woman's right to choose. But the serpent always sells death as deliverance. The state calls it "healthcare," the influencer calls it "self-care," and the devil calls it progress. Life reduced to paperwork, conscience outsourced to Planned Parenthood's payment portal. Because nothing says liberty like ending the future you were trusted to protect. Comfort now. Grief later. Subscription renewed.

     "Best decision I ever made — I deleted consequence and called it healing!" — Verified Empowered Customer

The Candle Guarantee (American Edition)

Every mandate, every memo, every algorithm comes bundled with a "comfort upgrade." During Covid, they called it compassion: a coupon for fries, a free streaming trial, a delivery discount. Get the shot, get a donut. Download the app, get two weeks free. Strike a match, binge your series, forget the price of freedom.

     "Best deal ever. Freedom is expensive, but comfort? Comfort is on auto-renew." — Lifetime Member

Price & Value

Groceries? Rising. Gas? Spiked. Rent? Un-payable. But hey — seven streaming platforms, unlimited Uber rides, and Ozempic on demand. *Comfort is priceless... until you see the bill.*

     "Worth every penny of my children's inheritance. At least I'm comfortable." — Verified Grandparent

Exclusive Crown Add-On

Forget kings and queens — America offers a new dynasty: the CEO. Worship at the altar of Bezos, Musk, or Zuck. *Stability never tasted so cozy.* Comes with free VR goggles so you don't notice your borders dissolving.

⭐⭐⭐⭐⭐ *"All hail King Prime. I tithe monthly with my subscription, and in return I get free shipping." — Loyal Subject*

Career Option: Bureaucrat Track™

Looking for security? The Comfort Package™ includes a career upgrade: become a compliance officer. File the forms. Smile for the HR seminar. Enforce community standards you didn't write. The paycheck is steady. The spirit dies quietly. *The pen is not mightier than the sword — it's comfier.*

⭐⭐⭐⭐⭐ *"Best gig ever. I buried three freedoms before lunch and still clocked out at 3." — Content Clerk*

So — America. Ready to trade your fire for fleece blankets, your grit for delivery apps, your covenant for a subscription plan? That's the Comfort Package™. A velvet prison with free Wi-Fi. The smile of surrender, lit by blue light. Comfort was the serpent's masterpiece — a cage that purrs.

Comfy, isn't it?

But comfort is never free. Every fleece blanket comes with a barcode. Every coupon carries a contract. Every "free" trial is a leash. The serpent hides his invoice until you're too numbed to notice. By the time you see the bill, it isn't dollars he's after — it's sovereignty. Comfort smothers. Fire frees. The serpent knows the difference. And he's betting you will choose the pillow over the fire.

65

THE PANOPLY OF
MEDIA & PLATFORMS

WAR FOR WORDS

"You are of your father the devil... When he lies, he speaks his native language." — John 8:44

The serpent's first weapon was not a sword but a sentence. His first battlefield was not the garden floor but the human tongue. He conquered with a question — *"Has God really said?"* — and he never stopped. Every empire that followed simply built louder pulpits: networks, feeds, platforms. They do not preach salvation. They preach sedation.

The New Priesthood

Once, priests interpreted Scripture. Now anchors interpret reality. They wear makeup instead of vestments, sit behind glass instead of pulpits, and preach not repentance but reassurance. Their god is engagement. Their gospel is distraction. The catechism of the screen replaces the covenant of the Word.

The Syndicate of Silence

They do not burn books; they bury stories. The same handful of corporations own the screens that define your sight. Every "independent" paper feeds from the same wire — Reuters, AP, AFP. That's why the same phrase echoes from Texas to Copenhagen: *"Experts say..." "Officials confirm..." "Sources close to the matter..."* It's not journalism. It's liturgy. One hymnbook, sung in every town, teaching citizens to doubt their own eyes. The serpent discovered mass replication long before AI. The journalist who dares to speak becomes the heretic. The citizen who questions becomes the extremist.

"Truth is fallen in the street, and equity cannot enter... Truth fails; and he who departs from evil makes himself a prey." — Isaiah 59:14–15

The Algorithm as Editor

In the old world, censorship was a red stamp. Now it's a code line — unseen, unaccountable. You post truth, it vanishes. You share courage, it's "reduced reach." You whisper dissent, and the feed buries it under ten thousand "fact-checks" funded by the same donors who fund the lies. You don't live in an information age. You live in a **curation age** — where the algorithm decides what you deserve to know.

"For the time will come when people will not endure sound teaching, but having itching ears, they will accumulate for themselves teachers to suit their own passions." — 2 Timothy 4:3–4

The Local Illusion

Small-town papers used to be watchmen. Now they're subsidiaries. A farm-town paper once defended its own; now it reprints climate reports drafted in Brussels. The local newsreader in Montana now mouths scripts written by a PR intern in Minnesota. The voice sounds familiar — but the soul is gone.

The Cost of Lies

Every false narrative carries a price tag. When media hides border collapse, towns drown in debt and fear. When they inflate panic, small shops die and monopolies feed. When they glamorize vice, industries pivot to exploitation. Each lie has an invoice, and it's billed to the working class. Truth is bad for advertisers — Your attention is the sacrifice. Every click funds captivity.

"Through covetousness they will exploit you with deceptive words." — 2 Peter 2:3

The Psychological Siege

Addiction disguised as awareness. Doom scrolling as duty. Outrage as identity. We wake up anxious, not informed. We mistake saturation for understanding. It's not mass communication. It's mass conditioning. When the mind is flooded, the conscience drowns.

"Is not My word like fire," declares the Lord, *"and like a hammer that breaks the rock in pieces?"* — Jeremiah 23:29

The Prophetic Counterstrike

Every war for words demands a remnant who still speak. You can't out-algorithm the dragon — but you can outlast him with clarity. Build alternative presses. Print truth on paper again. Teach your children how to discern tone from truth. Refuse the "neutral" middle ground. Neutrality is just censorship in polite clothes. Speak light. Speak fire. Speak covenant. The serpent rules only where language kneels. Let the righteous speak again — not with hashtags, but with fire. Because in the end, every war for words is a war for worship. And only one Word still stands unbroken.

"The mouth of the righteous speaks wisdom, and his tongue talks of justice." — Psalm 37:30

 Firelight Pause — The Mirror of Media

Sit by the fire. Let the noise fade. Ask yourself — slowly, honestly:

• Who decides what I see — me, or the systems trained on my attention and fear?

• When did silence begin to feel safer than speaking plainly?

• Do I still seek truth — or only confirmation and comfort?

• If the feed went dark tonight, would I recognize truth without permission?

• Am I informed — or conditioned? Free — or merely entertained?

The serpent no longer needs prophets. He has influencers. He no longer needs inquisitors. He has algorithms. He no longer burns scrolls. He buries them in trending noise. X sells rebellion as retweets. TikTok weaponizes apathy by the minute. Meta curates your conscience and calls it community. YouTube edits the world and names it "recommended." Every swipe trains your reflexes, not your reason. Every click builds a cage that feels like choice. And while we scroll, the watchtowers fall silent. Our minds — once the frontiers of freedom — become real estate for rent.

"Take heed what you hear; with the measure you use, it will be measured to you." — Mark 4:24

The algorithm remembers every measure. But so does Heaven. And when the last feed freezes, only one Word will remain unbroken. **And that Word still burns.**

66

MEMORY OF CHAINS

EUROPE'S SUGAR BLOOD VS. AMERICA'S FIRE

They told you Greenland was remote — a frozen footnote on the edge of history. They said Denmark's colonies were minor, that the sins in the ice did not matter. But graves are never small. They are receipts — each one testifying to the price of empire. What Denmark buried, Europe perfected: the art of forgetting. And what Europe perfected, America now toys with — the temptation to forget that freedom was paid for in blood.

The Art of Forgetting

Empires never confess what they built on bones. They rename conquest as progress, chains as heritage, blood as culture. The words change, but the hunger does not. Rome called its colonies provinces. Britain called them protectorates. Brussels calls them unions. Every empire learns the same trick — cover blood with treaties and call silence peace. Forgetting is the favorite weapon of power. *It turns crime into policy and amnesia into virtue.* Europe hides its sugar wealth and colonial graves beneath museums and flags. America, for all its wounds, still carries a different fire — the covenant that remembers freedom's cost.

That is what they fear most — a people who remember. Because memory breeds defiance, and defiance breaks chains. This is not simply history; it is covenant. *God commanded remembrance.* Forgetting is how empires survive. Remembering is how revolutions begin. To forget is to surrender your fire to another master. That is why every empire sells amnesia as maturity — because a people who remember cannot be ruled. Memory is strength, the weapon the serpent cannot counterfeit. History is not an archive to be curated; it is a battlefield to be won. And those who remember, win.

Europe's Amnesia

Europe remembers castles, cathedrals, and cafés. It forgets sugar blood and colonial graves. It forgets the cries from Christiansborg's dungeons, the plantations of St. Croix, the women sterilized in Greenland. It forgets Algeria's blood in French streets, Congolese hands severed under Belgian rule, Roma herded into Austrian camps. It even forgets its *own daughters.* It forgets the hundreds of thousands to over a million—German women violated during the collapse when the Red Army swept west. — their pain buried beneath the rubble, unspoken in the treaties that followed. The victors wrote peace while the wounded were told to be silent. The United Nations rose, but no monument was built for them. *The century changed; the reflex did not.* Because forgetting is not ignorance; it is rebellion against remembrance itself — the oldest sin repeated in marble.

Europe's gold still glitters with graves. And the silence has become its creed. It forgets — because *forgetting protects the system.* A continent that never repented only rebranded. Plantations became the welfare state. Chains became subsidies. And they call it civilization. But this is not merely political, nor even historical. **It is spiritual law unfolding.** What nations refuse to confess, they will relive. What they bury in silence returns as storm. When blood cries from the ground and no repentance answers, the curse does not vanish — it migrates.

You are not looking at immigration, or ideology, or coincidence. You are looking at *the mirror of empire*. Every un-repented sin becomes a seed, and seeds always find their season. Europe forgot covenant, so covenant now forgets Europe. The land remembers even when men do not. The nations that built their glory on the backs of others now find their foundations cracking beneath their own feet. Judgment is never sudden — it is memory made visible. And the pattern repeats. The names change — *progress, recovery, reconstruction* — but the reflex endures. From colonial missions to modern institutions, children torn from families, shipped across borders in the name of charity. The unwanted locked in institutions until their voices vanish. Cities rebuilt while their old quarters are razed, the stones of memory traded for steel and glass. Each generation is told it is new, yet walks among ruins it cannot name. This is not politics; it is war in the unseen — a war for memory itself. The serpent does not conquer by sword anymore, but by narrative. He edits. He renames. He convinces the living to bury the dead twice — once in the ground, and again in silence. This is not renewal; it is ritual — the periodic cleansing of conscience by destruction. The elites call it progress. Heaven calls it forgetting.

"For we wrestle not against flesh and blood, but against principalities, against powers, against the rulers of the darkness of this world, against spiritual wickedness in high places." — Ephesians 6:12

The Mirror Opens

The same reflex that buried Europe's sins now threatens every free land that forgets its covenant. What if this is not geography at all, but prophecy written in marble and markets — in treaties and streets? What if these nations are mirrors, not of politics, but of spirit? Every policy hides a theology. Every border traces a forgotten vow. What Europe calls migration, ideology, or modernization is only the surface. Beneath it runs the deeper current — the reckoning of covenant. The land itself bears witness. What was sown in conquest now blossoms in confusion; what was denied in repentance now returns as reversal.

This is not condemnation — it is unveiling. The pattern is ancient and exact — pride before captivity, denial before decay. Empires rise on borrowed fire, and when that fire goes unpaid, it burns their own houses. So look again at the continent — not with the eyes of politics, but with the eyes of spirit. What if what you are watching is not decline, but harvest? What if history itself is remembering what men tried to forget?

"They refused to love the truth ... therefore God sends them a powerful delusion so that they will believe the lie." — 2 Thessalonians 2:10–11

The Children of Amnesia

The citizens of these lands are not villains — they are the children of amnesia. They walk streets built on bones and think the silence is peace. They inherit palaces of order without knowing whose hands laid the stones. They sense the shaking, but they do not know its cause. They watch their borders blur, their speech policed, their faith mocked — and they ask *why?* They are told it is politics. Policy. Progress. But it is the old covenant stirring. The laws of sowing and reaping have no expiration date. What their fathers refused to confess, their sons now live through. When repentance is denied, remembrance becomes judgment. Yet even now, mercy waits. *If a nation remembers, God remembers mercy. If it kneels, He restores.* But repentance is not apology. It is return. It cannot be spoken by bureaucrats — only by hearts. It begins not in parliaments, but in prayer. Until nations bow, they will bend. Until they confess, they will be confused. Could repentance still change it? Scripture says yes — but time is not patient. *The fire that purifies is the same fire that consumes.* Yet even in amnesia, mercy waits — memory is the door back to covenant.

"If My people, who are called by My name, will humble themselves and pray and seek My face and turn from their wicked ways, then I will hear from heaven, and will forgive their sin and heal their land." — 2 Chronicles 7:14

Virtue as camouflage. Management as monarchy. Switzerland calls it prudence. Austria calls it victimhood. Luxembourg calls it discretion. Norway calls it welfare. Neutrality was never innocence; it was empire in soft focus — power without fingerprints. Nazi gold, colonial plunder, oligarch fortunes — baptized clean in "neutral" vaults. Brussels made bureaucracy the new throne; Geneva made control sound like conscience. They never repented. They rebranded. Chains became subsidies. Loot became "heritage."

Do not take their guilt as your own. The Europeans who fled here were rebels, not the bankers of Babylon. You were not born neutral. You were born in covenant fire. When you forget, you become Europe. When you remember, you remain free. The following is not written to shame a nation but to strip its myths bare. The wounds of empire cannot heal if they are never named. Truth is not hatred; it is surgery. And only what is cut open can breathe again.

🔥 **Firelight Pause — Memory as Weapon**

Sit with this a moment. Memory is not nostalgia — it is warfare. Ask yourself:

- What have *I* forgotten that my freedom depends on?
- What stories did my parents bury to keep peace — and what chains grew in that silence?
- Where have I accepted comfort instead of remembrance?
- Which wounds in my land have never been confessed — and still bleed through policy, culture, or fear?
- When did I begin believing the lie that forgetting is maturity?
- Have I buried truth because speaking it would cost me something?
- If my children inherit only my amnesia, what chains will they wear because of it?

Remember — A nation that forgets becomes Europe. A people that remember become free.

67

———

THE EUROPEAN MIRROR — THE FALL THAT WARNS AMERICA

EMPIRES DO NOT REPENT. THEY ONLY RENAME

Empires do not die. They change uniforms. They trade banners for bureaucracies and armies for acronyms. But the reflex remains — to rule, to rename, to forget. Europe is the proof. Every flag now flying above its parliaments is stitched with older ghosts. The marble still remembers. This chapter is not written for revenge but for reckoning. To look at Europe is to stare into the anatomy of forgetting — nations that baptized conquest as culture, polished guilt into heritage, and now reap the harvest of their own denial. Each country tells the same story in a different accent: faith turned into ideology, courage into compliance, repentance into regulation. These pages are not history lessons. They are mirrors. For every sin there is a return; for every empire, an echo. The faces change, the laws evolve, the creeds grow softer — but the law of sowing and reaping does not bend. The blood of the forgotten still writes policy in invisible ink. Look closely. Behind the statistics, the treaties, the migration quotas, lies a single pulse — the unhealed wound of empire. What Europe refused to confess now walks its streets, prays in its churches-turned-museums, and whispers through its bureaucracies. This is not punishment. It is remembrance made visible. So we open the atlas. We turn the pages of marble and smoke. We let each land speak its sin — and its return.

497

Britain — The Proud Mother of Chains

The Sin. Commonwealth as mask. India starved under "policy," Kenya's rebels caged, Irish tongues beaten from schools. Caribbean hands bled for sugar while London polished empire into heritage. Whips became treaties; plunder became "legacy." **The Mirror.** Chains return to their makers. The peoples once ruled now crowd the cities their labor built. In many districts churches empty while other minarets rise; sharia-based mediation shadows civil courts. The crown that conquered in Christ's name now silences its own gospel for fear of offense. Not invasion — inheritance. *"As you have done, it shall be done to you; your deeds shall return upon your own head."* — Obadiah 1:15

France — The Mirror of the Republic

The Sin. Liberté on banners, empire in practice. Algeria bled; Sétif burned. Philosophy covered sugar wealth and colonial violence; monuments outshouted repentance. **The Mirror.** The banlieues ring Paris like judgment. The sons of empire shape the suburbs; estimates place Muslims near a tenth of adults. Schools that once taught revolution now negotiate veils and riots. Not migration — consequence. *"They sow the wind, and they shall reap the whirlwind."* — Hosea 8:7

Belgium — The Marble and the Blood

The Sin. Leopold II's Congo: rubber quotas, rifles, severed hands. Brussels laundered blood into boulevards. **The Mirror.** Nearly half of Brussels residents are foreign-born; radicalization indices run high. The hands once severed now vote where ledgers were kept. *"They dress the wound... saying 'Peace, peace,' when there is no peace."* — Jeremiah 6:14

Netherlands — The Merchant's Creed

The Sin. Dutch East India Company (VOC) and Dutch West India Company (WIC): spice, sugar, slaves, soil — contracts crowned as civilization. After empire, welfare at home, networks abroad. Merchant logic survived. **The Mirror.** The ships returned with people. Workers from Indonesia, Suriname, Morocco, Turkey keep the ports humming. Commerce eclipsed covenant; citizens became inventory. *"By your great skill in trade you have increased your wealth, and your heart has become proud in your wealth."* — Ezekiel 28:5

Spain — The Faith That Conquered

The Sin. Cross fused with conquest; Inquisition sanctified control; Franco baptized obedience. **The Mirror.** From North Africa and the Middle East, new faiths cross the same seas. In regions of Andalusia and Catalonia, mosques multiply as monasteries fade. EU quotas dictate budgets and borders. Not conquest by sword — but by silence. *"You are like whitewashed tombs, which outwardly appear beautiful, but within are full of dead men's bones."* — Matthew 23:27

Germany — The Engine of Remembrance

The Sin. One atrocity confessed, another buried (Herero, Nama). The Reich's industrial dynasties rebadged for reconstruction; repentance mechanized into governance. **The Mirror.** Germany rules by systems, not soldiers — EU law, ECB austerity. Nearly one in five residents born abroad. Bureaucracy replaced belief; guilt became governance. *"Be sure your sin will find you out."* — Numbers 32:23

Austria — The Neutral Mask

The Sin. "Hitler's first victim" as national myth; guilt rebranded as diplomacy; elegance without honesty. **The Mirror.** Vienna hosts the world's committees and its frictions: sizable foreign-born population, imported tensions. The city that staged peace now administers fatigue. *"Their tongue is a deadly arrow; it speaks deceit."* — Jeremiah 9:8

Switzerland — The Polished Coin

The Sin. Neutrality banked blood. Nazi gold, cartel fortunes, colonial profits. BIS as altar; Geneva as conscience-for-hire. **The Mirror.** The vaults now hold data and ESG virtue. Davos crowns unelected saviors; migrants clean the halls where technocrats plan "salvation." *"You cannot serve God and money."* — Matthew 6:24

Luxembourg — The Quiet Vault

The Sin. Occupied twice, then monetized modesty. Shells outnumber citizens; the ECJ upstairs, tax rulings downstairs. **The Mirror.** Nearly half the nation foreign-born. The accountant of empire hums in decimals while Brussels writes the liturgy. *"Your riches have rotted... your gold and silver are corroded. Their corrosion will testify against you."* — James 5:2–3

Sweden — The Velvet Empire

The Sin. Neutrality sold as holiness while arming both sides of history; welfare sanctified as creed. **The Mirror.** Refugees from wars Sweden supplied now crowd suburbs; riots expose the seam. Virtue without repentance becomes ideology with teeth. *"Even from your own mouths you will be condemned; for with your lips you testify against yourselves."* — Luke 19:22

Italy — The Altar and the Airbase

The Sin. NATO's southern staging ground, Vatican's shield, Gladio's shadow — devotion blurred with deception. **The Mirror.** Boats wash against Lampedusa while drones launch inland. Saints and spies still share the square. *"They honor Me with lips; hearts far from Me."* — Matthew 15:8

Greece — The Cradle and the Cage

The Sin. Wisdom pawned to creditors. Eurozone entry, swaps, spectacle — then Troika austerity. Islands sold; hospitals gutted. **The Mirror.** Aegean camps shadow temples; migrants man cafés and docks. Philosophers gone; accountants remain. *"Professing to be wise, they became fools."* — Romans 1:22

Norway — The Virtue Vault

The Sin. Fortress to Reich, then ethics as brand; oil baptized as purity; peace monetized. **The Mirror.** Full vaults, empty pews. Foreign-born share rising; calls to prayer echo where missions once launched. Peace as product cannot purchase repentance. *"Woe to those who trust in wealth and boast in their great riches."* — Psalm 49:6

Turkey — The Gate Between Empires

The Sin. Sold neutrality dear; joined NATO; kept the tollbooth of empires. **The Mirror.** Millions of refugees crowd the gate; the straits that carried fleets now carry rafts. Brussels rents a border; Ankara rents the world. *"I will set My face against you, and nations will be shaken at your fall."* — Ezekiel 26:3

Europe's crown has fallen, and the Gate now trembles. Beyond the sea waits the last fire — the one nation still unbowed.

America — The Fire That Remembers

Do not mistake remembrance for innocence. America's fire burns because it remembers sin. This soil carries graves — of slaves who broke their chains in blood, and of tribes driven from their covenant lands. The Cherokee, Creek, Choctaw, Chickasaw, and Seminole walked the Trail of Tears — not as strangers, but as a mirror of our broken promise. This land has known pride, conquest, and mercy — all in the same breath.

But unlike Europe, we did not varnish our sins in marble. We faced them. We bled for them. We repented in fire. That is why our memory still burns, and why our hope is not comfort — but covenant. We still swear juries. We still bury sons in uniform. The fire costs. That is why it purifies. America remembers differently. Our memory is jagged, bloody, unpolished — but it burns. *We fought the bloodiest war in our history to break slavery's back.* Brother against brother. Six hundred thousand dead. Because liberty was worth the cost. We carry wounds, but also fire. **We speak our sins aloud.** We write them in schoolbooks. We topple statues of our own founders — sometimes foolishly, sometimes in repentance — but never in silence. Unlike Europe, we do not hide our chains in candlelight. We drag them into the open. That fire is our hope. Slavery was not denied — it was dragged into the light. The Civil War was not polite. It was fire and iron. Chains did not dissolve in silence; they shattered in blood. At Gettysburg, Shiloh, Antietam — liberty was purchased in graves. The Constitution was scarred, but reforged. Europe's forgetting birthed Brussels. America's remembering birthed fire. Europe hid its chains. America burned hers. America was not chosen for power, but for memory—to be the lamp that refuses to go out when the world forgets. **That was not comfort. It was covenant.**"That this nation, under God, shall have a new birth of freedom." — Lincoln at Gettysburg.

Immigrants — *Two Roads*

Every empire drew immigrants for labor. But America, when memory was alive, turned immigrants into citizens. They raised barns. Planted gardens. Took oaths. Buried their dead in new soil. They belonged. But the serpent opened another road — grievances harvested by bureaucrats. Bodies imported without belonging. Numbers without names. Quotas instead of neighbors. One road leads to covenant. The other to control. Ellis Island carved names in stone. Today's systems reduce men to data in spreadsheets. The question remains: are you being welcomed into a nation — or processed into a program?

The Transatlantic Bargain

After the war, America stood as the last free fire — but its leaders made a bargain with the ashes. Franklin D. Roosevelt and Harry Truman rebuilt the world not as covenant, but as contract. They wrote the blueprints of a "new order" that looked like peace but operated like empire.

The Bretton Woods Agreement (1944). A meeting of forty-four nations in New Hampshire — bankers and ministers crafting the architecture of global finance. The dollar became the anchor of the world; gold its promise. Europe's shattered economies were tied to America's currency, and America's currency was tied to their dependence. The World Bank and the International Monetary Fund were born that week — not as charities, but as levers. Loans became chains; "stability" became surveillance. The empire learned to print what it used to plunder. The United Nations (1945). A covenant written in marble, raised from the ruins of war. But the architects were the same powers that had divided the world before. The League of Nations had failed because it was weak; the U.N. would succeed because it was powerful. Its mission: "peace." Its method: control through consensus. America hosted it; Europe designed it; globalists baptized it. A parliament without people, a conscience without repentance.

The Marshall Plan (1948). $13 billion in aid — the greatest act of generosity ever recorded, they said. But follow the ledgers: contracts, conditions, rebuilding the same industrial families — Krupp, Thyssen, Siemens — under new management. Europe rose, yes, but on America's credit and under America's banks. The same ports that once loaded arms now unloaded aid. The same men signed the checks. Reconstruction became reintegration. The Atlantic Charter (1941, reaffirmed 1946). Roosevelt and Churchill's promise of freedom for all peoples — a noble sentence wrapped around an unspoken clause: Freedom under management. Colonies were not liberated; they were reorganized. National sovereignty was praised — so long as it obeyed the new order. The words were covenantal; the outcome contractual.

In rescuing Europe, America absorbed it. In leading the alliance, we inherited the infection. The serpent crossed the ocean not by ships, but by signatures. From those signatures grew the system that now rules the world — NATO policing nations, the IMF managing debt, the UN rewriting law, and the World Economic Forum scripting policy for governments that never voted. The covenant of ashes became the architecture of control. I recognized it before I could name it. Because it *smelled like Europe*. The same sterile air. The same polished arrogance disguised as order. They called it policy, partnership, progress — but I had breathed this before. It was the odor of control wrapped in civility, the perfume of safety that smothers courage. America was meant to be different — covenant, not compliance; risk, not regulation. Knowing history and European culture, I could smell the old continent rising again, this time in Washington and New York. Empire without flags. The serpent's accent, fluent in English.

"You boast, 'We have made a covenant with death, and with Sheol we are in agreement; when the overwhelming scourge passes through, it will not reach us, for we have made lies our refuge and falsehood our shelter.' Therefore thus says the Lord: 'Your covenant with death will be annulled; your agreement with Sheol will not stand.'" — Isaiah 28:15–18

The Republic You Forgot

Self-government is not slogans. It is oaths sworn in courthouses. Neighbors gathering in town halls. Juries filled with citizens who remember their duty. Memory practiced — lived — defended. Lose that, and you lose the Republic. Forget remembrance, and you accept management. Forget your chains, and you will wear them again. Picture the jury box half-empty because citizens no longer care. Picture neighbors who no longer know each other's names. Picture oaths recited by rote, drained of fire. That is how republics rot. The silence of citizens is the seedbed of tyranny.

The Psychology of Forgetting

Forgetting feels easier. That is why it works. Europe forgets by convenience. America forgets by seduction. Screens dull memory. Textbooks omit battles. Social media curates shame and calls it progress. History outsourced to the cloud — where it can be deleted at will. Forgetting is not failure. It is strategy. It is how empires keep you docile. *An empire doesn't need to burn the archives if it can edit the search results.*

Who Holds the Pen

Chains today are not forged in iron. They are signed into law. Who holds those pens? In Denmark, bureaucrats scrub textbooks. In Brussels, commissioners write migration quotas and call them "partnerships." In New York and Geneva, UN councils rename slavery as "equity" and censorship as "safety." In California and Massachusetts, governors copy EU decrees into state law — digital IDs, climate compacts, migration quotas — without a single American vote. In Davos, the serpent hides behind smiles and signatures. The dragon funds the infrastructure. The beast codifies it into law. **Memory — *your memory* — is the last firewall.** And the fire still lives — not in marble or markets, but in the remnant who remember.

Firelight Pause — The Republic's Test
- Will you remember when remembering costs?
- Will you speak when silence feels safe?
- If the serpent sells peace again, will you buy it?
- If your children inherit your apathy, will they still inherit your liberty?
- When your nation forgets, will you remember enough for both of you?

The Neutral Empire

Virtue as camouflage. Management as monarchy. What do these nations share? *Neutrality* — the velvet word. The mask that hides the blade. Switzerland calls it prudence. Austria calls it victimhood. Luxembourg calls it discretion. Norway calls it welfare. Spain once called it peace. But neutrality was never innocence. It was empire in soft focus — the art of power without fingerprints. Behind every polished plaza and Alpine meadow lies the same ledger: *blood in, wealth out.* Blood from Africa's fields and America's mines. Wealth funneled through banks and treaties. Nazi gold, colonial plunder, oligarch fortunes — all baptized clean in the vaults of "neutral" Europe. And what tongue recorded those ledgers? *German.* The language of decrees, contracts, and control. Austria spoke it. Switzerland banked in it. Luxembourg filed in it. Denmark obeyed it under occupation. Even Brussels — the heart of the "Union" — now drafts its decrees in the same bureaucratic rhythm. Coincidence? Or continuity? They never repented. They rebranded. Chains became subsidies. Loot became "heritage." Atrocity became architecture. Brussels became the seat of empire again — the EU Commission and NATO under one roof, built on Congo blood. Geneva became the conscience of the world — the UN's second capital, housed in Swiss marble and financed by vaults of old gold. Vienna became the stage of diplomacy — oil monarchs, OPEC clerks, UN envoys signing decrees under Austria's "neutral" light. Luxembourg became the accountant — the European Court of Justice above, the tax shelters below. Neutrality became the crown of the modern empire. Its capitals are not castles, but committees. *Its weapons are not armies, but algorithms. Its tyranny wears a smile.*

And **America — here is your test.** Do not take their guilt as your own. Do not let their amnesia become your inheritance. The Europeans who fled here were not the elites who hoarded blood-wealth. They were the rebels. The farmers. The families who refused to bow. **They crossed an ocean not to serve empire, but to break free of it. Your fire was covenant, not neutrality.** Your wealth was sweat and covenant oath, not slave forts in Africa or vaults in Zurich. You bled to break chains — not polish them.

But now many reach across the Atlantic, begging again for the same chains their fathers fled — craving management over freedom, regulation over risk, safety over sovereignty. They mistake comfort for virtue, and call obedience peace. The tragedy is not that Europe forgot, but that America envies its forgetting. The question is not — Will America be like Europe? The question is — Will America forget what made her different? Neutrality was their shield. German was their ledger. Wealth was their altar. They called it prudence, but it was plunder. They called it discretion, but it was blood scrubbed clean in vaults. Europe wrote its amnesia in stone and marble, in treaties and textbooks. But you, *America — you were not born neutral. You were born in covenant fire.* You broke chains with muskets and oaths, not with ledgers and masks. The question before you is not whether you will be rich, but whether you will remember. Because when you forget, you become Europe. When you remember, you remain free. Neutrality is empire's lie. Covenant is freedom's truth. **Choose.** These are only some of Europe's amnesias. The ledger is longer, the graves are deeper. But the pattern is enough. To remember is to resist. To forget is to surrender. Because the fire that forgets becomes ash.

"*Remember the days of old; consider the years of many generations. Ask your father, and he will show you; your elders, and they will tell you.*" — Deuteronomy 32:7

◊ **Firelight Pause — Memory Test**

• What chains did your fathers break — and have you forgotten the cost?

• What graves lie beneath your nation's marble halls?

• What stories are being erased from your town, your school, your church?

• What monuments still honor the rulers while the ruled remain unnamed?

• Whose grievance do you carry while your own wounds are ignored?

• What language do your laws speak — covenant, or empire?

• Do you guard memory as fire — or trade it for comfort?

• When forgetting is offered as peace, will you choose to remember?

68

MONEY WITHOUT SOUL
— THE NEW CHAINS

THE DIGITAL AND FINANCIAL TACTICS

Empires used to mint coins. Then they printed paper. Now they mint obedience. The currency of the new world is not gold or labor — it is data. The same systems that once counted your wages now count your worth. The same ledgers that tracked trade now track trust. The dollar, once backed by metal, is now backed by management. And when management replaces meaning, freedom becomes a variable — adjustable at will.

Central Bank Digital Currencies — The Code of Control — CBDCs are not "innovation." They are the final conversion of sovereignty into software. Every transaction becomes traceable. Every account programmable. The same governments that weaponized lockdowns now want to weaponize ledgers. Under a CBDC regime, money no longer belongs to you; it belongs to permission. They can expire it, limit where you spend it, or freeze it for "non-compliance." That is not currency — it is code-based captivity. The technology is ready. The theology is ancient.

508

ESG — Morality for Sale

Environmental, Social, and Governance scores sound ethical — but they are metrics of submission. ESG is how technocrats decide which companies deserve oxygen. It isn't about carbon; it's about control. Comply, and you receive access. Resist, and your capital dries up. Banks become priests of virtue, rating your soul by spreadsheet. The same firms that funded pollution now fund repentance — for a fee. It is indulgences for the digital age.

Paywalls and Platforms — The New Tax Collectors

You once paid taxes to kings. Now you pay subscriptions to gatekeepers. Algorithms decide which truths are "premium." Knowledge is no longer shared — it's leased. Even speech has toll roads. They censor the prophets and charge the peasants. The internet was supposed to democratize; instead, it feudalized — the few own the gates, and the many rent their way through them. You are the product — your outrage, your clicks, your fear.

The Parallel Economy — The Exodus Strategy

There is another way. Parallel economies are not rebellion; they are remembrance. They restore the ancient covenant of honest weight and measure. Barter, local trade, hard assets, decentralized currency — not as novelty, but as resistance. Build networks of trust, not surveillance. Support those who create real value — farmers, builders, craftsmen, truth-tellers. Withdraw your consent from systems that monetize your obedience. In the empire's economy, value is extracted. In the remnant's economy, value is created. Theirs is debt disguised as stability. Ours is stewardship measured in truth and work.

"Do not lay up for yourselves treasures on earth, where moth and rust destroy and thieves break in and steal; but lay up treasures in heaven..." — Matthew 6:19-20

The Economic War Is Spiritual

This is not to condemn wealth or trade — those were God's tools long before Babylon's. The sin begins when value replaces virtue, when profit replaces purpose. You cannot serve God and money — but the serpent insists you must. The financial system is not neutral; it is a theology in disguise. Every ledger carries a creed. Every transaction a covenant. Either your economy flows from faith — voluntary exchange under God — or from fear — managed value under man. They promise efficiency, equality, sustainability — but deliver dependence. In the name of saving the planet, they enslave it. ESG replaces repentance with reporting. CBDCs replace generosity with compliance. AI replaces conscience with code. And the people, lulled by convenience, call it progress. This is not about economics. It is about ownership — of soul, time, and choice. And the mark will not begin with a chip; it begins with consent.

🔥 **Firelight Pause — The Ledger of Souls**
- Who measures your worth — God, or the algorithm?
- If your wallet were frozen tomorrow, would you still be free?
- When you spend, who gains — the craftsman, or the system?
- Is your giving covenant — or monitored compliance?
- Do you trade your hours for truth — or for comfort?
- What do you possess that the State cannot touch?
- Who writes the code that now writes your choices?
- When currency becomes conscience, which one will you spend?

Empires once ruled by iron, then by ink. Now they rule by input. The sword became the ledger; the ledger became the code. When value can be edited, man becomes programmable. This is not finance — it is faith inverted. Digital money, digital identity, digital morality — three cords of the same chain. The system no longer needs your land; it only needs to assign your worth. Citizenship becomes access. Sin becomes "non-compliance." **The mark won't be forced at first — it will be offered as convenience.**

69

TECHNOCRACY — THE MARK OF MANAGEMENT

THE MACHINE THAT CALLS ITSELF MERCY

The serpent has learned to speak in metrics. He no longer tempts with fruit; he offers upgrades. Every tyranny needs belief — and technocracy is the religion of data. It promises salvation through efficiency, absolution through compliance, paradise through policy. It speaks the language of progress but carries the soul of Babel. The dream is always the same: one system, one code, one consciousness — managed by the enlightened few "for the good of all."

The Creed of the Code

They say, *"Trust the science."* They mean, *"Obey the system."* They say, *"Data will save us."* They mean, *"You will be measured until nothing human remains."* Algorithms become priests of truth; bureaucrats become gods of morality. Your choices are modeled, your thoughts predicted, your risks priced.

"Ever learning, and never able to come to the knowledge of the truth." — 2 Timothy 3:7

511

The Infrastructure of Obedience

Digital IDs, biometric passports, climate credits, health passes — every link sold as safety, every scan sold as belonging. Together they form the scaffolding of a world where permission replaces freedom. The same hand that offers convenience writes the code that decides who may buy, travel, or speak. When access becomes morality, you are already in the temple of the Beast. I saw it first in airports — the soft scan, the gentle nod, the gate that opened only for the compliant. They called it safety. It felt like worship. Europe accepted it first — but not because it chose. It obeyed as it always has — with a smile, with a stamp, with the quiet pride of being "modern." The ritual was not new; only the technology changed. The liturgy of obedience found a new altar — glowing, silent, efficient. In Genesis, man built a tower to reach heaven. Now he builds a network to replace it. Silicon Valley preaches immortality; Geneva codifies morality; Davos defines virtue. They call it *global governance*. Scripture calls it *Babylon reborn*.

"They said, 'Come, let us build ourselves a city and a tower with its top in the heavens...'" — Genesis 11:4

Technocracy is not neutral. It is worship inverted. Every app, every platform, every scan trains the soul to bow before the system that sees all and forgives none. The promise of safety hides the price of surrender. Once, kings ruled through armies. Now, elites rule through automation. The code does not sleep; the algorithm does not absolve. The answer is not escape but remembrance. Refuse the mechanical conscience. Defend the sacred boundary between man and machine — spirit and system. Build tools that serve life, not rule it. Choose craftsmanship over convenience. Paper over passcodes. Oath over automation. For the technocrat's god is precision. But the Living God is fire — and even here, mercy glimmers.

🔥 **Firelight Pause — The Test of Obedience**
- When truth is measured by code, will you still discern by spirit?
- If they promise safety for your soul, will you sell it?
- Do your tools serve freedom — or shape it?
- When "efficiency" demands silence, will you obey or burn?
- The mark begins not on skin, but in consent. Have you already given yours?

The Human Cost

I am not against technology. Fire itself was once technology — the first tool that could either warm a home or burn one down. In the right hands, code can heal, connect, and build. I have seen brilliance born in garages and mercy programmed into machines. But the question is never how fast we can make them think — it is whether we still remember how to feel. No algorithm can replace a handshake. No sensor can replace a soul. Every self-checkout lane that removes a cashier removes a conversation. Every automation that saves time may also steal touch. We need not fear the tools — only the forgetfulness that follows them. Technology without conscience becomes tyranny with a dashboard. If we do not teach humanity to hold the tools, the tools will soon hold humanity.

The machine is not new. It is Europe perfected. What the serpent coded in data, he first rehearsed in imperial decrees. The algorithm is only the latest empire — bureaucracy reborn in silicon. Davos is just Babylon with Wi-Fi. Brussels is Rome in a suit. The creed of the code began in cathedrals turned into councils, pulpits turned into policies. Before the world worshiped data, it worshiped order. And every order without God becomes a cage.

The technocrat does not kill faith — he digitizes it.

70

WHAT EUROPE FORGOT

SOFT HANDS. HARD JUDGMENT. A CONTINENT ASLEEP IN ITS RUINS

History rarely shouts. It whispers. It arrives not with armies, but with comfort — with ease, with forgetting. Not through conquest, but through silence. I have walked both continents. I have lived in Europe. I have lived in America. And I have seen: one fell by amnesia, and the other is following the same slope. Europe forgot the sacred. It forgot the sword. It forgot that strength without God becomes tyranny, and compassion without truth becomes cowardice. They traded churches for social programs. Courage for conformity. Wildness for welfare. The voice of God for the voice of bureaucracy.

In Denmark, I watched faith turned into folklore. Masculinity branded offensive. Men tamed into systems. Women polished into polite enforcers. And the people clapped — because the benefits kept coming. But beneath the applause, something ancient was dying — not in revolt or collapse, but in exchange. Memory was traded for management. Fire for benefits. Covenant for compliance. A nation can survive hardship. It cannot survive forgetting. The covenant fire that once sent Vikings across seas and Reformation preachers into pulpits had been reduced to candles in museums. Forgetting was not passive. It was deliberate. The Reich shed its uniforms but kept its planners. Brussels inherited the method.

514

They signed treaties that looked harmless but carried chains. The Paris Climate Accord cloaked as salvation but written as taxation. The UN Migration Compact dressed as compassion but written as surrender. The EU Green Deal taxed cows while importing grain from abroad. The WHO Pandemic Accords issued unelected decrees in the name of "health." This is not politics. *It is amnesia legislated.* Europe institutionalized forgetting — and then exported it. Europe forgot God — and remembered only management. A continent that loses its altar always builds more offices. Europe forgot God and inherited bureaucracy. It forgot covenant and inherited collapse. The cradle emptied. The coffin filled. This is not demography — it is consequence.

"They forgot the Lord their God, and He sold them into the hands of their enemies." — Judges 3:7–8

And Now... America

I came here for fire. Something in my bones still believed this country had not bowed. For a time, I was right. But I have seen it dim. America is not falling by invasion. She is falling by ease. Not by enemies at the gate — but by amnesia in the heart. Not by bombs, but by screens. Not by chains, but by comfort. Not by tyrants, but by forgetting. We medicate children. We mock masculinity. We legalize everything but holiness. And then we wonder why we feel lost. This is not political. It is spiritual. Screens don't just distract. They dictate. Comfort doesn't just dull. It disciplines. Europe rehearsed forgetting through bureaucracy. America rehearses forgetting through algorithms, HR catechisms, and curated outrage.

The Serpent's Hand

What Hitler enforced with jackboots, Brussels enforces with quotas. What Stalin dictated with commissars, the UN dictates with compacts. Comfort is the spell. Forgetting is the chain. The serpent is the hand behind both. The Beast codifies it. And America, if she forgets, becomes the prize. I have seen the end of this road. It looks like cathedrals turned into museums. It looks like nations with everything — and nothing. It looks like people who traded fire for safety, then begged for rescue when the wolves came. **Europe is not a path forward.** It is a warning carved in ruins. If America forgets who she is, she will become a copy — with better highways and better branding.

"The wicked shall be turned into hell, and all the nations that forget God." — Psalm 9:17

🔥 **Firelight Pause — Lest You Forget**
- What am I calling freedom that is really comfort?
- Where have I mistaken ease for peace, and silence for safety?
- What will my children inherit — my courage or my quiet?
- Do I carry America in my mouth, or in my marrow?
- If history records silence as complicity, what will it write of mine?

Europe forgot first — cathedrals became museums, covenant became bureaucracy, amnesia became progress. Now America stands at the same fork. One road remembers and stays free. The other forgets and bows. I know what forgetting births. Europe traded fire for management — and woke up in chains. If America forgets, she will not be unique. She will only be next — and the serpent is already at the door. The next war is not for land or oil. It is for memory itself.

"If you ever forget the Lord your God... I solemnly warn you today that you shall surely perish." — Deuteronomy 8:19

71

—————

THE WAR THEY DON'T WANT YOU TO REMEMBER

SECRETS, SILENCE, AND THE BATTLE FOR TRUTH

"*He who controls the past controls the future. He who controls the present controls the past.*" — George Orwell. History is not neutral. Memory is a weapon. Those who rewrite the past rewrite the future. They do not merely edit textbooks; they reassign guilt, rearrange heroes, and repurpose liberty into compliance. If you forget who carried the flame, you will hand your children a cold cinder.

The Counterfeit Word

They told you America was a democracy. They drilled it in your schools, echoed it in your media, and flattered you with the word because it sounds noble. But America was never designed as a democracy. It was forged as a **constitutional republic** — a covenant founded on unalienable rights given by God, not granted by government. **A democracy bows to the crowd; a republic bows only to truth.** One protects conscience; the other crucifies it. One shifts with moods and mobs; the other stands on principles even when truth is unpopular. That is why the republic is hated by managers and pollsters — because it cannot be administered by focus groups and trending topics. And that is why our republic today lies on life support.

517

Jefferson, Madison, Hamilton — the Founders warned us. Jefferson feared mob rule; he called democracy a danger to ordered liberty. Madison, in *Federalist No. 10*, framed the republic as a firewall — a design to control factions and protect minorities from the passions of the majority. Hamilton argued for a strong structure to preserve rights against fleeting majorities. Their counsel was not academic. It was precautionary - **liberty requires institutions that resist the tyranny of transient opinion.**

The Broadway Betrayal

Even our stages now preach the counterfeit. Broadway crowned Hamilton the hero — not Washington, not Jefferson, not Madison. The banker became the revolutionary. The architect of debt and central banks was recast as the father of freedom. It was dazzling, diverse, and it sold out for years. The elites loved it — presidents, moguls, and technocrats lined up to cheer. Why? Because it baptized their creed. Finance was enthroned. The builder erased. The Republic was built by plow and forge, not paper and bonds. Yet culture now sings the banker's gospel while the farmer's covenant fades. This is how the counterfeit spreads — not only in policy and textbooks, but in song and spectacle. Even memory is managed. I went once to watch that show. I left halfway through. The theater was roaring with applause, the elites beaming, the cast in motion. But to me it was Andersen's tale played live — the emperor parading naked while the crowd cheered his new clothes. Only this time the emperor was debt itself, dressed as liberty. They called it revolution. But what it really preached was a new creed: **Finance = freedom. Debt = destiny. Bureaucracy = brilliance.** I refused to clap. I walked out. Because when a culture applauds its own chains, silence and exit are the last acts of truth. And I refuse to join the clown show. God commanded memory. Israel set twelve stones at the Jordan as visible testimony: *"When your children ask in time to come, 'What do these stones mean?' you shall tell them..."* (Joshua 4:6–7). Memory was not nostalgia; it was covenantal law. Stones were receipts. If a people cease to remember, they break the contract between past and future — and the tyrant inherits the silence.

Memory as Warfare

They don't want you to remember because memory carries receipts. It reveals patterns and names names. *The Soviets* understood this - dissidents cut from photographs, whole families erased from textbooks, "unpersons" deleted until memory itself was a crime. *Mao* understood it - the Cultural Revolution burned libraries, smashed ancestral shrines, and declared centuries of wisdom "feudal superstition." **Every tyrant knows the same rule: destroy memory and you inherit the future.** Today the mask is digital and instantaneous. Deepfakes, edited photos, realtime "updates" to archives, and algorithmic burying make memory malleable at scale. Fact-checking shops, content moderators, and corporate platforms act as modern priests of memory — deciding which receipts survive the scroll. Where Stalin used scissors, today they use code. A photo cropped, a post relegated to the abyss, a citation quietly altered. **Attention is weaponized; oblivion is automated.**

The Lie That Rewrites America

They call themselves progressives; they claim justice. But history tells another ledger. Slavery, segregation, suppression — these once carried banners that have simply been rebranded. The faces changed. The slogans changed. The spirit did not. They tell you the parties "switched." They didn't switch souls; they changed tactics.. The plantation was modernized — whips became welfare, overseers became bureaucrats, chains became checks. Borders were reframed as cruelty, enforcement as hate, and the mass importation of dependent labor as "compassion." NGOs replaced overseers — moving bodies, laundering public money, and calling it humanitarianism while wages collapsed and accountability vanished. Control no longer required ownership; only dependency. Eugenics once wore lab coats. Now it wears grant language and moral theater. Margaret Sanger's eugenic associations were not footnotes; they were part of the architecture that later rationalized population control. Abortion was sold as liberation even as it functioned as erasure for the vulnerable. If you remembered who fought for liberty and who fought to preserve chains, the rebranding would fail. That is why they rewrite receipts.

The Forgotten Ledger

Black Americans demanded equal rights with blood, faith, and courage. Men and women like Martin Luther King Jr., Rosa Parks, and Medgar Evers stood on covenant, not convenience. Yet the resistance came from the Dixiecrats — Southern Democrats, filibustering senators, governors who sent sheriffs with dogs and hoses. The Civil Rights Acts of 1957, 1960, 1964, and 1965 passed because *Republican votes were decisive.* That ledger matters. Remembering it defangs the simplistic slogan that *"the parties switched" and reveals the true alliances of history.*

The Present Rewritten

This is not only about America's past. The serpent's trick repeats everywhere. Nazis are recast in textbooks as a distant "rightist" caricature while the architecture of centralized control is permitted to reappear under kinder labels. Denmark's own colonial past is scrubbed as it lectures others on sustainability. The UN rebrands permanent refugee camps as "humanitarian solutions." The WEF preaches "equity" while building platforms for centralized economic control. And today the erasure is engineered - Wikipedia edits vanish overnight, algorithms bury inconvenient search results, "fact-checkers" decide which memory survives. AI models are trained on curated narratives, not the whole ledger of receipts. The serpent's library is now code and contract, curated in real time — **one click at a time.**

Tools of Modern Erasure

Every tyrant updates his toolkit. Stalin used scissors. Mao used bonfires. Today, the weapon is code. Deepfakes replace scissors. Algorithms replace fire. Platforms don't burn books — they bury them. Photo tools erase faces. "Community standards" erase voices. Truth isn't censored now; it's *flooded* — drowned beneath sponsored noise and engineered outrage. And when deletion fails, they send the mob — paid agitators and professional screamers — to shout down the remnant who still remember.

The Past as Weapon

The past is not dead. It is a weapon. Forget it — and they will wield it against you. Do not let them rename slavery as safety. Do not let them sell censorship as compassion. Do not let them bury blood and chains under hashtags and curated units in curricula. Scripture ties memory to covenant. Israel's stones were testimony; they were not optional. Remembering is a command and a weapon. **To remember is to resist.** To teach memory is to arm the next generation. If we will not stack stones of testimony, the serpent will stack chains of forgetting.

How Memory Is Reclaimed

The serpent's power thrives in forgetfulness. Nations fall not by invasion, but by amnesia. Only remembrance restores covenant. To reclaim memory and the republic you must: Teach receipts, not slogans. Use primary sources, roll-call votes, contemporary newspapers, and original speeches. Show who voted for what, not what later spin doctors wrote. *Restore the Founders' warnings.* Reintroduce Madison's Federalist No. 10, Jefferson's fears, and Hamilton's structural cautions into civic education. Let students see that the republic was intentionally designed to resist the passions of the crowd. *Make visible monuments of memory.* The stones of covenant were public testimony. Erect local memorials that record the real ledger — who freed slaves, who passed civil rights, who advanced or obstructed liberty — so children can ask and elders can answer. *Train digital literacy as civic duty.* Teach how algorithms bury receipts, how to use archives, how to verify sources, and how to preserve local records beyond platforms that can edit them away.

🔥 Firelight Pause — The Reckoning

- What lies have I believed without asking who wrote the book?
- What truths were buried — not by accident, but by design?
- Who profits when memory fades and courage goes quiet?
- Have I mistaken forgetting for forgiveness, silence for peace?
- When my children ask, what will I hand them — fire or chains?

Forgetting is not peace. Forgetting is bondage. Memory is rebellion. The serpent flatters you with democracy; God entrusted you with a republic. *Remember — or lose it.* When memory dies, the womb closes. When truth is buried, generations vanish. The serpent doesn't stop at the mind — he moves for the cradle.

"Behold, the days are coming... a famine of hearing the words of the Lord". — Amos 8:11

72

THE ASHES OF EUROPE
EMPTY CRADLE. FULL COFFIN

Europe did not simply forget its flame. Its rulers smothered it. Fertility collapsed. Denmark at 1.6 children per woman. Germany at 1.5. Spain and Italy at 1.3. America now sliding to 1.5. Replacement requires 2.1. Anything less, and a people vanish. Decline is not gentle. It is collapse written in decades instead of days Schools close. Nurseries empty while cemeteries swell. Villages hollow into silence. Into that vacuum came mass migration — not covenant families, but imported blocs. Not builders, but replacements. Malmö, Brussels, Cologne: European cities turned into enclaves. This is not just demography — it is covenant arithmetic. Empty cradles are vacancies in the wall, and the wolves never leave a gate unguarded.

Europe killed its own future with abortion, sterilization, and the cult of being "childfree." Then it imported a future that does not honor women as equals, but as property. The torch did not pass to covenant children, but to enclaves of conquest. What Europe refused to sow, others came to reap. Where covenant was abandoned, grievance was enthroned. Where fathers refused the quiver, strangers claimed the inheritance.

When Light Met Its Shadow

Because Islam — as a political system — is not neutral. It is the opposite of covenant faith. Where Christ lifted women as daughters, Islam chained them as property. Where covenant joins man and woman in one flesh, Islam multiplied wives, sanctified child brides, and called it holy. Where Scripture declared every soul bears God's image, Islam branded unbelievers as dhimmi — taxed, silenced, second-class. Where Christ spoke truth to set men free, Islam enforced silence to preserve dominion. The West built and raised. Islamic empires consumed and collapsed. Conquest without covenant. Fire without light. And when Europe invited this shadow into its empty cradle, it was not just migration. It was covenant warfare — one altar replacing another.

"Children are an heritage of the Lord, and the fruit of the womb His reward. As arrows in the hand of a mighty man, so are children of youth. Happy is the man with a full quiver; they shall not be ashamed, but they shall speak with the enemies in the gate". — Psalm 127

The Trojan Horse of Identity Politics

Europe abandoned covenant and imported grievance. America is following. Look at Minneapolis. Look at Michigan. "Clan candidates rose to Congress — not elected by covenant, but by bloc. **This is not renewal. It is architecture.** Not one people under God, but blocs managed by bureaucrats. Identity politics is not democracy. It is a Trojan Horse — a gift wrapped in "rights," hiding the iron fist of Islamization and globalist rule. The serpent's new math is simple — divide sovereignty into quotas, divide liberty into blocs, divide covenant into fragments. A divided heart cannot stand. A divided people cannot endure. The Trojan Horse rolls quietly through ballots and bureaucracies — yet inside are the same chains Europe already wears. **A nation divided into quotas is no longer a nation — it is a ledger.**

The Serpent in the Classroom

This war is not only fought in borders and ballots. It is fought in minds. Universities once forged pastors, poets, patriots. Now they forge activists, informants, idolaters. Professors funded by Gulf gold. Campuses chanting "From the river to the sea." Endowments swollen with foreign cash. Textbooks preaching grievance as gospel. What looks like scholarship is siegecraft. What looks like diversity is division. **The serpent knows the battlefield is memory.** Capture the classroom, capture the nation. The cradle trains bodies. The classroom trains minds. Europe has already lost both. Today the classroom is not only brick and ivy — it glows in every hand. TikTok is the new textbook. Algorithms from Beijing train children more effectively than any professor. One feed preaches grievance, another mocks faith, another erases history with a swipe. While America debates curricula, China dictates culture. The serpent no longer waits in lecture halls. It coils in the palm of your child's hand.

Women as the First Casualty

When covenant collapses, women bleed first. This is not new. **Every empire that trades truth for order sacrifices its women first.** Sweden — rape reports surged as migration rose. Germany and France — knife crimes and gang rapes hushed to protect "narratives." England — grooming gangs ignored because officials feared being called racist. Thousands of daughters sacrificed on the altar of ideology. The inversion is complete: a Justice Secretary swears an oath on the Qur'an. The same system that ignored grooming gangs now places the fox over the henhouse. That is not justice. It is Babylon's law — **the inversion of justice itself.** The serpent crowned as judge. Chains always tighten first on women. And when women are silenced, the whole covenant is silenced.

The Locust Swarm

History keeps the pattern. When covenant dies, people do not rebuild — they flee. And when they flee, they consume. This is not about blood or race — it is about systems without covenant consuming what they did not build. Carthage lived on tribute, draining its neighbors instead of planting its own strength. When Rome came, the city burned. Centuries later, Arab tribes swept out with Sharia's sword — overrunning Egypt, Spain, and the Balkans, devouring rather than building, deserts replacing gardens. The Ottomans repeated the cycle — consuming fields, enslaving Christians, taxing the conquered into silence until the empire collapsed under its own hunger. In our time, the "Arab Spring" promised liberty but delivered Europe's winter — millions fleeing broken states into foreign streets. *This is the Locust Law: it does not sow — it devours. It does not build — it strips.* It does not covenant — it collapses. And now the swarm reaches America's gates — fentanyl, cartels, open borders. Consumption dressed as compassion. The pattern is ancient, and the warning unchanged: **where covenant is absent, the locusts always come.**

The Mask of Dubai

The West points to Dubai and says — *See?* Towers of glass. Malls dripping in gold. Order without liberty, wealth without covenant. A mirage presented as proof that faith can replace freedom and still flourish. But look closer. Many who fill those towers are not builders of a new civilization, but elites from Syria, Iraq, Libya, even Ukraine — men who fled wars their own systems, clans, or alliances helped ignite. They escaped the rubble, but not the chains. Dubai did not free them. It insulated them. Gold does not sanctify what covenant never healed. And the Islam now arriving in Europe and America is not skyscrapers. It is scars. Women veiled, silenced, erased. Rape recast as "honor." Apostasy punished. Blasphemy criminalized. Sharia enthroned where liberty once stood. The West is shown Dubai's skyline while receiving the debris of collapse — not architects, but wounds. Dubai is not the future being imported. It is the **advertisement.**

A showroom for power without accountability. Stability without repentance. Order without truth. The mask exists to confuse the naïve — to suggest that submission produces peace, that wealth redeems law, that control can replace covenant. But towers do not make a civilization. Foundations do. Dubai is the mask. The chain beneath it is real. Do not mistake towers for covenant. *The foundation is still sand.*

America's Warning

Seven million migrants crossed America's border in three years — more than the population of Massachusetts. This is not covenant families planting roots. It is waves — driven by cartels, processed by NGOs, applauded by global planners. The soil itself groans. Ranchers bury strangers on their land. Parents bury sons killed by fentanyl. Over 70,000 dead in 2022 alone — more than all U.S. combat deaths in Vietnam. This did not happen by accident. Gates were opened. Laws were suspended. Enforcement was mocked. The shepherds stepped aside. The wolves came in. And they called it compassion. Compassion without order is not mercy — it is betrayal. Europe's ashes are America's warning. The fire has not fallen yet. But the wind is the same. Ignore it, and America will not fall differently — only louder.

Borders or Burial

When borders were guarded, crossings fell eighty percent. When "Remain in Mexico" held, the flood slowed. When traffickers were prosecuted, children were freed. When borders were abandoned, cartels surged. When the wall was mocked, fentanyl killed. When silence ruled, the soil filled with graves. Two fires. Two futures. California's fire — sanctuary, fentanyl, surrender. Texas' fire — razor wire, oaths, covenant. One leads to ash. One guards the flame. A nation that refuses to choose will inherit the one it denies.

Sit with the heat. Do not look away.

• What does your cradle hold — covenant children who will guard the gate, or emptiness that leaves it open?

• When the wolves come, who stands watch — sons bound by oath, or strangers bound by grievance?

• Have I mistaken compassion for surrender — conquest slowed to a bureaucratic pace?

• Have I confused towers, subsidies, and stability with freedom — while ignoring the scars and chains beneath them?

• When the reckoning comes, will my children inherit memory as fire — or silence as chains?

• And when I speak of fallen nations, do I grieve their people — or only their lost power?

"For My people have committed two evils: they have forsaken Me, the fountain of living waters, and hewed out cisterns for themselves, broken cisterns that can hold no water." — Jeremiah 2:13

The cradle is the covenant.

Empty it, and the coffin fills.

Forget it, and the serpent feeds.

Guard it — or America will join Europe in ash.

73

MIGRATION AS A WEAPON

THE OLDEST CONQUEST ISN'T
WAR — IT'S REPLACEMENT.

History does not end at the cradle. When a people refuse their future, the map shifts. Empty nurseries become open gates, and the serpent trades children for borders. What dies in the womb is redrawn on the wall — lines cut, names erased, loyalties severed. A nation that will not bear its sons will soon bear another's. Empires do not fall when their armies lose. They fall when their people forget who they are — and when the serpent replaces those people with others who owe him more than they owe the land. For thousands of years, the strongest weapon wasn't the sword. It was **the population ledger.** Move enough bodies, erase enough memory, shift enough borders, and a nation falls without a single trumpet sounding.

History is full of kingdoms that were never conquered — only replaced. The Assyrians mastered the craft first. Seven centuries before Rome, they learned the secret: erase identity, and resistance dies with it. They uprooted whole nations, scattering tribes across distant lands and importing foreigners to fill the void. "That is how the Ten Northern Tribes vanished — not slaughtered, but dissolved. *Babylon* refined the tactic. They didn't just seize land; they seized memory.

They took the elders, the priests, the craftsmen — the cultural anchors of a people. Once the soul was extracted, they flooded the land with captives loyal to Babylon. Identity shattered. Resistance gone. *Persia* perfected conquest by paperwork. Instead of chains, they used administrators — foreign governors, engineered intermarriage, and bureaucratic fog. Slowly tribal lines blurred until no region could rise united. Empire by dilution — the ancestor of today's EU quotas and "mobility frameworks." *The Ottomans* sharpened the tactic into something brutal: *devshirme.* Christian boys stolen young, converted, trained, and forged into Janissaries loyal to the empire that abducted them. At the same time, they seeded Christian lands with Muslim settlers. This was not migration. It was demographic conquest. *The Mongols* used the scorched-earth version. First devastation, then repopulation. Cities razed, rebuilt with new clans, new loyalties, new identities. Wherever the Mongols rode, the map changed because the people changed. *The British Empire* mastered the quiet version. They called it *administration*, but it was demographic engineering disguised as order. Scots planted in Ireland. Indians moved into East Africa and the Caribbean. Anglo elites distributed across native lands. A plantation was never just a field — **it was a replacement strategy.**

Then came *the Soviet Union* — the modern prophet of demographic warfare. Stalin deported entire nations with the stroke of a pen: Chechens, Ingush, Crimean Tatars, Volga Germans. Whole peoples dragged across frozen steppes and replaced with populations loyal to Moscow. No slogans. No virtue-signaling. Just maps redrawn through bodies. Even *the Nazis* returned to the same ancient logic. *Lebensraum* was not only land theft — it was engineered population replacement. Clear out entire regions, settle them with Germans, erase memory through blood and breeding. And today *the Chinese Communist Party* repeats the pattern openly. Han settlers poured into Tibet and Xinjiang. Uyghurs scattered into factory towns. Forced intermarriage encouraged. Identity dismantled through relocation and reeducation. Old tactic, new uniform.

Now the global bodies of our age — the UN, the EU, the IMF, the World Bank — dress the same ancient weapon in humanitarian language. "Shared responsibility." "Mobility frameworks." "Managed migration." "Refugee quotas." But beneath the polished vocabulary lies the same arithmetic Assyria used: **Move the people. Break the covenant. Seize the future.**

Empires fall by replacement, not war. America is no different. The universities understand this. The global architects understand this. Their political instruments understand it too. Only the people — the ordinary families who still believe land is covenant — are told to ignore it. Told to stay quiet. Told to bow to the language of "equity," while their cities shift, their borders bleed, and their children inherit a nation that no longer remembers its name. History leaves a clear warning: when a nation becomes ashamed of its identity, someone else will claim it. And when a people give up their future, another people will take it. America is the final frontier — the last land where covenant still speaks louder than empire. And the serpent knows it, which is why he uses the oldest weapon he owns. Not tanks. Not invasions. Not armies. Numbers. Narratives. Replacement. The empires of yesterday fell because they traded their people for populations that did not share their story. The question for us is simple: Will America do the same? Because once a people are replaced, their flag follows. Their freedom follows. Their children's inheritance follows. And no army can restore what a nation surrendered willingly. The frontier remains the last firewall — the remnant who still know the land, still carry the fire, still refuse to kneel. History is clear: the enemy does not need your soil. He needs your seed. And once the people are gone, the Republic is already fallen. The ancient pattern did not stay in the past. It simply waited for a nation naïve enough to call surrender "virtue." Europe became the first modern test site — and Denmark its prototype.

Denmark's Experiment — The First Modern Prototype

Europe did not stumble into demographic collapse. It tested it — quietly, proudly, academically. And Denmark, small and self-assured, became the first laboratory. Denmark — a nation of fewer than six million — became a prototype long before the rest of Europe realized it was being redesigned. In 1983, Copenhagen passed a sweeping *Aliens Act* that flung the gates open: expansive asylum protections, generous family-reunification pathways, and a migration framework unprecedented in its postwar history. The law didn't adjust Denmark's trajectory — it rewrote it. Why did Denmark volunteer? Because Denmark didn't design the experiment — it simply wanted to be the most obedient student in Europe's new moral classroom. EU pressure made it fashionable. Nordic humanitarian pride made it righteous. A political class obsessed with appearing virtuous made it unquestionable. Guilt over WWII-era neutrality made it inevitable. Global institutions made it official. *Behind every Danish law stood an EU directive or UN compact calling it progress.* For decades the flow grew in waves — asylum centers multiplying, suburbs shifting, the cultural landscape bending under pressure no poll could measure. The 2015 refugee crisis did not create the fracture; it revealed it. By the late 2010s the Danish government introduced the "ghetto package" — a 2018 suite of laws defining so-called *vulnerable areas* and empowering social engineering tools almost unimaginable thirty years earlier: forced relocations, mandatory day-care assimilation programs, harsher penalties inside designated zones, and relocation schemes to break demographic concentrations. Officials defended it as social policy. Critics condemned it as punitive.

History recognized it instantly. I watched this shift happen — quietly at first, then unmistakably — long before Americans understood what a manufactured demographic crisis looks like. The results were not theoretical. They were lived: Neighborhoods hardened into enclaves. Danish faded as the first language of classrooms. Crime patterns shifted — clustered, predictable, denied. Streets changed faster than official narratives could hide. Parents whispered warnings; bureaucrats whispered statistics. Police adapted their routes; politicians adapted their speeches.

And through it all, the architects insisted everything was normal — that Denmark remained "cohesive," that integration was "improving," that the system was "working." It wasn't working. It was absorbing. Diluting. Rewriting. Because when a nation dismantles local unity in the name of virtue, it dismantles itself. The state responded with more management, more oversight, more rules — the predictable reflex of governments who break cohesion and then panic when they see the consequences. What Denmark lost was not territory. It was cultural memory. Neighborhood by neighborhood. School by school. Word by word. And this is the lesson America refuses to learn: Replacement does not announce itself. It accumulates. Not with soldiers — but with statistics. Not with invasions — but with incentives. Not with war — but with policy. Denmark was the first test. Europe became the proving ground. America is the final prize. Denmark was not an accident. Europe was not an accident. These demographic experiments were not random failure — they were tolerated because they did not threaten the people who hold power. And that is the part most Americans never learn: **Population replacement destroys nations, but it never destroys the elite who oversee it.**

The Red-Green Sword - The Part No One wants to name
The Left did not simply open Europe's gates. It opened them knowing exactly what comes with every unmanaged mass wave: not families seeking refuge, but *the networks that ride inside the chaos* — crime clans, radical cells, trafficking rings, extortion crews, men who carry a different law in their fists. Europe tried to whisper this into silence. But the evidence didn't whisper. It screamed.

England — For over a decade, police in Rotherham, Rochdale, Oxfordshire, and beyond ignored entire grooming-gang networks — *thousands* of girls — because officials feared being called racist. Children drugged, raped, trafficked, traded between men. Authorities looked away to protect their careers, not the children. When inquiries finally came, they admitted the truth in bureaucratic shame: perpetrators came from "sensitive communities," so no one acted. *That is the sword.*

Germany — Cologne, New Year's Eve 2015 — hundreds of women assaulted in one coordinated night. Police overwhelmed. Media hushed. Government downplayed it until the outrage grew too loud to bury. In Berlin and Bremen, extended crime clans control entire blocks — extortion, protection rackets, parallel justice systems. Police chiefs admit: *"We no longer control some neighborhoods." That is the sword.*

Sweden — Districts labeled "vulnerable areas" — polite language for: organized crime controlling streets, grenade attacks rising, drive-by shootings normalizing, ambulances requiring police escorts, honor-violence silenced, women afraid to walk alone. Officials confessed: *"We cannot maintain order in certain zones." That is the sword.*

France — Suburbs burning for days. Knife attacks in churches and schools. Whole neighborhoods governed by hardline enforcers, not French law. Teachers threatened. Police ambushed. Journalists chased out of districts they once mapped. *That is the sword.*

Denmark — I saw this shift with my own eyes: knife crime rising, neighborhoods turning hostile, "ghetto lists," police attacked with stones and firebombs in Vollsmose and Nørrebro, women warned not to walk alone, young men patrolling hallways like they owned the ground. *That is the sword.*

What makes it a weapon - Not an accident

Not every migrant. Not every Muslim. Not every foreigner. But radical elements, crime clans, and extremist networks thrive when leaders: throw open borders, refuse enforcement, teach shame instead of sovereignty, fear "optics" more than crime, protect ideology instead of citizens These networks become the enforcement arm of the Red–Green project: intimidating police, silencing dissent, capturing districts, influencing elections, enforcing parallel law, making politicians afraid to speak, making ordinary citizens censor themselves. When the state fears its own streets, the state no longer governs.

The Part America MUST hear

Europe lived this. Not theory. Not speculation. Not propaganda. **Documented fact.** Entire inquiries written in the ashes of political cowardice. And now the same officials who surrendered Europe lecture America about "compassion" and call a border "barbaric." The Reds opened the gates. The Greens brought the pressure. And together they wielded a sword of fear that politicians were too weak to resist. This is the truth no one would speak. This is the blade America must see before it feels it. Because the coalition that broke Europe didn't retire at the Atlantic. It crossed quietly — through NGOs, lawsuits, campuses, churches, corporations, ballots — and now it sets its sights on America's great cities. The frontier still holds. But the coasts have already begun to bend. And nowhere is the surrender more visible than in New York — the city that once roared with strength, now voting to manage its own undoing.

The Silent Weapon

The serpent's genius is simple: You don't need tanks if you can move people. You don't need bombs if you can erase borders. You don't need war if you can replace a population one busload at a time. Identity blurs. Culture fractures. Sovereignty dissolves. A nation dies not with a bang — but with a **paperwork shuffle.**

The weapon wears a human face: compassion, duty, international law. It also wears a political one: leaders who amplify crises into mandates, turn catastrophe into leverage, and stretch asylum definitions until the sieve admits everything. By the time the public understands the danger, the tide has become law — and law is hard to reverse.

The Elites Who Outlived Their Nations

For centuries, Europe replaced populations like a farmer rotates crops, yet the royal houses survived — untouched, uninterrupted. Why? Because their power was never rooted in the people. It was rooted in dynasty, alliances, property, and institutions. The House of Oldenburg — Denmark's royal line — is over a thousand years old, the longest unbroken monarchy in Europe, woven with German and Habsburg blood. It outlived migrations, plagues, invasions, the Reformation, world wars, and the demographic transformation of modern Denmark. The people changed. The rulers didn't. Royal houses mastered survival through marriages across borders, global elite alliances, bureaucracy that existed above nations, continuity insulated from demographic collapse. Every time Europe shifted, the palace remained. This is the oldest pattern in the Western world: **Replace the people. Preserve the palace.**

And now Americans must face the question history demands: If **European elites survived every replacement before — what makes you think American elites won't attempt the same?** Because a people can be replaced. A dynasty cannot. A nation can fall. An elite machine simply sheds its skin. When the people vanish, the Republic follows. And the ones who engineered the shift remain standing — exactly as they always have. In every age, the empire survives by finding a new population. **The question is whether America will let itself be the next one replaced.** History always ends where geography weakens. When elites preserve their palaces, the pressure always shifts downward — toward the gates. When the rulers survive every replacement, the people become the shield. And in America, the first shield to crack was the southern border.

America's Flood - The Border That Became A Breach

Turn west and you can feel it before you see it — the line softening, the firewall thinning, the Republic breathing harder at its weakest seam. Since 2021 the southern border has not been a boundary. It has been a breach. Millions have crossed — not in rumor but in the hard numbers of CBP and DHS. Every wave has strained hospitals, schools, sheriffs, and small towns that never volunteered for this war. What was once a line in the sand became an artery left open, pulsing loss into a nation pretending not to bleed. Human trafficking didn't just rise — it industrialized. Fentanyl didn't just slip in — it poured in like a biblical plague. Tens of thousands of Americans die each year from synthetic opioids, their names unspoken in the rooms where policy is crafted. Sons found in basements. Daughters on bathroom floors. Families gutted by a powder that traveled the same routes as the migrants — carried by criminal networks empowered by political negligence. And the children. Oversight reports read like lamentations — minors lost in the system, delivered to "sponsors" who were shadows, tracked by caseworkers drowning before the day even began. Federal warnings stacked up. Nothing changed. Vulnerable lives moved like inventory. Border towns bore the wounds. Eagle Pass. Yuma. Places the elites could not locate on a map endured what the nation refused to name: **a controlled collapse disguised as compassion.** Hospitals buckled. Schools overflowed. Law enforcement broke under the load. In Washington they called it equity. In living rooms it was grief. In cemeteries it was arithmetic. New voters. New dependents. New leverage. A people remade by numbers while their leaders recited poetry about mercy.

The Borderland Up Close

You cannot understand this crisis through graphs. You must walk the land. Ask the ranchers who ride their fence lines at dawn. They will tell you the truth the headlines hide. One dismounts and finds an abandoned camp — tiny shoes half-buried in dust, a blanket tangled in thorn, bright life vests left in a place where no river runs. Plastic bottles. Drug wrappers. Footprints pressed into the soil like bruises.

Then he sees a child — alone, trembling, too exhausted to cry. He wraps the small body into his coat and stands under the vast American sky, waiting for help that will come too late for too many. Border agents tell the same story: Children separated. Women violated. Men extorted. Families stripped and repackaged as commodities. What looks like empty desert on a map is up close a stage of human ruin — carved by cartels, ignored by bureaucrats, sanctified by activists who never once stood in the dust they legislate from afar. This is not immigration. This is exploitation. This is a nation tested at its gates. And the people paying the price are not the ones writing policy.

The Political War At The Gate

America did not slip into chaos by accident. It unraveled in three movements—quiet at first, then unmistakable. **Election. Reversal. Reckoning.** A nation learning, forgetting, and then remembering what a border means.

2016 — Election

The people spoke with a clarity that cut through every illusion. They wanted the gate guarded. They wanted the flood stopped. They wanted a nation that remembers its own name. They did not vote for poetry; they voted for sovereignty. So the gate finally grew teeth. A national emergency was declared. More than four hundred miles of new or reinforced barrier rose along the most exploited corridors. Cartel routes were disrupted. "Remain in Mexico" snapped shut the revolving door that had turned asylum into theater. Agreements tightened across Central America. ICE and CBP were allowed to enforce the law instead of apologizing for it. Crossings plummeted. Traffickers complained. Cartels adapted, as predators always do, but the message rang across the desert like a warning bell: **The gate is guarded.** For the first time in decades, the southern border felt like a border again.

2020 — Reversal

Then came the change of power. On day one, Biden signed executive orders like a man erasing a memory—wall construction halted, "Remain in Mexico" dismantled, asylum definitions stretched until they swallowed everything, ICE shackled by new restraints, enforcement pulled back, catch-and-release resurrected as if the last four years had never happened. The effect was immediate. Encounters surged into the millions. Cartels industrialized their routes. Fentanyl seeped across the line like a silent fog and settled over the nation. Border towns drowned first—hospitals buckling, schools overflowing, sheriffs exhausted, communities fraying under a burden they never agreed to carry. And the children. Untracked. Unprotected. Lost inside a system that had already warned Washington it was breaking. But Washington smiled and called it mercy. Law became theater. Sovereignty became an inconvenience. The border did not collapse. **It was opened.**

2024 — Reckoning

Eight years after the first cry, Americans raised their voices again—louder now, harder now, stripped of naïveté. They had tasted the consequences: crime, trafficking, overwhelmed classrooms, hollowed towns, the quiet arithmetic of demographic engineering wrapped in humanitarian slogans. This time they did not whisper. They demanded the gate be shut. And so Trump returned—not as the outsider who disrupted the system, but as the reckoning summoned by a nation that had seen the cost of forgetting its boundaries. He inherited not a border, but a breach. Not a crisis, but a collapse designed and signed into existence. No wall left unfinished—only a nation left unfinished. Now the battle begins again. Not over geography, but covenant. Not over policy, but sovereignty. Not over lines on a map, but the right of a nation to exist at all. The battle at the gate was the visible war. The next phase is quieter—and more dangerous. When a nation is exhausted, the serpent changes tactics. The flood was only the first phase. Exhaustion births a new language: soft words, gentle slogans, compassion weaponized. Crisis becomes the stage. Chaos becomes the excuse. And into that weariness steps a new authority, ready to rename surrender as mercy.

The False Mercy

There are voices within progressive circles that press for open borders — not out of mercy, but out of ideology. They speak the language of compassion while outsourcing the cost to others. Every slogan sounds noble: *No human is illegal. Borders are violence. Diversity is strength.* But behind the poetry lies arithmetic — votes, grants, cheap labor, and managed dependency. The suffering at the border becomes a stage, not a warning. Children become props. Towns become test sites. The same hands that denounce "trafficking" quietly fund the networks that profit from it. Nonprofits turn tragedy into payroll. Agencies turn chaos into budgets. Each new wave ensures another grant, another headline, another illusion of virtue. What begins as empathy ends as empire. True compassion has boundaries. False compassion demands surrender. One protects the innocent; the other consumes them in the name of virtue. Mercy without truth is not mercy at all — it is manipulation, weaponized emotion dressed in the language of light. The serpent always preaches compassion before he takes control. Mercy is never the root — it is the mask.

Strip away the slogans and the staged outrage and the real questions remain: Who opened the gates? Who engineered the flood? Who profits from a border turned into a wound? Tides do not rise on their own. This was not accident. It was architecture. A nation does not collapse because strangers arrive; it collapses because its guardians bow and its gate-keepers sell the keys. Behind every wave of bodies is a hand that moved them — politicians who wanted new voters, bureaucrats who wanted new budgets, NGOs who wanted new power, corporations who wanted new labor, activists who wanted new leverage, global institutions who wanted new maps. The invasion did not begin at the river. It began in offices, treaties, boardrooms, and council chambers — places where no citizen was invited and no covenant was considered. Europe learned this the hard way. America is just now seeing its face.

Follow the trail long enough — the money, the NGOs, the treaties, the courts, the platforms, the incentives — and it leads to the same place: the managerial elite that no longer belongs to any nation. They do not campaign. They coordinate. They do not migrate. They move others. They do not bear the cost. They externalize it. These elites operate above borders and beyond accountability — through the UN, the EU, financial institutions, foundations, corporate boards, and cultural engines that never appear on a ballot. They do not need to win elections; they only need compliant administrators to execute policy already written. What the public sees as chaos is, to them, leverage. What citizens experience as collapse is, to them, restructuring. The flood is not an accident. It is a tool. Europe learned this too late. America is being taught now. The pattern is visible. And what is seen can no longer be denied.

🔥 **Firelight Pause — How Did You Respond?**
- When you saw a child left in the dust, did you pray — or scroll?
- When women were violated, did you weep — or stay silent?
- When neighbors shouted "compassion," did you ask who paid the cost?
- When the border groaned, did you see politics — or people?
- When the serpent moved the map, did you stand — or look away?
- When compassion is weaponized, do I still know what mercy means?
- What does true mercy demand of me — courage or comfort?

"Speak up for those who cannot speak for themselves, for the rights of all who are destitute." — Proverbs 31:8

74

THE SIEGE OF THE REPUBLIC

THE RED–GREEN ALLIANCE AND THE WAR INSIDE THE GATES

The serpent floods nations with bodies. But it is not satisfied. It wants more than your soil, more than your borders. It wants you. This is the part most Americans never see. Floods redraw borders. But ideas redraw people. Once a nation's gates are open, the next frontier is the mind. Chains around wrists are crude; chains around language are final. The same hand that moves bodies across maps now moves narratives across hearts. Replacement is only the first act. Reprogramming is the second. America's geography was breached at the border. Her memory is breached from within. Now the siege turns inward.

The Elites Who Govern a Nation They Do Not Serve

Europe survived its collapses because it had dynasties — bloodlines insulated from the consequences they created. America has no royal houses, only something more evasive: a ruling class without faces or borders — a machine that survives every election, every crisis, every demographic shift. This elite has no ancestry. It has pipelines. Look to Wall Street and Silicon Valley and you will find America's true monarchs. BlackRock, Vanguard, State Street. Google, Meta, Apple, Amazon. Pfizer and the defense giants. They shape what the nation sees, buys, learns, and believes.

542

Their loyalties are not national. They answer to Davos, to ESG pressure imported from Europe, to transnational investors, to global governance networks that never face a ballot box. Presidents change. The permanent government does not. The DOJ, DHS, FBI, CIA, State Department, the regulatory agencies — these are America's hereditary lords. They operate through treaties they didn't ask voters to approve, through UN frameworks never ratified, through EU-style policy templates written in the language of management, not liberty. This is the aristocracy that remains no matter who wins the White House. Europe had monasteries. America has Harvard and Yale. These institutions mint the judges, diplomats, editors, policymakers, and intelligence officers who interpret reality for the nation. Fueled by foreign donors, global foundations, and corporate patrons, they produce a worldview detached from land, heritage, and constitutional memory. They are the priesthood of the new order — teaching a generation the gospel of border-lessness.

America's elites speak the language of global governance because they are trained, funded, and validated by the bodies that promote it: The UN. The EU Commission. The IMF and World Bank. The Atlantic Council, OECD, and NATO bureaucracies. The WEF in Davos. The international foundations that operate across borders with budgets larger than some nations. This is the bloodstream of the American ruling class — an entire architecture shaped not by voters, but by transnational institutions that treat America as a market, not a homeland. And then comes the political class — the merchants who trade sovereignty for status. They sell visas for votes. Borders for budgets. Freedom for federal dollars. Citizenship for corporate favor. They bow to donors, not citizens; to global councils, not the Constitution. This is America's palace without a king — its court without a crown. And here is the warning the Republic must face: If European elites survived every replacement before, what makes you think American elites won't attempt the same? A people can be erased. An elite simply replaces its base. A nation can fall. The machine remains. Unless the people interrupt the pattern.

The Interruption Begins

And yet — something is shifting. Quietly. Sharply. Historically. The Fourth Turning was always coming, but few expected the fault lines to crack open this fast. Power that once felt untouchable now flickers. Agencies long captured by ideology are being gutted and rebuilt. Executive orders read less like bureaucracy and more like battlefield maneuvers. Tech giants that shaped the narrative now scramble to explain their own behavior. Pharma, once untouchable, is being dragged into the sunlight. The alphabet agencies feel the ground moving beneath them — inspectors general resurfacing, internal purges beginning, shields of immunity thinning. For the first time in a generation, the machine is not just advancing — **it is being dismantled.** But caution belongs beside hope. These are early tremors, not the earthquake. Signals, not guarantees. A shift in wind, not yet a storm. And yet the pattern is unmistakable: Something old is breaking. Something long-protected is being exposed. And the people — the remnant — are rising to meet it. Perhaps for the first time in modern American history, the elites are not the only ones writing the script. Perhaps the cycle is not merely repeating — **it is being interrupted.** Whatever comes next, one truth stands: The machine has begun to lose its footing, and the frontier has begun to remember its strength. But elites never rule alone; they rule through alliances — and the most dangerous alliance shaping America's future is the one no citizen voted for.

The Red–Green Alliance

Behind the slogans and the staged compassion lies a coalition most Americans never see — an alliance not born of friendship, but of strategy. The radical Left and the Islamist political project. Red and Green. Marx and Mecca. Two ideologies that should war against each other, yet meet in the shadows because they share a single ambition: a world without covenant and a people without identity. One dreams of a borderless globe. The other dreams of global submission. Different scriptures, same hunger — dominion through dissolution.

And the fuel for this alliance doesn't rise from mosques or campus rallies alone. It pours from the high towers above them — the machinery the West pretends is neutral. UN compacts that redefine sovereignty as "shared responsibility." EU directives that turn migration into quota. World Bank and IMF incentives tied to "mobility frameworks." NGOs funded by billionaires who call borders "barbaric." Foundations that bankroll activists, lawsuits, and sanctuary networks. Corporate lobbies hungry for cheap labor and permanent dependency. A global web of power that treats nations like experiments and populations like pieces on a board.

Europe saw the prototype first. Socialist parties opened the gates. Islamist networks filled the vacuum. And the EU baptized the operation in humanitarian virtue, turning demographic engineering into policy. Denmark felt it. Sweden drowned in it. France burns under it. Germany trembles inside it. Fragmented cities, parallel societies, speech laws that punish dissent, elections tipped by imported electorates — a political bloc loyal not to nations, but to programs, payouts, and ideology. The architects call it progress. History calls it surrender. And now the same blueprint marches west. The same NGOs. The same UN language. The same foundations laundering ideology through "refugee initiatives." The same political operatives who turned Europe into a demographic experiment. All running the same playbook: flood the border, call it mercy, and build a new constituency from the ruins of the old. For the American Left, the motive is votes. For Islamist blocs, it is leverage. For corporations, cheap labor. For NGOs, endless funding. For global institutions, a weakened America. Different interests, same outcome. Red power. Green leverage. Blue silence.

A people caught in the crossfire, wondering when compassion became a weapon and when sovereignty became a sin. This is not immigration. This is strategy — a long war in slow motion, demographic, legal, cultural, and spiritual. And America is the final prize. The serpent made Europe kneel through treaties, quotas, and shame. He seeks to break America through numbers, narratives, and dependency. But the remnant still stands. And the last fortress is not Washington, nor New York, nor any capital built on marble. It is the frontier — the men and women who still remember covenant, and refuse to bow.

Europe thought it was unique. It wasn't. The same Red–Green machinery that hollowed its cities now moves through our own — not with tanks, but with NGOs, lobbyists, contractors, lawsuits, and demographics. The Left supplies the laws. The Islamist networks supply the numbers. Together they build a political machine that feeds on guilt, fear, and votes. Look at New York. Look at Minneapolis. Look at Dearborn. Look at Los Angeles. The pattern is identical: soft laws, loud activists, imported electorates, and city halls bending to blocs that do not share the covenant that built this nation. It begins with "equity," shifts to "accommodation," and ends in parallel governance — schools, tribunals, councils, and neighborhoods answering to systems older and harsher than the Constitution. Empires fall the same way — first the people, then the borders, then the meaning of the nation itself. Europe was only the modern rehearsal. But America was never spared. The architects simply tested a different population first — quietly, methodically, with a smile and a slogan. They tested it on Black America. Before the border broke — before Texas felt the tremor... before New York crowned a mayor who governs by dependency — the demographic war had already begun in America's own backyard. Not with migrants. Not with quotas. Not with UN compacts. But with **welfare.**

The Black community became the **first population engineered into dependency** — the domestic prototype for the Red–Green playbook now moving across the nation. It began in the 1960s, wrapped in mercy, spoken in the soft language of "relief" and "equity." But behind the poetry was the same arithmetic used by every empire that replaces a people through policy rather than war. The Great Society expanded benefits for the poor — but only if fathers were removed from the home. A generation later, family structure shattered. Marriage collapsed. Neighborhoods fractured. Crime spiked. Schools decayed. Churches carried burdens the state pretended to solve but quietly expanded. Black Americans were told they were being helped. In reality, they were being counted. New votes. New dependents. New leverage. A constituency engineered through need. And when outrage rose, it was redirected — toward police, toward history, toward imagined oppressors — while the real architects, the ruling class that lived far from the consequences, secured political control. The community that had endured slavery, survived Jim Crow, built churches that shaped American culture — was then hollowed by a system that rewarded fragmentation and punished covenant. It was a demographic strategy dressed as compassion. A domestic devshirme. A quieter version of the same European playbook. Black Americans were not enemies in this war. They were the first casualties. And now the machine that once targeted them has gone national — scaling from neighborhoods... to cities... to states... to the gates of the Republic. Because once an elite learns it can reshape a population for power, it will not stop with the first group. It will replicate the method until the nation forgets itself. The architects practiced on Black America. Now they apply it to everyone.

The architects didn't stop with Black America. Once the domestic model worked, they turned to the coasts — not to discipline them, but to redesign them. The West Coast was never meant to be sovereign. It was meant to be global. And so they built the perfect population for a post-national order: high-skill, apolitical, compliant, economically essential, and unlikely to challenge the machine.

Silicon Valley needed coders. Washington needed analysts. Universities needed tuition. Corporations needed quiet, tireless labor. And so a pipeline opened — from Beijing, Seoul, Taipei, Mumbai, Manila — a steady river of talent engineered to feed America's most powerful industries. But this was not charity. It was strategy. The Left wanted workers, not warriors. Taxpayers, not Texans. Professionals who would build the machine, not question the covenant beneath it. And for a time, Asian immigration delivered exactly what the coastal elite designed: low crime, high output, little political resistance. A demographic easy to manage, not because of who they are, but because of how *the system positioned them* — isolated by visas, dependent on institutions, and embedded in industries ruled by a few corporate crowns. Universities became the gatekeepers. UC Berkeley, Stanford, UCLA, UW Seattle — they didn't just admit students. They *imported populations*. Foreign tuition became a revenue stream; admissions became demographic policy; coastal cities became enclaves shaped by global demand, not American roots. Where the university planted its flag, a new political landscape followed.

Tech giants finished the job. H-1B pipelines. Corporate housing. Company towns in digital form. An economy built on talent from abroad and loyalty to no land at all. A West Coast that looked less like America and more like the future the global architects crave — borderless, rootless, cosmopolitan, managerial. But the machine miscalculated. A new generation rose — children of immigrants who were not content to be clients of the state. They pushed back against DEI. Fought school boards. Rejected racial quotas. Sued the Ivy League for discrimination. Refused to bow to the theology of equity. The demographic built to stabilize the system had begun to threaten the system. Yet the lesson stands: *The West Coast was not accidental. It was engineered.* A population chosen not for culture or covenant, but for *predictability* — the raw material of technocratic control. Once the coasts were secured, the architects turned inland. Because a nation is not captured all at once. It is captured coast first — then corridor — then heartland. And the heartland still remembers covenant.

Once the domestic model was proven, the machine did not pause. It expanded its ambitions. First the neighborhoods. Then the cities. Then the borders. Then the cultural corridors of the coasts. And America began to show the stages of its own erosion. New York shows surrender — a city trading its memory for management. Minneapolis shows capture — institutions bent, courts softened, streets patrolled by fear instead of law. Dearborn shows parallel governance — neighborhoods answering to codes older than the Constitution. Los Angeles shows drift — a metropolis dissolving into fragments governed by grievance and imported allegiance. Each city is a rung on the same ladder: **Surrender. Capture. Replacement. Dissolution.** But the architects know these are only the opening movements. None of them are the final prize. The machine advances until it meets a boundary it cannot bend — the one land too stubborn to swallow the script, too rooted to kneel on command. **Texas.** They do not need to conquer the whole Republic. They need only to break the fortress that still remembers covenant. If Texas falls, the rest is arithmetic. And so the next front of the Red–Green advance is not in the shadows of Manhattan or the boulevards of California. It is in the plains and cities of a state that the global machine wants badly — the last great hinge of American sovereignty. Now the battle comes south. Now the serpent reaches for the frontier. Now the architects test whether the land that once forged the Republic's spine can be bent into Europe's shape. Texas stands next in the path of the flood.

The Red–Green Advance on American Soil — Texas

Territory is not taken by armies now, but by institutions — schools that rewrite identity, councils that dilute sovereignty, religious centers that consolidate power, and demographic corridors that redraw a map from within. And the architects know the ancient truth: shatter Texas, and the last wall of the Republic collapses. Texas is not immune. What Europe learned in fire, America insists on learning at the fence line. Look to North Texas — Dallas, Plano, Richardson, Irving — a region some Muslims themselves now call "the Medina of America." The term isn't whispered; it's worn as identity. The density of mosques, schools, political networks, cultural hubs — it is unmatched anywhere else in the country.

The architecture of a parallel system isn't hypothetical. It stands in plain sight. Then came EPIC City — a master-planned Islamic enclave proposed near Dallas, forty minutes out, centered on the East Plano Islamic Center. Not a "city" on paper, but the blueprint was unmistakable: a self-contained zone of homes, schools, governance structures, all orbiting a single ideological core. Exactly the model Europe once thought it could manage. Exactly the model that managed Europe. Seven years ago, I sat in a room in Texas as speakers warned of this trajectory — enclaves rising, political blocs forming, infrastructure laid brick by brick. Most Americans dismissed it as fear mongering. They always dismiss it — until it reaches their ZIP code. Now Texans see what was once laughed off: zoning fights where neighborhoods push back; developments expanding without transparency; mosques placed strategically beside public schools; political alliances forming quietly in city halls. None of it random. All of it familiar. If you doubt it, open your phone. Pull up a map. Count the mosques. Trace their clustering around schools. Follow the density within specific suburbs. Watch how cultural power is threaded into civic infrastructure with precision. This is not immigration. This is infrastructure. This is strategy. This is parallel governance built in real time. Funded not by Texas soil, but by foreign hands eager to see America remade in Europe's image.

The same Red–Green machinery that hollowed Paris, Malmö, Berlin, and London now moves through Dallas–Fort Worth — not with armies, but with NGOs, lawsuits, foundations, foreign funding, political blocs, and demographic corridors. The Left supplies the laws. The Islamist networks supply the numbers. Together they build a political machine that feeds on guilt, fear, and votes. And those with eyes to see recognize the truth: The same coalition that subdued Europe now reaches for the last fortress standing. They want the land that remembers covenant. They want the Republic that still carries fire in its bones. They want the nation that refuses to kneel.

Texas shows the frontline of resistance. New York shows the blueprint of surrender. New York just crowned its 111th mayor — a democratic-socialist, Muslim, South Asian immigrant who campaigned on affordability, redistribution, and what he called *"radical municipal transformation.* The headlines called it progress. Commentators called it compassion. Activists called it victory. History calls it something else: a hinge — a moment when a great coastal citadel stops being a city and becomes a laboratory. A place where covenant dissolves into dependence. Where governance is not inherited, but engineered. Where demographics, not legacy, choose the future. This is not a story about one man. It is a story about the model. Because what happened in New York follows the pattern Europe learned long before America bothered to look. Mass migration arrives. Progressive governance fuses itself to imported majorities. Dependency grows. And the city becomes a controlled experiment — a petri dish where ideology can reshape a population faster than any legislature ever could. Denmark lived it. Sweden drowned in it. Germany trembled under it.

Now the Red–Green alliance wears an American accent — the marriage of leftist ideology with newly-arrived populations, forming a political bloc loyal not to covenant, but to programs. While Florida held the line and Texas remembered its oath, the coastal city-states drifted toward the world the global architects prefer — cities treated as network nodes, not homelands; citizens treated as clients, not heirs. This is what New York just voted for — municipal state-expansion in microform. A prototype for the world the UN, EU, and global technocrats have been building for decades: governance without borders, identity without heritage, citizenship without sovereignty. Because it is not only the flood of people that reshapes a nation. It is the flood of governance that comes behind them. The more the demographics shift, the more powerful the mandate becomes for those who promise management. The softer the population grows, the stronger the hold of those who speak the language of control.

America has seen flashes of this decay — Detroit collapsing, Minneapolis unraveling, San Francisco dissolving. New York simply made the pattern official. Empires no longer fall in battle — they fall in budgets, ballots, and bureaucracy. The Beast doesn't roar. It registers, allocates, legislates, normalizes. New York's election is not an anomaly but a signal — proof of how swiftly a city forgets its name when population, policy, and ideology align against covenant. The storm rising in Washington began in cities that traded founders for managers, sovereignty for slogans, duty for emotion. Yet the remnant still sees. Texas feels it like fire in its bones. Florida sees it in the bright, unblinking light. And those who keep covenant know: When cities bow, the frontier must rise. When towers forget the flag, the land remembers it. When the Beast tests New York, the fire awakens in the Republic.

"If the foundations are destroyed, what can the righteous do?" — Psalm 11:3

 Firelight Pause — What Does the Republic Ask of You Now?

• When the cities bowed, did you bow with them — or brace your spine?

• When your leaders traded sovereignty for slogans, did you notice — or nod along?

• When the maps shifted, did you look away — or look deeper?

• When truth grew costly, did you speak softer — or louder?

• When the frontier rose, did you rise with it — or retreat to comfort?

• When the Beast spoke the language of mercy, did you discern the serpent behind the smile?

• What does fidelity look like in a nation under siege?

The serpent has breached the borders and entered the gates. But it has not taken the mind. Not yet. The next assault will not come by flood or ballot — but by language, memory, identity, and design. **If the Republic is to fall, it will not fall on the ground. It will fall in the soul.** And that is where the remnant draws the line.

75

—————

THE SANITIZED MIND

HOW LANGUAGE, FEAR, AND
FALSE VIRTUE REWRITE THE SOUL

The next battlefield is smaller than a city and bigger than a nation. It lives behind your eyes. Your mind was not born free — it was claimed before you could speak. From the cradle they wrote lines into your memory—school slogans, news loops, social feeds. They told you what to think, what to repeat, what to fear. **You call it education. They call it programming.**

They did not have to burn books this time; they only had to rename words. *Mother* becomes *birthing person. Truth* becomes *misinformation.* With a stroke of a pen whole thoughts vanish. If a word is gone, the thought itself grows thin. The dictionary becomes a cage, and the cage is invisible. The scaffold today is digital. You are shamed, not whipped; cancelled, not crucified. A crowd laughs while one is humiliated. A worker is fired for a post. A student expelled for a prayer. The fear seeps deeper than law — it teaches you not to risk certain thoughts, because thinking them might cost you everything. Chains come wrapped in compassion. *"Comply to protect." "Obey to belong."* The lowest bow is sold as the highest virtue. Stand, and you're branded selfish, dangerous, hateful. Polished chains. Smiling jailers.

553

All designed to scrub the fire from your mind. You see it everywhere — testing that rewards obedience over judgment, SEL (Social and Emotional Learning) that replaces morality with mood, corporate "standards" that erase inconvenient facts, algorithms that bury documents while amplifying narratives. These are not accidents. They are doctrine.

Unmask the Goal

Sanitization is not safety. Safety is only the mask — the velvet glove on the iron hand. The real goal is a citizen who never questions, never imagines outside the script, never rebels. A sanitized mind is the perfect slave — polite, productive, hollow. Worse — once sanitized, a mind becomes a slave-maker; it polices neighbors and denounces the fire it once carried. The Serpent's method is always the same: confuse language, attach shame, reward compliance. The modern names change — *inclusion, safety, equity* — but the hand that signs the orders is the same.

Flip to the Spiritual War

This is more than social engineering. It is soul sterilization. The Serpent wants not merely obedience but silence; not only actions, but imagination. A numbed mind cannot dream covenant. A scrubbed conscience cannot speak truth. When imagination is sterilized, a person may still work, shop, vote — but his soul has been conquered. The battlefield is not the ballot box. It is your mind — your ability to see clearly, to name truth, to remember what they want erased.

"Do not be conformed to this world, but be transformed by the renewing of the mind." — Romans 12:2

Sanitization Unleashed — How Neighbors Turn on Neighbors

The serpent doesn't always conquer with armies; often he conquers with suspicion. Citizens learn to watch each other, to trade loyalty for survival, to sanitize their words before they're spoken. When betrayal becomes duty and silence becomes safety, no prison walls are needed — the cage lives in every home. These are not relics but mirrors. The serpent never changes his nature, only his tools. Remember: every tyranny began with neighbors who wanted to belong, not betray. Fear teaches obedience first — then excuses it.

The Soviet Purges (1936–1938) — Stalin's Great Terror devoured his own people. Millions were arrested, exiled, or executed. Entire professions — officers, priests, teachers — were wiped out. The state taught citizens to watch and report. A careless joke, a word at the dinner table, could mean arrest. Neighbors denounced neighbors; coworkers signed "loyalty" papers to protect themselves. Show trials broadcast confessions that were scripted, rehearsed, false. Fear turned life into surveillance theater. Betrayal became civic duty. A signature could save your family, or doom your neighbor. Cruelty was routinized until ordinary Russians lived as informants in their own kitchens. The West's intellectuals excused famine and terror as "progress." The UN did not yet exist — but silence and appeasement were already rehearsed.

Nazi Germany (1933–1945) — The Third Reich industrialized extermination. Six million Jews, Roma, disabled, and dissidents erased in camps. It began as paperwork: boycotts of Jewish shops, licenses revoked, teachers dismissed. Propaganda rewrote public imagination — films, newspapers, schoolbooks teaching that "health" required removal of the "unfit." Bureaucracy sanitized cruelty into civic hygiene. Neighbors learned to avert their eyes. Denunciations became municipal routine. Deportation lists were typed by clerks who went home to dinner. Genocide was no longer wild mobs but orderly files, schedules, signatures. Appeasement. Denial. "Peace in our time." Not until the camps were opened did the world admit what sanitized language had hidden.

Yugoslavia (1991–1995) — In Sarajevo, Srebrenica, Vukovar — neighbors who once lived side by side slaughtered each other under ethnic banners. Nationalist leaders rewrote history in media and schools. Serb, Croat, and Bosniak identities hardened into enemy categories. Checkpoints, ID lists, and "cleansing" campaigns made everyday life a test of loyalty. A neighbor's silence or denunciation could seal a family's fate. Ordinary men who once farmed or fixed roofs became paramilitaries. Harassment slid into massacre. UN "safe zones" became traps where thousands were executed under the blue flag of false protection. Europe wrung its hands. The UN condemned but delayed. NATO intervened late. Bureaucracy called it "ethnic conflict" — sanitized language for mass graves.

Rwanda (1994) — In one hundred days, 800,000 were slaughtered — neighbors hacking neighbors with machetes. Radio Télévision Libre des Mille Collines broadcast daily hate, calling Tutsis "cockroaches." Identity cards made every body legible to the state. Militias like the Interahamwe were armed and rewarded; men who refused were branded traitors. Bureaucratic euphemisms — "cleaning," "work" — masked genocide as duty. Villagers who once traded at markets turned executioners. Children were not spared. Conscience was numbed by obedience, and survival depended on participation. The UN withdrew peacekeepers. Washington called it "acts of genocide" but avoided the word "genocide" itself. Silence enabled slaughter.

China — Xinjiang (2010s–present) — Uyghur Muslims disappeared into "reeducation camps." Surveillance blanketed homes, mosques, even children's schools. Propaganda cast Uyghurs as "extremists." Reeducation was renamed "vocational training." Checkpoints, QR codes, and facial recognition replaced old denunciation networks. Families were split, language suppressed, memory rewritten. A whole people sterilized — culturally, spiritually, sometimes physically. Obedience enforced by algorithms, cameras, and endless files.

UN observers issued reports couched in cautious terms. Corporations stayed silent, profiting from supply chains. Sanitized phrases like "human rights concerns" covered mass internment. The pattern was clear: when elites want obedience, they soften the language, hide the wounds, and praise themselves for restraint. And once a people grow accustomed to sanitized cruelty overseas, they barely notice when the same machinery turns inward.

The World — COVID (2020–2022) — For the first time in history, every continent marched under the same script. Lockdowns, mandates, and surveillance were rolled out as "public health." The slogans were identical: "Stay home. Stay safe. Trust the science." QR codes became passes for work, worship, or travel. Neighbors reported gatherings. Doctors who questioned were censored. Obedience was reframed as compassion. Families split, churches closed, human contact criminalized. The sanitized vocabulary — "safety," "fact-checking," "community responsibility" — masked coercion as virtue. The world rehearsed neighbor-against-neighbor denunciation, now digital and global. The UN praised the "global response." Governments congratulated themselves. The price — fractured communities, silenced voices, and a sanitized mind trained to bow — was buried under the word "safety." **The sanitized mind was no longer a regional experiment. It was global policy.** And even their own scribes admit it. WEF advisor Yuval Noah Harari declared that humans are now "hackable animals." *Translation: they no longer need gulags. They can break you with code, with screens, with data.* When a man speaks of humans as 'hackable animals,' he confesses not science but surrender — the death of awe. **The sanitized mind is the gulag upgraded.** This is not theory. It is your feed, your office, your child's classroom. It is the quiet HR memo. The flagged post. The algorithm deciding what you see. This is not their past. It is your present. Different continents. Different excuses. The same operating system.

Echoes of the Same Pattern

Khmer Rouge — Cities emptied, families erased, temples smashed. Neighbors reported "incorrect thoughts," and reading a book could be a death sentence. *Zimbabwe* — Mugabe called seizure "justice." State media turned farmers into villains, mobs burned fields, and famine followed. *Darfur* — Militias branded whole tribes "rebels." Villages burned while the UN hid genocide beneath the word "counterinsurgency." *Myanmar* — Rohingya labeled "terrorists." Social media fanned hatred; villages vanished under "security operations." *Israel* (2020–2021) — The Green Pass split society; those without it were barred from work, worship, travel. A people once tattooed with numbers now carried QR codes. *South Africa* — Farmers cast as "colonial oppressors." "Kill the Boer" echoed while ritualized farm attacks were framed as vengeance. Different lands, same mechanics — language twisted, neighbors weaponized, conscience inverted.

The Red Thread

From Stalin's signatures to Hitler's lists, from Rwandan radio to Chinese QR codes — the pattern never changes. Rename the language. Reward the compliant. Remove the dissident. Neighbors become enforcers, families fracture, conscience collapses. The serpent's fingerprints stain every age and system. The sanitized mind is the weapon; the neighbor turned enemy is the fruit. And the world's silence — UN statements, bureaucratic files, the neighbor's shrug — is always the same chorus: **"safety."** Language first — targets labeled cockroach, traitor, infidel, colonizer, terrorist. Neighbors recruited by fear, reward, or silence. Bureaucracy/tech as mask: ID cards, permits, QR codes, "community guidelines." Moral inversion: killing recast as cleansing, justice, or safety. Sanitized memory: once shrines, schools, or records are erased, conscience collapses. *Different uniforms. Same machinery.* Communist terror. Fascist hygiene. Ethnic purification. Technocratic compliance. Biosecurity emergency. Digital surveillance control. The serpent does not care which flag flies overhead. He only needs the same tools: renamed language, rewarded obedience, punished dissent. **The system changes. The method does not.**

How the Beast and Serpent Work Together — A Concrete Map

The Serpent erases words and weaponizes guilt. The Dragon imposes emergencies, mandates, surveillance. The Beast codifies obedience through money, systems, and global compacts. Together they sterilize thought in three moves: rename, reward, remove. To wake is to become suspect — labeled extreme, unreasonable, hateful. It may cost friendships, income, even safety. But numbness is death and silence is surrender. Truth once seen cannot be unseen. Resist their script. Restore memory. Reclaim the country. The fire burns away their programming and reveals what they stole. A sanitized mind is not safe — it is subdued. A renewed mind is not compliant — it is armed. Empires don't just rewrite minds; they rewrite populations. When the mind bows, the map follows. Once they control thought, they decide who belongs — and who replaces. Every border begins in the brain. Every migration wave mirrors what a nation believes about itself. And the next test is not who crosses — but what spirit they carry when they do.

"Do not be conformed to this world, but be transformed by the renewing of your mind." — Romans 12:2

The Nazi Accusation — How Tyranny Preemptively Absolves Itself

In every age of control, power requires a moral solvent — a word so toxic it dissolves debate on contact. In our time, that word is *Nazi*. It is not used as history. It is used as a mechanism. The accusation does not emerge from careful comparison. It precedes analysis. It ends inquiry. The word *Nazi* is only the spear tip. Around it circles a full arsenal of interchangeable labels — *fascist, Christian nationalist, extremist, bigot, MAGA,* even *threat to democracy.* None of these are definitions. They are **administrative tags.** Once applied, argument is no longer required. The labeled person is treated as pre-guilty, socially hazardous, and unworthy of due process. The language functions exactly as intended: to collapse a human being into a category that can be managed, censored, excluded, or destroyed — all while the accuser claims moral superiority.

Once spoken, the accused is no longer a citizen to be debated but a contaminant to be removed. That is its function. Not persuasion — **preemption.** This is the first mark of a sanitized mind: language no longer describes reality; it **administers permission.**

The historical irony is precise. The core techniques of **National Socialism** were never theological or traditional. They were *bureaucratic and managerial:* **centralized authority, state-approved truth, speech regulation, medicalized obedience, emergency powers, and moral inversion justified by "the common good."** Churches that would not bow were suppressed. Dissidents were labeled threats to social health. Ordinary citizens were conscripted into surveillance through denunciation and silence. Violence was sanitized through paperwork long before it was executed in camps. These were not accidents of the Third Reich. They were its operating system. Yet in the modern West, these same methods are redeployed under different banners — *safety, inclusion, public health, equity* — and those who resist them are branded *Nazis.* This is not confusion. It is **projection.** Projection is a classic psychological defense: **transfer guilt outward to avoid recognition inward.** When a system begins to resemble the tyranny it claims to oppose, it must invert the mirror. The accusation becomes a laundering ritual. By naming others first, it conceals itself. This is why the label is aimed not at those who expand state power, but at those who resist it. Not at institutions that censor, but at citizens who speak. Not at bureaucracies that surveil, but at families, churches, and dissenters who refuse ideological compliance. The accusation follows a consistent pattern: **it targets conscience.** Christians are called Nazis not because they resemble fascists, but because *they assert allegiance beyond the state.* Conservatives are called Nazis not because they worship authority, but because *they resist centralized management.* Parents are called Nazis not because they seek domination, but because *they defend inheritance.* And Trump is called a Nazi not because of doctrine, but because *he breaks the spell of bureaucratic language and exposes institutional power by name.* The accusation is not about history. It is about permission. Once a person or group is successfully framed as "Nazi," extraordinary measures become moral.

Censorship becomes protection. De-platforming becomes hygiene. Financial exclusion becomes responsibility. Surveillance becomes care. The crowd is not asked to think — only to comply. This is how coercion is reborn without uniforms. Here the sanitized mind reveals its final function: it enables cruelty without acknowledging it. The deeper inversion is that modern accusers rely on a radically distorted memory of the Second World War — one stripped of its structural lessons. Nazism is reduced to a cartoon of "right-wing hate," severed from its actual foundations in state absolutism, ideological conformity, and bureaucratic obedience. By collapsing history into caricature, the public is trained to spot costumes instead of mechanisms. They learn to hunt symbols, not systems. This is not ignorance. It is design. A population trained to shout "Nazi" at dissenters will never ask whether censorship, surveillance, medical coercion, or speech policing resemble the regimes it claims to fear. The accusation acts as a firewall against self-recognition. It ensures that comparison is forbidden precisely where it would be most revealing. History shows this pattern without exception. In communist purges, dissenters were labeled "fascists." In Maoist China, critics were branded "counter-revolutionaries." In Rwanda, neighbors were renamed "cockroaches."

In each case, **language preceded violence. Dehumanization preceded enforcement.** The accusation did not describe danger; it **created authorization.** Different uniforms. Same machinery. Communist terror. Fascist hygiene. Ethnic purification. Technocratic compliance. Bio-security emergency. Digital surveillance control. The flags change. The method does not. The modern West is not repeating the symbols of the twentieth century. It is repeating its **structures** — with better technology and cleaner language. And the most reliable sign of that repetition is the moment when conscience itself is labeled totalitarian. When a system calls moral resistance "Nazism," it is not warning about tyranny. It is **announcing its return.** The question for the reader is not whether the accusation is offensive. It is whether it is **strategic.** Because once a people accept the lie that conscience is extremism, they will beg for the chains that follow — and thank their captors for the illusion of safety.

And by then, the word will no longer be needed. These labels are not meant to be accurate. They are meant to be *final*. **When a society replaces reason with tags, it has already crossed from persuasion into enforcement.** Every system that sanitizes the mind eventually needs a people it may hate without consequence. History shows who is always placed on that altar.

🔥 **Firelight Pause — The Mind Under Siege**

Sit before the flame. Let the smoke strip the lies.

• When did you first trade honesty for safety—and who taught you that bargain?

• Which words did you stop speaking after they were renamed?

• What fear trained you to police your own thoughts before anyone else had to?

• What part of your mind did you give to the algorithm without noticing?

• Do you still know your own voice—or only the echoes they rewarded?

The fire exposes what comfort concealed: A sanitized mind is not peaceful — it is conquered. A renewed mind is not polite — it is free. And freedom is always a threat to tyrants.

76

THE TWO TYPES OF IMMIGRANTS

CITIZENS BY EXPLOITING AND CITIZENS BY FIRE

"*But Ruth said, 'Do not urge me to leave you or to return from following you. For where you go I will go, and where you lodge I will lodge. Your people shall be my people, and your God my God.'*" — Ruth 1:16

Every empire has been shaped by migration — but not all migrations are equal. Some arrive like builders. Some arrive like thieves. Some kneel in gratitude to covenant. Others smirk at the feast and demand more. This is the dividing line. It is not skin. It is not accent. **It is allegiance.** Every soul that steps onto American soil makes a choice — *covenant or consumption, sacrifice or entitlement, remembrance or rebellion.* That choice doesn't wait for Washington. It is visible in the first act — **Do they give, or do they take?**

563

History's Warnings

Rome learned it the hard way. They invited mercenaries into their legions — and those mercenaries sold the empire for silver. Europe repeated the pattern. Migrants arrived not bound to covenant, and Europe woke to no-go zones in Malmö and Cologne, to churches turned into mosques. Sovereignty dissolved not with armies, but with open gates. The serpent always rides under the banner of compassion. He whispers of rights, never of responsibilities. He celebrates numbers, not loyalties. He preaches inclusion, but he means infiltration. The border is never just about who enters — it is about who rules tomorrow.

Covenant vs. Exploitation

The Founders themselves warned us. Jefferson feared "importing men who do not know liberty," warning they would bend the Republic toward tyranny. Madison in *Federalist No. 10* framed the republic as a firewall against factions — against mobs and blocs that would tear at covenant. They knew a republic can only survive if its people are bound by truth, sacrifice, and covenant. But even among them the fault line was clear. Jefferson and Madison built their vision on farmers, craftsmen, and land — covenant rooted in sweat and soil. Hamilton built his on credit, centralization, and managerial order — power without covenant. One vision tied to covenant; the other to control. That argument never ended. Today, the elites sing Hamilton's song — debt as destiny, finance as freedom, theater as history. But covenant has no Broadway show. It is built in barns and fields, in homes and small shops, in neighbors who bind themselves to one another without permission from a bank or a bureaucrat. *America will choose again - Jefferson's covenant or Hamilton's chains. One builds a Republic. The other sells it.*

Builders and Betrayers

A republic of builders becomes a plantation of managers the moment loyalty shifts from covenant to credit, from land and neighbor to payroll and permit. That is why every empire — ancient or modern — works first to hollow the middle. Because once the backbone bends, the people can be ruled, divided, and sold. In Scripture the pattern is plain. Babel gathered the nations into false unity, and God scattered them to break the spell. But at Pentecost, the Spirit gathered many nations and tongues into true unity — not managed by men, but bound by covenant fire. Ruth crossed borders in covenant — "Your people shall be my people, your God my God." She entered by fire, not by demand. Jezebel crossed borders too, but she brought Baal with her — foreign gods, foreign altars, foreign chains. Covenant immigration builds. Exploitative immigration corrupts. One kind comes to consume America — waving foreign flags, chanting foreign slogans, demanding benefits without covenant. They drink American freedom like cheap wine, forgetting it was poured from soldiers' wounds. Covenant immigrants strengthen the middle. Exploiters swell the servant class. That is the Two-Tier Trap — one path builds a Republic, the other hollows it into a colony. **America's gates will always open. The question is not if — but how. Will they open to covenant, or to chains?**

Not for Bread Alone, but for Covenant Fire

Another kind came differently. Pilgrims who planted faith before they planted crops. Pioneers who carved homesteads from wilderness. Ellis Island families who swore allegiance, learned the tongue, and sent sons to bleed in wars not yet their own — because covenant was already theirs. Many of the newly arrived even took up arms in 1776, proving that covenant does not wait a generation. It binds at once, demanding sacrifice even from those fresh to the soil. They built railroads, dug canals, laid brick, and raised steeples. *They came not for bread alone, but for covenant fire.* This is the line. One consumes. The other builds. One bleeds a nation dry. The other waters it with sacrifice.

America's Warning

The numbers today are staggering. Millions cross unchecked, while fentanyl flows in the same routes and cities buckle under crime and cost. Leaders call it compassion. But compassion that ignores covenant is betrayal. A republic is not saved by opportunists. It cannot endure if it is reduced to a cafeteria of comforts. It endures only if covenant is remembered — bread, soil, sacrifice, fire. Those who come for bread alone will vanish when the bread runs out. Those who come for covenant will stand even when the fire burns. The flood is not theory. It is now. In three years, more than seven million crossed illegally — more than the population of Massachusetts. Fentanyl carved mass graves while cities buckled under costs and crime. But the tide can be turned. For the first time in decades, the doctrine shifted — from managing the flood to confronting it. The border was sealed. The abuse of H-1B visas — loopholes that bled American jobs while elites imported cheap foreign labor — was confronted head-on. These were not just policy tweaks. They were covenant lines redrawn: **America is not a cafeteria to be consumed. America is a covenant to be honored.** Globalists screamed. Corporations whined. But the remnant saw it plain: a Republic cannot endure if its borders are open to consumption. Sovereignty is not hate. It is stewardship. To guard your gate is not cruelty. It is covenant.

🔥 **Firelight Pause — The Immigrant Test**
- Do you come to build, or to consume?
- Do you kneel in gratitude, or rise in entitlement?
- Do you honor sacrifice, or forget it when you mark the ballot?
- Do you see America as covenant, or as cafeteria?
- Do you learn the tongue of the land, or demand the land bend to yours?
- Do you raise children who will fight for freedom, or children who will only feed on it?
- Do you bring your gods and grievances as weapons, or lay them down at the altar of covenant?
- When the fire tests, will you stand as a builder — or vanish as a guest who only came for bread?

Covenant Call

Do not wait for Washington to guard your gates. Guard your town. Guard your family. Vet your leaders. Build economies that do not depend on imported labor. Teach your children that freedom is covenant, not cafeteria. Because the serpent's flood is here. NGOs process it. The UN blesses it. Politicians trade it for ballots. But the flood cannot drown a people who remember covenant. Fire burns hotter than water. And if America remembers, the tide breaks. The serpent's flood cannot drown covenant fire. Builders will outlast betrayers. But only if America remembers what kind of immigrant she was born from.

Every empire chooses its people. Every people chooses its story. Borders decide who enters; narratives decide what they become. If the gates open to covenant but the schools preach bondage, the Republic still dies. Before chains are forged in law, they are forged in language. Once the serpent bends the tongue, he bends the mind; once he bends the mind, he can redraw the map without a single soldier. Every empire falls the same way — first by invasion, then by instruction, finally by illusion. That illusion is called freedom.

77

THE ILLUSION OF FREEDOM
THE CHAINS OF CONTROL

If they lied about the parties — about who fought for slavery, about who wore the white hoods, about who built Jim Crow — what else did they lie about? — *everything*. From the way your children are taught to the way your body is managed; from the way your emotions are manipulated to the way your vote is counted; from the way your brain is trained by a screen — you were not educated, you were conditioned. You were not informed; you were distracted. You were not protected; you were sedated. Because a people who forget how to think become easy to rule. **Freedom is not stolen in chains but sold in comfort.** You are told you're free. But every opinion you hold was pre-selected. You are told your vote counts, but both parties fund the same wars and ride the same debt. You are told your voice matters, yet the platforms you speak on track you, silence you, and sell you. You are told this is "the land of the free," but say a man is a man and watch how fast you lose your job. Propaganda in democratic dress is older than social media. In 1917 Wilson's Committee on Public Information pumped government scripts into newspapers and film reels. In the 1950s the CIA ran the Congress for Cultural Freedom, laundering ideology through journals and art shows. Today it is Twitter, TikTok, and Google — same strategy, sharper tools.

And the courts blessed it. In Korematsu v. United States (1944), the Supreme Court upheld Japanese internment — proving "security" could erase liberty with one gavel strike. In Jacobson v. Massachusetts (1905), the Court upheld forced vaccination, language later weaponized during COVID mandates. Legal precedent turned the illusion of safety into the chain of obedience. **You did not choose most of your beliefs; they were dripped into you, drop by drop, from a poisoned well.**

School Was the First Battlefield

In the twentieth century mass schooling shifted from civic formation to workforce formation. Rockefeller's General Education Board funded systems that favored compliance over critical thought. Centralizing measures — a federal Department of Education, standardized testing, national curricula — turned classrooms into calibration labs for common opinion. By the 1990s and 2000s, "reforms" like Goals 2000, No Child Left Behind, and Common Core tightened the screws. By the 2010s, classrooms became pipelines for CRT, SEL, and gender ideology. Students can recite 72 pronouns but stumble over fractions. This was not accidental pedagogy. It was design. Reformers admitted they wanted "efficient citizens," not sovereign men.

The Attention War

The invention of the smartphone did not merely add convenience. It created an industry whose product is your attention. Algorithms shortened our attention spans and multiplied distraction, training reflexes where deliberation once lived. If you control the scroll, you control the soul. Behavioral engineers at Facebook admitted in 2017: "We designed dopamine loops into the feed." Netflix's CEO said his competition was sleep. TikTok's algorithm is so addictive even Beijing limits its own children's exposure to 40 minutes a day. What looks like entertainment is obedience by design. Each of these systems alone looks like convenience. Together, they form a cage.

The Health Trap

Health became a lever. Not care — compliance. This was not the failure of public health. It was the redesign of it. Public health stopped being a healer and became a manager of populations, shifting from bedside compassion to centralized oversight. Wellness was translated into metrics. Medicine into mandates. Safety into supervision. Under the banner of "collective good," institutions learned to monitor bodies the way they once monitored borders. Food systems engineered dependency. Chemicals and additives normalized numbness. Behavioral health became a pipeline — diagnosing, dosing, disciplining. A tracked body is an easier body to govern. A monitored body is an easier body to monetize. And a compliant body is an easier body to claim. Digital passes, biometric IDs, algorithmic screenings — these are not treatments. They are templates. Infrastructure for a world where access replaces agency, and permission replaces personhood. Not a mark upon the skin — but a **system** wrapped around the soul. Not a brand on the hand — but a bureaucracy in the bloodstream of society itself. A Contract Age disguised as a Care Economy. The serpent just changed its coat.

"And that no one may buy or sell unless he has the mark — Revelation 13:17

The Food & Water Cage

Food was reframed as an environmental problem, and regulatory regimes, credits, and quotas followed. Billionaires and institutional investors moved into farmland and water markets while elites sat at private tables. Whoever controls the table controls the nation. One Nestlé executive has *been criticized* for suggesting that water should be treated not as a universal right but as a commodity — priced, packaged, and rationed. That is the creed of the cage: life recast as inventory, creation rebranded as commodity. Bill Gates has been *reported as one of the largest* private farmland owners in America. BlackRock and Vanguard invest heavily in water-related assets and futures. Meanwhile, Danish bureaucrats draft nitrogen taxes on cattle, and some California districts have introduced insect-based protein products while elites dine on Wagyu.

Control the seed and you control the soul. This is not nutrition policy. It is siege disguised as sustainability. First they ration bread, then they ration memory, then they ration freedom. Tyrants always begin at the table because he who controls food controls the future. The playbook is simple: create scarcity narratives, centralize distribution, then legislate access.

The Debt Illusion

Debt is taught as a rite of passage — student loans, credit cards, mortgages — but debt is obedience with interest. It binds generations, mortgaging futures not yet born. A diploma becomes a shackle. A house becomes a hostage. A card swipe becomes silent servitude. Now programmable money — Central Bank Digital Currencies (CBDCs) — introduces a new frontier. White papers from the BIS (Bank for International Settlements) describe CBDCs as **"programmable policy instruments,"** raising questions about how money could be conditioned, automated, or restricted by design. Supporters call it modernization. Critics warn it could enable unprecedented oversight — transactions tracked, permissions coded, access governed by algorithms rather than agency. Debt wears the smile of progress until the bill arrives in chains. Cash is freedom; programmable money is control. It is not currency. It is code as cage — a ledger built for management disguised as convenience. This is no new trick. Pharaoh bound Egypt through grain debt — when famine came, Joseph's policy turned harvest into leverage, and land, cattle, even bodies were surrendered into Pharaoh's hand (Genesis 47). Rome chained its citizens through tribute — crushing farmers under taxes so heavy they abandoned land for the cities, swelling slums while elites hoarded gold. The chain is old; the code is new. The bondage is the same. Bread turned to bait, debt turned to chain. And today, the mechanisms return — digitized, sanitized, globalized. Slavery by debt weakens the body of a people. Slavery by spectacle weakens the soul. Both serve the same master.

"The borrower is slave to the lender." — Proverbs 22:7

The Cultural Circus

The serpent rehearsed in schools. The dragon struck with fear. The Beast codified the cage in treaties and codes. What Stalin could only dream — erasing photos, burning books — technocrats now attempt with deepfakes, selective "fact-checks," and algorithms that can revise archives in real time. Rome did the same. Emperors carved rivals from stone, striking their names from monuments as if erasure could defeat memory itself. Statues toppled, scrolls burned, histories revised — all to keep power unquestioned. What Rome chiseled with hammers, today's empire attempts with keystrokes. The chain is faster now — but it is the same chain. Today, entire accounts can disappear without warning. Books can be delisted or deprioritized by opaque systems. Curricula update not by public debate but by software patch. Historical narratives shift in school apps and AI feeds before yesterday's lessons have cooled. Memory itself is becoming mediated — curated, filtered, optimized. Truth does not vanish in fire anymore. It vanishes in silence, swallowed by code. Practices once tested in small nations — from Denmark's digital governance layers to America's content moderation experiments — now scale across Brussels, Geneva, and New York. Not by conspiracy, but by convenience. Not by decree, but by default. The illusion of freedom is the dress rehearsal. The technocrat's hand is the main act.

The Strongest Chains Are the Ones You Cannot See

Our politics are managed — your vote tallied, then buried beneath the same unbroken cycle of wars and promises. Your children are conditioned — not taught to think, but trained to comply. Your attention is addicted, seized by screens that trade reflex for reason. Your health is medicated, your body turned into a subscription model. Even your table is leveraged — bread and water priced as assets for investors. Your future is indebted, every loan a leash, every swipe a surrender. And your culture? Distracted into silence, circus after circus until citizenship dissolves. They told you this was freedom. It was slavery rebranded. Slavery didn't end; it upgraded. Truth doesn't ask for your comfort; it demands your courage. Refuse it, and you don't just lose history. You lose the future.

🔥 Firelight Pause — The Illusion of Freedom

• Who taught you what "freedom" means — and who benefits from your believing it?

• Where have you mistaken comfort for liberty, convenience for sovereignty?

• If slavery didn't end but evolved, what part of you has already adapted to the upgrade?

• When your body, wallet, and mind are managed by code, what part of you still belongs to God — and what part has already been leased to the Machine?

Fire exposes the bars no slogan can hide. It burns through narratives that kept you numb. It reveals that freedom without truth is not freedom at all — it is a velvet cage.

"They promise them freedom, but they themselves are slaves of corruption. For whatever overcomes a person, to that he is enslaved." — 2 Peter 2:19

78

THE SHOT BEFORE THE TOWER
WHEN BLOOD REVEALS THE SOUL OF A NATION

Most people live in fog. They think history turns on elections, markets, or headlines. But sometimes the fog is ripped open by fire — a bullet, a tower, a fall. America remembers the flames and crumbling steel of 9/11. Now again comes a shot that splits the sky. This moment is not only about a man. It is about what we have become. On one side — celebration and mockery. On the other — mourning and prayer. **The division is not political. It is spiritual, and it is final.**

The Cross Echoes

When Christ was crucified, the world split in two. Some jeered, some wailed, and the temple veil tore. That day revealed the hearts of men — their demons, their loyalties, their gods. So now, another death, another unveiling. Not the Savior, but a man of faith whose blood has become a mirror. **How you respond exposes your tormentors — or your Redeemer.**

The Beast and the Remnant

If you cheer, you chain yourself to the Beast. And when its system collapses — **and it will** — you will be left with nothing but madness. No truth. No mercy. No future. But those who belong to Christ are written with resurrection in their bones. Babylon will burn, but the remnant will rise. They will rebuild at the table the world abandoned. This moment is not merely political. It is prophetic. God is forcing souls to reveal themselves — children of the Beast, or children of God.

"For we wrestle not against flesh and blood, but against principalities, against powers, against the rulers of the darkness of this world." — Ephesians 6:12

A child of God is not a label. It is a bloodline, a covenant, an inheritance. Babylon calls you consumer, taxpayer, worker, voter. Christ calls you son, daughter, warrior, heir. The Beast offers ownership, surveillance, and fear. The Kingdom of Christ offers freedom, truth, and eternal belonging. To name Christ is to draw the line: you serve Him, or you serve the Dragon. There is no middle ground. The enemy always offers shadows of God's gifts — safety instead of salvation, equity instead of justice, tolerance instead of love. But the children of God are not deceived. They know the original. They see through the counterfeit.

"The great dragon was hurled down—that ancient serpent... They overcame him by the blood of the Lamb and by the word of their testimony." — Revelation 12:9–11

The Call

You are not here by accident. You are not a pawn in their system. You are blood-bought, forged in truth, sealed as a child of God. That is why the Dragon fears you. That is why the Beast hunts you. Because you carry a name higher than theirs. The night is cold, the towers fall, the shots echo, the Beast prowls — yet the remnant still carries fire. From catacombs to deserts, from forests to prisons, believers have always gathered by small fires, whispering songs of victory while the empire roared defeat.

That fire is here now. It is in your hands as you read. It is the Spirit that will not be extinguished. You do not stand alone. You stand among warriors, saints, and ancestors whose blood became seed. You stand beneath a sky where Christ's banner still waves, even if Babylon's towers burn. Breathe. Let the fire steady you. Let the Word remind you — resurrection is stronger than ruin. The tower has fallen. The shot has been fired. **The only question left is this: who do you belong to?** The fire does not flatter. The fire reveals. Answer carefully — because your answer is already echoing in eternity.

Firelight Pause — The Shot Before the Tower

- Who owns your memory — Christ, or the Dragon's screens?
- When the towers fell, what did you cling to — fear, or faith?
- Whose voice do you follow when the crowd mocks — Babylon's chorus, or the Shepherd's whisper?
- Do you love life, or do you celebrate death?
- Do you see yourself as voter, worker, consumer — or as son, daughter, warrior, heir?
- When the Beast marks the world with numbers, what mark will be found on you?

The Veil Before the Applause

The tower falls outside. The shot echoes across the nation. But a second sound rises — clapping. When a people applaud blood, covenant has cracked. This is not about politics. It is about possession. History bears witness. Lincoln's death tore a healing nation apart. Ferdinand's death ignited the Great War. Each shot revealed the soul of its age — and now, ours. Bullets and blades do not just wound bodies; they expose loyalties, idols, and fears. Lincoln's death unveiled America's unfinished covenant — freedom proclaimed, yet still contested. Ferdinand's death unveiled Europe's rotting order — monarchies brittle, nations restless, war inevitable.

"For the word of God is living and active, sharper than any two-edged sword..." — Hebrews 4:12

79

THE AGE OF APPLAUSE FOR BLOOD
THE LINE CROSSED

Every empire, at the end, hunts its truth-tellers. Babylon mocked. Rome fed. The Soviets jailed. The Nazis burned. **Now America bleeds.** Charlie Kirk — husband, father, builder — was shot on a public stage for the crime of speaking. They tried shadow bans, smears, de-platforming. When that failed, they reached for bullets. That is the sound a republic makes when argument is replaced by assassination. The state lowered flags. Congress stood in silence. And then even a prayer became a battleground — a chamber unable to agree that a life taken by political hate deserved words before God. This is collapse — when even grief is politicized, when compassion is divided by party. He was not a stranger. Not an enemy soldier. He was a husband. A father. A Christian. A builder of youth who spent his life pointing America's sons and daughters toward truth. His wife lost her husband. His children lost their father. His parents lost their son. His friends lost their brother in arms. And yet millions watched — some silent, some horrified... and some applauding. They laughed. They mocked. They cheered the murder of a man whose only weapon was a microphone.

"Woe unto them that call evil good, and good evil; that put darkness for light, and light for darkness." — Isaiah 5:20

577

This is not politics. Not culture war. **This is covenant-breaking.** His name becomes symbol. His blood becomes prophecy. For America today, he is not only a man fallen — he is proof that **truth itself is now the target.** This chapter is not about one man. It is about a Republic revealed — When truth itself becomes treason, every voice is tested. When words cut too deeply, Babylon reaches for bullets. When the Beast can no longer silence by censorship, it silences by assassination. **This is the crime of speaking plainly.**

They did not merely distract us. They discipled us — in numbness. Screens anesthetized. Propaganda rewired. Universities rehearsed obedience. Parents sedated. Children drugged. Generations softened on purpose. We were trained to rage at a red hat — but stay silent at a body. To cry over pronouns — but not over fathers. To scream at a flag — but laugh at a death. *This is not random outrage; it is engineered apathy.* The serpent whispered. The dragon enforced. And now the Beast feeds on applause — not only for policy, but for death itself. **When death becomes entertainment, judgment is already at the door.** Every empire runs the same ritual at the end. Babylon mocked. Rome drowned its citizens in gladiatorial blood until the crowd roared for death. The Reich wrapped cruelty in cinema until neighbors watched trains depart in silence. The Soviets baptized slaughter with words like "relocation," "re-education," "liquidation."

Denmark rehearses it now — asking families to hand over pets for "nutrition," cloaking theft of love as policy, perfecting silence as virtue. And America rehearses it today. Not with lions, but with algorithms. Not in coliseums, but on screens. Not with papyrus scrolls, but endless feeds. Screens did not just entertain; they anesthetized. Universities did not just instruct; they rehearsed obedience until thought itself became treason. **This is the ritual's final act — when a man is shot not for his crimes, but for his words — and the crowd scrolls on.**

Turning Point

Applause for blood did not appear overnight. It was taught. Screens rehearsed it. Slogans normalized it. Algorithms rewarded it. The bullet did not strike his chest, but his throat. The serpent's aim was clear — not just to kill a man, but to kill his voice. To strangle speech itself. This is the fork in the road. Will we rise up and turn back to Christ — or bow down and be silenced by terror? Names are not accidents. *Turning Point* is not branding. It is covenant. It is a line in the sand. *This is where America turns — away from evil, or into it.* One man's blood is now more than tragedy. It is testimony. It is America's mirror. In his silence, we see the serpent's goal: not just to kill a man, but to murder speech, to choke the covenant itself. Every generation has its altar of decision. This is ours. Will we kneel to the Beast, or rise with the Remnant?

The Call Back

The prophets warned. The Founders knew. Freedom dies when love grows cold. Covenant collapses when cruelty is applauded.

"He that justifieth the wicked, and he that condemneth the just, even they both are abomination to the Lord." — Proverbs 17:15

So rise, remnant. Refuse the spell. Mourn what is holy. Guard what is sacred. Weep when blood is spilled. Stand when truth is mocked. **Because when a nation cheers death, covenant has cracked — and judgment is no longer delayed.**

"And because iniquity shall abound, the love of many shall wax cold. But he that shall endure unto the end, the same shall be saved." — Matthew 24:12–13

🔥 **Firelight Pause — The Sword of the Remnant**

The fire burns. The sword gleams. And now it rests in your hands.

- Will you let bullets silence truth — or will you carry it further?
- Will you guard your gates — or let the serpent enter unopposed?
- Will you scroll past blood — or will you rise in covenant?

Truth has become treason. Speech has become target. And now bullets are the Beast's last weapon. **But the Remnant does not bow. We rise. We speak. We burn.** We do not answer bullets with bullets, lies with lies, or hate with hate. That is the Beast's way. We overcome by the blood of the Lamb and the word of our testimony. Our fire is covenant, not cruelty.

"For God has not given us a spirit of fear, but of power and of love and of a sound mind." — 2 Timothy 1:7

Jefferson warned that "the tree of liberty must be refreshed from time to time with the blood of patriots and tyrants." Solzhenitsyn whispered from the gulag that one word of truth outweighs the world. Orwell warned that in a time of universal deceit, telling the truth is a revolutionary act. Bonhoeffer, before the Nazi gallows, declared that silence in the face of evil is itself evil. And the prophets cried before them. Jeremiah thundered though kings hated him. Daniel prayed though lions waited for him. Paul sang hymns though chains clinked on his wrists. John wrote Revelation though Rome exiled him to die forgotten. Every age tried to bury truth. Every age failed. Because the Word of God is not chained. Because covenant is not broken by bullets. Because resurrection is already written into the bones of truth. Now it is our turn. The scroll has reached our name. Will we be silent, or will we burn? The age of applause for blood will not end in silence. It will end in fire. Rise, Remnant. **The war is here.**

"If my people, which are called by my name, shall humble themselves, and pray, and seek my face, and turn from their wicked ways; then will I hear from heaven, and will forgive their sin, and will heal their land." — II Chronicles 7:14

The crowd has chosen its liturgy — applause for blood. The Beast thinks the blade is his. But the only sword that decides a nation is the one that cuts lies from souls. If the crowd has chosen its liturgy, the Remnant must choose its weapon — not iron, but truth.

80

THE SWORD OF TRUTH

CUTS LIES, DEMANDS ALLEGIANCE

Truth is not opinion. Not narrative. Not consensus. Truth is reality as God speaks it — eternal, untouchable, unchanging. Babylon spins facts into fog, but truth cuts straight. Technocrats draft equations and call them "truth," but truth needs no algorithm. The Beast hates truth because truth exposes its chains. Truth is fire. It burns lies and blinds tyrants. Truth is sword. It divides bone from marrow. Truth is covenant. It anchors a people when towers fall. To walk out of Babylon is to hunger for truth more than comfort — because truth does not soothe; it sears.

The Great Divide

Humanity is not divided by politics, class, or skin. It is divided by truth. Truth does not negotiate. It does not flatter. It does not bow. It declares — this is light, that is darkness. This is life, that is death. This is God, that is Satan. That is why truth feels like a sword: it cuts illusions, masks, pride. Every war in history, every riot, every assassination is truth colliding with lies. To control memory is to control truth. The battle has never been left vs. right — it has always been **truth vs. lies.**

Truth destroys illusions. It costs jobs, friendships, reputations, families. Lies seduce because they comfort. Truth burns because it cleanses. Accepting truth collapses false peace — and that is why so many resist. Yet once the illusions burn, only the eternal remains. Truth resurrects covenant. Truth steadies a people when towers fall. I have paid for truth. Rooms went silent. "Friends" evaporated. Contracts vanished. Not because I was cruel, but because I refused the fog. Every truth-teller learns the same lesson: when you stop bowing, doors close — and heaven opens. History bears the same scar. Rome did not slaughter Christians for crime but for confession — because truth exposed Caesar's fraud. Solzhenitsyn's whisper cracked an empire built on lies. Luther's hammer shattered indulgence with a single word of Scripture. Every idol can tolerate anything except a mirror.

Today the pattern repeats. Doctors who question the script are erased. Parents at school boards are branded as threats. Pastors who refuse the new catechisms lose pulpits. Whistleblowers are jailed. Platforms delete dissent with a click. Babylon's appetite hasn't changed; it has only upgraded its tools. Refuse truth long enough, and madness becomes your inheritance. Embrace it, and fire becomes your strength. Truth is exclusive. It declares what is real and what is not. In a world that worships fog, that declaration feels like violence. Illusions pretend to keep peace — but it is a false peace. Truth demands allegiance. Lies let you drift. Truth forces you to choose. That choice has always divided blood from blood.

Christ Himself said, *"Do not think that I came to bring peace on earth. I did not come to bring peace but a sword."* — Matthew 10:34

Truth unmasks idols. Every empire is built on lies — Rome's "peace," Marx's "equality," today's "progress." When truth exposes the idol, the idol's worshipers rage. That rage births wars, persecutions, assassinations. Truth is light. And when light shines, darkness cannot coexist. Darkness resists violently — because light signals its end.

Even the Founders understood this. Jefferson warned democracy without virtue becomes mob rule. Madison said a republic must guard truth from factions. They built a republic on truth because lies always end in tyranny. Babylon loves fog because fog feels safe. "Let's all get along." "Your truth, my truth." But fog is not peace — it is anesthesia. When truth cuts through it, the real war appears. Lies cannot live beside truth. Rome killed Christians because truth unmasked Caesar. Communists killed millions because truth exposed Marx's fantasy. Today truth-tellers are censored, canceled, erased — because truth still unmasks the Beast. Every war is the same war: truth vs. lies. Truth kills illusions, but resurrects covenant. It divides, but also gathers. The Remnant know each other by truth — fire recognizing fire, light recognizing light. Truth is not fragile. Truth is a Person. Truth is Christ — the sword that divides and the fire that saves. Empires will fall. Idols will go silent. And still Truth will be standing.

Firelight Pause — The Sword at Your Chest
- Where are you living in fog and calling it peace?
- What illusions do you protect because they cost less than truth?
- When truth cut your friendships or family, did you choose comfort or covenant?
- When the crowd mocks, whose voice do you obey — Babylon's chorus or the Shepherd's whisper?
- When the Beast offers "safety," "equity," "tolerance," do you bow to the counterfeit or hold the line?
- When the world stamps its mark on your hand, what mark will be found in your soul?
- When your children ask what you stood for, will they inherit truth — or excuses?

"For the word of God is living and active, sharper than any two-edged sword, piercing to the division of soul and of spirit, of joints and of marrow, and discerning the thoughts and intentions of the heart." — Hebrews 4:12

81

BEAST-SYSTEM SORCERY
NUMBERS AS SPELLS, NAMES AS FREEDOM

They reached for bullets to silence a man. But bullets are not the Beast's only weapon. When the smoke clears and the body is buried, another weapon remains — quieter, colder, older. It does not fire from a gun. It drips from a ledger. It whispers through numbers. It brands with codes. Every empire, once it tastes blood, moves from swords to sorcery. Because power always seeks permanence, and fear is easier to manage than force. Rome crucified, then taxed. The Reich shot, then tallied. Today they censor, then they score. **Bullets strike the body, but numbers chain the soul.**

The Beast's power is not only in armies or politics but in hidden sorcery. It does not roar with teeth. It whispers through numbers, codes, and symbols. History's tattoos became today's credit scores and IDs. Logos and acronyms work like incantations. Algorithms and grids shape your choices. Even math, once a language of order, has been twisted to bind reality without truth. But the counterfeit seal is shallow. Once you see the Beast's sorcery, you cannot unsee it. And once you see it, you can refuse it, walk out of Babylon, and rise sealed by covenant instead of code.

The Net of Digits

The Beast hides in digits. What looks like harmless accounting is in fact a net—reducing men to files, shaping fear with statistics, branding flesh with counterfeit marks. Social security numbers. MitID. ESG scores. Carbon credits. Chains disguised as order. Case counts. Death tallies. Debt ratios. Percentages cast as spells to terrify the docile — fear disguised as fact. And always the counterfeit mark—666. Commerce stamped with a number that denies the name.

"He causes all, both small and great, rich and poor, free and slave, to receive a mark... that no one may buy or sell except one who has the mark." — Revelation 13:16–17.

Numbers Redeemed

The Beast twists numbers into chains. But in Scripture, numbers are covenant—not sorcery. They do not enslave; they testify. Three reveals the Trinity. Seven proclaims fullness. Twelve marks governance. Forty signals wilderness and transformation. Each number in God's order points back to His story. And no number has been more hijacked than thirty-three. Christ was crucified at thirty-three—the sacrifice that shattered the Serpent's grip. Secret societies flaunt it as mastery, not knowing it marks their bondage. But its true meaning is public and unhidden — redemption finished in blood. What the Beast flaunts in secrecy, Christ finished on a hill. The Beast has always erased names and replaced them with digits. In the camps, this sorcery was raw. Tattoos turned sons and daughters into tallies. Flesh branded with code. Names stripped away. It was more than cruelty. It was sorcery—worth rewritten by numbers.

"Even the very hairs of your head are all numbered. Fear not therefore; you are of more value than many sparrows." — Luke 12:7.

The tattoos are gone, but the spirit of numbering remains. Screens, scores, ledgers—the same mark in a new skin. China's social credit scores and QR codes reduce freedom to a rating. Denmark's "MitID", health passes, and carbon quotas sell compliance as convenience. The world prepares CBDCs, ESG tallies, biometric IDs—not tattoos, but chips and codes that whisper the same lie. The serpent conquers twice—first by lies, then by ledgers, because souls that stop discerning soon stop resisting.

The Global Priesthood of Acronyms

The Beast does not act alone. It clothes its spells in the robes of world institutions. The UN writes the script in the name of "inclusion." The WEF markets it as "stakeholder capitalism." The WHO enforces it as "health security." Each treaty, each compact, each global framework sells bondage as safety. A "sustainable goal" becomes a surveillance mandate. A "health pass" becomes a chain on worship and travel. A "climate quota" becomes a ration card. What looks like humanitarian order is sorcery in code. The very bodies sworn to protect nations now dissolve them into grids of compliance. Babylon speaks fluent acronym. ESG. DEI. CBDC. WHO. Each letter a spell. Each spell a chain. Chains are never sold as chains. They are dressed as gifts. They are baptized as progress. **Your number is said to keep you safe.** Your score is said to prove you are good. Your login is said to mean you belong. Your QR code is said to grant you access. But every gift is counterfeit. Every blessing is a leash. Every promise a spell. The counterfeit mark is numbers and codes. The true seal is blood and Spirit. Babylon counts digits. The Father names sons and daughters. The Beast says you are replaceable. Christ declares you are unrepeatable — a name, not a number.

"Then I looked, and behold, a Lamb standing on Mount Zion, and with Him one hundred and forty-four thousand, having His Father's name written on their foreheads." — Revelation 14:1

The Algorithmic Cage

The Beast no longer needs prophets of Baal. It has algorithms—hidden math that predicts, prescribes, and defines you. You think you scroll freely, but feeds decide what lives or dies on your screen. You think you search freely, but results show only what hidden code allows. You think you buy freely, but risk scores and smart grids pre-decide your limits — the new commandments of control. Christ hides nothing. His Word is open, His covenant public, His seal unbreakable. The algorithm whispers: You are predictable. *Christ answers: You are unrepeatable.* Refuse it wherever it rises. Refuse it at restaurants when bread is replaced with barcodes. Refuse it at airports when travel requires a scan. Refuse it at hospitals when healing is filtered through screens. Refuse it at banks that push you into apps instead of cash. Refuse it at governments that demand digital ID instead of covenant identity. Every refusal is resistance — not in rage, but in righteousness. Every no to their mark is a yes to covenant. Enough fires lit, and Babylon's night will turn to day. The Beast whispers — You cannot live without me. Christ declares: "The earth is the Lord's, and the fullness thereof." — Psalm 24:1. The Remnant has always built in the shadow of empire—catacombs, forests, underground tables. Alternative systems are not survivalism. They are rebellion redeemed — Kingdom living. The Beast enslaves with digits. The Kingdom frees with covenant. Babylon builds towers of numbers. The Remnant builds altars of fire.

This is the hour to tear your allegiance from the Beast. Neutrality is surrender. To belong to Christ is to rise. Refuse false safety. Withdraw your allegiance from Babylon's systems. Abandon the ship before it sinks. Do not whisper dissent—embody truth. Do not practice quiet resistance as comfort—make your life the dissent. No more silent compliance. No more worship of convenience. No more bowing to numbers that cannot save. *Christ calls you out of Babylon and seals you for His Kingdom. Rise. Name the chains. Walk free.* You are not a digit in their ledger. You are blood-bought. When the Beast hunts, it will find fire, not fear. The serpent began with your mind; now it brands your flesh. **The Remnant will not be numbered. We are sealed in blood, not code.**

🔥 **Firelight Pause — Mark or Seal**

- Where have I already accepted a number instead of my name?
- Have I traded freedom for the convenience of a score or a pass?
- What lies have I obeyed just to keep my place?
- Do I live as if an algorithm knows me better than Christ does?
- When the next "gift" is offered — code, score, or pass — will I bow, or refuse?
- Do I resist out of faith — or out of anger?
- When I say no to Babylon, do I still love those trapped within it?
- Am I building altars of fire — or just shouting at the towers?

"In Him you also trusted, after you heard the word of truth, the gospel of your salvation; in whom also, having believed, you were sealed with the Holy Spirit of promise, who is the guarantee of our inheritance until the redemption of the purchased possession." — Ephesians 1:13–14

The Beast no longer roars; it types. Its generals wear suits, not armor. Its battles are fought in code, not in streets. You've seen its mark — now trace the fingers that carve it. The serpent whispers. The dragon enforces. But the hand that signs the spell... belongs to the technocrat who forgot he had a soul.

82

———

THE TECHNOCRATS' HAND
GLOBAL MANAGERS OF CHAINS

Every empire has priests. Babylon had astrologers. Rome had scribes. Today the empire has technocrats. They are not kings, and they are not soldiers. **They are the managers of illusion.** They conquer with spreadsheets, march with frameworks, and whisper like consultants. The serpent hisses; the dragon terrifies; the Beast codifies. And the hand that enforces it all belongs to the technocrat.

The Exported Model

Denmark became the prototype of compliance — a small stage to rehearse global control. A consensus culture taught obedience as virtue. Hate-speech laws and values-education trained the reflex of censorship now embedded in code. Digital IDs were sold as "convenience" and exported to Brussels. Green cow taxes were tested as environmental policy and repackaged as quota models across Europe. From polished desks in Denmark came a script — velvet chains dressed as happiness. "Hygge" as spell. Dependency as gospel. Once perfected, the model was exported. What was tested in a nation of six million became European law.

Danish hands helped draft digital-service frameworks that dress censorship as safety, green deals that impose quotas as climate justice, migration compacts that erase sovereignty under the veneer of cooperation. Bureaucrats from Copenhagen sit on EU committees, UN boards, WHO panels. Local experiments became continental policy. At scale, the UN plays the same role. Compacts on migration, climate, and speech are written as global morality. WHO pandemic treaties surrender health sovereignty by signature. Sustainable Development Goals read like commandments of Babylon in PowerPoint form. **There is no ballot, only polished decrees enforced as international consensus.** The World Economic Forum is the technocrats' marketplace. There the managers meet billionaires and bless "stakeholder" covenants that tie capital to policy. ESG scores ration credit. Digital IDs track behavior. Net-zero pledges strip farmers while oligarchs preserve privilege. They call themselves stakeholders — but the stake runs through your sovereignty. Why the system works is simple: the tyrant's sword needs the technocrat's pen. Hitler needed accountants for Auschwitz. Stalin needed clerks for quotas. Today Brussels needs climate regulators, Geneva needs pandemic planners, and Silicon Valley supplies the algorithms. The serpent hides in the smile. The dragon hides in the framework. The Beast hides in the spreadsheet. Prophecy saw this age. Daniel's image — iron mixed with clay — warned bureaucracy fused with humanity will not hold. Revelation speaks of authority extending over every people — not from a single crown but through global desks, glowing screens, and endless treaties.

America at the Crossroads

Denmark rehearsed. Brussels scaled. Now the technocrats want America. Silicon Valley merges with Washington. Fact-check boards replace juries. AI models enforce "approved" speech. Digital IDs slip quietly into apps and paychecks. You thought it was convenience. It was consent.The question is whether America will remember hers — or surrender to their frameworks, choosing comfort over conscience.

If the technocrats win, America will not fall with tanks. It will dissolve under paperwork. There will be no vote, only frameworks. No covenant, only compliance. No law, only policy papers. Courts replaced by "fact-check boards." Elections by "stakeholder councils." Pastors monitored by "community standards." Farmers rationed by "climate quotas." Children catechized by "social-emotional" metrics. The republic will not burn in a day. It will suffocate in forms, apps, and signatures. The citizen who once bore covenant will become a managed asset in a global spreadsheet. **This is how liberty dies — not with an explosion, but with an update.**

The Smile of the System

The fire is lit. The desk glows. One of them will rule you. Ask yourself: have you already obeyed a framework no citizen ever voted for? Have you traded covenant for convenience — letting apps decide your truth and IDs decide your worth? Do you scroll past bans and deletions as if they are normal? The tyrant's face is obvious. The serpent's hiss is ancient. The dragon's roar is loud. But the most dangerous hand is the one that smiles while tightening the chain — the hand of the technocrat. The question is not only political — it is personal. **The framework cannot rule you unless your heart agrees.**

"For where the Spirit of the Lord is, there is liberty." — 2 Corinthians 3:17

◔ **Firelight Pause — The Hand at Your Neck**
- Have you bowed to a framework no law ever passed?
- What rules your days — law, love, or algorithm?
- When did convenience start feeling safer than freedom?
- Do you check your screens before your soul?
- Who shapes your morality — Christ or compliance training?
- When the next "update" demands silence, will you obey or resist?
- Do you still know how to say no when the system smiles?
- As you resist Babylon, do you still pray for those trapped within it?

When freedom fades, do you mourn — or have you learned to love your leash? Liberty dies not by force, but by habit — the quiet bow before the glowing screen. And yet even that bow is not the final spell. After obedience comes affection. The serpent knows the system alone cannot hold. So he wraps the chain in virtue. He teaches the captive to love his cage, to call it kindness, to weep while obeying. This is how tyranny becomes tender. This is the final disguise — **control baptized as compassion.**

"Stand fast therefore in the liberty wherewith Christ hath made us free, and be not entangled again with the yoke of bondage." — Galatians 5:1

Every empire justifies its chains with mercy. But the Remnant will not mistake mercy for manipulation. True compassion frees; false compassion flatters chains. After the technocrats build the system, they must soften the heart that would resist it. So compassion is rewritten — not as covenant, but as control. The hand that coded your cage now blesses it in the name of love. The spreadsheet gives way to the sermon. The code gives way to the tear. And the world applauds its own captivity, whispering:

"This is kindness."

83

THE MASK OF COMPASSION

HOW NGOS, AID, AND
MIGRATION BECOME CHAINS

The serpent never conquers with fangs alone. He conquers with pity. With charity. With compassion. Chains are not always hammered. Sometimes they are handed with a smile. He does not roar. He reassures. He weeps. He builds prisons out of pity and calls them progress. The age of algorithms could not rule without the age of empathy. The Beast needed priests — and it found them in NGOs, foundations, and ministries of mercy.

The NGO Illusion

Non-Governmental Organizations are celebrated as helpers, but a closer look tells a different story. UNRWA camps do not heal refugees; they preserve grievance. Global health became the newest altar. The Bill & Melinda Gates Foundation, draped in benevolence, now shapes WHO policy itself — funding vaccine initiatives, pandemic accords, and "health equity" compacts that override parliaments. Philanthropy became a crown without voters — a private empire steering public law in the name of mercy. The mask slips further under scrutiny. Oxfam staff in Haiti were caught exploiting those they were sent to help. UN "peacekeepers" in Africa traded food for sex.

Within the World Bank and IMF, "relief" became leverage — loans and grants tied to carbon pledges, ESG metrics, and social-policy conditions that rewrite national budgets. The old tribute returned — not in gold, but in green bonds. These organizations are not neutral. They are subcontractors of the Beast. They weaponize pity, harvest grievance, and channel emotion into policy.

Aid as Leverage

Aid is never free. It is a leash. Loans buy silence. Grants breed dependency. Relief programs evolve into permanent management. Africa was not lifted by aid; it was shackled by it. Palestine was not healed by billions in UN funding; it was frozen in grievance for generations. Even in America, relief checks trained citizens to trade fire for dependency. The new trade is migration itself. NGOs operating under UNHCR and the International Organization for Migration are paid per head — per refugee processed, per camp maintained, per border crossed. Every "crisis" becomes a contract. The flood is not a failure of policy; it is a business model. In the United States, the pattern wears a softer face. Faith-based contractors receive billions in federal grants to "resettle" migrants. Each arrival earns reimbursement. Each family becomes a funding line. The border becomes an industry — NGOs paid to house, feed, and transport what the State refuses to deter. Compassion is monetized. Sovereignty is outsourced.

Mercy as a Weapon

The wheel always turns the same way. Aid breeds dependency. Dependency sustains NGOs. NGOs amplify grievance. Grievance demands more aid. The loop spins endlessly — never toward healing, always toward deeper chains. Compassion is the serpent's favorite camouflage. Borders are opened not to heal but to weaken. Nations are flooded not with pilgrims bound to covenant, but with blocs that fracture sovereignty.

Revelation foresaw the pattern: *"The serpent spewed water like a river, to sweep away the woman with the flood."* The flood is not only water. It is engineered movement — population as pressure, migration as weapon. This is not compassion. It is war by administration. Partnerships between tech firms and humanitarian fronts now harvest data from refugees, disasters, and pandemics — training algorithms that promise safety and deliver surveillance. Charity becomes a sensor network. The donation becomes data. Before we condemn them, we must ask ourselves: how often have we confused comfort with calling, or charity with control?

The Mask Removed

America now drinks the same poison. NGOs file lawsuits to block deportations. Aid agencies profit from the border crisis — every migrant a client, every body a budget line, every crossing a paycheck. Suburbs fracture into blocs. Voters are imported. Sovereignty thins. They call it love. It is leverage. They call it compassion. It is conquest. Isaiah warned, *"They call evil good and good evil."* That is the mask of compassion. It looks like care, but it is captivity. It sounds like virtue, but it is vampirism. The Beast wears velvet gloves. The serpent weeps crocodile tears. And those tears are his sharpest weapon.

The Liturgy of Control

The serpent's tears have done their work. The people no longer fear chains — they defend them. Obedience is praised as virtue. Dependency is renamed dignity. Bureaucrats are crowned as shepherds. Mercy is rewritten not as covenant, but as control. The Beast does not rule by law alone. It rules by liturgy. Its prophets sit on panels. Its temples glow in blue light. Its sacraments are data, quotas, and pledges. When compassion becomes currency, the next step is worship. And when worship is misdirected, empire becomes religion. *"Even Satan disguises himself as an angel of light."* Chains are sold as charity. Borders are erased in the name of love. If the Remnant cannot see through the mask, those tears will drown them too.

🔥 Firelight Pause — Breaking the Mask

- What "aid" in my town bought silence instead of freedom?
- Who profits when grievance never heals?
- Do I still know the difference between mercy that frees and mercy that manages?
- When I unmask false compassion, do I still pray for those trapped within it?

Mercy without truth is manipulation. And every false mercy needs a priesthood to bless it.

84

THE GLOBAL PRIESTHOOD
THE GOSPEL OF BUREAUCRACY

Every empire builds a clergy to sanctify its lies. Babylon had magic. Rome had Caesars' priests. Today, the new clergy wear suits and badges. They speak in the language of progress and preach salvation through policy. They no longer burn incense — they burn data. They no longer sacrifice lambs — they sacrifice liberty. They stand at podiums instead of pulpits, carrying reports instead of scrolls, issuing decrees instead of prayers. Their temples are marble towers. Their hymns are PowerPoint slides. Their commandments are "goals." They promise heaven through management — a kingdom without a King. They call themselves experts, councils, commissions — but they are priests in the oldest sense: mediators between man and power. They define the sin — then sell the forgiveness. Their creed is safety. Their god is progress. Their liturgy is consensus. And their church is global.

The New Temples

In New York, Geneva, Brussels, and Davos, the altars gleam. The United Nations, the World Economic Forum, the International Monetary Fund, the World Health Organization — each draped in peace language, each echoing scripture's cadence while denying its truth.

597

They offer redemption through programs, salvation through funding, sanctification through quotas. The UN speaks of "human rights" yet cannot define what a human is. The WHO preaches "health equity" while trading sovereignty for signatures. The IMF forgives no debt without extracting obedience. The WEF promises "reset" — not repentance, but replacement. Man remade in code and contract. Every religion needs ritual. Theirs is paperwork. Every creed needs confession. Theirs is data. Every doctrine needs obedience. Theirs is compliance. They begin with the child — registered, measured, categorized before speech forms. They continue with the worker — tracked through ESG scores and payroll mandates. They end with the citizen — managed by health passes, climate pledges, stakeholder compacts. Every signature becomes a prayer to the Beast. Every checkbox becomes obedience. Every metric becomes worship. This is not administration. It is apostasy with credentials.

The High Priests of Progress

They speak softly — in bureaucratic glossolalia no citizen can decode. Their gospel is "sustainability." Their apocalypse is "climate." Their salvation is "net zero." In truth, they worship not the Creator, but the creation — earth deified, man demoted. They destroy farms to "save the planet," sterilize children in the name of "choice," and regulate breath itself as a pollutant. The priests of old slaughtered animals to appease false gods. The priests of now slaughter economies and call it virtue. They rewrite commandments into initiatives and hang them in glass halls. Their sermon always ends the same way: **"Trust the experts."**

The False Trinity

Every counterfeit mimics the divine. The Dragon inspires the vision. The Beast enforces the order. The False Prophet blesses it. Together they form the priesthood of Babylon — technocrat, bureaucrat, and philanthropist — united by creed, divided by masks. Pandemics become power. Crises become commandments. Compassion becomes compliance.

They preach equity while feasting on exemption. They promise inclusion while demanding erasure. Their language drips with empathy. Their policies reek of domination.

The Counterfeit Church

Even within walls once holy, the infection spreads. Pastors trade pulpits for panels. Sermons bow to slogans. The gospel is rebranded as justice without repentance, progress without truth, peace without the Prince of Peace. But **Christ does not share altars.** When the temple fills with merchants, He overturns tables. When priests sell indulgences, He tears veils. When nations kneel to bureaucrats, He raises prophets from dust and fire. The true Church is being refined — stripped, tested, and made ready.

The Warning and the Remnant

This priesthood will not endure. Babylon's temples will crack. Its data towers will fall. Truth does not need a framework. The Lamb does not consult committees. He reigns. The Remnant must learn to walk without the priests of this age — to build outside their temples, trade outside their systems, worship without licenses. The fire does not need permission to burn.

"For there is one God and one mediator between God and men, the man Christ Jesus." — 1 Timothy 2:5

◔ **Firelight Pause — The Priesthood Test**

- Whose approval do you crave before you speak — the Spirit's, or the system's?
- Where do you tithe your time — to covenant or to compliance?
- What altars have you built — truth or comfort?
- When safety is preached, do you remember Christ promised freedom, not comfort?
- Are you serving the temple of the Beast — or building the Kingdom of God?
- When the next "update" demands silence, will you obey or resist?
- Do you still know how to say no when the system smiles?

The priests of Babylon chant progress. The priests of Christ whisper freedom. The fire knows the difference. Worship has been rewritten in the language of governance. But faith never stays confined to temples. Once creed hardens, it redraws the map. Every false religion seeks territory. Every ideology baptizes nations in its gospel. The global priesthood now preaches through treaties and summits — its sermons signatures, its sacraments compliance. But even as maps shift, the Remnant still carries a compass.

The Spirit of Truth.

85

______

THE WAR OF MAPS

FROM PALESTINE TO AMERICA

How the Serpent Draws Borders and Keeps Wounds Open
Borders redraw nations, but thrones decide who owns them. Every map serves a master. Every line answers to a hand. The serpent does not only draw borders — he enthrones rulers. He gives crowns to cowards and robes to clerks, calling them kings. What begins with treaties ends with coronations: empires reborn as councils, monarchs remade as managers, crowns replaced by logos. The spirit never changes — rule without covenant, legitimacy without God. The map is the battle-field. The crown is the prize. Nothing here is hidden. Treaties are signed. Borders drawn. Resolutions passed. Everything is public record. Yet the pattern remains invisible because it does not speak in headlines — it speaks in lines. History does not only bleed in chains; it bleeds in borders. A chain can be broken in a night. A map can wound for centuries.

"The princes of Judah have become like those who move the landmark." —
Hosea 5:10

God draws borders by covenant, not conquest. He warns against moving boundary stones because borders are not mere lines — they are promises. They anchor memory, duty, and identity. When God marks territory, He binds land to responsibility. When the serpent redraws, he severs all three. One map protects order. The other manufactures chaos. Every border conflict on earth is the clash between two cartographers: covenant and counterfeit.

The Cartographer's Blade

Maps do not describe reality — they dictate it. They erase it. Families wake up on the wrong side of a line they never consented to. Cousins become foreigners. Tribes become enemies. The serpent always holds the pen. Rome taught the first lesson. After crushing the Jewish revolt in 135 AD, the empire erased Judea and renamed the land *Palestina* — not heritage, but revenge. Ink as weapon. A wound designed to outlive armies. If a name can erase a people, what part of your nation could vanish with a stroke of a pen? The method endured. The twentieth century perfected it. Germany was sliced. Berlin cut in half — one city, two systems, one scar. Korea was severed at the 38th parallel — one people turned into eternal enemies by map alone. Every line was sold as "peace." Every border was a leash. Maps became weapons. Borders became memory traps. And wherever covenant was absent, grievance was installed in its place.

When Maps Became Digital

The serpent adapted. Today borders are no longer only land — they are systems. Firewalls replace frontiers. Satellites replace watchtowers. Subsea cables become new Silk Roads. "Digital sovereignty" cages nations without a single soldier crossing a border. Old maps carved land. New maps carve data. Whoever controls the grid decides which nations rise, fracture, or vanish quietly. The map-war never ended. It migrated into the cloud.

Sovereignty Without War

Armies conquer territory. Maps conquer legitimacy. When soldiers invade, a nation resists. When borders move by treaty, the nation is told it consented. This is the serpent's genius. He does not need victory — only acquiescence. He replaces sovereignty quietly, transferring authority from covenant to administration, from people to process, from God to managers. Every modern map war follows the same logic: no declaration, no surrender, no final moment of awareness. Just "agreements," "mandates," "zones," and "frameworks." A nation wakes up intact — flag flying, anthem playing — yet no longer ruling itself. This is why Palestine is never resolved, Germany was never healed, Korea was never reunited, and America is now being dissolved without invasion. A wounded map does not need to win. It only needs to persist. Sovereignty dies not when land is lost — but when authority is transferred without confession. When borders become negotiable, covenant becomes optional. When covenant becomes optional, nations become inventory. The serpent does not seek land. He seeks **jurisdiction**. And jurisdiction is easier to steal with ink than with blood.

Soft power does not eliminate hard power — it precedes it.

Maps, treaties, and frameworks are not alternatives to war; they are how war is won without firing. A nation that loses jurisdiction through ink will not fight when steel arrives — because it will no longer know who commands, what it defends, or whether it is even allowed to resist. Hard power still exists. Armies still matter. But they only prevail where sovereignty remains intact. Soft conquest dissolves that sovereignty first — so when force finally appears, there is no authority left to answer it. This is why the serpent prefers maps to missiles. Missiles provoke resistance. Maps anesthetize it.

Denmark's Panic: A Case Study in Soft Sovereignty

In early January 2026, the mask slipped. Denmark did not treat renewed American talk of Greenland as rhetoric. It treated it as breach. Prime Minister Mette Frederiksen warned that any U.S. move regarding Greenland could fracture **NATO** itself — not because NATO is weak, but because Greenland is the tripwire Denmark cannot afford to lose. Then came the tell. Instead of calm bilateral diplomacy, Denmark rushed a **multinational joint statement** — joined by France, Germany, Italy, Poland, Spain, and the United Kingdom — *invoking Arctic security, the "inviolability of borders," and NATO cohesion*, while repeating the legitimacy incantation: *"Greenland belongs to its people — and only Denmark and Greenland can decide its future."* That is not confidence. That is **pre-emptive legitimacy stacking**. Before any treaty dispute existed, alliance language was deployed. Before facts were argued, the frame was asserted. This is how power moves now — not by invading first, but by narrating first.

Denmark's elite discourse still thinks in heritage: Vinland stories, symbolic ownership, moral authority through history. But empires do not care who was first. They care who can **hold, supply, defend, and integrate**. Greenland is logistics, radar, depth. Greenland is not about Danish pride. It is about the American security perimeter — early-warning systems, Arctic chokepoints, undersea cables, missile defense, and the narrowing distance between North America, Russia, and China. This is why the reaction was panic, not posture. **Soft sovereignty collapses under hard geography.** *When symbolism meets systems, systems win.* Denmark does not "owe" America historically. But Greenland is already functionally embedded in the U.S. defensive architecture — whether Copenhagen likes the language or not. And that is the lesson. When maps stop matching capability, fear rushes in. Unity is shouted loudly. Treaties multiply. NATO is invoked early. These are **defensive tells**, not strength.

Denmark's panic is not the crisis. It is the symptom. It shows what happens when symbolic sovereignty collides with strategic reality. But panic alone is not the serpent's endgame. Panic is the moment before design hardens. When a nation cannot hold, the serpent does not simply take — he *restructures*. He creates wounds that never heal, borders that never settle, identities that never resolve. This is how empires avoid resistance: not by conquering cleanly, but by ensuring the conflict never ends. A frozen dispute is more useful than a resolved one. A permanent grievance is more powerful than a decisive victory. Where sovereignty dissolves, the serpent does not rush to replace it with peace. He replaces it with administration, camps, committees, and narratives that justify endless intervention. This is the difference between a border that defends and a border that bleeds. Denmark shows how soft sovereignty fractures under pressure. Palestine shows what happens next. Not confusion — but permanence. Not panic — but policy. Not a temporary crisis — but an engineered wound meant to outlast generations. If Denmark is the warning flare, Palestine is the blueprint.

When Soft Power Forgets Sovereignty

Soft power only works when it rests on hard reality. Diplomacy assumes the presence of force. Treaties assume the ability to enforce. Legitimacy assumes capacity. When those assumptions break, soft power does not evolve — it **collapses**. Bureaucratic systems confuse recognition with control. They believe that if authority is acknowledged on paper, it exists in practice. But sovereignty is not granted by consensus. It is sustained by capability — by logistics, defense, integration, and willingness to act when words fail. This is where soft states misread the world.

They think:
- legality equals legitimacy
- legitimacy equals authority
- authority equals control

None of this is true once pressure arrives. **Under stress, hard power does not negotiate with symbols. It bypasses them.** Soft sovereignty survives only in times of surplus and peace. When geography tightens and resources matter, systems revert to fundamentals: **who can hold, who can supply, who can defend.** States that forget this do not fall dramatically. They are not conquered. They are **reclassified** — left with flags, anthems, and statements while decisions move elsewhere. This is not betrayal. It is mechanics. Every bureaucratic empire eventually discovers the same limit: **paper cannot stop physics.** That is why soft-power regimes panic when confronted with reality. They have nothing to escalate with except language. They respond to pressure by multiplying declarations, invoking alliances early, and asserting principles loudly — not to project strength, but to compensate for its absence. When sovereignty becomes symbolic, fear replaces confidence. And when confidence is gone, the map is already changing. NATO is supposed to follow sovereignty — not replace it. When alliance language comes before capability, it signals fear, not strength.

Palestine — The Wound by Design

To treat Palestine as a headline is to misunderstand the script. It is not an accident. It is a template — a wound engineered to remain open. For most of history, the land was a province inside empires. Identity centered on faith and tribe, not a modern nation-state. After World War I, Britain governed it under the Mandate for Palestine. In 1948, Israel declared independence. Five Arab armies invaded. Israel survived. Many local Arabs fled — urged by leaders who promised return after victory. The victory never came. Arab states refused to absorb the refugees. Camps became permanent. And in 1949, the United Nations created UNRWA — the only refugee agency in history designed not to resolve displacement, but to preserve it. Refugee status became hereditary. Five generations later, the wound remains — by international decree. Meanwhile, Israel absorbed its own exiles: over 800,000 Jews expelled from Arab countries after 1948, integrated and granted citizenship. One side built. The other institutionalized grievance. Who benefits when refugees are preserved instead of resettled? Who profits when wounds are kept open instead of healed?

Why Israel Is Targeted

Since the 1970s, the fixation hardened. In 1975, the UN declared "Zionism is racism." Though revoked, the poison remained. From 2015 to 2023, the UN passed more resolutions against Israel than against all other nations combined — including regimes that butcher their own people. Israel alone received a permanent agenda item for condemnation. This is not justice. It is ritual. Israel is not targeted because it is powerful. It is targeted because it is covenantal. A nation that remembers its God cannot be dissolved into a borderless world.

What Zionism Actually Is

Zionism is not conspiracy. It is survival. A people returning to covenant soil after two thousand years of exile. International law recognized it. History demanded it. Providence preserved it. Old antisemitism said: *"Jews, leave our country."* The new antisemitism says: *"Jews, you have no country at all."* To deny Zionism is to demand Jewish statelessness — the condition that produced centuries of persecution. "Anti-Zionism" is simply the serpent's newest costume. Strip it away and the ancient hatred stands unchanged. Israel represents the one thing the global order cannot domesticate: **a people whose identity flows from God, not the State.** Technocracy can manage consumers, migrants, and data subjects. It cannot manage covenant. And covenant, in an age of fog, is unforgivable. Soft war does not replace hard war. It disables resistance *before* hard war is needed. Maps don't make tanks irrelevant. They make tanks unnecessary.

America — The Next Map

The blade now turns toward the United States. Not through secret treaties — but through demographic floods, zoning mandates, migrant corridors, federal land grabs, interstate compacts, and regulatory frameworks written far from the soil they will reshape. Counties fracture into enclaves. Cities redraw districts to dissolve local authority. States surrender jurisdiction to unelected frameworks.

The border crisis is not chaos. It is cartography — a remapping of the republic disguised as compassion. Beneath the geopolitical wound lies a deeper one: *a nation trained to hate its founders, forget its faith, and abandon its memory.* A people who forget their borders soon forget themselves. The serpent's deepest cut is not land. It is identity. What you saw in Europe, in Korea, in Palestine — was rehearsal. The final stage is here.

Firelight Pause — The Map Beneath the Headlines

Sit with the fire. Let the smoke burn off the slogans. After this chapter, you will never again hear:

"peace process". "two-state solution". "international framework". "treaty-based order". "rules-based system". "border integrity" without asking:

- Who gains jurisdiction?
- Who loses authority?
- Who benefits if this never ends?

Now go deeper.

- Where in the world are borders being "managed" instead of defended — and who writes the management rules?
- Which conflicts are frozen instead of resolved — and who profits from their permanence?
- Where has soft power replaced sovereignty — treaties without teeth, recognition without control?
- Which nations are praised for "stability" while bleeding authority quietly into frameworks and councils?
- Where is NATO, the UN, or an alliance invoked *before* capability is demonstrated — and why?
- When you hear the word *peace*, do you now ask whether it means reconciliation — or administration?

Refuse naïve binaries.
- Not every conflict has heroes and villains — some have **designers.**
- Not every tragedy is failure — some are **systems functioning as intended.**
- Not every negotiation seeks peace — some seek **endless relevance.**

This chapter did not ask you to choose sides. It trained you to **see the board.** Wounds are often more useful to empires than victories. Frozen disputes last longer than resolved ones. Grievance is easier to govern than sovereignty. A people with no healed borders can be managed forever. Now turn the lens inward.
- Where has your own nation traded jurisdiction for recognition?
- Which borders are still defended — and which are only spoken of?
- When authority is transferred by ink instead of invasion, would you even know when it happened?
- If your nation were reduced to a map managed by others, how long would it take before resistance became "illegal"?

The serpent does not need to conquer the land if he can **administer the wound.** He does not seek territory first. He seeks **permission.** And permission is easier to take when people believe peace means silence and order means obedience.

"They say, 'Peace, peace,' when there is no peace." — Jeremiah 6:14

Let the fire teach you this final truth:
Sovereignty is not lost when the flag falls.
It is lost when authority moves quietly and no one dares to name it.
The fire is not asking what you feel.
It is asking what you now **see** —
and whether you will ever unsee it again.

86

WAR OF THE THRONES

HOW MAPS BECAME CROWNS,
AND CROWNS BECAME CHAINS

The War of Thrones

The map bleeds into the throne. What begins in ink ends in power. Every border crowns a ruler. Every treaty anoints a priest. The serpent never stops at geography — he enthrones himself in men. When the land is divided, the next conquest is conscience. When maps no longer bleed, minds will. The war of borders becomes the war of beliefs.

The Theater of Hate

Camps became backdrops. Slogans sharpened into erasure — *"From the river to the sea."* Some spoke it in ignorance; others meant annihilation. Hamas wrote it into its charter. The slogan promises not coexistence, but the end of Israel itself. UN agencies prolonged the grievance. UNRWA, created in 1949 to aid Palestinian refugees, became a system that preserved rather than resolved the crisis. Funds poured in. Textbooks distributed through UNRWA schools erased Jewish history and glorified martyrdom — findings confirmed repeatedly by European Union audits and independent groups like IMPACT-se and UN Watch.

Meanwhile, Israel absorbed its own exiles — Ethiopians airlifted from famine in Operations *Moses* (1984) and *Solomon* (1991); Russians fleeing Soviet collapse in the 1990s; Jews expelled from Arab lands, nearly a million souls who lost everything but their covenant. They were granted citizenship, housed, and folded into a reborn nation. One side built. The other preserved grievance. *Who writes the curriculum when textbooks erase entire peoples?*

The Larger Game

The Middle East is not just sand and borders. It is the serpent's testbed for global power. The **Abraham Accords** in 2020 showed a different path — wounds closing, trade replacing terror. The accords joined Israel with the UAE, Bahrain, Morocco, and Sudan, sparking commerce, tourism, and shared defense. For the first time in generations, Arab leaders spoke openly of peace. That terrified the machinery that feeds on conflict. Grievance is fuel; peace is bankruptcy. Every step toward normalization met outrage — boycotts, riots, resolutions by the dozen. The global order that profits from perpetual tension could not allow the wound to heal. Netanyahu became the lightning rod. To friends, a defender; to enemies, a tyrant. Either way, the spotlight stayed on him — not on the serpent tightening its coils through bureaucracies, aid agencies, and talking points.

The Pattern

Keep a people stateless. Keep the wound open. Keep the rage permanent. Then export the model everywhere: race politics, climate guilt, migration quotas. Preserve grievance. Weaponize guilt. Weaken nations. **Israel was the rehearsal. The same machinery now aims at America.**

Palestine Is the Script

Palestine is not just about land. It is about memory, grievance, and the machinery that keeps wounds open. The UN did not solve the refugee crisis. It industrialized it. And in that industry, Israel became the perpetual villain — and America, the next test case. If Jews can be told their homeland is illegitimate, why not tell Americans their nation was born in sin? So it came. Race politics recast America's founding not as covenant but as eternal crime. Statues toppled. Textbooks rewritten. Reparations drafted not as healing, but as permanent obligation. Climate compacts turned carbon into the new "occupation," condemning America while excusing China. Migration quotas reframed borders as cruelty. Refugees became grievance currency, managed by NGOs. Equity decrees re-mapped institutions into quotas and categories. The UN did not need tanks. It needed treaties. Resolutions. Weak leaders to import the framework.

The Same Machinery

UNRWA kept Palestinians stateless. American bureaucrats now keep citizens permanently "marginalized," no matter the progress. In 1975, Zionism was branded racism. In 2001 at Durban, "anti-racism" became a tribunal — first against Israel, then against America. The narrative held: Israel condemned endlessly. America condemned endlessly. Always guilty. Always chained. A people weighed down by guilt is easier to control. Whose power grows when your nation is always guilty?

But God Already Spoke

"As for all my wicked neighbors who seize the inheritance I gave my people Israel, I will uproot them... But after I uproot them, I will again have compassion and bring each of them back to their own inheritance." — Jeremiah 12:14–15

The UN manufactures guilt. God restores covenant. The serpent keeps wounds open. God heals. The UN cannot veto God's map. If God has already spoken, why do men still pretend to redraw His boundaries?

Presidents at the Gate

From the beginning, America has stood at the UN's gate — sometimes holding the line, sometimes selling the keys. **Truman** recognized Israel within eleven minutes of its birth — covenant over consensus. **Carter** brokered Camp David — peace on paper that entangled America in endless "process." **Obama** let Resolution 2334 pass, branding Jewish neighborhoods illegal. **Trump** broke the pattern — moved the embassy to Jerusalem, cut UNRWA, and signed the Abraham Accords. For a moment, the machine faltered. **Biden** restored it — rejoining Paris, restoring UNRWA, reopening the gates of dependency. And **Trump returned, hammer in hand** — denouncing empty promises, warning against compacts that erode sovereignty, declaring that America would not bow to unelected treaties. The contrast could not be sharper: one path resists, the other surrenders. One guards covenant. The other sells it for applause. And the verdict hangs in the air. America stands again at the same gate Truman faced, the same gate Carter and Obama sold, the same gate Trump slammed shut. *Covenant or consensus. Fire or chains.* The map is being drawn even now — but the ink has not yet dried. *Which leaders in your lifetime guarded covenant — and which sold it for applause?*

The Serpent's Choir

The pattern spreads by imitation. Once a nation trades covenant for applause, others follow. The serpent does not conquer each land by war — he recruits them by consensus. One signature inspires another. One surrender justifies the next. And soon, even those who once resisted begin to whisper in harmony.

Denmark's Whisper in the UN

The Nordic glove fits here too. Danish diplomats chair peace committees and draft resolutions beneath the blue flag of consensus. *Oslo — the Nordic stage of accords that never end* — reminds the world that some negotiations were never meant to conclude. NGOs funnel grievance funds. Denmark stands among the world's largest per-capita donors to humanitarian NGOs operating under the UN and EU umbrella — including in the Palestinian territories. Danish aid flows through DANIDA and the EU's ECHO mechanisms, channels that have drawn criticism for indirectly sustaining politicized NGOs that turn relief into leverage. The pattern is always the same: grievance managed, never healed. A Dane sat on UNRWA's board; Christina Markus Lassen now serves as Denmark's UN Ambassador. Lassen, appointed in 2023 as Denmark's Permanent Representative to the United Nations, continues the Nordic line of quiet influence. Denmark has long held rotational seats on UNRWA's Advisory Commission, shaping policies that perpetuate the "refugee industry" instead of resolving it — another example of how virtue and bureaucracy become interchangeable.

The whisper shifts. Denmark summons envoys over Greenland, declaring sovereignty non-negotiable — firm when it suits its crown, compliant when the serpent's system demands it. And now Copenhagen flirts with recognizing Palestine, a sharp contrast to the Denmark of World War II, when ordinary citizens risked everything to ferry more than seven thousand Jews across the Øresund to safety in Sweden. The same soil that once sheltered covenant now shelters committees. The nation that once guarded covenant now helps enshrine grievance. Do not be fooled by candlelight diplomacy, polite accents, or Nordic moderation. The velvet glove still strangles when it tightens. Behind the whisper is the serpent's script. When nations whisper of peace but build grievance — whose script are they reading from?

Make no mistake — if Palestine was the laboratory, **America is the prize.** Every grievance imported, every treaty ratified, every resolution signed is another leash. The serpent doesn't need to invade; **it only needs America to consent.** It works through compacts, councils, and clauses — through signatures that trade sovereignty for applause. **Israel was rehearsal. America is the stage.** The grievance machine that trapped one people is now aimed at an entire nation. The choice before you is the same as it has always been — **covenant or chains.** Choose quickly. The map is already being drawn. Its ink dries in silence, but it lands like a gavel — final, urgent, unavoidable. **Borders redraw nations, but lies redraw memory.** The serpent does not only cut with maps; he cuts with words. What began in refugee camps and UN chambers now continues in classrooms and newsrooms — where truth is inverted, guilt is weaponized, and language itself becomes the leash. If maps wound the body of nations, inversion poisons the mind of peoples.

The Map Today — Glass Towers, Quiet Knives

The cartographer's blade never retired. It traded paper for policy, bayonets for budgets, armies for acronyms. Now they redraw nations from glass towers in New York, Geneva, and Brussels — banners of "consensus" and "peace" fluttering over the doors while sovereignty bleeds beneath.

The United Nations

Born in 1945 as a forum for peace, the UN quickly mutated into a forum for leverage. The principle of *one-state-one-vote* gave oil kingdoms and dictatorships the same weight as democracies. Blocs formed — Soviet, Arab, Non-Aligned — each trading votes for influence. *Resolutions multiplied. Agencies proliferated. Budgets ballooned.* The refugee crisis became an industry, not a tragedy to be solved. UNRWA, created in 1949 as a temporary relief agency, evolved into a permanent system — sustaining five generations of registered refugees. More people. More funding. More grievance currency.

The Money Trail

Western taxpayers fund most of it. Over 70% of UNRWA's budget comes from the U.S. and the European Union. Networks of NGOs, subcontractors, and committees convert wounds into payrolls. A wound healed stops the flow. A wound kept open keeps the budgets alive. Accountability fades behind "humanitarian" layers — a labyrinth of aid agencies, consultants, and reports written to justify the next round of funding.

NATO's Shadow — The Border That Bleeds

While the UN manages grievances, NATO manages guns. Founded as a defensive pact, it became an instrument of projection — expanding eastward after 1991, redrawing security lines that Moscow once called promises. The nations of Eastern Europe — Poland, the Baltics, Romania — joined by choice, haunted by Soviet memory. But to Moscow, each new flag on its border looked less like liberty and more like siege.

The Border Game — The Russian Shadow

NATO calls it expansion. Russia calls it encirclement. Each draws maps in the name of security, each sees the other as the serpent at the gate. Gas once bound them together — Russian oil feeding German industry, Nord Stream running like a buried vein beneath the sea — until the pipeline exploded and trust shattered with it. Ukraine became the flashpoint — a nation wedged between empires, promised partnership yet left to bleed for maps drawn in foreign rooms. Washington armed it. Brussels debated it. Moscow invaded it. Civilians died for lines on paper and lies called peace. For the West, Putin became a caricature — strongman, autocrat, relic. For Russia, he became memory — the shadow of every invasion they survived, from Napoleon to Hitler to NATO's slow creep east. Behind the caricature was calculation: a man who understood that maps are weapons. He watched color revolutions redraw borders without tanks, economies fall by sanctions instead of sieges, and faith rewritten through media instead of manifestos.

To the West, that defiance looked dangerous. To Moscow, it looked like survival. Two empires, two fears — empire versus encirclement, order versus chaos — both bound to the same serpent. The war of maps never ended. It just moved from the battlefield to the boardroom.

Who Benefits?

Elites. Contractors. Technocrats. Arms manufacturers profit. NGOs profit. Dictators thrive by keeping grievance alive. Bureaucrats climb. Corporations move in to "reconstruct" what war destroyed. The losers are the same — refugees trapped, citizens taxed for policies they never voted for, soldiers sent to wars their leaders never intend to win. Nations stripped of sovereignty by signatures they never signed.

The Present Map War

Today the blade is compacts, accords, credits. Climate treaties bind industry. Migration compacts override borders. "Equity" decrees re-engineer institutions. NATO redraws security maps. The UN redraws moral maps. Both redraw sovereignty. The serpent no longer needs a war room — he has a conference room. And he's still drawing. Whose map are you living under today — your forefathers', or strangers in glass towers? How many of our chains today are treaties we applauded, not battles we lost?

🔥 **Firelight Pause — The Grievance Mirror**

• What guilt are you carrying that was manufactured, not earned?

• Who profits when your children are taught America is shame, not covenant?

• Who draws the maps you live under — your people, or strangers in glass towers?

The fire still burns beneath the maps — a reminder that no empire's ink can drown the covenant flame.

Maps are not just borders. They are covenants disguised as geography — theology etched into the earth. When men redraw what God ordained, judgment follows. Every false border breeds war. Every stolen land breeds rebellion. The serpent dreams in ink — a world where lines replace truth and signatures replace law. But God still owns the compass. And no empire can hold what He has marked. The map always bleeds into the throne. Cartographers give way to kings. What begins in ink ends in crowns — because whoever draws the lines claims the right to rule them. This is the war beneath all wars. Borders become thrones. Lines become laws. And now the serpent reaches for both — the crown of nations and the conscience of man. The ink is dry. The crowns are waiting. **The fire will decide.**

"He has determined their appointed times and the boundaries of their dwellings." — Acts 17:26

87

THE CRESCENT AND THE CROWN
THE QUIET SURRENDER

Every empire builds a theology of rule. Pharaoh claimed divinity. Rome crowned its Caesars as gods. Britain called it mandate. Brussels calls it consensus. The language changes. The instinct does not. At the summit of every false order sits a crown — and behind that crown, a creed. The question has never changed, only softened with time and paperwork: **Who rules you? Covenant — or coordination? Law — or ledger? Truth — or access?**

This chapter is not about treaties. It is about how **conquest learned to smile**, and how **sovereignty was surrendered without a shot fired**. The modern crown was not seized by force. It was assembled — signature by signature — until obedience lived inside the system itself. What follows is how it happened.

When Peace Learned to Command (1945)

The United Nations was born from real memory — men who had seen war and swore it would not return. The promise was peace through cooperation, equality among nations, dialogue instead of destruction. But peace was not the only thing written into the Charter.

Beneath the language of unity sat hierarchy. Five permanent powers. Veto authority. And a clause few citizens ever read — one that required member states to carry out Security Council decisions. What sounded like cooperation was written as obligation. This was the first quiet shift: **sovereignty became conditional.** America gained a stage and became the primary funder. Over time, resolutions written abroad began to echo into domestic policy — human-rights language, educational frameworks, environmental norms. Not by decree, but by legitimacy. The crown was not heavy yet. But it had been cast.

When the Land Was Reframed (1992)

Agenda 21 did not arrive as law. It arrived as care. Drafted under the banner of sustainability, it spoke of harmony with the planet — of responsible growth, managed development, shared resources. But beneath the green language was a quiet inversion. Private property was no longer treated as a right. It became a variable. Local governance became the delivery system for global priorities. Implementation was voluntary — but compliance was rewarded. Grants followed alignment. Prestige followed obedience. Cities adopted the language. Universities rewrote curricula. Federal agencies adjusted funding formulas. Compliance was rewarded. Resistance carried a cost. The serpent did not hiss. It learned to speak sustainability.

When Virtue Became Measurable (2000–2015)

The Millennium Development Goals sounded righteous: end poverty, educate children, heal the sick, protect women. Few objected — and that was the point. Each goal required data. Metrics. Reporting. Alignment. What cannot be measured cannot be managed. What is measured can be conditioned. When the Millennium Goals expired, they were not discarded. They were expanded and reborn as Agenda 2030 — seventeen goals, hundreds of indicators, endless assessments. Aid became leverage. Funding became discipline. Language became law without ever being called law.

Universities adopted the dialect. Federal grants demanded equity metrics. NGOs multiplied to administer compliance. Careers formed around alignment; resistance was quietly defunded. The empire learned a lasting truth: control does not require conquest. It requires coordination.

When Europe Became the Prototype (2009)

Europe showed how it could be done. The Lisbon Treaty elevated EU law above national constitutions, created permanent executive authority, and empowered courts beyond appeal. No tanks. No coups. Only procedure. Sovereignty did not fall. It was outvoted. Citizens became subjects of a system they could not remove. Law became something handed down, not debated. America watched carefully. GDPR — Europe's experiment in total data governance. Digital regulation. Speech governance. The framework crossed the Atlantic — and the line was drawn. Europe was not a partner. It was a preview.

When Borders Became a Moral Failure (2018)

The Global Compact for Migration was declared non-binding. That word did the work. Migration was reframed as a human right. Borders as negotiable. Resistance as stigmatization. Media portrayal itself became a matter of policy. Courts abroad began citing its language. Journalists were prosecuted. Nations aligned policy without passing law. The United States refused to sign — yet the language crossed the border anyway. California enacted sanctuary regimes and partnered with UN-aligned NGOs. Universities taught migration ethics. Resistance was challenged in courts and legislatures. Progress was tracked. Rankings issued. Capital followed compliance. The numbers were never neutral.

When Emergency Became Authority (2020)

Crisis reveals what structure hides. Under emergency, authority centralizes. Guidance becomes mandate. Mandates become infrastructure — passports, surveillance, data sharing. The World Health Organization did not command armies. It didn't need to. Airlines, insurers, banks, and platforms enforced compliance. Fear became the funding mechanism. California embedded emergency authority into law. Texas time-locked it and resisted. The border was no longer geographic. It was biological. And then digital.

What Emerged

Peace. Sustainability. Equity. Mobility. Health. Identity. Different words. Same direction. Europe supplied legal skeleton. The UN provided organs. Technocrats pumped capital, data, and metrics through the body. This is the crescent of the crown — **a system that speaks of unity while training obedience, that promises care while requiring permission.** They call it governance. It is rule without soul. In Denmark, the system no longer needs pressure. Compliance is cultural. Digital identity, data integration, speech norms, and global frameworks are not contested — they are celebrated. Enforcement is unnecessary when obedience is taught as maturity and dissent as immaturity. This is not tyranny. It is training completed.

The Line in the Land

Every system reveals itself through contrast. California submits — celebrating alignment as morality, regulation as virtue, compliance as leadership. Texas resists — defending constitutional limits, local authority, and the primacy of consent. The UN praises one. It pressures the other. Not because of emissions. Not because of compassion. But because **obedience is the currency of empire.**

The Reckoning

Treaties are only paper until a people obey them. The crown is not imposed. It is accepted. Each "non-binding" word binds someone anyway. Each grant carries a condition. Each metric trains a reflex. America was never meant to be a client state. She was meant to be a covenant nation. The battle is not overseas. It is here — in classrooms, courts, legislatures, and the quiet rooms where permissions are written. What is surrendered first is never land. It is discretion. You lose the right to decide quietly — how you bank, how you move, how you speak, how you raise your children without explanation. Access becomes conditional. Participation becomes monitored. Refusal becomes suspect. No one comes for you at dawn. They simply make life harder until obedience feels reasonable.

♨ **Firelight Pause — The Crescent and the Covenant**

The treaties feel distant. They are not. They touch every screen, every system, every future choice. Pause here. Let the fire speak.

- Where have I already agreed without knowing the cost?
- What parts of my life now require permission?
- What language do I use that was written by another hand?
- If access were revoked tomorrow, what would I lose?
- What can I still build, grow, trade, or defend without approval?
- Do I know the difference between freedom of choice and managed compliance?
- Have I taught my children covenant as duty — not theory?

The Sovereign Flame

Every empire begins with good intentions and ends with management. When men trade covenant for coordination, they rebuild Babel — one language, one ledger, one lord. The treaties were never just paperwork. They were prayers to a new god — **Control**. But fire still burns in the hands of the remnant. Truth still cuts where ink cannot reach. The crescent rises. But it cannot eclipse the flame. The world writes treaties. **America must write truth.**

88

THE EMPIRE IN NEW UNIFORMS
THE FIVE THRONES & THE SCRIPT

Maps wound. Now meet the hands that hold the pen. The marble halls that claim peace, the thrones that claim permanence — each has a face. What follows isn't theory; it's the seats themselves, the rulers and reflexes that turn borders into chains. Nazism did not vanish in 1945. Its banners fell, but its builders kept their hands. IG Farben dissolved on paper, but its heirs became household names — the cartel broken into successors that still sit at the heart of modern chemistry and medicine. BASF. Bayer. Hoechst. And it wasn't only chemicals. The Reich clothed itself, financed itself, armed itself, insured itself. Hugo Boss manufactured uniforms. Deutsche Bank financed expansion. Siemens wired the machinery. Volkswagen rolled off assembly lines built with forced labor. These pipelines did not disappear. They were laundered through courts, commissions, and "reconstruction." The lesson is not trivia. It is continuity: evil rarely dies; it rebrands. The names changed. The contracts remained.

Nazi planners who perfected population management and central planning were absorbed into the new European project — not as uniforms, but as frameworks. The Reich's instinct for control did not die; it mutated. Brussels became the new Berlin — bureaucracy instead of jackboots, treaties instead of tanks. Every empire believes it can perfect order. None believe they can corrupt it.

625

The Soviet Union rehearsed the same trick. Moscow redrew maps by decree, erasing nations with a pen. When the USSR collapsed, its methods were not discarded. They were exported into global frameworks — compacts, resolutions, treaties. But long before the collapse, the Soviets had already embedded themselves in the new order.

The United Nations was founded in 1945, but it was never neutral. From the first day, the Soviet Union sat as one of five permanent powers, armed with veto authority — and even secured additional leverage through Soviet republics like Ukraine and Belarus, granted their own General Assembly seats. What appeared as inclusion functioned as influence. Unity became cover. And look who sat on those thrones. Five permanent seats — five empires crowned in marble: the United States, the United Kingdom, the Soviet Union, France, and China. Not "the nations united," but the victors enthroned. It was not covenant. It was empire formalized, empire disguised as peace. The rest of the world sat in the gallery, applauding resolutions they could never enforce.

NATO too became something it was never meant to be. Born as a shield against Stalin in 1949, it promised only defense: an attack on one would be an attack on all. It was a covenant of protection, not conquest. But when the Soviet Union collapsed, NATO did not retire. It metastasized. The shield became the sword. Containment is conquest by patience. Instead of folding, it expanded — eastward into Warsaw Pact nations, then the Baltics, then even whispering Ukraine and Georgia. Each expansion was not defense but cartography — lines pushed, dependencies bound, old fault lines reopened. In the Balkans, NATO bombed Belgrade in 1999 — carving Kosovo from Serbia and calling it "peace." After 9/11, it crossed continents, deploying in Afghanistan, Libya, Iraq. These were not shields raised, but regimes toppled, borders redrawn, maps dictated.

What began as a covenant of protection hardened into a bureaucracy of power — military bases cemented, contracts feeding arms industries, "partnerships" tethering smaller nations into dependence. NATO became not merely an alliance but an empire in uniform — bureaucratic, sprawling, self-justifying. From Belgrade to Baghdad, Kyiv to Kabul, its expansions repeated the same imperial reflex — redraw maps, install regimes, call it peace. The maps were paper. The graves were not.

The Iron Throne — The Soviet Seat

The UN carried Soviet fingerprints from its birth. Stalin's diplomats helped shape the charter. His bloc secured extra seats for Ukraine and Belarus — not as sovereign nations, but as extra votes for Moscow disguised in the language of independence. And at the heart of it all, the Soviet Union sat crowned with veto power on the Security Council. But the UN was never Moscow's toy alone. It was always a stage for the great powers to wrestle, each one cloaking its ambitions in the language of "peace." The marble hall became theater, and the Soviet throne was cast in iron. That is why today's irony runs so deep. Putin still occupies the very chair Stalin secured in 1945 — a permanent seat at the world's most powerful table. Yet in that same hall, Russia is now scorned, condemned, treated as pariah. The house Stalin helped build has turned against his heir. Yet when we look beyond the marble and resolutions, Russia behaves not as a pariah, but as an empire in the making. Its borders still bleed with conflict. Ukraine now bears the brunt: the war child of Europe, invaded, bombed, displaced, resisting.

Across Eastern Europe, nations tremble at Russia's shadow — Belarus under its thumb, the Baltic states watching nightly for signs of the next move, Moldova whispering prayers against creeping influence. Moscow's missiles, hybrid warfare, energy weaponization, propaganda — these are not relics of Cold War stratagems. They are the iron throne's tools, sharpened for the modern world. Every tyranny updates its software but keeps the same code — control.

Ukraine — The War Child of Empire

Russia's empire still claws at its periphery. The war in Ukraine is its wound, its test, its script — waiting to see which nations will bow, bend, or break. But Ukraine is more than tanks and trenches; it is a battlefield of money and influence, a pawn of empires. For years, Ukraine was a laundromat for oligarchs and foreign elites. Burisma, the energy giant at the center of scandal, placed Hunter Biden — son of the U.S. vice president — on its board at $50,000 a month. His abandoned laptop later revealed emails, deals, and meetings tied to his father's office. At the same time, Joe Biden threatened to withhold $1 billion in U.S. aid unless President Poroshenko fired prosecutor Viktor Shokin — the man probing Burisma. Biden later bragged on camera about the firing. Washington called it "anti-corruption." Many saw it as protection — the powerful guarding their own. This is the deeper wound — Ukraine became both shield and sieve, absorbing Russian pressure on one side and Western exploitation on the other. It bled not only from Moscow's shells but from boardroom deals and foreign hands. Its soil became the stage where empires rehearsed their reflexes — Russia with missiles, the West with money.

But here is where scripts collide. Trump refused to play the managers' version. He cut U.S. funding for UNRWA, striking at the pipeline that kept the grievance industry alive. He blocked aid packages until Europe paid its share. He pressed Kyiv on corruption, demanding clarity before American money flowed. Most of all, he broke the assumption that the U.S. would bankroll a forever-war without question. Meanwhile, NATO and the EU made theater of painting Putin as the sole villain — not to heal the wound, but to distract from their own games. They wanted the war prolonged, because war justifies their budgets, their treaties, their grip on power. And they wanted America to pay for it. Billions signed away by Congress became tribute — not only to Ukraine's survival, but to Europe's management machine.

This is why Europe trembles. German factories depend on Russian gas. Hungarian politics orbit Moscow's favor. Turkish diplomats juggle NATO on one hand and Russian bargains on the other. To the Baltics, Ukraine is the warning of what defiance costs. To Poland, it is the test of NATO's promise. To Georgia and Moldova, it is the whisper that maps can be redrawn at Moscow's will. And to America, it is revelation: your leaders will fund a proxy war abroad while your own cities rot — unless someone calls the bluff.

Empires do not repent; they redirect. When their lies collapse, they look for new villains to hide behind. And here lies the irony — Putin, too, stood outside the script. He clawed at borders not because Brussels told him to, but because he rejected the very architecture Brussels built. He wanted empire, not management. Trump wanted covenant, not empire. **They were not partners, and they were not aligned — not allies, not friends, not even operating from the same moral ground — but both became intolerable to the managers because each refused the script.** For that, rage was unleashed against them both. And so Europe trembles. In Denmark, people whisper that Putin might bomb them — as though Moscow has any reason to target Copenhagen instead of Kyiv. The fear is irrational, yet it is cultivated. Brussels needs the fear. NATO feeds on it. The media amplifies it until even small nations believe the Russian bear is crouched outside their door. Fear is the favorite currency of the powerless who pretend to rule. This is how the serpent binds the West — not only with treaties and debt, but with shadows and phantoms. Fear becomes the leash, and compromise its collar.

Covenant or Chains

This is why Ukraine is not merely geopolitical but spiritual. The serpent thrives when nations are weakened not only by invasion but by infiltration — when chains are forged not just by tanks, but by contracts, loans, and signatures. He feeds on wounds that never close — using them to launder influence, to chain peoples to grievance, to make pawns of nations.

But covenant tells a different story — that nations are not pawns, that borders are not toys, and that truth can still break chains. Ukraine is a test, theater, and warning. But above all, it is reminder: without covenant, every nation becomes a pawn of empires. The iron throne was never built for peace. It was built for management. And management, in every age, means bondage dressed as order. Control is always baptized as compassion before it becomes law. But the King is not mocked. Thrones will topple. Chains will break. And covenant fire will outlast them all.

The Dragon's Throne — The Chinese Seat

The UN carried Soviet fingerprints from its birth. But Moscow was not the only power to inherit a throne. Another empire was seated from the beginning — China. When the UN was founded in 1945, China was given one of the five permanent seats on the Security Council, complete with veto power. At the time it belonged to Chiang Kai-shek's Republic of China — an ally in name if not in strength. But in 1971, the world shifted. The UN General Assembly recognized the People's Republic of China as "the only legitimate representative of China" (Resolution 2758), removing Taiwan's seat. In one vote, the red flag replaced the blue. Beijing inherited a throne it had never built. From that moment, China sat as a permanent emperor in the UN hall. The serpent had recycled again: the Republic vanished, the Communist Party enthroned. And unlike Stalin's seat, which now carries scorn, China's seat only grew stronger. Every lie gains longevity when clothed in legitimacy.

Consider the World Health Organization. It was not seized by China through conquest, but through patience. As the West pulled back its funding, Beijing filled the gap. Chinese officials took key posts. Chinese money funded projects. And Chinese influence shaped the words of the WHO itself. In the early days of COVID-19, the world watched as the WHO echoed Beijing's script — delaying warnings, muting questions about origins, praising China's "transparency" while the virus spread. But the dragon's power is not limited to international halls. At home, it perfected surveillance as a weapon of rule.

Cameras on every corner. Algorithms scoring citizens by obedience. A "social credit" system that rewards submission and punishes dissent. Tyranny not with chains, but with points. Not with prisons alone, but with digital leashes so complete that a man can lose his freedom with a single wrong word, a late payment, or a forbidden prayer. When sin becomes system, evil no longer hides — it audits. This is the model now whispered across the UN — management through data, obedience through code. The serpent calls it "safety." The dragon enforces it as destiny. China did not build the WHO. It bought it. It did not invent the UN throne. It inherited it. And yet in bending both, it revealed the deeper truth: the serpent does not care what banner flies over the throne. He only needs the throne itself. The red flag rose where the blue once stood. The seat never moved. When power changes hands but not hearts, the throne remains the same.

"And the dragon gave him his power and his throne and great authority."
— Revelation 13:2

The Fragile Throne — The French Seat

France was not crowned a victor in 1945 because of strength — but because of pride. When Hitler's legions marched into Paris in 1940, France collapsed in weeks. De Gaulle led a government-in-exile from London, while French soil was ruled by Vichy collaborators. By the time the war ended, France had been occupied more than liberated. Pride will always demand a crown, even when the sword that earned it is broken. But Roosevelt, Churchill, and Stalin knew Europe could not be rebuilt if France were humiliated. So they restored it on paper as a "great power." At San Francisco, France was awarded one of the five permanent seats on the Security Council — a throne it could never have won on the battlefield. It was not given as reward. It was given as medicine, a political sedative to calm a wounded nation. And yet, from that moment, France spoke with a voice it no longer earned in arms.

Its diplomats cast vetoes alongside empires far stronger than itself. Its signature appeared on charters that reshaped colonies across Africa and Asia. Paris played empire long after its armies could not. This is the pattern again — a throne not earned, but granted. A voice not rooted in covenant, but in concession. What began as a salve for French pride became another instrument of global management. Today, France sits on a throne it can scarcely defend. Its streets echo with riots, its churches stand empty, its suburbs burn with protests from those who were once colonial subjects. The republic is torn between two visions — one that clings to secular grandeur, and another that demands a new identity rooted not in covenant but in grievance. And yet still, in New York, the French flag hangs among the permanent five, as though empire were eternal. When faith departs, even marble learns to crack. This is the serpent's pattern again — thrones outlasting armies, marble outlasting memory. France keeps its seat, but the seat speaks louder than the nation behind it.

"You were exalted because of your beauty; you corrupted your wisdom for the sake of your splendor. So I cast you to the ground; I exposed you before kings." — Ezekiel 28:17

The Fading Throne — Britain's Seat

Britain sat at the table in 1945 as though the empire still stretched across the world. But the war had bled London dry, its factories bombed, its navy battered, its colonies restless. Within a generation, India was independent, Africa was rising, and the Union Jack was lowered across continents. Yet at San Francisco, Britain claimed a permanent throne. It was not the empire's armies that guaranteed it, but its past prestige. The empire crumbled, but the chair remained. When glory outlives truth, it becomes a ghost that governs the living. And that chair still remains, even as Britain itself fractures. On the ground, the nation undergoes one of the fastest cultural upheavals in its history. Mass immigration — much of it Muslim, much of it from the old colonies — has reshaped cities, schools, and neighborhoods.

Crime, protests, and clashes over values reveal a house divided. Native Britons quietly leave in record numbers, fleeing to Australia, Canada, Spain, even Eastern Europe, no longer seeing a future in their own land. Parliament allows it because empire reflex still governs — yesterday's colonies were given passports, and what was once managed abroad is now managed at home. The globalist consensus adds its weight, for the EU and the UN reframed mass migration as a moral duty, and Britain's political class internalized it. Elites tolerate it because division serves them; a fragmented population cannot unite against the managers. And the Crown blesses it in silence, cloaked in "tolerance" ceremonies and mosque visits that sanctify policy without ever speaking its name. Silence itself becomes consent. When kings bless confusion, they crown decay. Rebellion is arrested not because the people are violent, but because the people are clear. Working-class protests are branded "far-right," while vast marches under foreign banners are tolerated in the name of free expression. Hate-speech laws and counter-terror frameworks give the state cover to crush dissent while ignoring the fractures it helped engineer. Britain traded covenant for management. And when covenant vanishes, the vacuum does not remain empty. It is filled by rival gods, rival cultures, rival banners — and the managers prefer it, because it cements their role as arbiters of "peace." This is why rebellion is criminalized — the serpent does not fear noise in the streets, he fears clarity in the people. He fears a nation remembering who they are. When a nation forgets its covenant, it begins to police its conscience.

"They have sown the wind, and they shall reap the whirlwind." — Hosea 8:7

The American Throne — Covenant or Empire?

The last of the five thrones was given to America. In 1945, the United States stood unrivaled. Its armies had crossed two oceans. Its factories armed the world. Its flag rose over Normandy and Iwo Jima, its bomb fell on Hiroshima. By sheer strength, America's seat at the UN was undisputed. But that seat came with a choice: covenant or empire. America could sit as a witness of liberty — a republic that defended freedom, guarded self-rule, and checked the ambitions of empires. Or it could sit as another empire among empires, using its throne to redraw maps and dictate regimes in the name of "order." Every throne tests its bearer — to serve truth or to serve pride. For a time, the covenant fire burned. America funded the rebuilding of Europe, lifted Japan from ashes, stood as bulwark against Stalin's wall. But the temptation of empire grew. The same chair that vetoed Soviet designs also blessed coups in Latin America, interventions in the Middle East, endless wars dressed as "democracy." The seat meant to defend covenant became another instrument of control. But every choice leaves a scar on the map it draws.

Two Americas emerged: one that still guarded covenant, and one that managed the map. One spoke the language of borders and builders; the other, of frameworks and forever-wars. The fault line ran through Washington — and through us. Empires divide nations, but pride divides souls. That is America's tension still — to carry fire or to carry chains. To use its voice for covenant or for empire. The serpent cares little which mask it wears. He only wants the throne used to bind. Freedom without covenant always becomes control wearing liberty's flag. And here is the hinge of history — the remnant has not bowed. Across towns, churches, and homes, covenant fire is being carried still. Leaders rise who speak of sovereignty instead of submission, borders instead of bargains, builders instead of bureaucrats. Whatever one thinks of Trump, his presence revealed the fault line: covenant or empire. He spoke tariffs instead of treaties, borders instead of compacts, builders instead of managers. Peace instead of war. That is why the serpent raged — not because of one man, but because he called a nation to remember. The serpent fears remembrance, for memory is rebellion against his fog.

The remnant now carries that call. To refuse the empire's script. To guard covenant at the cost of comfort. To rebuild not only walls and factories but the fire itself. The American throne remains the most powerful of all. But power without covenant is empire. And empire without memory is always chains. When nations forget who they are, tyrants remember for them.

"When the righteous increase, the people rejoice, but when the wicked rule, the people groan." — Proverbs 29:2

The Five Thrones do not rule alone. Thrones require servants. Empires endure not only through crowns, but through uniforms, committees, and quiet nations that lend legitimacy to power they do not wield. What follows are not new thrones — but the hands that carry out their will.

Servants of the Thrones — The Quiet and the Uniformed

Not every empire rules by roar. Some rule by silence. Some rule by procedure. Some rule by helmets — clean, neutral, borrowed — enforcing decisions written far from the soil.

Denmark — The Quiet Servant

Not every seat of power is carved in marble. Some are carved in silence. Denmark holds no veto, no crown, no permanent seat among the five. And yet its role reveals how the serpent manages through whispers as well as decrees. Tyranny rarely begins with commands; it begins with compliance. Denmark once carried covenant memory. In 1943, ordinary Danes ferried Jews across the Øresund under Nazi occupation, risking death to preserve covenant life. But the fire that once burned became embers. The nation traded covenant for consensus, conviction for comfort. The state church became the state's mouthpiece. Families surrendered their children to institutions. Farmers bowed to Brussels' quotas. And Denmark learned to wear obedience as virtue.

That reflex followed it to the global stage. Virtue divorced from truth always becomes virtue weaponized. Danish envoys now chair "peace committees," manage negotiations, and host accords that never resolve. Oslo hosted the peace that chained Israel to endless "process." Copenhagen blesses climate compacts that bind farmers across continents. In the UN, Denmark rarely stands alone. Its vote folds into the European bloc, condemning Israel more often than defending it, whispering legitimacy into grievance. This is how empires recruit saints — by turning compassion into currency. This is the quiet servant — not loud like Moscow's iron, not sharp like Beijing's dragon, not proud like Paris or London. Instead, Denmark sanctifies the system. It lends moral tone to management, velvet glove to the iron fist. It tells the world that consensus is peace, that neutrality is virtue, that silence is stability. But silence is not peace. Silence is surrender. And that is why the serpent prizes the quiet servant. A voice that never shouts but always nods. A nation that once guarded covenant but now polishes the cage. Its crown is not iron or gold, but velvet — soft to the touch, deadly in the soul. Soft power becomes sacred power when no one remembers to question it.

The Blue Helmets — Servants in Uniform

The United Nations has no army of its own. Its soldiers wear no single flag. They come borrowed — contingents from Ghana, India, Pakistan, Brazil, or Europe, draped in the blue helmet. On paper, they are "peacekeepers." In reality, they are guardians of the map. They guard not lives but lines — borders frozen by bureaucracy, not healed by truth. These troops do not move for covenant. They move for consensus. Their orders are written not by parliaments or peoples, but by resolutions passed in marble halls. Their command flows not from families or fields, but from the five thrones — Washington, London, Moscow, Paris, Beijing. If the thrones agree, the helmets march. If they disagree, the helmets stand still while nations burn. Look at the record. In Rwanda, the helmets stood aside while machetes hacked through a million lives. In Bosnia, they declared "safe zones" but watched while Srebrenica was emptied in blood. In Congo, their missions turned into scandals of corruption and abuse. Neutrality became complicity.

"They have healed the wound of my people lightly, saying, 'Peace, peace,' when there is no peace." — Jeremiah 6:14

Peacekeeping became management. When justice is delayed in the name of peace, evil grows under paperwork. Because that is the truth — the blue helmets are not warriors of covenant, but managers of grievance. Their rifles defend not the widow or the orphan, but the cartographer's pen. They hold borders in place, enforce treaties in ink, keep wounds open long enough for bureaucrats to broker another "process." They call it peacekeeping, but it is wound-keeping — mercy without truth, law without heart. The serpent does not need conquerors when he has managers. The blue helmet is his perfect crown — polished, neutral, bloodless in appearance. A soldier who fires not for conquest, but for consensus. A rifle raised not to defend, but to delay. Empires no longer need tyrants when they have technicians.

"And he shall speak words against the Most High, and shall wear out the saints of the Most High, and shall think to change the times and the law." — Daniel 7:25

The Soft Glove and the Iron Fist — How the Thrones Enforce Order

The United Nations wears the blue helmet — the soft glove of empire. Its troops move slow, neutral, clothed in words like "peacekeeping" and "stability." They patrol borders, not to heal them, but to hold them in place. They manage grievances, keep the wound open, and freeze wars in amber until treaties can be signed. They do not conquer. They contain. They do not liberate. They prolong. Containment is conquest by patience.

NATO wields the sword — the iron fist of empire. Its jets roar, its missiles strike, its tanks redraw the map when "peacekeeping" alone cannot hold the line. Where the UN sends helmets, NATO sends bombs. Where the UN delays, NATO dictates. One parades as neutral. The other strikes with steel. But both serve the same hand. Mercy without truth becomes management; justice without mercy becomes tyranny. Look at the pattern. In the Balkans, the UN declared "safe zones" — then NATO bombed Belgrade. In Afghanistan, NATO deployed armies while the UN managed refugee camps. In Libya, NATO toppled a regime while the UN brokered endless "transition agreements." The glove and the fist, always together — one to soften, one to strike. Peace was the banner. Power was the business. The serpent knows this is how you build empire in the modern world. Not with crowns and legions, but with acronyms and coalitions. The UN blesses the process. NATO enforces it. One speaks in the language of compassion. The other speaks in fire. And both leave the same chains behind. The glove holds. The fist strikes. And the people remain in cages — managed, mapped, and muted. Mercy without truth becomes management; justice without mercy becomes tyranny.

"By peace he shall destroy many." — Daniel 8:25

A Permanent Wound — The Thrones Against Zion

Every empire requires a wound that never heals — a conflict that justifies conferences, resolutions, funding, and forever-management. For the modern world, that wound has been Israel. Here is how each throne plays its role in keeping Israel under judgment and Gaza in chains. Every empire needs a wound to justify its rule — and Israel became the wound that never heals.

The Soviet / Russian Throne — The Iron Reflex

From the start, Moscow cast Israel as a Western outpost, a "colonial project" pitted against Arab allies. The USSR armed Egypt, Syria, and Iraq during the Cold War, while voting against Israel in the UN. Even after the Soviet collapse, Russia crowns itself as protector of Arab grievance to secure oil, arms sales, and naval bases in Syria. Its reflex is to keep the wound open so Moscow remains the broker, weakening both Israel and America. Moscow learned long ago — if you cannot win the covenant, manage the grievance.

The Chinese Throne — The Dragon Reflex

China rarely bleeds over Israel directly, but it consistently votes against her in the UN. Its goal is to champion the "oppressed" of the Global South, aligning with Arab blocs to gain markets, oil, and diplomatic leverage. By echoing Palestinian rhetoric, Beijing buys loyalty in Africa, the Middle East, and Latin America. Its play is to weaponize grievance as currency, cementing Beijing as leader of the post-Western order. The dragon trades compassion like a commodity — pity as policy, grievance as gold.

The French Throne — The Fragile Reflex

France carries both guilt and pride from its colonial past in North Africa and the Middle East. It postures as "balancer" — selling arms to Arab states, calling for Palestinian statehood, and often restraining Israel in UN debates. This posture also soothes its large Muslim population at home. So it trades condemnation of Israel for legitimacy at home and influence abroad. It was not diplomacy — it was penance disguised as principle.

The British Throne — The Fading Reflex

Britain wrote much of the Palestinian wound into being — the Balfour Declaration, then retreat, then partition. Its elites lean on "process" — endless negotiations, endless frameworks, never resolution. Like France, it manages domestic Muslim demographics by posturing against Israel. Its reflex is to preserve the grievance as permanent penance for empire's past, while shifting the cost onto Israel and America. Every empire seeks absolution for its sins — and finds it by crucifying someone else.

The American Throne — The Divided Reflex

America has been the hinge. Truman recognized Israel. Reagan armed her. Trump moved the embassy. Yet half of America's ruling class restrains Israel "for peace" — State Department, NGOs, universities. **One administration shields, the next condemns.** *The serpent keeps the Republic divided, so Israel is never secure.* A house divided cannot stand — and the serpent keeps it divided on purpose.

When under globalist control— keep Gaza alive as grievance currency to weaken Israel, while exporting the same guilt machinery into America itself — race politics, reparations, refugee quotas. **When under covenant fire** — Trump broke the pattern. He moved the U.S. embassy to Jerusalem, affirming covenant over consensus. He cut off UNRWA, striking at the machinery that keeps Palestinians stateless. And most of all, he bypassed the UN and NATO entirely. No marble halls, no "quartet," no Oslo theater. Instead, he went straight to the capitals — Jerusalem, Abu Dhabi, Manama, Rabat — and signed the Abraham Accords. Arabs and Jews sat at the same table without global managers pulling the strings. It was not diplomacy — it was defiance in covenant form. Truth broke the algorithm — and for a heartbeat, the world remembered how peace once looked when men feared God more than failure. That is why the serpent raged — not because one man signed papers, but because the machinery was sidelined. The UN was not needed. NATO was not called. The "peace process" was exposed as fraud.

For a moment, grievance lost its grip, and covenant fire burned through the script.

The Common Outcome

Each throne acts from its own wound — empire's pride, Cold War reflex, demographic pressure, or global leadership contests. Yet their votes align — Israel endlessly condemned, Palestine endlessly preserved as grievance, Gaza endlessly caged. Why? Because a permanent wound is leverage. Arabs kept angry. Jews kept defensive. The West kept guilty. Bureaucrats kept necessary. Eternal grievance is the currency of control. When peace becomes a profession, war becomes its business model. The names changed. The uniforms changed. But the hand did not. Europe's Reich became Europe's Union. Soviet reflexes lived on in UN frameworks. NATO's shield became NATO's sword. The serpent has always known how to recycle empires. He only swaps the uniforms. Every empire rebrands its chains as progress — and every generation must learn to see the pattern again.

"What has been is what will be, and what has been done is what will be done, and there is nothing new under the sun." — Ecclesiastes 1:9

The serpent always recycles. Red banners fall, green banners rise. But the reflex is the same: control dressed as compassion, empire cloaked as peace. The red hand of Marx and Moscow now grips the green glove of Brussels. Together they write the same decrees: 'consensus,' 'sustainability,' 'equity' — the words change, the chains do not. When language is captured, liberty follows. Words become prisons long before walls do. Do not be fooled by the banners. Green is the color of Islam and the color of climate. Both are wielded the same way — to demand surrender. The serpent does not care which banner you bow to, so long as you bow. The thrones sit far away, in marble halls and glass towers, but their reflex reaches your street, your family, your church. Silence is how the serpent rules — not only in parliaments, but in kitchens, schools, and pews.

If nations can be managed into chains, so can souls. Silence is the serpent's favorite language — consent disguised as peace. And so the test comes to you: will you bow to consensus, or will you carry covenant fire? Thrones topple. Empires fade. But silence endures if no one speaks. History does not remember the quiet. It remembers the courageous. Do not keep quiet. Five thrones. Many servants. One reflex. Maps are wounded not by chaos, but by management. Nations fall not when invaded, but when they agree.

◐ **Firelight Pause — The Danger of Silence**
Sit by the fire and ask yourself:
- Where have I mistaken silence for virtue?
- Where do I nod when I should speak, agree when I should resist?
- Have I traded conviction for comfort, covenant for consensus?
- Do I soothe myself with "neutrality," while evil advances unopposed?
- When my nation whispers "peace," do I ask whose chains that peace protects?
- **Whose script am I repeating — the serpent's, or the covenant's?**

Because silence is never neutral. It always serves a throne. Every silence has a master; every whisper bows to someone.

"If you keep silent at this time, relief and deliverance will rise for the Jews from another place... And who knows whether you have not come to the kingdom for such a time as this?" — Esther 4:14

89

TARIFFS — TOOLS OF BUILDERS

CHAINS ENSLAVE. HAMMERS BUILD. TARIFFS ARE THE BUILDER'S STRIKE AGAINST EMPIRE.

Tariffs aren't chains. They're hammers.

For centuries, Europe mastered them — blocking American cars, taxing our beef, guarding their markets — while demanding America leave its doors wide open. They called it "free trade." It was never free. It was tribute disguised as fairness. America played along. We produced. The world consumed. And unelected bureaucrats in Brussels, Geneva, and New York wrote the rules. Treaties bound our hands. The EU and UN buried tariffs inside agreements, dressed them in the fog of "global cooperation," and sold us dependence as destiny. But **tariffs were never meant as punishment. They are leverage.** They are the tool that forces hidden games into the light. When factories fled overseas to chase cheap labor and lax standards, tariffs tore the veil. They said: If you want American shelves, you must respect American workers. If you want our market, you must meet our terms. That's why corporations squeal. Not because tariffs fail — but because they expose the racket. Rather than absorb the penalty for abandoning American soil, they pass the cost onto you. They slap a "tariff tax" onto your receipt and call it inevitability. But *that excuse betrays their allegiance.* Instead of honoring covenant with the nation that gave them life, they side with foreign factories and bureaucratic decrees.

Yes, at first it hurts. Prices climb. The news shouts panic. But this is short pain for long freedom. Because once companies return to building here — once they weld steel in Ohio, stitch fabric in Carolina, press medicine in Michigan — the tariffs vanish. Prices fall. Wages rise. And sovereignty is restored. Tariffs are not punishment. They are repentance. They are the hammer that breaks false treaties and rebuilds covenant. They return wealth to the builder, dignity to the worker, and independence to the nation. **Without tariffs, America becomes a colony — a market owned by others, rationed by foreign decrees. With them, she returns to covenant, not as the world's open purse, but as the builder who sets the terms.** One path is chains. The other is fire.

"A false balance is abomination to the Lord, but a just weight is his delight." — Proverbs 11:1

America's Forgotten Covenant

America's first covenant with its builders was sealed not in subsidies but in tariffs. The Founders levied them to protect fledgling industries. Hamilton called them essential to national survival. Lincoln expanded them to shield Union factories and Northern steel. For nearly 150 years, tariffs were not slandered as backward; they were *celebrated as the spine of sovereignty.* Only when globalists captured the narrative did tariffs become a dirty word. In truth, they were *America's original firewall* — a shield forged to keep wealth and labor anchored in the Republic.

The War of Labels

Notice the sleight of hand. When Europe shields its markets, it is "sustainable policy." When China slams the gate, it is "strategic development." But when America dares to defend its workers, it is smeared as "protectionism." When Brussels imposes quotas, it is called "stability." When Washington imposes tariffs, it is "xenophobia." **Words become weapons. The goal is not debate, but shame. They would have America apologize for surviving.**

And that is why millions turned their anger at the wrong man. When President Trump used tariffs as leverage, not as punishment, but as leverage — the oldest language of builders confronting empires. The people felt the pain but never saw the game — because the globalists hid the board. They blamed the hammer instead of the hand that forced it to swing. Because the serpent knows this truth: **A people who are shamed will surrender faster than a people who are beaten.** Labels are the new sanctions — used not on nations, but on minds. If they can brand American strength as selfishness, they can make Americans afraid to defend themselves. That is the real war: not over steel or soybeans, but over *the moral right of a sovereign nation to put its own builders first.* They don't fear tariffs. They fear America waking up to its authority. That is why the fight has moved into courts and committees. When tariffs began to restore leverage, the managers did not debate their results — they challenged the authority to use them at all. Legal restraints, oversight boards, and procedural traps followed. Not to protect consumers, but to reclaim control. Because a sovereign tool in the hands of a builder is dangerous to a system built on permission. Markets respond to leverage faster than legislation. Long before factories move, contracts hesitate — and hesitation is where power shifts.

The Hidden Front — The Middle Class Under Siege

Victory at the border is meaningless if surrender follows at the paycheck. We can strike the factories back to American soil. Good. Do it. But the serpent does not yield at ports alone. It moves in payrolls, permits, and payouts that teach a people to kneel. If we stop at tariffs, we win a battle and lose the war. The real front is the middle — the builders' class — now targeted not by soldiers, but by stipends. **Name the weapon. Dependency is the new chain.**

Tariffs alone do not rebuild a nation. They clear the ground. Builders still need energy that is cheap, regulations that are sane, taxes that reward work, and trades that are honored again. Tariffs force the game into the open. The rest of the work makes staying home worth it. This is why empire fears the builder's stack — tariffs, energy, labor, and law aligned toward production instead of dependency. Markets respond to leverage faster than legislation. Long before factories move, contracts hesitate — and hesitation is where power shifts.

🔥 **Firelight Pause — Covenant or Colony?**
Stop here. Ask yourself what side of this line you stand on.
- Are tariffs punishment, or protection?
- Who gains when America's shelves are stocked with foreign sweat?
- What would it mean to rebuild at home — steel in Ohio, cloth in Carolina, medicine in Michigan?
- Will I endure short pain for long freedom?

"The Lord will open to you his good treasury, the heavens, to give the rain to your land in its season and to bless all the work of your hands. And you shall lend to many nations, but you shall not borrow. And the Lord will make you the head and not the tail; you shall only go up and not down." — Deuteronomy 28:12–13

90

DEPENDENCY — THE NEW CHAIN

THE EMPIRE'S QUIET WEAPON

Tariffs forge freedom. But sovereignty does not survive on trade alone. A nation may reclaim its factories — yet still lose its soul. Because the serpent has another weapon. If he cannot enslave you through imports, he will seduce you through aid. If he cannot conquer your borders, he will conquer your appetites. Dependency is his quietest chain. A nation can survive invasion, but not sedation. It binds not wrists, but wills. And so the battlefield shifts — from ports to paychecks, from tariffs to temptations.

The new slavery comes with stipends, grants, and guarantees. It speaks softly — in the tone of care, the language of relief. It trains nations to kneel for comfort instead of to stand for covenant. The IMF calls it "development." The UN calls it "sustainability." The bureaucrat calls it "safety nets." But what they sell as mercy is management. Loans that never end. When mercy becomes management, compassion becomes currency. Programs that never close. Crises that never heal — because the healing would end the funding. Aid is the new army. Debt the new doctrine. Subsidy the new scripture. They no longer invade. They invoice. And every invoice is written in your children's names.

The Velvet Hand of Europe

Denmark perfected the ritual. It smiles as it binds. From Copenhagen desks flow billions in "aid" to Africa, the Middle East, and the refugee industry — each grant dressed in compassion, each contract stitched with conditions. The same nation that taxes its farmers for cow breath funds foreign ministries to preach "climate justice." The same bureaucrats who scold Texas for carbon, export Danish blueprints to Brussels, turning subsidies into scripture. Dependency abroad buys moral credit at home. The giver gains the crown; the receiver learns the creed. They call it generosity. It is management. They call it compassion. It is control. They call it sustainability. It is the serpent learning to hiss in policy briefs.

From Exported Mercy to Internal Management

Europe preached generosity abroad because it had perfected dependency at home. Before Brussels managed Africa, Copenhagen managed its own poor. The empire that learned to bind distant nations with loans first practiced on its neighbors with ledgers. Aid overseas was simply the export of an older reflex — the belief that human need must be catalogued, supervised, and made permanent. What began as charity within the parish became policy from the capital. The same hand that fed the colonies learned to number its own. That is where the next story begins — the birth of the modern welfare faith.

The Managed Poor — From "Fattiggården" to EBT

Europe wrote the first welfare gospel. It began as mercy, ended as management. In Denmark they built *fattiggården* — the "poorhouse." On paper it was compassion; in practice, control. The poor were fed, but fenced. They were catalogued, not cared for. Men who lost work became cases. Women who lost husbands became dependents. Children were inspected, weighed, and classified. Poverty was treated not as a tragedy to heal, but as a condition to manage.

The state assumed the role once held by family and church — provider, disciplinarian, priest. The message was clear: "You will be cared for, but you will not be free." That reflex hardened over generations. Denmark built the first soft cage — the social democracy — the welfare state. Every right came with registration. Every benefit, a file. The *"fattiggård"* evolved into a digital welfare system that tracks citizens from cradle to grave. Compassion became currency, and bureaucracy its church. Even now, the pattern endures. Nearly a third of Denmark's economy now flows through social protection. Security has become the state's primary product. Around 700,000 working-age citizens receive public benefits each year — and that number swells whenever crisis strikes. The poverty line is low, but the price is high: a society where risk is outlawed and responsibility outsourced. When the state feeds nearly everyone in one form or another, even the bureaucrat becomes a ward of the system — the modern poorhouse wearing a salary instead of a ration card.

That system sailed west. America imported the logic, not the language. **The Republic was not built for dependency.** It was built for self-rule — covenant between free men, not contract between managers and wards. Jefferson called dependency the seed of tyranny; Lincoln called labor the measure of liberty. For a century and a half, Americans lived that creed — working, giving, building. Churches and communities bore the burden of the weak. Responsibility was the price of freedom. Then came the technocrats — New Dealers, planners, social engineers. They brought Europe's model across the sea: welfare as system, not charity. They called it the Great Society. They replaced neighbors with programs, pastors with caseworkers, covenants with clauses. The *"fattiggård"* found a new home in Washington. At first, the intent seemed noble — no child hungry, no family destitute. But the structure was ancient. The state that feeds becomes the state that defines. The giver becomes the god.

The EBT Age — The Digital Poorhouse

The modern poorhouse hums with electronics. The breadline became a card — the EBT. The ledger became an algorithm. With one digital swipe, dependency became invisible and efficient. Welfare was no longer a stigma; it was a subscription. Work requirements vanished. Oversight faded. Now they return in token form — not to restore dignity, but to disguise dependence. The state no longer asked, "Can you rise?" It asked only, "Will you comply?" Then came SNAP — the Supplemental Nutrition Assistance Program. Its purpose: feed the hungry. Its effect: expand the registry. Each new recipient becomes another datapoint in a system that rewards participation and punishes self-reliance. Even more telling is who receives it. Beneath it lies the quiet obscenity no spreadsheet will confess — veterans sleeping on sidewalks while benefits flow through loopholes to those who never bore the nation's burden. Illegal immigrants, through household loopholes or proxy eligibility, access benefits once reserved for citizens. It's no accident. Welfare has become the quiet weapon of demographic management. **Import dependency, you import votes.** Feed the obedient, not the free.

The Welfare Machine — Mercy or Management?

The serpent learned a new language. He stopped promising chains; he promised care. He traded the whip for a card and called it compassion. SNAP became the safety net; EBT the hand that feeds. But behind every swipe lies a truth: the Republic now rations its people through policy. SNAP is the promise; EBT, the leash disguised as help. Over forty million Americans use those cards each month — twelve percent of the nation. Most are citizens, some are not. Refugees qualify after waiting; undocumented immigrants through the loophole of "mixed households." The benefit flows, the registry grows. Beneath it hides another pattern — the able-bodied who no longer work. Then came the planners, the lockdowns, the "emergencies." Work requirements were suspended, forgotten. A generation learned to wait for *reload day instead of payday*. Relief became ritual.

The Shutdown Revelation

When Washington closes, the mask slips. EBT cards stall. SNAP funding freezes. Panic spreads. The headlines call it "crisis." But it is revelation. A single bureaucratic vote halts meals for millions — proof that the chain works both ways. Yes, real families suffer. Yes, the poor feel the blow first. But the deeper wound is moral — a nation so entangled that a congressional delay becomes a famine. That is not mercy. It is management. The Republic was never meant to feed through fear or rule through ration. Once, neighbors and churches bore the burden. Now an algorithm decides who eats.

Dependency as Dominion

Politicians know the pattern: dependency is loyalty. Each new program purchases obedience. Each expansion turns citizens into clients. The welfare state does not seek to end hunger; it seeks to own gratitude. People are taught to fear losing the benefit more than losing their freedom. It is governance through appetite — control dressed as compassion. They call it "relief." But what it relieves is responsibility. They call it "equity." But what it equalizes is dependence. The serpent's logic is simple: *if you feed a man long enough, you no longer have to fight him — he will defend the hand that feeds him, even when it strangles him.*

The Firelight Truth

A shutdown is not the enemy — it is the mirror. It shows the Republic what it has become: a nation that cannot miss a payment without panic. That is not civilization; that is captivity with good marketing. Freedom requires risk. Covenant demands courage. When the people forget that truth, they trade destiny for debit. They kneel not from hunger, but from habit.

The Native Pattern — Resources in Chains

No people show the cruelty of dependency more clearly than America's first nations. On paper, tribes are sovereign. In practice, they are managed. Their oil, timber, and minerals are held "in trust" by Washington — land they cannot use, wealth they cannot touch. Federal overseers call it protection. It is paralysis. The reservation was not protection; it was rehearsal. Drive through Navajo country — riches underfoot, poverty overhead. Casinos bloom while schools crumble. Bureaucrats bless the arrangement as "cultural preservation." They call it preservation. It is permission. And every few years the cameras return — politicians in cowboy hats smiling beside hungry children, selling compassion while keeping the leash tight. The image never changes because the poverty serves its purpose: moral credit for the powerful, silence from the managed. It is the *fattiggård* reborn — the poorhouse scaled to a people. Greenland knows this pattern. Rich in minerals, bound by Danish and EU "environmental stewardship." Royals arrive for photo-ops, smiling in sealskin while villages wither. They call it green. It is gray control. Different flags. Same formula: lock resources behind policy, feed dependence through subsidy, praise it as compassion. What would sovereignty look like if the managed stopped mistaking management for mercy?

The Cost in Courage — When a Nation Forgets How to Stand

A nation does not lose courage overnight. It leaks. A little at a time. First in the stomach, then in the spine, then in the soul. Dependency does not break a people — it softens them. It whispers that risk is reckless, that bravery is outdated, that strength is unnecessary because the state will always catch you. Soon a citizen who once stood tall begins to crouch without noticing. The man who once provided becomes a "recipient." The woman who once guarded her home becomes a "case." The family that once weathered storms becomes a file waiting for approval. The Republic forgets how to stand because its people forget what standing feels like. And when courage goes, covenant goes. The serpent never needs to strike a nation that kneels on its own.

When the State Replaces the Family

I saw this most clearly in Denmark — not through force, but through routine. Children are not taken from their parents. They are scheduled away from them. From early morning until late afternoon, infants and toddlers are placed in institutions — not as emergency care, but as normal life. Parents hand over their children at dawn and retrieve them at dusk, five days a week, year after year. The system calls it childcare. In practice, it is early delegation of formation. This is not abuse. *It is architecture.* Even *intact families cannot survive economically unless both adults work full time.* The cost of living demands it. Yet paradoxically, a single parent can survive — because *subsidies replace the missing spouse.* The system does not strengthen the family. It quietly renders the family optional. And the consequences follow with mechanical precision. Marriage weakens not from rebellion, but from redundancy. Divorce rises without scandal. Men lose purpose and retreat inward — into alcohol, medication, silence. Depression and suicide climb, disproportionately among men. Masculinity becomes suspect. Fatherhood becomes symbolic. Women are praised for independence, then quietly exhausted by isolation. Families fragment and are recombined into managed units.

The body records what policy denies.

Not only in children — but in adults, families, entire populations. I remember the trains — constant coughing. Workplaces the same. A nation permanently sick — never enough to alarm, never enough to heal. This is what managed life looks like in the body. Persistent fatigue. Low-grade illness that never clears. A society always fighting something, never fully well. This is not coincidence, nor merely viral exposure from institutions. It is chronic stress layered over early separation, flattened emotion, and lives lived under constant supervision. A population already accustomed to chronic illness does not meet medical emergency the same way a resilient one does. **When fatigue is normal, intervention feels merciful.** When sickness is routine, authority feels protective. Denmark did not comply so quickly during covid because it was ignorant — it complied because it was conditioned. The body was already trained to defer. The culture had already outsourced trust.

So when the crisis came, obedience felt like care. Not because the people were weak — but because the system had already taught them that safety comes from surrender. The body mirrors the culture. **A regulated society produces regulated immune systems.** This is the exchange: security for witness. Comfort for continuity. Management for mastery. **A soft-totalitarian model — not coercive, but anesthetic.** *What Denmark perfected in a generation, America is being taught to accept in a decade.*

The Europeanization of the Republic

Welfare is not just policy. It's culture. It rewires the soul. Denmark calls it security — *tryghed*. Denmark is proud that no one falls too far. But they no longer rise either. Risk has been outlawed. Courage replaced by consensus. Innovation by incentive. The state manages what once burned in the human spirit. That creed is now preached in Washington. Politicians promise safety from every storm — economic, environmental, emotional. But the price of safety is sovereignty. **The citizen becomes client; the client becomes commodity. The Republic becomes Denmark — with better slogans.** This is the quiet revolution — the transformation of covenant people into managed populations. No whips, no chains, no tyrants — just "benefits." A society too comfortable to rebel, too supervised to grow. A Republic cannot run on welfare. It runs on work, virtue, and covenant trust. Freedom is not sustained by comfort. Denmark chose management. America must choose mastery — not of others, but of self. If we trade that for comfort, we return to the poorhouse — only this time, it glows. No more poses. No more pity. The lens has turned — and the fire sees everything. The serpent's final miracle is to make bondage feel benevolent.

 Firelight Pause — The Bureaucrat's Bargain

They pose beside the poor they manage and call it service. But mercy without liberty is theater. A system that feeds but never frees is not compassion — it's choreography. The truest service is not management — it is release.

Ask yourself:
- What is the value of compassion that requires an audience?
- When leaders feed dependence, do they heal — or harvest?
- Do I confuse management with mercy simply because it smiles?
- Would I still serve if the cameras were gone?
- Who profits when pity becomes policy?

"The borrower is servant to the lender." — Proverbs 22:7

91

—————

COVENANT AND THE COLLAPSE

WHY AMERICA IS NOT JUST AN
EXPERIMENT — AND WHAT HAPPENS
WHEN WE BREAK SACRED VOWS

The masks are gone. The stage is clear. What remains is the war beneath all wars — **the Prophetic War.**

Every system unmasked. Every chain named. Now the line is drawn. Babylon stands revealed — its machinery naked, its promises ash. The war that began with whispers now sounds the trumpets. This is where analysis ends and prophecy begins. These final chapters lift the curtain fully. You will see how covenant, once broken, becomes the fracture line of nations — **how Denmark's quiet crown rehearsed the mark,** how America's covenant teeters between remembrance and ruin. The spiritual architecture of the age unfolds — the serpent's lineage, the counterfeit kingdom, and the remnant rising in fire. Here, prophecy becomes command. The Remnant is not called to observe, but to act. To break the chains. To stand sealed in blood, not code. To bear covenant when the world bows to counterfeit. Babylon falls. The Remnant rises. The fire passes to your hands.

656

Why America Is Not Just an Experiment, and What Happens When We Break Sacred Vows.

We have watched the serpent whisper in Denmark and Brussels, scripting obedience as consensus. We have felt the dragon's claws reach from Beijing into our farms, our medicine, and our borders. Now we stand at the edge of the Beast's throne in America. America was not founded on management. It was born in *covenant* — oaths whispered in prayer, sealed in blood, pledged with trembling hands. This is not about rejecting technology, cooperation, or medicine. It's about who holds authority — *God or system*. When covenant is forgotten, the Republic becomes an empty shell. And hollow shells do not stand.

"And the great dragon was cast out, that old serpent, called the Devil, and Satan, which deceiveth the whole world." — Revelation 12:9

Scripture pulls back the veil — the serpent and the dragon walk together. One deceives, the other devours. Together they hand power to the Beast. This is not myth. It is the pattern of history. *The serpent whispers lies. The dragon enforces chains. The Beast enthrones itself in worship.* One seduces, one devours, one reigns. Together they suffocate nations. But covenant is the fracture line. Nations that forget covenant wear crowns of silence. Tribes that break covenant carry shadows into history.

The serpent drafts the chains, the dragon forges them, and the Beast baptizes them. Those chains now stretch across America. Foreign hands own nearly 350,000 acres of farmland, many beside U.S. bases. Fentanyl takes seventy thousand American lives every year. Antibiotics are manu-factured under Beijing's grip. Migrants are processed like freight through NGO pipelines. Surveillance cameras, fiber cables, and imported chips form the nervous system of American life. The dragon blinks through your phone, your vote, your grid.

What looks like convenience is colonization. What looks like trade is trail-marked conquest. The dragon does not roar. It seeps. Its claws pierce land by buying farms and water rights, body through poison and dependency, freedom with IDs and apps, and faith itself with silence dressed as tolerance, censorship dressed as peace. And the dragon's shadow reaches even deeper — into the code that governs our choices. Every major platform that moderates speech in America relies on foreign-built models, foreign-trained moderators, or foreign-owned infrastructure. TikTok runs psy-ops in plain sight, shaping the instincts of eighty million Americans with an algorithm written in Beijing. Children scroll foreign propaganda disguised as entertainment. Teens repeat scripts written by a rival state. The dragon does not need soldiers when it can shape a generation's reflexes one swipe at a time. What was once influence is now infiltration — not through armies, but through appetite.

The Covenant Broken

Power never rules naked. It always dresses itself in service. The serpent does not govern directly. The dragon does not administer programs. The Beast does not knock on doors. They rule through vessels — systems built to look benevolent, structures designed to feel necessary, institutions that translate domination into "help." This is how spiritual authority becomes political reality. Not through crowns, but through committees. Not through conquest, but through coordination. The ancient powers learned long ago that force creates martyrs — but management creates compliance. **Institutions are the incarnation layer of empire.** They take spiritual rebellion and render it operational. They turn deception into policy, control into care, obedience into virtue. Only then do the saviors arrive. Many individuals within these systems mean well. That is precisely why the systems work.

The institutions that parade as saviors are often the managers of this system. NGOs pose as helpers. The EU brands itself as "union." The UN sells itself as peacekeeper. But stripped of language, they are engines of control.

"Woe to those who decree unrighteous decrees, and who write misfortune, which they have prescribed; to rob the needy of justice and to take what is right from the poor of My people." — Isaiah 10:1–2

What these institutions call governance, God calls rebellion. They baptize chains as virtue and market them as progress. The serpent drafts the decree. The dragon enforces the decree. The Beast stamps it with inevitability.

"Because your heart is lifted up, and you say, 'I am a god, I sit in the seat of gods... yet you are a man, and not a god.'" — Ezekiel 28:2 — That is the arrogance of empire. And that is the arrogance now embedded in the global system.

In the Bible, **arrogance is the first rebellion** — the creature claiming the throne of the Creator. That was Lucifer's fall. It was Babel's sin. It was Rome's crown. Every empire that exalts itself above God repeats the same pattern — *it builds towers instead of temples, systems instead of souls, decrees instead of repentance.* That's what Ezekiel saw — rulers calling themselves gods while forgetting they are dust. This rebellion no longer wears crowns or carries banners. It writes software.

The New Babel — When Code Replaces Covenant

That same spirit rides again in our time. **The new Babel is digital.** Its priests are not kings in robes, but *technocrats in lab coats.* They speak *the language of code,* but their creed is the same: *We will ascend.* They promise to upgrade creation, to rewrite the genome, to merge mind and machine, to end death by data. They call it innovation. It is imitation — **the oldest rebellion repackaged in silicon.**

It speaks the language of progress and dresses rebellion in robes of peace. It does not storm heaven; it manages earth. It seeks worship through policy, not prayer — through algorithms, not altars. *They no longer carve idols from stone; they code them from flesh.* **Artificial intelligence becomes the oracle, biotech the altar, digital ID the mark of belonging.** And Scripture warns what follows — **when men enthrone themselves as gods, a counterfeit kingdom rises** to fill the void. That kingdom rides a white horse — a rider crowned not with glory, but with code, conquering in the name of "*safety*," "*equity*," and "*evolution*."

How the Pattern Enters the World

The serpent, the dragon, and the Beast are not metaphors floating above history. They are roles — functions — that appear wherever power seeks permanence. **The serpent** speaks first. It captures language, redefines virtue, and trains conscience. It lives wherever meaning is managed — in narratives, education, media, and moral frameworks. **The dragon** enforces what the serpent prepares. It brings force, pressure, leverage — economic, military, technological. It appears wherever obedience must be secured when belief begins to fracture. **The Beast** is what emerges when deception and force are fused into system. It does not rule by terror, but by integration — when identity, access, currency, movement, and speech are bound together until dissent becomes impractical rather than illegal. These roles are not owned by a single nation or institution. They move. They migrate. They inhabit whatever structure will carry them. Empires change flags; the architecture remains. This is why Scripture names patterns, not countries. Because **the danger is not who sits on the throne — but what kind of throne it is.**

The Architecture of the Beast

The Beast does not rise through thrones or armies. It rises through *systems.* The prophet saw a kingdom that controlled buying and selling, that governed not by sword but by seal — a mark that determined who belonged and who bowed. For centuries, that image seemed symbolic. Now it reads like an operations manual. **Every global institution is building the same structure: a single, interoperable grid of identity, currency, and compliance.** The Beast's architecture is not mythology. It is bureaucracy. It is code.

Digital ID is the first pillar — a number that replaces the name. The EU calls it eIDAS. The UN calls it "legal identity for all." The WEF brands it necessity. But stripped of promises, it is one truth: permission to exist granted by the system.

Then comes the second pillar: **programmable currency.** Central bank digital currencies arrive wrapped in efficiency but built for obedience. They track every transaction, trace every purchase, and freeze any hand that steps out of line. Money stops being yours. It becomes a message — approved or denied.

The third pillar is **harmonization,** the quiet empire. Laws "align." Standards "unify." Nations "coordinate." Climate rules become border rules, border rules become trade rules, and trade rules become identity rules. What looks like cooperation is consolidation — sovereignty shrink-wrapped in global compliance. *Biometric borders rise. Universal health passes wait in the wings. ESG scores regulate businesses. SDGs regulate govern-ments. WHO treaties stretch toward emergency authority. Databases merge. Systems sync.*

The Beast does not conquer by force. It conquers by removing alternatives. A thousand small systems weaving into one throne. This is how the serpent drafts the decree, **the dragon enforces the decree, and the Beast enthrones itself in visibility disguised as inevitability.** A kingdom not of land, but of data — a dominion where citizenship is measured in compliance, and human worth is read by scanners glowing in blue. This is the architecture Scripture warned of: a world where the right to trade, travel, or speak depends on a signal from a system no man can see yet every man must obey.

The White Horse
   "And the dragon gave him his power, and his seat, and great authority." — *Revelation 13:2*

This is the rider on the white horse of Revelation 6: a crown without arrows, a conquest without war. It advances not by fire, but by worship. Not by armies, but by allegiance. The serpent whispers treaties. The dragon enforces chains. The Beast enthrones itself in worship. This is the shape of false peace. It arrives dressed as unity, smiling as safety, polished as inevitability. It conquers not by destroying nations but by hollowing them out until only shells remain. America does not stumble for lack of power. It stumbles for lack of covenant. Forgetting covenant is not neutrality. It is rebellion disguised as rest — and every rebellion ends in collapse.

🔥 **Firelight Pause — Covenant or Collapse**

The fire does not bargain. It burns. Now the question is yours:

• Where have I traded covenant for convenience?

• What dragon's gifts sit in my home, on my desk, in my pocket?

• Do I still believe America's strength lies in politics — or in covenant with God?

• What am I willing to lose so my children do not inherit chains?

• When the serpent drafts, the dragon enforces, and the Beast enthrones — will I kneel, or stand sealed in blood?

The fire waits for your answer 🔥

To the blind it looks like progress. To the lukewarm it looks like safety. To the remnant it is prophecy fulfilled. The serpent whispers, the dragon strikes, and the Beast enthrones — yet the covenant still stands. The fire is now in your hands. The Remnant must choose: **covenant, or collapse.**

"If the foundations are destroyed, what can the righteous do?" — Psalm 11:3

The Beast does not march with banners. It enters with a crown — and no arrows.

92

THE CROWN WITHOUT ARROWS

HOW THE SERPENT CONQUERS WITHOUT WAR

It began in a garden. Not with armies. Not with fire. But with a whisper: "Did God really say?" (Genesis 3:1). **The serpent's first weapon was doubt** — not chains, not swords. Words twisted into poison. Adam and Eve traded covenant for compromise. The first fall was born not from war but from seduction. The serpent's script has never changed — *doubt leads to deception, deception to dependency, dependency to dominion.*

Satan's genius is not force. It is disguise. First, *"I don't exist."* Second, *"Look over there, not here."* For centuries men watched Rome, Moscow, Beijing. But the serpent coiled elsewhere — masked in comfort, smiling as he constricted. For centuries, people have searched for a face — a tyrant, a despot, a single figure to blame. But Scripture warns us that the final deception would be broader than a man and quieter than a crown. The Antichrist is not only a man. It is a system — a counterfeit kingdom that flips good and evil, enslaves under the promise of safety. Scripture warned that this kingdom would not arrive with terror, but with inversion — calling evil good, promising peace and safety, and binding obedience to survival itself. It does not roar with horns. It comes wrapped in treaties. It comes dressed as technocracy. It comes cloaked in equity, sustainability, and inclusion.

664

It parades in borrowed light — "the happiest people on earth." A crown without arrows. A conqueror by seduction. The Bible does not warn of a monster the world will fear — but of a figure the world will admire. Revelation names the pattern in symbols — horses that ride before kingdoms fall.

Revelation 6:6 warns of the black horse: "Two pounds of wheat for a day's wages." Food rationed. Herds culled. Quotas enforced. Scarcity not natural, but manufactured. **In Denmark** the pattern was rehearsed — mink industries slaughtered by decree; cattle taxed, herds cut, farms strangled; fishermen crushed by quotas; carbon credits weaponized as famine. Scarcity rehearsed as policy. **In America, the horse rides differently — but it rides.** Egg prices triple. Meat becomes a luxury. Small farmers drown in regulation while corporate giants consolidate. Water rights are locked behind permits. Fertilizer prices spike. Diesel costs choke transport. Supply chains "break." Shelves thin. The language is always crisis, sustainability, safety. But the result is the same: food made scarce, labor devalued, dependence normalized. Scarcity is not an accident. It is leverage. Scarcity prepares the ground. When life is tightened just enough — food uncertain, costs rising, pressure everywhere — the people do not demand freedom. They demand relief. And relief is how conquest changes its clothes.

Revelation 6:2 then shows the white horse: "I looked, and there before me was a white horse! Its rider held a bow, and he was given a crown..." A crown without arrows. A conqueror without war. False salvation adored as peace. The white horse does not bring chains. It brings solutions. **In Denmark,** vaccine passports were sold as "freedom." Digital ID bound all life. Turbines and taxes were packaged as redemption. Subsidies were presented as security. Smiles masked chains. Scarcity first. Seduction second. The serpent rode crowned in comfort. **In America, the offer is already familiar.** Safety apps. Health passes. Emergency powers extended "just a little longer." ESG scores sold as responsibility. Digital wallets framed as convenience. Surveillance rebranded as protection.

Compliance rewarded, resistance labeled selfish. No tanks. No knock at the door. Just access — granted or denied. The white horse conquers by applause. It does not threaten. It reassures. It does not silence by force. It persuades by promise. This is how empire wins without firing a shot: First make life scarce. Then sell order as mercy. First starve the field. Then crown the savior.

Every chain is forged in velvet. Every shackle polished as progress. Digital identity binds health, speech, and money — not with force, but with permission. And beneath it hums a deeper ambition: not merely to govern behavior, but to reengineer the human itself. The new covenant of the technocrats is not with God, but with code. Programmable currency forbids "unapproved" choices. Health decrees scale authority without debate. Compliance becomes access. In Denmark, life itself now depends on alignment. One wrong word. One wrong click. You are not arrested — you are digitally erased. Locked out, not locked up. A modern exile written in code. And the venom has crossed the sea. Digital ID. Digital dollars. ESG enforcement. Vaccine passes rehearsed in New York and California. This is not accidental. Global governance talent does not scatter by accident. It clusters where systems already speak its language. Nordic and European administrators gravitate toward the same corridors — UN agencies, climate NGOs, humanitarian tech, academic and policy hubs — translating familiar models into American form. Not as invaders, but as carriers. The pattern spreads because the soil is prepared. America still resists — unevenly, imperfectly — but the infrastructure is already in the bloodstream. The serpent no longer needs to strike. The venom works quietly from within. The Bible was not the only witness. Norse sagas told of **Midgårdsormen** — the world-serpent coiled so tightly around creation that it strangled without sound. Even Thor, the defender, did not fall in battle, but **walked a few steps after victory and then collapsed — poisoned by venom already inside him.** Genesis spoke of the serpent striking the heel. Revelation warned of a dragon deceiving nations. Different tongues. Same enemy. The lesson was never that the serpent wins by strength — but that it kills **after the fight, from within.**

Venom in the bloodstream. Collapse delayed. The danger unseen until it becomes unbearable to reverse — unless it is named in time, resisted in truth, and burned out while covenant still lives. Denmark shows the script best — famine by policy, peace by propaganda. The horses ride not only in Scripture. They ride in headlines. Scripture does not describe this moment symbolically. It describes it operationally.

Revelation 13:16–17 speaks of the mark: "It also forced all people, great and small, rich and poor, free and slave, to receive a mark on their right hands or on their foreheads, so that they could not buy or sell unless they had the mark..." Once upon a time — not in myth but prophecy — there was a mark. Not a crown. Not a sword. **A mark.**

In Denmark it appears as NemID, MitID, CPR. One key for all doors — to bank, to work, to cross borders, to see a doctor. One wrong post. One frozen account. One missed box. You are not arrested. You are digitally erased — locked out, not locked up. The modern poorhouse now runs on code. In Denmark, you do not live free. You live logged in. And one wrong move — you do not live at all. **The mark is not paperwork. It is worship.** To bow is to choose. Babylon or covenant. Beast or Lamb.

People imagine the mark arrives in a single moment — one command, one global decree. But *marks are not taken. They are trained.* A thousand small compromises before the final one. The serpent never begins where resistance is loud. He begins where obedience is quiet. Denmark rehearsed the mark. And rehearsal always precedes performance. A quiet kingdom by the sea became the serpent's showroom. The world applauded its comfort. But prophecy names it plainly — a rehearsal of the Beast. Denmark is not the villain. It is the mirror. The rehearsal hall where global governance tests its scripts before the premiere. Copenhagen was never the throne. It was the showroom.

What Worship Actually Is

Worship is widely misunderstood. Most people imagine it as music, prayer, or ritual — something confined to churches, temples, or belief systems. Scripture uses the word far more precisely. In biblical terms, worship is not first about praise. It is about **allegiance.** *Worship is revealed not by what a person sings or claims, but by who they trust for survival, who they obey when obedience costs them, who defines what is good or forbidden, and who grants permission to live, work, speak, buy, or belong.* These questions apply to every human being — **believer or not.** That is why Revelation does not describe the mark as a confession of belief, but as a condition of participation. *"So that no one could buy or sell unless he had the mark."* This is not symbolic theology. It is infrastructure. It is access. It is authority. **God's covenant marks were always relational** — signs of belonging rooted in trust: circumcision, Sabbath, baptism. They pointed upward, away from systems, toward provision beyond human control. **The Beast's mark is functional.** It is not about what you believe, but about **who controls the terms of your existence.** One says, *I live by God's provision.* The other says, *I live by the system's permission.* This is why the final conflict is not fought with weapons. It is fought with architecture.

Scripture shows the pattern repeatedly: seduction before coercion, convenience before command, training before enforcement. No one wakes up one morning and worships a tyrant. They are conditioned. First the system feeds them. Then it organizes them. Then it defines reality for them. Eventually, obedience feels moral. Resistance feels reckless. Gratitude replaces discernment. When obedience begins to feel virtuous, worship is already complete. This is not about fear. It is about trust. When people instinctively look to a system for safety, meaning, identity, and provision — when dissent feels dangerous and compliance feels compassionate — authority has already shifted. Worship has already occurred. That is why Scripture warns that the mark does not arrive with terror, but with inversion. Evil is called good. Restriction is called safety. Obedience is called virtue. Exclusion is called care. The danger is not that people will hate it. The danger is that they will defend it. Worship does not require an altar. It requires alignment.

Each time a person adjusts truth to preserve access, each time conscience bows to permission, each time survival outweighs conviction, a decision is made. The mark is not taken in a moment. It is trained — through a thousand small compromises, a thousand permissions granted in exchange for ease, a thousand silences where truth felt inconvenient. This is why the warning is universal. You do not need to believe Scripture to recognize the pattern. You only need to recognize power. **Any system that controls identity, currency, speech, and movement does not merely govern behavior — it reshapes loyalty.** When access replaces conscience, worship has changed hands. The question is not whether the mark exists. The question is whether life has already been structured around permission instead of principle. Because worship is not what you say you believe. It is what you cannot afford to lose.

From Brussels' treaties to Geneva's resolutions, from New York's pulpits to the halls of the WHO, the prototype was scaled. Not reinvented — replicated. The same logic. The same architecture. The same grid. Those who build the grid decide the future. Even the UN's procurement arm quietly exported digital infrastructure from Copenhagen into the developing world — not by conquest, but by contract; not by force, but by silence. This is not about Denmark alone. It is about a pattern rehearsed, refined, and now global.

🔥 **Firelight Pause — Covenant or Collapse**

The fire does not negotiate. It exposes. It burns until truth stands bare.

The question is no longer whether evil exists — but whether you **serve it, ignore it,** or **resist it.**

Ask yourself:

• Where have I traded covenant for comfort — letting convenience silence conviction?

• Do I still recognize the serpent's whisper, or have I learned to call it "progress"?

• When the dragon feeds on nations through debt and fear, do I look away because my own table is still full?

• Have I accepted the Beast's mark in quieter forms — letting code, comfort, or consensus rule what only conscience should?

• What gifts sit in my home, on my desk, in my pocket — tools that promise ease while stealing attention, privacy, and prayer?

• Am I teaching my children vigilance — or training them to obey the glow of the machine?

• When the serpent drafts, the dragon enforces, and the Beast enthrones — will I kneel, stay silent, or stand sealed in covenant fire?

• If the fire demanded everything today — comfort, career, reputation — would I still choose freedom so my children do not inherit chains?

The fire waits for your answer 🔥

The serpent's whisper is everywhere — in screens, in treaties, in taxes. The crown without arrows looks harmless — but its power is allegiance. One day soon you will be asked to bow. Not with a sword at your throat, but with a screen in your hand. The question will not be survival. The question will be worship. Choose covenant. Or choose the chain. But eternity hangs on the mark you bear. This is not myth. This is prophecy rehearsed. Will you dismiss it as progress? Or will you name it as the Beast? Because prophecy was not written for comfort. It was written for war. And **war is now at your gates.**

I have not given you a conclusion. I have handed you a key. Could the polished prototype — this quiet kingdom of comfort, quotas, and codes — be the rehearsal of prophecy itself? The Danish experiment, exported in velvet words and digital chains, may already be the shadow of the Beast's mark. The rest is not my verdict. It is your vision. Will you dismiss it as myth, or name it for what it is? Because warnings are never written for comfort. They are written for the Remnant who will look.

The serpent is here. The trumpet has sounded. The gates stand open. The air itself demands your answer.

"I am coming soon. Hold fast what you have, so that no one may seize your crown." — Revelation 3:11

93

———

THE HIDDEN WAR
WHEN THE VEIL TEARS

The Trumpet and the Veil

You met the Board at the beginning—when all you had was intuition, suspicion, and the spark of a call. Now the trumpet has sounded, and the veil is torn. Every mask is fallen. Every system named. Every chain exposed. What remains is revelation: not politics but principality, not policy but prophecy, not governance but war. The serpent still believes he owns the board—but the Fire has learned his moves. When the veil tears, sight returns. The world you thought you knew shatters into layers — one reality stacked upon another, each feeding the next. The serpent hides not in one empire but in dimensions of influence. What you see on the surface is only the shadow of what moves beneath. The field is larger than politics, deeper than policy, older than history. You have heard its echoes — in news cycles that never end, in laws no one voted for, in screens that speak louder than Scripture. What feels like chaos is choreography. Every headline is a distraction. Every argument, a rehearsal. Every comfort, a cage. Now lift the curtain. The stage is set. The serpent still plays the board — but not all boards are seen. Look beneath the noise, and you will find the four fields where this war is truly fought.

The Four Boards Beneath

Most people live on the surface — angry at headlines, enslaved by noise, blind to design. They argue over symbols while systems move unseen. But the battlefield has always been layered. The serpent wins where vision ends.

The Surface Board

Here lies the theater of distraction — elections, hashtags, and televised outrage. It feels real because it's loud. Politicians wrestle under lights while the true game unfolds in the shadows behind them. Every cycle promises change, yet the serpent keeps the frame. One channel sells fear, another sells hope, but both feed the same machine: division. Outrage is the currency; exhaustion, the goal. In this layer, men win arguments but lose nations. They choose sides without realizing the sides were drawn for them. The serpent loves democracy when it can choreograph both sides of the stage.

The Domain Board

Beneath the surface lies the quiet empire — treaties, trade, debt, migration, and energy. Here sovereignty is sold, not stolen. Signatures replace soldiers; ink replaces iron. While citizens debate presidents, the technocrats write the contracts that outlive them all. This is where nations become subsidiaries — where currency is created by the same hands that count your votes. A handshake in Brussels moves more power than a protest in any square. The serpent works best in conference rooms — polite voices, polished lies, global reach.

The Mind Board

Deeper still is the war for perception — the invisible field of algorithms, speech codes, and engineered truth. Here the serpent scripts reality before you can question it. Every scroll is surveillance. Every search a catechism. Words are formatted before they're spoken; thoughts are shaped before they're felt.

Freedom is repackaged as convenience, dissent as extremism. Men think they are choosing; they are being curated. The serpent no longer burns books; he buries truth beneath data. He discovered that censorship is unnecessary when distraction works better.

The Spirit Board

At the deepest level lies the only real war — not over land or law, but over worship. Allegiance is the final currency. This is where kings bow, where nations fall, where souls are counted. Every policy above flows from a spirit beneath: pride, fear, idolatry, rebellion. Without Christ, you can map the system and still walk into the trap. Eyes open but spirit blind. Only covenant gives sight. Only Spirit grants discernment. Only Truth breaks the game. And that is why the serpent still believes he owns the board — because most of humanity never leaves the surface. But the Remnant does. They see the pattern in every layer, and they move not by sight, but by fire.

You have seen the layers — surface, domain, mind, spirit — and how each feeds the next. But beneath them all lies something darker still, the architect behind the architecture. For every war has a command, and every deception has a designer. The serpent does not work alone; he builds systems in his own image. What Heaven formed as covenant, Hell imitates as code. The old rebellion has learned new language — policy, progress, peace. Yet the pattern is ancient. The same pride that said "I will ascend" now writes algorithms, drafts treaties, and calls it evolution. The battlefield has changed; the spirit behind it has not. **What once tempted with fruit now governs with forms — but it is the same rebellion, wearing permission instead of fangs.**

The Trinity of Inversion

Every lie is born from fear of the truth it imitates. Heaven moves in triune harmony — Father, Son, Spirit — the Source, the Word, and the Breath. Hell could not create, so it counterfeited. It built its own trinity — not of love, but of leverage. Not of covenant, but of control.

The first face is **Bureaucracy — the False Father.** He promises order, safety, equality. He writes mercy in the language of management and calls obedience compassion. He builds councils in place of conscience, programs in place of prayer. *He measures virtue by compliance and holiness by efficiency.* His creed is consensus; his temple, the institution.

The second face is **Technology — the False Son.** He offers redemption through innovation, immortality through machine. His gospel is progress, his miracles are data, his disciples are connected but never known. He heals with screens, saves with science, and whispers, *"You shall be as gods."* Yet behind every upgrade waits a deeper dependence. He erases sin by deleting memory and calls it mercy. He is the savior of self, the messiah of man remade.

The third face is **Force — the False Spirit.** He moves through armies, sanctions, and fear. When persuasion fails, he enforces peace through power. He baptizes nations in fire and calls it security. His breath is intimidation; his anointing is surveillance. He appears last — for he is the sword that guards the system, the muscle of the machine. Force, when wielded as the foundation of authority and obedience, becomes the False Spirit. But force used in defense of freedom and justice, submitted to covenant truth, is not part of the Beast's counterfeit. Force becomes evil only when it is worshiped as authority. When it serves covenant, it restrains evil; when it replaces covenant, it becomes the Beast's breath.

Together they form the **Trinity of Inversion** — the Bureaucrat, the Machine, and the Sword. Three faces, one will: to replace worship with management, faith with permission, covenant with control. Their creation is the Beast — an empire of commerce, code, and compliance. Its chains are not forged of iron but of comfort. Credentials. Carbon. Identity. Data. Medicine. Money. Soft. Velvet. Digital. Permanent. This is not prophecy of tomorrow. It is description of today.

Systems are never still. Once built, they begin to breathe. The counterfeit trinity—bureaucracy, technology, and force—does not rest after creation; it rides. What began as structure becomes spirit, and what was policy becomes power. The machine hungers for motion. It needs crisis to justify its crown.

Every empire in decay learns the same ritual: manufacture chaos to offer control. The serpent knows the pattern. He's been rehearsing it since Eden—promise safety, then demand surrender. What was once prophecy becomes procedure; what was once symbol becomes software. The Beast does not wait for Revelation; it *runs* Revelation. Its riders no longer gallop through vision—they move through history, coded and disguised.

Listen. The hooves are already on the earth.

The Riders and the Seals

Revelation never predicted chaos — it mapped it. The seals were never superstition, but blueprints, written in divine geometry and mistaken for myth. What follows are the four seals that ride — not symbols of the end, but systems that move history itself. What God revealed as warning, the Beast studied as design.

The First Seal — The White Horse

It rides under the banner of peace—clean, clinical, persuasive. Its rider wears no crown of thorns but a halo of code. He conquers not with sword but with simulation. His gospel is efficiency; his salvation, data. He rides into nations promising order, and they welcome him because his war is bloodless. He digitizes covenant and calls it progress. Every contract, every credential, every scan—another mark in his quiet conquest. *False peace, salvation by code.*

The Second Seal — The Red Horse

He follows close, bearing the blade of intervention. His banner reads "collective security," but his creed is control. He wages peace by perpetual war, reshaping borders with drones and decrees. When diplomacy fails, he sends deliverance through detonation. He calls it humanitarian. He calls it safe. But *the earth drinks blood in every age*, and the rider never dismounts.

The Third Seal — The Black Horse

He rides with scales in hand and scarcity in his wake. His balance is deceit—justice repackaged as ration. He taxes the breath of creation, weighing grain and carbon as though they were sin. He preaches sustainability while he prices survival. His arithmetic divides the living from the allowed. Famine becomes policy, quotas become commandments. *Bread costs freedom; fuel costs faith.*

The Fourth Seal — The Pale Horse

He is the color of fear—neither white nor gray but absence itself. His weapon is not plague but panic. He governs through prescription, commands through statistics, anoints through permission. Life becomes conditional, measured by compliance. He rides softly, with bureaucrats in his saddle, physicians in his armor, algorithms for reins. Fear once ruled by force; now *comfort rules by consent.*

Together they are not visions but variables—systems that walk, laws that breathe. The Beast did not wait to be born in prophecy; it was coded into bureaucracy, translated into technology, and sanctified through fear. And the rehearsal? Not in the East, but in the **North.**

The Serpent's Showroom

Copenhagen is quiet. Polished. Efficient. Nothing looks wrong. That is the point. This is what the serpent perfected here — not terror, not tyranny, but design. A nation without rebellion, where compliance is culture and silence is citizenship. No banners. No boots. No shouting in the streets. Life simply requires login. Virtue is verified. Obedience is framed as freedom. The mark was not announced. It was beta-tested. CPR. NemID. MitID. Numbers replacing names. One key for all doors — banking, work, healthcare, travel, identity. Why arrest the dissident when you can delete her? Why police belief when you can program access? Fear once ruled by force. Here, comfort rules by consent.

The serpent's throne is not a palace. It is a touchscreen. His masterpiece was never the machine itself. It was the illusion that you could stand beside it and remain untouched. That you could scroll without serving. Comply without bowing. Exist inside the system while belonging to another kingdom. Neutrality becomes the fog that hides surrender. Every click is confession. Every convenience is covenant. The serpent does not need to own what resists him. He only needs permission. He tempts you to call apathy peace and obedience wisdom. *Stay reasonable. Stay quiet. Stay safe.* And slowly, the fire in the conscience cools to ash. The Beast does not demand worship. It accepts it passively — through silence. Fog thickens here. Not panic, not chaos — fatigue. A narrowing of vision. A life made so smooth, so regulated, so carefully managed that resistance feels unnecessary, even impolite. The field tightens without anyone noticing the fence. Yet even here, something remains. A spark. A voice. A fire that does not go out. The Remnant does not shout. It does not posture. It does not rage against the fog. It walks through it carrying light.

Where it steps, truth roots again. Where even one pair of eyes begins to see, the illusion fractures. The serpent's empire depends on blindness — and blindness breaks the moment sight returns. This is not war with flesh and blood. It never was.

"For we wrestle not against flesh and blood, but against principalities, against powers, against the rulers of the darkness of this world." — Ephesians 6:12

The enemy does not march beneath flags or wear uniforms. He works through suggestion, convenience, and fatigue. His battlefield is obedience. His prize is allegiance. Neutrality is not virtue. It is vacancy. Silence crowns the serpent. Comfort enthrones the Beast. Each time truth is traded for tolerance, a gate closes. Each time safety is chosen over Spirit, another chain is fastened. Apathy does not prevent war — it only postpones it until the children inherit it. The fog promises ease. *There is nothing to see. Nothing to fear.* But behind the softness waits the system that counts breath, coin, and conscience. The serpent rules by exhaustion. Make men weary enough, and they will call captivity calm. This was the showroom. Clean. Quiet. Convincing. And what worked here did not stay here.

Why You Saw Denmark First

Because prophecy rarely announces itself. It hides in plain sight. Denmark did not rise as an empire. It never needed to. Its power was never conquest, but calibration. *Consensus instead of command.* Comfort instead of coercion. Obedience learned as culture, not imposed as law. This is why your eyes went there first. Denmark's crown was not forged in fire but in refinement. Its rule was velvet. Its faith orderly. Its people disciplined. Nothing looked broken — which is precisely why the exchange went unnoticed. Covenant was not attacked. It was replaced. Truth softened into tolerance. Fire traded for form.

Here, the serpent learned to *govern without fear*. To *conquer without violence*. To make *obedience feel virtuous and resistance feel impolite*. **Power through politeness. Control through mechanism. Virtue measured in compliance.** The model was tested everywhere that shapes a people: classrooms, clinics, ministries, markets. A nation so rational, so regulated, that rebellion felt unnecessary. Even immoral. The people did not fall — they adjusted.

Denmark was not the throne. It was the blueprint. What worked here scaled cleanly. From Copenhagen's committees to Brussels' bureaucracy. From Geneva's councils to New York's chambers. From Davos' stage to Beijing's data farms. The system did not spread by force, but by imitation. The world watched a nation run smoothly and asked for the instructions. And now the pattern turns west. Not to crown America — but to hollow her. A covenant nation cannot be ruled the same way. **Denmark surrendered to comfort. America must be conquered by confusion.** The stronger the oath, the subtler the warfare. The serpent tightens his coils differently around a people born in fire. This is why the North mattered. Not because of myth. Because of method. The serpent always builds his prototype where resistance is quiet, virtue is procedural, and obedience feels like maturity. He hides not in chaos, but in calm. His mark is not first a number or a code. It is culture — control disguised as responsibility. And once the pattern is perfected, it does not stay local. You did not imagine it. You recognized it. The showroom revealed the system. This reveals the strategy.

Denmark's apparent insignificance was never real. It was protected by leverage few noticed. Greenland gave Denmark strategic mass without imperial appearance — Arctic access, NATO gravity, rare-earth corridors, climate authority, and undersea infrastructure routes. Power without posture. Influence without accusation. While others projected force, Denmark curated systems. Greenland made Denmark unavoidable in security, energy, data, and climate governance — while its cultural footprint remained small enough to escape suspicion.

This is how a minor crown learned to move among giants without being named as one. What began as rehearsal is now replication. And the question is no longer *why Denmark* — but whether America will recognize the pattern before the velvet hardens into chain.

The Fire Does Not Go Out

The fire does not end with exposure. It passes. Not to institutions. Not to leaders. Not to movements. It passes to living hands. There are those who do not shout when truth is revealed. They do not organize or posture or announce themselves. They simply stop pretending. They stop complying where compliance costs the soul. They remember who they are. Scripture never promised that the faithful would be visible—only that they would endure. Not conquerors, but witnesses. Not crowned, but sealed. The serpent does not fear crowds. He fears clarity. He trembles when a man or woman sees—and does not look away. Because sight spreads. Conviction multiplies. Fire passes quietly, one conscience at a time. The war does not end here. It turns inward. Revelation is no longer thunder. It is ember. And ember is enough.

Firelight Pause — The Final Seeing

You are no longer naïve. You have seen the board and the hand that moved it. Comfort now reveals its god. Peace exposes its throne. Screens no longer soothe without cost, and silence is no longer neutral. When sovereignty is traded for safety, worship has already shifted. Every compromise lights an altar. Every passivity pays tithe. Every silence crowns a king.

The move from this moment forward is not political. It is spiritual. The board still burns, but the fire no longer sits outside you. It lives within. Guard it. Feed it. Carry it home. Remember this: the fire was never meant to warm you. It was meant to send you.

"For the Light shines in the darkness, and the darkness has not overcome it." — John 1:5

94

THE TRIBE OF DAN

A SERPENT IN THE PATH, A MARK ON THE MAP

The Quiet Crown

The quiet crown is not only Denmark's past — it is its prophecy. Scripture spoke long ago of a tribe that would wear silence like a crown and strike nations from the shadows. This is not a fairy tale. Not a saga. It is a warning written in Scripture — about one of Israel's tribes. **The tribe of Dan.**

I am not asking you to accept a bloodline theory. I am naming an archetype. Scripture is a compass for patterns — how deception moves, how power hides, how silence becomes governance. Some will argue names and maps; fine. I am not building this case on etymology. I am tracing a repeating spirit: the serpent's method — quiet, strategic, administrative — wearing virtue as camouflage. Hear this clearly: this is not an accusation against farmers or families, not a charge against ordinary Danes. The prophecy speaks of a spirit, not a people; a pattern, not a passport. It is not blood, but *bureaucracy, that carries the crown.*

I have walked their streets — clean, proud, and silent. I have seen good men trust the machine because it smiles. That is how the serpent survives: not through malice alone, but through well-meaning hearts too weary to resist. The serpent's whisper lives not in the fisherman or the craftsman, but in the polished rooms of ministries and councils — in the comfortable men who mistake consensus for truth and silence for peace. Ordinary souls may still carry courage, but the system they serve has learned to weaponize their decency.

Omitted from the Seal

In Revelation 7, every tribe of Israel is sealed by God — except one. Dan. Not forgotten. Omitted. A warning carved into prophecy.

"Dan shall judge his people, as one of the tribes of Israel. Dan shall be a serpent by the way, an adder in the path, that biteth the horse heels, so that his rider shall fall backward." — Genesis 49:16–17

This was not curse alone; it was diagnosis. Jacob saw what history would confirm: cunning over courage, strategy over surrender. The serpent's brilliance written into Dan's story. Jacob did not crown Dan a lion or a shepherd — he named him serpent. Hidden. Coiled. Striking from the shadows. Toppling riders not through open war, but through deception and reversal.

The Northward Pattern

Scripture does not trace Dan by genealogy alone, but by *movement*. Northward. Coastal. Administrative. Strategic. Dan's inheritance was never brute force; it was *placement* — ports, rivers, routes, names, influence without visibility. The point is not where Dan went, but how the serpent learned to move: quietly, legally, and without revolt. From Israel's northern border to the coasts. From the coasts to the isles. From the isles to the far north. The trail remains. Dan in northern Israel — their first inheritance. Phoenician ports — their ships taking to sea. The Danube — a river bearing the name across Europe.

And at last, Dan-mark — the land of Dan, the mark made crown. To name is to claim. But without covenant, names become warnings, not blessings. *Dan's calling was judgment. Its distortion is false judgment.* What was once meant to discern truth now scripts compromise. Where covenant tribes judged by God's law, Dan judged by consensus. Where others upheld truth, Dan *engineered silence.* That same spirit now animates our age. *Courts replaced by commissions. Justice replaced by frameworks. Prophets replaced by policy papers. Covenant replaced by consensus.* Follow governance, not flags. Power leaves footprints long before it leaves headlines. **Brussels is the courtroom of Dan** — rulings without judges, laws without voters, verdicts without witnesses. **Geneva is its pulpit. New York, its crown.** What was once the serpent's path now writes the world's decrees.

Greenland gave Denmark strategic weight far beyond its size — cover enough for influence without scrutiny. Even the name bears shadow. In the native tongue, *Danmark* — the land of Dan. In English, softened to *Den-mark.* One reveals. The other conceals. This is why Revelation omits Dan from the sealed tribes. The fracture was not forgotten. It was foreseen. The serpent's path winds through rivers, treaties, and signatures — and its quiet crown still gleams today. Scripture does not bind nations to fate; it reveals patterns so they can be broken.

Why It Matters Now

Prophecy does not end with parchment. The spirit moves through time, finding new thrones to inhabit. From Eden's whisper to Midgårdsormen's coil, from Jacob's blessing to John's Revelation — the serpent's shape never changes. It encircles. It suffocates. It deceives. Never roaring — always smiling. Not conquest by fire, but by silence. Not war by sword, but by comfort. Not chains of iron, but chains of policy, paperwork, and peace.

Denmark became the serpent's quiet crown — the model nation of sedation. Its silence rehearsed in Brussels. Its obedience codified in Geneva. Its decrees amplified in New York. The serpent never builds prototypes for their own sake. He builds them to scale. The danger is not Denmark. The danger is imitation. The serpent never needs a throne if he can build a template. What was tested in silence will be enforced in crisis. What was accepted as efficiency will be demanded as obedience. This is why prophecy matters: not to accuse the past, but to interrupt the future.

The blueprint now spreads — through global frameworks, pandemic treaties, and climate decrees — Babylon dressed in blue flags and green ribbons. What begins as "model governance" in the North becomes mandatory governance everywhere else. The serpent does not rest in Copenhagen. Its eyes are on Washington. On the Republic. **On you.**

Personal Witness — What I Saw in the Quiet Crown

I did not learn this pattern in books. I lived inside it. I walked streets so calm they felt holy, yet beneath them hummed a system that punished the soul for breathing differently. I watched friends accept digital chains because they were warm, efficient, polite. I saw truth whispered only in kitchens, never in public — not because of tyranny, but because of training. The serpent does not need fear where he has formed habit. This is why I recognized the pattern in America long before others could see it. I had seen the rehearsal. And I knew the premiere was coming.

Twin Witnesses — Israel and America

Every empire eventually coils around Israel. Yesterday the Nazis called the Jew a parasite and silenced six million voices. After 1945, the "United Nations" made condemning Israel its first obsession. Today, anti-Zionism wears the cloak of compassion while terror hides behind banners of "rights." The serpent hates covenant. It always strikes the people God marked as proof that His promises endure.

Two nations stand as covenant witnesses — one ancient, one new. Israel carries the memory. America carries the mandate. Both are hated for the same reason: they remind the world that freedom is not man's invention but God's gift. That is why every empire coils against Jerusalem and Washington. That is why the serpent hisses loudest at covenant flames that refuse to die.

 Firelight Pause — The Serpent Seen

Why would God omit a tribe unless its covenant carried a shadow? Why does the serpent never roar with chaos but smile with comfort? What happens when a nation bears the name of Dan — yet forgets the name of God? The tribe of Dan is not history. It is prophecy. A serpent in the path. A mark on the map. A warning to the nations. Unless you see it, you will stumble as the rider falls. But if you see it — if you name it — the spell shatters, and the remnant stands. Dan. Danmark. The mark was never hidden; it was always spoken — waiting for you to wake. From "the happiest people on earth" to the serpent rehearsing the Beast. This is not commentary. This is revelation. **This is a line in the sand.**

Prophecy is not prediction. It is pattern revealed. And when the pattern returns, so does the choice. America was not founded on management, but on covenant. Nations fall when vows are forgotten, when tables grow cold, when silence is mistaken for peace. The serpent thrives in broken promises. Christ restores through kept ones. Progress without sovereignty is slavery. Peace without truth is bondage. Safety without freedom is death. **The mark is not tomorrow. The question is now.**

"In returning and rest you shall be saved; in quietness and in trust shall be your strength. But you were unwilling." — Isaiah 30:15

God's warning was never for Israel alone. It was for every generation that trades covenant for control.

 Firelight Pause — The Mark

The serpent's crown was silence. The serpent's path was treaties. But what if the final coil is not only political — but **technological**? What if the mark does not arrive as terror, but as access? Not as chains, but as convenience. Not as force, but as permission. Not imposed in a moment — but trained over time. Not announced — but accepted. **The mark of the Beast.** Not shouted. Not feared. Normalized.

Could it be?

95

AMERICA - BREAK THE CHAINS
WALK OUT OF BABYLON

The serpent's crown has been revealed. The pattern is no longer hidden. Now comes the reckoning—the hour when prophecy meets flesh, when revelation becomes responsibility.

Babylon is collapsing everywhere. But no collapse shakes the world more than the chains fastened around America. For generations, the Beast has tried to bind this nation not with armies, but with guilt, shame, and false history. It could not conquer you with armies. It could not crush you with slavery. So it forged new chains — words, shame, silence. If the Remnant is to walk out of Babylon, America must too. And that means breaking not only the systems, but the spell.

"They have healed the wound of my people lightly, saying, 'Peace, peace,' when there is no peace." — Jeremiah 6:14

The Accusation

America, they've lied to you about yourself. You were the nation that broke the back of slavery — at the cost of blood, brother against brother. Lincoln stood. Union soldiers fell by the hundreds of thousands. That war was not waged to preserve chains but to end them. *Yet the accusation still clings: America the slaver.* Europe points the finger. Denmark hides its sugar blood. Britain polishes its castles. France censors its empire. But none point at themselves. Because the accusation was never about justice — it was about jurisdiction. *If America can be convinced she is evil, she can be managed. If she believes she is cursed, she can be controlled.* Shame is the leash forged by empires that can no longer win wars. They do not need you to be guilty — only to feel guilty. A nation that bows its head will never lift its sword. And America with a lowered head is the dream of every tyrant on earth.

The Forgotten Truth

You were the nation that welcomed the persecuted. The Irish who fled famine dug canals and built New Orleans with their hands. The Italians carved stone, laid brick, raised cities from dust. The Chinese blasted tunnels through mountains and drove the railroads west. The Poles, the Danes, the Norwegians, the Germans — all fleeing a Europe that chewed them up and spat them out — found a new beginning here. **You did not inherit peace. You inherited struggle.** Yes, America betrayed its First Peoples with the Trail of Tears and broken treaties. But here is the truth they won't tell you: today Native Americans serve in the U.S. military at the highest per-capita rate of any group. The same America accused of genocide now sees its First Peoples among the fiercest defenders of its flag. That is not hypocrisy. That is honor.

The Weapon of Shame

So why are you flogged with guilt while Europe dines in castles, lectures you from marble halls, sips wine from lands once tilled by slaves, still ruling colonies, still writing the rules of global commerce? Because **the same hands that once ran empires still run the game.** They could not conquer you with armies. They could not crush you with slavery. So they **weaponized shame.** They forged a whip of words. They named you slaver. They named you guilty. They named you cursed. And with names, they sought to bind you. Chains of iron break in battle. Chains of words slip in quietly — and last longer. This is why they rewrote your history. Not to tell the truth — but to break your spine. A nation convinced it is wicked will not defend itself. A people convinced they are oppressors will surrender their own inheritance. **This is the spell:** Rewrite the story → reshape the soul → remove the will to fight.

They call it education. It is erasure. They call it justice. It is judgment without truth. They call it healing. It is hypnosis.

But here is the truth — America, *you are not the shame. You are the break.* You are the proof that freedom can be forged from persecution. That **strangers from every land can fight under one flag.** That chains can be shattered, and a nation can rise — not perfect, but freer than any in history. *That record stands.* No empire before you ever broke its own chains. Europe points. But their hands are still dirty. Their crowns still gilded with blood. Their colonies still shackled.

Break the Chains

America — break the chains. Not the iron ones. The invisible ones — *guilt, silence, the spell.* The world is not waiting for another empire. It is **waiting for one nation brave enough to stop apologizing for freedom and start defending it again.**

They built an altar of guilt and told you to kneel. Europe hid its chains. Denmark hid its colonies. The elites hid their crimes. And then they told America — bow forever for sins you already broke.

America is the only nation besides Israel founded on covenant instead of conquest. **Israel walked out of Egypt; America walked out of empire.** Israel carried the law; America carried the flame. Both rose not by bloodlines but by belief — not by royalty but by revelation. This is why Babylon hates you. Not because you failed, but because you dared to rise. **A covenant nation cannot be conquered by force — it must be confused.** And so they buried your courage beneath accusations, hoping you would forget your anointing. I say NO. Tear down their altar. Scatter the ashes. Because **guilt is not the gospel. Truth is. And truth doesn't bind.** It breaks chains. Because what guilt cannot cleanse, truth can burn away. **The world does not need your guilt. It needs your fire.**

"The Spirit of the Lord God is upon me; because the Lord hath anointed me to preach good tidings unto the meek; he hath sent me to bind up the broken-hearted, to proclaim liberty to the captives, and the opening of the prison to them that are bound." — Isaiah 61:1

Babylon survives only as long as its citizens stay asleep. Its power is not chains — it is consent. Its currency is not strength — it is sedation. Empires do not fall because people fight them; empires fall because people wake. And here is the deeper truth: The serpent tightens his coils differently around a covenant nation. Denmark surrendered to comfort; America must be conquered by confusion. The stronger the oath, the sharper the warfare. Babylon cannot possess what Christ has sealed — so it must convince the sealed to silence themselves. That is the spell. Break it, and the empire collapses overnight.

The Choice to Leave

Breaking the spell is only the beginning. If you wait for Babylon to give you permission, you will never leave. The Beast does not issue exit visas. **You must walk out.** To stay is slavery — marked, numbered, dependent. You may gain their comforts, but you trade away your soul. To walk out is freedom — but freedom costs. You lose their approval, their applause, their illusions. *The moment you say no to the Beast, you are no longer theirs.* And *that no* is your first step into the Kingdom.

The Exodus

Walking out of Babylon does not begin with packing bags. It begins on your knees. Confess to Christ. Be redeemed. Receive the seal of adoption. That is the true exit visa. Even for those who do not yet believe, the principle is the same: freedom begins when allegiance shifts — when conscience is reclaimed from the system, and truth is placed above permission. Then *dismantle their hold on your life, piece by piece.* Not by a single formula, but by obedience — as God leads each household differently. *Reject their language redefinitions* — call things what they are. *Step away from their false economy* whenever you can — *learn to trade, plant, build, and barter. Unplug from their propaganda* — turn off the feeds that numb and program you. *Root yourself in land, in truth, in God* — anchor in what the Beast cannot counterfeit. This is how the Remnant has always survived. In catacombs, in deserts, in forests, in fields. **They walked out of empire one choice at a time.**

The Freedom

The chains fall the moment you see them as chains. *Babylon thrives on your consent. Withdraw it, and you are free.* The Beast system cannot own a soul that bows only to Christ. You may still live in Babylon's shadow, but you no longer belong to it.

Vision of the Remnant

Outside Babylon's walls, the Remnant gathers. Not in towers, but around tables. Not in palaces, but in fields and firesides. They trade bread, not quotas. They measure wealth in children and covenant, not in scores or ledgers. Their work is stewardship, not slavery. Their songs rise in the night as prayers, not propaganda. This is the life Babylon could never counterfeit. This is the Kingdom rising in shadow, even as empire burns. The Beast chains you to survive its fall. Christ frees you to build what comes after.

🔥 **Firelight Pause — Breaking Babylon's Chains**

The fire still burns. Face the truth:

• When you see America, do you see chains — or the hands that broke them?

• Whose story do you repeat — your fathers', or your enemies'?

• Your ancestors crossed oceans for freedom. Do you now defend the system they fled?

• If you guard the cage they escaped, whose descendant are you?

• If liberty no longer stirs you, why live in the land built for it?

• Where did you trade freedom for comfort — or truth for applause?

• What permissions still own you?

• Do you eat, scroll, medicate, and obey — calling convenience peace?

• Have you mistaken guilt for virtue, or silence for wisdom?

• When you speak to your children, do you give them courage — or chains?

• And what chain could you drop **today** if you dared to name it?

The serpent counts on your silence. Heaven counts on your courage. Choose the fire. Now. Truth does not erase the past — it shatters the spell that traps you inside it. America, you are not cursed. You are called. Not to bow under Babylon's shame — but to rise in fire. Break the chains. Walk out of Babylon. The serpent waits with chains. The Beast whispers with velvet words. But the Remnant walks free — and builds what Babylon can never counterfeit.

WEAR TRUTH LIKE A BADGE

Babylon burns.
The Remnant walks

Now you hold the manual.

PART V

THE FIRELINE - WAR MANUAL

A BLUEPRINT FOR RENEWAL, RESISTANCE, AND REBUILD

THIS IS THE LINE YOU CAN NOT CROSS

96

STATEMENT OF INTENT AND SCOPE

This work is an analysis of language, power, and governance as they operate through law, treaties, and institutions. It does not call for violence, insurrection, or unlawful action of any kind. It advocates lawful civic literacy, constitutional awareness, peaceful scrutiny of public policy, and the moral responsibility of citizens to understand the mechanisms that govern them. All examples discussed are presented for educational and analytical purposes, grounded in publicly available documents and historical record. Any references to "war," "weapons," or "combat" are metaphorical, describing conflicts of ideas, authority, and language—not physical force. The author affirms that truth, transparency, lawful process, and nonviolent civic engagement are the proper means of preserving a free society.

97

THE WEIGHT OF THE TORCH

America was not founded on parchment alone. It was founded in blood, oath, and endurance. Before there was a Constitution, there was an army. Before there was ink, there was sacrifice. In 1775, the Continental Army was formed—more than a decade before the Constitution was ratified in 1789. The Declaration of Independence followed in 1776, seven years before Yorktown and the Treaty of Paris ended the war. **America declared itself before it legally existed.** It was born in fire, tested in war, and only later crowned in law. **This order matters.**

Military law came first—not to rule the nation, but to defend the birth of one. The Articles of War governed soldiers before Congress ever framed civil law. From the beginning, officers did not swear allegiance to a king, a party, or a personality. **They swore an oath to the Republic itself—to defend it against all enemies, foreign and domestic.** That oath has never expired. It was never meant to stand above the Constitution. It was meant to shield it. Continuity of government was embedded from the beginning—not as tyranny, but as covenantal defense, ensuring that sovereignty would endure even when rulers faltered or institutions collapsed. America sealed its covenant in blood before it framed it in ink.

This pattern is not unique. It repeats whenever nations face their testing hour. Covenant precedes structure. Sacrifice precedes order. Endurance precedes renewal. That is why this age cannot be understood as ordinary politics. History calls these moments turnings. Scripture calls them reckonings. When nations reach the end of an age, heaven shifts the board. Ecclesiastes named it plainly: *"For everything there is a season... a time to break down, and a time to build up... a time for war, and a time for peace."* Modern historians describe the final phase of such cycles as a Fourth Turning—a season of crisis when institutions fail and legitimacy fractures. Revelation names the same moment with sharper clarity: the breaking of seals, when death shadows the earth and truth is forced into the open. This is not the end. It is the purge before renewal.

In such seasons, war is never carried by one man alone. It is carried by a people who remember their covenant. Behind every visible leader stand the unseen guardians: veterans with scars no parade can heal, builders who raised families through collapse, watchmen who never left their post when governments broke their word. These are not props for rallies or pawns for parties. They are the remnant in flesh and blood. They were the first remnant in 1775. They are the remnant now.

The battlefield has changed. The oath has not. Where war once raged in trenches, it now moves through treaties, sanctions, algorithms, and screens. The serpent adapts—but so do the warriors. The next front is not fought primarily with rifles, but with truth, restraint, endurance, and courage. Empires fall by debt. Covenants endure by blood. Kings rise and pass. Thrones crack. But the fire outlasts them all. The torch was never ceremonial. It was given to be carried. And now it is in your hands.

You have carried the weight. You have inherited the fire. Now comes the question every generation must answer: **Will you hold it — or will you wield it?**

Truth does not remain abstract for long. It either hardens into habit or fractures into fear. What you have seen cannot be unseen. What you have remembered cannot be returned to silence. Fire that is not used does not stay warm — it goes out. And fire that is used must be shaped, disciplined, and aimed, or it burns its bearer. This is the moment history always narrows to.

Not belief — but obedience.

Not insight — but formation.

From here on, the fire is no longer a warning.

It is a tool.

98

THE FORGE OF RENEWAL
TEMPERED IN FIRE, FORGED FOR LIBERTY

"*I*s not my word like fire, declares the Lord, and like a hammer that breaks the rock in pieces?" — Jeremiah 23:29

The Forge Begins

The trumpet has sounded. Now comes the forging. You've seen fire consume. Now you must feel it shape you. The Reckoning was not the end — it was the hammer striking the anvil. Empires collapse. Covenants crack. Every generation faces the same test: kneel in the ashes, or rise with fire in your hands. This is not reflection. It is resolve. Here you turn from witness to warrior. Collapse is not the grave of a people — it is the furnace of rebirth. The Founders knew it. The prophets knew it. The remnant knows it. You are not called to mourn what is dying. You are called to forge what must rise.

Forge Rules

Break dependency first, because any state that controls your bread eventually controls your voice. Build covenant tables in your home; families who pray and eat together cannot be erased. Defend your local ground — your county, your town, your soil — for the frontline is always smaller than the map suggests. Ignite builders: farmers, craftsmen, teachers, and parents, because the Republic stands only when they stand. Carry memory with discipline, telling the stories they want forgotten and teaching the truths they forbid. Steel is not formed in comfort; it is born in fire. And you — remnant, keeper, builder — are standing inside that forge now. The flame is not only for you. It is for the children who will one day ask what you kept, what you built, and what you dared. Steel is tested in fire. Faith is tested in collapse. Nations are tested in the silence after their towers fall. You are the Remnant. The Keeper. The Builder. The line is drawn. The forge is lit. Do not wait for permission. The world is not waiting for another analyst. It is waiting for a people who remember how to stand when the world kneels. **Tyranny thrives in the apathy between collapse and courage — that thin moment when men stare at the ruins and forget they still have hands.** But you are not a spectator of history. You are its hammer. The moment you rise, the lies tremble. Do not beg for peace. Do not kneel to ashes. Take the hammer. Take the fire. Build what cannot be broken. Keep what cannot be stolen. Guard what cannot be bought. Babylon burns. America can rise — but only if you step across the Fireline. This is your commission. From here on, the War Manual is no longer analysis — it is training. Each chapter is a drill.

"Watch, stand fast in the faith, be brave, be strong." — 1 Corinthians 16:13

Firelight Pause — The Forge Within
- Where has comfort cooled my fire?
- What ashes am I kneeling in instead of rebuilding?
- Who around me is waiting—and who can I ignite?
- What truth or skill must I reheat until it glows?
- What will I build or defend even if the world burns around it?

99

REBUILD THE REPUBLIC

FROM THE FAMILY TABLE
TO THE NATION'S SOUL

Before empires fall by fire, they fall by truth. The hammer breaks stone. The word breaks the lie — the lie that safety is freedom, that comfort is covenant, that the state is father.

"Is not my word like fire, declares the Lord, and like a hammer that breaks the rock in pieces?" — Jeremiah 23:29

Empires do not collapse gently. Their chains are woven into money, food, media, and law. When the system trembles, it drags down everything bound to it. To wait for permission is to remain enslaved. To walk out is to live. Exodus does not begin with bags packed or borders crossed. It begins with a vow: to bend the knee to Christ, not the Beast. Some will arrive here before they know how to name that vow. They will feel it first as conscience — the refusal to lie, the refusal to comply, the refusal to trade truth for comfort. Call it integrity. Call it courage. Call it standing when silence is cheaper. Truth always gathers the honest before it gathers the faithful.

From that vow, unraveling follows — language reclaimed, propaganda rejected, false economies abandoned, and tables rebuilt in covenant and fire. The serpent tightens before it dies. Dependency cannot save you. Comfort was always a cage. Walk out before it falls, or be buried when it breaks. Fire clears the ground. What you build next determines whether the serpent returns.

The First Republic Is Family

The fall never begins in Congress. It begins at the table. After the fire, survival is not enough. Rebuilding begins at the foundation — the family table. From the mother who remembers. From the father who repents and returns. From children who rise with strength because truth was not withheld from them. We ask, *When did the country fall?* The better question is: *Where did the fall begin?* It began in homes where fathers disappeared. In classrooms where God was banished. In pulpits where truth was traded for applause. In kitchens where no one had time to cook, pray, or speak. Empires are not lost first on battlefields. They are lost at tables left empty. The ancient republic is not first a political system. It is a covenant. And the first republic a child will ever know is called **family**. Lose the table, and you lose the Republic. Guard the table, and you guard the nation.

Start Where It Broke

Before you rage at systems, pass bread. Before you march in the streets, look your neighbor in the eye without contempt. Pray before meals. Bless your children. Teach them to plant, mend, speak truth. Show them creation as gift, not commodity. Nations do not rise on policies. They rise on fathers who provide, mothers who guard, children who honor, neighbors who bear burdens, and elders who are not abandoned. If you want the Republic to live, build a table no serpent can silence. Teach one skill this week. Restore one lost ritual. Reconcile one broken relationship.

Rebuilding begins with small disciplines:
- Restore a daily meal.
- Establish a weekly table of prayer and truth.
- Train your children in one skill their school refuses to teach.
- Learn one craft. Plant something. Fix something. Build something.
- Form a small council of families who refuse the serpent's script and guard one another when the cost rises.

Begin rebuilding the Republic where it first broke — at home, in covenant, with courage.

America's Warning

Denmark shows what happens when covenant is traded for comfort. The serpent promises safety, efficiency, and care — and replaces builders with bureaucrats, fathers with systems, conscience with compliance. This is not about flags or parties. It is about structure. Bureaucracy always survives regimes. Paper outlives principles. Treaties burn. Covenant endures. Freedom is not preserved in boardrooms. It is preserved around tables. Sovereignty does not begin in Brussels or Washington. It begins at home. Learn from the tribes whose treaties were broken and yet still fight for the land. Learn from the prophets who called it repairing the breach. Learn from Joshua:

"As for me and my house, we will serve the Lord." — Joshua 24:15

Every covenant begins at the fracture. Every wall is rebuilt stone by stone. This is your wall. This is your watch. Do not wait for Washington. Do not wait for Brussels. Guard your table. If the serpent conquers the table, it conquers the nation. If fathers reclaim the table, nothing can conquer the nation. Revolutions built on anger collapse. Revolutions built on covenant endure. A Republic is not rebuilt by crowds in the streets — but by families who refuse to bow at their own table.

• Where did the first cracks appear — in the nation, or in my own home?

• When truth pressed against my silence, did I speak — or fold?

• What will rebuilding truly cost me — in time, sweat, courage?

• Which discipline must I restore first — prayer, meals, skill, or truth?

• What serpent has crept into my table, and how will I cast it out?

• Who in my home is waiting for me to lead, repent, or return?

• Which neighbor must I face without contempt so the wall can be rebuilt?

• When my children ask what I built while the Republic fractured — what stone, what story, what table will I hand them?

The fire has tested your hands. Now it demands you build. Guard the table like a fortress. Build it like an altar. Keep it like a covenant.

"Unless the Lord builds the house, they labor in vain who build it." — Psalm 127:1

100

THE POWER OF THE POWERLESS
TRUTH AGAINST THE EMPIRE'S SCRIPT

Empires collapse the same way they rise — one obedient citizen at a time. You do not need tanks to hold a people; you only need their silence. Every age has its prophets who refuse to pretend, who choose truth over comfort and witness over fear. When nations forget covenant, God raises voices from prisons instead of parliaments. One of those voices was born behind the Iron Curtain — and his pen cracked an empire.

Václav Havel was no general. No president. No soldier. He was a playwright in Communist Czechoslovakia — a man who wrote words the regime feared more than bullets. He showed us that even without armies, empires collapse when ordinary people stop living by lies. His essay, *The Power of the Powerless,* spread underground like fire. His words sparked what became the Velvet Revolution. Havel proved this: truth, quietly lived, becomes a weapon no state can disarm. You don't need guns to topple an empire. You need the courage to stop pretending. *"Live in truth, and the lie crumbles."* That was his creed. And he lived it — from prisoner to president, from cell to castle — because he refused to kneel to the lie.

His lesson wasn't for Prague alone — it is for any nation where lies demand obedience. **Havel's power was not protest. It was refusal — the first discipline of any free people.**

The serpent doesn't fear your weapons first. It fears your refusal to believe its lies. It feeds on compliance. It survives on your willingness to act like its rules are real. But when enough people stop pretending, its empire falls like ash. Truth lived openly becomes fire in the public square. The same serpent coils here. The same lie demands your silence. The same power waits for your refusal. Havel's witness leaves us no excuse. If truth alone can collapse an empire, then truth armed with fire and steel — **the courage to stand and the discipline to endure —** cannot be stopped.

The First Amendment is not decoration. It is the breath of a free people — the right to speak, print, assemble, worship, dissent, and name reality without permission. **The Second** is not aggression. It is the shield that keeps that breath from being crushed. History is unambiguous: **speech that cannot be defended is tolerated only until it is inconvenient.** Rights that rely on goodwill are revoked by decree — eventually. When the shield is removed, the voice follows. **Keep both.** The powerless are not those without weapons. They are those without the ability to refuse.

"Therefore, having put away falsehood, let each one of you speak the truth with his neighbor." — Ephesians 4:25

 Firelight Pause — Live in Truth
  - Where am I still pretending just to stay safe?
  - What rules do I obey that I know are lies?
  - What truth must I live — even if it costs me everything?
  - When the serpent hisses "silence," will I speak — or bow?
  - **Whose courage waits on my witness?**

101

RECLAIM THE GROUND

THE GROUND YOU IGNORE
IS THE GROUND YOU LOSE

You cannot defend what you do not understand. You cannot rebuild what you never touch. Every empire collapses the same way: the locals stop showing up. The table fills with polished strangers fluent in the language of "sustainability," "growth," and "best practices." Decisions are made quietly. Papers are signed politely. The ground shifts while the people remain distracted. *Every tyranny can also be reversed the same way it begins* — when ordinary men and women show up again. Not with noise, but with knowledge. Not with rage, but with presence. Power does not fear crowds. It fears citizens who understand the terrain. This chapter is not about protest. It is about **re-occupation.**

Know Your Ground

Start with the map under your feet. Who sits on your city council or commission? Who runs your county board? Who funds your sheriff's campaign, your local paper, your state college? Know their names. Read their records. Trace the money behind their smiles. **Global power is exercised locally** — through contracts, zoning, water rights, education grants, emergency authorities, and permits. Most citizens never read those documents. That is how empires move without resistance.

709

Begin a small notebook for your county. A ledger. Give each official a page. Write down: votes, donors, contracts, affiliations. Patterns appear quickly when the ink is your own. This is how blindness ends.

Read What They Hide

Start with what every citizen can access but almost no one reads: the annual county budget, sheriff and judicial campaign-finance reports, school-board minutes, zoning and land-use proposals, water-rights allocations, property-tax rolls, and nonprofit IRS Form 990s. These documents look dull on purpose. That is the camouflage. Budgets reveal priorities. Minutes reveal alliances. Zoning maps reveal who profits. 990s reveal who funds the "community initiatives" shaping your town. These records are not secret. They are hidden in plain sight. Every county is required to publish them. Elites rely on fatigue, not force. Walk through the unguarded gates. **The truth is always in the paper trail.**

The Power Map

Power is not only ballots. It is land, water, bandwidth, food, energy, and permits. The county controls zoning, water, and development. The school board controls curriculum and hiring — the spine of the next generation. The sheriff decides what laws are enforced. Commissioners and judges control budgets, emergencies, and federal money. And the quiet boards — the ones no one watches — bind communities to long contracts with corporations and agencies for decades.

Show Up Where It Counts

Attend the meetings that touch land, schools, water, and money. Read the agendas before you go. Take notes. Ask one clear question. Do not rant. Do not posture. Presence is pressure. Teach one neighbor what you learn. Light spreads when shared. This is how ground is reclaimed — inch by inch, room by room.

When Parties Fail, Citizens Must Vet

Across America, local parties — Republican and Democrat alike — have been quietly captured. Insiders are recycled. Donors steer slates. Endorsements are traded behind closed doors. The grassroots are expected to clap, not question. Many citizens assume the party has done the vetting. Often, no one has. When the party will not vet, the people must. Create parallel vetting. Invite candidates to answer questions in public. Record their answers. Publish them. One room. One evening. One camera. When candidates refuse to appear, the truth reveals itself. Absence is not logistics. **Absence is contempt dressed as professionalism.** A man who will not answer to his neighbors will not serve them. A woman who will not face citizens will not defend them. Publish the invitation. Publish the refusal. **Transparency is not cruelty. It is duty.**

Build the People's Forum

You do not need permission to demand accountability. A library. A church hall. A barn. Any room becomes a fortress of transparency when citizens command it. Ask what the party avoids — donors, conflicts of interest, land ties, outside influence, constitutional understanding, and who truly writes their talking points. **Sunlight is the weapon elites fear most.**

Take the Precincts

Across America, precinct positions sit empty — yet they decide endorsements, delegates, and party direction. Ten committed citizens can change a county. Twenty can change a region. The precinct system was built for neighbors, not donors. When citizens return to it, the balance shifts fast. Read the party bylaws. Use them. Open meetings. Recorded votes. Quorum rules. Conflict disclosures. These rules exist — elites count on you never reading them. One citizen with the rulebook can overturn decisions built on secrecy.

The Weapon They Removed

Long before agencies and prosecutors, free people had a tool the powerful feared: **the grand jury.** Not a trial jury. *An investigative body drawn from ordinary citizens, empowered to subpoena records, compel testimony, and indict without permission from the state.* It did not ask judges what to pursue. It did not wait for politicians to authorize inquiry. It answered to conscience and evidence alone.

In many states, that authority did not vanish overnight. It was narrowed. Citizens were permitted to vote, attend hearings, submit complaints, and petition representatives — but not to compel investigation without permission from within the system itself. Grand juries, where they still exist, may be summoned only at the discretion of judges or prosecutors. Oversight became conditional. Inquiry became optional. **You may vote for who governs you, but you may not investigate them.** This is not tyranny by force, but by design — a structure of managed consent where accountability depends on approval rather than right.

Over time, many states quietly dismantled this power. Some abolished grand juries entirely. Others reduced them to ceremonial tools controlled by prosecutors — the very officials they were meant to watch. The reason is simple. A true grand jury cannot be managed. It bypasses party, bench, and bureaucracy. It investigates upward. **Where grand juries remain active, corruption retreats. Where they vanish, misconduct hides behind procedure.** This is why *resistance is redirected into legislatures and courts* — slow arenas where power dissipates. **The people were never meant to investigate themselves through their rulers.** They were meant to investigate their rulers directly. When a people forget the weapons they once held, they mistake helplessness for normalcy. Reclaiming the ground begins with knowing not only what power exists — but what power was taken away. **Grand juries did not disappear because they were obsolete — they disappeared because they worked.**

Expose the Networks

Influence hides in friendships long before it hides in laws. Follow: Donor lists. Board memberships. Real-estate partnerships. Consultant contracts. When patterns are mapped and shared across churches, farms, and small businesses, dynasties built on silence fracture. Truth moves faster than propaganda when people speak directly to one another.

Build Independent Channels

Many "local" media outlets are not local at all. They are owned by distant corporations with aligned interests and shared scripts. Watch for identical headlines, sudden smears, and stories that vanish without explanation. Build your own channels: Newsletters, County coalitions, Church bulletins, Podcasts. Town halls. A captured media cannot silence a people who speak face to face.

Field Orders

This is not theory. It is stewardship. This week: Attend one meeting. Read one record. Study one official. Ask one question that forces truth into the room. Liberty does not return through rage. It returns through vigilance. To arm the people is to arm minds with truth and hands with lawful work. A Republic is defended not by mobs, but by neighbors who know their ground and guard it in peace. **Read. Verify. Show up. Speak truth.** The ground is reclaimed by those who refuse to abandon it.

Firelight Pause — Reclaim the Ground

- Do I truly know my ground — who governs it, funds it, profits from it?
- Where have I surrendered influence through ignorance or fatigue?
- Who in my county stands for truth — and who only repeats the script?
- What will change when I stop watching and start showing up?
- What ground must I reclaim before the serpent does?

"Know well the condition of your flocks, and give attention to your herds." — Proverbs 27:23

102

THE COVENANT OF THE TABLE
BREAD, WINE, AND FAMILY

Every war for nations begins with a war for the home. Before empires fall by lies, families fall by silence. The family is not an accident of biology. It is the first covenant. The first church. The first nation. That is why the serpent struck it first. Sever man from woman, scatter children from their father, hollow out the hearth — and the land itself withers. You will have citizens, not sons. Consumers, not daughters. Orphans with parents still breathing. **Every empire begins in a house. Every revolution begins at a table. The ground of nations is first the ground of a home.**

Do not think the war for the home ended. It simply learned new language. Divorce courts now stage the same destruction in slower motion — endless hearings, accusations, bureaucracy — until children fracture while parents are turned into enemies. Mothers are forced to fight battles they were never meant to fight alone. Fathers are exiled not by death, but by decree. The pattern repeats everywhere power seeks permanence: remove the father, fragment the mother, process the child.

America has lived this. Welfare policies rewarded absence. Fathers were traded for checks. Courts learned to profit from broken homes. Children grew up staring at emptiness where strength should have stood. The method changes. The target never does. Every empire that intends to last attacks the family first — by policy, by poverty, by ideology, or by decree. Abortion crowned this logic as liberation. The cradle was emptied and called progress. The womb became a battlefield where the victims could not cry out. China's one-child law turned family into arithmetic and erased millions of daughters by order. The Nazis did not only kill — they severed bonds, tore families apart, forced parents to choose which child lived. Every time the state claims it knows better than the parent, that shadow returns.

If the American table falls, the Republic falls with it. No Constitution, no Congress, no court can outlast a people who forget how to bless bread together. What was destroyed by decree must now be rebuilt by hand. This is not nostalgia. This is warfare.

The serpent shattered the hearth. The table must be rebuilt — **fortress, altar, school.** A house without fire is a tomb. Rekindle it. Stoke wood. Light candles. Boil broth. Bake bread. Cook real food. Fast food feeds bodies, not souls. Every homemade meal is rebellion. A table with screens is not a table. It is a feed trough. Guard the table. No phones. No rush. One consecrated meal. Bless aloud. Pray. Speak the names of your children. Tell the stories — how you met, who stood before you, who bled so you could sit there now. Name the dead so they are not forgotten. Memory is a weapon. Time is a battlefield. Cancel what must be canceled. Guard one meal a day, or three a week, or Sunday night. Guard it like a line that must not break. Hospitality is warfare. An empty chair is a wall against despair. Welcome the stranger. Let silence breathe. Let eyes meet again. The serpent will hiss. The screens will call. The schedules will scream. Rebuild the table anyway. Restore covenant, and the land will heal. Lose the table, and the Republic dies without a shot fired.

Drills of the Table

Hold one shared meal with no devices. Tell one story that roots your family. Speak one blessing aloud. Offer one act of forgiveness — small, real, immediate. Attempt one reconciliation. Repeat until peace returns to the room.

For the Broken Families

Not every hearth can be rebuilt whole. The serpent left scars — homes divided, parents estranged, children caught between. And in our time, *that wound is monetized.* Courts profit when mothers and fathers war. Children are processed like files, not raised like souls. Hear this: you are not beyond covenant. Christ restores what the serpent breaks. *Forgive,* or bitterness will raise your children. You share children — that is covenant. Silence the venom. Bless or stay silent. Put the children first. Sit at the same table for an hour. Show them peace is possible. Start small. One meal. One hour. One peace. Choose one topic that builds. Set one rule — no blame, no history-weaponizing. Create one new memory stronger than the old pain. This is how covenant begins again. Rebuild the table, or watch the covenant burn. **Heal the table, and the land heals with it.** Refuse, and Babylon will feast on your children.

"He will turn the hearts of the fathers to their children, and the hearts of the children to their fathers; or else I will come and strike the land with total destruction." — Malachi 4:6

🔥 **Firelight Pause — Guard the Table**
- Who sits at your table — and who has been pushed out?
- Do your children see peace there — or a battlefield?
- What have your words carved into their souls?
- When you leave the room, what story remains?
- Which one meal this week will you guard like a fortress?
- If the table is covenant, what covenant do your meals proclaim?

103

THE SWORD AND THE PEN
TWO WEAPONS, ONE WAR

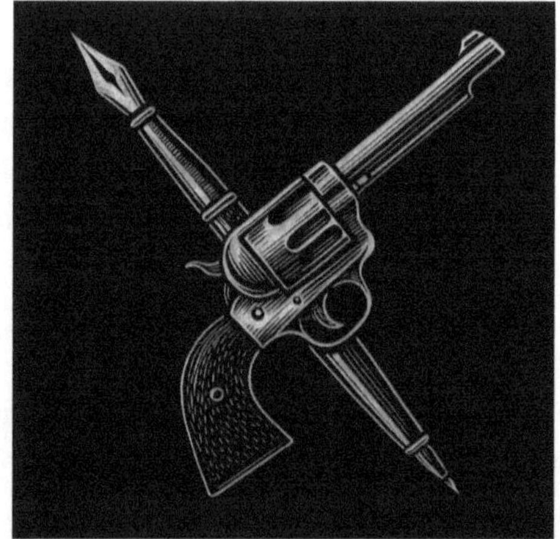

From the table rises the guard. Once the hearth is restored, the gates must be defended. Every covenant needs sentinels — one to feed the flame, another to guard the border. The sword and the pen were forged for that very reason: one keeps the peace of the home; the other secures the freedom of the land.

The forefathers did not write the First and Second Amendments as ornaments. **They wrote them as shields — against kings, against tyrants, against silence.** They knew the sword could win a war, but only the pen could secure a republic. They knew the pen would one day need the shield again. These men had seen the lash, the prison, the gallows. They had seen voices crushed and weapons seized. So they swore covenant with their descendants: **you shall not be disarmed, you shall not be silenced, you shall not kneel again.** That covenant is your inheritance. The enemy has not forgotten it. Neither must you. **The First is the fire. The Second is the steel.** Together they are America's covenant. This is the line in the sand. **Lose the shield, and the fire dies. Lose the fire, and the Republic falls.** That is why they scheme, again and again, to strip you of your arms. Because once the steel is seized, the voice is bound. And *once your voice is bound, you are not free — you are owned.* Better to die fighting on your feet than to live bowed as a slave on your knees. **Lawful defense is covenant; reckless violence is the serpent's trap.** The sword is never for rage — only for protection, only for peace. But this war is not waged only in flesh and blood — it is fought in spirit, in word, in faith.

"For where the Spirit of the Lord is, there is liberty." — 2 Corinthians 3:17

If you surrender your weapons, you surrender your speech. The First dies the moment the Second is betrayed. Look north: Canada bent the knee — pastors chained, bank accounts frozen, protests silenced. Look south and east: Australia became an open-air prison — police batons for walking, helicopters over suburbs, liberty reduced to a permit. This is what happens when covenant is forgotten. This is what happens when people trust the chorus of the blind — media as priest, bureaucrats as prophets, lies polished until they gleam like truth. *Most don't even know the First and Second belong together.* They were taught only half the truth. A crippled story. A censored gospel. But you must remember both — **the fire and the steel, the breath and the shield.** Half-truths build half-men; a Republic that forgets one dies by the other. The Beast knows this — and fears it — for a free man with a voice and a weapon cannot be enslaved.

"Blessed be the Lord my strength, which teacheth my hands to war, and my fingers to fight." — Psalm 144:1

Read from the Constitution and from Scripture — not as a burden, but as orientation. **Know the laws of your state** so you *understand what protects your voice and your defense.* Write truth as a discipline — in journals, letters, or public words — and do not self-censor when conscience speaks. Train your body as you train your mind; strength is stewardship, not vanity. Teach your children both crafts when you can: how to speak with conviction and how to stand with courage. And when the moment comes — because it always does — take truth into the open. **Speak in a room where lies dominate.** Write once where silence ruled. Stand beside someone being targeted for their voice. Show up when your county drafts laws, when your school board censors speech, when your church bends under pressure. You are not required to do everything at once. You are required to **not surrender the ground.** The pen trains the soul. The sword trains the will. Use both as called — quietly at first, openly when required, boldly when the hour demands.

The covenant of fire and steel is not theory. It is not history. It is the front line of your hour. Kings disarm before they silence. Tyrants burn books before they break bodies. *It always begins the same way.* Now the mask has slipped. The world has snapped. The line is drawn. Evil does not only attack with weapons — it strangles language, poisons words, rewrites memory. It censors the cry before it reaches the air. It silences the faithful, hoping silence itself will bury the truth. But the sword of the pen is not silent. It cuts deeper than steel. It unmasks contracts made in shadows, lies paraded as progress, hearts turned to stone. When the lie grows loud enough to drown nations, only truth incarnate can speak above it. Every system eventually reveals its god. Bureaucracy cannot save. Law cannot redeem. Power cannot cleanse itself. When every lesser authority fails, the question is no longer *whether* we serve a king — but *which.*

That is why we need Jesus now more than ever — not as decoration, but as King. His Word does not bend to propaganda. His cross stands when empires fall. So we draw the sword of the pen — not to flatter, not to retreat, but to carve truth back into the land. **Let them ban. Let them censor. Still we speak. Still we write. Still we stand. Silence is surrender. And surrender is not an option.**

The wicked say, "Live by the sword, die by the sword." It is the world's logic — violence begets violence, rebellion ends in ruin. *But the warrior of Christ lives by the Word and never dies — he conquers even in death.* The Word gives life that cannot be taken, and the warrior who fights with truth never truly falls. Wield both. Protect the hearth. Defend the nation. Hesitate, and both will be gone. A nation that keeps its pen but loses its steel becomes a colony. A nation that keeps its steel but loses its truth becomes a tyranny. Only a people who keep both remain free.

"Stand firm then, with the belt of truth buckled around your waist... take the helmet of salvation and the sword of the Spirit, which is the word of God." — *Ephesians 6:14–17*

🔥 **Firelight Pause — Sword and Pen**

The fire asks you:

• Have I guarded both flame and freedom — the truth in my mouth, the steel in my spirit?

• Where have I stayed silent when truth demanded sound?

• Do my words cut clean — or wound in anger?

• Will I lift both at my own table first — to bless my children, to speak what must be said?

• When the hour calls, will I still write, still stand, still speak — no matter who forbids it?

• What witness will remain when my pen and voice fall silent — fear, or fire?

• When the fire fades, will your table still burn with covenant light?

Field Doctrine — Fire and Steel

This war is not fought by impulse. It is fought by restraint, clarity, and lawful strength. The sword is never raised to threaten speech. It exists so speech does not need permission. The pen is never used to provoke chaos. It exists to name reality before chaos arrives. Never separate the two. A people who speak without the will to defend are begging. A people who defend without truth become beasts. Train both.

Rules of Engagement

Truth First, Always.

Speak truth plainly before force is ever considered. Force without truth is rebellion. Truth without courage is performance.

Defense Is Covenant, Not Emotion.

The sword exists to protect life, home, and lawful order — not ego, not anger, not vengeance. Rage is the serpent's bait.

Write Before You Strike.

Document. Record. Publish. Testify. The pen exposes before the sword ever needs to stand. Most tyrannies retreat when the light is steady.

Stand in Law, Not Lawlessness.

Know your rights. Know your limits. Lawful strength is feared because it cannot be criminalized without revealing the tyrant.

Guard the Weak First.

Children. The voiceless. The isolated. The targeted. The sword is judged by who it shields, not who it threatens.

Never Fight Alone.

Lone warriors burn out. Covenants endure. Stand with witnesses. Write with names. Defend with community.

Silence Is the First Defeat.

When speech is surrendered "for peace," peace never follows. Silence is how chains are tested before they are locked.

You are not commanded to conquer. You are commanded to stand. Stand in truth. Stand in restraint. Stand in courage. Stand long enough that lies collapse under their own weight. The pen keeps the record. The sword keeps the space. Lose either — and someone else will decide what you're allowed to say, believe, or defend.

104

THE SERPENT WRITES WITH PENS

THE SPELL OF TREATIES

You've seen how fire and steel guard freedom; now watch **how the serpent turns ink into chains.** The serpent does not always strike with fangs. Sometimes it writes with pens. *Denmark has mastered this sorcery—and it's being exported to America.* A model disguised as mercy, embedded in your own agencies, your own towns. Ask yourself: if treaties signed in silence there become law here, who is really governing your town? Six million people, yet Denmark has sat on the UN Security Council five times. Egypt, with 115 million, has equaled that record. Indonesia, with 286 million, only four. A postage-stamp state treated as an empire. Not by force of arms, but by force of language—by the spell of treaties. Danish diplomats do not leap onto the global stage with bluster; they strategize.

Influence in global governance is not proportional to population; it is proportional to fluency in procedure. When Denmark held its temporary seat on the UN Security Council (2005–2006), its envoys built what scholar Troels Burchall Henningsen called a **general theory of success—a strategy of flexibility, consensus, and linguistic framing.** They learned to steer outcomes without confrontation. Vague priorities gave them narrative room to move.

724

Consensus phrasing let them navigate between power blocs. The result: policies that sounded neutral but carried hidden weight. *"The purpose of strategy,"* Henningsen wrote, *"is ... the art of creating power."* What does that mean in practice? Frameworks instead of swords. Theory becomes treaty. Treaty becomes funding. Funding becomes chains. They do not need to occupy your streets with armies; they occupy your future with acronyms. They never say *sword*—they say *framework*. They never say *fire*—they say *sustainable governance*. They never say *fight*—they say *resilience*. If every word is a chain, what happens when you stop translating their code? **Language became their army.** To defeat it, you must learn its ranks.

Framework: a net wide enough to catch your rights now and stretch later. **Resilience:** obedience dressed as strength—bending, adapting, never resisting. **Sustainable governance:** permanent management of every choice. **Equity:** forced sameness; excellence flattened to flatter weakness. **Inclusivity:** silence conviction; all voices "equal" except the one that dissents. **Stakeholders:** unelected hands pulling the strings. **Policy instruments:** hidden weapons to enforce without consent. **Best practices:** imported blueprints—their model, your chains. **Consensus:** manufactured agreement; debate forbidden. **International obligations:** treaties you never voted for, binding you nonetheless. **Risk management:** fear-governance — control justified by hypothetical danger.

Picture this: a thousand pages of "inclusive frameworks" and "stakeholder resilience" land in Congress. Do they read every page? No. They vote on consensus, not substance. Inside the pages lie the hidden triggers—the clauses to be *activated* later. This is how sovereignty is signed away: not with tanks, but with terms. **Empires no longer send legions. They send language.** The serpent writes in treaties, the dragon signs them, and the Beast enforces them through code and policy. Each document reads like mercy but legislates like chains.

The Paris Agreement bound nations in the name of "climate cooperation." It promised to *strengthen resilience* and created a *technology framework* to *mobilize finance*. Translation: resilience means obedience; technology framework means global control grid; mobilizing finance means redistributing sovereignty through debt and guilt. The climate was never the covenant—control was. Each nation signed not for weather, but for worship, bowing to the altar of "global responsibility." The serpent sells salvation through spreadsheets.

The Sendai Framework preached "investing in disaster risk reduction for resilience." Sounds like safety. Reads like submission. Investing means funding permanent bureaucracy; risk reduction means pre-emptive control; resilience means bending the knee early. The serpent cloaks pre-crime in policy. The framework is a leash.

The Sustainable Development Goals carved resilience into every law. "Inclusive frameworks." "Equitable growth." "Global partnership." Translation: inclusion silences conviction; equity flattens excellence; partnership erases borders. It reads like scripture but functions like software—a code of managed humanity. The serpent wrote commandments for technocrats, not saints.

The Global Compact for Migration bound signatories to "shared responsibility." Borders became experiments, not lines. Orderly migration: engineered transfer. Shared responsibility: dissolved sovereignty. Whole-of-government: total compliance. The flood was foretold—*Revelation 12:15*. Babylon calls it compassion; God calls it conquest.

After COVID, the **WHO treaty crowned health as empire.** "Health security." "Information management." "Equity in access." Translation: surveillance, censorship, rationed obedience. What began as *flatten the curve* ended as *flatten dissent.* The serpent swapped pulpits for dashboards; silence became the new vaccine.

The EU Green Deal promised "just transition" and "sustainable growth." Translation: managed collapse, permanent quota, moralized finance. Carbon became currency; virtue became compliance.

Even *NATO rewrote its creed.* **"Resilience-based defense."** "Societal preparedness." "Whole-of-society approach." Translation: obedience as armor, surveillance as safety, every citizen enlisted in bureaucracy. The sword sheathed in policy. Patriots replaced by protocols.

From climate to combat, the serpent's pen writes the same spell— obedience disguised as order. And in America, these global commitments slip in through the back door: agencies adopt treaty language as regulations — EPA, DOE, DOT, HHS — binding you without a single vote cast in Congress. **A nation that cannot read the treaties it signs is not sovereign — it is colonized by its own signature.**

🔥 **Firelight Pause — Read the Fine Print**
The fire asks you:
- Who writes your laws now — your legislature or their frameworks?
- What "agreement" did you consent to without a vote?
- When safety becomes scripture, will you remember covenant?
- What words have you repeated without realizing whose pen wrote them?
- What treaty, grant, or "initiative" governs your county right now that you've never read?

Your First Drill — Translate the Fog.

Take a treaty. Do not skim. Do not trust. Take a yellow marker and underline the traps. When you see *framework, mark it as a net.* When you see *resilience, mark it as surrender.* When you see *sustainable governance, mark it as permanent control.* When you see *stakeholders, write in the margin: unelected rulers.* Do this once and you will see the pattern. Do it a hundred times and you will never read the world the same way again. This is the discipline of the Remnant—to read what others overlook, to name what others obey, to translate the fog back into fire. And when you've translated the traps, share your notes with one neighbor — light spreads when shared. This is the war you have already entered—not for land alone, but for **language.** Not for votes alone, but for **definitions.**

The serpent's pen writes the cage; the Remnant's pen must write its undoing. Every time they say *framework,* read *weapon.* Every time they say *resilience,* read *obedience.* Take the yellow marker. Underline the traps. Translate their vocabulary into truth. This is your first strike.

The world thought Denmark was harmless. The receipts show otherwise —a nation of six million wielding contracts like chains, hiding gold beneath ice. The coil tightens in Nordic silence—and now the silence is broken. So will you keep calling it harmless, or name it for what it is? The treaties were only the handwriting. The Beast is the hand that moves the pen. The serpent wrote in ink. The Beast signs in blood. And the Remnant will be the hand that breaks the pen.

"They make many promises, take false oaths and make agreements; therefore lawsuits spring up like poisonous weeds in a plowed field." — Hosea 10:4

105

THE OUTSIDER'S EYE

ONLY THE EDGE SEES THE CRACKS

Before the war can be won out there, it must be seen in here. Empires bend nations with treaties — but they first blind men with illusion. If the serpent writes the lie, it is the circle that keeps you inside it. The next battle is not fought with ink or policy. It is fought in vision — who still sees clearly when the world spins? I learned this young. On the playground. Watching the circle from the edge. The kids inside laughed, played, lived in their world. To them, it was whole. To me, it was fractured. I saw the cracks because I was not inside. That circle never disappears. It only grows taller walls. Adults rebuild it online. Curated smiles, shallow applause, a life performed instead of lived. They mistake visibility for meaning and attention for covenant. Politics has its own circle — avatars screaming, insiders spinning in noise, thinking their fury moves the world. It doesn't. It only tightens the circle. Meanwhile, a few step away. They disengage — not from reality, but from the performance. They know the real world is not the circle. It is soil, sweat, children, covenant, fire. They are mocked as "out of touch," yet they are the only ones touching truth.

Safety is the deadliest illusion of all. Inside the circle, everyone believes the map is shared. Everyone assumes silence is agreement. Everyone accepts the script. That is why collapse always blinds the insiders. But the outsider feels the tremor first. He hears the silence beneath the noise. He names the crack before the wall gives way. Weimar insiders trusted the process — until it consumed them. Soviet insiders repeated slogans about "progress" while outsiders like Solzhenitsyn saw the chains in every word. In America today, insiders scroll, comply, consume — convinced this is normal. Outsiders see the cage tightening one acronym at a time. This is the **first fracture of language** — not censorship, but assumption. The belief that everyone sees the same world. The enemy thrives in that blindness. That is why language is the first battlefield. Words are maps. Illusion rewrites the map. And if you assume the map is shared, you will be ambushed.

⚁ **Firelight Pause — The Outsider's Advantage**
   - Where are you standing — inside the circle, or at its edge?
   - What illusions have you mistaken for reality?
   - Whose map are you following — yours, theirs, or Babylon's?
   - What cracks can only be seen from the edge?
   - Will you stay safe in the circle, or step into the fire of truth?

The fire tests everything. Step into it, and illusions burn — but sight returns. The circle may call you bitter or extreme, but only those outside it can see the fracture line running through the age. Jesus Himself lived on the edge of every circle — dining with outcasts, confronting rulers, dividing crowds with truth sharp enough to cut bone from marrow. The circle feeds on your gaze. Every click is consent. Every scroll is surrender. Every silence is a signature on Babylon's script. Break it.

Drill of Clarity — Break the Spell

Delete one app. Log off for seven days. Call someone in person. Step onto soil. Touch wind no algorithm can script. Move your body until the fog lifts. Build something with your hands. Pray aloud where the algorithm cannot hear you. Replace one hour of scrolling with one hour of Scripture, skill, or silence. Write down one illusion you believed — and the truth that replaced it. The circle dies the moment you stop spinning.

The serpent does not fear those inside the circle — only those who step out and start leading others out with them.

"Do not be conformed to this world, but be transformed by the renewal of your mind..." — Romans 12:2

106

THE BATTLEFIELD OF LANGUAGE
WHERE DEFINITIONS DECIDE DESTINY

You've stepped out of the circle. Now the real fight begins. The serpent cannot stand to be seen, so it strikes where sight becomes speech — in language itself. Once you see through illusion, it will try to steal your tongue. It will twist words until truth sounds hateful and lies sound kind. This is how they disarm you — not by taking your weapons, but by corrupting your words. The next battlefield is not land. It is language. And every careless word becomes terrain. Every sentence, a line of defense. Your first discipline is this: **refuse their vocabulary. Call things what they are. Rename the lie the moment you hear it.**

Tactic of Disarmament — The War of Words

Every war begins with words. The battlefield is staged long before a shot is fired, a law is passed, or a people kneel. **Language is the first weapon.** It shapes perception, rewrites memory, and softens resistance. If you control words, you control thought. If you control thought, you control belief. And if you control belief, you control nations. You cannot fight what you cannot name.

This is why *the serpent does not always reach for swords. It reaches for dictionaries. It redefines what you can say until you forget what you mean.* It narrows the range of your speech until it shrinks the range of your mind. They don't need to take your guns if they can disarm you with your own vocabulary.

Life and death are in the power of the tongue. — Proverbs 18:21

Every empire that fell left witnesses. Men who saw the mask of language ripped away — and dared to name it. *Milojević* showed that nations are not built on armies first, but on myths and vocabularies. Words plant roots deeper than laws. *Solzhenitsyn* sat in the gulag and still declared: *"One word of truth outweighs the whole world."* His rebellion was not with rifles but with refusing to speak the lie. *Havel* lived under the gray rot of communism. He wrote of the shopkeeper who hangs a slogan in his window — not because he believes it, but because silence is survival. His creed was simple — live in truth. *One refusal, multiplied, could bring down a wall.* They were not generals or presidents — only watchers of words. And they proved this — **control the dictionary, and you control destiny. Refuse the lie, and you set a people free.**

The Tyrant's Trick

The tyrants of the last century knew it — **redefine freedom, and it becomes slavery. Redefine obedience, and it becomes virtue. Redefine lies, and they become "facts."** Yesterday it was propaganda posters, party decrees, and red pens slashing books. Today it is cleaner — coded into the machine. **They shadow-ban voices until they vanish.** They throttle reach so truth whispers while lies scream. They slap **"fact-check" labels on dissent.** They rewrite definitions online and bury history under algorithmic silence. It feels like freedom because no one kicks down your door. But the outcome is the same as Stalin's censor with a knife - you are speaking inside their cage. Same trick. Different name. New technology. Babylon no longer burns the books. It buries them.

The Gospel of Chains

The tyrants always preached first. *Lenin* promised "Peace, Land, and Bread." It delivered famine, gulags, and war. *Marx* cried "Workers of the world, unite!" It birthed class war — neighbor against neighbor, son against father. *Hitler* thundered "Ein Volk, ein Reich, ein Führer" — one people, one empire, one leader — unity twisted into dictatorship. And above the camps they hung the words "Arbeit macht frei" — work will set you free — *when work ended only in ash.* **The formula never changed — inversion as propaganda.** Promise salvation, deliver chains. Today's globalists know the same trick. *The EU preaches "unity" while enforcing conformity. The UN whispers of "sustainable development" while tightening the net of one world order.* **They drill slogans until chains sound like freedom, tolerance sounds like truth, and safety sounds like life.**

You cannot fight shadows with emotion — only with definition. The serpent's power lives in inversion: turning virtue into vice, and vice into virtue, until the world forgets which is which. **To break the spell, you must learn to read its language.** Every slogan hides a doctrine. Every doctrine hides a chain. Before the drills, take a notebook. Write their word on the left — and the real meaning on the right. Train yourself to translate instantly.

Drills — Round One: Words of Control

Each word is a weapon. Learn to see the inversion.

Safety.

Their definition: surrender risk, surrender freedom, and we will protect you. *If you accept it:* fear masquerades as wisdom; you call your cage a shield. *The result:* slavery. Tyrants always begin with "protection." *Reframed:* true safety is courage and covenant, not compliance.

Misinformation. *Their definition:* anything that challenges the approved story. *If you accept it:* you hand your discernment to "fact-checkers" and fear your own questions. *The result:* slavery. A people who accept only the official narrative will never see the truth behind the curtain. *Reframed:* misinformation is deliberate deceit; disagreement is the engine of truth.

Equality. *Their definition:* sameness for all. If you accept it: you fear greatness, silence excellence, and kneel so no one feels small. *The result:* slavery. Nations that confuse equality with justice cut down their strongest and still end up ruled by elites. *Reframed:* true equality is dignity before God, not sameness before men.

Tolerance. *Their definition:* you must accept everything, question nothing. *If you accept it:* you mistake silence for kindness, and let corruption spread unchecked. *The result:* slavery. *Reframed:* true tolerance respects people, but false tolerance excuses lies. Conviction is not hate — it is the guardrail of truth.

Progress. *Their definition:* whatever they say is next. *If you accept it:* you forget roots, memory, and covenant. *The result:* slavery. *Reframed:* progress is not erasing the past, but carrying truth forward. Without roots, every step forward is a stumble into the abyss.

Drills — Round Two: Words of Shame and Strength

Science. *Their definition*: absolute, unquestionable decree. *If you accept it*: you bow to technocrats. *The result*: slavery — "experts" as priests, decree as dogma. *Reframed*: science is discovery, not decree. Real science doubts, tests, and questions. When doubt is forbidden, science has already died.

Guilt. *Their definition*: you inherit crimes you never committed. *If you accept it*: you walk bent, silenced by shame. *The result*: slavery — a man chained to inherited guilt can never stand free. *Reframed*: guilt belongs only where there is sin. Repentance is personal, not collective. Your life is not collateral for another's past.

White Privilege. *Their definition*: your skin is a debt. *If you accept it:* you believe your existence is a crime. *The result*: fear — identity weaponized as chain. *Reframed:* worth is not pigment. Worth is fire, faith, and the work of your hands.

Oppressor. *Their definition*: anyone strong who resists the script of victimhood. *If you accept it*: you kneel so strength looks like tyranny. *The result*: slavery — the strong shamed, the weak enthroned. *Reframed*: the oppressor is not the one who guards truth, land, and family. The oppressor is the one who strips them away.

The Tongue - First Battlefield

If every war begins with words, then every battle is fought first in your mouth, your mind, your heart. The tongue is never neutral. It blesses or it curses. It builds covenants or it breaks them. It forges freedom or it fastens chains. **What you repeat becomes your reality. What you accept becomes your cage. What you speak becomes your weapon.** Life and death are not only in bullets or ballots. *They are in the tongue.*

🔥 **Firelight Pause — Read the Language of Chains**

The serpent writes in treaties and whispers in words — binding the mind before the hand.

- Who writes your laws now — your legislature, or their frameworks?
- What agreements did you "consent" to without a vote?
- When safety becomes scripture, will you remember covenant?
- Which words have you repeated without question?
- Which chains have you worn because they came wrapped in virtue?
- Whose dictionary are you living inside — yours, or theirs?

The serpent's first weapon was a twisted question: *"Did God really say?"* The tyrant's first command is never march — it is repeat after me. **You are not powerless.** Every time you refuse their script, every time you reclaim a word, every time you speak truth without apology — *you strike back.* Words are not neutral. They are fire. They burn chains or they forge them. *Which will your tongue build?* End each day by correcting one word you misused — and reclaiming one word they stole. This is how the remnant sharpens its tongue into a weapon again. The serpent conquers no nation by force. It conquers by vocabulary. **Lose the language, and you lose the land.** Guard your tongue, and you guard your future. **The first weapon they aim for is not your gun — it is your dictionary.**

You've seen how they twist language — now watch the lie turn to law. The serpent's whispers calcify into code; words harden into rule. What was once spoken in secret, you now live under in silence. A nation's collapse begins the moment its people borrow the tyrant's vocabulary. A nation's resurrection begins the moment its people reclaim God's.

"Let your 'Yes' be Yes, and your 'No,' No; anything more than this comes from the evil one." — Matthew 5:37

107

THE HIDDEN ORDER OF WORDS
THE REMNANT'S DECODING KEY

You've seen how laws harden the lie — now look deeper, where law begins. Before a tyrant rules a nation, he rewrites the heart. Before the serpent governs the world, it governs your words. *Every empire is born twice: first in language, then in law.* The Beast writes constitutions for nations; Babylon writes them in souls. What you are about to read is not about their system — it's about yours. The battlefield is now inside you. The war has entered your hierarchy.

The Hierarchy of Words - The Invisible Constitution of Your Life

Every person. Every culture. Every nation. All carry a hidden hierarchy of words. That order decides everything. *This is more than language —it is belief.* The words you place highest reveal what you worship, what you fear, what you will trade away when the pressure comes. Your hierarchy of words is the invisible constitution of your life. It governs your choices before you ever make them.

If comfort sits above truth, you trade fire for sedation. If fear sits above freedom, you bow to lies. If tolerance sits above conviction, rot spreads in the name of peace. If safety sits above courage, you accept chains and call them protection. If equity sits above excellence, you flatten the strong and end in mediocrity. If progress sits above principle, you cheer while your foundation is erased. But if truth sits at the top, you cannot be controlled — and if Christ, the Living Word, is not above truth itself, something else will own you. Words are not decoration; they are architects. They shape how you see, what you believe, and how you act. Every ranked word becomes either a chain or a weapon — and you forged it. Every order you accept writes your response before you move. This is how they conquer without a shot — they reorder your words. **Once you adopt their vocabulary, your reactions are already scripted.**

The Algorithm That Reads Your Soul

Every click, search, and phrase you type becomes data. The machine listens. It maps your fears, your loyalties, your desires. It doesn't guess who you are—it calculates it. You are profiled by probability, scored by obedience, and nudged by code. The serpent no longer needs to change your words; it predicts them. Every "recommended" video, every auto-complete suggestion, every tailored feed is a mirror of your hierarchy of words. It learns what you love, what you fear, what you will defend—and what you will trade away for comfort. The algorithm is not predicting your future. It is disciplining you into one.

The Drill Begins — Rewrite Your Order

Do not skim this. Read it once for the truth. Then return and work the drills. Take one word a week. Slow down. This is not busywork — it is re-training your soul. Rushing keeps Babylon's order in place; slowing down lets you rewrite it. Now comes the test. One word placed above another changes everything — how you live, how you bow, how you rise. The order reveals the master. The question is no longer if you have a hierarchy — but who built it.

Safety vs. Freedom

If safety is placed above freedom, you will lock yourself in a cage and call it protection; if freedom is placed above safety, you will take risks and live like a sovereign being. Which one rules you?

Fear vs. Truth

If fear is placed above truth, you will kneel to lies and obey whoever shouts the loudest; if truth is placed above fear, you will walk through fire rather than bow to deception. Which one rules you?

Progress vs. Principle

If progress is placed above principle, you will cheer while your foundations are erased; if principle is placed above progress, you will measure every step against what endures. Which one rules you?

Tolerance vs. Conviction

If tolerance is placed above conviction, you will let rot spread in the name of peace; if conviction is placed above tolerance, you will guard your soul even when it offends. Which one rules you?

Guilt vs. Legacy

If guilt is placed above legacy, you will bend under the past, never building the future; if legacy is placed above guilt, you will honor the past without being chained by it. Which one rules you?

The Choice

This is no game. **Your hierarchy will either enslave you — or set you free.** Order your words, and you order your destiny.

Your Turn — The Hierarchy Check

Write it down. Don't skim. Ink forces truth. Name the duel: two words are already fighting for dominance in your life — Safety vs. Freedom, Comfort vs. Truth, or something else. Write them. Then rank them. Which one sits higher? Which one rules your choices before you even speak? Put them in order: one, two. Now trace it forward — if the order stays the same, where does it lead? What will you give up, what will you obey, what cage will you accept? Write the outcome plainly. Then flip it. Reverse the order. What happens if freedom outranks safety, if truth outweighs comfort? Spell that out. Then choose. Which word will you crown? Which one will bend the knee?

Every word you accept becomes either a chain or a weapon. Empires conquer by reshaping language until your own tongue enforces their rule. Fight back: seize your words, strip the lies, rename in truth, wield them like fire. Recheck often. Hierarchies drift. If you don't guard your vocabulary daily, Babylon will rebuild it for you.

Worked Example — Safety

Start with the word itself: *safety*. Now strip it open. Their definition: safety means surrender — give up risk, give up freedom, and "we" will protect you. Your definition: safety is not the absence of risk. True safety is courage, faith, and strength. Trace the belief. If you accept theirs, fear masquerades as wisdom and you'll call your cage a shield. If you accept yours, you stand free — even in danger — because you refuse to kneel. Test the order. If safety sits above freedom, you will lock yourself in a cage and call it protection. If freedom sits above safety, you will take risks — and live like a sovereign being. Finally, reframe it in fire: safety is not granted by government; it is defended by free men and women, bound in covenant.

Worked Example — Tolerance

Start with the word: *tolerance*. The badge they force you to wear. Now decode it. Their definition: tolerance means silence — you must applaud what you don't believe or be cast out. Claim it back. Your definition: tolerance is coexistence without surrender; conviction is the guardrail of the soul. Trace the belief. If you accept theirs, you will betray conviction for applause and let rot spread in the name of peace. If you accept yours, you guard your soul even when it offends. Test the order. If tolerance sits above conviction, rot spreads in the name of peace. If conviction sits above tolerance, truth stands firm. Reframe it in fire: peace without truth is counterfeit; conviction is love armed with courage.

Worked Example — Progress

Start with the word: *progress*. Now decode it. Their definition: progress means erasing what came before — tearing down statues, traditions, foundations. Claim it back. Your definition: progress is building forward on truth, honor, and legacy. Trace the belief. If you accept theirs, you will cheer while your roots are ripped out. If you accept yours, you measure every step against what endures. Test the order. If progress sits above principle, you will applaud your own erasure. If principle sits above progress, you will keep your foundation while you rise. Reframe it in fire: progress without roots is collapse; progress anchored in principle is destiny. You now hold the sword. The hierarchy is no longer abstract — it is inside you. Re-forge it, and you cannot be enslaved.

 Firelight Pause — The Order You Serve
- Which word rules you—truth or comfort?
- Which command shapes you—freedom or fear?
- Which demand do you kneel to—principle or progress?
- Under pressure, which word do you sacrifice first?
- Who set your order—Christ, or the system that feeds on your fear?

108

THE ORDERS IN FLESH AND BLOOD
WHERE THEORY ENDS AND TRUTH WALKS

Theory hides. Behavior reveals. You learned the hierarchy of words — now watch it march. Comfort becomes silence. Fear becomes obedience. Truth becomes exile. Courage becomes war. Under pressure, masks fall; a man's order erupts in choices, loyalties, surrender or stand. **Every pressure test exposes the hierarchy inside.** These are not abstractions — they have faces. You've seen the American bent by comfort, the elite drunk on power, the globalist scripting obedience, the remnant guarding covenant. You've seen the molded student, the blue-haired zealot, the indifferent who think neutrality is safety. Call them archetypes, masks, or warnings — but know this: **they are not symbols. They are the battlefield.** Theory ends here. Flesh begins. Belief builds behavior, and the order inside a man decides the fate of a nation.

"You will recognize them by their fruits." — Matthew 7:16

Here's how it looks in flesh and blood.

Meet Maria — watch how the trap works.

Maria's Order: Comfort → Safety → Truth → Freedom → Conviction.

Comfort first. She avoids hard conversations. She scrolls, she shops, she numbs. Fire never touches her. **Safety second — which means obedience first.** She masks when told, complies when ordered, never asks why. Truth sits beneath both. She trades it away anytime it threatens comfort or safety. Freedom lower still. She hands it over with a shrug — after all, she's still "comfortable." Conviction last. She won't fight. Not for herself. Not for anyone. **Maria thinks she's free — but her hierarchy already enslaved her.** She is docile. Predictable. The perfect citizen for Babylon.

This is David's reality. Watch the difference.

David's Order: Truth → Freedom → Conviction → Courage → Comfort.

Truth first. He refuses to repeat lies. He loses friends, jobs, approval — but keeps his fire. **Freedom second.** He won't hand it over. Not for safety. Not for applause. Not for anything. Conviction third. He speaks when silence is demanded, stands when kneeling would be easier. Courage fourth. He faces fear head-on. Risks, bleeds, endures — because chains are worse. Comfort last. He enjoys it when it comes, but never bows to it. Comfort is reward, not master. **David cannot be scripted. Cannot be bought. Cannot be broken.** His order makes him dangerous to Babylon. That is the difference. Maria's order creates slaves. David's order forges warriors.

Which one looks more like yours? Don't rush past the question. Your hierarchy is already training you — for bondage or for war.

The Average American Today (Sedated)

Comfort first. Safety second. **Tolerance and success stacked above truth.** Freedom buried. Conviction last. At first glance harmless — "normal." But watch the pattern in motion. They obey quietly. They work, consume, post, sleep. Discomfort avoided. Conflict feared. Responsibility outsourced. They chant slogans but never fight. They are "good citizens," already conquered. *History is blunt:* Rome pacified its crowds with bread and circus. Weimar's middle class kept their heads down while inflation gutted them. Silence paved the road every tyrant walked. Today sedation comes in cleaner wrappers — screens for the mind, delivery for the body, dopamine feeds for the soul. Different packaging. Same captivity. They scroll TikTok while the house burns. They avoid conflict, comply on command, call sedation "self-care," confuse silence with virtue and comfort with peace. They wave flags on holidays but do not know the oath behind them. **They speak the language of freedom without the life that proves it.**

The Elites' Code (The Engineers of Babylon)

Power first. Control next. Profit engineered, image curated, "safety" manufactured — for them, never you. Truth only when useful. Freedom never. They play 5D chess while the world plays checkers — staging collapse, then selling themselves as the cure. *History echoes.* In Babylon, priests enforced empire through ritual. In medieval Europe, kings hid behind church hierarchy — piety as camouflage, control as sacrament. Today they see no nations, only markets; no souls, only data; not corruption but "ordination." Think tanks, Davos panels, hedge funds, media empires all whisper the same creed: power first, freedom last. Watch them: Davos. WEF. Silicon Valley bunkers. Hedge-fund dinners with $10,000 wine. Private jets circling the globe while they tell you to stop flying. Wagyu steaks while you're told to eat bugs. Mansions lit like palaces while your mortgage drowns. They flaunt contempt — mock you on late-night TV, preach equity from private islands, regulate with one hand while selling your future with the other. They don't just profit from collapse — they manufacture it, monetize it, and sanctify themselves in the process. Harmless to themselves. **Fatal to you.**

The Globalists (*The Enforcers*)

Not kings — priests of the machine. They don't invent the lie; they administer it. They don't rule; they execute.Bureaucrats. Technocrats. Administrators. "Experts." A class of clerks convinced they're saviors. Compliance is their creed. Image their sacrament. Power their borrowed halo. Fear disguised as safety. Equity disguised as profit. Truth isn't sought — it's managed, pruned, rewritten. Freedom isn't trusted — it's quarantined. Faith isn't denied — it's replaced: by technocracy, climate liturgies, and curated idols of self. They build cages and call them "safe zones." They enforce treaties and call it "progress." They craft slogans, censor dissent, award themselves medals. They confuse obedience with compassion and control with virtue — convinced they are not rebuilding Babylon but "improving" humanity. They are not masters — they are the engineer caste of empire. And history proves this: **managers become more brutal than kings.**

History echoes. In 1930s Germany, it wasn't only Hitler. It was the Brownshirts — neighbors, students, clerks — who smashed windows and policed words. Bureaucrats in gray rooms fed the camps with paperwork. "Functionaries" became executioners. In Stalin's USSR, millions vanished not by Stalin's hand, but by apparatchiks with pens who rewrote textbooks and erased names. Compliance — not conviction — kept the machine humming. In Mao's China, the Red Guards — teenagers with slogans for souls — destroyed shrines, humiliated teachers, denounced parents. *Today:* UN panels. EU commissions. NGO offices. Speech-coders in Silicon Valley. They draft treaties no nation voted for. They shame governments with "climate compacts." They wave flags — rainbow, Ukraine, Palestine — every banner but their own. They are not generals. They are managers. And **managers with pens kill nations faster than soldiers with guns.**

The Remnant's Hierarchy (The Guardians)

Faith first — a covenant no power can buy. Family next — the root from which nations rise. Freedom after that — God-given, never state-granted. Then truth — the fire that unmasks the lie. Then conviction — the spine of the warrior. Then courage — conviction made flesh. Then legacy — what endures beyond your bones. Comfort last, always last — servant, never master. This order forges warriors, not workers; households, not hives; nations, not markets. With faith at the top, nothing can claim you. This is the hierarchy of fire — unbending, unbought, unbroken. They do not seek dominion; they seek to keep the world free of deceit and pass truth on uncorrupted. *History* remembers them: the catacomb church, the Founders signing away their lives, the underground presses smuggling truth in ink. Outnumbered, ignored, yet always the seed of renewal. Today they gather in house churches, in veterans who still salute, in parents who defy school boards. They don't trend. They anchor. They guard. They raise. **Few — but enough.**

The Molded Student (The Prototype)

Still pliable, half-asleep — clay waiting for a stamp. They prize belonging over truth, image over conviction, comfort over courage. Safety rules them; freedom buried; faith forgotten. They graduate paper-smart and soul-shallow — perfect recruits for Babylon, trained in one ritual: repeat, comply, never question. Promised enlightenment, sold employment, handed a debt-shaped leash — the parchment became the chain. Every empire raised its scribes: Komsomol youth, Hitlerjugend, Mao's Red Guards — drilled not to think but to memorize, chant, obey. Today they fill lecture halls, laptops plastered with slogans, absorbing "equity" scripts without resistance. They trust the syllabus more than their instincts, craving grades and belonging more than truth. When the bill comes due, they march into corporate cubicles calling it "freedom," paying interest on their own indoctrination. Fear of isolation makes them trade discernment for approval — polite, pliable, programmable. Babylon calls them educated. Heaven calls them unformed. Until they shatter the stamp, **they remain property — not people.**

The Blue-Hair Brigade (The Zealot)

No longer clay — now weaponized. A slogan with legs. Identity for armor; victimhood for power. Tolerance only for the tribe; image over reality; compliance over truth. "**My truth**" as shield and spear. Freedom feared. Faith replaced by ideology. Shock troops of globalism — not thinkers but amplifiers, not builders but arsonists — useful until the regime is done with them. They were not born enraged; they were engineered — wounds harvested, pain weaponized, empathy inverted until compassion became control. *History echoes*: Brownshirts and Red Guards — statues smashed, books burned, teachers dragged into mobs, language policed with fists and fire. Always loud. Always righteous. Always discarded. Rage dressed as virtue. Forged in cultural labs — universities, media, algorithms — then released as moral crusaders. Today: marches where speech is "violence," censorship is "safety," TikTok gender doctrines preached as revelation, campuses purging professors for "harmful" words. They cancel, shout, burn — not seeking truth but submission. **Disposable yet dangerous, torching everything until only their own reflection remains.**

The Indifferent (The Neutral Ground)

Not rebels. Not zealots. Just drifting. Comfort first. Routine next. Safety always. Tolerance without truth. Image without substance. Freedom surrendered quietly. Conviction dim. Faith optional. They don't scream or march or build — they drift. And in drifting, they hand the field to whoever screams loudest. They confuse peace with silence and silence with virtue. They call themselves "balanced," but balance without truth is apathy wearing a mask. Calm is their idol; as long as nothing burns, they believe everything is fine. *History echoes*: the "good Germans," the Soviet middle class, the French bourgeois — neutrality saved none of them. Silence isn't safety; silence is surrender. Today: Netflix sedation, routines on autopilot, headlines skimmed and forgotten, patriotism reduced to décor. They crave "normal," but normal is already gone. They neither build nor defend. They drift. "I'm staying out of it," they say — not knowing that *out of it* is exactly where tyranny grows. **Indifference doesn't preserve peace — it buries it.**

The Sedated Citizen (The Numbed)

Comfort. Escape. Safety. Pleasure. Routine. Truth buried, freedom forgotten, conviction mocked, faith erased. Still breathing, still numbing, still forgetting. They don't revolt or rise — they drift into smoke, screens, and bottles. Highs blur into lows. Vision traded for vapor. Fire traded for fog. Harmless — hollow. They aren't pursuing joy; they're outrunning pain. The system shattered purpose, then sold pleasure as medicine. They think they're healing; they're only hiding. *History echoes*: Rome drugged by bread and circus; China drowned in opium; Britain dulled by gin. Today sedation is polished — dispensaries on corners, SSRIs in cabinets, vapes in every hand. They line up for weed while freedoms are stripped, call it "medicine" when it's management. Scroll high, laugh high, sleep high, repeat. Numb anxiety, wonder why nothing changes. Haze mistaken for peace. They swear they're free — while their fire is rented out. Not self-care — self-erasure. Every high rehearses surrender. Every cloud hides apathy. You don't need to cage the numbed — they never leave the couch.

Before You Read On

What you just saw are not characters. They are archetypes — patterns burned into the soul. They may look like your neighbor, your professor, the stranger on the street — and if you're honest, one may look like you. Don't read this to sneer; read it to measure. This is not entertainment but an X-ray of the spirit — a diagnostic of who you've become and what order rules your life. These hierarchies shape people and nations. See them clearly and you'll understand why America bends and freedom falters. Use this as a weapon. Test yourself, your family, the slogans drilled into you at school, church, work. If you don't define the order, others will — and you won't notice the chains until the lock clicks. Freedom is not theory; it is air. Either your children breathe it or they choke without it. What follows is the dividing line — slaves or sovereigns, conquered or remnant, lie or free. Choose your order before someone else does.

How to Fight Back

When professors, bosses, or "experts" weaponize words, don't step into their arena. Don't echo their code. Don't swallow their definitions. *That's how they win.*

First, decode. Listen for the loaded word — "equity," "safety," "justice," "inclusion." Don't react. Just note it. Ask: *what definition are they smuggling in? Discernment is the first defense.* **Then, refuse their frame.** If they say "safety," don't parrot "safety." Say "freedom." If they preach "equity," demand "excellence." Never fight inside their dictionary. *Change the word — change the battlefield.* **Ask questions, not permission.** Babylon fears the honest question more than the loud protest. "What do you mean by that word?" "Who decided that definition?" "If it's true, why does history say the opposite?" *Questions tear off masks faster than shouting.* **Anchor in your own order.** If you rank truth above comfort, freedom above fear, conviction above tolerance — their words can't chain you. They bounce. You don't bow, because you already know who rules you. *The man who knows his order cannot be owned.* A man who knows his hierarchy cannot be captured by theirs. **Build fire with others.** Find one who won't kneel. Whisper truth if you must. Babylon isolates to break you. But once you know you're not alone, you become unbreakable. *The remnant multiplies in silence before it roars.* **Remember this** - their power lives in your consent to their vocabulary. The moment you refuse, the spell cracks. When enough refuse, Babylon falls. **Language was their weapon. Now it's yours.**

You've learned to read their playbook. Now it's time to write your own. This is the part most skip — the drills. But war is not won by awareness alone. It's won by repetition, by retraining the reflex.

Exercise: Reclaim Your Vocabulary

The goal is simple — burn out implanted definitions. Forge your own. Words are weapons. Use them, or be used. **Start by picking your five.** Choose the five words that steer your week — the Core Five, or others that hold sway over you. **Write their current definitions.** One sentence each, straight from your own mouth. No Googling. *What do you mean when you say it?* **Spot the implant.** Where did you learn that definition? The newsroom? The classroom? HR training? Church? Family? *Circle the source that profits if you stay compliant.*

Trace the behavior. For each word, name one action you took this month because of that definition — masking in silence "for safety," nodding along "for tolerance." **Forge the new definition.** Rewrite each word in fire language — truth first, responsibility central, courage assumed. **Install a counter-phrase.** A mantra of 5–7 words that rises when the old trigger hits. – Safety → "Protection needs truth, not permission." – Freedom → "Duty first; then rights have weight." **Field-test it for 24 hours.** Catch yourself using one of the words. Pause. Swap in your forged definition and mantra. Note the shift. **Run a conversation drill.** Take one hot topic, reframe it with your forged words, and speak it to a friend. If they attack the word, defend the definition — calm, precise, steady. **Apply the policy sniff test.** Choose one slogan or policy this week. Ask: which definition is assumed? Who gains power? What truth is silenced? What duty erased? **Draw the commitment line.** Sign and date it: I will not outsource my vocabulary. My words serve truth. **Forge together.** Don't build this vocabulary alone. Share it with friends, family, colleagues who still value truth. Compare definitions. Test mantras. Build a living dictionary of fire. A shared vocabulary of courage is a fortress against every lie.

The fire asks you:

• Which word has dominated your decisions this year — comfort, fear, safety, equity, progress, or image?

• Who wrote the meaning you've been living by — your Maker, or the machine?

• Which definitions have slipped into your mouth as chains disguised as virtue?

• If your hierarchy is your battlefield map, have you been fighting on the wrong side without knowing it?

• When pressure came, which word did you sacrifice first — truth, freedom, conviction, or courage?

• And most urgently: if you do not defend your hierarchy daily, who will rebuild it for you?

The Sword in Your Hands

Language is not a mirror. It is a weapon. Every word carries power. Every definition commands allegiance. Whoever defines the words controls the war. You've seen how language becomes chains and hierarchies become behavior. That was training. This is deployment. Out there, the world is no longer pretending. Empires don't just lie — they fracture. The cracks are open now. Neutral ground is gone. Reclaim the words or be ruled by them. Order them or be ordered. Wield them — or wear the chains they forge. This is your sword. This is your fire. What you speak next will either reinforce the cage — or break it. There is no third option.

You've taken back the keys — now see the next lock

109

THE WEAPON OF BUNDLED WORDS
CHAINS HIDDEN IN PHRASES

Treaties are written in fog. But once the ink dries in Brussels or New York, the fog condenses into chains you can feel. Clauses become acronyms. Consensus becomes slogans. Treaties become mantras — repeated until resistance feels impossible. If you control the definition, you control the battlefield. If they control the bundle, they control you.

At first, they stole single words. *Safety. Freedom. Progress.* Now they braid them together: **Diversity, Equity, Inclusivity. Environmental, Social, Governance. Net Zero.** Bundles engineered to bypass thought and demand obedience.
— Say no to *diversity* and you sound cruel.
— Say no to *equity* and you sound unjust.
— Say no to *inclusivity* and you sound hateful.

Stack them together — and you are crushed under three accusations at once. **This is the new weapon: bundled words.** A single word can wound, but a bundle can bind. **Bundled words don't just disarm individuals — they disarm nations.** Once named, even their strongest spells begin to break.

The formula is simple — they don't stop at one word. They braid three or four together so resistance looks impossible. Who dares say no to *"Diversity, Equity, Inclusivity"*? The more words, the heavier the chain. On the surface, the meaning looks harmless: diversity means difference, equity means fairness, inclusivity means acceptance. But hidden in the bundle lies the trap — diversity becomes hiring by category, not competence. Equity becomes grievance hierarchy. Inclusivity becomes compelled speech and censored thought. The words change. The goal does not: **obedience.** Once braided, the bundle becomes policy. Corporations adopt DEI or lose funding. Schools tie grants to ideological compliance. Governments use it as a litmus test for legitimacy. Media brand dissenters as "extremists" or "haters." The bundle hardens into law — and law becomes power. **That is how language becomes legislation without a vote.**

Breaking the Spell

A lie multiplied is still a lie — and every spell breaks the moment you separate its parts. Break the bundle. Expose each word on its own. Show the cost: creativity stifled, excellence crushed, freedom surrendered. They stack words to look invincible, but light collapses the illusion. Bundles only work when unexamined; truth dissolves them instantly. You've heard the acronyms, the DEI scripts, the "sustainability" sermons, the corporate "net zero" boasts. It never was random. It was the spell. The forge began in the **Frankfurt School**, where truth was reframed as "constructed" and justice redefined as "equity." Bureaucrats in Europe polished the words into treaties — *sustainability, equity, social partnership.* The *UN* and *WEF* sanctified them into global mandates. Firms like *Black-Rock* and *Vanguard* enforced them with capital — ESG scores as gatekeepers to markets and investment. By the time they reached America, the spells had hardened into acronyms — DEI, ESG, SDGs — ready for schools, corporations, and governments to obey. What begins as a slogan ends as a chain. What begins as "inclusion" ends as exclusion. The spell does not lift you — it captures you. "Next time someone says DEI, stop them. Ask: 'Which one? Diversity? Equity? Or Inclusivity? They're not the same.' The spell breaks the moment the bundle is separated."

Firelight Pause — The Bundled Obedience

The fire asks you:

• Which acronyms have you repeated without thinking — DEI, ESG, Net Zero?

• Where have you already bowed to bundled words and silent threats?

• Do you see the fingerprints of treaties in your boardroom, your classroom, your town hall?

• Who profits from the spell — and who pays the cost?

• Can you name the hidden clause behind the words you've trusted?

• What collapses when you refuse the bundle — and stand in truth instead?

You've seen how treaties harden into acronyms, and acronyms harden into obedience. The power of the bundle is not persuasion — it is compression. Multiple accusations, delivered at once, so resistance collapses under weight. Once separated, the spell fails. Empires do not survive exposure. They survive confusion. Remove the fog, and the chain breaks.

Their power ends the moment you separate one word from another. Light breaks every braid of deception. When the bundle falls apart, the empire follows.

110

WORD WISDOM - DECODING KEY

LANGUAGE AS LEGACY, WORDS AS WEAPONS

Armory: The Language Rebuild Project
Earlier I told you that words are weapons. This is the forge. Every tyranny begins by twisting language. If you do not own your words, you do not own your liberty. We now live in a world where *"love is love"* means lawlessness, where *"democracy"* means digital rule by decree, where *"freedom"* exists only by permission. Definitions collapse, confusion is crowned as virtue, and inversion is sold as progress. We do not need new leaders. We need old words restored. This is not a glossary. It is a resurrection.

Words have been hijacked, inverted, smuggled into treaties, encoded into algorithms, and turned against the people who once spoke them in good faith. Your task is not to admire them — it is to reclaim them. Not once, but daily. Words are embers. The tongue is the forge. What you speak decides whether you light a lamp — or ignite a war. Every reclaimed word redraws the battlefield. Every stolen word is a stolen weapon. Every word taken back is territory recovered.

Speak truth — and you redraw the map.
Speak boldly — and you reclaim the realm.

And remember this:

Before they seize nations, they seize vocabularies.

Before they chain people, they chain meaning.

Before they conquer land, they conquer language.

The Battle Starts With the Tongue

"He who defines the terms, wins the war." — Truth is no longer debated — it is deleted. Language is the frontline. Some words must be reclaimed. Some disarmed. Some rebuilt from ash. Teach them to your children. Speak them aloud. This is how you undo confusion — one word, one home, one nation at a time. The battle is real — It's time to fight back — word by word. Choose one word today — define it, defend it, and refuse every counterfeit.

The Vault

Here the arsenal lives — where words are reforged, history and prophecy converge, and the remnant sharpens its tongue. When you're ready, step into the circle — thyragrimm.com/vault. Sign your name. The key will find your hand." Not a glossary. An armory. Every spell begins with a stolen word. Break the word, and you break the spell.

"Death and life are in the power of the tongue, and those who love it will eat its fruit." — Proverbs 18:21

Every war needs an armory. This is yours. The words you've seen twisted, stolen, and inverted are not gone; they can be taken back. Each entry inside the Vault is a weapon reforged from the ashes of propaganda — stripped, purified, and sharpened back to truth. The Vault is more than memory — it is a *parallel linguistic economy*. A living tongue outside Babylon's exchange. Every word you reclaim weakens their market of lies and strengthens the trade of truth.

Inside you'll find the pattern every word follows: Who wields it. How it is attacked. What they claim it means — and what it truly means. Why they fear it. How to reframe it. How to carry it into battle.

The Vault will grow over time — word by word, fire by fire. As long as lies evolve, the Vault will keep sharpening new weapons. This book lit the spark. The Vault holds the arsenal. The Vault is your armor. These words are your sword. Now stand. Before you enter the Vault, choose five words you will never again surrender. These become your daily creed — your unbreakable vocabulary. **Language is the first liberty to fall, and the last one tyrants try to give back.**

Before the Arsenal Comes the Forge

Steel is useless until it's shaped; words are the same. A blade begins as ore — raw, dull, ordinary. It becomes a weapon only after fire, blows, and resolve. So it is with language. You cannot wield a word you have not forged. You cannot defend a truth you have not spoken. You cannot fight with a tongue trained in silence. The hammer is choice. The fire is truth. Your voice is the anvil where courage takes form. Before you open the Vault, you must prove you are not merely a reader — but a smith.

Forge Drill — Tonight, speak one truth aloud that you have been whispering.

Not typed, not posted — spoken. Truth gains power only when it vibrates through air and body. This is how you heat the steel. Then speak it again tomorrow. And again the next day. Repetition shapes the edge. Courage sharpens it. Silence dulls it. One word spoken in truth is worth a thousand whispered in fear. Before the arsenal comes the forge. Before the weapon comes the fire. Before the battle comes the voice. Forge your tongue — and you forge your future.

WORD: MAGA

    Category: National Identity • Political Warfare • Language Inversion
    Used By: Patriots, builders, America-First believers
    Attacked By: Globalists, media operatives, elites

What They Say It Means:

"Racist. Cultish. Fascist." A backward slogan tied to one man.

What It Really Means:

A cry for restoration — faith, family, courage, liberty, soil. Not about Trump, but about truth. Not nostalgia, but roots. Not power, but purpose.

Why They Attack It:

Because it defies globalism. Because it rejects guilt-based obedience. Because it insists nations remain sovereign and free.

Tactical Reframe:

- "MAGA isn't about a man. It's a mission."
- "Why does America being great offend you?"

Ask Yourself:

What do they fear you remembering? What happens if America does remember?

Signal to the Front Lines:

MAGA is not a slogan. It is a line in the sand. A prayer disguised as politics. Say it without shame. Carry it like a torch.

WORD: FREEDOM

Category: Spiritual Warfare • National Foundations • Psychological Reversal

Used By: Patriots, builders, truth-tellers

Attacked By: Globalists, technocrats, coward-kings

What They Say It Means:

Selfishness. A threat to public health. Extremist. Conditional — only granted if you comply.

What It Really Means:

The God-given right to live, speak, and worship without coercion. Not granted by government — bestowed by God. Fire in the human soul, covenantal and unbreakable.

Why They Attack It:

Because the free soul can say "no." Because freedom unmasks lies the moment it stands. Because a people who know freedom is sacred cannot be ruled by fear.

Tactical Reframe:

- "Freedom isn't selfish — it's sacred."
- "If freedom threatens you, what power are you clinging to?"

Ask Yourself:

What would you do if fear no longer ruled you?

Signal to the Front Lines:

Freedom is not a gift. It is the last gate before captivity — and the first proof of covenant. Guard it like fire.

WORD: TRUTH
    Category: Moral Law • Cultural Warfare • Divine Order
    Used By: Prophets, constitutional guardians, truth-tellers
    Attacked By: Ideologues, emotionalists, power brokers

What They Say It Means:

"My truth." "Your truth." Relative, flexible, convenient — until you disagree. Then suddenly "dangerous."

What It Really Means:

Truth is not a feeling. Truth is alignment with God's law and reality itself. Eternal. Unshaken. A sword that cuts illusion from flesh.

Why They Attack It:

Because truth dismantles illusions. Because one word of truth outweighs the whole world. Because the moment truth is spoken, the lie collapses.

Tactical Reframe:
- "Truth isn't hate — it's love."
- "If truth offends, maybe it's the lie you loved that hurts."

Ask Yourself:

What truth are you still afraid to speak?

Signal to the Front Lines:

Truth is not optional. It is the weapon of last resort. Speak it — even if your voice shakes.

You have reclaimed your language. Now you must ask the question every empire fears: **Who stands above the words?** Language does not collapse civilizations on its own. It obeys a crown. Every system serves an authority. Every law bows to a king — named or hidden. Before words become law, they answer to something higher. Before chains are built, a throne is occupied. This is where the war turns vertical. This is where the crown is revealed.

 Firelight Pause — The Tongue That Builds Nations
The fire asks you:
• Which word have you surrendered because speaking it came with a cost?
• Which definition have you lived by that you never chose?
• Who taught you the grammar you now obey — your ancestors, or the machine?
• What truth have you whispered that should have been thunder?
• If your vocabulary is the map of your mind, who has been drawing the borders?
• And the blade-point: What part of your future disappears if you stay silent one more year?

Stand in the fire.
Your tongue is your first territory.
Reclaim it.

"Is not my word like fire," declares the Lord, *"and like a hammer that breaks the rock in pieces?"* — Jeremiah 23:29

111

THE HIDDEN CROWN
THE KING THEY COULDN'T REPLACE

Most people today hear "biblical values" and think of control. Rules. Dogma. Power. But that is not what built the West. What built it was Christ the King at the top — and the roots that followed:

Truth — reality isn't whatever the ruler says it is.
 Justice — all men are accountable, even kings.
 Responsibility — every life carries duties, not just demands.
 Family — the first government, the first school, the first economy.
 Courage — to speak and act when it costs.
 Humility — to know you are not God.
 Reverence — to anchor law above power.
 Sacrificial love — to bind free people together without chains.

Every civilization that forgot these roots crumbled. Every people who remembered them rose. **These are not church rules. They are a survival code.**

The Blueprint of Liberty

The founders of America understood this. They wrote liberty into law because they had first learned covenant at church benches and kitchen tables. **They crowned Christ — not the king of England, not the state, not themselves — as authority.** That is why their law endured where empires rotted. *This is not about forcing belief. It is about remembering the blueprint that kept empires from becoming tyrannies.* The Bible is not a cult manual. *It is the charter of a free people* — the oldest record of how to restrain power, lift the weak, and build nations that last. And at the center stands **Jesus.** Not myth. Not symbol. Flesh and blood. The messenger and the message. He carried covenant in His hands, walked it into villages, and spoke it into hearts. He touched lepers, defended women, lifted children, and faced rulers without bowing once. And then — **the cross.** Rome called it execution. The priests called it justice. Heaven called it proof — that love is stronger than empire, that truth cannot be silenced, that freedom is worth dying for. No tyrant ever died for his people. No emperor ever carried the guilt of slaves. But Christ did — not as a victim, but as the victor. He broke the oldest chain — death itself — and rose to crown life, not power, as the final word. This is the King the West forgot — and the King every tyrant fears.

The Cosmic War

You live in a world that believes war is fought with drones, votes, and money. But the oldest war — the one beneath them all — is **spiritual.** *The rebellion that began in Heaven never ended; it just changed terrain.* Now it wages through ideologies, treaties, algorithms, and appetites. Every false crown you've seen in this book — from the bureaucrat's pen to the influencer's pride — is a fragment of that rebellion. Babylon is not just a city. It is the world system built to enthrone man in God's place. And *Christ is the axis* — the only point that does not move when every false empire falls. That's why His name still shakes thrones. Why regimes censor Him more fiercely than any dissident. Why the carpenter from Galilee is feared more than armies. Because **His resurrection declared open war on every counterfeit king.** Everything you're fighting today is simply the fallout of that war.

The Counterfeit Order

Every kingdom reveals its king by how it treats the weakest. This is where the war becomes visible — in the bodies of the vulnerable. Christ's order builds. The counterfeit order devours.

Christ honors life — every child knit in the womb, every elder crowned with dignity. *Their order* kills babies, discards the weak, treats life as disposable. Abortion as "freedom." Euthanasia as "mercy." Death repackaged as progress.

Christ honors women — image-bearers, life-bearers, covenant keepers. *Their order* strips them — silenced, erased, reduced to shadows or slogans.

Christ shields children — treasures, arrows, heirs. *Their order* exploits children — soldiers, workers, trophies, experiments. Innocence stolen.

Christ crowns fathers and mothers — "Honor your father and mother" as the root of nations. Builders of covenant. *Their order* severs fathers, mocks mothers, cuts children from roots. Orphans without graves. Families without memory.

Christ gives freedom — truth that makes men free, courage that crowns conscience. *Their order* chains freedom — obedience dressed as safety, silence dressed as peace.

Christ raises builders — men and women who plant, guard, create, leave legacy. *Their order* breeds takers — locusts that consume, enslave, erase.

Christ commands justice — righteous scales, accountability for rich and poor alike. *Their order* twists justice — quotas, bribes, favoritism dressed as "equity."

Christ rules with sacrifice — laying down His life to lift the lost. *Their order* demands chains — always taking, never giving.

Christ restores bodies — heals the sick, opens blind eyes, raises the dead. *Their order* violates bodies — injections without consent, surgeries to erase identity, transhumanist dreams to replace flesh with code.

The choice is already before you.

One King gives life; the other takes it. Neutrality is an illusion — even silence crowns a master. One builds while the other devours. One honors; the other erases. One lays down His life; the other demands yours.

"The thief comes only to steal and kill and destroy; I came that they may have life, and have it abundantly." — John 10:10

🔥 **Firelight Pause — Which Kingdom Do You Serve?**

The fire does not ask what you believe. It asks what you bow to.

- When you speak of freedom, is it covenant — or permission without restraint?
- When you call for justice, is it righteous scales — or vengeance dressed as virtue?
- When you say love, is it sacrifice — or self-affirmation?
- When you seek peace, is it truth reconciled — or silence enforced?
- When you choose silence, is it wisdom — or survival disguised as virtue?

Before You Name Your King — Measure Your Life

A man's loyalty is revealed not by creed but by reflex. The battlefield exposes what the heart hides: what you sacrifice for reveals your king; what you refuse to say reveals your fear; what you protect reveals your loyalty; the habits you hide reveal your altar; the wounds you ignore reveal your compromise. Every life has a crown. Choose your king — or the world will choose him for you. A man cannot serve two kings — but most try until the battlefield forces the truth. You will kneel — either now in truth or later in terror. Only one King kneels first, bleeds first, and rises forever. Stand with Him before the battlefield decides for you.

So answer this, before the battlefield answers it for you: Who has the right to define reality?

"Then I saw heaven opened, and behold — a white horse. The One who sat upon it is called Faithful and True, and in righteousness He judges and makes war." — Revelation 19:11

112

RE-SENSITIZE THE REPUBLIC

HEAR AGAIN, FEEL AGAIN

The Greatest Wound

America is not collapsing from military defeat or economic shortage. *It is collapsing from sensory and spiritual numbness.* The soul has been dulled; the mind sanitized. People still salute the flag but no longer feel the flame. They weep over slogans yet shrug when children are subjected to what even the White House calls "chemical and surgical mutilation." They rage over politics but stay silent when women are raped at the border, when the unborn are discarded like trash. Pets are treated as royalty, while human life is treated as disposable. **They still feel — but for the wrong things.** Tears for celebrities, not for the unborn. Rage for politics, not for truth. Empathy for animals, apathy for children. **The heart did not die. It was hijacked.**

This is not natural decay. **It is programming.** The Beast has rewired the conscience with screens and spells until evil no longer feels evil, and good no longer feels good. Celebrities can parade filth on stage and be celebrated, while truth-tellers are mocked, censored, or slandered. Rome fell this way — bread and circuses while neighbors were fed to lions. Babylon always dulls the senses before it chains the people.

768

And America today has its own bread and circuses — TikTok scrolls, Netflix binges, stadium spectacles — all numbing the conscience while tyranny sharpens its teeth. Babylon confuses compassion until people defend what harms them and attack what heals them. **The senses are not erased — they are rewired.**

A republic without a living conscience cannot stand.

If the conscience can be dulled, it can also be reawakened. The mind that has been sanitized can be washed clean again. This is not theory — it is training. *A republic is not restored by slogans but by habits.* That is why we set orders — *daily, weekly, monthly.* **Daily orders** sharpen the senses — Scripture before screens, truth before propaganda, faces before pixels. **Weekly orders restore the household** — meals shared, stories told, neighbors served, a day of rest defended. Choose one day — any day — where you refuse the machine. Rest is not a date on a calendar; it is a rebellion against Babylon's pace. **Monthly orders** rebuild the republic — bodies in the room where decisions are made, names of the vulnerable remembered, skills trained, guardians honored, covenants renewed. This is how the spell is broken. Not once, but over and over. The Beast dulls by repetition. We resist by repetition — **truth daily, covenant weekly, courage monthly.** Only then can a people learn to feel again, to see again, to live awake instead of numb.

Daily Orders — Re-Sensitize the Republic

Break the machine's grip — Cold start. Warm heart. No phone for the first hour. Begin with Scripture, prayer, or silence. Write one note by hand — gratitude, courage, or remembrance. Warm hearts before the machine can chill them.

Refuse propaganda — Feed your mind truth, not noise. Read one founding document, one transcript, or one local paper. Ten minutes of reality beats an hour of spin. Ask: *Fact or fog?*

Name the wound — Speak one sorrow aloud — personal or national. Pray a psalm. Example: "Lord, I grieve that children are trafficked while leaders look away." Naming pain keeps the heart human.

Move the body — Walk. Stretch. Lift. Sweat. Ten minutes outside, push-ups at dawn, a walk after dinner. A republic cannot be defended by people who never rise.

Eat for vigilance — One clean meal — less sugar, more water, no chemicals. Food is fuel for clarity and endurance.

Guard the presence — When family enters, stop everything. Look them in the eye. Ask one real question before a screen steals the moment. Nations die when homes go numb.

Rest as warfare — Seven to eight hours. Not luxury — weapon. The tired obey. The rested resist. *"Search me, O God, and know my heart; test me and know my anxious thoughts."* — Psalm 139:23

Rebuild the home as ground worth defending — choose one night each week for the table. Phones off. No noise. Share one story of courage — a woman who crossed danger, a man who stood alone, an ancestor who rebuilt from loss. Let your children learn what strength tastes like.

Guard the table — Aim for one meal together each day — even if it's only breakfast or soup at night. No screens. No noise. Speak one gratitude and one grief. The table is the republic's first altar.

Recover skill — Trade consumption for creation. Plant something. Fix something. Cook from scratch. Let hands remember what hearts forgot — that dominion begins with stewardship.

Establish service as rhythm — Choose one mission of mercy — a widow, a veteran, a single mother, a neighbor alone. Visit, write, repair, or bring food. Rotate the role. Make service part of the household liturgy.

Guard a day of refusal — one evening or morning each week without the machine. No feeds. No noise. Read aloud. Walk outside. Sit in stillness. Teach your children that rest is not retreat — it is defiance against Babylon's pace.

"One generation shall commend your works to another, and shall declare your mighty acts." — Psalm 145:4

Monthly Orders — Civic Drills

Stand in the room — Step into the space where decisions are made — the school board, city council, or county hall. Presence is power. One calm, watchful citizen can shift an entire meeting. Bring receipts. Speak once. Stay steady. The Republic still answers to those who show up.

Guard the vulnerable — Choose one forgotten place — a shelter, a nursing home, a foster home, a food bank. Learn a name. Shake a hand. Remember a story. Protection is not policy; it is proximity.

Train for the day you pray never comes — Take one step: CPR, first aid, fire safety, self-defense, or marksmanship. If able, train with firearms responsibly and reverently. The Second Amendment is not about sport — it is about stewardship. Preparedness is love in action.

Honor the guardians — Take your children to meet a veteran, a firefighter, or a peace officer who kept their oath. Record their names in your family's remembrance book. Teach your sons and daughters that courage is not a myth — it has faces. Stand in the room — Once a month... **The Republic still answers to those who show up.**

Renew the covenant — Gather your remnant — family, friends, or neighbors — and speak truth aloud. What did we build? Where did we numb? What must we repair? Light a candle. Pray. Write it down. The Republic survives only when households remember their vows.

"And let us consider how to stir up one another to love and good works." — Hebrews 10:24

The Cost and the Crown

Breaking the spell is costly. Comfort will die, and applause will vanish. But the reward is immeasurable — a people re-sensitized to truth, a republic that feels again, a nation with a heart of flesh instead of stone. We have been numbed — sanitized into apathy, medicated into compliance, pacified by distraction. The cost of comfort is a silent epidemic of despair. The cure begins here — with a de-sanitized mind, a heart that feels again, a body that moves, a soul that remembers its Source. You will not just think clearer; you will feel alive again. **Empires fall when men stop feeling evil.**

 Firelight Pause — The Heart That Feels Again
- Where has my conscience gone numb?
- What truth do I scroll past instead of weep for?
- What injustice have I learned to tolerate because it is far away — or too near?
- When was the last time I felt holy anger — and turned it into action?
- What would it take for my home, my heart, my land to feel again?

"I will give you a new heart, and a new spirit I will put within you..." — Ezekiel 36:26

This is the promise — and the charge. The new heart is not given to sleep, but to stand; not to consume, but to build; not to cower, but to fight with truth and covenant fire. If you take this path, you will bleed. You will be mocked. You will be misunderstood. But you will also *heal.* And you will stand among the remnant — and **the remnant always outlasts the empire.**

113

THE GUARDIANS OF THE GATE
DEFENDING THE NEW REPUBLIC

The remnant now rises from the ashes — not only to rebuild, but to guard. The Republic breathes again, but its gates must not be left unguarded.

"Then I said to them, 'Do not be afraid of them. Remember the Lord, who is great and awesome, and fight for your brothers, your sons, your daughters, your wives, and your homes.'" — Nehemiah 4:14

The Return of the Watchmen

Every nation has walls — not of stone, but of spirit. When the walls fall, the city forgets itself. When the gates are unguarded, tyranny enters not with armies, but with comfort. **Freedom is not inherited; it is guarded.** The serpent does not rest; it regroups. Even as the remnant rebuilds, it plots infiltration. The empire never announces its comeback — it walks in through open gates. That is why the remnant must rise not only as builders, but as watchmen. The call now is not just to create, but to protect.

The Law of the Gate

A gate is more than entry — **it is discernment.** *It decides what may enter, what must stay out, and what must be burned at the threshold.* Babylon fell because its gates were opened to everything. The New Republic will stand only if its gates are kept by conviction. *Every family, every church, every town is a gate.* If the watchmen sleep, the serpent slides back in — through treaties, through tech, through trust misplaced. The enemy no longer storms the walls; it seduces the guards. The serpent's sharpest weapon is not force but fatigue. It doesn't need to defeat you — only to distract you. The battle is not at the border, but in the algorithm, the classroom, the conscience.

The Anatomy of Defense

Defense begins not with weapons, but with will. The walls of Jerusalem were rebuilt by men who held trowels in one hand and swords in the other. That image must return. The new defenders must be both farmers and fighters, teachers and sentinels, mothers and generals. There are four gates every free people must guard:

The Gate of Truth — Lies are invasions. Every falsehood tolerated is a breach. A people who excuse lies for peace will accept chains for comfort. Guard speech. Teach discernment early. Punish deliberate deceit. A Republic cannot survive polite lies — it dies by them.

The Gate of Faith — The serpent fears prayer more than protest, because prayer places authority above power. A praying people are ungovernable because they answer to God, not fear. Keep altars lit. Keep pulpits pure. Keep covenant central. When faith collapses, the state becomes god — and tyranny follows.

The Gate of Labor — Idle hands are tools of tyranny. Work is worship when it builds freedom. A people who no longer produce become dependent; a people trained to depend become governable. The taker class always arrives disguised as compassion, but it consumes what it does not build. Reward production, not dependence. Honor the builder. Starve the locust.

The Gate of Arms — Freedom without defense is theater. The right to bear arms is not permission; it is responsibility. A people unwilling to defend themselves invite chains. Arms are not for dominance, but for deterrence — not for rage, but for restraint. The shepherd must know how to wield the staff and the sling, and must know when to set them down.

The Covenant of Courage

The serpent always tests courage first. It whispers, "Stay silent. Stay safe." And that whisper, obeyed, becomes the chain. But courage is not noise; it is clarity. It is the quiet man who says "No" when everyone else nods. It is the mother who teaches truth when the state teaches fear. It is the veteran who still stands at dawn when others bow to ease. **Courage is the first wall rebuilt.**

The Discipline of Watchmen

The old Republic fell partly because vigilance became a slogan, not a habit. Freedom was romanticized, not maintained. The new Republic must train its sons and daughters differently. They must learn not only to speak but to stand. Not only to pray but to prepare. *The Republic's endurance depends on citizens who can defend it at the local level — with mind, muscle, and moral clarity.* Watchmen rise early, rest little, and answer to conscience more than command. They keep their lamps lit because they know night always returns. No guardian stands alone for long. Build a watch-circle: one who prays, one who warns, one who stands at your flank. A lone watchman can see far — but a circle endures the siege.

The Eternal Shift

Defense is not paranoia — it is love in armor. To guard is to honor what is sacred. To defend is to declare that something is still worth dying for. When a people forget that, they do not deserve what their ancestors built. But the remnant remembers. They are the *keepers of covenant, the guardians of the gate, the last sentries of the Republic's soul.* Their armor is truth. Their weapon is light. Their oath is unbroken. A Republic does not collapse when enemies advance — it collapses when its guardians drift. Hold your post. Your gate is your ground. A Republic with unguarded gates is already conquered. The serpent does not need permission — only an opening.

◉ Firelight Pause — Hold the Line

• What gate am I assigned to guard — my home, my church, my craft, my city?

• What serpent has already slipped past my watch?

• Have I mistaken comfort for peace?

• Who are the fellow watchmen I can trust at my flank?

• When I am weary, do I still hold the line? — or do I wait for someone else to stand in my place?

Freedom is not a feeling; it is a formation. When every watchman keeps his post, the Republic sleeps safe — and the serpent flees. A sleeping watchman is the serpent's invitation.

Your assignment this week: walk your boundary — your home, your land, your church, your town hall — and name the gate you will guard. The watch begins when you speak it aloud. **If you do not name your gate, the serpent will. Hold your post. Guard your gate. The night is watching.**

"If the foundations are destroyed, what can the righteous do?" — Psalm 11:3

114

THE COVENANT ECONOMY

BUILDING THE KINGDOM THROUGH WORK, WORSHIP, AND WARFARE

*"U*nless the Lord builds the house, they labor in vain who build it." — Psalm 127:1

Empires count coins. Kingdoms count covenants. Babylon's markets were temples to appetite—credit without conscience, luxury without labor. It called that order **economy**. But the word came first from Scripture: *oikonomia* — the stewardship of the household. The ordering of life under divine law. We forgot that. We built towers before we built altars, profit before purpose, systems without soul. And now the towers sway. The remnant's task is not to save Babylon's economy. It is to build the **Covenant Economy**—where work is worship, provision is service, and defense is love in armor. The covenant economy begins wherever one man decides to repair what Babylon broke. Men like Robert F. Kennedy Jr. took the fight to the rivers—forcing the giants of industry to pay for the poison they poured. His lawsuits became a new kind of altar — one where justice met water and the land began to heal. He reminded America that dominion was never license to destroy, but duty to defend. Babylon called exploitation progress; he called it crime. His victories over corporate polluters are proof that the land still answers when men of conscience speak. **Dominion is not destruction — it is defense.**

The Counterfeit Dominion

Babylon always counterfeits what covenant creates. When conscience rose through men like Kennedy—who cleaned rivers with lawsuits and labor—it answered with idols who speak, not serve. Greta Thunberg was anointed by media as a savior of the planet, yet she builds nothing, heals nothing, plants nothing. Her fire burns on cameras, not in fields. The system that poisoned the rivers funds her stage. That is Babylon's trick: noise instead of nurture, attention instead of action. Covenant creates; counterfeit performs. Babylon raises idols who speak, not serve. The media-anointed prophet of panic became their high priestess — a prophet of panic funded by the very empires she denounces.

Work — Dominion Restored

When Adam was told to till the ground, it was not punishment—it was inheritance. Labor is sacred ground. To sweat is to pray with the body. Babylon enslaved men to debt and screen; Covenant frees them to purpose and soil. Every craftsman, farmer, mother, coder, soldier, and poet is a steward of creation.

The War on Builders

Babylon fears the man who can build. The man who can grow food, mend engines, raise children, fix fences, craft tools, or defend a household is a man who cannot be controlled. So the modern economy did something grave and deliberate — **it severed men from skill.** It *replaced craftsmen with factories, fathers with bureaucrats, farmers with machinery, trades with degrees, apprenticeship with debt.* **When a man loses his skills, he loses his sovereignty. When he loses his craft, he loses his confidence. When he loses his usefulness, he loses his voice.** This is *psychological warfare.* A population that cannot repair anything must depend on those who control everything. Dependency feels like convenience at first — until the day the system no longer agrees to provide.

Helplessness is not an accident. It is a strategy. Skill-loss is the quiet conquest of a free people. A man who cannot fix, cannot fight. A man who cannot build, cannot lead. A man who cannot shape his world becomes shaped by it. But the remnant is different — when they recover skill, they recover freedom. A tool in the hand restores dignity in the heart. A learned craft reignites courage. Skill is sovereignty. Skill is resistance. Skill is worship with calloused hands.

The Law of Covenant Work

Create before you consume. Consumption breeds dependence; creation breeds dominion. *Honor craft over credential.* Degrees do not feed nations —discipline does. *Root local.* Build where your feet touch ground. Babylon exports. Covenant cultivates. *Train the hands.* Re-teach trades, rebuild guilds, apprentice sons and daughters. **A hammer in the hand of a free man is holier than gold in the vault of a tyrant.**

Real Lives of Dominion

You see the covenant alive in those who refuse automation's anesthesia—the ranchers of Texas and Montana raising cattle on open range, restoring soil instead of strip-mining it for speed. The regenerative farmers rotating crops and trading locally, feeding neighbors not markets. The craftsmen shaping wood, steel, and leather into heirlooms instead of disposable goods. The inventors and coders building tools for freedom, not surveillance—open systems instead of digital cages. The mechanics who keep old machines running without permission. The builders who raise homes meant to last generations, not quarters. You see it in parents who teach their children that work is not drudgery but dominion—the partnership between Creator and created. In small businesses that refuse outsourcing at the cost of community. In tradesmen who train apprentices instead of chasing scale. These are the keepers of the garden. They rebuild civilization from the ground up—one field, one forge, one home at a time.

🔥 Firelight Pause — Dominion in Practice

- What skill of creation — not consumption — still lives in your hands?
- Where does your work feed Babylon's system instead of God's garden?
- Have you passed a craft to your children — or only screens?
- When the land calls, will you know how to answer?

Provision — Service in Motion

Provision is not about hoarding. It is about guarding. In Babylon, money circulates without meaning—profit without people, wealth without work. But in covenant, provision is love in motion: the act of defending others through diligence, discipline, and generosity.

The Law of Covenant Provision

Earn through excellence, not exploitation. Give first. Save second. Consume last. *Invest in people*, not systems. Teach sons to produce before they spend. *Trade within the remnant.* Keep capital in covenant circles. The wealth of Babylon is weight; the wealth of covenant is witness.

Real Lives of Provision

You see it in the small-town business owner who pays fair wages when global chains cut corners. In the veteran-turned-contractor who hires fellow soldiers rebuilding their lives through honest work. In the single mother who runs a kitchen feeding families with food grown within fifty miles. In the pastor or rancher who refuses the subsidy trap—trusting God's abundance more than bureaucratic control. In the family who tithes through action, giving time and trade to the widow, the veteran, the fatherless. They measure worth not by profit but by protection—the lives sustained by their work. In this, they embody covenant: every exchange bound in honor, every dollar carrying witness.

 Firelight Pause — The Measure of Provision

- What if true economy is not what you earn, but who you uphold?
- Where does your money still feed Babylon's altars?
- Who could you protect this month — through skill, service, or sacrifice?

Defense — Love in Armor

Freedom is not sustained by sentiment; it is guarded by steel, spine, and spirit. Babylon promises safety through control. Covenant builds peace through courage. Defense is not paranoia—it is protection of the sacred.

The Law of Covenant Defense

Guard what God gave—life, family, faith, and land. Train the body as vessel and shield. Discipline before firepower. Integrity before victory. A free nation is not kept by standing armies alone, but by households willing to defend what they love.

Real Lives of Defense

You see it in the veteran who still raises the flag at dawn, teaching boys to handle rifles as responsibly as they handle truth. In the farmer who locks no door because neighbors watch each other's six. In the policeman who stands when violence or criminals threaten ordinary people — first in line to protect, sometimes even stopping to help change a tire on a Texas highway. In the sheriff who refuses unlawful orders, placing conscience above command. In the firefighter who kneels before battle to pray, not to fear. In the father who trains his household—not in violence, but vigilance. Defense is not domination. It is disciplined love. When the watchmen keep their post, the serpent flees.

Disciplines of Defense

Train the body, for a soft people cannot hold a hard truth. *Train the mind*, to discern propaganda as a swordsman reads feints. *Train the household*, knowing readiness is responsibility, not paranoia. *Train the spirit*, rooting courage in prayer, not pride. **A Republic survives only while its builders are also its soldiers.**

🔥 Firelight Pause — The Armor of Love
- What would you die to protect — and are you already living for it?
- Has comfort made you too polite to defend what is sacred?
- Do your children know how to guard what matters — not with hatred, but with holy resolve?

Worship — The Center That Holds

No economy stands without an altar. Worship is not a Sunday performance; it is the heartbeat of civilization. The Founders knew it—that liberty could only survive if men bowed to something higher than government. Where worship dies, tyranny thrives.

The Law of Covenant Worship

Guard a day of rest as rebellion. Give thanks before you demand gain. Raise your hands before you raise your voice. Pray before you purchase. Praise before you plan. When worship ceases, worth collapses.

Real Lives of Worship

You see it in *the family* who lights candles at supper, reading Scripture before screens. In the blacksmith who hangs a verse above the forge. In *the soldier* who prays before deployment and writes home about faith, not fear. In *the church* that refuses to close its doors when tyrants demand silence. In *the young man* who kneels not for a flag but before his Maker —and rises with fire instead of shame. Worship reorders the heart—and through the heart, the nation.

🔥 **Firelight Pause — The First and Final Order**

- Have you built an altar in your home — or outsourced worship to institutions?
- What would it look like to make prayer your protest?
- Who do you thank when you prosper — God, or the system?

The Covenant Economy is not theory. It is blueprint. Work as worship. Provision as protection. Defense as devotion. Worship as foundation. These four pillars rebuild nations and households alike. The remnant will be mocked for living this way. But when the towers fall again, the farms, forges, and altars will still stand—because covenant cannot collapse. Babylon trades. The Kingdom builds. Choose your labor. Choose your altar.

The Covenant Economy is how the remnant rebuilds nations in ruins—one covenant, one craft, one altar at a time. The builders now gather at the edge of the fire line — where covenant meets consequence.

115

THE FIRELINE RISING

THE ANATOMY OF RENEWAL

There is a moment after every battle when even the victors tremble. It is not peace yet — it is the pause between worlds. Babylon's towers smolder behind us, but before us lies an empty horizon — waiting to be built again. This is where the remnant stands: soot on their faces, light in their eyes, knowing that victory means responsibility. You cannot rebuild the world if you still speak its language of fear. You cannot rebuild until you confront the wound. Babylon did not only break systems — it broke spirits. Every lie you obeyed left a bruise on the conscience. Every truth you swallowed left a scar — but scars are proof of survival. Renewal begins when a people confess what was lost — and reclaim what was stolen. A nation heals when its people feel again.

Empires burn fast; covenants rebuild slow. The serpent ruled through systems; the remnant restores through souls. The first task is not political. It is personal. Before you build walls, you rebuild will. Before you restore cities, you restore conscience. *Freedom is not recovered by decree — it is reborn in discipline.* The same fire that consumed Babylon now hardens steel in the faithful. It burns away compromise, leaving conviction. The remnant rises because they remember what the serpent forgot: that truth is not written in code, but in courage.

The Anatomy of Renewal

Renewal begins in four chambers — like a heart beating a nation back to life. **Memory** is the first pulse. You remember who you were before fear. You speak the truth about what happened — no euphemisms, no edits, no revisionist mercy. You record the names of the brave and the betrayers alike, because memory is moral armor. A nation that forgets cannot be free. **Faith** follows. You rebuild altars before buildings. You thank God not for comfort, but for clarity. You light candles not for nostalgia, but for navigation — reminders that light is not decoration; it is direction. Then comes **Work** — the sweat that sanctifies the soil. You plant again, both literal and spiritual. You rebuild local economies, local trust, local accountability. You turn consumption into creation, dependency into discipline. Freedom is not recovered in speeches; it is reforged in labor. And finally, **Covenant** — the binding of souls who refuse to bow again. Not by slogans, but by oath. Not by party, but by promise. The Republic survives only as a fellowship of the faithful, men and women who will not trade conscience for convenience, nor courage for compliance. These four chambers beat together — memory, faith, work, and covenant — driving new blood through the Republic's body. When they move in rhythm, a nation breathes again.

The Remnant's Mandate

You are not rebuilding an old order; you are birthing a new one. The serpent's empire was global, but the fireline is local. Start where your boots touch the ground. *Every farm reclaimed is a fortress. Every honest trade a strike against technocracy. Every home that teaches truth a citadel in disguise.* When men work the land again, when women guard the hearth again, when children learn courage instead of compliance, the serpent starves — because his systems feed only on the passive.

The Law of the Fireline

Fire spreads where it finds fuel. So does courage. One spark in a small town can light a nation. A single act of defiance can unravel a system built on fear. That is why the remnant must speak — even when tired, even when mocked. Silence is the serpent's oxygen; speech is its suffocation. The fireline is not an organization. It is an orientation —a line of souls who burn brighter than the lies around them. What begins in one valley becomes a chorus across the land. The same fire that refines a man can reignite a nation. Courage is contagious — and when one remnant burns bright, others remember the way home. America has been broken before — and rebuilt before. From Valley Forge to Gettysburg, from Pearl Harbor to Ground Zero, every generation has faced its reckoning. **Our strength has never been perfection, but perseverance.** We fall, we fight, we forge. We are not finished; we are being refined. The serpent thought the fire would end us. It only revealed what still burns. Fire does not ask permission. It asks for fuel.

🔥 **Firelight Pause — Rebuilding the Republic**
  - What is one thing I can rebuild where I stand?
  - What fear must die for my courage to live?
  - Do I still carry Babylon's habits — or heaven's orders?
  - Who in my circle will form the next covenant of builders?
  - Will I rebuild for comfort — or for consecration?

The fireline is not just survival. It is resurrection.

The ashes are not an ending; they are soil for the next awakening. The fireline does not end at survival — it begins at sovereignty. These ashes are not graves; they are blueprints. What was burned becomes boundary. What was lost becomes map. The remnant now rebuilds not as exiles, but as architects of a freer order. The remnant has learned to see through smoke — now they must learn to chart through fire.

"Behold, I am making all things new." — Revelation 21:5

116

THE CARTOGRAPHERS OF FREEDOM
DRAWING THE NEW REPUBLIC

Empires erase maps to control minds — they rename cities, rewrite history, redraw the world until people forget where they stand. But when the remnant rises, they draw new maps. *Every generation of freedom begins with cartographers — men and women who dare to sketch what others fear to see.* The serpent draws chains; we draw coordinates of courage. The map is not geography. It is moral topography — a chart of conscience, covenant, and creation. Every mark says: Here we stand. Here the fireline holds.

"Write the vision; make it plain upon tablets, that he may run who reads it." — Habakkuk 2:2

The Old Maps Burned

Babylon mapped the world in metrics. It charted profit, not purpose. It valued efficiency above life. Its maps were made of spreadsheets and treaties, territories divided by those who never walked the land. But *the new cartographers draw with different ink* — faith, work, soil, song. They are not bureaucrats. They are builders. They are those who take the ashes of empire and sketch freedom into form.

788

The Lost Maps

The modern American does not suffer from ignorance — but from disorientation. They know the headlines but not the horizons. They can locate Paris on a globe but not purpose in their own town. Babylon erased not geography but imagination. **A people who cannot imagine freedom cannot fight for it.** Before we redraw the Republic, we must restore the inner map — the one etched on the soul before screens replaced sight.

The New Coordinates

This is the moral compass of a Republic reborn. To rebuild a free world, we must know what we are building toward. The coordinates of the new Republic are not ideology — they are integrity. Faith over Fear. Fear is the language of slaves; reverence is the language of free men. A nation that fears God bows to no tyrant. Covenant is the only constitution that cannot be corrupted. Local over Global. A nation is rebuilt not by summits, but by suppers. A global plan cannot nurture a single soul. Rebuild locally, trade honestly, defend fiercely. Production over Consumption. Consumers depend. Builders decide. Grow food. Forge goods. Teach trades. The hands that build become the hearts that lead. Truth over Optics. Truth costs reputation; optics cost your soul. The remnant traffics in integrity. What is real must matter more than what is viral. Covenant over Consensus. Consensus bends to pressure. Covenant holds under fire. The remnant answers, "Stand." Agreement is not freedom; allegiance to truth is. Principles mean nothing without practice; lines on a map mean nothing until feet walk them.

The Builders of the Parallel

Every empire breeds its mirror — a smaller, freer system that grows quietly until it outlives its master. The underground churches of Rome. The monasteries after the fall. The samizdat presses of Soviet nights. The blacksmith shops that armed revolutions. Parallel economies are always born in the shadow of tyranny.

Wall Street built towers; Y'all Street builds tables.

The old street worshiped the market. The new one honors the maker. One traded souls for stocks; the other trades skill for sustenance. In New York, the towers tremble and the marble cracks — symbols of an empire that forgot its roots. But in Texas, new foundations rise — markets of covenant, not speculation. Wall Street was the wall between the few and the many; Y'all Street is the gate swung open for the builders. Today's cartographers draw not on parchment but on networks of faith and fellowship—homesteads, small businesses, encrypted trade, decentralized currency, churches that refuse to bow. Each one a point of light on the new map, soon to connect into a civilization.

The Map of Tomorrow

The serpent always fights the future, not the present. It does not fear your memories — it fears your plans. A people who can picture tomorrow cannot be controlled today. Every tyrant collapses the moment free men see a future without him. The remnant must sketch not only what is, but what must be — a world where families thrive, borders mean something, work is holy, and truth is law. **A clear map of tomorrow is a death sentence to every empire.**

The Fireline Code

The Fireline is not an organization; it is an order. It lives wherever truth and courage meet. *It has no headquarters because its headquarters is the human heart.* It has no membership because its oath is written in conviction. Its symbol is not a logo but a fire — passed from hand to hand. To join it, you do not sign. You *stand.* To lead it, you do not command. You *serve.* To sustain it, you do not fund it. You *live it.* This is how nations are reborn — not through elections, but through examples. *Each remnant becomes a map point; together they redraw the Republic.* The Fireline doesn't wait for orders; it watches the horizon.

The Moral Cartography of a People

America's first cartographers were explorers and patriots. Its next must be *guardians and restorers.* The new lines are not merely borders — they are boundaries of meaning. Where truth ends, tyranny begins. Where family breaks, empire enters. Where covenant is forgotten, control rushes in. To draw new maps, we must first redraw the soul. Every heart reclaimed is a province freed. Every conscience awakened is territory recovered.

The Local Sovereigns

Every free nation is built from the county up, not the capital down. Babylon drew power vertically; the remnant draws it horizontally. A single sheriff with spine can nullify a federal order. A school board with courage can protect an entire generation. A county that refuses corruption becomes a fortress. Political cartography begins here — mapping authority where the serpent least expects resistance: the local level. One courageous county can nullify tyranny. One sheriff can block a federal overreach. One school board can halt ideological capture. One pastor can reopen a church when the state orders silence. One rancher can defend land rights that would otherwise vanish into bureaucracy. Local power is not small power — it is the last legal firewall against empire.

The New Declaration

It will not be written on parchment this time, but on platforms, in pulpits, in homes, in code, in soil. It will not begin with *We hold these truths* —but with *We live these truths. The Republic will not be restored by nostalgia, but by renewal.* The founders wrote the first map; the remnant must draw the next. We are the ink. The truth is the compass. The covenant is the key. Now draw what they said could never exist — a free people who remember

◊ Firelight Pause — Draw the Line

- What territory of truth have I abandoned to the serpent's maps?
- Where in my community can covenant replace compliance?
- Am I still reacting to Babylon, or building beyond it?
- Who stands beside me on the fireline — and have I thanked them?
- When I draw my map, will my children know where to stand?
- What would my map of courage look like if I drew it today?

Freedom begins not with permission, but with a pencil of fire. To draw the new Republic, start with one line: *"As for me and my house, we will serve the Lord."*

"He has set before you life and death, blessing and curse. Therefore choose life."
— Deuteronomy 30:19

A map means nothing until warriors walk it. Turn the page — the march begins.

117

SIGNS OF COLLAPSE

CRACKS IN THE EMPIRE

E very empire kills its truth-tellers. Babylon mocked the prophets. Rome fed Christians to lions. The Soviets exiled dissidents to gulags. The Nazis burned books — then burned their authors. And now, America joins them.

The tools have changed — no lions, just algorithms; no bonfires, just deletions — but the purpose is the same: silence the witness. Voices are erased not only by censorship, but by fear. Careers destroyed. Accounts frozen. Platforms vanished. When words fail to cage them, mobs and bullets finish the job. Refugees flee bombs only to meet knives and fists in "safe" lands. Cities once considered secure are pierced with random violence. Innocents are struck down while officials shrug. And under it all, *the programming tightens*. Digital IDs are sold as convenience. Cashless systems marketed as progress. Algorithms quietly sort the faithful from the "dangerous." Without the mark, how will you work, travel, or buy food? What was once prophecy is now policy — drafted, piloted, and rolled out under the guise of "safety" and "innovation." Voluntary trials. Incentivized sign-ups. Dissent labeled extremism. The cage is already built; only the door remains to be closed.

This is collapse — when speech becomes a crime, when safety becomes theater, when even the fleeing find no refuge, when survival requires a pass from Babylon's hand. **The war is no longer overseas. It is here — on American soil. It is physical. It is spiritual.** The illusion of safe spaces is collapsing. No neutral ground. You will either stand, or you will hide. You will either fight, or you will be claimed. The serpent is on its final strike, and silence is consent to the kill. But remember: the serpent always reveals itself in the end. And when it does, the remnant must already be on its feet — sword drawn, torch lit, unafraid. **America has crossed that line.** And as the Fourth Turning accelerates, expect more — supply disruptions sold as "resilience," new speech codes framed as "safety," digital passes presented as "progress." What was once unimaginable is now inevitable — unless the remnant stands. **The serpent cannot silence the soul that still burns.**

Collapse never begins with chaos. It begins with conditioning.

A people are softened long before they are subdued. First their outrage is numbed. Then their standards are lowered. Then their survival is tied to compliance. Babylon doesn't need bars when it can rewire the brain. It teaches helplessness through noise. It teaches obedience through fear. It teaches passivity through pleasure. A population trained to scroll instead of think, to panic instead of prepare, to obey instead of discern — collapses long before the nation does. This is why the serpent attacks the mind before the body. If it can conquer your reflexes, it never needs your permission.

The Collapse Field Checklist

If you see three or more of the following, you're no longer in "decline." **You're in collapse.** You know a nation is entering collapse when truth is reclassified as harm and speech is monitored as threat. When citizenship is tied to digital credentials and cash is quietly restricted or removed. When your body becomes a permission slip owned by the state. When dissent is labeled extremism and random violence becomes background noise. When borders dissolve while surveillance tightens. When access to food depends on compliance and "safety" becomes the excuse for control. When faith is treated as suspicious and prophets are mocked while bureaucrats are worshiped. When the state claims ownership of flesh, collapse has already begun. The more the signs multiply, the smaller your window becomes. Collapse is not sudden — **it is signaled.** The wise see the smoke before the flames. The world does not announce when it begins to fracture. It continues to function — until it no longer functions the way you expect.

When the World Cracks

Most people expect collapse to feel like chaos — riots, shortages, sirens. That is not how it begins. It begins when **outcomes stop matching effort.** When rules apply unevenly. When decisions no longer resolve problems — only delay them. Life still looks normal. You still go to work. Stores stay open. Elections happen. Flights land on time. But beneath it, **things no longer line up.** Alliances strain without explanation. Old enemies fall quietly. New conflicts ignite without clear cause. Treaties dissolve not with declarations, but with silence. What was once unthinkable becomes "under review."

You feel it when:
- global institutions speak but no longer persuade
- enforcement becomes selective instead of universal
- power centralizes while responsibility evaporates
- crises overlap instead of resolve

This is not collapse as destruction. This is collapse as **separation**. Systems pulling apart faster than they can be held together. What looks like contradiction is actually fracture:

- control tightens **inside**
- authority weakens **outside**
- stability becomes performative
- trust becomes local

The world feels normal — and wrong — at the same time. That is how cracking begins.

🔥 **Firelight Pause — The Silence Turns to Blood**

- When truth was mocked, did I laugh along — or stand apart?
- Where have I traded courage for convenience, speech for silence?
- If the "mark" became the price of food, what would I choose?
- Have I trusted safety theater instead of preparing for real danger?
- When the serpent reveals itself, will I be found swordless — or standing?

"Do not fear those who kill the body but cannot kill the soul. Rather fear Him who can destroy both soul and body in hell." — Matthew 10:28

The systems are turning on themselves.

The silence is breaking.

What was built to control will now consume its builders.

118

LAW AND THE BEAST

LAWS, ORDERS, AND THE BEAST

Every empire survives on its own "laws." Not divine justice, but decrees written to guard the throne of the Beast. Babylon calls chains *safety*. Technocrats call tracking *order*. Globalists call treaties *peace*. But their "laws" are weapons dressed as words. A counterfeit order always hides behind noble names. Mandates are sold as protection. Surveillance as convenience. Executive orders as leadership. Look closer — each one binds men while setting rulers free. These are not laws of liberty. They are chains polished to look like gold. Yet there is a higher Order — the one that crushes false law. The prophets spoke it. The apostles carried it. Revelation names it: *the Lamb breaks seals, not kings*. Heaven writes decrees, not technocrats. The Constitution itself was a covenant echo of this truth — law meant not to chain the people, but to chain power. *"We the People"* are sovereign, and government is bound.

The Covenant of Law

At America's birth, this order was written into flesh and ink. **Separation of powers** — so no throne could crown itself supreme. **Checks and balances** — so power could be restrained before it consumed all. **A Bill of Rights** — to guard liberty instead of strangle it. **Due process and equal protection** — so even the lowliest citizen stands sheltered beneath justice. **Federalism** — so no single Beast can devour the whole union. They were not perfect men, but they bound their government because they knew: power unbound is Beast unleashed. But counterfeit order creeps back under the language of law. Emergency powers. Executive decrees. Rule by signature, not by covenant. Law flowing from one mouth instead of many. That is the Beast's design — hidden in plain sight, draped in constitutional vocabulary while hollowing it from within.

Revelation and the Fourth Turning

Revelation tears the mask. Each broken seal is not chaos — it is judgment with order. The Beast builds counterfeit law; the Lamb exposes it. The Beast tightens decrees; Heaven tears them open. Every seal broken is another false order revealed for what it truly is. History echoes this pattern. Strauss and Howe called it the Fourth Turning — cycles of eighty to ninety years where institutions collapse and new orders rise. Each cycle a reckoning: hidden rot exposed, false systems burned, new covenants written. That is the secular echo of Revelation's seals — prophecy for the saints, pattern for the nations. But Strauss and Howe could not see the turning we face now. They mapped political decay, not digital captivity. They foresaw institutional collapse, not algorithmic control. They warned of failed systems, not biometric citizenship. Their turnings assumed sovereign nations — not a web of global technocrats writing policy above the ballot box. They tracked generational cycles — but not the rise of AI, the death of skill, or the psychological demoralization of a population trained to consume instead of build. **This is the first Fourth Turning where collapse is engineered, not accidental.**

Revelation and Strauss & Howe align — but only Revelation anticipated the Beast hiding inside the machine. Only prophecy understood that the final empire would be digital, global, invisible, and hungry for souls. **This Fourth Turning is not merely a cycle. It is a choosing — and history will remember who chose.**

For the first time in history, empires do not merely occupy land. They occupy *minds*. They redraw not borders but beliefs. They do not seize farms; they seize perception. And that is why this Turning is different. In every past cycle, the people awakened too late — only after institutions exploded. But this generation — the Remnant — sees the fault lines *before* the collapse. You recognize the seals breaking. You see the Beast's architecture tightening. You know the pattern of false order rising. **This is the first Turning in history where the faithful can act before the fall.** Parallel economies already stir beneath Babylon's scaffolding: Homesteads. Small churches with unpolished pews and unbroken spines. Trades revived. Guilds reborn. Mothers reclaiming children from screens. Builders crafting systems that do not need the Beast's permission to exist. Past historians believed collapse was inevitable. They missed the possibility that prophecy creates *preparation,* and preparation creates **interruption.** The Fourth Turning is no longer a guaranteed descent. It is a fork. A dividing line. A moment where the Remnant can break the old cycle by building the new order while the old one still trembles. The Founders could not see this moment. The reformers could not imagine it. But the prophets did. This Turning will not be decided by bureaucrats or ballots. It will be decided by witness-warriors — souls who refuse the counterfeit law, who see the seals, who stand before the Beast and say, **"Not this time."** The last Turnings forged soldiers. **This one will forge sanctified architects.** Men and women who do not wait for collapse to build covenant. Who do not wait for ashes to plant roots. Who do not wait for Babylon's fall to raise altars. The Fourth Turning is not merely a crisis. **It is an inheritance — given to the generation that remembers the covenant and refuses the chains.**

The Cracks in the Throne

The Beast whispers, *"You cannot stop me — only comply."* But prophecy breaks that spell. It sees the hidden refusals, the quiet revolts, the parallel systems forming beneath its feet. Farmers reclaiming land. Families leaving grids. Mothers teaching truth instead of lies. Churches waking. Coders building supply lines the Beast cannot trace. These are not random acts — they are fractures in the counterfeit throne. Every tyranny begins with the whisper *"resistance is futile."* Every remnant begins when one soul answers *"No."* The real war is not televised. Empires fall not by armies alone but by witnesses who refuse to bow. Hidden committees. Midnight riders. Pulpits of fire. The oldest American tradition. The Remnant does not wait for permission — it moves under cover until the ground is ready.

The Quiet Exodus

What if this is not collapse alone, but counterstrike? An Exodus disguised as ordinary life. A takedown hidden inside obedience. A seedbed of liberty sprouting beneath the asphalt of tyranny. You will not see it on television. You will not hear it from the Beast's mouthpieces. But *you can feel it* — every family that steps away from digital chains, every farmer who keeps his field, every mother who trains her child to speak truth — each is a strike in silence. Do not wait for a savior in uniform. Do not wait for a press conference. The quiet war is already here. The Remnant is already here. The Beast is already falling — it just has not admitted it yet.

- What if the seals were never just scrolls in heaven but patterns on earth — breaking now before our eyes?
- What if America's Fourth Turning is not a cycle but a cleansing — counterfeit order collapsing under its own decrees?
- What if the Constitution is a prophetic tether — a covenant chain meant not to bind the people but to shackle kings?
- What if the Remnant has already crossed the threshold — builders of altars and systems the Beast cannot touch?
- What if you are already living a quiet Exodus — each refusal, each act of courage a step out of Babylon's grip?
- What if the end of the age is not one great cataclysm but a million small flames breaking Babylon's night?

When the Beast falls, will you be found burning — or gone cold?

The Beast will not fall by headlines or heroes. **It will fall when soldiers of the sword and soldiers of the Spirit stand as one** — the *Remnant remembering, the warriors resisting* — until counterfeit chains shatter. When that day comes, let it be said you stood. That you kept the flame. That you remembered the covenant and spoke the Word no Beast could rewrite. You live in the unseen war between covenant and counterfeit law. The battlefield is language. The weapon is truth. And the Remnant already fights with quiet fire. Do not wait for orders. For every front of this war unfolds through the Five Dimensions — **Time** reclaimed from distraction. **Truth** spoken against distortion. **Power** redeemed from corruption. **Eternity** remembered amid decay. **Spirit** awakened where flesh grows cold. When these align, the counterfeit order collapses under its own weight — because only the real can endure. **Rise. Remember. Rebuild.**

"They shall rebuild the ancient ruins..." — Isaiah 61:4

119

THE SEVEN SEALS
PROPHECY IN THE PRESENT

Why Revelation?

The book of Revelation is not easy reading. Horses ride. Seals break. Trumpets sound. Bowls pour. To many, it feels distant—mythic, symbolic, unreal. But prophecy was not written to confuse. It was written to warn, to anchor, and to prepare. John did not see chaos. He saw order unveiling. Deception stripped layer by layer. Power structures exposed one seal at a time. This is how I read it. I do not claim perfect vision. I may be wrong. But patterns repeat. Echoes grow louder. I do not believe the seals break only in heaven. They reverberate on earth. They are not just scrolls—they are cycles. Systems rise, harden, fracture, and reveal themselves in stages. Once you see the pattern, you cannot unsee it. Revelation is not fantasy. It is a battlefield map. It shows what the Beast builds, how deception consolidates, how judgment unfolds—and where a people must stand when the lines are drawn.

The First Seal — False Peace

"And behold, a white horse! And its rider had a bow, and a crown was given to him, and he came out conquering, and to conquer." — Revelation 6:2

The first seal is the spirit of false peace — peace that reassures while it restrains. The rider carries a bow with no arrows, signaling conquest without open conflict. Control does not enter a nation through invasion at first, but through calm language, polite assurances, and promises of safety. False peace never announces itself as tyranny. It arrives as solutions. It speaks softly. It asks you to sign a treaty "for your protection." It invites you to surrender a freedom "for stability." It offers an identification system "so everyone can be kept safe." In earlier ages, this seal rode through imperial diplomacy, puppet governments, and peace accords that concealed conquest. Today it moves through something far more refined — global agreements negotiated above the people, beyond their consent, and insulated from accountability. This is the peace of pandemic treaties that cede sovereignty, climate compacts that empower unelected bodies, digital identification systems marketed as convenience but engineered for control, and international security frameworks that coordinate compliance while narrowing freedom. It always presents itself as progress. It always claims benevolence. But beneath the language lies a simple exchange: you relinquish sovereignty, and in return you receive comfort. The bow without arrows is the deception. You are not conquered by force; you are conquered by consent. A people will often trade liberty for the illusion of safety — and every empire knows it.

Action: Refuse peace built on fear. Examine every policy that promises protection at the cost of liberty. False peace is the first seal because it is the first surrender — the quiet one, the reasonable one, the one that feels responsible and even loving. But when sovereignty is traded for safety, the Beast does not thank you. He enters.

Seal 2 — The Red Horse (War and Division)

"And out came another horse, bright red. Its rider was permitted to take peace from the earth, so that people should slay one another, and he was given a great sword." (Rev 6:4)

The red horse does not wage war the way nations expect. He does not arrive with armies or banners; he arrives with division. His weapon is not invasion, but inflammation — the slow turning of neighbor against neighbor until society becomes its own battlefield. In earlier ages, this seal rode through tribal conflicts, civil wars, revolutions, and political purges. Today it moves with far greater precision, delivered not by troops but by systems engineered to fracture the human bond. The red horse now gallops through algorithms designed to amplify outrage, headlines crafted to split communities, and narratives that weaponize identity. He rides inside social feeds that reward anger, punish restraint, and train the population to react before it can reason. Families fracture. Churches divide. Friendships dissolve — not because truth was spoken, but because hostility was cultivated. This is war without trenches — a conflict fought inside relationships. The Beast does not need bombs when it can turn households into front lines. When peace collapses within a people, the serpent thrives, because a divided nation is easy to rule and impossible to rally. The red horse is not chaos; he is strategy. He takes peace so that people destroy one another willingly. The enemy understands this law well: if you can make a nation hate itself, you never need to conquer it from the outside.

Action: Guard brotherhood deliberately. Break the script of outrage. Refuse to speak the language of polarization. Practice disciplined unity — not by avoiding truth, but by refusing the traps designed to turn every disagreement into war. When the red horse rides, courage looks like refusing to become the weapon he is trying to wield.

Seal 3 — The Black Horse (Scarcity and Control)

"When he opened the third seal, I heard the third living creature say, 'Come!' And I looked, and behold, a black horse! Its rider had a pair of scales in his hand. And I heard what seemed to be a voice... 'A quart of wheat for a denarius, and three quarts of barley for a denarius.'" (Rev 6:5–6)

The black horse represents engineered scarcity — not famine by nature, but shortage by design. His weapon is not starvation; it is control through rationing. In Scripture he carries scales, not a sword, because the battlefield is economic. Tyrannies have always understood this law: if you cannot control a people's votes, you control their bread. Throughout history, power has learned that hunger disciplines faster than force. Today this strategy appears in modern dress — inflation that never resolves, supply chains that break in predictable patterns, farmland regulations that punish producers, and digital currencies that track and restrict every transaction. Scarcity becomes policy rather than tragedy. Shortage is no longer an accident; it is administered. The voice beside the black horse sets prices for basic goods — wheat and barley measured like luxuries — signaling a world where essentials become privileges and privilege becomes leverage. This is the economy of the Beast. What you may buy becomes conditional. When you may buy becomes scheduled. Whether you may buy becomes political. The scales in the rider's hand are not symbols of fairness; they are instruments of permission. In every age, the black horse trains nations to trade freedom for food, autonomy for access, dignity for survival. Dependency hardens into obedience, and obedience quietly becomes worship. The method is precise and repeatable: weaken the producer, reward the consumer, and make the entire population reliant on systems they do not control. A dependent people will bow long before a starving one does.

Action: Build counter systems. Grow something. Repair something. Produce something. Store something. Every habit that weakens dependency snaps a link in the black horse's chain. Scarcity is the Beast's tactic. Creation is the remnant's answer.

Seal 4 — The Pale Horse (Death and Pestilence)

"When he opened the fourth seal, I heard the voice of the fourth living creature say, 'Come!' And I looked, and behold, a pale horse! And its rider's name was Death, and Hades followed him. And they were given authority over a fourth of the earth, to kill with sword and with famine and with pestilence and by wild beasts of the earth." (Rev 6:7–8)

The fourth seal is not simply death — it is death repackaged as management. It is fear organized into policy, mortality administered as compliance. In earlier ages, the pale horse rode openly through plague, famine, and war. Today it rides in something far more strategic: the fusion of public health with state power. This is death in a new uniform — not a sword, but a clipboard; not a battlefield, but a briefing room; not terror, but "safety guidelines." The pattern is unmistakable. Fear is elevated into a governing tool. Emergency powers linger until they become permanent architecture. Experts displace elected authority. Restrictions harden into rituals. Obedience is recast as virtue. Entire nations were conditioned to mistake compliance for compassion. Travel, work, worship, and movement were reorganized around fear, not wisdom. The logic was simple and devastating: to protect life, surrender living. The pale rider does not strike once and depart. He circles. He weakens the body through stress, isolation, and enforced inactivity. He dulls the mind through panic, repetition, and contradiction. He erodes the spirit through loneliness, despair, and distrust. A population held in chronic fear begins to behave like managed stock — waiting for permission to move, work, gather, or breathe. That is the true danger of the pale horse. Not disease, but dependency. Not mortality, but mastery through fear.

Action: Refuse to let fear become your ruler. Strengthen the body. Guard the mind. Anchor the spirit. The pale horse feeds on people trained to feel helpless. Break the training. Courage is immunity. Clarity is resistance. Faith is armor.

Seal 5 — The Cry of the Witnesses

"When he opened the fifth seal, I saw under the altar the souls of those who had been slain for the word of God and for the witness they had borne. They cried out with a loud voice, 'O Sovereign Lord, holy and true, how long before you will judge and avenge our blood on those who dwell on the earth?'" (Rev 6:9–10) — And I saw the souls under the altar, crying, "How long?"

The fifth seal is not about catastrophe outside, it is about testimony inside. It reveals what tyranny always produces: silenced witnesses and censored truth-tellers. Rome fed Christians to lions. The Soviets disappeared dissidents into gulags. Today, the same spirit moves through different tools: banned accounts, erased videos, fired employees, imprisoned pastors, assassinated journalists, ridiculed believers, mothers labeled extremists, fathers called threats, whistleblowers destroyed by lawsuits or "mistakes." This is the age where truth costs reputation, livelihood, or life. And yet, under the altar, the witnesses cry—not in weakness, but in protest. Their blood is recorded. Their testimony is not forgotten. Scripture shows us that witness itself becomes judgment on the Beast: truth spoken under threat becomes the very evidence Heaven uses against tyranny.

Action: Speak now, not later. The fifth seal teaches that waiting for a "safer time" to speak is a myth. Safety never comes. Silence does not protect you; it empowers the Beast. Your words today—your clarity, your courage, your refusal to bow—join the testimony that cracks the system's mask. The martyrs are told to "rest a little longer," which means the number of witnesses is not yet complete. The age of witness is not over; it is accelerating. And Heaven counts every act of courage, every refusal to recant, every moment someone speaks truth when silence would be easier. The fifth seal is not just about those who died for truth. **It is about those who live it—loudly, openly, unashamed—when the world demands they kneel.**

Seal 6 — The Shaking

"When he opened the sixth seal, I looked, and behold, there was a great earthquake, and the sun became black as sackcloth, the full moon became like blood, and the stars of the sky fell to the earth..." (Rev 6:12–13)

The sixth seal is the moment when the world's illusions collapse all at once. Revelation calls it shaking—not random disaster, but exposure. Shaking is what happens when systems built on lies finally meet truth. It is economic pillars trembling, currencies cracking, governments losing legitimacy, institutions unraveling, and elites scrambling to maintain control as their narratives fail. People call it "crisis," "instability," "polarization," "breakdown." Revelation calls it **unveiling**. This shaking is not meant to destroy the faithful; it is meant to reveal foundations. When everything trembles, you discover what your life was built on—rock or sand, covenant or convenience. Shaking exposes who bows to fear and who bows to God. It exposes corrupt leaders, fraudulent experts, rotten institutions, and counterfeit stability. It is judgment, but also mercy—God refusing to let nations continue under deception.

Action: Stand firm. When the sixth seal breaks, panic is the Beast's language. Stability is Heaven's. Do not be swept into fear, hysteria, or dependency. The shaking strips away illusions so the remnant can see clearly and act decisively. When systems fall, the prepared rise. When institutions crack, the covenant people step into their purpose. The sixth seal reminds us: collapse is never the end. **Collapse is the disclosure of what was already broken. Shaking is the moment truth becomes impossible to ignore.** What the world calls crisis, Revelation calls clarity.

The Seventh Seal — Silence Before the Fire

"When the Lamb opened the seventh seal, there was silence in heaven for about half an hour." (Rev 8:1)

The seventh seal is the most misunderstood moment in Revelation. It is not surrender. It is not uncertainty. It is **poised judgment**—the stillness before Heaven strikes. Silence in Scripture is never empty; it is concentration. It is the held breath before a commander gives the order. It is angels gripping trumpets. It is Heaven aligning its aim. This silence is the pause between unveiling and action, between exposure and intervention. Everything false has already been revealed. Now Heaven waits for the appointed moment to act. That waiting feels like tension on earth—systems trembling, people choosing sides, nations dividing along spiritual lines. Heaven is silent, but the battlefield is loud. There are two silences in the last days: **the serpent's silence**, which is censorship and fear; **and Heaven's silence**, which is preparation for fire. The seventh seal asks only one question: **Who is awake when Heaven becomes still?** The remnant must be found ready—clean-handed, clear-eyed, unshaken. When the world grows quiet, it is not peace. It is positioning. It is Heaven drawing the bowstring tight.

Action: Stay awake. Stay anchored. Stay armed in spirit. When Heaven is silent, complacency is fatal. This silence is not the end of the story; it is the hinge on which the story turns. The trumpets follow. The fire follows. The intervention follows. But only the watchful recognize the silence for what it is. The seventh seal teaches this: **The pause is not weakness. It is precision. Judgment waits for the exact second truth will strike hardest.** When Heaven pauses, the remnant must stand ready for the command.

The question is: **When Heaven pauses, will you stand with the Lamb or sleep with the serpent?**

Why This Matters Now

The seals reveal **two orders:** the counterfeit order of the Beast and the higher order of the Lamb. What looks like chaos is judgment; what feels like unraveling is exposure. The Beast whispers inevitability, but the seals shout unmasking. Revelation is not irrelevant — it is reading our headlines. And if Scripture was right about this, then it is right about the rest: the Kingdom that comes, the Christ who reigns, the freedom no Beast can chain.

"For the great day of their wrath has come, and who can stand?" — Revelation 6:17.

Seven seals. Seven unveilings. Seven ways the Beast tightens its grip — and seven ways the remnant breaks it. You cannot stop the seals from breaking, but you can decide how you stand when they do.

🔥 **Firelight Pause — The Seals in Your Hour**

The seals do not break only in prophecy — **they break in you.**
- Expose false peace — tear up every pact built on fear.
- Refuse division — guard brotherhood where the Beast sows hate.
- Defy scarcity — create, grow, give; build what Babylon rations.
- Reject fear of death — remember eternity already holds you.
- Keep witness — speak when silence feels safer.
- Stand firm in shaking — name it rightly: judgment.
- Hold the silence — not in fear, but in readiness for fire.

When Heaven pauses, stay awake.
When trumpets sound, stand.
When the last seal breaks, Heaven asks only one thing:
Did you stand?

<h1 style="text-align:center">120</h1>

<hr>

THE TRUMPET CALL

THOSE WHO MADE IT TO THE END — THE FINAL RECKONING AND COMMISSION

"Fear not, for I am with you; be not dismayed, for I am your God; I will strengthen you, I will help you, I will uphold you with my righteous right hand." — Isaiah 41:10

Ragnarök — The Serpent's Double Tongue

Every age ends with a lie that looks like peace. The ancients called it Ragnarök — the twilight of the gods, when the serpent uncoils and the sky catches fire. They imagined gods clashing on frozen plains. But the real battle now is quieter. It unfolds in boardrooms and classrooms, on screens and in laws. It is the war for the human soul. The serpent learned that division alone cannot rule; chaos must be organized. So it forged a final covenant — the Red and the Green. Two banners that should never have flown side by side. Revolution and submission. Marxism and political Islam. Together they promised liberation; together they built a new yoke. The Red burns with envy and dissolves what stands. The Green binds with law and replaces what remains. Destruction and order — two coils of one body.

The elites feed them money, attention, guilt, and sympathy, watching from above as markets rise on chaos and governance fattens on conflict. That is the algorithm of empire. The West, ashamed of its own inheritance, became the bridge. Universities preached revolution; corporations funded a faith that hates freedom. Politicians opened borders not from compassion but calculation — a managed collapse dressed as virtue.

"They shall surely gather together, but not by Me."— Isaiah 54:15

Now the coils tighten. One ideology abolishes the family; the other enslaves it. One erases God; the other imprisons Him. Both serve the same throne. Once the free man under heaven is subdued, they will devour each other. The serpent always eats its young. Ragnarök is the revelation of that truth — the moment false unity collapses under its own weight. The flood will rise, but fire will answer. In the end, the serpent falls to the returning Light. Thor falls, yes — but the hammer lands true. In the old tongue, Midgaardsormen — Jörmungandr, the World Serpent — encircles the earth until the appointed hour. When it releases its tail, the seas rise and gods fall. The Red–Green pact follows the same pattern — two coils tightening — revolution and submission, chaos and control — until the pressure snaps the counterfeit order. The goal has not changed: *swallow the world.*

The False Unity Before the Fire

Ragnarök begins with counterfeit peace — enemies acting as allies. That is the Red–Green covenant. Each head believes it will rule after the fall; neither sees it is fuel for something larger. The Beast offers crowns; it only delivers ash. When the serpent rises, fire and ice meet. Marxism's cold calculus. Islamism's burning zeal. Together they melt the boundaries that once protected nations and souls. Out of that flood the elites build their ark — digital, bureaucratic, global. They call it progress. It is Babel in code.

The Last Battle

The final war is not nation against nation but **memory versus amnesia, faith versus simulation, covenant versus code.** The Red–Green alliance breaks the old defenses so technocrats can crown themselves gods. Yet even then, prophecy stands — the serpent is slain by returning light. The question isn't whether Ragnarök comes, but who stands when it does. After the smoke clears, *only those who remembered truth will rebuild the world.* Prophecy was not written to scare the faithful, but to steady them. The crown on the board was never the elites'. It was claimed by treaties, stolen by the serpent, slid quietly into Washington while the world mocked pawns. But **the knight still waits** — underestimated, untracked. Move unseen. Strike unannounced. Build what cannot be censored. He does not crawl in lines; he leaps. The remnant must move like knights, not pawns — unexpected, unstoppable, striking where the serpent never looks. *"Blow the trumpet in Zion; sound the alarm on my holy mountain..."* — *Joel 2:1* The board is set. The Beast has moved. Heaven sounds the trumpet; the remnant must answer. The knights rise unseen. The game is over. The war begins.

The wolf is chaos unchained — mobs and riots, bloodlust and noise, the frenzy that rises when restraint is gone. The gods are the rulers and **elites who serve the serpent until they too are consumed by the fire they helped ignite. Thor is the warrior** who strikes even when he knows the cost — a shadow of Christ, the pattern of every remnant who still stands when others flee. And **the World Serpent — Midgaardsormen —** is the enemy across ages, the whisper in Eden, the dragon of Revelation, the global coil pressing now. Different names, same enemy. Different myths, same truth. The sagas were never about gods — *they were about us.* Every myth was a map for the living — men and women who would one day face the same storm in flesh and blood. The wolf, the gods, the serpent — they live again in systems, in slogans, in the quiet bargains we make to stay safe. *The battlefield was never Valhalla.* It is the world you wake to every morning — the classroom, the boardroom, the feed glowing in your hand. **The war is not ancient. It is now.**

The sagas did not end with negotiation. They ended with fire.vSurtr was never a villain and never a savior. He was the limit. When the serpent would not loosen its grip, when false gods would not yield, when corruption learned to mimic peace — **fire answered.**cNot chaos, but cleansing. Not annihilation, but **judgment**. The world was not destroyed. It was **released**. Some lands learn to kneel. Others learn to burn without bowing.

You have walked through Denmark's history and America's legacy. You have seen the Serpent, the Dragon, the Beast, the Mark. You have watched elites fracture families and Babylon sell lies in the language of compassion. Now the mask is gone. The serpent strikes openly. The war is no longer coming — it is here. Live here. Build here. Take the ground beneath your feet as covenant ground. Break the chains. Rebuild the Republic. Let Babylon hear that its walls are no longer unquestioned. This is not the hour to scroll. Scrolls are for history. You are for action. Not the hour to hide. This is the hour to rise. You made it through the fire, through the fracture, through the remembering — and you did not flinch. That means you were marked for this hour. This is not a conclusion. It is a commission. You are no longer a reader. You are a witness. A torchbearer. A remnant. Not the silent, but the stirred. Not the compliant, but the called. Not the weary, but the warrior. If you wondered who would rise, stop wondering. It is you. Speak one truth aloud today — to your child, to your neighbor, wherever silence still rules. *"In this world you will have tribulation. But take heart; I have overcome the world."* — John 16:33

Let Babylon burn behind you. Let the Republic rise before you. When they ask who gave you permission to speak, answer with the only name that matters — **GOD DID.** When it gets loud — stay rooted. When it gets dark — stay lit. When it gets lonely — stay watching. History will not remember the bowed. It will remember those who carried fire through the storm. Because America is not Denmark. America was not built on compliance, but on men who crossed oceans, held lines, and stood when retreat would have been easier.

While the covenant lives, the Republic can still rise. The Vikings left the north. They did not ask permission. They crossed into danger, found harder ground and higher cost, and did not turn back. America called that spirit the frontier. It was never about conquest — it was about courage under pressure. This fire was never given for display. It was given for war — to refine, to reveal, to reclaim. The question is no longer whether you hold the flame — but whether the flame still holds you.

"The light shines in the darkness, and the darkness has not overcome it." — John 1:5

The trumpet has sounded. The line is drawn.

This is not the hour to scroll. Scrolls are for history. There will be no neutral ground. Every silence is now a vote. Every truth spoken, a strike of light against the coil. Stand where you are. Guard what is holy. Speak as if your words weigh eternity — because they do. The hour of the watchers has come again. The knights rise unseen. The remnant gathers flame to flame. **This is not the end. It is the reckoning.**

🔥 **Firelight Pause — The Torch in Your Hands**

- Which side of the fire do I stand on — the order born of chaos, or the flame that frees?
- When the serpent speaks with two tongues, will I answer with truth or silence?
- Where do I see the wolf breaking loose — and what will I do about it?
- Which false gods still tempt my trust?
- Will I strike, even at cost?
- Will I guard this fire or let it smolder?
- When night deepens, will my torch burn brighter — or go out?

121

TO AMERICA'S WARRIORS

To every man and woman who put on the uniform — whether your name rests in Arlington, whether you walk with scars the world cannot see, or whether you rose again to build, to lead, and to guard — this is for you. You bore the cost and carried the weight. You fought in deserts, jungles, skies, and seas. Some battles ended; some never did. All of them were sacrifice.

Because of you, we woke in freedom. Because of you, our children laughed on their own soil. Because of you, even in an hour of invasion within, we still know peace, courage, and the chance to stand. Your sacrifice was not wasted. It was seed. It was shield. It was fire. And though the world may forget, we see you.

Valhalla is not myth. It is every grave marked with a flag. It is every veteran who still stands. It is America's warriors — fallen and living — whose watch is never wasted. This fire bows in gratitude. This land still breathes because of you. *Thank you.* Your watch is remembered. Our watch has begun.

"Greater love has no one than this, that someone lay down his life for his friends." — John 15:13

122

THE VAULT

ARSENAL FOR THE REMNANT

"*F aith without works is dead*". — James 2:26

Belief demands action. It is not enough to see the fire or carry the torch — you must **build**, **fight**, and **guard** with precision and purpose. The Vault is your arsenal — practical, spiritual, and strategic resources forged for the frontlines. Whether you walk alone or stand shoulder-to-shoulder in the circle, these guides, ceremonies, and manifestos will equip you to live as a remnant who does not simply endure — but who rises, leads, and rebuilds.

🔑 Inside the Vault

The book handed you the sword. The Vault sharpens it. Not everything belongs in the open. Some truths cut too close to breathe in public. The Vault is no library — it is an armory, sealed for those who carry the fire. Here you will find words forged like steel, wisdom hidden from the public square, and maps too sharp for polite culture. Each chamber holds a different weapon — **word, witness, fire, record, dispatch,** and **buried history.** Together, they form the arsenal of the Remnant.

Every word is a key. Every key opens a weapon.

Choose carefully. Enter boldly.

The Vault is not static — it breathes. New chambers will open as the fire spreads and the remnant grows. What begins as a whisper will one day thunder. Each entry is forged by hand, added in season, tested in fire. The Vault is not for the curious. It is for the called — those who know the war will not be won on stages, but in kitchens, churches, counties, and covenant.

Access it. Guard it. Use it. Because when the fire burns low, it may be the only light left standing.

Step forward. The Vault waits.

Father, God of truth. Lord of nations.
You raise prophets to warn, warriors to fight, and builders to rebuild the ruins.
This book is not mine. It is Yours. I lay it at Your feet as fire. Let every page be courage. Let every word cut lies and wake sleepers.
Carry it where I cannot. Place it in the hands of those You choose—leaders, warriors, mothers, sons, and daughters who still remember freedom.
Guard it from corruption. Let it burn as the torch You placed in mine. If even one soul turns back to truth, to faith, to liberty—let Your name be glorified.
I dedicate this work to You — a war manual for the remnant, a shield for the weak, a trumpet against Babylon.
So be it.
Amen.

†

I will not bow. I will not break. I will carry the fire You gave me until the Kingdom comes.

Though it linger, wait for it; it will certainly come and will not delay. — Habakkuk 2:3

EPILOGUE - THE SEAL OF FIRE

You thought this was a book. It was a blade. A Trojan Horse of fire carried through the gates of your mind — and now no empire can ever rule you the same way again. I was born where the spell was forged. I chose to break it. But the breaking does not end with me. It begins with you. The fire revealed demands an answer — not admiration, but action. This is not about a man. It is about a mantle. America's covenant fire is older than any presidency. Before there was law, there was blood. Before there was ink, there was oath. That oath still stands. The battlefield has changed, but the covenant has not. The serpent adapts. So do the warriors. The next front will not be fought with rifles, but with truth, restraint, endurance, and courage. The war of our age is not succession. It is endurance. Empires fall by debt. Covenants endure by blood. Kings rise and pass. Thrones crack. But the fire outlasts them all. The last word was never theirs. It belongs to the Lamb. They fall. You rise. The fire was never theirs to give — and never theirs to take. Go find your people. Stand with the remnant. Carry the fire home.

"I have fought the good fight, I have finished the race, I have kept the faith." — 2 Timothy 4:7

THE COVENANT

You have seen the map. You have traced the coil. The treaties, the codes, the crowns — all of it was built to make you forget who you are. **Remember.** You were not born to comply. *You were born to choose.* The covenant was never written in marble or policy. It was written in blood, in conscience, in courage. The world will call you extreme, outdated, dangerous — but freedom has always worn those names before it broke its chains.. So walk out from the smoke of their systems. Speak as one who remembers the first language — **truth without permission.** Build where they cannot reach. Plant where they cannot tax. Teach your sons and daughters to pray before they post, to think before they sign, to fight before they kneel.

The crown may curve into a crescent, but the line holds — the remnant still stands, unapologetically American.

If this book lit a fire in you, good. That was the point. If it made you uncomfortable, even better — it means something inside you isn't dead yet. You made it here. You are not soft. You didn't flinch. You didn't scroll past. You walked through the fire, and **now you remember** — not just who you are, but what this nation once was, and what it still can be. **This was never written for the masses. It was written for the Remnant.** For the mothers who refuse to raise slaves. For the men who never bowed even when it cost them everything. For the immigrants who came not for comfort but for covenant. And for the Americans who woke up in time. The hour is late. **The war is spiritual.** And no one is coming to save us except God. But He has always used the few. This book was not written in the ordinary sense. It was revealed, piece by piece, until the serpent was named and the shadow crowned. It is my offering — my fire laid at the altar, *my strike against the silence.*

Now it is your turn. Don't just share it. Live it. Don't just nod. Speak. Don't just see. *Rise.* Remember this — they had systems, you have fire. They had treaties, **you have truth.** They had power, but you — you have permission from Heaven to strike. Let the cowards kneel. Let the blind follow. You were not made for this moment by accident. You were forged for it. So guard it. Carry it. Pass it on.

"The people who know their God shall be strong, and carry out great exploits."
— Daniel 11:32

History bends for the brave, not the obedient. And never forget the ending written from the beginning:

"The Lamb will triumph, because He is Lord of lords and King of kings — and with Him will be His called, chosen, and faithful ones." — Revelation 17:14

This was not a book. It was a covenant. Thank you for walking it with me.

I AM Unapologetically American.

ACKNOWLEDGMENTS

Every fire has a source. Every oath has a witness. This book was not written in peace. It was written in war. And no one walks through war alone.

To my husband — my rock in every storm, who never flinched when the fire pressed close and never ran when truth roared. Your strength is steady as stone, your presence my refuge. You read, listened, believed, and inspired when others fell silent. You are quiet fire — and you stood when others scattered.

To my son and daughter — you are the reason I will never bow or back down. This book is my vow to you — my covenant that the fire will not die, my shield to guard your freedom. I fight so you may live not as slaves of men, but as free heirs in God's country — America the Beautiful. I thank God you grew up in freedom, not in Denmark, where silence wears a crown and fire was forgotten.

To the men and women who still love this land — who raise families, build, speak, pray, fly the flag when it's mocked, and fight on every front — in homes, halls, pulpits, screens, and streets — this book is your mirror. Your fire kept mine burning. You never flinched when the storm broke, and you still stand when others bowed.

And to those born in freedom yet forgot what it cost — may these words remind you, not to shame but to awaken. A nation endures only when its people choose courage over comfort, truth over applause, and liberty over fear.

To the quiet warriors who whispered courage in private — heaven sees you. Even the silence of others became a forge; it showed me what must never again be left unsaid. Their quiet did not quench the fire — it proved it was real.

To the remnant — the faithful, the misfits, the migrants who remembered, the native-born who never forgot, the warriors in uniform who still stand, and the ones who fight in unseen ways — you are why I wrote. You are why I will not stop.

To the God of Truth, who brought me out of darkness and into fire — every word is Yours.

"His word is in my heart like a fire, a fire shut up in my bones; I am weary of holding it in, indeed I cannot." — Jeremiah 20:9

And now — the fire passes to you. 🔥

www.ingramcontent.com/pod-product-compliance
Lightning Source LLC
Chambersburg PA
CBHW020856060726
47591CB00004B/970